Internetworking With TCP/IP
Volume I
Principles, Protocols, and Architecture
Fifth Edition

Internetworking With TCP/IP

Volume I

Principles, Protocols, and Architecture

Fifth Edition

DOUGLAS E. COMER

Cisco Systems
Boxborough, MA 01719

and

Department of Computer Sciences
Purdue University
West Lafayette, IN 47907

PEARSON
Prentice
Hall

UPPER SADDLE RIVER, NEW JERSEY 07458

Library of Congress Cataloging-in-Publication Data

CIP Data Available.

Vice President and Editorial Director, ECS: Marcia Horton
Senior Acquisitions Editor: Tracy Dunkelberger
Editorial Assistant: Christianna Lee
Executive Managing Editor: Vince O'Brien
Managing Editor: Camille Trentacoste
Production Editor: Irwin Zucker
Director of Creative Services: Paul Belfanti
Art Director: Heather Scott
Managing Editor, AV Management and Production: Patricia Burns
Art Editor: Gregory Dulles
Manufacturing Manager: Alexis Heydt-Long
Manufacturing Buyer: Lisa McDowell
Marketing Manager: Pamela Hersperger
Marketing Assistant: Barrie Reinhold

 © 2006, 2000, 1995, 1991, 1987 by Pearson Education, Inc.
Pearson Prentice Hall
Pearson Education, Inc.
Upper Saddle River, NJ 07458

The author and publisher of this book have used their best efforts in preparing this book. These efforts include the development, research, and testing of the theories and programs to determine their effectiveness. The author and publisher make no warranty of any kind, expressed or implied, with regard to these programs or the documentation contained in this book. The author and publisher shall not be liable in any event for incidental or consequential damages in connection with, or arising out of, the furnishing, performance, or use of these programs.

TRADEMARK INFORMATION: Cisco is a registered trademark of Cisco Systems, Inc. EUI-64 is a trademark of the Institute for Electrical and Electronic Engineers (IEEE). IEEE is a registered trademark of the Institute of Electrical and Electronics Engineers, Inc. Linux is a registered trademark of Linus Torvalds. UNIX is a registered trademark of The Open Group in the United States and other countries.Windows, Windows NT, Windows CE, and/or other Microsoft products referenced herein are either trademarks or registered trademarks of Microsoft Corporation in the United States and/or other countries.Additional company and product names used in this text may be trademarks or registered trademarks of the individual companies, and are respectfully acknowledged.
Printed in the United States of America

10 9 8 7 6 5 4 3

ISBN 0-13-187671-6

Pearson Education Ltd., London
Pearson Education Australia Pty. Ltd., Sydney
Pearson Education Singapore, Pte. Ltd.
Pearson Education North Asia Ltd., Hong Kong
Pearson Education Canada, Inc., Toronto
Pearson Educación de Mexico, S.A. de C.V.
Pearson Education-Japan, Tokyo
Pearson Education Malaysia, Pte. Ltd.
Pearson Education, Inc., Upper Saddle River, New Jersey

To Chris

Contents

Chapter 4   Classful Internet Addresses ·   41

Chapter 5   Mapping Internet Addresses To Physical Addresses (ARP)   57

Chapter 6   Internet Protocol: Connectionless Datagram Delivery (IPv4)   71

Chapter 7   Internet Protocol: Forwarding IP Datagrams   93

Chapter 8   Internet Protocol: Error And Control Messages (ICMP)   109

Chapter 9   Classless And Subnet Address Extensions (CIDR)   127

Chapter 10   Protocol Layering   155

Chapter 11   User Datagram Protocol (UDP)   175

Chapter 12   Reliable Stream Transport Service (TCP)   187

Chapter 13   Routing Architecture: Cores, Peers, And Algorithms   235

Chapter 14   Routing Between Peers (BGP)   249

Chapter 15   Routing Within An Autonomous System (RIP, OSPF)   271

Chapter 16   Internet Multicasting   297

Chapter 17   IP Switching And MPLS   327

Chapter 18   Mobile IP   339

Chapter 19   Private Network Interconnection (NAT, VPN)   349

Chapter 20   Client-Server Model Of Interaction   363

Chapter 21   The Socket Interface   373

Chapter 22   Bootstrap And Autoconfiguration (DHCP)   403

Chapter 23   The Domain Name System (DNS)   **419**

Chapter 24   Remote Login And Desktop (TELNET, SSH)   **445**

Chapter 30   Internet Security And Firewall Design (IPsec, SSL)   **543**

Chapter 31   A Next Generation IP (IPv6)   **561**

Foreword

Here, better than ever, is the fifth edition of a landmark book, the book that signaled the coming of age of the Internet.

Development of the protocols for the Internet started around 1974. The protocols had been in limited but real use starting in the early 80's, but as of 1987, there was still no good introduction to how they worked or how to code them. The standards documents for TCP, IP and the other protocols existed, of course, but the true truth — the collection of knowledge and wisdom necessary to implement a protocol stack and actually expect it to work — was a mystery, known only to a small band of the initiated. This lack of knowledge was not a good thing, and the initiated knew it. But it takes a lot of effort to pull all the right stuff together and write it down. We waited, knowing that a good book explaining TCP/IP would be an important step towards the broad acceptance of our protocols.

And then Doug wrote the book. The Internet took a big step on its way from a small guild to a global community.

Of course, knowing that this was a landmark book back then is not enough to make you buy it now. Collectors might want to find the first edition, but 18 years ago is a long time in Internet years, and a lot has changed since then. We have learned a lot more, the field has grown up, whole new protocols have emerged, and Doug has rewritten the book four times. That is a measure both of how much and how fast the field changes, and how much work must go into keeping this book current. This book has all the new stuff, and our best current knowledge about all the old stuff. It is much more than simply TCP and IP. The book will give you an introduction to network technology like Ethernet, the design principles of the Internet, addressing and routing, programming over TCP, and examples of applications like email and the world wide web. This book has been updated with such things as an introduction to IP switching and MPLS, an updated discussion of mobile IP, private network interconnection, and secure alternatives to older protocols. Lots of sections have been revised to make sure that the reader gets the very latest information, as well as the basic understanding that has always been the hallmark of this book.

Other things have changed since the first edition. Not only has the Internet grown up, but some of our heroes have grown old, and some have died. The foreword to the first edition was written by Jon Postel, one of the true Internet pioneers, who died in the fall of 1998. Below, we have reprinted the foreword he wrote for the first edition. Much is the same, but much has changed. In 1987, Jon wrote "Computer communication systems and networks are currently separated and fragmented. The goal of interconnection and internetworking, to have a single powerful computer communication network, is fundamental to the design of TCP/IP.'' Only 18 years ago, networks were fragmented; today, the Internet unites the world. And TCP/IP is still the glue at the core of the Internet that makes all this work. And this is still the book to read to learn about it.

David Clark
Massachusetts Institute of Technology

May, 2005

Foreword To The First Edition
By The Late Jon Postel

In this book, Professor Douglas Comer has provided a long sought overview and introduction to TCP/IP. There have been many requests for "the" article, report, or book to read to get started on understanding the TCP/IP protocols. At last, this book satisfies those requests. Writing an introduction to TCP/IP for the uninitiated is a very difficult task. While combining the explanation of the general principles of computer communication with the specific examples from the TCP/IP protocol suite, Doug Comer has provided a very readable book.

While this book is specifically about the TCP/IP protocol suite, it is a good book for learning about computer communications protocols in general. The principles of architecture, layering, multiplexing, encapsulation, addressing and address mapping, routing, and naming are quite similar in any protocol suite, though, of course, different in detail (See Chapters 3, 10, 17, and 18)†. Computer communication protocols do not do anything themselves. Like operating systems, they are in the service of applications processes. Processes are the active elements that request communication and are the ultimate senders and receivers of the data transmitted. The various layers of protocols are like the various layers in a computer operating system, especially the file system. Understanding protocol architecture is like understanding operating system architecture. In this book, Doug Comer has taken the "bottom up" approach — starting with the physical networks and moving up in levels of abstraction to the applications.

Since application processes are the active elements using the communication supported by the protocols, TCP/IP is an "interprocess communication" (IPC) mechanism. While there are several experiments in progress with operating system style message passing and procedure call types of IPC based on IP, the focus in this book is on more traditional applications that use the UDP datagram or TCP logical connection forms of IPC (See Chapters 11, 12, 17, 18, and 19).

One of the key ideas inherent in TCP/IP and in the title of this book is "internetworking." The power of a communication system is directly related to the number of entities in that system. The telephone network is very useful because (nearly) all of the telephones are in (as it appears to the users) one network. Computer communication systems and networks are currently separated and fragmented. The goal of interconnection and internetworking, to have a single powerful computer communication network, is fundamental to the design of TCP/IP. Essential to internetworking is addressing (See

---

†Editor's note: chapter numbers have changed since the first edition.

Chapters 4, 5, and 6), and a universal protocol — the Internet Protocol (See Chapters 7, 8, and 9).

To have an internetwork the individual networks must be connected. The connecting devices are called gateways. Further, these gateways must have some procedures for forwarding data from one network to the next. The data is in the form of IP datagrams and the destination is specified by an IP address, but the gateway must make a routing decision based on the IP address and what it knows about the connectivity of the networks making up the Internet. The procedures for distributing the current connectivity information to the gateways are called routing algorithms, and these are currently the subject of much study and development (See Chapters 13, 14, 15, and 16).

Like all communication systems, the TCP/IP protocol suite is an unfinished system. It is evolving to meet changing requirements and new opportunities. Thus, this book is, in a sense, a snapshot of TCP/IP circa 1987. And, as Doug Comer points out, there are many loose ends (See Chapter 20).

Most chapters end with a few pointers to material "for further study." Many of these refer to memos of the RFC series of notes. This series of notes is the result of a policy of making the working ideas and the protocol specifications developed by the TCP/IP research and development community widely available. This availability of the basic and detailed information about these protocols, and the availability of the early implementations of them, has had much to do with their current widespread use. This commitment to public documentation at this level of detail is unusual for a research effort, and has had significant benefits for the development of computer communication (See Appendix 3).

This book brings together information about the various parts of the TCP/IP architecture and protocols and makes it accessible. Its publication is a very significant milestone in the evolution of computer communications.

Jon Postel,
Internet Protocol Designer and
Deputy Internet Architect

December, 1987

Preface

Readers around the world have asked for a new edition, and many have suggested topics that need to be emphasized. The new addition responds to suggestions by refocusing the discussion on protocols and technologies that are currently used in the Internet. Thus, much of the history has been reduced or removed. A new chapter on IP switching and MPLS has replaced the chapter on ATM. Sections on protocols such as RARP and BOOTP that are no longer used in the Internet have been reduced. The discussion of GGP has been removed along with sections on the now-defunct routing arbiter system; the Classful addressing scheme is discussed as a historical fact, and the Internet is presented as using classless addressing throughout.

All chapters have been updated to reflect the latest versions of the protocols and the latest terminology. For example, the chapter on TCP now discusses Selective ACKnowledgements (SACK), Explicit Congestion Notification (ECN), and the set of fast retransmit schemes. In addition, new sections on traffic management discuss queuing and scheduling mechanisms, and a rewrite of the security chapter discusses stateful firewalls†.

Like earlier editions, which have been extremely popular, the entire text focuses on the concept of internetworking in general and the TCP/IP internet technology in particular. Internetworking is a powerful abstraction that allows us to deal with the complexity of multiple underlying communication technologies. It hides the details of network hardware and provides a high level communication environment. The text reviews both the architecture of network interconnections and the principles underlying protocols that make such interconnected networks function as a single, unified communication system. It also shows how an internet communication system can be used for distributed computation.

After reading this book, you will understand how it is possible to interconnect multiple physical networks into a coordinated system, how internet protocols operate in that environment, and how application programs use the resulting system. As a specific example, you will learn the details of the global TCP/IP Internet, including the architecture of its router system and the application protocols it supports. In addition, you will understand some of the limitations of the internet approach.

Designed as both a college text and as a professional reference, the book is written at an advanced undergraduate or graduate level. For professionals, the book provides a comprehensive introduction to the TCP/IP technology and the architecture of the Internet. Although it is not intended to replace protocol standards documents, the book is an excellent starting point for learning about internetworking because it provides a uniform

---

†In addition to other changes, the author has reluctantly agreed to replace the term *datagram routing* with *datagram forwarding*.

overview that emphasizes principles. Moreover, it gives the reader perspective that can be extremely difficult to obtain from individual protocol documents.

When used in the classroom, the text provides more than sufficient material for a single semester network course at either the undergraduate or graduate level. Such a course can be extended to a two-semester sequence if accompanied by programming projects and readings from the literature. For undergraduate courses, many of the details are unnecessary. Students should be expected to grasp the basic concepts described in the text, and they should be able to describe or use them. At the graduate level, students should be expected to use the material as a basis for further exploration. They should understand the details well enough to answer exercises or solve problems that require them to explore extensions and subtleties. Many of the exercises suggest such subtleties; solving them often requires students to read protocol standards and apply creative energy to comprehend consequences.

At all levels, hands-on experience sharpens the concepts and helps students gain intuition. Thus, I encourage instructors to invent projects that force students to use Internet services and protocols. The semester project in my graduate Internetworking course at Purdue requires students to build an IP router. We supply hardware and the source code for an operating system, including device drivers for network interfaces; students build a working router that interconnects three networks with different MTUs. The course is extremely rigorous, students work in teams, and the results have been impressive (many industries recruit graduates from the course). Although such experimentation is safest when the instructional laboratory network is isolated from production computing facilities, we have found that students exhibit the most enthusiasm, and benefit the most, when they have access to the Internet.

The book is organized into four main parts. Chapters 1 and 2 form an introduction that provides an overview and discusses existing network technologies. In particular, Chapter 2 reviews physical network hardware. The intention is to provide basic intuition about what is possible, not to spend inordinate time on hardware details. Chapters 3-12 describe the TCP/IP Internet from the viewpoint of a single host, showing the protocols a host contains and how they operate. They cover the basics of Internet addressing and routing as well as the notion of protocol layering. Chapters 13-19 and 31 describe the architecture of an internet when viewed globally. They explore routing architecture and the protocols routers use to exchange routing information. Finally, Chapters 20-30 discuss application level services available in the Internet. They present the client-server model of interaction, and give several examples of client and server software.

The chapters have been organized bottom up. They begin with an overview of hardware and continue to build new functionality on top of it. This view will appeal to anyone who has developed Internet software because it follows the same pattern one uses in implementation. The concept of layering does not appear until Chapter 10. The discussion of layering emphasizes the distinction between conceptual layers of functionality and the reality of layered protocol software in which multiple objects appear at each layer.

A modest background is required to understand the material. The reader is expected to have a basic understanding of computer systems, and to be familiar with data structures like stacks, queues, and trees. Readers need basic intuition about the organization of computer software into an operating system that supports concurrent programming and application programs that users invoke to perform computation. Readers do not need sophisticated mathematics, nor do they need to know information theory or theorems from data communications; the book describes the physical network as a black box around which an internetwork can be built. It states design principles clearly, and discusses motivations and consequences.

I thank all the people who have contributed to versions of this book. Dan Ardelean and Max Martynov provided extensive assistance with this edition, including reading RFCs and suggesting updates. Dave Roberts and Fernando Lichtschein read early drafts. Special thanks go to my wife and partner, Chris, whose careful editing and suggestions made many improvements throughout.

Douglas E. Comer

May, 2005

What Others Have Said About The Fifth Edition Of Internetworking With TCP/IP

"This is the book I go to for clear explanations of the basic principles and latest developments in TCP/IP technologies. It's a 'must have' reference for networking professionals."

Dr. Ralph Droms
Cisco Systems
Chair of the DHCP working group

"When the Nobel committee turns its attention to the Internet, Doug gets the prize for literature. The new fifth edition of this classic is the best way to master Internet technology."

Dr. Paul V. Mockapetris
Inventor of the Domain Name System

"The best-written TCP/IP book I have ever read. Dr. Comer explains complex ideas clearly, with excellent diagrams and explanations. With this edition, Dr. Comer makes this classic textbook contemporary."

Dr. John Lin,
Bell Laboratories

"The Internet continues to evolve and so does Comer's comprehensive coverage of the protocol architecture of this global communication system. As the convergence of voice and data networks continues apace, understanding the Internet is all the more important for the 21st century telecommunications engineer. The fifth edition of Comer's classic continues to serve as the premiere guide."

Dr. Vinton Cerf
SVP Technology Strategy, MCI
and co-inventor of TCP/IP

"*Internetworking with TCP/IP* has always been the definitive reference for the Internet's key technologies. This new edition is an important update that confirms Doug Comer's reputation for clear and accurate presentation of essential information for every Internet professional."

> *Dr. Lyman Chapin,*
> *Interisle Consulting Group*
> *Former IAB Chair*

"One of the greatest books I have read. True genius is when you are not only fluent in your field, but can get your point across simply. Thank you Dr. Comer for writing a great book!"

> *Marvin E. Miller*
> *CIO, The ACS Corporation*

". . . a true masterpiece."

> *Mr. Javier Sandino*
> *Systems Engineer*

About The Author

Douglas Comer, Distinguished Professor of Computer Science at Purdue University and Visiting Faculty at Cisco Systems Inc., is an internationally recognized expert on computer networking, the TCP/IP protocols, and the Internet. The author of numerous refereed articles and technical books, he is a pioneer in the development of curriculum and laboratories for research and education.

A prolific author, Comer's popular books have been translated into 16 languages, and are used in industry as well as computer science, engineering, and business departments around the world. His landmark three-volume series *Internetworking With TCP/IP* revolutionized networking and network education. His textbooks and innovative laboratory manuals have and continue to shape graduate and undergraduate curricula.

The accuracy and insight of Dr. Comer's books reflect his extensive background in computer systems. His research spans both hardware and software. He has created a complete operating system, written device drivers, and implemented network protocol software for conventional computers as well as network processors. The resulting software has been used by industry in a variety of products.

Comer has created and teaches courses on network protocols and computer technologies for a variety of audiences, including courses for engineers as well as academic audiences. His innovative educational laboratories allow him and his students to design and implement working prototypes of large, complex systems, and measure the performance of the resulting prototypes. He continues to teach at industries, universities, and conferences around the world. In addition, Comer consults for industry on the design of computer networks and systems.

For over eighteen years, Professor Comer has served as editor-in-chief of the research journal *Software — Practice and Experience*. He is a Fellow of the ACM, a Fellow of the Purdue Teaching Academy, and a recipient of numerous awards, including a Usenix Lifetime Achievement award.

Additional information can be found at:

www.cs.purdue.edu/people/comer

and information about Comer's books can be found at:

www.comerbooks.com

Chapter Contents

1

Introduction And Overview

1.1 The Motivation For Internetworking

Internet communication has become a fundamental part of life. The World Wide Web contains information about such diverse subjects as atmospheric conditions, crop production, stock prices, and airline traffic. Groups establish electronic mailing lists so they can share information of common interest. Professional colleagues exchange business correspondence electronically, and relatives exchange personal greetings.

Although it appears to operate as a unified network, the Internet is not engineered from a single networking technology because no technology suffices for all uses. Instead, networking hardware is designed for specific situations and budgets. Some groups need high-speed networks to connect computers in a single building. Because low-cost hardware that works well inside a building cannot span large geographic distances, an alternative must be used to connect machines thousands of miles apart.

In the past twenty-five years, a technology has been created that makes it possible to interconnect many disparate physical networks and operate them as a coordinated unit. Known as *internetworking*, the technology forms the basis for the Internet by accommodating multiple, diverse underlying hardware technologies, providing a way to interconnect the networks, and defining a set of communication conventions that the networks use to interoperate. The internet technology hides the details of network hardware, and permits computers to communicate independent of their physical network connections.

The internet technology described in this book is an example of *open system interconnection*. It is called *open* because, unlike proprietary communication systems available from one specific vendor, the specifications are publicly available. Thus, anyone can build the software needed to communicate across an internet. More important, the

1

entire technology has been designed to foster communication among machines with diverse hardware architectures, to use almost any packet switched network hardware, to accommodate a wide variety of applications, and to accommodate arbitrary computer operating systems.

1.2 The TCP/IP Internet

U.S. government agencies realized the importance and potential of internet technology many years ago, and funded research that made possible a global Internet†. This book discusses principles and ideas that resulted from research funded by the *Defense Advanced Research Projects Agency* (*DARPA‡*). The DARPA technology includes a set of network standards that specify the details of how computers communicate, as well as a set of conventions for interconnecting networks and forwarding traffic. Officially named the *TCP/IP Internet Protocol Suite* and commonly referred to as *TCP/IP* (after the names of its two main standards), it can be used to communicate across any set of interconnected networks. For example, TCP/IP can be used to interconnect a set of networks within a single building, within a physical campus, or among a set of campuses.

Although the TCP/IP technology is noteworthy by itself, it is especially interesting because its viability has been demonstrated on a large scale. It forms the base technology for the global Internet that connects over 650 million individuals in homes, schools, corporations, and government labs in virtually all populated areas. An outstanding success, the Internet demonstrates the viability of the TCP/IP technology and shows how it can accommodate a wide variety of underlying hardware technologies.

1.3 Internet Services

One cannot appreciate the technical details underlying TCP/IP without understanding the services it provides. This section reviews internet services briefly, highlighting the services most users access, and leaves to later chapters the discussion of how computers connect to a TCP/IP internet and how the functionality is implemented.

Much of our discussion of services will focus on standards called *protocols*. Protocols like TCP and IP provide the syntactic and semantic rules for communication. They contain the details of message formats, describe how a computer responds when a message arrives, and specify how a computer handles errors or other abnormal conditions. Most important, protocols allow us to discuss computer communication independent of any particular vendor's network hardware. In a sense, protocols are to communication what algorithms are to computation. An algorithm allows one to specify or understand a computation without knowing the details of a particular CPU

---

†We will follow the usual convention of capitalizing *Internet* when referring specifically to the global Internet, and use lower case to refer to private internets that use TCP/IP technology.

‡At various times, *DARPA* has been called the *Advanced Research Projects Agency* (*ARPA*).

instruction set. Similarly, a communication protocol allows one to specify or understand data communication without depending on detailed knowledge of a particular vendor's network hardware.

Hiding the low-level details of communication helps improve productivity in several ways. First, because programmers deal with higher-level protocol abstractions, they do not need to learn or remember as many details about a given hardware configuration. Thus, they can create new programs quickly. Second, because programs built using higher-level abstractions are not restricted to a particular computer architecture or a particular network hardware, the programs do not need to be changed when computers or networks are replaced or reconfigured. Third, because application programs built using higher-level protocols are independent of the underlying hardware, they can provide direct communication between an arbitrary pair of computers. Programmers do not need to build a special version of application software for each type of computer or each type of network. Instead, software built to use protocols is general-purpose; the same code can be compiled and run on an arbitrary computer.

We will see that the details of each service available on the Internet are given by a separate protocol. The next sections refer to protocols that specify some of the application-level services as well as those used to define network-level services. Later chapters explain each of these protocols in detail.

1.3.1 Application Level Internet Services

From a user's point of view, the Internet appears to consist of a set of application programs that use the underlying network to carry out useful communication tasks. We use the term *interoperability* to refer to the ability of diverse computing systems to cooperate in solving computational problems. Internet application programs exhibit a high degree of interoperability. Most users that access the Internet do so merely by running application programs without understanding the types of computers being accessed, the TCP/IP technology, the structure of underlying internets, or even the path the data travels to its destination; they rely on the application programs and the underlying network software to handle such details. Only programmers who write network application programs need to view a TCP/IP internet as a network and need to understand some of the technology.

The most popular and widespread Internet application services include:

- *World Wide Web*. The Web allows users to view documents that contain text and graphics, and to follow hypermedia links from one document to another. The Web grew to become the largest source of traffic on the global Internet between 1994 and 1995, and continues to be a major source of traffic.

- *Electronic Mail* (*e-mail*). Electronic mail allows a user to compose a memo and send a copy to individuals or groups. Another part of the mail application allows users to read memos that they have received. E-mail allows users to include "attachments" with a mail message that consist of arbitrary files. Electronic mail has been so successful that many Internet users depend on it for most correspondence. One reason for the popularity of Internet e-mail arises from a careful design: the protocol makes delivery reliable. Not only does the mail system on the sender's computer contact the mail system on the receiver's computer directly, but the protocol specifies that a message cannot be deleted by the sender until the receiver has successfully placed a copy on permanent storage.

- *File Transfer.* The file transfer application allows users to send or receive a copy of a data file. File transfer is one of the oldest, and still among the most heavily used application services in the Internet.

- *Remote Login And Remote Desktop.* Remote login and remote desktop services allow a user sitting at one computer to connect to a remote machine and use the remote machine as if it were local. That is, keystrokes are sent to the remote machine, and the display from the remote machine appears on the user's screen (either in a window or across the entire screen).

We will return to these and other applications in later chapters and examine them in more detail. We will see exactly how applications use the underlying TCP/IP protocols, and why having standards for application protocols has helped ensure that they are widespread.

1.3.2 Network-Level Internet Services

A programmer who creates application programs that use TCP/IP protocols has an entirely different view of an internet than a user who merely executes applications like electronic mail. At the network level, an internet provides two broad types of service that all application programs use. While it is unimportant at this time to understand the details of these services, they cannot be omitted from an overview of TCP/IP:

- *Connectionless Packet Delivery Service.* This service, explained in detail throughout the text, forms the basis for all internet services. Connectionless delivery is an abstraction of the service that most packet-switching networks offer. It means simply that a TCP/IP internet forwards small messages from one computer to another based on address information carried in the message. Because the connectionless service forwards each packet separately, it does not guarantee reliable, in-order delivery. Because it usually maps directly onto the underlying hardware, the connectionless service is extremely efficient. More important, having connectionless packet delivery as the basis for all internet services makes the TCP/IP protocols adaptable to a wide range of network hardware.

- *Reliable Stream Transport Service.* Most applications need much more than packet delivery because they require the communication software to recover automatically from transmission errors, lost packets, or failures of intermediate switches along the path between sender and receiver. The reliable transport service handles such problems. It allows an application on one computer to establish a "connection" with an application on another computer, and then to send a large volume of data across the connection as if it were a permanent, direct hardware connection. Underneath, of course, the communication protocols divide the stream of data into small messages and send them, one at a time, waiting for the receiver to acknowledge reception.

Many networks provide basic services similar to those outlined above, so one might wonder what distinguishes TCP/IP services from others. The primary distinguishing features are:

- *Network Technology Independence.* Although TCP/IP is based on conventional packet switching technology, it is independent of any particular brand or type of hardware; the global Internet includes a variety of network technologies. TCP/IP protocols define the unit of data transmission, called a *datagram*, and specify how to transmit datagrams on a particular network.

- *Universal Interconnection.* A TCP/IP internet allows any pair of computers to which it attaches to communicate. Each computer is assigned an *address* that is universally recognized throughout the internet. Every datagram carries the addresses of its source and destination. Intermediate switching devices use the destination address to make forwarding decisions.

- *End-to-End Acknowledgements.* The TCP/IP internet protocols provide acknowledgements between the original source and ultimate destination instead of between successive machines along the path, even if the source and destination do not connect to a common physical network.

- *Application Protocol Standards.* In addition to the basic transport-level services (like reliable stream connections), the TCP/IP protocols include standards for many common applications including electronic mail, file transfer, and remote login. Thus, when designing application programs that use TCP/IP, programmers often find that existing software provides the communication services they need.

Later chapters will discuss the details of the services provided to the programmer as well as many of the application protocol standards.

1.4 History And Scope Of The Internet

Part of what makes the TCP/IP technology so exciting is its universal adoption as well as the size and growth rate of the global Internet. DARPA began working toward an internet technology in the mid 1970s, with the architecture and protocols taking their current form around 1977-79. At that time, DARPA was known as the primary funding agency for packet-switched network research, and pioneered many ideas in packet-switching with its well-known *ARPANET*. The ARPANET used conventional point-to-point leased line interconnections, but DARPA also funded exploration of packet-switching over radio networks and satellite communication channels. Indeed, the growing diversity of network hardware technologies helped force DARPA to study network interconnection, and pushed internetworking forward.

The availability of research funding from DARPA caught the attention and imagination of several research groups, especially those researchers who had previous experience using packet switching on the ARPANET. DARPA scheduled informal meetings of researchers to share ideas and discuss results of experiments. Informally, the group was known as the *Internet Research Group*. By 1979, so many researchers were involved in the TCP/IP effort that DARPA created an informal committee to coordinate and guide the design of the protocols and architecture of the emerging Internet. Called the *Internet Control and Configuration Board* (*ICCB*), the group met regularly until 1983, when it was reorganized.

The global Internet began around 1980 when DARPA started converting machines attached to its research networks to the new TCP/IP protocols. The ARPANET, already in place, quickly became the backbone of the new Internet and was used for many of the early experiments with TCP/IP. The transition to Internet technology became complete in January 1983 when the Office of the Secretary of Defense mandated that all computers connected to long-haul networks use TCP/IP. At the same time, the *Defense Communication Agency* (*DCA*) split the ARPANET into two separate networks, one for further research and one for military communication. The research part retained the name ARPANET; the military part, which was somewhat larger, became known as the *military network*, (*MILNET*).

To encourage university researchers to adopt and use the new protocols, DARPA made an implementation available at low cost. At that time, most university computer science departments were running a version of the UNIX operating system available in the University of California's *Berkeley Software Distribution*, commonly called *Berkeley UNIX* or *BSD UNIX*. By funding Bolt Beranek and Newman, Incorporated (*BBN*) to implement its TCP/IP protocols for use with UNIX and funding Berkeley to integrate the protocols with its software distribution, DARPA was able to reach over 90% of university computer science departments. The new protocol software came at a particularly significant time because many departments were just acquiring second or third computers and connecting them together with local area networks. The departments needed communication protocols that provided application services such as file transfer.

Besides a set of utility programs, Berkeley UNIX provided a new operating system abstraction known as a *socket* that allowed application programs to access communication protocols. A generalization of the UNIX mechanism for I/O, the socket interface has options for several types of network protocols in addition to TCP/IP. The introduction of the socket abstraction was important because it allowed programmers to use TCP/IP protocols with little effort. The socket interface has become a de facto standard, now used in most operating systems.

Realizing that network communication would soon be a crucial part of scientific research, the National Science Foundation (*NSF*) took an active role in expanding the TCP/IP Internet to reach as many scientists as possible. In the late 1970s, NSF funded a project known as the *Computer Science NETwork* (*CSNET*), which had as its goal connecting all computer scientists. Starting in 1985, NSF began a program to establish access networks centered around its six supercomputer centers, and in 1986 expanded networking efforts by funding a new wide area backbone network, known as the *NSFNET backbone*. NSF also provided seed money for regional networks, each of which connected major scientific research institutions in a given area.

Within seven years of its inception, the Internet had grown to span hundreds of individual networks located throughout the United States and Europe. It connected nearly 20,000 computers at universities, government, and corporate research laboratories. Both the size and the use of the Internet continued to grow much faster than anticipated. By late 1987, it was estimated that the growth had reached 15% per month. By 2005, the global Internet reached nearly 300 million computers in 209 countries.

Early adoption of TCP/IP protocols and growth of the Internet was not limited to government-funded projects. Major computer corporations connected to the Internet as did many other large corporations including: oil companies, the auto industry, electronics firms, pharmaceutical companies, and telecommunications carriers. Medium and small companies began connecting in the 1990s. In addition, many companies used TCP/IP protocols on their internal corporate intranets even if they chose not to be part of the global Internet.

1.5 The Internet Architecture Board

Because the TCP/IP internet protocol suite did not arise from a specific vendor or from a recognized professional society, it is natural to ask, ''who set the technical direction and decided when protocols became standard?'' The answer is a group known as the *Internet Architecture Board* (*IAB*†) that was formed in 1983 when DARPA reorganized the Internet Control and Configuration Board. The IAB provided the focus and coordination for much of the research and development underlying the TCP/IP protocols, and guided the evolution of the Internet. It decided which protocols were a required part of the TCP/IP suite and set official policies.

1.6 The IAB Reorganization

By the summer of 1989, both the TCP/IP technology and the Internet had grown beyond the initial research project into production facilities upon which thousands of people depended for daily business. It was no longer possible to introduce new ideas by changing a few installations overnight. To a large extent, the hundreds of

---

†IAB originally stood for *Internet Activities Board*.

commercial companies that offer TCP/IP products determined whether products would interoperate by deciding when to incorporate changes in their software. Researchers who drafted specifications and tested new ideas in laboratories could no longer expect instant acceptance and use of the ideas. It was ironic that the researchers who designed and watched TCP/IP develop found themselves overcome by the commercial success of their brainchild. In short, TCP/IP became a successful, production technology and the market place began to dominate its evolution.

To reflect the political and commercial realities of both TCP/IP and the Internet, the IAB was reorganized in the summer of 1989. Researchers were moved from the IAB itself to a subsidiary group known as the *Internet Research Task Force* (*IRTF*), and a new IAB board was constituted to include representatives from the wider community. Responsibility for protocol standards and other technical aspects passed to a group known as the *Internet Engineering Task Force* (*IETF*).

The IETF existed in the original IAB structure, and its success provided part of the motivation for reorganization. Unlike most IAB task forces, which were limited to a few individuals who focused on one specific issue, the IETF was large — before the reorganization, it had grown to include dozens of active members who worked on many problems concurrently. Following the reorganization, the IETF was divided into over 20 *working groups*, each of which focused on a specific problem.

Because the IETF was too large for a single chairman to manage, it has been divided into approximately ten areas, each with its own manager. The IETF chairman and the area managers constitute the *Internet Engineering Steering Group* (*IESG*), the individuals responsible for coordinating the efforts of IETF working groups. The name ''IETF'' now refers to the entire body, including the chairman, area managers, and all members of working groups.

1.7 Internet Request For Comments

We have said that no vendor owns the TCP/IP technology nor does any professional society or standards body. Thus, the documentation of protocols, standards, and policies cannot be obtained from a vendor. Instead, the documentation is placed in on-line repositories and made available at no charge.

Documentation of work on the Internet, proposals for new or revised protocols, and TCP/IP protocol standards all appear in a series of technical reports called Internet *Requests For Comments*, or *RFCs*. RFCs can be short or long, can cover broad concepts or details, and can be standards or merely proposals for new protocols. There are references to RFCs throughout the text. While RFCs are not refereed in the same way as academic research papers, they are edited. For many years, a single individual, the late Jon Postel, served as RFC editor. The task of editing RFCs now falls to area managers of the IETF; the IESG as a whole approves new RFCs.

The RFC series is numbered sequentially in the chronological order RFCs are written. Each new or revised RFC is assigned a new number, so readers must be careful to obtain the highest numbered version of a document; an RFC index is available to help identify the correct version. In addition, preliminary versions of RFC documents, which are known as *Internet drafts*, are available.

RFCs and Internet Drafts can be obtained from:

www.ietf.org

1.8 Future Growth And Technology

Both the TCP/IP technology and the Internet continue to evolve. New protocols are being proposed; old ones are being revised. The most significant demand on the underlying technology does not arise from added network connections, but from additional traffic. As new users connect to the Internet and new applications appear, traffic patterns change. For example, when users began to browse information using services like the *World Wide Web*, traffic increased dramatically. Later, when file sharing became popular, traffic patterns changed again. More changes are occurring as the Internet is used for telephone and video services.

Figure 1.1 summarizes expansion of the Internet, and illustrates an important component of growth: much of the change in complexity has arisen because multiple groups now manage various parts of the whole. Because the technology was developed when a single person at DARPA had control of all aspects of the Internet, the designs of many subsystems depended on centralized management and control. As the Internet grew, responsibility and control were divided among multiple organizations. In particular, as the Internet became global, the operation and management needed to span multiple countries. Much of the effort since the early 1990s was directed toward finding ways to extend the design to accommodate decentralized management.

	number of networks	number of computers	number of users	number of managers
1980	10	10^2	10^2	10^0
1990	10^3	10^5	10^6	10^1
2000	10^5	10^7	10^8	10^2
2005	10^6	10^8	10^9	10^3

Figure 1.1 Growth of the Internet. In addition to increases in traffic, complexity has resulted from decentralized management.

1.9 Organization Of The Text

The material on TCP/IP has been written in three volumes. This volume presents the TCP/IP technology, applications that use it, and the architecture of the global Internet in more detail. It discusses the fundamentals of protocols like TCP and IP, and shows how they fit together in an internet. In addition to giving details, the text highlights the general principles underlying network protocols, and explains why the TCP/IP protocols adapt easily to so many underlying physical network technologies. Volume II discusses protocols in more depth, and explains the internal organization of protocol software. It presents code from a working system to illustrate how the individual protocols work together. Volume III shows how distributed applications use TCP/IP for communication. It focuses on the client-server paradigm, the basis for all distributed programming. It discusses the interface between programs and protocols†, and shows how client and server programs are organized. In addition, Volume III describes the remote procedure concept, middleware, and shows how programmers use tools to build client and server software.

So far, we have talked about the TCP/IP technology and the Internet in general terms, summarizing the services provided and the history of their development. The next chapter provides a brief summary of the type of network hardware used throughout the Internet. Its purpose is not to illuminate nuances of a particular vendor's hardware, but to focus on the features of each technology that are of primary importance to an internet architect. Later chapters delve into the protocols and the Internet, fulfilling three purposes: they explore general concepts and review the Internet architectural model, they examine the details of TCP/IP protocols, and they look at standards for high-level services like electronic mail and electronic file transfer. Chapters 3 through 12 review fundamental principles and describe the network protocol software found in any machine that uses TCP/IP. Later chapters describe services that span multiple machines, including the propagation of routing information, name resolution, and applications like electronic mail.

An appendix that follows the main text contains an alphabetical list of terms and abbreviations used throughout the literature and the text. Because beginners often find the new terminology overwhelming and difficult to remember, they are encouraged to use the alphabetical list instead of scanning back through the text.

1.10 Summary

An internet consists of a set of connected networks that act as a coordinated whole. The chief advantage of an internet is that it provides universal interconnection while allowing individual groups to use whatever network hardware is best suited to their needs. We will examine principles underlying internet communication in general and the details of one internet protocol suite in particular. We will also discuss how internet protocols are used in an internet. Our example technology, called TCP/IP after its two main protocols, was developed by the Defense Advanced Research Projects Agency. It

---

†Volume III is available in three versions: one that uses the Linux *socket interface*, a second that uses the *Windows Sockets Interface* defined by Microsoft, and a third that uses the *Transport Layer Interface* (*TLI*).

provides the basis for the global Internet, an internet that connects individuals, businesses, governments, and other organizations in countries around the world. The global Internet is expanding rapidly.

FOR FURTHER STUDY

Cerf's *A History Of The ARPANET* [1989] and *History of the Internet Activities Board* [RFC 1160] provide fascinating reading and point the reader to early research papers on TCP/IP and internetworking. Denning [Nov-Dec 1989] provides a different perspective on the history of the ARPANET. Jennings et. al. [1986] discusses the importance of computer networking for scientists. Denning [Sept-Oct 1989] also points out the importance of internetworking and gives one possible scenario for a world-wide Internet. The U.S. Federal Coordinating Committee for Science, Engineering and Technology (*FCCSET*) suggested networking should be a national priority.

The IETF (*ietf.org*) publishes minutes from its regular meetings. The World Wide Web Consortium (*w3c.org*) produces protocols and standards for Web technologies. Finally, the reader is encouraged to remember that the TCP/IP protocol suite and the Internet continue to evolve; new information can be found in RFCs and at conferences such as the annual ACM SIGCOMM Symposium.

EXERCISES

1.1 Explore application programs at your site that use TCP/IP.

1.2 Plot the growth of TCP/IP technology and Internet access at your organization. How many computers, users, and networks were connected each year?

1.3 TCP/IP products account for billions of dollars per year in gross revenue. Read trade publications to find a list of vendors offering such products.

Chapter Contents

2

Review Of Underlying
Network Technologies

2.1 Introduction

It is important to understand that the Internet is not a new kind of physical network. It is, instead, a method of interconnecting physical networks and a set of conventions for using networks that allow the computers they reach to interact. While network hardware plays only a minor role in the overall design, understanding the internet technology requires one to distinguish between the low-level mechanisms provided by the hardware itself and the higher-level facilities that the TCP/IP protocol software provides. It is also important to understand how the interfaces supplied by underlying packet-switched technology affect our choice of high-level abstractions.

This chapter introduces basic packet-switching concepts and terminology, and then reviews some of the underlying network hardware technologies that have been used in TCP/IP internets. Later chapters describe how these networks are interconnected and how the TCP/IP protocols accommodate vast differences in the hardware. While the list presented here is certainly not comprehensive, it clearly demonstrates the variety among physical networks over which TCP/IP operates. The reader can safely skip many of the technical details, but should try to grasp the idea of packet switching and try to imagine building a homogeneous communication system using such heterogeneous hardware. Most important, the reader should look closely at the details of the physical address schemes the various technologies use; later chapters will discuss in detail how high-level protocols use physical addresses.

2.2 Two Approaches To Network Communication

Whether they provide connections between one computer and another or between a terminal and a computer, communication networks can be divided into two basic types: *connection-oriented* (sometimes called *circuit-switched*) and *connectionless* (sometimes called *packet-switched*†). Connection-oriented networks operate by forming a dedicated *connection* or *circuit* between two points. Traditional telephone systems use a connection-oriented technology — a telephone call establishes a connection from the originating phone through the local switching office, across trunk lines, to a remote switching office, and finally to the destination telephone‡. While a connection is in place, the phone equipment samples the microphone repeatedly, encodes the samples digitally, and transmits them across the connection to the receiver. The sender is guaranteed that the samples can be delivered and reproduced because the connection provides a guaranteed data path of 64 Kbps (thousand bits per second), the rate needed to send digitized voice. The advantage of connection-oriented networking lies in its guaranteed capacity: once a circuit is established, no other network activity will decrease the capacity of that circuit. One disadvantage of connection-oriented technology arises from cost: circuit costs are fixed, independent of use. For example, one pays a fixed rate for a phone call, even when the two parties do not talk.

Connectionless networks, the type often used to connect computers, take an entirely different approach. In a connectionless network, data to be transferred across a network is divided into small pieces called *packets* that are multiplexed onto high capacity intermachine connections. A packet, which usually contains only a few hundred bytes of data, carries identification that enables the network hardware to know how to send it to the specified destination. For example, a large file to be transmitted between two machines must be broken into many packets that are sent across the network one at a time. The network hardware delivers the packets to the specified destination, where software reassembles them into a single file again. The chief advantage of packet-switching is that multiple communications among computers can proceed concurrently, with intermachine connections shared by all pairs of computers that are communicating. The disadvantage, of course, is that as activity increases, a given pair of communicating computers receives less of the network capacity. That is, whenever a packet switched network becomes overloaded, computers using the network must wait before they can send additional packets.

Despite the potential drawback of not being able to guarantee network capacity, connectionless networks have become extremely popular. The motivations for adopting packet switching are cost and performance. Because multiple computers can share the network bandwidth, fewer connections are required and cost is kept low. Because engineers have been able to build high-speed network hardware, capacity is not usually a problem. So many computer interconnections use connectionless networks that, throughout the remainder of this text, we will assume the term *network* refers to a connectionless network unless otherwise stated.

---

†Hybrid technologies are also possible.

‡IP-based telephony is replacing traditional telephone technology.

2.3 Wide Area And Local Area Networks

Data networks that span large geographical distances (e.g., the continental U.S.) are fundamentally different from those that span short distances (e.g., a single room). To help characterize the differences in capacity and intended use, packet switched technologies are often divided into two broad categories: *Wide Area Networks* (*WANs*) and *Local Area Networks* (*LANs*). The two categories do not have formal definitions. Instead, vendors apply the terms loosely to help customers distinguish among technologies.

WAN technologies, sometimes called *long haul networks*, provide communication over long distances. Most WAN technologies do not limit the distance spanned; a WAN can allow the endpoints of a communication to be arbitrarily far apart. For example, a WAN can span a continent or can join computers across an ocean. Usually, WANs operate at slower speeds than LANs, and have much greater delay between connections. Typical speeds for a WAN range from 1.5 Mbps (million bits per second) to 2.4 Gbps (billion bits per second). Delays across a WAN can vary from a few milliseconds to several tenths of a second†.

LAN technologies provide the highest speed connections among computers, but sacrifice the ability to span long distances. For example, a typical LAN spans a small area like a single building or a small campus, and operates between 100 Mbps and 10 Gbps. Because LAN technologies cover short distances, they offer lower delays than WANs. The delay across a LAN can be as short as a few tenths of a millisecond or as long as 10 milliseconds.

We have already stated the general tradeoff between speed and distance: technologies that provide higher speed communication operate over shorter distances. There are other differences among the technologies as well. In LAN technologies, each computer usually contains a device known as a *Network Interface Card* (*NIC*) that connects the machine directly to the network. The network itself need not contain much intelligence; it can depend on electronic interface devices in the attached computers to generate and receive the complex electrical signals. In WAN technologies, a network usually consists of a series of complex computers called *packet switches* interconnected by long-distance communication lines. The size of the network can be extended by adding a new switch and another communication line. Attaching a user's computer to a WAN means connecting it to one of the packet switches. Each switch along a path in the WAN introduces delay when it receives a packet and forwards it to the next switch. Thus, the larger the WAN becomes the longer it takes to forward traffic across it.

This book discusses protocol software that hides the technological differences among networks and makes interconnection independent of the underlying hardware. To appreciate design choices in the software, it is necessary to understand how it relates to network hardware. The next sections present examples of network technologies that have been used in the Internet, showing some of the differences among them. Later chapters show how the TCP/IP software isolates such differences and makes the communication system independent of the underlying hardware technology.

---

†Such long delays result from WANs that communicate by sending signals to a satellite orbiting the earth.

2.3.1 Network Hardware Addresses

Each network hardware technology defines an *addressing mechanism* that computers use to specify the destination for a packet. Every computer attached to a network is assigned a unique address, usually an integer. A packet sent across a network includes a *destination address field* that contains the address of the intended recipient. The destination address appears in the same location in all packets, making it possible for the network hardware to examine the destination address easily. A sender must know the address of the intended recipient, and must place the recipient's address in the destination address field of a packet before transmitting the packet.

Each hardware technology specifies how computers are assigned addresses. The hardware specifies, for example, the number of bits in the address as well as the location of the destination address field in a packet. Although some technologies use compatible addressing schemes, many do not. This chapter contains a few examples of hardware addressing schemes; later chapters explain how TCP/IP accommodates diverse hardware addressing schemes.

2.4 Ethernet Technology

Ethernet is the name given to a popular packet-switched LAN technology invented at Xerox PARC in the early 1970s. Xerox Corporation, Intel Corporation, and Digital Equipment Corporation standardized Ethernet in 1978; IEEE released a compatible version of the standard using the standard number *802.3*. Ethernet has become the most popular LAN technology; it now appears in virtually all corporate and personal networks. Because Ethernet is so popular, many variants exist. The original wiring scheme, which consisted of a coaxial cable to which all computers attached, has been superseded. The current technology is known as *twisted pair Ethernet* because it allows a computer to access an Ethernet using conventional unshielded copper wires similar to the wires used to connect telephones†. The chief advantages of using twisted pair wiring (which is known as *category 5 cable*) are that it reduces costs and is easier to install than coaxial cable.

Formally known as *10Base-T*, the first twisted pair Ethernet operated at 10 Mbps, exactly like the original Ethernet. A set of eight wires (four pairs) is used to connect each computer to a central Ethernet *hub* or *switch*, as Figure 2.1 shows. Only four of the eight wires are used: one pair carries data from the computer to the hub, and another pair carries data from the hub to the computer.

---

†The term *twisted pair* arises because conventional telephone wiring uses the technique of twisting the wires to avoid interference.

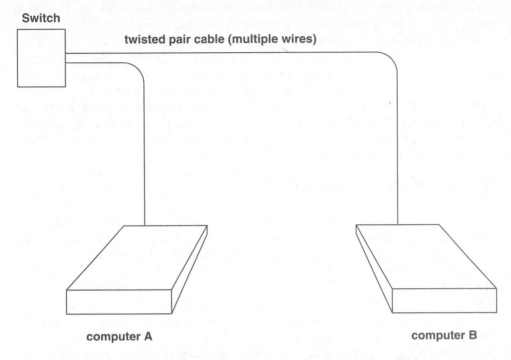

Switch

twisted pair cable (multiple wires)

computer A   computer B

Figure 2.1 An illustration of Ethernet using twisted pair wiring. Each computer connects to a switch using a cable with multiple twisted pairs.

The hub is an electronic device that simulates the signals on an Ethernet cable. Physically, a hub consists of a small box that usually resides in a wiring closet; a connection between a hub and a computer must be less than 100 meters long. A hub requires power, and can allow authorized personnel to monitor and control its operation over the network. To a computer, a network interface card that connects to a hub appears to operate as an I/O device that can be used to send or receive data.

2.4.1 Ethernet Capacity

Although the wiring scheme evolved from the original coaxial cable to twisted pair, much of the original Ethernet design remained the same. In particular, the initial twisted pair Ethernet design operated at the same rate as the original Ethernet: data could be transmitted at 10 million bits per second. Although a computer can generate data at Ethernet speed, raw network speed should not be thought of as the rate at which two computers can exchange data. Instead, network speed should be thought of as a measure of total traffic capacity. Think of a network as a highway connecting multiple cities, and think of packets as cars on the highway. High bandwidth makes it possible to carry heavy traffic loads, while low bandwidth means the highway cannot carry as much traffic. A 10 Mbps Ethernet, for example, can handle a few computers that generate heavy loads, or many computers that generate light loads.

In the late 1970s when Ethernet was standardized, a LAN operating at 10 Mbps had more than sufficient capacity for many computers because the available CPU speeds and network interface hardware prohibited a given computer from transmitting data rapidly. By the mid 1990s, however, CPU speeds had increased dramatically as had the use of networks. Consequently, an Ethernet operating at 10 Mbps did not have sufficient capacity to act as a central corporate backbone for even a moderate sized corporation — Ethernet had become a bottleneck.

2.4.2 Fast And Gigabit Ethernet

To overcome the throughput limitation of Ethernet, engineers designed faster versions of Ethernet. A version marketed as *Fast Ethernet* operates at 100 million bits per second, and *Gigabit Ethernet* (*GigE*) operates at 1000 million bits per second. Known formally as *100Base-T*, and *1000Base-T*, the faster versions use the same category 5 twisted pair wiring that is used for 10Base-T; the increase in speed is achieved by using more of the wires to carry data and changing the signaling mechanism.

In addition to Gigabit Ethernet over copper wiring, IEEE has defined a standard for Ethernet over optical fiber. Known as *1000Base-X*, the technology converts an Ethernet packet into pulses of light, which are then transferred across a fiber. The chief advantages of optical fiber are: higher capacity and immunity to electrical interference. The capacity of fiber is sufficient to support bit rates much higher than 1 Gbps. Thus, engineers are already developing 10 and 40 Gbps Ethernet technologies.

To understand the significance of increase in capacity, it is important to understand two facts. First, although computers have become faster, few computer systems can transmit data at a sustained rate of 1 Gbps. Second, the new versions of Ethernet did not change other parts of the standard. In particular, the maximum packet size remains the same as for 10Base-T. These two facts imply that higher-speed Ethernet technologies were not optimized to provide the highest possible throughput between a pair of computers. Instead, the design is optimized to allow more stations and more total traffic.

2.4.3 10/100/1000 Ethernet

Soon after the invention of Fast Ethernet, manufacturers began to build devices that could accept either a 10 or 100 Mbps connection; modern Ethernet can operate at 10, 100, or 1000 Mbps. The technology, known as *10/100/1000 Ethernet* is available for NICs as well as for switches. More important, a 10/100/1000 device automatically negotiates when it is first connected to determine the types of cable (straight through or cross-over) and the maximum speed that the other side of the connection can support.

In essence, the hardware interjects extra signals that the other side of the connection can use to determine the correct configuration.

Automatic negotiation and retention of the original packet format means that a computer can be moved between a 10 Mbps Ethernet switch to a Gigabit switch without reconfiguring the software or changing the device driver. From a protocol point of view, the underlying hardware and wiring only changes the speed with which packets can be sent; the packets themselves are interchangeable across Ethernet technologies.

2.4.4 Power Over Ethernet

In addition to other innovations, engineers have developed a technology known as *Power over Ethernet* (*PoE*) that can send a small amount of electrical power over the same copper cable used for Ethernet. The important point is that the technology is arranged so the presence of power does not degrade data transmission. Although the amount of power that PoE supplies is insufficient for a computer, the innovation is particularly important for small devices such as an IP telephone because it means the device needs only one cable.

2.4.5 Properties of an Ethernet

Ethernet was designed to be a shared bus technology that supports broadcast, uses best-effort delivery semantics, and has distributed access control. The topology is called a *shared bus* because all stations connect to a single, shared communication channel; it is called a *broadcast technology* because all stations receive every transmission, making it possible to transmit a packet to all stations at the same time. The methods used to direct packets from one station to just one other station or a subset of all stations will be discussed later. Ethernet is called a *best-effort delivery* mechanism because the hardware provides no information to the sender about whether the packet was delivered. For example, if the destination machine happens to be powered down, packets sent to it will be lost and the sender will not be notified. We will see later how the TCP/IP protocols accommodate best-effort delivery hardware.

Ethernet access control is distributed because, unlike some network technologies, Ethernet has no central authority to grant access. The Ethernet access scheme is called *Carrier Sense Multiple Access* with *Collision Detect* (*CSMA/CD*). It is *CSMA* because multiple machines can access an Ethernet simultaneously and each machine determines whether the network is idle by sensing whether a carrier wave is present. When a host interface has a packet to transmit, it listens to see if a message is being transmitted (i.e., performs carrier sensing). When no transmission is sensed, the host interface starts transmitting. Each transmission is limited in duration because there is a maximum packet size. Furthermore, the hardware must observe a minimum idle time between transmissions, which means that no single pair of communicating machines can use the network without giving other machines an opportunity for access.

2.4.6 Collision Detection And Recovery

When a station begins transmission, the signal does not reach all parts of the network simultaneously. Instead it travels along copper wires at approximately 70% of the speed of light. Thus, it is possible for two stations to both sense that the network is idle and begin transmission simultaneously. When the two electrical signals cross they become scrambled, meaning that neither remains meaningful. Such incidents are called *collisions*.

The Ethernet handles collisions in an ingenious fashion. Each station monitors the cable while it is transmitting to see if a foreign signal interferes with its transmission. Technically, the monitoring is called *collision detection* (*CD*), making the Ethernet a CSMA/CD network. When a collision is detected, the host interface aborts transmission, waits for activity to subside, and tries again. Care must be taken or the network could wind up with all stations busily attempting to transmit and every transmission producing a collision. To help avoid such situations, Ethernet uses a binary exponential backoff policy where a sender delays a random time after the first collision, doubles the range if a second attempt to transmit also produces a collision, quadruples the range if a third attempt results in a collision, and so on. The motivation for exponential backoff is that in the unlikely event many stations attempt to transmit simultaneously, a severe traffic jam could occur. In such a jam, there is a high probability two stations will choose random backoffs that are close together. Thus, the probability of another collision is high. By doubling the range of the random delay, the exponential backoff strategy quickly spreads the stations' attempts to retransmit over a reasonably long period of time, making the probability of further collisions extremely small.

2.4.7 Wireless Networks And Ethernet

IEEE has developed a series of standards for wireless networks that are closely related to Ethernet. The most well-known, which has IEEE standard number *802.11b* and is marketed under the name *Wi-Fi*, is available on many laptop computers. Wi-Fi provides bandwidth up to 11 Mbps, but typically operates between 2.5 to 4 Mbps; alternatives that operates up to 54 Mbps have numbers *802.11a* and *802.11g*† Each of the three standards can be used in two forms: as access technologies in which a single base station (called an *access point*) accommodates multiple clients (e.g., users with laptops), and in a point-to-point configuration used to connect exactly two access points. IEEE has also defined a higher-speed technology intended primarily for point-to-point interconnections. Marketed as *Wi-Max* and assigned the standard number *802.16*, the technology is of most interest to network providers or corporations that need to connect two sites. Finally, IEEE has plans to introduce an *802.11n* wireless standard for 540 Mbps and an *802.11i* standard for security.

---

†802.11g can interoperate with 802.11b.

2.4.8 Ethernet Hardware Addresses

Ethernet defines a 48-bit addressing scheme that has become a standard for the industry. Each network interface card is assigned a unique 48-bit number known as an *Ethernet address*. To assign an address, Ethernet hardware manufacturers purchase blocks of Ethernet addresses† and assign them in sequence as they manufacture Ethernet interface hardware. Thus, no two hardware interfaces have the same Ethernet address.

Usually, the Ethernet address is fixed in machine readable form on the host interface hardware. Because each Ethernet address belongs to a hardware device, they are sometimes called *hardware addresses*, *physical addresses*, *media access (MAC) addresses*, or *layer 2 addresses*. Note the following important property of Ethernet physical addresses:

> *An Ethernet address is associated with the interface hardware, not the computer; moving the hardware interface to a new machine or replacing a hardware interface that has failed changes the machine's physical address.*

Knowing that Ethernet physical addresses can change will make it clear why higher levels of the network software are designed to accommodate such changes.

Recall that when computers connect to a hub, each computer receives a copy of every packet that passes through a hub — even those addressed to other machines. The host interface hardware uses the destination address field in a packet as a filter. The interface ignores those packets that are addressed to other machines, and passes to the host only those packets addressed to it. Although the computer's central processor could perform the check, doing so in the host interface keeps traffic on the Ethernet from slowing down processing on all computers.

A 48-bit Ethernet address can do more than specify a single destination computer. An address can be one of three types:

- The physical address of one network interface (a *unicast address*)
- The network *broadcast address*
- A *multicast address*

By convention, the broadcast address (all 1s) is reserved for sending to all stations simultaneously. Multicast addresses provide a limited form of broadcast in which a subset of the computers on a network agree to listen to a given multicast address. The set of participating computers is called a *multicast group*. To join a multicast group, a computer must instruct its host interface to accept the group's multicast address. The advantage of multicasting lies in the ability to limit broadcasts: every computer in a multicast group can be reached with a single packet transmission, but computers that choose not to participate in a particular multicast group do not receive packets sent to the group.

---

†The Institute for Electrical and Electronic Engineers (IEEE) manages the Ethernet address space and assigns addresses as needed.

To accommodate broadcast and multicast addressing, Ethernet interface hardware must recognize multiple addresses. An interface accepts at least two kinds of packets: those addressed to the interface's physical (i.e., unicast) address and those addressed to the network broadcast address. Some interfaces can be configured to accept specific multicast addresses, an alternate physical address, or all packets (known as *promiscuous mode* and used for monitoring). When a computer boots, the operating system initializes and configures the interface, by specifying the addresses to accept. The interface then examines the destination address field in each packet, passing on to the computer only those packets allowed by the configuration.

2.4.9 Ethernet Frame Format

Ethernet should be thought of as a link-level connection among machines. Thus, we say that an Ethernet transmits a *frame*†. Ethernet frames are of variable length, with no frame smaller than 64 octets‡ or larger than 1518 octets (header, data, and CRC). As in all packet-switched networks, each Ethernet frame contains a field that holds the address of its destination. Figure 2.2 shows that the Ethernet frame format contains the physical source address as well as the destination address.

Preamble	Destination Address	Source Address	Frame Type	Frame Data	CRC
8 octets	6 octets	6 octets	2 octets	46–1500 octets	4 octets

Figure 2.2 The format of an Ethernet frame (packet). The frame is preceded by a preamble and followed by an inter-packet gap. Fields are not drawn to scale.

In addition to identifying the source and destination, each frame transmitted across the Ethernet contains a *preamble, type field, data field,* and *Cyclic Redundancy Check* (*CRC*). The preamble consists of 64 bits of alternating *0*s and *1*s to help receiving interfaces synchronize. The 32-bit CRC helps the interface detect transmission errors: the sender computes the CRC as a function of the data in the frame, and the receiver recomputes the CRC to verify that the packet has been received intact.

The frame type field contains a 16-bit integer that identifies the type of data being carried in the frame. From the Internet point of view, the frame type field is essential because it means Ethernet frames are *self-identifying*. When a frame arrives at a given machine, the operating system uses the frame type to determine which protocol software module should process the frame. The chief advantages of self-identifying frames are that they allow multiple protocols to be used together on a single computer and they allow multiple protocols to be intermixed on the same physical network without interference. For example, one can have an application program on a computer using Internet

---

†The term *frame* derives from communication over serial lines in which the sender "frames" the data by adding special characters before and after the transmitted data.

‡Technically, the term *byte* refers to a hardware-dependent character size; networking professionals use the term *octet*, because it refers to an 8-bit quantity on all computers.

protocols while another application on the same computer uses a local experimental protocol. The operating system examines the type field of each arriving frame to decide how to process the contents. We will see that the TCP/IP protocols use self-identifying Ethernet frames to distinguish among several protocols.

2.4.10 Extending An Ethernet With Bridges

An *Ethernet bridge* is a device that connects two Ethernets and passes frames between them. A bridge does not replicate noise, errors, or malformed frames; the bridge must receive a completely valid frame from one segment before the bridge will accept and transmit it on the other segment. Furthermore, each connection between a bridge and an Ethernet network follows the CSMA/CD rules, so collisions and propagation delays on one segment remain isolated from those on the other. As a result, an (almost) arbitrary number of Ethernets can be connected together with bridges. Bridging is used in many network systems. For example, a typical *cable modem* and *Digital Subscriber Line* (*DSL*) connections used for broadband Internet service implement bridging — Ethernet frames sent at the residence are bridged to the ISP, and vice versa.

From our point of view, the most important point to understand about bridging is:

> *Bridges hide the details of interconnection: a set of bridged segments acts like a single Ethernet.*

That is, bridged networks are classified as *transparent* because a computer does not know how many bridges connect segments of the network. The computer uses exactly the same hardware, frame format, and procedures to communicate with a computer across a bridge as it uses to communicate with a computer on a local hub.

Most bridges do much more than replicate frames from one wire to another: they make intelligent decisions about which frames to forward. Such bridges are called *adaptive* or *learning* bridges. An adaptive bridge consists of a computer with two Ethernet interfaces. The software in an adaptive bridge keeps two address lists, one for each interface. When a frame arrives from Ethernet E_1, the adaptive bridge adds the 48-bit Ethernet *source* address to the list associated with E_1. Similarly, when a frame arrives from Ethernet E_2, the bridge adds the source address to the list associated with E_2. Thus, over time the adaptive bridge will learn which machines lie on E_1 and which lie on E_2.

After recording the source address of a frame, the adaptive bridge uses the destination address to determine whether to forward the frame. If the address list shows that the destination lies on the Ethernet from which the frame arrived, the bridge does not forward the frame. If the destination is not in the address list (i.e., the destination is a broadcast or multicast address or the bridge has not yet learned the location of the destination), the bridge forwards the frame to the other Ethernet.

The advantages of adaptive bridges should be obvious. Because the bridge uses addresses found in normal traffic, it is completely automatic — humans need not configure the bridge with specific addresses. Because it does not forward traffic unnecessarily, a bridge helps improve the performance of an overloaded network by isolating traffic on specific segments. Bridges work exceptionally well if a network can be divided physically into two segments that each contain a set of computers that communicate frequently (e.g., each segment contains a set of workstations along with a server, and the workstations direct most of their traffic to the server). To summarize:

> *An adaptive Ethernet bridge connects two Ethernet segments, forwarding frames from one to the other. It uses source addresses to learn which machines lie on which Ethernet segment, and it combines information learned with destination addresses to eliminate forwarding when unnecessary.*

From the TCP/IP point of view, bridged Ethernets are merely another form of physical network connection. The important point is:

> *Because the connection among Ethernets provided by a bridge is transparent to machines using the Ethernet, we think of multiple Ethernet segments connected by bridges as a single physical network system.*

Most commercial bridges are much more sophisticated and robust than our description indicates. When first powered up, they check for other bridges and learn the topology of the network. They use a distributed spanning-tree algorithm to decide how to forward frames. In particular, the bridges decide how to propagate broadcast packets so only one copy of a broadcast frame is delivered to each wire. Without such an algorithm, Ethernets and bridges connected in a cycle would produce catastrophic results because they would forward broadcast packets in both directions simultaneously.

2.5 Switched Ethernet

An *Ethernet switch* is a device that incorporates and extends the concept of bridging. A switch provides multiple connections, called *ports*, into which devices connect. Like a bridge, a switch uses the source address and destination address in each incoming frame when forwarding the frame. The switch uses the source address to determine which computer attaches to each port on the switch, and uses the destination address in the frame to determine where the frame should be sent. Thus, an Ethernet switch can be viewed as analogous to a multi-port bridge.

2.6 Asynchronous Transfer Mode

Asynchronous Transfer Mode (ATM) is the name given to a connection-oriented networking technology that is intended for use in both local area and wide area networks. ATM was designed to permit high-speed data switching. To achieve high transfer speeds, ATM uses special-purpose hardware and software techniques. First, an ATM network consists of one or more high-speed switches that each connect to computers and to other ATM switches. Second, the lowest layers of an ATM network use fixed-size frames called *cells*. Because each cell is exactly the same size, ATM switch hardware can process cells quickly.

2.6.1 ATM Cell Size

Surprisingly, each ATM cell is only 53 octets long. The cell contains 5 octets of header followed by 48 octets of data. Later chapters will show, however, that when using ATM to send IP traffic, the 53 octet size is irrelevant — an ATM network accepts and delivers much larger packets.

2.6.2 Connection-Oriented Networking

ATM differs from the packet-switching networks described earlier because it offers *connection-oriented* service. Before a computer connected to an ATM switch can send cells, a connection must be established manually or the host must first interact with the switch to specify a destination. The interaction is analogous to placing a telephone call†. The requesting computer specifies the remote computer's address, and waits for the ATM switch to find a path through the network and establish a connection. If the remote computer rejects the request, does not respond, or the ATM switches between the sender and receiver cannot currently establish a path, the request to establish communication fails.

Once a connection succeeds, the local ATM switch chooses an identifier for the connection, and passes the connection identifier to the computer along with a message that informs the computer of success. The computer uses the connection identifier when sending or receiving cells.

When it finishes using an ATM connection, a computer again communicates with the ATM switch to request that the connection be broken. The switch then disconnects the two computers. Disconnection is equivalent to hanging up a telephone at the end of a telephone call; after a disconnection, the computers cannot communicate until they establish a new connection. Furthermore, identifiers used for a connection can be recycled; once a disconnection occurs, the switch can reuse the connection identifier for a new connection.

---

†Because ATM arose from phone companies interested in carrying voice as well as data, a strong relationship exists between the ATM design and a telephone system.

2.6.3 Wide Area Point-To-Point Networks

Although WAN services such as ATM, *Switched Multimegabit Data Service* (SMDS) and *X.25* exist, modern WANs are formed by leasing data circuits from a telephone company and using the circuits to interconnect network elements. Phone companies originally designed digital circuits to carry digitized voice calls; only later did their use in data networks become important. Consequently, the data rates of available circuits are not powers of ten. Instead, they have been chosen to carry multiples of 64 Kbps because a digitized voice call uses an encoding known as *Pulse Code Modulation* (*PCM*) which produces 8000 samples per second, where each sample is 8 bits.

The table in Figure 2.3 lists a few common data rates used in North America and Europe.

Name	Bit Rate	Voice Circuits	Location
–	0.064 Mbps	1	
T1	1.544 Mbps	24	North America
T2	6.312 Mbps	96	North America
T3	44.736 Mbps	672	North America
T4	274.760 Mbps	4032	North America
E1	2.048 Mbps	30	Europe
E2	8.448 Mbps	120	Europe
E3	34.368 Mbps	480	Europe
E4	139.264 Mbps	1920	Europe

Figure 2.3 Example data rates available on digital circuits leased from a telephone company. The rates were chosen to encode multiple voice calls.

Higher-rate digital circuits require the use of fiber. In addition to standards that specify the transmission of high data rates over copper, the phone companies have developed standards for transmission of the same rates over optical fiber. The table in Figure 2.4 contains examples. Of course, circuits that operate at such high data rates are considerably more expensive than circuits that operate at lower rates.

From TCP/IP's point of view, any communication system that connects exactly two computers is known as a *point-to-point network*. Thus, a leased data circuit between two computers is an example of a point-to-point network. Of course, using the term ''network'' to describe a connection between two computers stretches the concept. However, we will learn that viewing a connection as a network helps maintain consistency. For now, we only need to note that a point-to-point network differs from a conventional network in one significant way: because only two computers attach, no hardware addresses are needed. When we discuss internet address binding, the lack of hardware addresses will make point-to-point networks an exception.

Standard Name	Optical Name	Bit Rate	Voice Circuits
STS-1	OC-1	51.840 Mbps	810
STS-3	OC-3	155.520 Mbps	2430
STS-12	OC-12	622.080 Mbps	9720
STS-24	OC-24	1,244.160 Mbps	19440
STS-48	OC-48	2.488 Gbps	38880
STS-96	OC-96	4.976 Gbps	64512
STS-192	OC-192	9.952 Gbps	129024
STS-256	OC-256	13.271 Gbps	172032

Figure 2.4 Example data rates of high-capacity circuits that can be leased from phone companies. Optical fiber is used to achieve the high rates over long distances.

2.6.4 Dialup IP

Dialup internet access provides another example of a point-to-point network. A dialup modem in a computer is used to place a phone call to another modem. Typically the call originates at a residence and terminates at an ISP. Once the phone connection is in place, the two modems use audio tones to send data. From the TCP/IP view, dialing a telephone call is equivalent to running a wire. Once the call has been answered by a modem on the other end, there is a connection from one computer directly to another, and the connection stays in place as long as needed.

2.7 Summary

We have reviewed several network hardware technologies used by the TCP/IP protocols, ranging from inexpensive Local Area Network technologies like Ethernet to expensive leased digital circuits that are used for Wide Area connections. While the details of specific network technologies are not important, a general idea has emerged:

The TCP/IP protocols are extremely flexible; almost any underlying technology can be used to transfer TCP/IP traffic.

FOR FURTHER STUDY

Early computer communication systems employed point-to-point interconnection, often using general-purpose serial line hardware that McNamara [1988] describes. Metcalfe and Boggs [1976] introduces the Ethernet with a 3 Mbps prototype version. Digital *et. al.* [1980] specifies the original 10 Mbps Ethernet standard; the IEEE standard is numbered 802.3. Information about Ethernet cabling is available on-line. Shoch, Dalal, and Redell [1982] provides an historical perspective of the Ethernet evolution. Related work on the ALOHA network is reported in Abramson [1970], with a survey of technologies given by Cotton [1980].

For more information on the ARPANET see Cerf [1989] and BBN [1981]. Lanzillo and Partridge [January 1989] describes dial-up IP. De Prycker [1995] describes Asynchronous Transfer Mode and its use for wide area services. Partridge [1994] surveys many gigabit technologies, including ATM, and describes the internal structure of high-speed switches.

EXERCISES

2.1 Find out which network technologies your site uses.

2.2 If Ethernet frames are sent over an OC-192 leased circuit, how long does it take to transmit the largest possible frame? The smallest possible frame? (Note: exclude the preamble from your calculations.)

2.3 Study Ethernet switch technology. How does a switch differ from a hub?

2.4 If your site uses switched Ethernet technology, find out how many connections can be attached to a single switch and how switches are interconnected.

2.5 Read about VLAN Ethernet switches. What capability does a VLAN switch add to a conventional switch?

2.6 Read the Ethernet standard to find exact details of the inter-packet gap and preamble size. What is the maximum steady-state rate at which Ethernet can transport data?

2.7 What characteristic of a satellite communication channel is most desirable? Least desirable?

2.8 Find a lower bound on the time it takes to transfer a 5 megabyte file across a network that operates at: 28.8 Kbps, 1.54 Mbps, 10 Mbps, 100 Mbps, and 2.4 Gbps.

2.9 Does the processor, disk, and internal bus on your computer operate fast enough to send data from a disk file at 2 gigabits per second?

Chapter Contents

3

Internetworking Concept And Architectural Model

3.1 Introduction

So far we have looked at the low-level details of transmission across individual data networks, the foundation on which all computer communication is built. This chapter makes a giant conceptual leap by describing a scheme that allows us to collect the diverse network technologies into a coordinated whole. The primary goal is a system that hides the details of underlying network hardware while providing universal communication services. The primary result is a high-level abstraction that provides the framework for all design decisions. Succeeding chapters show how we use this abstraction to build the necessary layers of internet communication software and how the software hides the underlying physical transport mechanisms. Later chapters also show how applications use the resulting communication system.

3.2 Application-Level Interconnection

Designers have taken two different approaches to hiding network details, using application programs to handle heterogeneity or hiding details in the operating system. Early heterogeneous network interconnections provided uniformity through application-level programs called *application gateways*. In such systems, an application-level program, executing on each computer in the network, understands the details of the network connections for that computer, and interoperates across those connections with application programs on other computers. For example, some electronic mail systems consist of mail programs that are each configured to forward a memo to a mail program on the next computer. The path from source to destination may involve many different networks, but that does not matter as long as the mail systems on all the machines cooperate by forwarding each message.

Using application programs to hide network details may seem natural at first, but such an approach results in limited, cumbersome communication. Adding new functionality to the system means building a new application program for each computer. Adding new network hardware means modifying existing programs (or creating new programs) for each possible application. On a given computer, each application program must understand the network connections for the computer, resulting in duplication of code.

Users who are experienced with networking understand that once the interconnections grow to hundreds or thousands of networks, no one can possibly build all the necessary application programs. Furthermore, success of the step-at-a-time communication scheme requires correctness of all application programs executing along the path. When an intermediate program fails, the source and destination remain unable to detect or control the problem. Thus, systems that use intermediate applications programs cannot guarantee reliable communication.

3.3 Network-Level Interconnection

The alternative to providing interconnection with application-level programs is a system based on network-level interconnection. A network-level interconnection provides a mechanism that delivers small packets of data from their original source to their ultimate destination without using intermediate application programs. Switching small units of data instead of files or large messages has several advantages. First, the scheme maps directly onto the underlying network hardware, making it extremely efficient. Second, network-level interconnection separates data communication activities from application programs, permitting intermediate computers to handle network traffic without understanding the applications that are sending or receiving. Third, using network connections keeps the entire system flexible, making it possible to build general purpose communication facilities. Fourth, the scheme allows network managers to add new network technologies by modifying or adding a single piece of new network-level software, while application programs remain unchanged.

The key to designing universal network-level interconnection can be found in an abstract communication system concept known as *internetworking*. The internetwork, or *internet*, concept is extremely powerful. It detaches the notions of communication from the details of network technologies and hides low-level details from the user. More important, it drives all software design decisions and explains how to handle physical addresses and routes. After reviewing basic motivations for internetworking, we will consider the properties of an internet in more detail.

We begin with two fundamental observations about the design of communication systems:

- No single network hardware technology can satisfy all constraints.
- Users desire universal interconnection.

The first observation is an economic as well as technical one. Inexpensive Local Area Networks that provide high-speed communication only cover short distances; wide area networks that span long distances cannot supply local communication cheaply. Because no single network technology satisfies all needs, we are forced to consider multiple underlying hardware technologies.

The second observation is self-evident. Ultimately, users would like to be able to communicate between any two points. In particular, we desire a communication system that is not constrained by the boundaries of physical networks.

The goal is to build a unified, cooperative interconnection of networks that supports a universal communication service. Within each network, computers will use underlying technology-dependent communication facilities like those described in Chapter 2. New software, inserted between the technology-dependent communication mechanisms and application programs, will hide the low-level details and make the collection of networks appear to be a single, large network. Such an interconnection scheme is called an *internetwork* or *internet*.

The idea of building an internet follows a standard pattern of system design: researchers imagine a high-level computing facility and work from available computing technology, adding layers of software until they have a system that efficiently implements the imagined high-level facility. The next section shows the first step of the design process by defining the goal more precisely.

3.4 Properties Of The Internet

The notion of universal service is important, but it alone does not capture all the ideas we have in mind for a unified internet because there can be many implementations of universal services. In our design, we want to hide the underlying internet architecture from the user. That is, we do not want to require users or application programs to understand the details of hardware interconnections to use the internet. We also do not want to mandate a network interconnection topology. In particular, adding a new network to the internet should not mean connecting to a centralized switching point, nor should it mean adding direct physical connections between the new network and all existing networks. We want to be able to send data across intermediate networks even though they are not directly connected to the source or destination computers. We want all computers in the internet to share a universal set of machine identifiers (which can be thought of as *names* or *addresses*).

Our notion of a unified internet also includes the idea of network independence in the user interface. That is, we want the set of operations used to establish communication or to transfer data to remain independent of the underlying network technologies and the destination computer. Certainly, a user should not have to understand the network interconnection topology when creating or using application programs that communicate.

3.5 Internet Architecture

We have seen how computers connect to individual networks. The question arises, "How are networks interconnected to form an internetwork?" The answer has two parts. Physically, two networks can only be connected by a computer that attaches to both of them. A physical attachment does not provide the interconnection we have in mind, however, because such a connection does not guarantee that the computer will cooperate with other machines that wish to communicate. To have a viable internet, we need special computers that are willing to transfer packets from one network to another. Computers that interconnect two networks and pass packets from one to the other are called *internet gateways* or *internet routers*†.

Consider an example consisting of two physical networks shown in Figure 3.1. In the figure, router *R* connects to both network *1* and network *2*. For *R* to act as a router, it must capture packets on network *1* that are bound for machines on network *2* and transfer them. Similarly, *R* must capture packets on network *2* that are destined for machines on network *1* and transfer them.

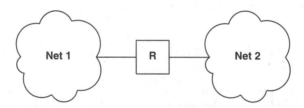

Figure 3.1 Two physical networks interconnected by *R*, a router (IP gateway).

In the figure, clouds are used to denote physical networks because the exact hardware is unimportant. Each network can be a LAN or a WAN, and each may have many computers attached or a few computers attached.

---

†The original literature used the term *IP gateway*. However, vendors have adopted the term *IP router* — the two terms are used interchangeably throughout this text.

3.6 Interconnection Through IP Routers

Although it illustrates the basic connection strategy, Figure 3.1 is quite simplistic. In an actual internet that includes many networks and routers, each router needs to know about the topology of the internet beyond the networks to which it connects. For example, Figure 3.2 shows three networks interconnected by two routers.

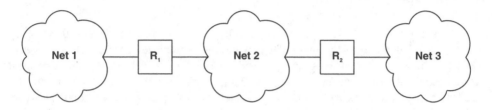

Figure 3.2 Three networks interconnected by two routers.

In this example, router R_1 must transfer from network *1* to network *2* all packets destined for computers on either network *2* or network *3*. For a large internet composed of many networks, the router's task of making decisions about where to send packets becomes more complex.

The idea of a router seems simple, but it is important because it provides a way to interconnect networks, not just computers. In fact, we have already discovered the principle of interconnection used throughout an internet:

> *In a TCP/IP internet, special computers called* IP routers *or* IP gateways *provide interconnections among physical networks.*

You might suspect that routers, which must each know how to forward packets toward their destination, are large machines with enough primary or secondary memory to hold information about every computer in the internet to which they attach. In fact, routers used with TCP/IP internets are usually small computers. They often have little disk storage and modest main memories. The trick to building a small internet router lies in the following concept:

> *Routers use the destination network, not the destination computer, when forwarding a packet.*

If packet forwarding is based on networks, the amount of information that a router needs to keep is proportional to the number of networks in the internet, not the number of computers.

Because routers play a key role in internet communication, we will return to them in later chapters and discuss the details of how they operate and how they learn about routes. For now, we will assume that it is possible and practical to have correct routes for all networks in each router in the internet. We will also assume that only routers provide connections between physical networks in an internet.

3.7 The User's View

Remember that TCP/IP is designed to provide a universal interconnection among computers independent of the particular networks to which they attach. Thus, we want a user to view an internet as a single, virtual network to which all machines connect despite their physical connections. Figure 3.3a shows how thinking of an internet instead of constituent networks simplifies the details and makes it easy for the user to conceptualize communication. In addition to routers that interconnect physical networks, software is needed on each computer to allow application programs to use an internet as if it were a single, physical network.

The advantage of providing interconnection at the network level now becomes clear. Because application programs that communicate over the internet do not know the details of underlying connections, they can be run without change on any computer. Because the details of each machine's physical network connections are hidden in the internet software, only the internet software needs to change when new physical connections are added or existing connections are removed. In fact, it is possible to optimize the internal structure of the internet by altering physical connections while application programs are executing.

A second advantage of having communication at the network level is more subtle: users do not have to understand, remember, or specify how networks connect or what traffic they carry. Application programs can be written that communicate independent of underlying physical connectivity. In fact, network managers are free to change interior parts of the underlying internet architecture without changing application software in most of the computers attached to the internet (of course, network software must be reconfigured when a computer moves to a new network).

As Figure 3.3b shows, routers do not provide direct connections among all pairs of networks. It may be necessary for traffic traveling from one computer to another to pass through several routers as the traffic crosses intermediate networks. Thus, networks participating in an internet are analogous to highways in the U.S. interstate system: each net agrees to handle transit traffic in exchange for the right to send traffic throughout the internet. Typical users are unaffected and unaware of extra traffic on their local network.

3.8 All Networks Are Equal

Chapter 2 reviewed examples of the network hardware used to build TCP/IP internets, and illustrated the great diversity of technologies. We have described an internet
as a collection of cooperative, interconnected networks. It is now important to understand a fundamental concept: from the internet point of view, any communication system capable of transferring packets counts as a single network, independent of its delay
and throughput characteristics, maximum packet size, or geographic scale. In particular,
Figure 3.3b uses the same small cloud shape to depict each physical network because
TCP/IP treats them equally despite their differences. The point is:

> *The TCP/IP internet protocols treat all networks equally. A Local
> Area Network like an Ethernet, a Wide Area Network used as a back-
> bone, or a point-to-point link between two computers each count as
> one network.*

Readers unaccustomed to internet architecture may find it difficult to accept such a
simplistic view of networks. In essence, TCP/IP defines an abstraction of "network"
that hides the details of physical networks; we will learn that such abstractions help
make TCP/IP extremely powerful.

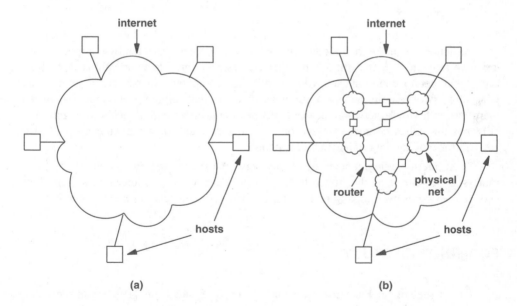

(a)   (b)

Figure 3.3 (a) The user's view of a TCP/IP internet in which each computer
appears to attach to a single large network, and (b) the structure
of physical networks and routers that provide interconnection.

3.9 The Unanswered Questions

Our sketch of internets leaves many unanswered questions. For example, you might wonder about the exact form of internet addresses assigned to computers or how such addresses relate to the physical hardware addresses such as the Ethernet addresses described in Chapter 2. The next two chapters confront these questions. They describe the format of IP addresses and illustrate how software on a computer maps between internet addresses and physical addresses. You might also want to know exactly what a packet looks like when it travels through an internet, or what happens when packets arrive too fast for some computer or router to handle. Chapter 6 answers these questions. Finally, you might wonder how multiple application programs executing concurrently on a single computer can send and receive packets to multiple destinations without becoming entangled in each other's transmissions or how internet routers learn about routes. All of these questions will be answered as well.

Although it may seem vague now, the direction we are following will let us learn about both the structure and use of internet protocol software. We will examine each part, looking at the concepts and principles as well as technical details. We began by describing the physical communication layer on which an internet is built. Each of the following chapters will explore one part of the internet software, until we understand how all the pieces fit together.

3.10 Summary

An internet is more than a collection of networks interconnected by computers. Internetworking implies that the interconnected systems agree to conventions that allow each computer to communicate with every other computer. In particular, an internet will allow two computers to communicate even if the communication path between them passes across a network to which neither connects directly. Such cooperation is only possible when computers agree on a set of universal identifiers and a set of procedures for moving data to its final destination.

In an internet, interconnections among networks are formed by computers called IP routers, or IP gateways, that attach to two or more networks. A router forwards packets between networks by receiving them from one network and sending them to another.

FOR FURTHER STUDY

Our model of an internetwork comes from Cerf and Cain [1983] and Cerf and Kahn [1974], which describe an internet as a set of networks interconnected by routers and sketch an internet protocol similar to that eventually developed for the TCP/IP protocol suite. More information on the connected Internet architecture can be found in Postel [1980]; Postel, Sunshine, and Cohen [1981]; and in Hinden, Haverty, and

Sheltzer [1983]. Shoch [1978] presents issues in internetwork naming and addressing. Boggs *et. al.* [1980] describes the internet developed at Xerox PARC, an alternative to the TCP/IP internet we will examine. Cheriton [1983] describes internetworking as it relates to the V-system.

EXERCISES

3.1   What processors have been used as routers in the connected Internet? Does the size and speed of early router hardware surprise you? Why?

3.2   Approximately how many networks constitute the internet at your site? Approximately how many routers?

3.3   Consider the internal structure of the example internet shown in Figure 3.3b. Which routers are most crucial? Why?

3.4   Changing the information in a router can be tricky because it is impossible to change all routers simultaneously. Investigate algorithms that guarantee to either install a change on a set of computers or install it on none.

3.5   In an internet, routers periodically exchange information from their routing tables, making it possible for a new router to appear and begin routing packets. Investigate the algorithms used to exchange routing information.

3.6   Compare the organization of a TCP/IP internet to the style of internet designed by Xerox Corporation.

Chapter Contents

4

Classful Internet Addresses

4.1 Introduction

The previous chapter defines a TCP/IP internet as a virtual network built by inter-connecting physical networks with routers. This chapter begins a discussion of address-ing, an essential part of the design that helps TCP/IP software hide physical network de-tails and makes the resulting internet appear to be a single, uniform entity.

4.2 Universal Identifiers

A communication system is said to supply *universal communication service* if the system allows any host computer to communicate with any other host. To make our communication system universal, it needs a globally accepted method of identifying each computer that attaches to it.

Often, host identifiers are classified as *names*, *addresses*, or *routes*. Shoch [1978] suggests that a name identifies *what* an object is, an address identifies *where* it is, and a route tells *how* to get there†. Although these definitions are intuitive, they can be misleading. Names, addresses, and routes really refer to successively lower-level representations of host identifiers. In general, people usually prefer pronounceable names to identify machines, while software works more efficiently with compact representations of identifiers that we think of as addresses. Either could have been chosen as the TCP/IP universal host identifiers. The decision was made to standardize on compact, binary addresses that make computations such as the selection of a route efficient. For now, we will discuss only binary addresses, postponing until later the questions of how to map between binary addresses and pronounceable names, and how to use addresses for forwarding packets.

---

†An identifier that specifies where an object can be found is also called a *locator*.

4.3 The Original Classful Addressing Scheme

Think of an internet as a large network like any other physical network. The difference, of course, is that an internet is a virtual structure, imagined by its designers, and implemented entirely in software. Thus, the designers are free to choose packet formats and sizes, addresses, delivery techniques, and so on; nothing is dictated by hardware. For addresses, the designers of TCP/IP chose a scheme analogous to physical network addressing in which each host on the internet is assigned a 32-bit integer address called its *Internet Protocol address* or *IP address*. The clever part of internet addressing is that the integers are carefully chosen to make forwarding efficient. Specifically, an IP address encodes the identification of the network to which a host attaches as well as the identification of a unique host on that network. We can summarize:

> *Each host on a TCP/IP internet is assigned a unique 32-bit internet address that is used in all communication with that host.*

The details of IP addresses help clarify the abstract ideas. For now, we give a simplified view and expand it later. In the simplest case, each host attached to an internet is assigned a single 32-bit universal identifier as its internet address. A prefix of an IP address identifies a network. That is, the IP addresses in all hosts on a given network share a common prefix.

Conceptually, each address is a pair (*netid*, *hostid*), where *netid* identifies a network, and *hostid* identifies a host on that network. In practice, however, the partition into prefix and suffix is not uniform throughout the entire internet because the designers did not specify a single boundary. In the original addressing scheme, which is known as *classful*, each IP address had one of the first three forms shown in Figure 4.1†.

In the classful addressing scheme, each address is said to be *self-identifying* because the boundary between prefix and suffix can be computed from the address alone, without reference to external information. In particular, the class of an address can be determined from the three high-order bits, with two bits being sufficient to distinguish among the three primary classes. Class *A* addresses, used for the handful of networks that have more than 2^{16} (i.e., 65,536) hosts, devote 7 bits to netid and 24 bits to hostid. Class *B* addresses, used for intermediate size networks that have between 2^8 (i.e., 256) and 2^{16} hosts, allocate 14 bits to the netid and 16 bits to the hostid. Finally, class *C* addresses, used for networks that have less than 2^8 hosts, allocate 21 bits to the netid and only 8 bits to the hostid. Note that the IP address was originally defined in such a way that it was possible to extract the hostid or netid portions quickly. Efficiency was especially important for routers, which use the netid portion of an address when deciding where to send a packet. We will return to the discussion of efficient route lookup after examining recent changes and extensions to the addressing scheme.

---

†The fourth form, reserved for internet multicasting, will be described later; for now, we will restrict our comments to the forms that specify addresses of individual objects.

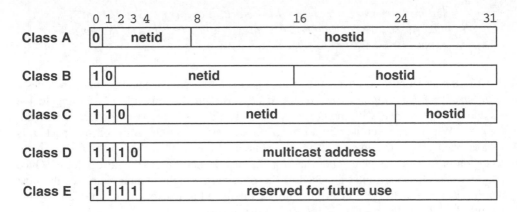

Figure 4.1 The five forms of Internet (IP) addresses used with the original classful addressing scheme. The three primary classes, *A*, *B* and *C*, can be distinguished by the first three bits.

4.4 Addresses Specify Network Connections

To simplify the discussion, we said that an internet address identifies a host, but that is not strictly accurate. Consider a router that attaches to two physical networks. How can we assign a single IP address if the address encodes a network identifier as well as a host identifier? In fact, we cannot. A similar situation exists for a conventional computer that has two or more physical network connections (such computers are known as *multi-homed hosts*): each of the machine's network connections must be assigned an address. The idea is a fundamental part of IP addressing:

> *Because IP addresses encode both a network and a host on that network, an address does not specify an individual computer, but a connection to a network.*

Thus, a router connecting *n* networks has *n* distinct IP addresses, one for each network connection.

4.5 Network And Directed Broadcast Addresses

We have already cited the major advantage of encoding network information in internet addresses: it makes efficient forwarding possible. Another advantage is that internet addresses can refer to networks as well as hosts. By convention, hostid *0* is never assigned to an individual host. Instead, an IP address with hostid portion equal to zero is used to refer to the network itself. In summary:

> *Internet addresses can be used to refer to networks as well as indivi-
> dual hosts. By convention, an address that has all bits of the hostid
> equal to 0 is reserved to refer to the network.*

Another significant advantage of the internet addressing scheme is that it includes a
directed broadcast address that refers to all hosts on the network. According to the
standard, any address with the hostid consisting of all *1s* is reserved for directed broad-
cast†. When a packet is sent to such an address, a single copy of the packet is
transferred across the internet from the source. Routers along the path use the netid
portion of the address when choosing a path; they do not look at the host portion. Once
the packet reaches a router attached to the final network, that router examines the host
portion of the address to determine how to deliver the packet. If it finds all *1s*, the
router broadcasts the packet to all hosts on the network.

On some network technologies (e.g., Ethernet), broadcasting is as efficient as unicast transmission; on others, software implements broadcast by sending an individual
copy to each host on the network. Thus, having an IP directed broadcast address does
not guarantee the availability or efficiency of broadcast delivery. In summary,

> *IP addresses can be used to specify a directed broadcast in which a
> packet is sent to all computers on a network; such addresses map to
> hardware broadcast, if available. By convention, a directed broad-
> cast address has a valid netid and has a hostid with all bits set to 1.*

4.6 Limited Broadcast

The broadcast address we just described is known as *directed* because it contains
both a valid network ID and the broadcast hostid. A directed broadcast can be sent
across an internet because routers along the path use only the netid portion of the address when deciding how to forward the datagram. Directed broadcast addresses provide a powerful (and somewhat dangerous) mechanism that allows a remote system to
send a single packet that will be broadcast on the specified network. To avoid potential
problems, many sites configure routers to reject all directed broadcast packets.

From an addressing point of view, the chief disadvantage of directed broadcast is
that it requires knowledge of the network address. Another form of broadcast address,
called a *limited broadcast address* or local network broadcast address, provides a broadcast address for the local network independent of the assigned IP address. The local
broadcast address consists of thirty-two *1s* (hence, it is sometimes called the "all *1s*"
broadcast address). As we will see, a host can use the limited broadcast address as part
of a startup procedure before it learns its IP address or the IP address prefix for the local network. Once the host learns the correct IP address for the local network, however,
directed broadcast is preferred.

---

†An early release of TCP/IP code that accompanied Berkeley UNIX incorrectly used all zeroes for broadcast. Because the error still survives, TCP/IP software often includes an option that allows a site to use all
zeroes for directed broadcast.

As a general rule, TCP/IP protocols restrict broadcasting to the smallest possible set of machines. We will see how this rule affects multiple networks that share addresses in the chapter on subnet addressing.

4.7 The All-0s Address

An address that consists of thirty-two zero bits is reserved for cases where a host needs to communicate, but does not yet know its IP address (i.e., temporarily during startup). In particular, we will see that to obtain an IP address, a host sends a datagram to the limited broadcast address, and uses address *0* to identify itself. The receiver understands that the host does not yet have an IP address, and the receiver uses a special method to send a reply.

4.8 Subnet And Classless Extensions

The addressing scheme described so far requires a unique network prefix for each physical network. Although that was, indeed, the original plan, it did not last long. In the 1980s as LAN technologies became popular and networks proliferated, it became apparent that requiring a unique prefix for each physical network would exhaust the address space quickly. Consequently, an addressing extension was developed to conserve network prefixes. Known as *subnet addressing*, the scheme allows multiple physical networks to share a single network prefix.

In the 1990s, a second extension was devised that relaxed the classful hierarchy and allowed the division between prefix and suffix to occur at an arbitrary point in the address. Called *classless addressing*, the scheme allows more complete utilization of the address space.

Chapter 9 will consider details of the subnet and supernet addressing extensions. For now, it is only important to know that the addressing scheme has been extended, and that the original classful scheme described in this chapter is no longer the most widely used.

4.9 IP Multicast Addresses

In addition to *unicast delivery*, in which a packet is delivered to a single computer, and *broadcast delivery*, in which a packet is delivered to all computers on a given network, the IP addressing scheme supports a special form of multipoint delivery known as *multicasting*, in which a packet is delivered to a specific subset of hosts. IP multicasting is especially useful for networks where the hardware technology supports multicast delivery. Chapter 16 discusses multicast addressing and delivery in detail. For now, it is sufficient to understand that Class *D* addresses are reserved for multicasting.

4.10 Weaknesses In Internet Addressing

Encoding network information in an internet address does have some disadvantages. The most obvious disadvantage is that addresses refer to network connections, not to the host computer:

> *If a host computer moves from one network to another, its IP address must change.*

To understand the consequences, consider a traveler who wishes to disconnect his or her personal computer, carry it on a trip, and reconnect it to the Internet after reaching the destination. The personal computer cannot be assigned a permanent IP address because an IP address identifies the network to which the machine attaches. Chapter 18 shows how the IP addressing scheme makes *mobility* a complex problem.

Another weakness of the scheme arises from early binding — once a prefix size is chosen, the maximum number of hosts on the network is fixed. If the network grows beyond the original bound, a new prefix must be selected and all hosts on the network must be renumbered. While *renumbering* may seem like a minor problem, changing network addresses can be incredibly time-consuming and difficult to debug.

The most important flaw in the internet addressing scheme will not become fully apparent until we examine forwarding. However, its importance warrants a brief introduction here. We have suggested that forwarding will be based on internet addresses, with the netid portion of an address used to make forwarding decisions. Consider a host with two connections to the internet. We know that such a host must have more than one IP address. The following is true:

> *Because forwarding uses the network portion of the IP address, the path taken by packets traveling to a host with multiple IP addresses depends on the address used.*

The implications are surprising. Humans think of each host as a single entity and want to use a single name. They are often surprised to find that they must learn more than one name and even more surprised to find that packets sent using multiple names can behave differently.

Another surprising consequence of the internet addressing scheme is that merely knowing one IP address for a destination may not be sufficient; it may be impossible to reach the destination using that address. Consider the example internet shown in Figure 4.2. In the figure, two hosts, A and B, both attach to network 1, and usually communicate directly using that network. Thus, users on host A should normally refer to host B using IP address I_3. An alternate path from A to B exists through router R, and is used whenever A sends packets to IP address I_5 (B's address on network 2). Now suppose B's connection to network 1 fails, but the machine itself remains running (e.g., a wire breaks between B and network 1). Users on A who specify IP address I_3 cannot reach B, although users who specify address I_5 can. These problems with naming and addressing will arise again in later chapters when we consider forwarding and name binding.

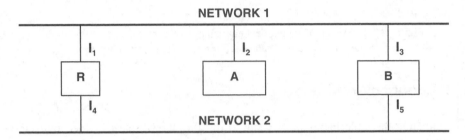

Figure 4.2 An example internet with a multi-homed host, B, that demonstrates a disadvantage of the IP addressing scheme. If interface I_3 becomes disconnected, A must use address I_5 to reach B, sending packets through router R.

4.11 Dotted Decimal Notation

When communicated to humans, either in technical documents or through application programs, IP addresses are written as four decimal integers separated by decimal points, where each integer gives the value of one octet of the IP address†. Thus, the 32-bit internet address

$$10000000 \quad 00001010 \quad 00000010 \quad 00011110$$

is written

$$128.10.2.30$$

We will use dotted decimal notation when expressing IP addresses throughout the remainder of this text. Indeed, most TCP/IP software that displays or requires a human to enter an IP address uses dotted decimal notation. For example, application programs such as a web browser allow a user to enter a dotted decimal value instead of a computer name. As an example of dotted decimal, the table in Figure 4.3 summarizes the dotted decimal values for each address class.

---

†Dotted decimal notation is sometimes called *dotted quad notation.*

Class	Lowest Address	Highest Address
A	1.0.0.0	127.0.0.0
B	128.0.0.0	191.255.0.0
C	192.0.0.0	223.255.255.0
D	224.0.0.0	239.255.255.255
E	240.0.0.0	255.255.255.254

Figure 4.3 The range of dotted decimal values that correspond to each IP address class. Some values are reserved for special purposes.

4.12 Loopback Address

Although the table in Figure 4.3 shows the IP address space divided into classes, not all values in a class are assigned. For example, the lowest prefix in class B (128.0.0.0) was not assigned; the first class B prefix is 128.1.0.0. Similarly, the lowest assigned class C prefix is 192.0.1.0. More important, the network prefix 127.0.0.0, a value from the class A range, is reserved for *loopback*, and is intended for use in testing TCP/IP and for inter-process communication on the local computer. When a program uses the loopback address as a destination, the protocol software in the computer processes the data without sending traffic across any network; a datagram sent to a network 127 address should never appear on any network. Furthermore, a host or router should never propagate routing or reachability information for network number *127*; it is not a network address.

4.13 Summary Of Special Address Conventions

In practice, IP uses only a few combinations of *0*s or *1*s to form special addresses. Figure 4.4 lists the possibilities. As the notes in the figure mention, using all *0*s for the IP address is only allowed during initial startup to permit a computer to send a datagram without knowing its address. Once the machine learns its correct network and IP address(es), it must not use network prefix *0*. In any case, the all 0s address is never used as a destination address.

4.14 Internet Addressing Authority

Each network address prefix used within a given TCP/IP internet must be unique. An organization that uses TCP/IP technology to build a completely private internet (i.e., one that is not connected to the global Internet) can assign address prefixes without considering the assignments made by other organizations. However, an organization that connects to the global Internet must not use address prefixes assigned to another organization.

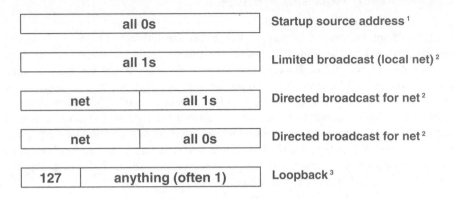

| all 0s | Startup source address [1] |

| all 1s | Limited broadcast (local net) [2] |

| net | all 1s | Directed broadcast for net [2] |

| net | all 0s | Directed broadcast for net [2] |

| 127 | anything (often 1) | Loopback [3] |

Notes: [1] Never a valid destination
[2] Never a valid source
[3] Should not appear on a network

Figure 4.4 Special forms of IP addresses.

To ensure that the network portion of an address is unique in the global Internet, all Internet addresses are assigned by a central authority. Originally, the *Internet Assigned Number Authority* (*IANA*) had control over numbers assigned, and set the policy. From the time the Internet began until the fall of 1998, a single individual, Jon Postel, ran the IANA and assigned addresses. In late 1998, after Jon's untimely death, a new organization was created to handle address assignment. Named the *Internet Corporation For Assigned Names and Numbers* (*ICANN*), the organization sets policy and assigns values for names and other constants used in protocols as well as addresses.

Most organizations never interact with the central authority directly. Instead, to connect its networks to the global Internet, an organization usually contracts with a local *Internet Service Provider* (*ISP*). In addition to providing a connection between the organization and the rest of the Internet, an ISP obtains a valid address prefix for each of the customer's networks. Many local ISPs are, in fact, customers of larger ISPs — when a customer requests an address prefix, the local ISP merely obtains a prefix from a larger ISP. Thus, only the largest ISPs need to contact one of the *address registries* that ICANN has authorized to administer blocks of addresses (*ARIN*, *RIPE*, *APNIC*, *LATNIC*, or *AFRINIC*).

Note that the central authority only assigns the network portion of an address. That is, once an organization obtains a prefix for a network, the organization can choose how to assign a unique suffix to each host on the network without contacting the central authority.

4.15 Reserved Address Prefixes

How should addresses be assigned on a private intranet (i.e., on an internet that does not connect to the global Internet)? In theory, arbitrary addresses can be used. For example, on the global Internet, the class A address 9.0.0.0 has been assigned to IBM Corporation, and address 12.0.0.0 has been assigned to AT&T. Although such addresses can be used on a private network, experience has shown that doing so is dangerous because packets that leak onto the global Internet appear to come from valid sources. To avoid conflicts between addresses used on private internets and addresses used on the global Internet, the IETF reserved several address prefixes and recommends using them on private internets. The set of reserved prefixes includes both classful and classless values, and is described in Chapter 9.

4.16 An Example

To clarify the IP addressing scheme, consider an example of two networks in the Computer Science Department at Purdue University. Figure 4.5 shows the network addresses, and illustrates how routers interconnect the networks.

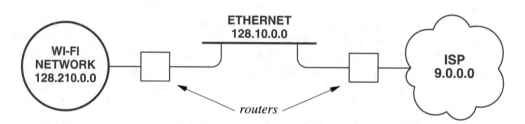

Figure 4.5 The logical connection of two networks to the Internet backbone. Each network has been assigned an IP address.

The example shows three networks and the network numbers they have been assigned: the Internet Service Provider (9.0.0.0), an Ethernet (128.10.0.0), and a Wi-Fi network (128.210.0.0). According to the table in Figure 4.3, the ISP address is class *A*, and the other two are each in class *B*.

Figure 4.6 shows the same networks with host computers attached and Internet addresses assigned to each network connection. In the figure, four hosts, labeled *Arthur*, *Merlin*, *Guenevere*, and *Lancelot*, attach to the networks; *Taliesyn* is a router that connects the Ethernet and Wi-Fi networks; and *Glatisant* is a router that connects the site to an ISP.

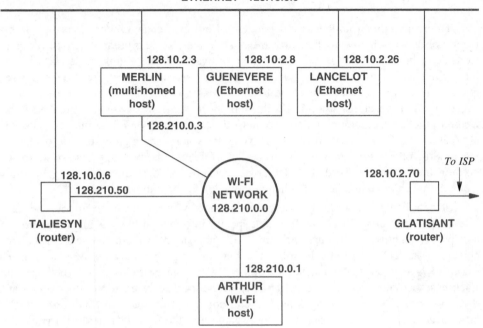

ETHERNET   128.10.0.0

Figure 4.6 Example IP address assignment for routers and hosts attached to the three networks in the previous figure.

Host *Merlin* has connections to both the Ethernet and the Wi-Fi network, so it can reach destinations on either network directly. The distinction between a router (e.g., *Taliesyn*) and a multi-homed host (e.g., *Merlin*) arises from the configuration: a router is configured to forward packets between the two networks whereas a host can use either network, but does not forward packets.

As Figure 4.6 shows, an IP address must be assigned to each network connection. *Lancelot*, which connects only to the Ethernet, has been assigned 128.10.2.26 as its only IP address. *Merlin* has address 128.10.2.3 for its connection to the Ethernet and 128.210.0.3 for its connection to the Wi-Fi network; whoever made the address assignment chose the same value for the low-order byte of each address. The addresses assigned to router *Taliesyn* do not follow the convention. For example, *Taliesyn's* addresses, 128.10.2.6 and 128.210.0.50, are two unrelated strings of digits. IP does not care whether any of the bytes in the dotted decimal form of a computer's addresses are the same or different. However, network technicians, managers, and administrators may need to use addresses for maintenance, testing, and debugging. Choosing to make all of a computer's addresses end with the same octet makes it easier for humans to remember or guess the address of a particular interface.

4.17 Network Byte Order

To create an internet that is independent of any particular vendor's machine architecture or network hardware, the software must define a standard representation for data.
Consider what happens, for example, when software on one computer sends a 32-bit
binary integer to another computer. The physical transport hardware moves the sequence of bits from the first machine to the second without changing the order. However, not all architectures store 32-bit integers in the same way. On some (called *Little
Endian*), the lowest memory address contains the low-order byte of the integer. On others (called *Big Endian*), the lowest memory address holds the high-order byte of the integer. Still others store integers in groups of 16-bit words, with the lowest addresses
holding the low-order word, but with bytes swapped. Thus, direct copying of bytes
from one machine to another may change the value of the number.

Standardizing byte-order for integers is especially important in an internet because
internet packets carry binary numbers that specify information like destination addresses
and packet lengths. Such quantities must be understood by both the senders and receivers. The TCP/IP protocols solve the byte-order problem by defining a *network
standard byte order* that all machines must use for binary fields in internet packets.
Each host or router converts binary items from the local representation to network standard byte order before sending a packet, and converts from network byte order to the
host-specific order when a packet arrives. Naturally, the user data field in a packet is
exempt from this standard because the TCP/IP protocols do not know what data is being
carried — application programmers are free to format their own data representation and
translation. When sending integer values, many application programmers do choose to
follow the TCP/IP byte-order standards. Of course, users who merely invoke application programs never need to deal with the byte order problem directly.

The internet standard for byte order specifies that integers are sent with the most
significant byte first (i.e., *Big Endian* style). If one considers the successive bytes in a
packet as it travels from one machine to another, a binary integer in that packet has its
most significant byte nearest the beginning of the packet and its least significant byte
nearest the end of the packet. Many arguments have been offered about which data
representation should be used, and the internet standard still comes under attack from
time to time. In particular, proponents of change argue that although most computers
were big endian when the standard was defined, most are now little endian. However,
everyone agrees that having a standard is crucial, and the exact form of the standard is
far less important.

4.18 Summary

TCP/IP uses 32-bit binary addresses as universal machine identifiers. Called Internet Protocol addresses or IP addresses, the identifiers are partitioned into two parts: a
prefix identifies the network to which the computer attaches, and the suffix provides a
unique identifier for a computer on that network. The original IP addressing scheme is

known as classful, with each prefix assigned to one of three primary classes. Leading bits define the class of an address; the classes are of unequal size. The classful scheme provides for 127 networks with over a million hosts each, thousands of networks with thousands of hosts each, and over a million networks with up to 254 hosts each. To make such addresses easier for humans to understand, they are written in dotted decimal notation, with the values of the four octets written in decimal, separated by decimal points.

Because the IP address encodes network identification as well as the identification of a specific host on that network, forwarding is efficient. An important property of IP addresses is that they refer to network connections. Hosts with multiple connections have multiple addresses. One advantage of the internet addressing scheme is that the form includes an address for a specific host, a network, or all hosts on a network (broadcast). The biggest disadvantage of the IP addressing scheme is that if a machine has multiple addresses, knowing one address may not be sufficient to reach it when no path exists to the specified interface (e.g., because a particular network is unavailable).

To permit the exchange of binary data among machines, TCP/IP protocols enforce a standard byte ordering for integers within protocol fields. A host must convert all binary data from its internal form to network standard byte order before sending a packet, and it must convert from network byte order to internal order upon receipt.

FOR FURTHER STUDY

The internet addressing scheme presented here can be found in Reynolds and Postel [RFC 1700]; further information can be found in Kirkpatrick et. al. [RFC 1166].

Several important additions have been made to the Internet addressing scheme over the years; later chapters cover them in more detail. Chapter 9 discusses an important extension called *classless addressing* that permits the division between prefix and suffix to occur at an arbitrary bit position. In addition, Chapter 9 examines an essential part of the Internet address standard called *subnet addressing*. Subnet addressing allows a single network address to be used with multiple physical networks. Chapter 16 continues the exploration of IP addresses by describing how class D addresses are assigned for internet *multicast*.

Cohen [1981] explains bit and byte ordering, and introduces the terms "Big Endian" and "Little Endian."

EXERCISES

4.1   Exactly how many class *A*, *B*, and *C* networks can exist? Exactly how many hosts can a network in each class have? Be careful to allow for broadcast as well as class *D* and *E* addresses.

4.2   A machine readable list of assigned addresses is sometimes called an internet *host table*. If your site has a host table, find out how many class *A*, *B*, and *C* network numbers have been assigned.

4.3   How many hosts are attached to each of the local area networks at your site? Does your site have any local area networks for which a class *C* address is insufficient?

4.4   What is the chief difference between the IP addressing scheme and the U.S. telephone numbering scheme?

4.5   The address registries around the world cooperate to hand out blocks of IP addresses. Find out how they ensure no ISP is given addresses that overlap with those given to another ISP.

4.6   Does network standard byte order differ from your local machine's byte order?

4.7   How many IP addresses would be needed to assign a unique IP address to every house in your country? the world? Is the IP address space sufficient?

Chapter Contents

5

Mapping Internet Addresses
To Physical Addresses
(ARP)

5.1 Introduction

The previous chapter describes the TCP/IP address scheme in which each host is assigned a 32-bit address, and states that an internet behaves like a virtual network, using only the assigned addresses when sending and receiving packets. Chapter 2 reviews several network hardware technologies, and notes that two machines on a given physical network can communicate *only if they know each other's physical network address*. What we have not mentioned is how a host or a router maps an IP address to the correct physical address when it needs to send a packet across a physical net. This chapter considers that mapping, showing how it is implemented for the two most common physical network address schemes.

5.2 The Address Resolution Problem

Consider two machines A and B that connect to the same physical network. Each has an assigned IP address I_A and I_B and a physical address P_A and P_B. Ultimately, communication must be carried out by physical networks using whatever physical address scheme the underlying network hardware supplies. Our goal, however, is to devise software that hides physical addresses and allows higher-level programs to work only

57

with Internet addresses. For example, assume machine A needs to send a datagram to machine B across the physical network to which they both attach, but A only knows B's Internet address I_B. The question arises: how does A map B's Internet address to B's physical address, P_B?

Address mapping must be performed at each step along a path from the original source to the ultimate destination. In particular, two cases arise. First, at the last step of delivering a datagram, the datagram must be sent across a physical network to the ultimate destination. The computer sending the datagram must map the final destination's Internet address to the destination's physical address before transmission is possible. Second, at any point along the path from the source to the destination other than the final step, the datagram must be sent to an intermediate router. Thus, the sender must map the intermediate router's Internet address to a physical address.

The problem of mapping high-level addresses to physical addresses is known as the *address resolution problem*, and has been solved in several ways. Some protocol suites keep tables in each machine that contain pairs of high-level and physical addresses. Other protocols solve the problem by encoding hardware addresses in high-level addresses. Using either approach exclusively makes high-level addressing awkward at best. This chapter discusses two techniques for address resolution used by TCP/IP protocols, and shows when each is appropriate.

5.3 Two Types Of Physical Addresses

There are two basic types of physical addresses: large, fixed addresses, such as those used with Ethernet, and small, easily configured addresses. TCP/IP can accommodate each, but the popularity of Ethernet means that almost all network hardware currently uses large addresses. Therefore, the chapter will consider small addresses briefly, and concentrate on large addresses.

5.4 Resolution Through Direct Mapping

Consider network hardware that uses small, configurable integers as hardware addresses. Whenever a new computer is added to such a network, the system administrator chooses a hardware address and configures the computer's network interface card. The only important rule is that no two computers can have the same address. To make assignment easy and safe, an administrator typically assigns addresses sequentially: the first computer on the network is assigned address 1, the second computer is assigned address 2, and so on.

The key to making address resolution work with such network hardware lies in observing that as long as one has the freedom to choose both IP and physical addresses, the addresses can be selected such that parts of them are identical. In particular, the IP address of a computer can have the hostid portion equal to the hardware address. For example, suppose the prefix for a network is 192.5.48.0 with the network prefix occupying the first three octets. The first computer on the network is assigned hardware address 1 and IP address 192.5.48.1, the second computer is assigned hardware address 2 and IP address 192.5.48.2, and so on. In essence, each IP address on the network encodes the computer's hardware address in the low-order octet.

If the IP address encodes the hardware address, address resolution is trivial. In the example above, if software is given the IP address of a computer on the network (e.g., 192.5.48.3), the corresponding hardware address can be computed by extracting the low-order octet. We say that resolution is performed by *direct mapping*. Because it requires only a few machine instructions, the example mapping is computationally efficient, and does not involve references to external data. Finally, new computers can be added to the network without changing existing assignments or propagating information to existing computers.

Mathematically, direct mapping means selecting a function f that maps IP addresses to physical addresses, and resolving IP address I_A means computing

$$P_A = f(I_A)$$

Although it is possible to choose mappings other than the example above, we want the computation of f to be efficient, and we want choices to be easy for a human to understand. Thus, a scheme is preferred in which the relationship between the IP address and hardware address is obvious.

5.5 Resolution Through Dynamic Binding

Although it is efficient, direct mapping cannot be used for hardware technologies that use Ethernet addressing. To see why, recall from Chapter 2 that each Ethernet NIC is assigned a 48-bit physical address when the device is manufactured. As a consequence, when hardware fails and requires that an Ethernet interface be replaced, the machine's physical address changes. Furthermore, because the Ethernet address is 48 bits long, there is no hope it can be encoded in a 32-bit IP address†.

Designers of TCP/IP protocols found a creative solution to the address resolution problem for networks like Ethernet that have broadcast capability. The solution allows new hosts or routers to be added to the network without recompiling code, and does not require maintenance of a centralized database. To avoid maintaining a centralized database, the designers chose to use a low-level protocol to bind addresses dynamically. Named the *Address Resolution Protocol* (*ARP*), the protocol provides a mechanism that is both reasonably efficient and easy to maintain.

As Figure 5.1 shows, the idea behind dynamic resolution with ARP is simple: when host A wants to resolve IP address I_B, it broadcasts a special packet that asks the host with IP address I_B to respond with its physical address, P_B. All hosts, including B, receive the request, but only host B recognizes its IP address and sends a reply that con-

---

†Because direct mapping is more convenient and efficient than dynamic binding, the next generation of IP is being designed to allow 48-bit hardware addresses to be encoded in IP addresses.

tains its physical address. When *A* receives the reply, it uses the physical address to send the internet packet directly to *B*. We can summarize:

> *The Address Resolution Protocol, ARP, allows a host to find the physical address of a target host on the same physical network, given only the target's IP address.*

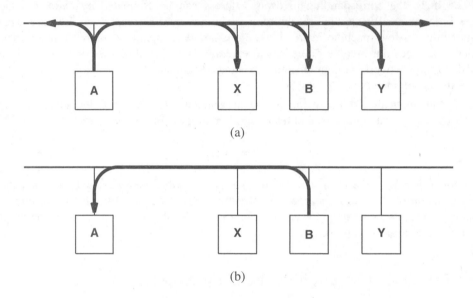

Figure 5.1 The ARP protocol. To determine P_B, *B*'s physical address, from I_B, its IP address, (a) host *A* broadcasts an ARP request containing I_B to all machines on the net, and (b) host *B* responds with an ARP reply that contains the pair (I_B, P_B).

5.6 The Address Resolution Cache

It may seem silly that for *A* to send a packet to *B* it first sends a broadcast that reaches *B*. Or it may seem even sillier that *A* broadcasts the question, "how can I reach you?" instead of just broadcasting the packet it wants to deliver. But there is an important reason for the exchange. Broadcasting is far too expensive to be used every time one machine needs to transmit a packet to another because every machine on the network must receive and process the broadcast packet.

5.7 ARP Cache Timeout

To reduce communication costs, computers that use ARP maintain a cache of recently acquired IP-to-physical address bindings. That is, whenever a computer sends an ARP request and receives an ARP reply, it saves the IP address and corresponding hardware address information in its cache for successive lookups. When transmitting a packet, a computer always looks in its cache for a binding before sending an ARP request. If it finds the desired binding in its ARP cache, the computer need not broadcast on the network. Thus, when two computers on a network communicate, they begin with an ARP request and response, and then repeatedly transfer packets without using ARP for each one. Experience shows that because most network communication involves more than one packet transfer, even a small cache is worthwhile.

The ARP cache provides an example of *soft state*, a technique commonly used in network protocols. The name describes a situation in which information can become "stale" without warning. In the case of ARP, consider two computers, A and B, both connected to an Ethernet. Assume A has sent an ARP request, and B has replied. Further assume that after the exchange B crashes. Computer A will not receive any notification of the crash. Moreover, because it already has address binding information for B in its ARP cache, computer A will continue to send packets to B. The Ethernet hardware provides no indication that B is not on-line because Ethernet does not have guaranteed delivery. Thus, A has no way of knowing when information in its ARP cache has become incorrect.

To accommodate soft state, responsibility for correctness lies with the owner of the information. Typically, protocols that implement soft state use timers, with the state information being deleted when the timer expires. For example, whenever address binding information is placed in an ARP cache, the protocol requires a timer to be set, with a typical timeout being 20 minutes. When the timer expires, the information must be removed. After removal there are two possibilities. If no further packets are sent to the destination, nothing occurs. If a packet must be sent to the destination and there is no binding present in the cache, the computer follows the normal procedure of broadcasting an ARP request and obtaining the binding. If the destination is still reachable, the binding will again be placed in the ARP cache. If not, the sender will discover that the destination is off-line.

The use of soft state in ARP has advantages and disadvantages. The chief advantage arises from autonomy. First, a computer can determine when information in its ARP cache should be revalidated independent of other computers. Second, a sender does not need successful communication with the receiver or a third party to determine that a binding has become invalid; if a target does not respond to an ARP request, the sender will declare the target to be down. Third, the scheme does not rely on network hardware to provide reliable transfer. The chief disadvantage of soft state arises from delay — if the timer interval is N seconds, a sender may not detect that a receiver has crashed until N seconds elapse.

5.8 ARP Refinements

Several refinements of ARP have been included in the protocol. First, observe that if host *A* is about to use ARP because it needs to send to *B*, there is a high probability that host *B* will need to send to *A* in the near future. To anticipate *B*'s need and avoid extra network traffic, *A* includes its IP-to-physical address binding when sending *B* a request. *B* extracts *A*'s binding from the request, saves the binding in its ARP cache, and then sends a reply to *A*. Second, notice that because *A* broadcasts its initial request, all machines on the network receive it and can extract *A*'s IP-to-physical address binding, and use the information to update the binding in their cache. Third, when a computer has its host interface replaced, (e.g., because the hardware has failed), its physical address changes. Other computers on the net that have stored a binding in their ARP cache need to be informed so they can change the entry. The computer can notify others of a new address by broadcasting a *gratuitous ARP request* when it boots†.

The following rule summarizes ARP refinements:

> *The sender's IP-to-physical address binding is included in every ARP broadcast; receivers update the IP-to-physical address binding information in their cache before processing an ARP packet.*

5.9 Relationship Of ARP To Other Protocols

ARP provides one possible mechanism to map from IP addresses to physical addresses; we have already seen that hardware technologies that support direct mapping do not need ARP. The point is that ARP would be completely unnecessary if we could make all network hardware recognize IP addresses. Thus, ARP merely imposes a new address scheme on top of whatever low-level address mechanism the hardware uses. The idea can be summarized:

> *ARP is a low-level protocol that hides the underlying network physical addressing, permitting one to assign an arbitrary IP address to every machine. We think of ARP as part of the physical network system, and not as part of the internet protocols.*

5.10 ARP Implementation

Functionally, ARP is divided into two parts. The first part maps an IP address to a physical address when sending a datagram, and the second part answers requests from other machines. Address resolution for outgoing datagrams seems straightforward, but small details complicate an implementation. Given a destination IP address, the software consults its ARP cache to see if it knows the mapping from IP address to phy-

---

†Typically, the booting machine sends a request for its own IP address as a way to verify that no other computer has accidentally been assigned the same IP address.

sical address. If it does, the software extracts the physical address, places the data in a frame using that address, and sends the frame. If it does not know the mapping, the software must broadcast an ARP request and wait for a reply.

Broadcasting an ARP request to find an address mapping can become complex. The target machine can be down or too busy to accept the request. If so, the sender may not receive a reply or the reply may be delayed. Because the Ethernet is a best-effort delivery system, the initial ARP broadcast request can also be lost (in which case the sender should retransmit, at least once). Meanwhile, the host must store the original outgoing packet so it can be sent once the address has been resolved†. In fact, the host must decide whether to allow other application programs to proceed while it processes an ARP request (most do). If so, the software must handle the case where an application generates datagrams that require resolution of the same address without broadcasting multiple requests for a given target.

Finally, consider the case where machine *A* has obtained a binding for machine *B*, but then *B*'s hardware fails and is replaced. Although *B*'s address has changed, *A*'s cached binding has not, so *A* uses a nonexistent hardware address, making successful reception impossible. This case shows why it is important to have ARP software treat its table of bindings as a cache and remove entries after a fixed period. Of course, the timer for an entry in the cache must be reset whenever an ARP broadcast arrives containing the binding (but it is not reset when the entry is used to send a packet).

The second part of the ARP code handles ARP packets that arrive from the network. When an ARP packet arrives, the software first extracts the sender's IP address and hardware address pair, and examines the local cache to see if it already has an entry for the sender. If a cache entry exists for the given IP address, the handler updates that entry by overwriting the physical address with the physical address obtained from the packet. The receiver then processes the rest of the ARP packet.

A receiver must handle two types of incoming ARP packets. If an ARP request arrives, the receiving machine must see if it is the target of the request (i.e., some other machine has broadcast a request for the receiver's physical address). If so, the ARP software forms a reply by supplying its physical hardware address, and sends the reply directly back to the requester. The receiver also adds the sender's address pair to its cache if the pair is not already present. If the IP address mentioned in the ARP request does not match the local IP address, the packet is requesting a mapping for some other machine on the network and can be ignored.

The other interesting case occurs when an ARP reply arrives. Depending on the implementation, the handler may need to create a cache entry, or the entry may have been created when the request was generated. In any case, once the cache has been updated, the receiver tries to match the reply with a previously issued request. Usually, replies arrive in response to a request, which was generated because the machine has a packet to deliver. Between the time a machine broadcasts its ARP request and receives the reply, application programs or higher-level protocols may generate additional requests for the same address; the software must remember that it has already sent a request and not send more. Usually, ARP software places the additional packets on a

---

†If the delay is significant, the host may choose to discard the outgoing datagrams(s).

queue. Once the reply arrives and the address binding is known, the ARP software removes packets from the queue, places each packet in a frame, and uses the address binding to fill in the physical destination address. If it did not previously issue a request for the IP address in the reply, the machine updates the sender's entry in its cache, and then simply stops processing the packet.

5.11 ARP Encapsulation And Identification

When ARP messages travel from one machine to another, they must be carried in physical frames. Figure 5.2 shows that the ARP message is carried in the data portion of a frame.

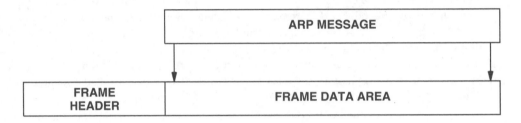

Figure 5.2 An ARP message encapsulated in a physical network frame.

To identify the frame as carrying an ARP message, the sender assigns a special value to the type field in the frame header, and places the ARP message in the frame's data field. When a frame arrives at a computer, the network software uses the frame type to determine its contents. In most technologies, a single type value is used for all frames that carry an ARP message — network software in the receiver must further examine the ARP message to distinguish between ARP requests and ARP replies. For example, on an Ethernet, frames carrying ARP messages have a type field of 0806_{16}. This is a standard value assigned by the authority for Ethernet; other network hardware technologies use other values.

5.12 ARP Protocol Format

Unlike most protocols, the data in ARP packets does not have a fixed-format header. Instead, to make ARP useful for a variety of network technologies, the length of fields that contain addresses depend on the type of network. However, to make it possible to interpret an arbitrary ARP message, the header includes fixed fields near the beginning that specify the lengths of the addresses found in succeeding fields. In fact, the ARP message format is general enough to allow it to be used with arbitrary physical addresses and arbitrary protocol addresses. The example in Figure 5.3 shows the 28-octet ARP message format used on Ethernet hardware (where physical addresses are 48-bits or 6 octets long), when resolving IP protocol addresses (which are 4 octets long).

Figure 5.3 shows an ARP message with 4 octets per line, a format that is standard throughout this text. Unfortunately, unlike most of the remaining protocols, the variable-length fields in ARP packets do not align neatly on 32-bit boundaries, making the diagram difficult to read. For example, the sender's hardware address, labeled *SENDER HA*, occupies 6 contiguous octets, so it spans two lines in the diagram.

0	8	16	24	31
HARDWARE TYPE		PROTOCOL TYPE		
HLEN	PLEN	OPERATION		
SENDER HA (octets 0-3)				
SENDER HA (octets 4-5)		SENDER IP (octets 0-1)		
SENDER IP (octets 2-3)		TARGET HA (octets 0-1)		
TARGET HA (octets 2-5)				
TARGET IP (octets 0-3)				

Figure 5.3 An example of the ARP/RARP message format when used for IP-to-Ethernet address resolution. The length of fields depends on the hardware and protocol address lengths, which are 6 octets for an Ethernet address and 4 octets for an IP address.

Field *HARDWARE TYPE* specifies a hardware interface type for which the sender seeks an answer; it contains the value *1* for Ethernet. Similarly, field *PROTOCOL TYPE* specifies the type of high-level protocol address the sender has supplied; it contains 0800_{16} for IP addresses. Field *OPERATION* specifies an ARP request (*1*), ARP response (*2*), RARP† request (*3*), or RARP response (*4*). Fields *HLEN* and *PLEN* allow ARP to be used with arbitrary networks because they specify the length of the hardware address and the length of the high-level protocol address. The sender supplies its hardware address and IP address, if known, in fields *SENDER HA* and *SENDER IP*.

When making a request, the sender also supplies the target hardware address (RARP) or target IP address (ARP), using fields *TARGET HA* or *TARGET IP*. Before the target machine responds, it fills in the missing addresses, swaps the target and sender pairs, and changes the operation to a reply. Thus, a reply carries the IP and hardware addresses of the original requester, as well as the IP and hardware addresses of the machine for which a binding was sought.

---

†The next section describes RARP, a protocol that uses the same message format.

5.13 Automatic ARP Cache Revalidation

It is possible to use a technique that avoids introducing *jitter* (i.e., variance in packet transfer times). To understand the situation, observe that whenever an ARP timer expires, the next datagram sent to the address will experience extra delay because the datagram waits in a queue until the ARP software sends a request and receives a response. Furthermore, expiration can occur at any time, possibly during a period of steady traffic. Although such delays are usually negligible, they do introduce jitter.

The key to avoiding jitter arises from *early revalidation*. That is, the implementation associates two counters with each entry in the ARP cache: the traditional timer and a revalidation timer. When the revalidation timer expires, the software examines the entry. If datagrams have recently used the entry, the software sends an ARP request and continues to use the entry. When it receives the request, the target station replies, and both timers are reset. If no reply arrives, the traditional timer expires, and datagrams are held while ARP attempts to obtain a response. In most cases, however, a revalidation can reset the timer without interruption.

5.14 Reverse Address Resolution (RARP)

We saw above that the operation field in an ARP packet can specify a *Reverse Address Resolution* (*RARP*) message. RARP is no longer important in the Internet, but was once an essential protocol used to *bootstrap* systems that did not have stable storage. In essence, RARP allows a system to obtain an IP address at startup. The procedure is straightforward: when it boots, the system broadcasts a *RARP request* and waits for a response. Another computer on the network must be configured to listen for RARP requests and generate a *RARP reply* that contains the requester's IP address. Once the reply arrives, the system continues to boot, and uses IP for all communication.

When it makes a RARP request, a system must identify itself so the computer receiving the request can place the correct IP address in the reply. Although any unique hardware identification suffices (e.g., the CPU serial number), RARP uses an obvious ID: the system's MAC address. That is, a booting system places its MAC address in the RARP request, and receives its IP address in the RARP reply.

Interestingly, RARP uses the same packet format as ARP†. A RARP request is formed by filling in the target protocol address field, changing the message type from *request* to *reply*, and sending the reply back directly to the machine making the request.

Like an ARP message, a RARP message is sent from one machine to another encapsulated in the data portion of a network frame. For example, an Ethernet frame carrying a RARP request has the usual preamble, Ethernet source and destination addresses, and packet type fields in front of the frame. The frame type contains the value 8035_{16} to identify the contents of the frame as a RARP message.

---

†The ARP packet format can be found on page 65.

5.15 Summary

IP addresses are assigned independent of a machine's physical hardware address. To send an internet packet across a physical net from one computer to another, the network software must map the IP address into a physical hardware address and use the hardware address to transmit the frame. If hardware addresses are smaller than IP addresses, a direct mapping can be established by having the machine's physical address encoded in its IP address. Otherwise, the mapping must be performed dynamically. The Address Resolution Protocol (ARP) performs dynamic address resolution, using only the low-level network communication system. ARP permits machines to resolve addresses without keeping a permanent record of bindings.

A machine uses ARP to find the hardware address of another machine by broadcasting an ARP request. The request contains the IP address of the machine for which a hardware address is needed. All machines on a network receive an ARP request. If the request matches a machine's IP address, the machine responds by sending a reply that contains the needed hardware address. Replies are directed to one machine; they are not broadcast.

To make ARP efficient, each machine caches IP-to-physical address bindings. Because internet traffic tends to consist of a sequence of interactions between pairs of machines, the cache eliminates most ARP broadcast requests; early revalidation can be used to eliminate jitter.

An older protocol related to ARP, RARP, allows a computer to obtain an IP address at system startup. Chapter 22 discusses a replacement.

FOR FURTHER STUDY

The address resolution protocol used here is given by Plummer [RFC 826], and has become a TCP/IP internet protocol standard. The details of RARP are given in Finlayson, *et. al.* [RFC 903]. Dalal and Printis [1981] describes the relationship between Ethernet and IP addresses, and Clark [RFC 814] discusses addresses and bindings in general. Parr [RFC 1029] discusses fault tolerant address resolution. Kirkpatrick and Recker [RFC 1166] specifies values used to identify network frames in the Internet Numbers document. Volume 2 of this series presents an example ARP implementation, and discusses the caching policy.

EXERCISES

5.1   Given a small set of physical addresses (positive integers), can you find a function f and an assignment of IP addresses such that f maps the IP addresses 1-to-1 onto the physical addresses and computing f is efficient? (Hint: look at the literature on perfect hashing).

5.2 In what special cases does a host connected to an Ethernet not need to use ARP or an ARP cache before transmitting an IP datagram?

5.3 One common algorithm for managing the ARP cache replaces the least recently used entry when adding a new one. Under what circumstances can this algorithm produce unnecessary network traffic?

5.4 Read the standard carefully. Should ARP update the cache if an old entry already exists for a given IP address? Why or why not?

5.5 Should ARP software modify the cache even when it receives information without specifically requesting it? Why or why not?

5.6 Any implementation of ARP that uses a fixed-size cache can fail when used on a network that has many hosts and much ARP traffic. Explain how.

5.7 ARP is often cited as a security weakness. Explain why.

5.8 Suppose machine C receives an ARP request sent from A looking for target B, and suppose C has the binding from I_B to P_B in its cache. Should C answer the request? Explain.

5.9 ARP can prebuild a cache for all possible hosts on an Ethernet by iterating through the set of possible IP addresses and sending an ARP request for each. Is doing so a good idea? Why or why not?

5.10 Should early revalidation send a request for all possible IP address on the local network, all entries in the ARP cache, or only for destinations that have experienced traffic recently? Explain.

5.11 How can a workstation use ARP when it boots to find out if any other machine on the network is impersonating it? What are the disadvantages of the scheme?

5.12 Explain how sending IP packets to nonexistent addresses on a remote Ethernet can generate broadcast traffic on that network.

Chapter Contents

6

Internet Protocol: Connectionless Datagram Delivery (IPv4)

6.1 Introduction

Previous chapters review pieces of network hardware and software that make internet communication possible, explaining the underlying network technologies and address resolution. This chapter explains the fundamental principle of connectionless delivery and discusses how it is provided by the *Internet Protocol* (*IP*), which is one of the two major protocols used in internetworking (TCP being the other). We will study the format of IP packets, and see how they form the basis for all internet communication. The next two chapters continue our examination of the Internet Protocol by discussing packet forwarding and error handling.

6.2 A Virtual Network

Chapter 3 discusses internet architecture in which routers connect multiple physical networks. Looking at the architecture may be misleading, because the focus should be on the interface that an internet provides to users, not on the interconnection technology.

> *A user thinks of an internet as a single virtual network that intercon-*
> *nects all hosts, and through which communication is possible; its*
> *underlying architecture is both hidden and irrelevant.*

In a sense, an internet is an abstraction of physical networks because, at the lowest level, it provides the same functionality: accepting packets and delivering them. Higher levels of internet software add most of the rich functionality users perceive.

6.3 Internet Architecture And Philosophy

Conceptually, a TCP/IP internet provides three sets of services as shown in Figure 6.1; their arrangement in the figure suggests dependencies among them. At the lowest level, a connectionless delivery service provides a foundation on which everything rests. At the next level, a reliable transport service provides a higher-level platform on which applications depend. We will soon explore each of these services, understand what they provide, and see the protocols associated with them.

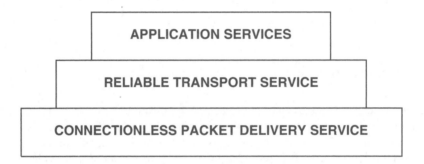

Figure 6.1 The three conceptual layers of internet services.

6.4 The Conceptual Service Organization

Although we can associate protocol software with each of the services in Figure 6.1, the reason for identifying them as conceptual parts of the internet is that they clearly point out the philosophical underpinnings of the design. The point is:

> *Internet software is designed around three conceptual networking ser-*
> *vices arranged in a hierarchy; much of its success has resulted be-*
> *cause this architecture is surprisingly robust and adaptable.*

One of the most significant advantages of the conceptual separation is that it becomes possible to replace one service without disturbing others. Thus, research and development can proceed concurrently on all three.

6.5 Connectionless Delivery System

The most fundamental internet service consists of a packet delivery system. Technically, the service is defined as an unreliable, best-effort, connectionless packet delivery system, analogous to the service provided by network hardware that operates on a best-effort delivery paradigm. The service is called *unreliable* because delivery is not guaranteed. The packet may be lost, duplicated, delayed, or delivered out of order, but the service will not detect such conditions, nor will it inform the sender or receiver. The service is called *connectionless* because each packet is treated independently from all others. A sequence of packets sent from one computer to another may travel over different paths, or some may be lost while others are delivered. Finally, the service is said to use *best-effort delivery* because the internet software makes an earnest attempt to deliver packets. That is, the internet does not discard packets capriciously; unreliability arises only when resources are exhausted or underlying networks fail.

6.6 Purpose Of The Internet Protocol

The protocol that defines the unreliable, connectionless delivery mechanism is called the *Internet Protocol*. Because the current version of the protocol is version 4, it is usually referred to by the acronym *IPv4*; when the version is unambiguous, it is referred to as *IP*. IP provides three important definitions. First, the IP protocol defines the basic unit of data transfer used throughout a TCP/IP internet. Thus, it specifies the exact format of all data as it passes across the internet. Second, IP software performs the *forwarding* function, choosing a path over which a packet will be sent. Third, in addition to the precise, formal specification of data formats and forwarding, IP includes a set of rules that embody the idea of unreliable delivery. The rules characterize how hosts and routers should process packets, how and when error messages should be generated, and the conditions under which packets can be discarded. IP is such a fundamental part of the design that the Internet is sometimes called an *IP-based technology*.

We begin our consideration of IPv4 by looking at the packet format it specifies. We leave until later chapters the topics of packet forwarding and error handling.

6.7 The IPv4 Datagram

The analogy between a physical network and a TCP/IP internet is strong. On a physical network, the unit of transfer is a frame that contains a header and data, where the header gives information such as the (physical) source and destination addresses. The internet calls its basic transfer unit an *Internet datagram*, usually abbreviated *IP datagram* or merely *datagram*. Like a typical physical network frame, a datagram is divided into header and data areas. Also like a frame, the datagram header contains the source and destination addresses and a type field that identifies the contents of the datagram. The difference, of course, is that the datagram header contains IP addresses whereas the frame header contains physical addresses. Figure 6.2 shows the general form of a datagram:

DATAGRAM HEADER	DATAGRAM DATA AREA

Figure 6.2 General form of an IP datagram, the TCP/IP analogy to a network frame. IP specifies the header format including the source and destination IP addresses. IP does not specify the format of the data area; it can be used to transport arbitrary data.

6.7.1 Datagram Format

Now that we have described the general layout of an IP datagram, we can look at the contents in more detail. Figure 6.3 shows the arrangement of fields in a datagram:

Because datagram processing occurs in software, the contents and format are not constrained by any hardware. For example, the first 4-bit field in a datagram (*VERS*) contains the version of the IP protocol that was used to create the datagram. It is used to verify that the sender, receiver, and any routers in between them agree on the format of the datagram. All IP software is required to check the version field before processing a datagram to ensure it matches the format the software expects. If standards change, machines will reject datagrams with protocol versions that differ from theirs, preventing them from misinterpreting datagram contents according to an outdated format. For IPv4, the version field contains *4*.

The header length field (*HLEN*), also 4 bits, gives the datagram header length measured in 32-bit words. As we will see, all fields in the header have fixed length except for the *IP OPTIONS* and corresponding *PADDING* fields. The most common header, which contains no options and no padding, measures 20 octets and has a header length field equal to *5*.

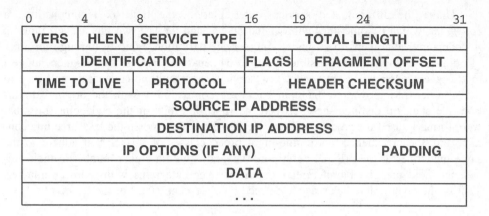

Figure 6.3 Format of an Internet datagram, the basic unit of transfer in a TCP/IP internet.

The *TOTAL LENGTH* field gives the length of the IP datagram measured in octets, including octets in the header and data. The size of the data area can be computed by subtracting the length of the header (*HLEN*) from the *TOTAL LENGTH*. Because the *TOTAL LENGTH* field is 16 bits long, the maximum possible size of an IP datagram is 2^{16} or 65,535 octets. In most applications this is not a severe limitation. It may become more important in the future if higher speed networks can carry data packets larger than 65,535 octets.

6.7.2 Datagram Type Of Service And Differentiated Services

Informally called *Type Of Service* (*TOS*), the 8-bit *SERVICE TYPE* field specifies how the datagram should be handled. The field was originally divided into subfields that specified the datagram's precedence and desired path characteristics (low delay or high throughput). In the late 1990s, the IETF redefined the meaning of the field to accommodate a set of *differentiated services* (*DiffServ*). Figure 6.4 illustrates the resulting definition.

0	1	2	3	4	5	6	7
CODEPOINT						UNUSED	

Figure 6.4 The differentiated services (DiffServ) interpretation of the *SERVICE TYPE* field in an IP datagram.

Under the differentiated services interpretation, the first six bits constitute a *codepoint*, which is sometimes abbreviated *DSCP*, and the last two bits are left unused. A codepoint value maps to an underlying service definition, typically through an array of pointers. Although it is possible to define 64 separate services, the designers suggest that a given router will only need a few services, and multiple codepoints will map to each service. Moreover, to maintain backward compatibility with the original definition, the standard distinguishes between the first three bits of the codepoint (bits that were formerly used for precedence) and the last three bits. When the last three bits contain zero, the precedence bits define eight broad classes of service that adhere to the same guidelines as the original definition: datagrams with a higher number in their precedence field are given preferential treatment over datagrams with a lower number. That is, the eight ordered classes are defined by codepoint values of the form:

$$xxx000$$

where **x** denotes either a zero or a one.

The differentiated services design also accommodates another existing practice — the widespread use of precedence 6 or 7 for high-priority routing traffic. The standard includes a special case to handle these precedence values. A router is required to implement at least two priority schemes: one for normal traffic and one for high-priority traffic. When the last three bits of the *CODEPOINT* field are zero, the router must map a codepoint with precedence 6 or 7 into the higher-priority class and other codepoint values into the lower-priority class. Thus, if a datagram arrives that was sent using the original TOS scheme, a router using the differentiated services scheme will honor precedence 6 and 7 as the datagram sender expects.

The 64 codepoint values are divided into three administrative sets as Figure 6.5 illustrates.

Pool	Codepoint	Assigned By
1	xxxxx0	Standards organization
2	xxxx11	Local or experimental
3	xxxx01	Local or experimental

Figure 6.5 The three administrative pools of codepoint values.

As the figure indicates, half of the values (i.e., the 32 values in pool *1*) must be assigned interpretations by the IETF. Currently, all values in pools *2* and *3* are available for experimental or local use. However, if the standards bodies exhaust all values in pool *1*, they may also choose to assign values in pool *3*.

The division into pools may seem unusual because it relies on the low-order bits of the value to distinguish pools. Thus, rather than a contiguous set of values, pool *1* contains every other codepoint value (i.e., the even numbers between 2 and 64). The division was chosen to keep the eight codepoints corresponding to values **xxx000** in the same pool.

Whether the original TOS interpretation or the revised differentiated services interpretation is used, it is important to realize that forwarding software must choose from among the underlying physical network technologies at hand and must adhere to local policies. Thus, specifying a level of service in a datagram does not guarantee that routers along the path will agree to honor the request. To summarize:

> *We regard the service type specification as a hint to the forwarding algorithm that helps it choose among various paths to a destination based on local policies and its knowledge of the hardware technologies available on those paths. An internet does not guarantee to provide any particular type of service.*

6.7.3 Datagram Encapsulation

Before we can understand the next fields in a datagram, it is important to consider how datagrams relate to physical network frames. We start with a question: "How large can a datagram be?" Unlike physical network frames that must be recognized by hardware, datagrams are handled by software. They can be of any length the protocol designers choose. We have seen that the IPv4 datagram format allots 16 bits to the total length field, limiting the datagram to at most 65,535 octets.

More fundamental limits on datagram size arise in practice. We know that as datagrams move from one machine to another, they must always be transported by the underlying physical network. To make internet transportation efficient, we would like to guarantee that each datagram travels in a distinct physical frame. That is, we want our abstraction of a physical network packet to map directly onto a real packet if possible.

The idea of carrying one datagram in one network frame is called *encapsulation*. To the underlying network, a datagram is like any other message sent from one machine to another. The hardware does not recognize the datagram format, nor does it understand the IP destination address. Thus, as Figure 6.6 shows, when one machine sends an IP datagram to another, the entire datagram travels in the data portion of the network frame†.

---

†A field in the frame header usually identifies the data being carried; Ethernet uses the type value 0800_{16} to specify that the data area contains an encapsulated IP datagram.

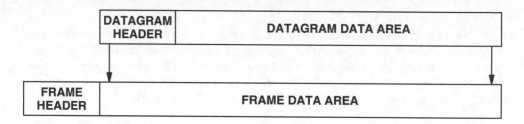

Figure 6.6 The encapsulation of an IP datagram in a frame. The physical network treats the entire datagram, including the header, as data.

6.7.4 Datagram Size, Network MTU, and Fragmentation

In the ideal case, the entire IP datagram fits into one physical frame, making transmission across the physical net efficient. To achieve such efficiency, the designers of IP might have selected a maximum datagram size such that a datagram would always fit into one frame. But which frame size should be chosen? After all, a datagram may travel across many types of physical networks as it moves across an internet to its final destination.

To understand the problem, we need a fact about network hardware: each packet-switching technology places a fixed upper bound on the amount of data that can be transferred in one physical frame. For example, Ethernet limits transfers to 1500† octets of data. We refer to the limits as the network's *maximum transfer unit* or *MTU*. MTU sizes can be larger than 1500 or smaller: some hardware technologies limit transfers to 128 octets. Limiting datagrams to fit the smallest possible MTU in the internet makes transfers inefficient when datagrams pass across a network that can carry larger size frames. However, allowing datagrams to be larger than the minimum network MTU in an internet means that a datagram may not always fit into a single network frame.

The choice should be obvious: the point of an internet is to hide underlying network technologies and make communication convenient for the user. Thus, instead of designing datagrams that adhere to the constraints of physical networks, TCP/IP software chooses a convenient initial datagram size and arranges a way to divide large datagrams into smaller pieces when the datagram needs to traverse a network that has a small MTU. The small pieces into which a datagram is divided are called *fragments*, and the process of dividing a datagram is known as *fragmentation*.

As Figure 6.7 illustrates, fragmentation usually occurs at a router somewhere along the path between the datagram source and its ultimate destination. The router receives a datagram from a network with a large MTU and must send it over a network for which the MTU is smaller than the datagram size.

---

†The limit of 1500 octets comes from the Ethernet specification; when used with a SNAP header the IEEE 802.3 standard limits data to 1492 octets.

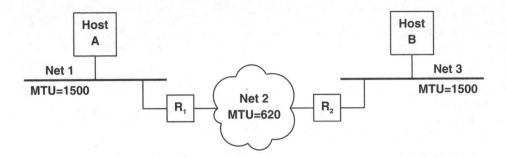

Figure 6.7 An illustration of where fragmentation occurs. Router R_1 fragments large datagrams sent from A to B; R_2 fragments large datagrams sent from B to A.

In the figure, both hosts attach directly to Ethernets which have an MTU of 1500 octets. Thus, both hosts can generate and send datagrams up to 1500 octets long. The path between them, however, includes a network with an MTU of 620. If host A sends host B a datagram larger than 620 octets, router R_1 will fragment the datagram. Similarly, if B sends a large datagram to A, router R_2 will fragment the datagram.

Fragment size is chosen so each fragment can be shipped across the underlying network in a single frame. In addition, because IP represents the offset of the data in multiples of eight octets, the fragment size must be chosen to be a multiple of eight. Of course, choosing the multiple of eight octets nearest to the network MTU does not usually divide the datagram into equal size pieces; the last piece is often shorter than the others. Fragments must be *reassembled* to produce a complete copy of the original datagram before it can be processed at the destination.

The IP protocol does not limit datagrams to a small size, nor does it guarantee that large datagrams will be delivered without fragmentation. The source can choose any datagram size it thinks appropriate; fragmentation and reassembly occur automatically, without the source taking special action. The IP specification states that routers must accept datagrams up to the maximum of the MTUs of networks to which they attach. In addition, a router must always handle datagrams of up to 576 octets. (Hosts are also required to accept, and reassemble if necessary, datagrams of at least 576 octets.)

Fragmenting a datagram means dividing it into several pieces. It may surprise you to learn that each piece has the same format as the original datagram. Figure 6.8 illustrates the result of fragmentation.

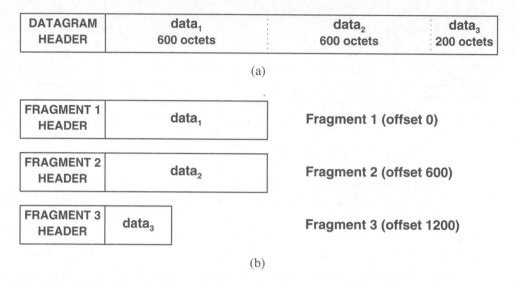

Figure 6.8 (a) An original datagram carrying 1400 octets of data and (b) the three fragments for a network MTU of 620. Headers 1 and 2 have the *more fragments* bit set. Offsets shown are decimal octets; they must be divided by 8 to get the value stored in the fragment headers.

Each fragment contains a datagram header that duplicates most of the original datagram header (except for a bit in the *FLAGS* field that shows it is a fragment), followed by as much data as can be carried in the fragment while keeping the total length smaller than the MTU of the network over which it must travel.

6.7.5 Reassembly Of Fragments

Should a datagram be reassembled after passing across one network, or should the fragments be carried to the final host before reassembly? In a TCP/IP internet, once a datagram has been fragmented, the fragments travel as separate datagrams all the way to the ultimate destination where they must be reassembled. Preserving fragments all the way to the ultimate destination has two disadvantages. First, because datagrams are not reassembled immediately after passing across a network with small MTU, the small fragments must be carried from the point of fragmentation to the ultimate destination. Reassembling datagrams at the ultimate destination can lead to inefficiency: even if some of the physical networks encountered after the point of fragmentation have large MTU capability, only small fragments traverse them. Second, if any fragments are lost, the datagram cannot be reassembled. The receiving machine starts a *reassembly timer* when it receives an initial fragment. If the timer expires before all fragments arrive, the receiving machine discards the surviving pieces without processing the datagram. Thus, the probability of datagram loss increases when fragmentation occurs because the loss of a single fragment results in loss of the entire datagram.

Despite the minor disadvantages, performing reassembly at the ultimate destination works well. It allows each fragment to be forwarded independently, and does not require intermediate routers to store or reassemble fragments.

6.7.6 Fragmentation Control

Three fields in the datagram header, *IDENTIFICATION*, *FLAGS*, and *FRAGMENT OFFSET*, control fragmentation and reassembly of datagrams. Field *IDENTIFICATION* contains a unique integer that identifies the datagram. Recall that when a router fragments a datagram, it copies most of the fields in the datagram header into each fragment. Thus, the *IDENTIFICATION* field must be copied. Its primary purpose is to allow the destination to know which arriving fragments belong to which datagrams. As a fragment arrives, the destination uses the *IDENTIFICATION* field along with the datagram source address to identify the datagram. Computers sending IP datagrams must generate a unique value for the *IDENTIFICATION* field for each datagram†. One technique used by IP software keeps a global counter in memory, increments it each time a new datagram is created, and assigns the result as the datagram's *IDENTIFICATION* field.

Recall that each fragment has exactly the same format as a complete datagram. For a fragment, field *FRAGMENT OFFSET* specifies the offset in the original datagram of the data being carried in the fragment, measured in units of 8 octets‡, starting at offset zero. To reassemble the datagram, the destination must obtain all fragments starting with the fragment that has offset *0* through the fragment with highest offset. Fragments do not necessarily arrive in order, and there is no communication between the router that fragmented the datagram and the destination trying to reassemble it.

The low-order two bits of the 3-bit *FLAGS* field control fragmentation. Usually, application software using TCP/IP does not care about fragmentation because both fragmentation and reassembly are automatic procedures that occur at a low level in the operating system, invisible to end users. However, to test internet software or debug operational problems, it may be important to test sizes of datagrams for which fragmentation occurs. The first control bit aids in such testing by specifying whether the datagram may be fragmented. It is called the *do not fragment* bit because setting it to *1* specifies that the datagram should not be fragmented. An application may choose to disallow fragmentation when only the entire datagram is useful. For example, consider a bootstrap sequence in which a small embedded system executes a program in ROM that sends a request over the internet to which another machine responds by sending back a memory image. If the embedded system has been designed so it needs the entire image or none of it, the datagram should have the *do not fragment* bit set. Whenever a router needs to fragment a datagram that has the *do not fragment* bit set, the router discards the datagram and sends an error message back to the source.

---

†In theory, retransmissions of a packet can carry the same *IDENTIFICATION* field as the original; in practice, higher-level protocols perform retransmission, resulting in a new datagram with its own *IDENTIFICATION*.

‡To save space in the header, offsets are specified in multiples of 8 octets.

The low order bit in the *FLAGS* field specifies whether the fragment contains data from the middle of the original datagram or from the end. It is called the *more fragments* bit. To see why such a bit is needed, consider the IP software at the ultimate destination attempting to reassemble a datagram. It will receive fragments (possibly out of order) and needs to know when it has received all fragments for a datagram. When a fragment arrives, the *TOTAL LENGTH* field in the header refers to the size of the fragment and not to the size of the original datagram, so the destination cannot use the *TOTAL LENGTH* field to tell whether it has collected all fragments. The *more fragments* bit solves the problem easily: once the destination receives a fragment with the *more fragments* bit turned off, it knows this fragment carries data from the tail of the original datagram. From the *FRAGMENT OFFSET* and *TOTAL LENGTH* fields, it can compute the length of the original datagram. By examining the *FRAGMENT OFFSET* and *TOTAL LENGTH* of all fragments that have arrived, a receiver can tell whether the fragments on hand contain all pieces needed to reassemble the original datagram.

6.7.7 Time to Live (TTL)

In principle, field *TIME TO LIVE* specifies how long, in seconds, the datagram is allowed to remain in the internet system. The idea is both simple and important: whenever a computer injects a datagram into the internet, it sets a maximum time that the datagram should survive. Routers and hosts that process datagrams must decrement the *TIME TO LIVE* field as time passes and remove the datagram from the internet when its time expires.

Estimating exact times is difficult because routers do not usually know the transit time for physical networks. A few rules simplify processing and make it easy to handle datagrams without synchronized clocks. First, each router along the path from source to destination is required to decrement the *TIME TO LIVE* field by *1* when it processes the datagram header. Furthermore, because routers were initially slow, the original standard specified that if a router holds a datagram for *K* seconds, the router should decrement the *TIME TO LIVE* by *K*.

Although once important, the notion of a router delaying a datagram for many seconds is now outdated — current routers and networks are designed to forward each datagram within a few milliseconds at most. If the delay becomes excessive, the router simply discards the datagram. Thus, in practice, the *TIME TO LIVE* acts as a "hop limit" rather than an estimate of delay. Each router along the path (i.e., each *hop*) decrements the value by 1.

Whenever a *TIME TO LIVE* field reaches zero, the router discards the datagram and sends an error message back to the source. The idea of keeping a timer for datagrams is interesting because it guarantees that datagrams cannot travel around an internet forever, even if routing tables become corrupt and routers forward datagrams in a circle. Thus, the *TIME TO LIVE* field can be viewed as a fail-safe mechanism.

6.7.8 Other Datagram Header Fields

Field *PROTOCOL* is analogous to the type field in a network frame; the value specifies which high-level protocol was used to create the message carried in the *DATA* area of the datagram. In essence, the value of *PROTOCOL* specifies the format of the *DATA* area. The mapping between a high-level protocol and the integer value used in the *PROTOCOL* field must be administered by a central authority to guarantee agreement across the entire Internet.

Field *HEADER CHECKSUM* ensures integrity of header values. The IP checksum is formed by treating the header as a sequence of 16-bit integers (in network byte order), adding them together using one's complement arithmetic, and then taking the one's complement of the result. For purposes of computing the checksum, field *HEADER CHECKSUM* is assumed to contain zero.

It is important to note that the checksum only applies to values in the IP header and not to the data. Separating the checksum for headers and data has advantages and disadvantages. Because the header usually occupies fewer octets than the data, having a separate checksum reduces processing time at routers which only need to compute header checksums. The separation also allows higher-level protocols to choose their own checksum scheme for the data. The chief disadvantage is that higher-level protocols are forced to add their own checksum or risk having corrupted data go undetected.

Fields *SOURCE IP ADDRESS* and *DESTINATION IP ADDRESS* contain the 32-bit IP addresses of the datagram's sender and intended recipient. Although the datagram may be forwarded through many intermediate routers, the source and destination fields never change; they specify the IP addresses of the original source and ultimate destination†.

The field labeled *DATA* in Figure 6.3 shows the beginning of the data area of the datagram. Its length depends, of course, on what is being sent in the datagram. The *IP OPTIONS* field, discussed below, is variable length. The field labeled *PADDING*, depends on the options selected. It represents bits containing zero that may be needed to ensure the datagram header extends to an exact multiple of 32 bits (recall that the header length field is specified in units of 32-bit words).

6.8 Internet Datagram Options

The *IP OPTIONS* field following the destination address is not required in every datagram; options are included primarily for network testing or debugging. Options processing is an integral part of the IP protocol, however, so all standard implementations must include it.

The length of the *IP OPTIONS* field varies depending on which options are selected. Some options are one octet long; they consist of a single octet *option code*. Other options are variable length. When options are present in a datagram, they appear con-

---

†An exception is made when the datagram includes the source route options listed below.

tiguously, with no special separators between them. Each option consists of a single octet option code, which may be followed by a single octet length and a set of data octets
for that option. The option code octet is divided into three fields as Figure 6.9 shows.

0	1	2	3	4	5	6	7
COPY	OPTION CLASS		OPTION NUMBER				

Figure 6.9 The division of the option code octet into three fields of length 1,
2, and 5 bits.

The fields of the *OPTION CODE* consist of a 1-bit *COPY* flag, a 2-bit *OPTION CLASS*,
and a 5-bit *OPTION NUMBER*. The *COPY* flag controls how routers treat options during fragmentation. When the *COPY* bit is set to *1*, it specifies that the option should be
copied into all fragments. When set to *0*, the *COPY* bit means that the option should
only be copied into the first fragment and not into all fragments.

The *OPTION CLASS* and *OPTION NUMBER* bits specify the general class of the
option and a specific option in that class. The table in Figure 6.10 shows how option
classes are assigned.

Option Class	Meaning
0	Datagram or network control
1	Reserved for future use
2	Debugging and measurement
3	Reserved for future use

Figure 6.10 Classes of IP options as encoded in the *OPTION CLASS* bits of
an option code octet.

The table in Figure 6.11 lists examples of options that can accompany an IP datagram and gives their *OPTION CLASS* and *OPTION NUMBER* values. As the list
shows, most options are used for control purposes.

Option Class	Option Number	Length	Description
0	0	-	End of option list. Used if options do not end at end of header (see header padding field for explanation).
0	1	-	No operation. Used to align octets in a list of options.
0	2	11	Security and handling restrictions (for military applications).
0	3	var	Loose source route. Used to request routing that includes the specified routers.
0	7	var	Record route. Used to trace a route.
0	8	4	Stream identifier. Used to carry a SATNET stream identifier (obsolete).
0	9	var	Strict source route. Used to specify an exact path through the internet.
0	11	4	MTU Probe. Used for path MTU discovery.
0	12	4	MTU Reply. Used for path MTU discovery.
0	20	4	Router Alert. Router should examine this datagram even if not an addressee.
2	4	var	Internet timestamp. Used to record timestamps along the route.
2	18	var	Traceroute. Used by traceroute program to find routers along a path.

Figure 6.11 Examples of IP options with their numeric class and number codes. The value *var* in the length column stands for *variable*.

6.8.1 Record Route Option

The route and timestamp options are the most interesting because they provide a way to monitor or control how internet routers forward datagrams. The *record route* option allows the source to create an empty list of IP addresses and arrange for each router that handles the datagram to add its IP address to the list. Figure 6.12 shows the format of the record route option.

As described above, the *CODE* field contains the option class and option number (*0* and *7* for record route). The *LENGTH* field specifies the total length of the option as it appears in the IP datagram, including the first three octets. The fields starting with the one labeled *FIRST IP ADDRESS* constitute the area reserved for recording internet addresses. The *POINTER* field specifies the offset within the option of the next available slot.

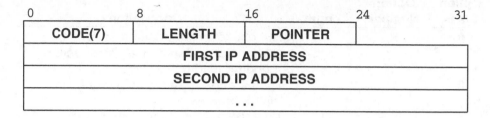

Figure 6.12 The format of the record route option in an IP datagram. The option begins with three octets immediately followed by a list of addresses. Although the diagram shows addresses in 32 bit units, they are not aligned on any octet boundary in a datagram.

Whenever a machine handles a datagram that has the record route option set, the machine adds its address to the record route list (enough space must be allocated in the option by the original source to hold all entries that will be needed). To add itself to the list, a machine first compares the pointer and length fields. If the pointer is greater than the length, the list is full, so the machine forwards the datagram without inserting its entry. If the list is not full, the machine inserts its 4-octet IP address at the position specified by the *POINTER* and increments the *POINTER* by four.

When the datagram arrives, the destination machine can extract and process the list of IP addresses. Usually, a computer that receives a datagram ignores the recorded route. Using the record route option requires two machines that agree to cooperate; a computer will not automatically receive recorded routes in incoming datagrams after it turns on the record route option in outgoing datagrams. The source must agree to enable the record route option, and the destination must agree to process the resultant list.

6.8.2 Source Route Options

Another idea that network builders find interesting is the *source route* option. The idea behind source routing is that it provides a way for the sender to dictate a path through the internet. For example, to test the throughput over a particular physical network, *N*, system administrators can use source routing to force IP datagrams to traverse network *N* even if routers would normally choose a path that did not include it. The ability to make such tests is especially important in a production environment, because it gives the network manager freedom to forward users' datagrams over networks that are known to operate correctly while simultaneously testing other networks. Of course, source routing is only useful to people who understand the network topology; the average user has no need to know or use it.

IP supports two forms of source routing. One form, called *strict source routing*, specifies a routing path by including a sequence of IP addresses in the option as Figure 6.13 shows.

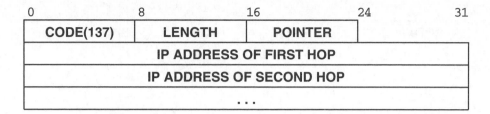

Figure 6.13 The strict source route option specifies an exact route by giving a list of IP addresses the datagram must follow.

Strict source routing means that the addresses specify the exact path the datagram must follow to reach its destination. The path between two successive addresses in the list must consist of a single physical network; an error results if a router cannot follow a strict source route. The other form, called *loose source routing*, also includes a sequence of IP addresses. It specifies that the datagram must follow the sequence of IP addresses, but allows multiple network hops between successive addresses on the list.

Both source route options require routers along the path to overwrite items in the address list with their local network addresses. Thus, when the datagram arrives at its destination, it contains a list of all addresses visited, exactly like the list produced by the record route option.

The format of a source route option resembles that of the record route option shown above. Each router examines the *POINTER* and *LENGTH* fields to see if the list has been exhausted. If it has, the pointer is greater than the length, and the router forwards the datagram to its destination as usual. If the list is not exhausted, the router follows the pointer, picks up the IP address, replaces it with the router's address†, and forwards the datagram using the address obtained from the list.

6.8.3 Timestamp Option

The *timestamp option* works like the record route option in that the timestamp option contains an initially empty list, and each router along the path from source to destination fills in one item in the list. Each entry in the list contains two 32-bit items: the IP address of the router that supplied the entry and a 32-bit integer timestamp. Figure 6.14 shows the format of the timestamp option.

---

†A router has one address for each interface; it records the address that corresponds to the network over which it forwards the datagram.

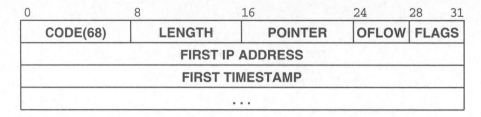

Figure 6.14 The format of the timestamp option. Bits in the FLAGS field control the exact format and rules routers use to process this option.

In the figure, the *LENGTH* and *POINTER* fields are used to specify the length of the space reserved for the option and the location of the next unused slot (exactly as in the record route option). The 4-bit *OFLOW* field contains an integer count of routers that could not supply a timestamp because the option was too small.

The value in the 4-bit *FLAGS* field controls the exact format of the option and tells how routers should supply timestamps. The values are:

Flags value	Meaning
0	Record timestamps only; omit IP addresses.
1	Precede each timestamp by an IP address (this is the format shown in Figure 6.14).
3	IP addresses are specified by sender; a router only records a timestamp if the next IP address in the list matches the router's IP address.

Figure 6.15 The interpretation of values in the FLAGS field of a timestamp option.

Timestamps give the time and date at which a router handles the datagram, expressed as milliseconds since midnight, Universal Time†. If the standard representation for time is unavailable, the router can use any representation of local time provided it turns on the high-order bit in the timestamp field. Of course, timestamps issued by independent computers are not always consistent even if represented in universal time; each machine reports time according to its local clock, and clocks may differ. Thus, timestamp entries should always be treated as estimates, independent of the representation.

It may seem odd that the timestamp option includes a mechanism to have routers record their IP addresses along with timestamps because the record route option already provides that capability. However, recording IP addresses with timestamps eliminates

---

† Universal Time was formerly called Greenwich Mean Time; it is the time of day at the prime meridian.

ambiguity. Having an address recorded along with each timestamp is also useful because it allows the receiver to know exactly which path the datagram followed.

6.8.4 Processing Options During Fragmentation

The idea behind the *COPY* bit in the option *CODE* field should now be clear. When fragmenting a datagram, a router replicates some IP options in all fragments, while it places others in only one fragment. For example, consider the option used to record the datagram route. We said that each fragment will be handled as an independent datagram, so there is no guarantee that all fragments follow the same path to the destination. If all fragments contained the record route option, the destination might receive a different list of routes from each fragment. It could not produce a single, meaningful list of routes for the reassembled datagram. Therefore, the IP standard specifies that the record route option should only be copied into one of the fragments.

Not all IP options can be restricted to one fragment. Consider the source route option, for example, that specifies how a datagram should travel through the internet. Source routing information must be replicated in all fragment headers, or fragments will not follow the specified route. Thus, the code field for source route specifies that the option must be copied into all fragments.

6.9 Summary

The fundamental service provided by TCP/IP internet software is a connectionless, unreliable, best-effort packet delivery system. The Internet Protocol (IP) formally specifies the format of internet packets, called *datagrams*, and informally embodies the ideas of connectionless delivery. This chapter concentrated on datagram formats; later chapters will discuss IP forwarding and error handling.

Analogous to a physical frame, the IP datagram is divided into header and data areas. Among other information, the datagram header contains the source and destination IP addresses, fragmentation control, precedence, and a checksum used to catch transmission errors. Besides fixed-length fields, each datagram header can contain an options field. The options field is variable length, depending on the number and type of options used as well as the size of the data area allocated for each option. Intended to help monitor and control an internet, options allow one to specify or record route information or to gather timestamps as the datagram traverses an internet.

FOR FURTHER STUDY

Postel [1980] discusses possible ways to approach internet protocols, addressing, and forwarding. In later publications, Postel [RFC 791] gives the standard for the Internet Protocol. Braden [RFC 1122] further refines the standard. Hornig [RFC 894] specifies the standard for the transmission of IP datagrams across an Ethernet. Clark [RFC 815] describes efficient reassembly of fragments; Kent and Mogul [1987] discusses the disadvantages of fragmentation.

Nichols et. al. [RFC 2474] specifies the differentiated service interpretation of the service type bits in datagram headers, and Blake et. al. [RFC 2475] discusses an architecture for differentiated services. In addition to the packet format, many constants needed in the network protocols are also standardized; the values can be found in the Official Internet Protocols RFC, which is issued periodically.

An alternative internet protocol suite known as *XNS*, is given in Xerox [1981]. Boggs *et. al.* [1980] describes the PARC Universal Packet (PUP) protocol, an abstraction from *XNS* closely related to the IP datagram.

EXERCISES

6.1 What is the single greatest advantage of having the IP checksum cover only the datagram header and not the data? What is the disadvantage?

6.2 Is it ever necessary to use an IP checksum when sending packets over an Ethernet? Why or why not?

6.3 What is the MTU size for a Frame Relay network? An 802.11 network? A Hyperchannel?

6.4 Do you expect a high-speed local area network to have larger or smaller MTU size than a wide area network?

6.5 Argue that fragments should have small, nonstandard headers.

6.6 Find out when the IP protocol version last changed. Is having a protocol version number useful?

6.7 Extend the previous exercise by arguing that if the IP version changes, it makes more sense to assign a new frame type than to encode the version number in the datagram.

6.8 Can you imagine why a one's complement checksum was chosen for IP instead of a cyclic redundancy check?

6.9 What are the advantages of doing reassembly at the ultimate destination instead of doing it after the datagram travels across one network?

6.10 What is the minimum network MTU required to send an IP datagram that contains at least one octet of data?

6.11 Suppose you are hired to implement IP datagram processing in hardware. Is there any rearrangement of fields in the header that would make your hardware more efficient? Easier to build?

6.12 If you have access to an implementation of IP, revise it and test your locally available implementations of IP to see if they reject IP datagrams with an out-of-date version number.

6.13 When a minimum-size IP datagram travels across an Ethernet, how large is the frame?

6.14 The differentiated services interpretation of the *SERVICE TYPE* field allows up to 64 separate service levels. Argue that fewer levels are needed (i.e., make a list of all possible services that a user might access).

6.15 The differentiated service definition was chosen to make it backward compatible with the original type-of-service priority bits. Will the backward compatibility force implementations to be less efficient than an alternative scheme? Explain.

Chapter Contents

7

Internet Protocol: Forwarding IP Datagrams

7.1 Introduction

We have seen that all internet services use an underlying, connectionless packet delivery system, and that the basic unit of transfer in a TCP/IP internet is the IP datagram. This chapter adds to the description of connectionless service by describing how routers forward IP datagrams and deliver them to their final destinations. We think of the datagram format from Chapter 6 as characterizing the static aspects of the Internet Protocol. The description of forwarding in this chapter characterizes the operational aspects. The next chapter completes our basic presentation of IP by describing how errors are handled. Chapter 9 then describes extensions for classless and subnet addressing, and later chapters show how other protocols use IP to provide higher-level services.

7.2 Forwarding In An Internet

Traditionally, the term *routing* was used with packet switching systems such as the Internet to refer to the process of choosing a path over which to send packets, and the term *router* was used to describe the system making such a choice. More recently, engineers have adopted the term *forwarding* to refer to the process of choosing the path for a packet, but have retained the term router to refer to the system making the choice. We will follow popular usage, and use the term *forwarding*.

Forwarding occurs at several levels. For example, within a switched Ethernet that spans multiple physical chassis, the switches are responsible for forwarding Ethernet frames from the time a frame first enters until the frame is delivered to the destination host. Such internal forwarding is completely self-contained inside the network. Machines on the outside cannot participate in decisions; they merely view the network as an entity that accepts and delivers packets.

Remember that the goal of IP is to provide a virtual network that encompasses multiple physical networks and offers a connectionless datagram delivery service. Thus, we will focus on *IP forwarding*, (which was traditionally called *IP routing*). The information used to make forwarding decisions is known as *IP forwarding information*. Like forwarding within a single physical network, IP forwarding chooses a path over which a datagram should be sent. Unlike forwarding within a single network, the IP forwarding algorithm must choose how to send a datagram across multiple physical networks.

Forwarding in an internet can be difficult, especially among computers that have multiple physical network connections. Ideally, the forwarding software would examine network load, datagram length, the data being carried, or the type of service specified in the datagram header when selecting the best path. Most internet forwarding software is much less sophisticated, however, and selects routes based on fixed assumptions about shortest paths.

To understand IP forwarding completely, we must review the architecture of a TCP/IP internet. First, recall that an internet is composed of multiple physical networks interconnected by systems called *routers*. Each router has direct connections to two or more networks. By contrast, a host computer usually connects directly to one physical network. We also know that it is possible to have a multi-homed host connected directly to multiple networks.

Both hosts and routers participate in forwarding an IP datagram to its destination. When an application program on a host attempts to communicate, the TCP/IP protocols eventually generate one or more IP datagrams. The host must make an initial forwarding decision when it chooses where to send the datagrams. As Figure 7.1 shows, hosts must make forwarding decisions even if they have only one network connection.

The primary purpose of routers is to make IP forwarding decisions. What about multi-homed hosts? Any computer with multiple network connections can act as a router, and as we will see, multi-homed hosts running TCP/IP have all the software needed to forward datagrams. In fact, sites that cannot afford separate routers sometimes use general-purpose computers as both hosts and routers. However, the TCP/IP standards draw a sharp distinction between the functions of a host and those of a router, and sites that try to mix host and router functions on a single machine sometimes find that their multi-homed hosts engage in unexpected interactions. For now, we will distinguish hosts from routers, and assume that hosts do not perform the router's function of transferring packets from one network to another.

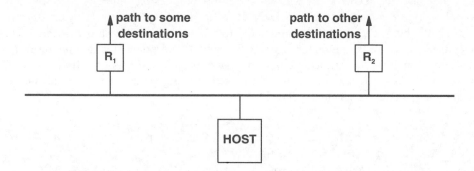

Figure 7.1 An example of a singly-homed host that must forward datagrams. The host must choose to send a datagram either to router R_1 or to router R_2, because each router provides the best path to some destinations.

7.3 Direct And Indirect Delivery

Loosely speaking, we can divide forwarding into two forms: *direct delivery* and *indirect delivery*. Direct delivery, the transmission of a datagram from one machine across a single physical network directly to another, is the basis on which all internet communication rests. Two machines can engage in direct delivery only if they both attach directly to the same underlying physical transmission system (e.g., a single Ethernet). *Indirect delivery* occurs when the destination is not on a directly attached network, forcing the sender to pass the datagram to a router for delivery.

7.3.1 Datagram Delivery Over A Single Network

We know that one machine on a given physical network can send a physical frame directly to another machine on the same network. To transfer an IP datagram, the sender encapsulates the datagram in a physical frame as described in Chapter 6, uses the ARP protocol described in Chapter 5 to map the destination IP address into a physical address, and uses the network hardware to transfer the frame. Thus, we have examined all the pieces needed to understand direct delivery. To summarize:

> *Transmission of an IP datagram between two machines on a single physical network does not involve routers. The sender encapsulates the datagram in a physical frame, binds the destination IP address to a physical hardware address, and sends the resulting frame directly to the destination.*

How does the sender know whether the destination lies on a directly connected network? The test is straightforward. Each IP address is divided into a network-specific prefix and a host-specific suffix. To determine if a destination lies on one of the directly connected networks, the sender extracts the network portion of the destination IP address and compares the extracted bits to the network portion of its own IP address(es). A match means the datagram can be sent directly. Here we see one of the advantages of the Internet address scheme, namely:

> *Because the internet addresses of all machines on a single network include a common network prefix and extracting that prefix requires only a few machine instructions, testing whether a machine can be reached directly is efficient.*

From an internet perspective, it is easiest to think of direct delivery as the final step in any datagram transmission, even if the datagram traverses many networks and intermediate routers. The final router along the path between the datagram source and its destination will connect directly to the same physical network as the destination. Thus, the final router will deliver the datagram using direct delivery. We can also think of direct delivery between the source and destination as a special case of general purpose forwarding – in a direct route the datagram does not pass through intervening routers.

7.3.2 Indirect Delivery

Indirect delivery is more difficult than direct delivery because the sender must identify an initial router to which the datagram can be sent. The router must then forward the datagram on toward the destination network.

To visualize how indirect forwarding works, imagine a large internet with many networks interconnected by routers, but with only two hosts at the far ends. When a host has a datagram to send, the host encapsulates the datagram and sends it to the nearest router. We know that the host can reach a router because all physical networks are interconnected, so there must be a router attached to each network. Thus, the originating host can reach a router using a single physical network. Once the frame reaches the router, software extracts the encapsulated datagram, and the IP software selects the next router along the path toward the destination. The datagram is again placed in a frame and sent over the next physical network to a second router, and so on, until it can be delivered directly. The concept can be summarized:

> *Routers in a TCP/IP internet form a cooperative, interconnected structure. Datagrams pass from router to router until they reach a router that can deliver the datagram directly.*

How can a router know where to send each datagram? How can a host know which router to use for a given destination? The two questions are related because they both involve IP forwarding. We will answer the questions in two stages, considering a basic table-driven forwarding algorithm in this chapter and postponing a discussion of how routers learn about destinations until Chapters 13 - 15.

7.4 Table-Driven IP Forwarding

The IP forwarding algorithm employs a data structure on each machine that stores information about possible destinations and how to reach them. The data structure is known formally as an *Internet Protocol routing table* or *IP routing table*, and informally as simply a *routing table*†.

Because both hosts and routers route datagrams, both have IP routing tables. Whenever the IP forwarding software in a host or router needs to transmit a datagram, it consults the routing table to decide where to send the datagram.

What information should be kept in a routing table? If every routing table contained information about every possible destination address, it would be impossible to keep the tables current. Furthermore, because the number of possible destinations is large, small special-purpose systems could not connect to the Internet because they would not have sufficient space to store the information.

Conceptually, it is desirable to use the principle of information hiding and allow machines to make forwarding decisions with minimal information. For example, we would like to isolate information about specific hosts to the local environment in which they exist and arrange for machines that are far away to forward packets to them without knowing such details. Fortunately, the IP address scheme helps achieve this goal. Recall that IP addresses are assigned to make all machines connected to a given physical network share a common prefix (the network portion of the address). We have already seen that such an assignment makes the test for direct delivery efficient. It also means that routing tables only need to contain network prefixes and not full IP addresses.

7.5 Next-Hop Forwarding

Using the network portion of a destination address instead of the complete host address makes forwarding efficient and keeps routing tables small. More important, it helps hide information, keeping the details of specific hosts confined to the local environment in which the hosts operate. Typically, a routing table contains pairs (N, R), where N is the IP address of a destination *network*, and R is the IP address of the "next" router along the path to network N‡. Router R is called the *next hop*, and the idea of using a routing table to store a next hop for each destination is called *next-hop forwarding* or *next-hop routing*. Thus, the routing table in a router R only specifies one

---

†Engineers sometimes use the term *IP forwarding table* as a synonym for *IP routing table*.

‡In practice, a routing table entry also specifies a network interface to use when sending to the next router as well as administrative information such as a count of the times it has been used.

step along the path from *R* to a destination network – the router does not know the complete path to a destination.

It is important to understand that each entry in a routing table points to a router that can be reached across a single network. That is, all routers listed in machine *M*'s routing table must lie on networks to which *M* connects directly. When a datagram is ready to leave *M*, IP software locates the destination IP address and extracts the network portion. *M* then uses the network portion to make a forwarding decision, selecting a router that can be reached directly.

In practice, we apply the principle of information hiding to hosts as well. We insist that although hosts have IP routing tables, they must keep minimal information in their tables. The idea is to force hosts to rely on routers for most forwarding.

Figure 7.2 shows a concrete example that helps explain routing tables. The example internet consists of four networks connected by three routers. The table in the figure corresponds to the routing table for router *R*. Because *R* connects directly to networks 20.0.0.0 and 30.0.0.0, it can use direct delivery to send to a host on either of these networks (possibly using ARP to find physical addresses). Given a datagram destined for a host on network 40.0.0.0, *R* routes it to the address of router *S*, 30.0.0.7. *S* will then deliver the datagram directly. *R* can reach address 30.0.0.7 because both *R* and *S* attach directly to network 30.0.0.0.

As Figure 7.2 demonstrates, the size of the routing table depends on the number of networks in the internet; the table only grows when new networks are added. That is, the table size and contents are independent of the number of individual hosts connected to the networks. We can summarize the underlying principle:

> *To hide information, keep routing tables small, and make forwarding decisions efficient, IP forwarding software only keeps information about destination network addresses, not about individual host addresses.*

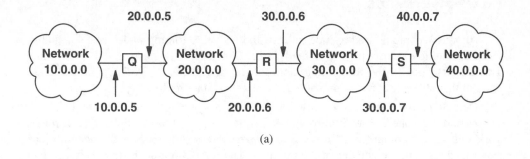

(a)

TO REACH HOSTS ON NETWORK	ROUTE TO THIS ADDRESS
20.0.0.0	DELIVER DIRECTLY
30.0.0.0	DELIVER DIRECTLY
10.0.0.0	20.0.0.5
40.0.0.0	30.0.0.7

(b)

Figure 7.2 (a) An example internet with 4 networks and 3 routers, and (b) the routing table in *R*.

Choosing routes based on the destination network ID alone has several consequences. First, in most implementations, it means that all traffic destined for a given network takes the same path. As a result, even when multiple paths exist, they may not be used concurrently. Also, in the simplest case, all traffic follows the same path without regard to the delay or throughput of physical networks. Second, because only the final router along the path attempts to communicate with the destination host, only it can determine if the host exists or is operational. Thus, we need to arrange a way for the final router to send reports of delivery problems back to the original source. Third, because each router forwards traffic independently, datagrams traveling from host *A* to host *B* may follow an entirely different path than datagrams traveling from host *B* back to host *A*. We need to ensure that routers cooperate to guarantee that two-way communication is always possible.

7.6 Default Routes

Another technique used to hide information and keep routing table sizes small consolidates multiple entries into a default case. The idea is to have the IP forwarding software first look in the forwarding table for the destination network. If no route appears in the table, the forwarding software sends the datagram to a *default router*.

Default forwarding is especially useful when a site has a small set of local addresses and only one connection to the rest of the internet. For example, default routes work well in host computers that attach to a single physical network and reach only one router leading to the remainder of the internet. The forwarding decision consists of two tests: one for the local net and a default that points to the only router. Even if the site contains a few local networks, the forwarding is simple because it consists of tests for the local networks plus a default for all other destinations.

7.7 Host-Specific Routes

Although we said that all forwarding is based on networks and not on individual hosts, most IP forwarding software allows per-host routes to be specified as a special case. Having per-host routes gives the local network administrator more control over network use, permits testing, and can also be used to control access for security purposes. When debugging network connections or routing tables, the ability to specify a special route to one individual machine turns out to be especially useful.

7.8 The IP Forwarding Algorithm

Taking into account everything we have said, the original algorithm used to forward IP datagrams with classful addressing was†:

---

†Chapter 9 discusses the modified algorithm currently used with classless IP addresses.

Algorithm:

ForwardDatagram (Datagram , RoutingTable)

Extract destination IP address, D, from the datagram;
if the table contains a host-specific route for D
  send datagram to next-hop specified in table and quit;
compute N, the network prefix of address D;
if N matches any directly connected network address
  deliver datagram to destination D over that network;
  (This involves resolving D to a physical address,
  encapsulating the datagram, and sending the frame.)
else if the table contains a route for network prefix N
  send datagram to next-hop specified in table;
else if the table contains a default route
  send datagram to the default router specified in table;
else declare a forwarding error;

Figure 7.3 The original algorithm IP used to forward a datagram. Given an IP datagram and a routing table, the algorithm selects the next hop to which the datagram should be sent. All routes must specify a next hop that lies on a directly connected network.

7.9 Forwarding With IP Addresses

It is important to understand that except for decrementing the time to live and recomputing the checksum, IP forwarding does not alter the original datagram. In particular, the datagram source and destination addresses remain unaltered; they specify the IP address of the original source and the IP address of the ultimate destination†. When IP executes the forwarding algorithm, it selects a new IP address, the IP address of the machine to which the datagram should be sent next. The new address is most likely the address of a router. However, if the datagram can be delivered directly, the new address is the same as the address of the ultimate destination.

We said that the IP address selected by the IP forwarding algorithm is known as the *next hop* address because it tells where the datagram must be sent next. Where does IP store the next hop address? Not in the datagram; no place is reserved for it. In fact, IP does not store the next hop address at all. After executing the forwarding algorithm, IP passes the datagram and the next hop address to the network interface software responsible for the physical network over which the datagram must be sent. The net-

---
†The only exception occurs when the datagram contains a source route option.

work interface software binds the next hop address to a physical address, forms a frame using that physical address, places the datagram in the data portion of the frame, and sends the result. After using the next hop address to find a physical address, the network interface software discards the next hop address.

It may seem odd that routing tables store the IP address of a next hop for each destination network when those addresses must be translated into corresponding physical addresses before the datagram can be sent. If we imagine a host sending a sequence of datagrams to the same destination address, the use of IP addresses will appear incredibly inefficient. IP dutifully extracts the destination address in each datagram and uses the routing table to produce a next hop address. It then passes the datagram and next hop address to the network interface, which recomputes the binding to a physical address. If the routing table used physical addresses, the binding between the next hop's IP address and physical address could be performed once, saving unneeded computation.

Why does IP software avoid using physical addresses when storing and computing routes? As Figure 7.4 illustrates, there are two important reasons.

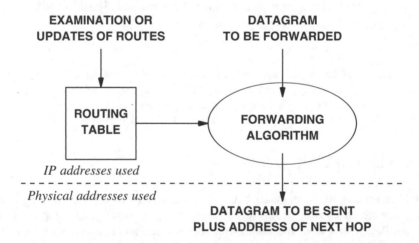

Figure 7.4 IP software and the routing table it uses reside above the address
boundary. Using only IP addresses makes routes easy to examine
or change and hides the details of physical addresses.

First, the routing table provides an especially clean interface between IP software that forwards datagrams and high-level software that manipulates routes. To debug forwarding problems, network managers often need to examine the routing tables. Using only IP addresses in the routing table makes it easy for managers to understand and to determine whether software has updated the routes correctly. Second, the goal of the Internet Protocol is to build an abstraction that hides the details of underlying networks.

Figure 7.4 shows the *address boundary*, the important conceptual division between low-level software that understands physical addresses and internet software that only uses high-level addresses. Above this boundary, all software can be written to communicate using internet addresses; knowledge of physical addresses is relegated to a few small, low-level routines. We will see that observing the boundary also helps keep the implementation of remaining TCP/IP protocols easy to understand, test, and modify.

7.10 Handling Incoming Datagrams

So far, we have discussed IP forwarding by describing how forwarding decisions are made about outgoing datagrams. It should be clear, however, that IP software must process incoming datagrams as well.

When an IP datagram arrives at a host, the network interface software delivers the datagram to the IP module for processing. If the datagram's destination address matches the host's IP address, IP software on the host accepts the datagram and passes it to the appropriate higher-level protocol software for further processing. If the destination IP address does not match, a host is required to discard the datagram (i.e., hosts are forbidden from attempting to forward datagrams that are accidentally forwarded to the wrong machine).

Unlike hosts, routers perform forwarding. When an IP datagram arrives at a router, it is delivered to the IP software. Again, two cases arise: the datagram has reached its final destination, or it may need to travel further. As with hosts, if the datagram destination IP address matches the router's own IP address, the IP software passes the datagram to higher-level protocol software for processing†. If the datagram has not reached its final destination, IP forwards the datagram using the standard algorithm and the information in the local routing table.

Determining whether an IP datagram has reached its final destination is not quite as trivial as it seems. Remember that a router has multiple physical connections, each with its own IP address. When an IP datagram arrives, the receiving machine must compare the destination internet address to the IP address for each of its network connections. If any match, it keeps the datagram and processes it. A machine must also accept datagrams that were broadcast on the physical network if the destination IP address is the limited IP broadcast address or the directed IP broadcast address for that network. As we will see in Chapters 9 and 16, classless, subnet, and multicast addresses make address recognition even more complex. In any case, if the address does not match any of the local machine's addresses, IP decrements the time-to-live field in the datagram header, discarding the datagram if the count reaches zero, or computing a new checksum and forwarding the datagram if the count remains positive.

Should every machine forward the IP datagrams it receives? Obviously, a router must forward incoming datagrams because that is its main function. We said that some sites also configure general-purpose computers to operate as routers, and such computers must be configured to forward datagrams. However hosts not designated to be

---

†Usually, the only datagrams destined for a router are those used to test connectivity or those that carry router management commands, but a router also receives a copy of any datagram that is broadcast on the network.

routers should *not* forward datagrams; if such a host receives a datagram that does not match any of the host's addresses, the host must discard the datagram.

There are four reasons why a host not designated to serve as a router should refrain from performing any router functions. First, when such a host receives a datagram intended for some other machine, something has gone wrong with internet addressing, forwarding, or delivery. The problem may not be revealed if the host takes corrective action by forwarding the datagram. Second, forwarding will cause unnecessary network traffic (and may steal CPU time from legitimate uses of the host). Third, simple errors can cause chaos. Suppose that every host forwards traffic, and imagine what happens if one machine accidentally broadcasts a datagram that is destined for a host, *H*. Because it has been broadcast, every host on the network receives a copy of the datagram. Every host forwards its copy to *H*, which will be bombarded with many copies. Fourth, as later chapters show, routers do more than merely forward traffic. As the next chapter explains, routers use a special protocol to report errors, while hosts do not (again, to avoid having multiple error reports bombard a source). Routers also propagate information to ensure that their routing tables are consistent and correct. If hosts forward datagrams without participating fully in all router functions, unexpected anomalies can arise.

7.11 Establishing Routing Tables

We have discussed how IP forwards datagrams based on the contents of routing tables, without saying how systems initialize their routing tables or update them as the network changes. Later chapters deal with these questions and discuss protocols that allow routers to keep routes consistent. For now, it is only important to understand that IP software uses the routing table whenever it decides how to forward a datagram, so changing routing tables will change the paths datagrams follow.

7.12 Summary

IP software forwards datagrams; the computation consists of deciding where to send a datagram based on its destination IP address. Direct delivery is possible if the destination machine lies on a network to which the sending machine attaches; we think of this as the final step in datagram transmission. If the sender cannot reach the destination directly, the sender must forward the datagram to a router. The general paradigm is that hosts send indirectly forwarded datagrams to the nearest router; the datagrams travel through the internet from router to router until they can be delivered directly across one physical network.

IP keeps information needed for forwarding in a table known as a routing table. When IP looks up a route, the algorithm produces the IP address of the next machine (i.e., the address of the next hop) to which the datagram should be sent; IP passes the datagram and next hop address to network interface software. Transmission of a datagram from one machine to the next always involves encapsulating the datagram in a physical frame, mapping the next hop internet address to a physical address, and sending the frame using the underlying hardware.

The internet forwarding algorithm only uses IP addresses; the binding between IP address and hardware address is not part of the IP forwarding function. Although it is possible for a routing table to contain a host-specific destination address, most routing tables contain only network addresses to keep routing tables small. Using a default route can also keep a routing table small, especially for hosts that access only one router.

FOR FURTHER STUDY

Forwarding is an important topic. Frank and Chou [1971] discusses forwarding in general; Postel [1980] discusses Internet forwarding. Baker [RFC 1812] provides a summary of how Internet routers handle IP datagrams. Narten [1989] contains a survey of Internet forwarding. Fultz and Kleinrock [1971] analyzes adaptive forwarding schemes; and McQuillan, Richer, and Rosen [1980] describes the ARPANET adaptive forwarding algorithm.

The idea of using policy statements to formulate rules about forwarding has been considered often. Leiner [RFC 1124] considers policies for interconnected networks. Braun [RFC 1104] discusses models of policy forwarding for internets, Rekhter [RFC 1092] relates policy forwarding to the second NSFNET backbone, and Clark [RFC 1102] describes using policy forwarding with IP.

EXERCISES

7.1   Complete routing tables for all routers in Figure 7.2. Which routers will benefit most from using a default route?

7.2   Examine the forwarding algorithm used on your local system. Are all forwarding cases mentioned in the chapter covered? Does the algorithm allow anything not mentioned?

7.3   What does a router do with the *time to live* value in an IP header?

7.4   Consider a machine with two physical network connections and two IP addresses I_1 and I_2. Is it possible for that machine to receive a datagram destined for I_2 over the network with address I_1? Explain.

7.5   In the above exercise, what is the appropriate response if such a situation arises?

7.6   Consider two hosts, A and B, that both attach to a common physical network, N. Is it ever possible, when using the forwarding algorithm discussed in Figure 7.3, for A to receive a datagram destined for B? Explain.

7.7   Modify the forwarding algorithm to accommodate the IP source route options discussed in Chapter 6.

7.8   An IP router must perform a computation that takes time proportional to the length of the datagram header each time it processes a datagram. Explain.

7.9   A network administrator argues that to make monitoring and debugging his local network easier, he wants to rewrite the forwarding algorithm in the chapter so it tests host-specific routes *before* it tests for direct delivery. How can he use the revised algorithm to build a network monitor?

7.10   Is it possible to address a datagram to a router's IP address? Does it make sense to do so?

7.11   Consider a modified forwarding algorithm that examines host-specific routes before testing for delivery on directly connected networks. Under what circumstances might such an algorithm be desirable? undesirable?

7.12   Play detective: after monitoring IP traffic on a local area network for 10 minutes one evening, someone notices that all frames destined for machine *A* carry IP datagrams that have destination equal to *A*'s IP address, while all frames destined for machine *B* carry IP datagrams with destination *not* equal to *B*'s IP address. Users report that both *A* and *B* can communicate. Explain.

7.13   How could you change the IP datagram format to support high-speed packet switching at routers? Hint: a router must recompute a header checksum after decrementing the time-to-live field.

Chapter Contents

8

Internet Protocol: Error And Control Messages (ICMP)

8.1 Introduction

The previous chapter shows how the Internet Protocol software provides an unreliable, connectionless datagram delivery service by arranging for each router to forward datagrams. A datagram travels from router to router until it reaches one that can deliver the datagram directly to its final destination. If a router cannot forward or deliver a datagram, or if the router detects an unusual condition that affects its ability to perform forwarding (e.g., network congestion), the router needs to inform the original source to take action to avoid or correct the problem. This chapter discusses a mechanism that Internet routers and hosts use to communicate such control or error information. We will see that routers use the mechanism to report problems and hosts use it to test whether destinations are reachable.

8.2 The Internet Control Message Protocol

In the connectionless system we have described so far, each router operates autonomously, forwarding or delivering datagrams that arrive without coordinating with the original sender. The system works well if all hosts and routers operate correctly and agree on routes. Unfortunately, no large communication system works correctly all the time. Besides failures of communication lines and processors, IP fails to deliver datagrams when the destination machine is temporarily or permanently disconnected from the network, when the time-to-live counter expires, or when intermediate routers become so congested that they cannot process the incoming traffic. The important difference between having a single network implemented with homogeneous, dedicated hardware and an internet implemented with multiple, independent systems is that in the former, the designer can arrange for the underlying hardware to inform attached hosts when problems arise. In an internet, which has no such hardware mechanism, a sender cannot tell whether a delivery failure resulted from a local malfunction or a remote one. Debugging becomes extremely difficult. The IP protocol itself contains nothing to help the sender test connectivity or learn about such failures.

To allow routers in an internet to report errors or provide information about unexpected circumstances, the designers added a special-purpose message mechanism to the TCP/IP protocols. The mechanism, known as the *Internet Control Message Protocol (ICMP)*, is considered a required part of IP and must be included in every IP implementation†.

Like all other traffic, ICMP messages travel across the internet in the data portion of IP datagrams. The ultimate destination of an ICMP message is not an application program or user on the destination machine, however, but the Internet Protocol software on that machine. That is, when an ICMP error message arrives, the ICMP software module handles it. Of course, if ICMP determines that a particular higher-level protocol or application program has caused a problem, it will inform the appropriate module. We can summarize:

> *The Internet Control Message Protocol allows routers to send error or control messages to other routers or hosts; ICMP provides communication between the Internet Protocol software on one machine and the Internet Protocol software on another.*

Initially designed to allow routers to report the cause of delivery errors to hosts, ICMP is not restricted to routers. Although guidelines restrict the use of some ICMP messages, an arbitrary machine can send an ICMP message to any other machine. Thus, a host can use ICMP to correspond with a router or another host. The chief advantage of allowing hosts to use ICMP is that it provides a single mechanism used for all control and information messages.

8.3 Error Reporting Vs. Error Correction

Technically, ICMP is an *error reporting mechanism*. It provides a way for routers that encounter an error to report the error to the original source. Although the protocol specification outlines intended uses of ICMP and suggests possible actions to take in response to error reports, ICMP does not fully specify the action to be taken for each possible error. In short:

---

†When it is necessary to indicate that ICMP is part of IP version 4, we write *ICMPv4*.

> *When a datagram causes an error, ICMP can only report the error condition back to the original source of the datagram; the source must relate the error to an individual application program or take other action to correct the problem.*

Most errors stem from the original source, but others do not. Because ICMP reports problems to the original source, however, it cannot be used to inform intermediate routers about problems. For example, suppose a datagram follows a path through a sequence of routers, R_1, R_2, ..., R_k. If R_k has incorrect routing information and mistakenly forwards the datagram to router R_E, R_E cannot use ICMP to report the error back to router R_k; ICMP can only send a report back to the original source. Unfortunately, the original source has no responsibility for the problem or control over the misbehaving router. In fact, the source may not be able to determine which router caused the problem.

Why restrict ICMP to communication with the original source? The answer should be clear from our discussion of datagram formats and forwarding in the previous chapters. A datagram only contains fields that specify the original source and the ultimate destination; it does not contain a complete record of its trip through the internet (except for unusual cases where the record route option is used). Furthermore, because routers can establish and change their own routing tables, there is no global knowledge of routes. Thus, when a datagram reaches a given router, it is impossible to know the path it has taken to arrive there. If the router detects a problem, IP cannot know the set of intermediate machines that processed the datagram, so it cannot inform them of the problem. Instead of silently discarding the datagram, the router uses ICMP to inform the original source that a problem has occurred, and trusts that host administrators will cooperate with network administrators to locate and repair the problem.

8.4 ICMP Message Delivery

ICMP messages require two levels of encapsulation as Figure 8.1 shows. Each ICMP message travels across the internet in the data portion of an IP datagram, which itself travels across each physical network in the data portion of a frame. Datagrams carrying ICMP messages are forwarded exactly like datagrams carrying information for users; there is no additional reliability or priority. Thus, error messages themselves may be lost or discarded. Furthermore, in an already congested network, the error message may cause additional congestion. An exception is made to the error handling procedures if an IP datagram carrying an ICMP message causes an error. The exception, established to avoid the problem of having error messages about error messages, specifies that ICMP messages are not generated for errors that result from datagrams carrying ICMP error messages.

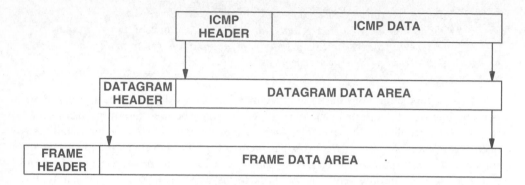

Figure 8.1 Two levels of ICMP encapsulation. The ICMP message is encapsulated in an IP datagram, which is further encapsulated in a frame for transmission. To identify ICMP, the datagram protocol field contains the value *1*.

It is important to keep in mind that even though ICMP messages are encapsulated and sent using IP, ICMP is not considered a higher-level protocol — it is a required part of IP. The reason for using IP to deliver ICMP messages is that they may need to travel across several physical networks to reach their final destination. Thus, they cannot be delivered by the physical transport alone.

8.5 ICMP Message Format

Although each ICMP message has its own format, they all begin with the same three fields: an 8-bit integer message *TYPE* field that identifies the message, an 8-bit *CODE* field that provides further information about the message type, and a 16-bit *CHECKSUM* field (ICMP uses the same additive checksum algorithm as IP, but the ICMP checksum only covers the ICMP message). In addition, ICMP messages that report errors always include the header plus additional octets from the datagram that caused the problem†.

The reason ICMP returns more than the datagram header alone is to allow the receiver to determine more precisely which protocol(s) and which application program were responsible for the datagram. As we will see later, higher-level protocols in the TCP/IP suite are designed so that crucial information is encoded in the first 64 bits following the IP header.

The ICMP *TYPE* field defines the meaning of the message as well as its format. Figure 8.2 lists possible ICMP message types:

---

†To keep error messages small and avoid fragmentation, it is not possible to include the entire datagram that caused the problem.

Type Field	ICMP Message Type
0	Echo Reply
3	Destination Unreachable
4	Source Quench
5	Redirect (change a route)
6	Alternate Host Address
8	Echo Request
9	Router Advertisement
10	Router Solicitation
11	Time Exceeded for a Datagram
12	Parameter Problem on a Datagram
13	Timestamp Request
14	Timestamp Reply
15	Information Request
16	Information Reply
17	Address Mask Request
18	Address Mask Reply
30	Traceroute
31	Datagram Conversion Error
32	Mobile Host Redirect
33	IPv6 Where-Are-You
34	IPv6 I-Am-Here
35	Mobile Registration Request
36	Mobile Registration Reply
37	Domain Name Request
38	Domain Name Reply
39	SKIP
40	Photuris

Figure 8.2 Values that can appear in the TYPE field of an ICMP message and the meaning of each. Values not listed are unassigned or reserved.

The next sections describe each of these messages, giving details of the message format and its meaning.

8.6 Testing Destination Reachability And Status (Ping)

TCP/IP protocols provide facilities to help network managers or users identify network problems. One of the most frequently used debugging tools invokes the ICMP *echo request* and *echo reply* messages. A host or router sends an ICMP echo request message to a specified destination. Any machine that receives an echo request formulates an echo reply and returns it to the original sender. The request contains an optional data area; the reply contains a copy of the data sent in the request. The echo request and associated reply can be used to test whether a destination is reachable and responding. Because both the request and reply travel in IP datagrams, successful receipt of a reply verifies that major pieces of the transport system work. First, IP software on the source computer must forward the datagram. Second, intermediate routers between the source and destination must be operating and must forward the datagram correctly. Third, the destination machine must be running (at least it must respond to interrupts), and both ICMP and IP software must be working. Finally, the routing tables in all routers along the return path must contain information that forms a viable path.

On many systems, the command users invoke to send ICMP echo requests is named *ping*†. Some versions of ping send a fixed number of request packets and await replies; other versions send a series of ICMP echo requests, capture responses, and provide statistics about datagram loss. Most versions allow the user to specify the length of the data being sent and the interval between requests. Sending a large ping packet is useful for testing fragmentation and reassembly.

8.7 Echo Request And Reply Message Format

Figure 8.3 shows the format of echo request and reply messages.

0	8	16	31
TYPE (8 or 0)	CODE (0)	CHECKSUM	
IDENTIFIER		SEQUENCE NUMBER	
OPTIONAL DATA			
. . .			

Figure 8.3 ICMP echo request or reply message format.

The field listed as *OPTIONAL DATA* is a variable length field that contains data to be returned to the sender. An echo reply always returns exactly the same data as was received in the request. Fields *IDENTIFIER* and *SEQUENCE NUMBER* are used by the sender to match replies to requests. The value of the *TYPE* field specifies whether the message is a request (*8*) or a reply (*0*).

---

†Dave Mills once suggested that *PING* is an acronym for *Packet InterNet Groper*.

8.8 Reports Of Unreachable Destinations

When a router cannot forward or deliver an IP datagram, it sends a *destination un-reachable* message back to the original source, using the format shown in Figure 8.4.

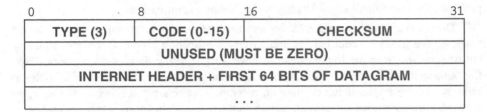

0	8	16	31
TYPE (3)	CODE (0-15)	CHECKSUM	
UNUSED (MUST BE ZERO)			
INTERNET HEADER + FIRST 64 BITS OF DATAGRAM			
. . .			

Figure 8.4 ICMP destination unreachable message format.

The *CODE* field in a destination unreachable message contains an integer that further describes the problem. Possible values are given in Figure 8.5.

Code Value	Meaning
0	Network unreachable
1	Host unreachable
2	Protocol unreachable
3	Port unreachable
4	Fragmentation needed and DF set
5	Source route failed
6	Destination network unknown
7	Destination host unknown
8	Source host isolated
9	Communication with destination network administratively prohibited
10	Communication with destination host administratively prohibited
11	Network unreachable for type of service
12	Host unreachable for type of service
13	Communication administratively prohibited
14	Host precedence violation
15	Precedence cutoff in effect

Figure 8.5 Possible values for the CODE field in an ICMP destination un-reachable message.

Although IP is a best-effort delivery mechanism, discarding datagrams should not be taken lightly. Whenever an error prevents a router from forwarding or delivering a datagram, the router sends a destination unreachable message back to the source and then *drops* (i.e., discards) the datagram. Network unreachable errors imply forwarding failures at intermediate points; host unreachable errors imply delivery failures†. Because the ICMP error message contains a short prefix of the datagram that caused the problem, the source will know exactly which address is unreachable.

Destinations may be unreachable because hardware is temporarily out of service, because the sender specified a nonexistent destination address, or (in rare circumstances) because the router does not have a route to the destination network. Note that although routers report failures they encounter, they may not know of all delivery failures. For example, if the destination machine connects to an Ethernet network, the network hardware does not provide acknowledgements. Therefore, a router can continue to send packets to a destination after the destination is powered down without receiving any indication that the packets are not being delivered. To summarize:

> *Although a router sends a destination unreachable message when it encounters a datagram that cannot be forwarded or delivered, a router cannot detect all such errors.*

The meaning of protocol and port unreachable messages will become clear when we study how higher-level protocols use abstract destination points called *ports*. Most of the remaining messages are self explanatory. If the datagram contains the source route option with an incorrect route, it may trigger a *source route* failure message. If a router needs to fragment a datagram but the ''do not fragment'' bit is set, the router sends a *fragmentation needed* message back to the source.

8.9 Congestion And Datagram Flow Control

Because IP is connectionless, a router cannot reserve memory or communication resources in advance of receiving datagrams. As a result, routers can be overrun with traffic, a condition known as *congestion*. It is important to understand that congestion can arise for two entirely different reasons. First, a high-speed computer may be able to generate traffic faster than a network can transfer it. For example, imagine a supercomputer generating internet traffic. The datagrams may eventually need to cross a slow-speed dialup connection, even though the supercomputer itself attaches to a high-speed local area net. Congestion will occur in the router that attaches the high-speed network to the slow dialup line because datagrams arrive faster than they can be sent. Second, if many computers simultaneously need to send datagrams through a single router, the router can experience congestion, even though no single source causes the problem.

---

†The IETF recommends only reporting host unreachable messages to the original source, and using routing protocols to handle other forwarding problems.

When datagrams arrive too quickly for a host or router to process, it enqueues them in memory temporarily. If the datagrams are part of a small burst, such buffering solves the problem. If the traffic continues, the host or router eventually exhausts memory and must discard additional datagrams that arrive. A machine uses ICMP *source quench* messages to report datagram discard to the original source. A source quench message is a request for the source to reduce its current rate of datagram transmission. Usually, congested routers send one source quench message for every datagram that they discard. Routers may also use more sophisticated congestion control techniques. Some monitor incoming traffic and quench sources that have the highest datagram transmission rates. Others attempt to avoid congestion altogether by arranging to send requests as their queues start to become long, but before they overflow†.

There is no ICMP message to reverse the effect of a source quench. Instead, a host that receives source quench messages for a destination, *D*, lowers the rate at which it sends datagrams to *D* until it stops receiving source quench messages; it then gradually increases the rate as long as no further source quench requests are received. In practice, most implementations ignore source quench and rely on higher-layer protocols such as TCP to react to congestion.

8.10 Source Quench Format

In addition to the usual ICMP *TYPE*, *CODE*, *CHECKSUM* fields, and an unused 32-bit field, source quench messages have a field that contains a datagram prefix. Figure 8.6 illustrates the format. As with most ICMP messages that report an error, the datagram prefix field contains a prefix of the datagram that triggered the source quench request.

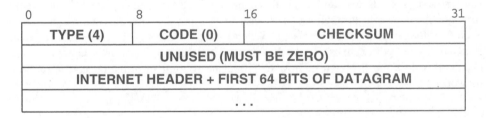

Figure 8.6 ICMP source quench message format. A congested router sends one source quench message each time it discards a datagram; the datagram prefix identifies the datagram that was dropped.

---

†Chapter 12 discusses an alternative congestion management scheme known as RED.

8.11 Route Change Requests From Routers

Internet routing tables usually remain static over long periods of time. Hosts initialize them from a configuration file at system startup, and system administrators seldom change routes during normal operations. As we will see in later chapters, routers are more dynamic — they exchange routing information periodically to accommodate network changes and keep their routes up-to-date. Thus, as a general rule:

> *Routers are assumed to know correct routes; hosts begin with minimal routing information and learn new routes from routers.*

To help follow this rule and to avoid duplicating information in the configuration file on each host, the initial host route configuration specifies the minimum possible route information needed to communicate (e.g., the address of a single router). Thus, the host begins with minimal information and relies on routers to update its routing table. In one special case, when a router detects a host using a nonoptimal route, it sends the host an ICMP message, called a *redirect*, requesting that the host change its route. The router also forwards the original datagram on to its destination.

The advantage of the ICMP redirect scheme is simplicity: it allows a host to boot knowing the address of only one router on the local network. The initial router returns ICMP redirect messages whenever a host sends a datagram for which there is a better route. The host routing table remains small, but still contains optimal routes for all destinations in use.

Because they are limited to interactions between a router and a host on a directly connected network, redirect messages do not solve the problem of propagating routing information in a general way. Figure 8.7 illustrates the limitation. In the figure, assume source S sends a datagram to destination D. Assume that router R_1 incorrectly forwards the datagram through router R_2 instead of through router R_4 (i.e., R_1 incorrectly chooses a longer path than necessary). When router R_5 receives the datagram, it cannot send an ICMP redirect message to R_1 because it does not know R_1's address. Later chapters explore the problem of how to propagate routing information across multiple networks.

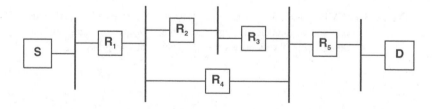

Figure 8.7 ICMP redirect messages do not propagate route changes among routers. In this example, router R_5 cannot redirect R_1 to use the shorter path for datagrams from S to D.

In addition to the requisite *TYPE*, *CODE*, and *CHECKSUM* fields, each redirect message contains a 32-bit *ROUTER INTERNET ADDRESS* field and an *INTERNET HEADER* field, as Figure 8.8 shows.

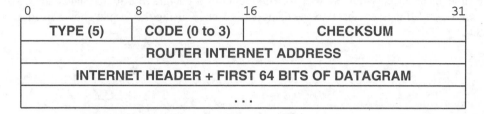

Figure 8.8 ICMP redirect message format.

The *ROUTER INTERNET ADDRESS* field contains the address of a router that the host is to use to reach the destination mentioned in the datagram header. The *INTER-NET HEADER* field contains the IP header plus the next 64 bits of the datagram that triggered the message. Thus, a host receiving an ICMP redirect examines the datagram prefix to determine the datagram's destination address. The *CODE* field of an ICMP redirect message further specifies how to interpret the destination address based on values assigned as follows:

Code Value	Meaning
0	Redirect datagrams for the Net (now obsolete)
1	Redirect datagrams for the Host
2	Redirect datagrams for the Type of Service† and Net
3	Redirect datagrams for the Type of Service and Host

As a general rule, routers only send ICMP redirect requests to hosts and not to other routers. We will see in later chapters that routers use other protocols to exchange routing information.

8.12 Detecting Circular Or Excessively Long Routes

Because internet routers compute a next hop using local tables, errors in routing tables can produce a *routing cycle* for some destination, *D*. A routing cycle can consist of two routers that each forward a datagram for destination *D* to the other, or it can consist of several routers. When several routers form a cycle, they each forward a datagram for destination *D* to the next router in the cycle. If a datagram enters a routing cycle, it will pass around the cycle endlessly. As mentioned previously, to prevent datagrams from circling forever in a TCP/IP internet, each IP datagram contains a time-

---

†Recall that each IP header specifies a type of service that can be used for forwarding.

to-live counter, sometimes called a *hop count*. Whenever it processes a datagram, a router decrements the time-to-live counter and discards the datagram when the count reaches zero.

Whenever it discards a datagram because its hop count has reached zero or because a timeout occurred while waiting for fragments of a datagram, a router sends an ICMP *time exceeded* message back to the datagram's source, using the format shown in Figure 8.9.

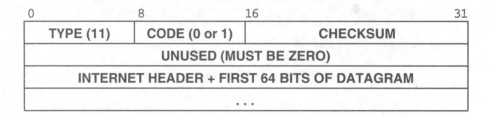

Figure 8.9 ICMP time exceeded message format. A router sends this message whenever a datagram is discarded because the time-to-live field in the datagram header has reached zero or because its reassembly timer expired while waiting for fragments.

ICMP uses the *CODE* field in each time exceeded message (value zero or one) to explain the nature of the timeout being reported:

Code Value	Meaning
0	Time-to-live count exceeded
1	Fragment reassembly time exceeded

Fragment reassembly refers to the task of collecting all the fragments from a datagram. When the first fragment of a datagram arrives, the receiving host starts a timer, and considers it an error if the timer expires before all the pieces of the datagram arrive. Code value *1* is used to report such errors to the sender; one message is sent for each error.

8.13 Reporting Other Problems

When a router or host finds problems with a datagram not covered by previous ICMP error messages (e.g., an incorrect datagram header), it sends a *parameter problem* message to the original source. One possible cause of such problems occurs when arguments to an option are incorrect. The message, formatted as shown in Figure 8.10, is only sent when the problem is so severe that the datagram must be discarded.

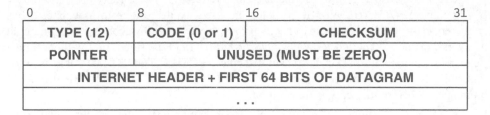

Figure 8.10 ICMP parameter problem message format. Such messages are only sent when the problem causes the datagram to be dropped.

To make the message unambiguous, the sender uses the *POINTER* field in the message header to identify the octet in the datagram that caused the problem. Code *1* is used to report that a required option is missing (e.g., a security option in the military community); the *POINTER* field is not used for code *1*.

8.14 Clock Synchronization And Transit Time Estimation

Although machines on an internet can communicate, they usually operate independently, with each machine maintaining its own notion of the current time. Clocks that differ widely can confuse users or distributed systems software. The TCP/IP protocol suite includes several protocols that can be used to synchronize clocks. One of the simplest techniques uses an ICMP message to obtain the time from another machine. A requesting machine sends an ICMP *timestamp request* message to another machine, asking that the second machine return its current value for the time of day. The receiving machine returns a *timestamp reply* back to the machine making the request. Figure 8.11 shows the format of timestamp request and reply messages.

```
0                 8                 16                              31
+-----------------+-----------------+--------------------------------+
| TYPE (13 or 14) |    CODE (0)     |          CHECKSUM              |
+-----------------+-----------------+--------------------------------+
|          IDENTIFIER               |      SEQUENCE NUMBER           |
+-----------------------------------+--------------------------------+
|                      ORIGINATE TIMESTAMP                           |
+-------------------------------------------------------------------+
|                       RECEIVE TIMESTAMP                            |
+-------------------------------------------------------------------+
|                      TRANSMIT TIMESTAMP                            |
+-------------------------------------------------------------------+
```

Figure 8.11 ICMP timestamp request or reply message format.

The *TYPE* field identifies the message as a request (*13*) or a reply (*14*); the *IDEN-TIFIER* and *SEQUENCE NUMBER* fields are used by the source to associate replies with requests. Remaining fields specify times, given in milliseconds since midnight Universal Time†. The *ORIGINATE TIMESTAMP* field is filled in by the original sender just before the packet is transmitted, the *RECEIVE TIMESTAMP* field is filled immediately upon receipt of a request, and the *TRANSMIT TIMESTAMP* field is filled immediately before the reply is transmitted.

Hosts use the three timestamp fields to compute estimates of the delay time between them and to synchronize their clocks. Because the reply includes the *ORIGINATE TIMESTAMP* field, a host can compute the total time required for a request to travel to a destination, be transformed into a reply, and return. Because the reply carries both the time at which the request entered the remote machine as well as the time at which the reply left, the host can compute the network transit time, and from that, estimate the differences in remote and local clocks.

In practice, accurate estimation of round-trip delay can be difficult and substantially restricts the utility of ICMP timestamp messages. Of course, to obtain an accurate estimate of round trip delay, one must take many measurements and average them. However, the round-trip delay between a pair of machines that connect to a large internet can vary dramatically, even over short periods of time. Furthermore, recall that because IP is a best-effort technology, datagrams can be dropped, delayed, or delivered out of order. Thus, merely taking many measurements may not guarantee consistency; sophisticated statistical analysis is needed to produce precise estimates.

8.15 Older ICMP Messages No Longer Needed

Originally, ICMP defined a set of messages that a host used at startup to determine its IP address, the address of a router, and the address mask used on the network. Currently, a protocol known as *DHCP* provides all the necessary information in a single exchange‡, and the older ICMP messages are no longer used.

Information Request And Reply Messages. ICMP's information request and reply messages (types *15* and *16*) were intended to allow hosts to discover their internet address at system startup. The IETF has declared them obsolete, so they should not be used.

Address Mast Request And Reply Messages. ICMP's address mask request and reply messages (types *17* and *18*) were intended to allow a host to obtain the address mask used on the local network. A request was broadcast, and routers on the network sent a reply.

Router Solicitation And Advertisement Messages. ICMP's router solicitation and router advertisement messages were intended to allow a host to discover routers currently available on a local network. Unlike DHCP, which uses a configuration file to provide the address of a router, the ICMP router discovery mechanism provides direct communication — a host receives advertisements directly from routers.

---

†Universal Time was formerly called Greenwich Mean Time; it is the time of day at the prime meridian.

‡Chapter 9 explains address masks, and Chapter 22 describes how DHCP returns masks along with other information.

Although no longer used, ICMP router discovery does offer two conceptual differences from DHCP. First, because the information is obtained directly from the router itself, the information is never stale. Second, ICMP router discovery uses a *soft state* technique with timers to prevent hosts from retaining a routing table entry after a router crashes — routers advertise their information periodically, and a host discards a route if the timer for the route expires.

8.16 Summary

The Internet Control Message Protocol is a required and integral part of IP that is used for extranormal communication (i.e., to report abnormal conditions or to send control information). In most cases, ICMP error messages originate from a router in the Internet; ICMP messages always go back to the original source of the datagram that caused the error.

ICMP includes *source quench* messages that retard the rate of transmission, *redirect* messages that request a host to change its routing table, and *echo request/reply* messages that hosts can use to determine whether a destination can be reached. A set of older ICMP messages that were intended to supply information to a host that booted are no longer used.

An ICMP message travels in the data area of an IP datagram and has three fixed-length fields at the beginning of the message: an ICMP message *type* field, a *code* field, and an ICMP *checksum* field. The message type determines the format of the rest of the message as well as its meaning.

FOR FURTHER STUDY

For a discussion of clock synchronization protocols see Mills [RFCs 956, 957, and 1305].

The Internet Control Message Protocol described here is a TCP/IP standard defined by Postel [RFC 792] and updated by Braden [RFC 1122]. Nagle [RFC 896] and Prue and Postel [RFC 1016] discuss ICMP source quench messages and how routers should use them to handle congestion control. Nagle [1987] argues that congestion is always a concern in packet switched networks. Mogul and Postel [RFC 950] discusses subnet mask request and reply messages, and Deering [RFC 1256] discusses the solicitation and advertisement messages that were used in router discovery.

EXERCISES

8.1   Devise an experiment to record how many of each ICMP message type appear on your local network during a day.

8.2   Experiment to see if you can send packets through a router fast enough to trigger an ICMP source quench message.

8.3   Devise an algorithm that synchronizes clocks using ICMP timestamp messages.

8.4   See if your local computer system contains a *ping* command. How does the program interface with protocols in the operating system? In particular, does the mechanism allow an arbitrary user to run a copy of the *ping* program, or does such a program require special privilege? Explain.

8.5   Assume that all routers send ICMP time-exceeded messages and that your local TCP/IP software will return such messages to an application program. Use the facility to build a *traceroute* command that reports the list of routers between the source and a particular destination.

8.6   If you connect to the Internet, try to ping host 128.10.2.1 (a machine at Purdue).

8.7   Should a router give ICMP messages priority over normal traffic? Why or why not?

8.8   Consider an Ethernet that has one conventional host, *H*, and 12 routers connected to it. Find a single (slightly illegal) frame carrying an IP packet that, when sent by host *H*, causes *H* to receive exactly 24 packets.

8.9   Compare ICMP source quench packets with Jain's 1-bit scheme used in DECNET. Which is a more effective strategy for dealing with congestion? Why?

8.10 There is no ICMP message that allows a machine to inform the source that transmission errors are causing datagrams to arrive corrupted. Explain why.

8.11 In the previous question, under what circumstances might such a message be useful?

8.12 Should ICMP error messages contain a timestamp that specifies when they are sent? Why or why not?

8.13 If routers at your site participate in ICMP router discovery, find out how many addresses each router advertises on each interface.

8.14 Try to reach a server on a nonexistent host on your local network. Also try to communicate with a nonexistent host on a remote network. In which case do you receive an error message? Why?

8.15 Try using *ping* with a network broadcast address. How many computers answer? Read the protocol documents to determine whether answering a broadcast request is required, recommended, not recommended, or prohibited.

Chapter Contents

9

Classless And Subnet Address Extensions (CIDR)

9.1 Introduction

Chapter 4 discusses the original Internet addressing scheme and presents class A, B, and C unicast addresses. This chapter examines four extensions of the IP address scheme that are designed to conserve network prefixes: anonymous point-to-point links, proxy ARP, subnet addressing, and classless addressing. The chapter considers the motivation for each extension, and describes the basic mechanism. Two of the techniques, subnet and classless addressing, are especially important because they are now used throughout the Internet.

9.2 Review Of Relevant Facts

Chapter 4 discusses addressing in internetworks and presents the original address scheme used with IPv4. Each address is divided into two parts; the designers envisioned the prefix as defining the network portion of an internet address and the remainder as a host portion. The consequence of importance to us is:

> *In the original IP addressing scheme, each physical network is assigned a unique network address; each host on a network has the network address as a prefix of the host's individual address.*

The chief advantage of dividing an IP address into two parts arises from the size of the routing tables required in routers. Instead of keeping one routing entry per destination host, a router can keep one routing entry per network, and examine only the network portion of a destination address when making forwarding decisions.

Recall that the original IP addressing scheme used classful addressing to determine the boundary between prefix and suffix. Class *A* partitioned an address into an 8-bit network portion and a 24-bit host portion, class *B* partitioned an address into 16-bit portions, and class *C* partitioned the address into a 24-bit network portion and an 8-bit host portion.

9.3 Minimizing Network Numbers

The original classful IP addressing scheme seems to handle all possibilities, but it has a minor weakness. Because they worked in a world of expensive mainframe computers, the designers failed to anticipate the growth of the Internet. They envisioned an Internet with hundreds of networks and thousands of hosts; personal computers did not appear for several years after TCP/IP was designed. Since its inception, the connected Internet has doubled in size every nine to fifteen months. Eventually, the IPv4 address space will be exhausted†. In the early 1980s, as Ethernet gained popularity, it became apparent that the classful addressing scheme would have insufficient network addresses, especially class B prefixes. The question arose, "How can the technology accommodate growth without abandoning the original classful addressing scheme?"

Several technologies were proposed to answer the question, including three that have survived: unnumbered point-to-point links, proxy ARP, and subnet addressing. In each case, the basic motivation was the same: reduce the number of network prefixes used. Later in the history of the Internet, the ideas used in subnet addressing were extended to network prefixes, and the concept of classless addressing was created. The next sections examine each technology.

9.4 Proxy ARP

The terms *proxy ARP*, *promiscuous ARP*, and *the ARP hack* refer to a technique in which a single network prefix is used for two physical networks. The technique, which only applies to networks that use ARP to bind internet addresses to physical addresses, can best be explained with an example. Figure 9.1 illustrates the situation.

---

†Although there were many predictions that the IPv4 address space would be exhausted before the year 2000, it now appears that with careful allocation and the techniques described in this chapter, IPv4 addresses will suffice until around the year 2019.

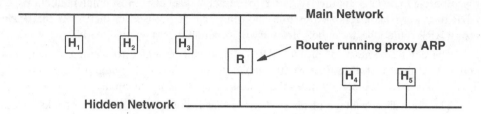

Figure 9.1 Proxy ARP technique (the ARP hack) allows one network address to be shared between two physical nets. Router R answers ARP requests on each network for hosts on the other network, giving its hardware address and then forwarding datagrams correctly when they arrive. In essence, R lies about IP-to-physical address bindings.

In the figure, two networks share a single IP network address. Imagine that the network labeled *Main Network* was the original network, and that the second, labeled *Hidden Network*, was added later. The router connecting the two networks, R, is configured to know which hosts lie on which physical network, and uses ARP to maintain the illusion that only one network exists. To make the illusion work, R keeps the location of hosts completely hidden, allowing all other machines on the networks to communicate as if they are directly connected on a single network. In our example, when host H_1 needs to communicate with host H_4, it first invokes ARP to map H_4's IP address into a physical address. Once it has a physical address, H_1 can send the datagram directly to that physical address.

Because it runs proxy ARP software, R captures the broadcast ARP request from H_1, decides that the machine in question lies on the other physical network, and responds to the ARP request by sending its own physical address. H_1 receives the ARP response, installs the mapping in its ARP table, and then uses the mapping to send datagrams destined for H_4 to R. When R receives a datagram, it searches a special routing table to determine how to forward the datagram. R must forward datagrams destined for H_4 over the hidden network. To allow hosts on the hidden network to reach hosts on the main network, R performs the proxy ARP service on that network as well.

Routers using the proxy ARP technique are taking advantage of an important feature of the ARP protocol, namely, trust. ARP is based on the idea that all machines cooperate and that any response is legitimate. Most hosts install mappings obtained through ARP without checking their validity and without maintaining consistency. Thus, it may happen that the ARP table maps several IP addresses to the same physical address, but that does not violate the protocol specification.

Some implementations of ARP are not as lax as others. In particular, ARP implementations designed to alert managers to possible security violations will inform them whenever two distinct IP addresses map to the same physical hardware address. The purpose of alerting the manager is to warn about *spoofing*, a situation in which one machine claims to be another in order to intercept packets. Host implementations of ARP that warn managers of possible spoofing cannot be used on networks that have proxy ARP routers because the software will generate messages frequently.

The chief advantage of proxy ARP is that it can be added to a single router on a network without disturbing the routing tables in other hosts or routers on the network. Thus, proxy ARP completely hides the details of physical connections.

The chief disadvantage of proxy ARP is that it does not work for networks unless they use ARP for address resolution. Furthermore, it does not generalize to a more complex network topology (e.g., multiple routers interconnecting two physical networks), nor does it support a reasonable form of forwarding. In fact, most implementations of proxy ARP rely on managers to maintain tables of machines and addresses manually, making it both time consuming and prone to errors.

9.5 Subnet Addressing

A second technique that allows a single network address to span multiple physical networks is called *subnet addressing*, *subnet forwarding*, or *subnetting*. Because it is the most general and has been standardized, subnetting is the most widely used of the three address extension techniques. In fact, subnetting is a required part of IP addressing.

To understand subnetting, it is important to realize that individual sites have the freedom to modify addresses and routes as long as the modifications remain invisible to other sites. That is, a site can choose to assign and use IP addresses in unusual ways internally as long as:

- All hosts and routers at the site agree to honor the site's addressing scheme.

- Other sites on the Internet can treat addresses as a network prefix and a host suffix.

The easiest way to understand subnet addressing is to imagine that a site has a single class *B* IP network address assigned to it, but it has two or more physical networks. Only local routers know that there are multiple physical nets and how to forward traffic among them; all other routers in the Internet forward traffic as if there were a single physical network at the site. Figure 9.2 shows an example.

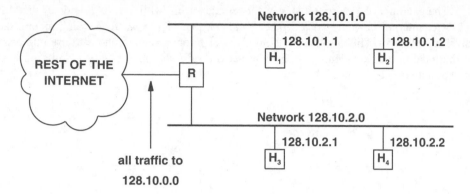

Figure 9.2 A site with two physical networks using subnet addressing to label them with a single class *B* network address. Router *R* accepts all traffic for net 128.10.0.0, and chooses a physical network based on the third octet of the address.

In the example, the site is using the single class *B* network address *128.10.0.0* for two networks. Except for router *R*, all routers in the Internet forward traffic as if there were a single physical net at the site. Once a packet reaches *R*, the packet must be sent across the correct physical network to its destination. To make the choice of physical network efficient, the local site has chosen to use the third octet of the address to distinguish between the two networks. The manager assigns machines on one physical net addresses of the form *128.10.1.X*, and machines on the other physical net addresses of the form *128.10.2.X*, where *X*, the final octet of the address, contains a small integer used to identify a specific host. To choose a physical network, *R* examines the third octet of the destination address and forwards datagrams with value *1* to the network labeled *128.10.1.0* and those with value *2* to the network labeled *128.10.2.0*.

Conceptually, adding subnets only changes the interpretation of IP addresses slightly. Instead of dividing the 32-bit IP address into a network prefix and a host suffix, subnetting divides the address into a *network portion* and a *local portion*. The interpretation of the network portion remains the same as for networks that do not use subnetting. As usual, when making a forwarding decision, routers in the Internet only examine the network prefix. Thus, interpretation of the local portion of an address is left up to the site (within the constraints of the formal standard for subnet addressing). To summarize:

> *When using subnet addressing, we think of a 32-bit IP address as having an internet portion and a local portion, where the internet portion identifies a site, possibly with multiple physical networks, and the local portion identifies a physical network and host at that site.*

The example of Figure 9.2 shows subnet addressing with a class *B* address that has a 2-octet internet portion and a 2-octet local portion. To make forwarding among the physical networks efficient, the site administrator in our example chose to use one octet of the local portion to identify a physical network and the other octet to identify a host on that network, as Figure 9.3 shows.

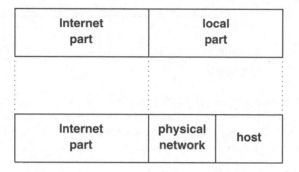

Figure 9.3 (a) Conceptual interpretation of a 32-bit IP address in the original IP address scheme, and (b) conceptual interpretation of addresses using the subnet scheme shown in Figure 9.2. The local portion is divided into two parts that identify a physical network and a host on that network.

The result is a form of *hierarchical addressing* that leads to corresponding *hierarchical routing*. The top level of the hierarchy (i.e., other autonomous systems in the Internet) uses the first two octets when forwarding, and the next level (i.e., the local site) uses an additional octet. Finally, the lowest level (i.e., delivery across one physical network) uses the entire address.

Hierarchical addressing is not new; many systems have used it before. The best example is the U.S. telephone system, where a 10-digit phone number is divided into a 3-digit area code, 3-digit exchange, and 4-digit connection. The advantage of using hierarchical addressing is that it accommodates large growth because it means a given router does not need to know as much detail about distant destinations as it does about local ones. One disadvantage is that choosing a hierarchical structure is complicated, and it often becomes difficult to change once a hierarchy has been established.

9.6 Flexibility In Subnet Address Assignment

The TCP/IP standard for subnet addressing recognizes that not every site will have the same needs for an address hierarchy; it allows sites flexibility in choosing how to assign them. To understand why such flexibility is desirable, imagine a site with five networks interconnected, as Figure 9.4 shows. Suppose the site has a single class *B* network address that it wants to use for all physical networks. How should the local part be divided to make forwarding efficient?

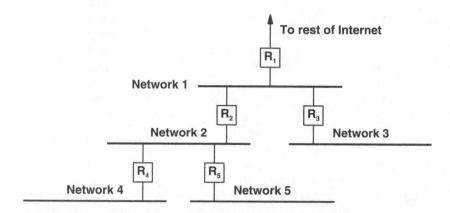

Figure 9.4 A site with five physical networks arranged in three "levels." The simplistic division of addresses into physical net and host parts may not be optimal for such cases.

In our example, the site will choose a partition of the local part of the IP address based on how it expects to grow. Dividing the 16-bit local part into an 8-bit network identifier and an 8-bit host identifier as shown in Figure 9.3 allows up to 256 networks, with up to 256 hosts per network†. Figure 9.5 illustrates the possible choices if a site uses the *fixed-length subnetting* scheme described above and avoids the all 0s and all 1s subnet and host addresses.

---

†In practice, the limit is 254 subnets of 254 hosts per subnet because the all 1s and all 0s host addresses are reserved for broadcast, and an all 1s or all 0s subnet is not recommended.

Subnet Bits	Number of Subnets	Hosts per Subnet
0	1	65534
2	2	16382
3	6	8190
4	14	4094
5	30	2046
6	62	1022
7	126	510
8	254	254
9	510	126
10	1022	62
11	2046	30
12	4094	14
13	8190	6
14	16382	2

Figure 9.5 The possible fixed-length subnets sizes for a class B number, with 8 subnet bits being the most popular choice; an organization must choose one line in the table.

As the figure shows, an organization that adopts fixed-length subnetting must choose a compromise. If the organization has a large number of physical networks, the networks cannot contain many hosts; if the number of hosts on a network is large, the number of physical networks must be small. For example, allocating 3 bits to identify a physical network results in up to 6 networks that each support up to 8190 hosts. Allocating 12 bits results in up to 4094 networks, but restricts the size of each to 14 hosts.

9.7 Variable-Length Subnets

We have implied that choosing a subnet addressing scheme is synonymous with choosing how to partition the local portion of an IP address into physical net and host parts. Indeed, most sites that implement subnetting use a fixed-length assignment. It should be clear that the designers did not choose a specific division for subnetting because no single partition of the local part of the address works for all organizations — some need many networks with few hosts per network, while others need a few networks with many hosts attached to each. The designers realized that the same problem can exist within a single organization. To allow maximum autonomy, the TCP/IP subnet standard provides even more flexibility than indicated above. An organization may select a subnet partition on a per-network basis. Although the technique is known as *variable-length subnetting*, the name is slightly misleading because the value does not "vary" over time — once a partition has been selected for a particular network, the partition never changes. All hosts and routers attached to that network must follow the decision; if they do not, datagrams can be lost or misrouted. We can summarize:

To allow maximum flexibility in choosing how to partition subnet addresses, the TCP/IP subnet standard permits variable-length subnetting in which the partition can be chosen independently for each physical network. Once a subnet partition has been selected, all machines on that network must honor it.

The chief advantage of variable-length subnetting is flexibility: an organization can have a mixture of large and small networks, and can achieve higher utilization of the address space. However, variable-length subnetting has serious disadvantages. Most important, values for subnets must be assigned carefully to avoid *address ambiguity*, a situation in which an address is interpreted differently depending on the physical network. For example, an address can appear to match two different subnets. As a result, invalid variable-length subnets may make it impossible for all pairs of hosts to communicate. Routers cannot resolve such ambiguity, which means that an invalid assignment can only be repaired by renumbering. Thus, network managers are discouraged from using variable-length subnetting.

9.8 Implementation Of Subnets With Masks

The subnet technology makes configuration of either fixed or variable length easy. The standard specifies that a 32-bit *mask* is used to specify the division. Thus, a site using subnet addressing must choose a 32-bit *subnet mask* for each network. Bits in the subnet mask are set to *1* if machines on the network treat the corresponding bit in the IP address as part of the subnet prefix, and *0* if they treat the bit as part of the host identifier. For example, the 32-bit subnet mask:

11111111   11111111   11111111   00000000

specifies that the first three octets identify the network and the fourth octet identifies a host on that network. A subnet mask should have *1*s for all bits that correspond to the network portion of the address (e.g., the subnet mask for a class *B* network will have *1*s for the first two octets plus one or more bits in the last two octets).

The interesting twist in subnet addressing arises because the standard does not restrict subnet masks to select contiguous bits of the address. For example, a network might be assigned the mask:

11111111   11111111   00011000   01000000

which selects the first two octets, two bits from the third octet, and one bit from the fourth. Although such flexibility makes it possible to arrange interesting assignments of addresses to machines, doing so makes assigning host addresses and understanding routing tables tricky. Thus, it is recommended that sites use contiguous subnet masks and that they use the same mask throughout an entire set of physical nets that share an IP address.

9.9 Subnet Mask Representation

Specifying subnet masks in binary is both awkward and prone to errors. Therefore, most software allows alternative representations. Sometimes, the representation follows whatever conventions the local operating system uses for representation of binary quantities, (e.g., hexadecimal notation).

Most IP software uses dotted decimal representation for subnet masks; it works best when sites choose to align subnetting on octet boundaries. For example, many sites choose to subnet class *B* addresses by using the third octet to identify the physical net and the fourth octet to identify hosts as on the previous page. In such cases, the subnet mask has dotted decimal representation *255.255.255.0*, making it easy to write and understand.

The literature also contains examples of subnet addresses and subnet masks represented in braces as a 3-tuple:

{ <network number> , <subnet number> , <host number> }

In this representation, the value *-1* means ''all ones.'' For example, if the subnet mask for a class *B* network is *255.255.255.0*, it can be written *{-1, -1, 0}*.

The chief disadvantage of the 3-tuple representation is that it does not accurately specify how many bits are used for each part of the address; the advantage is that it abstracts away from the details of bit fields and emphasizes the values of the three parts of the address. To see why address values are sometimes more important than bit fields, consider the 3-tuple:

{ 128.10 , -1, 0 }

which denotes an address with a network number *128.10*, all ones in the subnet field, and all zeroes in the host field. Expressing the same address value using other representations requires a 32-bit subnet mask as well as a 32-bit IP address, and forces readers to decode bit fields before they can deduce the values of individual fields. Furthermore, the 3-tuple representation is independent of the IP address class or the size of the subnet field. Thus, the 3-tuple can be used to represent sets of addresses or abstract ideas. For example, the 3-tuple:

{ <network number>, -1, -1 }

denotes ''addresses with a valid network number, a subnet field containing all ones, and a host field containing all ones.'' We will see additional examples later in this chapter.

9.10 Forwarding In The Presence Of Subnets

The standard IP forwarding algorithm must be modified to work with subnet addresses. All hosts and routers attached to a network that uses subnet addressing must use the modified algorithm, which is called *subnet forwarding* or *subnet routing*. What may not be obvious is that unless restrictions are added to the use of subnetting, other hosts and routers at the site may also need to use subnet forwarding. To see how a problem arises without restrictions, consider the example set of networks shown in Figure 9.6.

In the figure, physical networks *2* and *3* have been (illegally) assigned subnet addresses of a single IP network address, *N*. Although host *H* does not directly attach to a network that has a subnet address, it must use subnet forwarding to decide whether to send datagrams destined for network *N* to router R_1 or router R_2. It could be argued that *H* can send to either router and let them handle the problem, but that solution means not all traffic will follow a shortest path. In larger examples, the difference between an optimal and nonoptimal path can be significant.

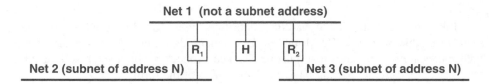

Figure 9.6 An example (illegal) topology with three networks where Nets *2* and *3* are subnets of a single IP network address, *N*. If such topologies were allowed, host *H* would need to use subnet forwarding even though Net *1* does not have a subnet address.

In theory, a simple rule determines when machines need to use subnet forwarding. The subnet rule is:

> *To achieve optimal forwarding, a machine* M *must use subnet forwarding for an IP network address* N, *unless there is a single path* P *such that P is a shortest path between* M *and every physical network that is a subnet of* N.

Unfortunately, understanding the theoretical restriction does not help in assigning subnets. First, shortest paths can change if hardware fails or if routing protocols redirect traffic around congestion. Such dynamic changes make it difficult to use the subnet rule except in trivial cases. Second, the subnet rule fails to consider the boundaries of sites or the difficulties involved in propagating subnet masks. It is impossible to propagate subnet information beyond the boundary of a given organization because the

routing protocols discussed later do not provide for it. Realistically, it becomes extremely difficult to propagate subnet information beyond a given physical network.
Therefore, the designers recommend that if a site uses subnet addressing, that site
should keep subnetting as simple as possible. In particular, network administrators
should adhere to the following guidelines:

> *All subnets of a given network IP address must be contiguous, the
> subnet masks should be uniform across all networks, and all machines
> should participate in subnet forwarding.*

The guidelines pose special difficulty for a large corporation that has multiple sites each
connected to the Internet, but not connected directly to one another. Such a corporation
cannot use subnets of a single network address for all its sites because the physical networks are not contiguous.

9.11 The Subnet Forwarding Algorithm

Like the standard IP forwarding algorithm, the algorithm used with subnets
searches a table of routes. Recall that in the standard algorithm, per-host routes and default routes are special cases that must be checked explicitly; table lookup is used for all
others. A conventional routing table contains entries of the form:

(network address, next hop address)

where the *network address* field specifies the IP address of a destination network, *N*,
and the *next hop address* field specifies the address of a router to which datagrams destined for *N* should be sent. The standard forwarding algorithm compares the network
portion of a destination address to the *network address* field of each entry in the routing
table until a match is found. Because the *next hop address* field is constrained to specify a machine that is reachable over a directly connected network, only one table lookup
is ever needed.

The standard algorithm knows how an address is partitioned into network portion
and local portion because the first three bits encode the address type and format (i.e.,
class *A*, *B*, *C*, or *D*). With subnets, it is not possible to decide which bits correspond to
the network and which to the host from the address alone. Instead, the modified algorithm used with subnets maintains additional information in the routing table. Each
table entry contains one additional field that specifies the address mask used with the
network in that entry:

(address mask, network address, next hop address)

When choosing routes, the modified algorithm uses the *address mask* to extract bits of
the destination address for comparison with the table entry. That is, it performs a bit-
wise Boolean *and* of the full 32-bit destination IP address and the *address mask* field
from an entry, and it then checks to see if the result equals the value in the *network ad-*

dress field of that entry. If so, it forwards the datagram to the address specified in the *next hop address* field† of the entry.

9.12 A Unified Forwarding Algorithm

Observant readers may have guessed that if we allow arbitrary masks, the subnet forwarding algorithm can subsume all the special cases of the standard algorithm. It can handle routes to individual hosts, a default route, and routes to directly connected networks using the same masking technique it uses for subnets. In addition, masks can handle routes to conventional classful addresses. The flexibility comes from the ability to combine arbitrary 32-bit values in a *subnet mask* field and arbitrary 32-bit addresses in a *network address* field. For example, to install a route for a single host, one uses a mask of all *1*s and a network address equal to the host's IP address. To install a default route, one uses an address mask of all *0*s and a network address of all *0*s (because any destination address *and* zero equals zero). To install a route to a (nonsubnetted) class *B* network, one specifies a mask with two octets of *1*s and two octets of *0*s. If entries in the table are sorted by longest masks first, the forwarding algorithm contains fewer special cases as Figure 9.7 shows.

Algorithm:

Forward_IP_Datagram (datagram, routing_table)

Extract destination IP address, I_D, from datagram;
If prefix of I_D matches address of any directly connected
      network send datagram to destination over that network
      (This involves resolving I_D to a physical address,
      encapsulating the datagram, and sending the frame.)
else
    for each entry in routing table do
      Let N be the bitwise-and of I_D and the subnet mask
      If N equals the network address field of the entry then
        forward the datagram to the specified next hop address
    endforloop
If no matches were found, declare a forwarding error;

Figure 9.7 The unified IP forwarding algorithm. Given an IP datagram and a routing table sorted by mask length, the algorithm selects a next hop router to which the datagram should be sent. The next hop must lie on a directly connected network.

---

†As in the standard forwarding algorithm, the next hop router must be reachable by a directly connected network.

In fact, most implementations eliminate the explicit test for destinations on directly connected networks. To do so, one must add a table entry for each directly connected network. Like other entries, each entry for a directly connected network contains a mask that specifies the number of bits in the prefix.

9.13 Maintenance Of Subnet Masks

How are subnet masks assigned by an administrator, and how are subnet masks propagated to hosts and routers? The second question will be answered later. We will see that a host obtains subnet mask information at boot time and that routers pass subnet masks to other routers when they use routing protocols to exchange routing information.

The first question is more difficult to answer. Each site is free to choose subnet masks for its networks. When making assignments, managers attempt to balance sizes of networks, numbers of physical networks, expected growth, and ease of maintenance. Difficulty arises because nonuniform masks give the most flexibility, but make possible assignments that lead to ambiguous routes. Or worse, they allow valid assignments that become invalid if more hosts are added to the networks. There are no easy rules, so most sites make conservative choices. Typically, a site selects contiguous bits from the local portion of an address to identify a network, and uses the same partition (i.e., the same mask) for all local physical networks at the site. For example, many sites simply use a single subnet octet when subnetting a class *B* address.

9.14 Broadcasting To Subnets

Broadcasting is more difficult in a subnet environment. Recall that in the original IP addressing scheme, an address with a host portion of all *1*s denotes broadcast to all hosts on the specified network. From the viewpoint of an observer outside a subnetted site, broadcasting to the network address still makes sense. That is, the address:

$$\{ \text{ network, -1, -1 } \}$$

means "deliver a copy to all machines that have *network* as their network addresses, even if they lie on separate physical networks." Operationally, broadcasting to such an address makes sense only if the routers that interconnect the subnets agree to propagate the datagram to all physical networks†. Of course, care must be taken to avoid forwarding loops. In particular, a router cannot merely propagate a broadcast packet that arrives on one interface to all interfaces that share the subnet prefix. To prevent such loops, routers use *reverse path forwarding (RPF)*. The router extracts the source of the broadcast datagram, and looks up the source in its routing table. The router then discards the datagram unless it arrived on the interface used to forward to the source (i.e., arrived from the shortest path).

---

†For security reasons, most sites prohibit directed broadcast.

Within a set of subnetted networks, it becomes possible to broadcast to a specific subnet (i.e., to broadcast to all hosts on a physical network that has been assigned one of the subnet addresses). The subnet address standard uses a host field of all ones to denote subnet broadcast. That is, a subnet broadcast address becomes:

{ network, subnet, -1 }

Considering subnet broadcast addresses and subnet broadcasting clarifies the recommendation for using a consistent subnet mask across all networks that share a subnetted IP address. As long as the subnet and host fields are identical, subnet broadcast addresses are unambiguous. More complex subnet address assignments may or may not allow broadcasting to selected subsets of the physical networks that constitute a subnet.

9.15 Anonymous Point-To-Point Networks

In the original IP addressing scheme, each network was assigned a unique prefix. In particular, because IP views a point-to-point connection between a pair of machines as a "network," the connection was assigned a network prefix and each computer was assigned a host suffix. When addresses became scarce, the use of a prefix for each point-to-point connection seemed absurd. The problem was especially severe for organizations that have many point-to-point connections. For example, an organization with multiple sites might use leased digital circuits (e.g., OC3 circuits) to form a backbone that interconnects a router at each site to routers at other sites.

To avoid assigning a prefix to each point-to-point connection, a simple technique was invented. Known as *anonymous networking*, the technique is often applied when a pair of routers is connected with a leased digital circuit. The technique simply avoids numbering the leased line, and does not assign a host address to the routers at each end. No hardware address is needed, so the interface software is configured to ignore the next hop address when sending datagrams. Consequently, an arbitrary value can be used as the next-hop address in the IP routing table.

When the anonymous networking technique is applied to a point-to-point connection, the connection is known as an *unnumbered network* or an *anonymous network*. The example in Figure 9.8 will help explain forwarding in unnumbered networks.

To understand why unnumbered networks are possible, one must remember that hardware used for point-to-point connections does not operate like shared-media hardware. Because there is only one possible destination — the computer at the other end of the circuit — the underlying hardware does not use physical addresses when transmitting frames. Consequently, when IP hands a datagram to the network interface, any value can be specified as a next hop because the hardware will ignore it. Thus, the next-hop field of the IP routing table can contain an arbitrary value (e.g., zero).

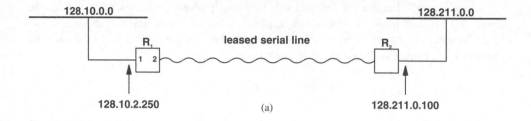

Figure 9.8 (a) An unnumbered point-to-point connection between two routers,
and (b) the routing table in router R_1.

The routing table in Figure 9.8b does not have a zero in the next hop field. Instead, the example demonstrates a technique often employed with unnumbered networks. Rather than leaving the next hop empty, it is filled with one of the IP addresses
assigned to the next-hop router (i.e., an address assigned to another of the router's interfaces). In the example, the address of R_2's Ethernet connection has been used.

We said that the hardware ignores the next hop address, so it may seem odd that a
value has been assigned. It may seem even more odd that the next-hop refers to a network not directly reachable from R_1. In fact, neither IP nor the network interface code
uses the value in any way. The only reason for specifying a non-zero entry is to make
it easier for humans to understand and remember the address of the router on the other
end of the point-to-point connection. In the example, we chose the address assigned to
R_2's Ethernet interface because R_2 does not have an address for the leased line interface.

9.16 Classless Addressing And Supernetting

We said that subnet addressing and unnumbered point-to-point links both arose in
an attempt to conserve the IP address space. By 1993, it became apparent that those
techniques alone would not prevent Internet growth from quickly exhausting the address
space, and preliminary work began on defining an entirely new version of IP with larger
addresses. To accommodate growth until the new version of IP could be standardized
and adopted, a temporary solution was invented.

Known as *classless addressing*, the addressing scheme extends the idea used in subnet addressing to permit a network prefix to be an arbitrary length. In addition to a new addressing model, the designers invented forwarding and route propagation techniques. As a result, the entire technology has become known as *Classless Inter-Domain Routing*, (*CIDR*).

To understand the impact of CIDR, one needs to know three facts. First, the classful scheme did not divide network addresses into equal size classes — although fewer than seventeen thousand class B numbers exist, more than two million class C network numbers exist. Second, because class C prefixes only suffice for small networks and are not amenable to subnetting, demand for class C prefixes was much smaller than demand for class B prefixes. Third, studies showed that at the rate class B numbers were being assigned, class B prefixes would be exhausted quickly.

One of the first uses of classless addressing was known as *supernetting*. To understand how supernetting works, consider a medium-sized organization that joins the Internet. Under the classful scheme, such an organization would request a class B prefix. The supernetting scheme allows an ISP to assign the organization a block of class C addresses instead of a single class B number. The block must be large enough to number all the networks in the organization and (as we will see) must lie on a boundary that is a power of 2. For example, suppose the organization expects to have 200 networks. Supernetting can assign the organization a block of 256 contiguous class C numbers.

9.17 CIDR Address Blocks And Bit Masks

Although the motivation for CIDR is easy to understand when viewed as a way to use multiple class C addresses instead of a class B address, the proposers designed it to be used in a broader context. They envisioned a hierarchical addressing model in which each commercial *Internet Service Provider* (*ISP*) could be given a large block of Internet addresses that the ISP could then allocate to subscribers. Because it permits the network prefix to occur on an arbitrary bit boundary, CIDR allows an ISP to assign each subscriber a block of addresses appropriate to the subscriber's needs.

Like subnet addressing, CIDR uses a 32-bit *address mask* to specify the boundary between prefix and suffix. Contiguous 1 bits in the mask specify the size of the prefix, and 0 bits in the mask correspond to the suffix. For example, suppose an organization is assigned a block of 2048 contiguous addresses starting at address 128.211.168.0. The table in Figure 9.9 shows the binary values of addresses in the range.

	Dotted Decimal	**32-bit Binary Equivalent**
lowest	128.211.168.0	10000000 11010011 10101000 00000000
highest	128.211.175.255	10000000 11010011 10101111 11111111

Figure 9.9 An example CIDR block of 2048 addresses. The table shows the lowest and highest addresses in the range expressed as dotted decimal and binary values.

For the range shown, a CIDR address mask has 21 bits set, which means that the division between prefix and suffix occurs after the 21st bit:

$$11111111 \quad 11111111 \quad 11111000 \quad 00000000$$

9.18 Address Blocks And CIDR Notation

Because identifying a CIDR block requires both an address and a mask, a shorthand notation was devised to express the two items. Called *CIDR notation* but known informally as *slash notation*, the shorthand represents the mask length in decimal and uses a slash to separate it from the address. Thus, in CIDR notation, the block of addresses in Figure 9.9 is expressed:

$$128.211.168.0 / 21$$

where */21* denotes an address mask with 21 bits set to 1. The table in Figure 9.10 lists dotted decimal values for all possible CIDR masks. The /8, /16, and /24 prefixes correspond to traditional class *A*, *B*, and *C* divisions.

CIDR Notation	Dotted Decimal	CIDR Notation	Dotted Decimal
/1	128.0.0.0	/17	255.255.128.0
/2	192.0.0.0	/18	255.255.192.0
/3	224.0.0.0	/19	255.255.224.0
/4	240.0.0.0	/20	255.255.240.0
/5	248.0.0.0	/21	255.255.248.0
/6	252.0.0.0	/22	255.255.252.0
/7	254.0.0.0	/23	255.255.254.0
/8	255.0.0.0	/24	255.255.255.0
/9	255.128.0.0	/25	255.255.255.128
/10	255.192.0.0	/26	255.255.255.192
/11	255.224.0.0	/27	255.255.255.224
/12	255.240.0.0	/28	255.255.255.240
/13	255.248.0.0	/29	255.255.255.248
/14	255.252.0.0	/30	255.255.255.252
/15	255.254.0.0	/31	255.255.255.254
/16	255.255.0.0	/32	255.255.255.255

Figure 9.10 Dotted decimal mask values for all possible CIDR prefixes.

9.19 A Classless Addressing Example

The table in Figure 9.10 illustrates one of the chief advantages of classless addressing: complete flexibility in allocating blocks of various sizes. With CIDR, the ISP can choose to assign each customer a block of an appropriate size. If it owns a CIDR block of N bits, an ISP can choose to hand customers any piece of more than N bits. For example, if the ISP is assigned 128.211.0.0/16, the ISP may choose to give one of its customers the 2048 address in the /21 range that Figure 9.9 specifies. If the same ISP also has a small customer with only two computers, the ISP might choose to assign another block 128.211.176.212/30, which covers the address range that Figure 9.11 specifies.

	Dotted Decimal	**32-bit Binary Equivalent**
lowest	128.211.176.212	10000000 11010011 10110000 11010100
highest	128.211.176.215	10000000 11010011 10110000 11010111

Figure 9.11 An example of CIDR block 128.211.176.212/30. The use of an arbitrary bit mask allows more flexibility in assigning a block size than the classful addressing scheme.

One way to think about classless addresses is as if each customer of an ISP obtains a (variable-length) subnet of the ISP's CIDR block. Thus, a given block of addresses can be subdivided on an arbitrary bit boundary, and a separate route can be entered for each subdivision. As a result, although the group of computers on a given network will be assigned addresses in a contiguous range, the range does not need to correspond to a predefined class. Instead, the scheme makes subdivision flexible by allowing one to specify the exact number of bits that correspond to a prefix. To summarize:

> *Classless addressing, which is now used throughout the Internet, treats IP addresses as arbitrary integers, and allows a network administrator to partition addresses into contiguous blocks, where the number of addresses in a block is a power of two.*

9.20 Data Structures And Algorithms For Classless Lookup

The fundamental criterion used to judge the algorithms and data structures used with routing tables is speed. There are two aspects: the primary consideration is the speed of finding a next hop for a given destination, while a secondary consideration is the speed of making changes to values in the table.

The introduction of classless addressing had a profound effect on forwarding in the Internet because it fundamentally changed lookup. In the classful world where each address is *self-identifying* (i.e., the size of the prefix can be computed from the address itself, a hash table works well for IP lookup. In a classless world, however, hashing does not work well. Thus, an alternative must be used.

9.20.1 Searching By Mask Length

The key to understanding CIDR lies in observing that the address block an ISP assigns to a subscriber always has a longer address mask than the block owned by the ISP. Thus, the goal of route lookup is *longest prefix match* (*LPM*). That is, given a destination address, D, find the entry in the routing table that has the longest prefix of bits that match the bits of D.

The simplest LPM algorithm iterates over all possible divisions between prefix and suffix. That is, given a destination address, D, the algorithm first tries matching all 32 bits of D, then 31 bits, and so on. For each possible size, M, the router extracts M bits from D, assumes the extracted bits form a network prefix, and looks up the prefix in the table. The algorithm stops once a match has been found.

The disadvantage of trying all possible lengths should be obvious: doing so is extremely slow because the algorithm performs up to 21 lookups for each datagram. The worst case occurs when no route exists, but even when it finds a route, the iterative approach searches the table many times. Except in cases where a routing table contains host-specific routes, the algorithm wastes time checking host bits. More important, the algorithm performs 31 unnecessary lookups before it can decide to follow a default route (in many routing tables, the default route is heavily used).

9.20.2 Binary Trie Structures

To avoid inefficient searches, a hierarchical data structure is used for classless lookup. The most popular data structures are variants of a *binary trie* in which the value of successive bits in the address determine a path from the root downward.

A binary trie is a tree with paths determined by the data stored. To visualize a binary trie, imagine that a set of 32-bit addresses is written as binary strings and redundant suffixes are removed. What remains is a set of prefixes that uniquely identify each item. For example, Figure 9.12 shows a set of seven addresses written in binary and the corresponding unique prefixes.

As Figure 9.12 illustrates, the number of bits required to identify an address depends on the values in the set. For example, the first address in the figure can be uniquely identified by two bits because no other addresses begin with *00*. However, five bits are required to identify the last item in the table because the 4-bit prefix *1011* is shared by more than one item.

32-Bit Address	Unique Prefix
00110101 00000000 00000000 00000000	00
01000110 00000000 00000000 00000000	0100
01010110 00000000 00000000 00000000	0101
01100001 00000000 00000000 00000000	011
10101010 11110000 00000000 00000000	1010
10110000 00000010 00000000 00000000	10110
10111011 00001010 00000000 00000000	10111

Figure 9.12 A set of 32-bit binary addresses and the corresponding set of prefixes that uniquely identify each.

Once a set of unique prefixes has been computed, it can be used to define a binary trie. Figure 9.13 illustrates a trie for the seven prefixes in Figure 9.12.

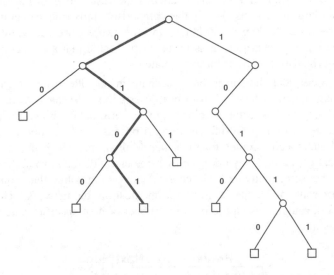

Figure 9.13 A binary trie for the seven binary prefixes listed in Figure 9.12. The path through the trie for prefix *0101* is shown darkened.

Each interior node in the trie (shown as a circle) corresponds to two or more prefixes, and each exterior node (shown as a square) corresponds to one unique prefix. The search algorithm stops when it reaches an exterior node or when no path exists for the specified prefix. For example, a search for address

10010010 11110000 00000000 00000001

fails because there is no branch with label *0* at the node corresponding to *10*.

> *To make lookup efficient, forwarding software that handles classless routes must use data structures and algorithms that differ from those used for classful lookup. Many systems use a scheme based on a binary trie to accommodate classless lookup.*

9.21 Longest-Match And Mixtures Of Route Types

Our brief description of binary tries only gives a sketch of the data structure used in practice. For example, we said that a trie only needs to store a unique prefix for each route in the table, without stating that the prefix must cover the entire network portion of the route. To guarantee that a router does not forward datagrams unless the entire network prefix in the destination matches the route, each exterior node in the trie must contain a 32-bit address, A, and a 32-bit mask, M, that covers the entire network portion of A. When the search reaches an exterior node, the algorithm computes the logical *and* of M with the destination address, and compares the result to A in the same way that conventional lookup algorithms do. If the comparison fails, the datagram is rejected (also like conventional lookup algorithms). In other words, we can view the trie as a mechanism that quickly identifies items in the routing table that are potential candidates rather than a mechanism that finds an exact match.

Even if we consider the trie to be a mechanism that identifies potential matches, another important detail is missing from our description. We have assumed that each entry in a routing table has a unique binary prefix. In practice, however, the entries in most routing tables do not have unique prefixes because routing tables contain a mixture of general and specific routes for the same destination. For example, consider any routing table that contains a network-specific route and a different route for one particular subnet of the same network. Or consider a routing table that contains both a network-specific route and a special route for one host on that network. The binary prefix of the network route is also a prefix of the subnet or host-specific route. Figure 9.14 provides an example.

Prefix	Next Hop
128.10.0.0 / 16	10.0.0.2
128.10.2.0 / 24	10.0.0.4
128.10.3.0 / 24	10.1.0.5
128.10.4.0 / 24	10.0.0.6
128.10.4.3 / 32	10.0.0.3
128.10.5.0 / 24	10.0.0.6
128.10.5.1 / 32	10.0.0.3

Figure 9.14 An example set of routes without unique prefixes. The situation occurs frequently because many routing tables contain a mixture of general and specific routes for the same network.

To permit overlapping prefixes, the trie data structure described above must be modified to follow the *longest-match* paradigm when selecting a route. One possible implementation allows each interior node to contain an address / mask pair, and modifies the search algorithm to check for a match at each node. A match that occurs later in the search (i.e., a match that corresponds to a more specific route) must override any match that occurs earlier because a later match corresponds to a longer prefix.

9.21.1 PATRICIA And Level Compressed Tries

Our description of binary tries also omits details related to optimization of lookup. The most important involves "skipping" levels in the trie that do not distinguish among routes. For example, consider a binary trie for the set of routes in Figure 9.14. Because each route in the list begins with the same sixteen bits (i.e., the value 10000000 00001010), a binary trie for the routes will only have one node at each of the first sixteen levels below the root.

In this instance, it would be faster to examine all sixteen bits of a destination address at once rather than extracting bits one at a time and using them to move through the trie. Two modified versions of tries use the approach to optimize performance. The first, a *PATRICIA tree*, allows each node to specify a value to test along with a number of bits to skip. The second, a *level compressed trie*, provides additional optimization by eliminating one or more levels in the trie that can be skipped along any path.

Of course, data structure optimizations represent a tradeoff. Although the optimizations improve search speed, they require more computation when creating or modifying a routing table. In most cases, however, such optimizations are justified because one expects a routing table to be modified much less frequently than it is searched.

9.22 CIDR Blocks Reserved For Private Networks

Chapter 4 stated that the IETF had designated a set of prefixes to be reserved for use with private networks. Reserved prefixes will never be assigned to networks in the global Internet. Collectively, the reserved prefixes are known as *private addresses* or *nonroutable addresses*. The latter term arises because routers in the global Internet understand that the addresses are reserved; if a datagram destined to one of the private addresses is accidentally forwarded onto the global Internet, a router in the Internet will be able to detect the problem.

In addition to blocks that correspond to classful addresses, the set of reserved IPv4 prefixes contains a CIDR block that spans multiple classes. Figure 9.15 lists the values in CIDR notation along with the dotted decimal value of the lowest and highest addresses in the block. The last address block listed, *169.254.0.0 / 16*, is unusual because it is used by systems that *autoconfigure* IP addresses.

Prefix	Lowest Address	Highest Address
10.0.0.0/8	10.0.0.0	10.255.255.255
172.16.0.0/12	172.16.0.0	172.31.255.255
192.168.0.0/16	192.168.0.0	192.168.255.255
169.254.0.0/16	169.254.0.0	169.254.255.255

Figure 9.15 The prefixes reserved for use with private internets not connected to the global Internet. If a datagram sent to one of these addresses accidentally reaches the Internet, an error will result.

9.23 Summary

This chapter examines four techniques that have been invented to conserve IP addresses. The first technique, called proxy ARP, arranges for a router to impersonate computers on another physical network by answering ARP requests on their behalf. Proxy ARP is useful only on networks that use ARP for address resolution, and only for ARP implementations that do not complain when multiple IP addresses map to the same hardware address. The second technique, a TCP/IP standard called subnet addressing, allows a site to share a single IP network address among multiple physical networks. All hosts and routers connected to networks using subnetting must use a modified forwarding scheme in which each routing table entry contains a subnet mask. The modified scheme can be viewed as a generalization of the original forwarding algorithm because it handles special cases like default routes or host-specific routes. The third technique allows a point-to-point link to remain unnumbered (i.e., have no IP prefix).

The fourth technique, known as classless addressing (CIDR), represents a major shift in IP technology. Instead of adhering to the original addressing scheme, classless addressing allows the division between prefix and suffix to occur on an arbitrary bit boundary. CIDR allows the address space to be divided into blocks, where the size of each block is a power of two. One motivation for CIDR arises from the desire to combine multiple class C prefixes into a single supernet block. Because classless addresses are not self-identifying like the original classful addresses, CIDR requires significant changes to the algorithms and data structures used by IP software on hosts and routers to store and look up routes. Many implementations use a scheme based on the binary trie data structure.

FOR FURTHER STUDY

The standard for subnet addressing comes from Mogul [RFC 950] with updates in Braden [RFC 1122]. Clark [RFC 932], Karels [RFC 936], Gads [RFC 940], and Mogul [RFC 917] all contain early proposals for subnet addressing schemes. Mogul [RFC 922] discusses broadcasting in the presence of subnets. Postel [RFC 925] considers the use of proxy ARP for subnets. Atallah and Comer [1998] presents a provably optimal algorithm for variable-length subnet assignment. Carl-Mitchell and Quarterman [RFC 1027] discusses using proxy ARP to implement transparent subnet routers. Rekhter and Li [RFC 1518] specifies classless IP address allocation. Fuller, Li, Yu, and Varadhan [RFC 1519] specifies CIDR and supernetting. Rekhter et. al. [RFC 1918] specifies address prefixes reserved for private networks.

EXERCISES

9.1   If routers using proxy ARP use a table of host addresses to decide whether to answer ARP requests, the routing table must be changed whenever a new host is added to one of the networks. Explain how to assign IP addresses so hosts can be added without changing tables. Hint: think of subnets.

9.2   Although the standard allows all-0's to be assigned as a subnet number, some vendors' software does not operate correctly. Try to assign a zero subnet at your site and see if the route is propagated correctly.

9.3   Show that proxy ARP can be used with three physical networks that are interconnected by two routers.

9.4   Consider a fixed subnet partition of a class *B* network number that will accommodate at least 76 networks. How many hosts can be on each network?

9.5   Does it ever make sense to subnet a class *C* network address? Why or why not?

9.6   A site that chose to subnet their class *B* address by using the third octet for the physical net was disappointed that they could not accommodate 255 or 256 networks. Explain.

9.7   Design a subnet address scheme for your organization assuming that you have one class *B* address to use.

9.8   Is it reasonable for a single router to use both proxy ARP and subnet addressing? If so, explain how. If not, explain why.

9.9   Argue that any network using proxy ARP is vulnerable to "spoofing" (i.e., an arbitrary machine can impersonate any other machine).

9.10 Can you devise a (nonstandard) implementation of ARP that supports normal use, but prohibits proxy ARP?

9.11 Analyze the differences between an Ethernet learning bridge that connects two Ethernet segments and a system using proxy ARP to connect two Ethernet segments.

9.12 One vendor decided to add subnet addressing to its IP software by allocating a single subnet mask used for all IP network addresses. The vendor modified its standard IP routing software to make the subnet check a special case. Find a simple example in which this implementation cannot work correctly. (Hint: think of a multi-homed host.)

9.13 Characterize the (restricted) situations in which the subnet implementation discussed in the previous exercise will work correctly.

9.14 Read the standard to find out more about broadcasting in the presence of subnets. Can you characterize subnet address assignments that allow one to specify a broadcast address for all possible subnets?

9.15 The standard allows an arbitrary assignment of subnet masks for networks that comprise a subnetted IP address. Should the standard restrict subnet masks to cover contiguous bits in the address? Why or why not?

9.16 Find an example of variable length subnet assignments and host addresses that produces address ambiguity.

9.17 Carefully consider default forwarding in the presence of subnets. What can happen if a packet arrives destined for a nonexistent subnet?

9.18 Compare architectures that use subnet addressing and routers to interconnect multiple Ethernets to an architecture that uses bridges as described in Chapter 2. Under what circumstances is one architecture preferable to the other?

9.19 Consider a site that chooses to subnet a class *B* network address, but decides that some physical nets will use *6* bits of the local portion to identify the physical net while others will use *8*. Find an assignment of host addresses that makes destination addresses ambiguous.

9.20 The subnet forwarding algorithm in Figure 9.7 uses a sequential scan of entries in the routing table, allowing a manager to place host-specific routes before network-specific or subnet-specific routes. Invent a data structure that achieves the same flexibility but uses hashing to make the lookup efficient. [This exercise was suggested by Dave Mills.]

9.21 Although much effort has been expended on making routers operate quickly, software for classless route lookup still runs slower than the hashing schemes used with classful lookup. Investigate data structures and lookup algorithms that operate faster than a binary trie.

9.22 A binary trie uses one bit to select among two descendants at each node. Consider a trie that uses two bits to select among four descendants at each node. Under what conditions does such a trie make lookup faster? Slower?

9.23 If all Internet service providers use classless addressing and assign subscribers numbers from their block of addresses, what problem occurs when a subscriber changes from one provider to another?

Chapter Contents

10

Protocol Layering

10.1 Introduction

Previous chapters review the architectural foundations of internetworking, describe how hosts and routers forward Internet datagrams, and present mechanisms used to map IP addresses to physical network addresses. This chapter considers the structure of the software found in hosts and routers that carries out network communication. It presents the general principle of layering, shows how layering makes Internet Protocol software easier to understand and build, and traces the path of datagrams through the protocol software they encounter when traversing a TCP/IP internet.

10.2 The Need For Multiple Protocols

We have said that protocols allow one to specify or understand communication without knowing the details of a particular vendor's network hardware. They are to computer communication what programming languages are to computation. It should be apparent by now how closely the analogy fits. Like assembly language, some protocols describe communication across a physical network. For example, the details of the Ethernet frame format, network access policy, and frame error handling constitute a protocol that describes communication on an Ethernet. Similarly, like a high-level language, the Internet Protocol specifies higher-level abstractions (e.g., IP addressing, datagram format, and the concept of unreliable, connectionless delivery).

Complex data communication systems do not use a single protocol to handle all transmission tasks. Instead, they require a set of cooperative protocols, sometimes called a *protocol family* or *protocol suite*. To understand why, think of the problems that arise when machines communicate over a data network:

• *Hardware Failure.* A host or router may fail either because the hardware fails or because the operating system crashes. A network transmission link may fail or accidentally be disconnected. The protocol software needs to detect such failures and recover from them if possible.

• *Network Congestion.* Even when all hardware and software operates correctly, networks have finite capacity that can be exceeded. The protocol software needs to arrange ways that a congested machine can suppress further traffic.

• *Packet Delay Or Loss.* Sometimes, packets experience extremely long delays or are lost. The protocol software needs to learn about failures or adapt to long delays.

• *Data Corruption.* Electrical or magnetic interference or hardware failures can cause transmission errors that corrupt the contents of transmitted data. Protocol software needs to detect and recover from such errors.

• *Data Duplication Or Inverted Arrivals.* Networks that offer multiple routes may deliver data out of sequence or may deliver duplicates of packets. The protocol software needs to reorder packets and remove any duplicates.

Taken together, the problems seem overwhelming. It is difficult to understand how to write a single protocol that will handle them all. From the analogy with programming languages, we can see how to conquer the complexity. Program translation has been partitioned into four conceptual subproblems identified with the software that handles each subproblem: compiler, assembler, link editor, and loader. The division makes it possible for the designer to concentrate on one subproblem at a time, and for the implementor to build and test each piece of software independently. We will see that protocol software is partitioned similarly.

Two final observations from our programming language analogy will help clarify the organization of protocols. First, it should be clear that pieces of translation software must agree on the exact format of data passed between them. For example, the data passed from a compiler to an assembler consists of a program defined by the assembly programming language. The translation process involves multiple representations. The analogy holds for communication software because multiple protocols define the representations of data passed among communication software modules. Second, the four parts of the translator form a linear sequence in which output from the compiler becomes input to the assembler, and so on. Protocol software also uses a linear sequence.

10.3 The Conceptual Layers Of Protocol Software

Think of the modules of protocol software on each machine as being stacked vertically into *layers*, as in Figure 10.1. Each layer takes responsibility for handling one part of the problem.

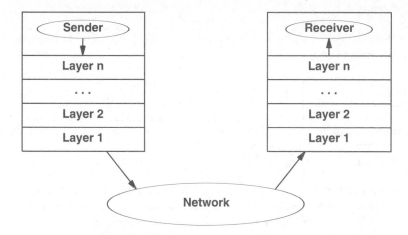

Figure 10.1 The conceptual organization of protocol software in layers.

Conceptually, sending a message from an application program on one machine to an application program on another means transferring the message down through successive layers of protocol software on the sender's machine, forwarding the message across the network, and transferring the message up through successive layers of protocol software on the receiver's machine.

In practice, the protocol software is much more complex than the simple model of Figure 10.1 indicates. Each layer makes decisions about the correctness of the message and chooses an appropriate action based on the message type or destination address. For example, one layer on the receiving machine must decide whether to keep the message or forward it to another machine. Another layer must decide which application program should receive the message.

To understand the difference between the conceptual organization of protocol software and the implementation details, consider the comparison shown in Figure 10.2. The conceptual diagram in Figure 10.2a shows an internet layer between a high-level protocol layer and a network interface layer. The realistic diagram in Figure 10.2b shows that the IP software may communicate with multiple high-level protocol modules and with multiple network interfaces.

Although a diagram of conceptual protocol layering does not show all details, it does help explain the general concept. For example, Figure 10.3 shows the layers of protocol software used by a message that traverses three networks. The diagram shows only the network interface and Internet Protocol layers in the routers because only those layers are needed to receive, look up a next hop, and send datagrams. We understand that any machine attached to two networks must have two network interface modules, even though the conceptual layering diagram shows only a single network interface layer in each machine.

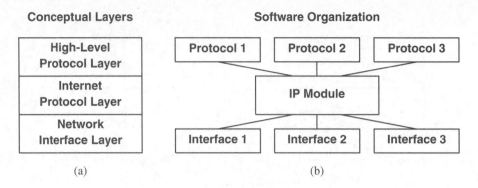

Figure 10.2 A comparison of (a) conceptual protocol layering and (b) a realistic view of software organization showing multiple network interfaces below IP and multiple protocols above it.

As Figure 10.3 shows, a sender on the original machine transmits a message which
the IP layer places in a datagram and sends across network *1*. On intermediate routers,
the datagram passes up to the IP layer which sends it back out again (on a different network). Only when it reaches the final destination machine, does IP extract the message
and pass it up to higher layers of protocol software.

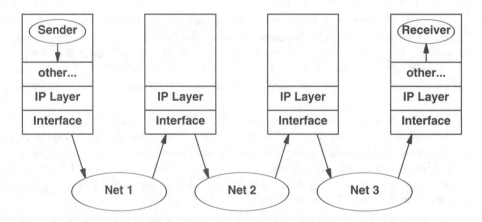

Figure 10.3 The path of a message traversing the Internet from the sender
through two intermediate routers to the receiver. Intermediate
routers only send the datagram to the IP software layer.

10.4 Functionality Of The Layers

Once the decision has been made to partition the communication problem and organize the protocol software into modules that each handle one subproblem, the question arises: "What functionality should reside in each module?" The question is not easy to answer for several reasons. First, given a set of goals and constraints governing a particular communication problem, it is possible to choose an organization that will optimize protocol software for that problem. Second, even when considering general network-level services such as reliable transport, it is possible to choose from among fundamentally distinct approaches to solving the problem. Third, the design of network (or internet) architecture and the organization of the protocol software are interrelated; one cannot be designed without the other.

10.4.1 ISO 7-Layer Reference Model

Two ideas about protocol layering dominate the field. The first, based on early work done by the International Organization for Standardization (ISO), is known as ISO's *Reference Model of Open System Interconnection*, often referred to as the *ISO model*. The ISO model contains 7 conceptual layers organized as Figure 10.4 shows.

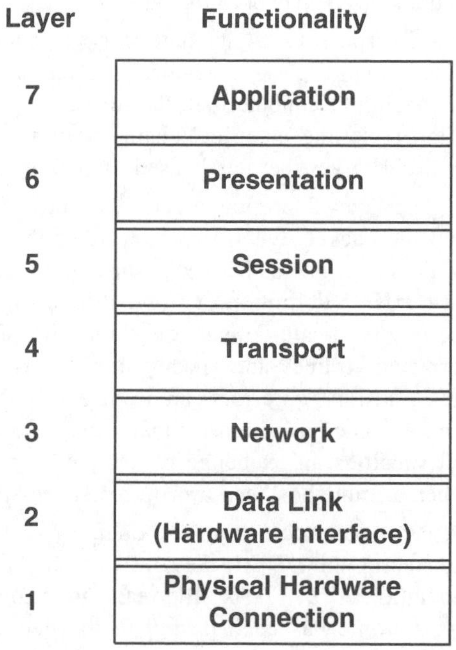

Layer	Functionality
7	Application
6	Presentation
5	Session
4	Transport
3	Network
2	Data Link (Hardware Interface)
1	Physical Hardware Connection

Figure 10.4 The ISO 7-layer reference model for protocol software.

The ISO model, built to describe protocols for a single network, does not contain a specific layer for internetwork forwarding in the same way TCP/IP protocols do.

10.5 X.25 And Its Relation To The ISO Model

Although it was designed to provide a conceptual model and not an implementation guide, the ISO layering scheme has been the basis for several protocol implementations. Among the protocols commonly associated with the ISO model, the suite of protocols known as X.25 is probably the most recognized and widely used. X.25 was established as a recommendation of the *International Telecommunications Union (ITU)*, formerly the *CCITT*, an organization that recommends standards for international telephone services. X.25 was adopted by public data networks, and became especially popular in Europe. Considering X.25 will help explain ISO layering.

In the X.25 view, a network operates much like a telephone system. An X.25 network is assumed to consist of complex packet switches that contain the intelligence needed to route packets. Hosts do not attach directly to communication wires of the network. Instead, each host attaches to one of the packet switches using a serial communication line. In one sense, the connection between a host and an X.25 packet switch is a miniature network consisting of one serial link. The host must follow a complicated procedure to transfer packets onto the network.

• *Physical Layer.* X.25 specifies a standard for the physical interconnection between host computers and network packet switches, as well as the procedures used to transfer packets from one machine to another. In the reference model, layer *1* specifies the physical interconnection including electrical characteristics of voltage and current. A corresponding protocol, X.21, gives the details used by public data networks.

• *Data Link Layer.* The layer *2* portion of the X.25 protocol specifies how data travels between a host and the packet switch to which it connects. X.25 uses the term *frame* to refer to a unit of data as it passes between a host and a packet switch (it is important to understand that the X.25 definition of *frame* differs slightly from the way we have defined it). Because raw hardware delivers only a stream of bits, the layer *2* protocol must define the format of frames and specify how the two machines recognize frame boundaries. Because transmission errors can destroy data, the layer *2* protocol includes error detection (e.g., a frame checksum). Finally, because transmission is unreliable, the layer *2* protocol specifies an exchange of acknowledgements that allows the two machines to know when a frame has been transferred successfully.

One commonly used layer *2* protocol, named the *High Level Data Link Communication*, is best known by its acronym, *HDLC*. Several versions of HDLC exist, with the most recent known as *HDLC/LAPB*. It is important to remember that successful transfer at layer *2* means a frame has been passed to the network packet switch for delivery; it does not guarantee that the packet switch accepted the packet or was able to forward it.

• *Network Layer.* The ISO reference model specifies that the third layer contains functionality that completes the definition of the interaction between host and network. Called the *network* or *communication subnet* layer, this layer defines the basic unit of transfer across the network and includes the concepts of destination addressing and forwarding. Remember that in the X.25 world, communication between host and packet switch is conceptually isolated from the traffic that is being passed. Thus, the network might allow packets defined by layer 3 protocols to be larger than the size of frames that can be transferred at layer 2. The layer 3 software assembles a packet in the form the network expects, and uses layer 2 to transfer it (possibly in pieces) to the packet switch. Layer 3 must also respond to network congestion problems.

• *Transport Layer.* Layer 4 provides end-to-end reliability by having the destination host communicate with the source host. The idea is that even though lower layers of protocols provide reliable checks at each transfer, the end-to-end layer double checks to make sure that no machine in the middle failed.

• *Session Layer.* Higher layers of the ISO model describe how protocol software can be organized to handle all the functionality needed by application programs. The ISO committee considered the problem of remote terminal access so fundamental that they assigned layer 5 to handle it. In fact, the central service offered by early public data networks consisted of terminal to host interconnection. On its networks, a carrier provided a special purpose host computer with dialup access called a *Packet Assembler And Disassembler* (*PAD*). Subscribers, often travelers with portable computers, used a modem to dial up the local PAD, made a network connection to a host computer, and logged in.

• *Presentation Layer.* ISO layer 6 is intended to include functions that many application programs need when using the network. Typical examples include standard routines that compress text or convert graphics images into bit streams for transmission across a network. For example, an ISO standard known as *Abstract Syntax Notation 1* (*ASN.1*), provides a representation of data that application programs use. One of the TCP/IP protocols, SNMP, also uses ASN.1 to represent data.

• *Application Layer.* Finally, ISO layer 7 includes application programs that use the network. Examples include electronic mail or file transfer programs.

10.5.1 The TCP/IP 5-Layer Reference Model

The second major layering model did not arise from a standards body, but came instead from research that led to the TCP/IP protocol suite. Now that TCP/IP protocols have become popular, proponents of the older ISO model have attempted to stretch the ISO model to accommodate TCP/IP, but the fact remains that the original ISO model did not provide for internetworking.

Broadly speaking, TCP/IP protocols are organized into five conceptual layers — four new layers that build on a fifth layer of conventional hardware. Figure 10.5 shows the conceptual layers as well as the form of data as it passes between them.

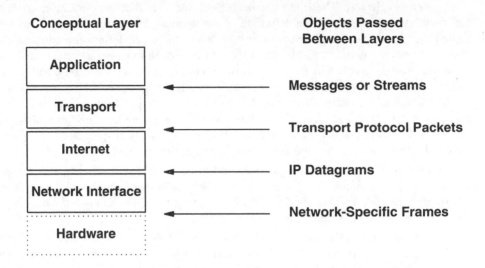

Figure 10.5 The 4 conceptual layers of TCP/IP software above the hardware
layer, and the form of objects passed between layers. The layer
labeled *network interface* is sometimes called the *data link* layer.

• *Application Layer.* At the highest layer, users invoke application programs that
access services available across a TCP/IP internet. An application interacts with one of
the transport layer protocols to send or receive data. Each application program chooses
the style of transport needed, which can be either a sequence of individual messages or
a continuous stream of bytes. The application program passes data in the required form
to the transport layer for delivery.

• *Transport Layer.* The primary duty of the transport layer is to provide communication from one application program to another. Such communication is often called
end-to-end. The transport layer may regulate flow of information. It may also provide
reliable transport, ensuring that data arrives without error and in sequence. To do so,
transport protocol software arranges to have the receiving side send back acknowledgements and the sending side retransmit lost packets. The transport software divides the
stream of data being transmitted into small pieces (sometimes called *packets*) and passes
each packet along with a destination address to the next layer for transmission.

Although Figure 10.5 uses a single block to represent the application layer, a general purpose computer can have multiple application programs accessing an internet at
one time. The transport layer must accept data from several user programs and send it
to the next lower layer. To do so, it adds additional information to each packet, including codes that identify which application program sent it and which application program
should receive it, as well as a checksum. The receiving machine uses the checksum to
verify that the packet arrived intact, and uses the destination code to identify the application program to which it should be delivered.

• *internet Layer*. As we have already seen, the internet layer handles communication from one machine to another. It accepts a request to send a packet from the transport layer along with an identification of the machine to which the packet should be sent. It encapsulates the packet in an IP datagram, fills in the datagram header, uses the forwarding algorithm to determine whether to deliver the datagram directly or send it to a router, and passes the datagram to the appropriate network interface for transmission. The internet layer also handles incoming datagrams, checking their validity, and uses the forwarding algorithm to decide whether the datagram should be processed locally or forwarded. For datagrams addressed to the local machine, software in the internet layer deletes the datagram header, and chooses from among several transport protocols the one that will handle the packet. Finally, the internet layer sends and receives ICMP error and control messages as needed.

• *Network Interface Layer*. The lowest-layer TCP/IP software comprises a network interface layer, responsible for accepting IP datagrams and transmitting them over a specific network. A network interface may consist of a device driver (e.g., when the network is a local area network to which the machine attaches directly) or a complex subsystem that uses its own data link protocol.

10.6 Locus Of Intelligence

TCP/IP requires protocol software on hosts to participate in almost all of the network protocols. We have already mentioned that hosts actively implement end-to-end error detection and recovery. They also participate in forwarding because they must choose a router when sending datagrams, and they participate in network control because they must respond to ICMP control messages. Thus, unlike a telephone network, a TCP/IP internet can be viewed as a relatively simple packet delivery system to which intelligent hosts attach. The idea is fundamental:

> *TCP/IP protocols place much of the network intelligence in hosts —
> routers in the Internet forward datagrams, but do not participate in
> higher-layer services.*

10.7 The Protocol Layering Principle

Independent of the particular layering scheme used or the functions of the layers, the operation of layered protocols is based on a fundamental idea. The idea, called the *layering principle*, can be summarized succinctly:

> *Layered protocols are designed so that layer* n *at the destination receives exactly the same object sent by layer* n *at the source.*

The layering principle explains why layering is such a powerful idea. It allows the protocol designer to focus attention on one layer at a time, without worrying about how other layers perform. For example, when building a file transfer application, the designer considers only two copies of the application program executing on two computers, and concentrates on the messages they need to exchange for file transfer. The designer assumes that the application on one host receives exactly the data that the application on the other host sends.

Figure 10.6 illustrates how the layering principle works:

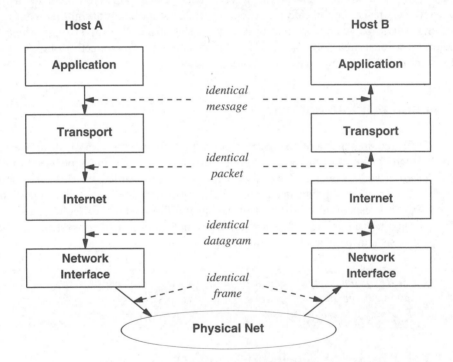

Figure 10.6 The path of a message as it passes from an application on one host to an application on another. Layer n on host B receives exactly the same object that layer n on host A sent.

10.7.1 Layering in a TCP/IP Internet Environment

Our statement of the layering principle is somewhat vague, and the illustration in Figure 10.6 skims over an important issue because it fails to distinguish between transfers from source to ultimate destination and transfers across multiple networks. Figure 10.7 illustrates the distinction, showing the path of a message sent from an application program on one host to an application on another through a router.

As the figure shows, message delivery uses two separate network frames, one for the transmission from host A to router R and another from router R to host B. The network layering principle states that the frame delivered to R is identical to the frame sent by host A. By contrast, the application and transport layers deal with end-to-end issues and are designed so the software at the source communicates with its peer at the ultimate destination. Thus, the layering principle states that the packet received by the transport layer at the ultimate destination is identical to the packet sent by the transport layer at the original source.

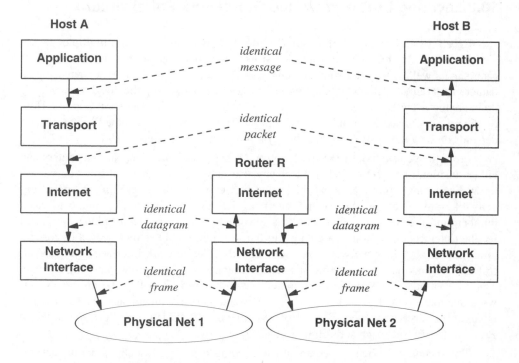

Figure 10.7 The layering principle when a router is used. The frame delivered to router R is exactly the frame sent from host A, but differs from the frame sent between R and B.

It is easy to understand that in higher layers, the layering principle applies across end-to-end transfers, and that at the lowest layer, it applies to a single machine transfer. It is not as easy to see how the layering principle applies to the internet layer. On one hand, we have said that hosts attached to the Internet should view it as a large, virtual network, with the IP datagram taking the place of a network frame. In this view, datagrams travel from original source to ultimate destination, and the layering principle guarantees that the ultimate destination receives exactly the datagram that the original source sent. On the other hand, we know that the datagram header contains fields, like a *time to live* counter, that change each time the datagram passes through a router. Thus, the ultimate destination will not receive exactly the same datagram as the source sent. We conclude that although most of the datagram stays intact as it passes across a TCP/IP internet, the layering principle only applies to datagrams across single machine transfers. To be accurate, we should not view the internet layer as providing end-to-end service.

10.8 Layering In The Presence Of Network Substructure

Recall from Chapter 2 that some wide area networks contain multiple packet switches. For example, a WAN can consist of routers that connect to a local network at each site as well as to other routers using leased serial lines. When a router receives a datagram, it either delivers the datagram to its destination on the local network, or transfers the datagram across a serial line to another router. The question arises: "How do the protocols used on serial lines fit into the TCP/IP layering scheme?" The answer depends on how the designer views the serial line interconnections.

From the perspective of IP, the set of point-to-point connections among routers can either function like a set of independent physical networks, or they can function collectively like a single physical network. In the first case, each physical link is treated exactly like any other network in the Internet. The link is assigned a unique network number, and the two hosts that share the link each have a unique IP address assigned for their connection†. Routes are added to the IP routing table as they would be for any other network. A new software module is added at the network interface layer to control the new link hardware, but no substantial changes are made to the layering scheme. The main disadvantage of the independent network approach is that it proliferates network numbers (one for each connection between two machines) and causes routing tables to be larger than necessary. Both *Serial Line IP* (*SLIP*) and the *Point to Point Protocol* (*PPP*) treat each serial link as a separate network.

The second approach to accommodating point-to-point connections avoids assigning multiple IP addresses to the physical wires. Instead, it treats all the connections collectively as a single, independent IP network with its own frame format, hardware addressing scheme, and data link protocols. Routers that use the second approach need only one IP network number for all point-to-point connections.

---

†The only exception arises when using the anonymous network scheme described in Chapter 9; leaving the link unnumbered does not change the layering.

Using the single network approach means extending the protocol layering scheme to add a new intranetwork forwarding layer between the network interface layer and the hardware devices. For machines with only one point-to-point connection, an additional layer seems unnecessary. To see why it is needed, consider a machine with several physical point-to-point connections, and recall from Figure 10.2(b) how the network interface layer is divided into multiple software modules that each control one network. We need to add one network interface for the new point-to-point network, but the new interface must control multiple hardware devices. Furthermore, given a datagram to send, the new interface must choose the correct link over which the datagram should be sent. Figure 10.8 shows the organization.

The internet layer software passes to the network interface all datagrams that should be sent on any of the point-to-point connections. The network interface passes them to the intranet forwarding module that must further distinguish among multiple physical connections and forward the datagram across the correct one.

The programmer who designs the intranet forwarding software determines exactly how the software chooses a physical link. Usually, the algorithm relies on an intranet routing table. An intranet routing table is analogous to an internet routing table in that it specifies a mapping of destination address to next hop. The table contains pairs of entries, (D, L), where D is a destination host address and L specifies the physical line used to reach that destination.

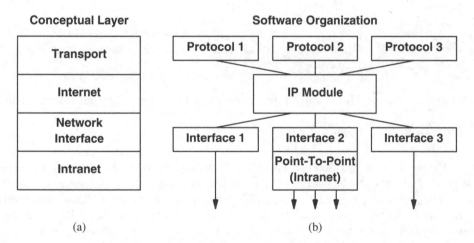

Figure 10.8 (a) Conceptual position of an intranet protocol for point-to-point
connections when IP treats them as a single IP network, and (b)
detailed diagram of corresponding software modules. Each ar-
row corresponds to one physical device.

The difference between an internet routing table and an intranet routing table is that intranet routing tables are quite small. They only contain forwarding information for hosts directly attached to the point-to-point network. The reason is simple: the internet layer maps an arbitrary destination address to a specific router address before passing the datagram to a network interface. The intranet layer is asked only to distinguish among machines on a single point-to-point network.

10.9 Two Important Boundaries In The TCP/IP Model

The conceptual protocol layering includes two boundaries that may not be obvious: a protocol address boundary that separates high-level and low-level addressing and an operating system boundary that separates the system from application programs.

10.9.1 High-Level Protocol Address Boundary

Now that we have seen the layering of TCP/IP software, we can be precise about an idea introduced in Chapter 7: a conceptual boundary partitions software that uses low-level (physical) addresses from software that uses high-level (IP) addresses. As Figure 10.9 shows, the boundary occurs between the network interface layer and the internet layer. That is,

> *Application programs as well as all protocol software from the internet layer upward use only IP addresses; the network interface layer handles physical addresses.*

Thus, protocols like ARP belong in the network interface layer. They are not part of IP.

10.9.2 Operating System Boundary

Figure 10.9 shows another important boundary as well, the division between software that is generally considered part of the operating system and software that is not. While each implementation of TCP/IP chooses how to make the distinction, many follow the scheme shown. Because lower layers of the protocol stack lie inside the operating system, passing data between lower layers of protocol software is much less expensive than passing it between an application program and a transport layer. Chapter 21 discusses the problem in more detail, and describes an example of the interface an operating system might provide.

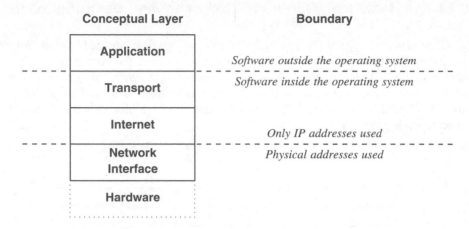

Figure 10.9 The relationship between conceptual layering and the boundaries for operating system and high-level protocol addresses.

10.10 The Disadvantage Of Layering

We have said that layering is a fundamental idea that provides the basis for protocol design. It allows the designer to divide a complicated problem into subproblems and solve each one independently. Unfortunately, the software that results from strict layering can be extremely inefficient. As an example, consider the job of the transport layer. It must accept a stream of bytes from an application program, divide the stream into packets, and send each packet across the underlying internet. To optimize transfer, the transport layer should choose the largest possible packet size that will allow one packet to travel in one network frame. In particular, if the destination machine attaches directly to one of the same networks as the source, only one physical net will be involved in the transfer, so the sender can optimize packet size for that network. If the software preserves strict layering, however, the transport layer cannot know how the internet module will forward traffic or which networks attach directly. Furthermore, the transport layer will not understand the datagram or frame formats nor will it be able to determine how many octets of header will be added to a packet. Thus, strict layering will prevent the transport layer from optimizing transfers.

Usually, implementors relax the strict layering scheme when building protocol software. They allow information like route selection and network MTU to propagate upward. When allocating buffers, they often leave space for headers that will be added by lower-layer protocols and may retain headers on incoming frames when passing them to higher-layer protocols. Such optimizations can make dramatic improvements in efficiency while retaining the basic layered structure.

10.11 The Basic Idea Behind Multiplexing And Demultiplexing

Communication protocols use the techniques of *multiplexing* and *demultiplexing* throughout the layered hierarchy. When sending a message, the source computer includes extra bits that encode the message type, originating program, and protocols used. Eventually, all messages are placed into network frames for transfer and combined into a stream of packets. At the receiving end, the destination machine uses the extra information to guide processing.

Consider an example of demultiplexing shown in Figure 10.10.

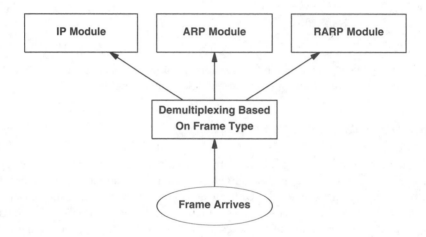

Figure 10.10 Demultiplexing of incoming frames based on the type field found in the frame header.

The figure illustrates how software in the network interface layer uses the frame type to select a procedure to handle the incoming frame. We say that the network interface *demultiplexes* the frame based on its type. To make such a choice possible, software in the source machine must set the frame type field before transmission. Thus, each software module that sends frames uses the type field to specify frame contents.

Multiplexing and demultiplexing occur at almost every protocol layer. For example, after the network interface demultiplexes frames and passes those frames that contain IP datagrams to the IP module, the IP software extracts the datagram and demultiplexes further based on the transport protocol. Figure 10.11 demonstrates demultiplexing at the internet layer.

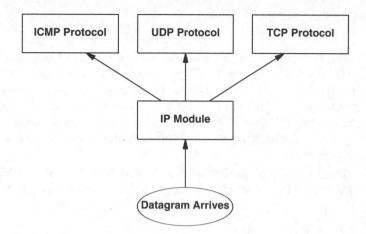

Figure 10.11 Demultiplexing at the internet layer. IP software chooses an appropriate procedure to handle a datagram based on the protocol type field in the datagram header.

To decide how to handle a datagram, IP software examines the header of a datagram and selects a protocol handler based on the datagram type. In the example, the possible datagram types are: *ICMP*, which we have already examined, and *UDP* and *TCP*, which we will examine in later chapters.

10.12 Summary

Protocols are the standards that specify how data is represented when being transferred from one machine to another. Protocols specify how the transfer occurs, how errors are detected, and how acknowledgements are passed. To simplify protocol design and implementation, communication problems are segregated into subproblems that can be solved independently. Each subproblem is assigned a separate protocol.

The idea of layering is fundamental because it provides a conceptual framework for protocol design. In a layered model, each layer handles one part of the communication problem and usually corresponds to one protocol. Protocols follow the layering principle, which states that the software implementing layer n on the destination machine receives exactly what the software implementing layer n on the source machine sends.

We examined the 5-layer Internet reference model as well as the older ISO 7-layer reference model. In both cases, the layering model provides only a conceptual framework for protocol software. In practice, protocol software uses multiplexing and demultiplexing to distinguish among multiple protocols within a given layer, making protocol software more complex than the layering models suggest.

FOR FURTHER STUDY

Postel [RFC 791] provides a sketch of the Internet Protocol layering scheme, and Clark [RFC 817] discusses the effect of layering on implementations. Saltzer, Reed, and Clark [1984] argues that end-to-end verification is important. Chesson [1987] makes the controversial argument that layering produces intolerably bad network throughput. Volume 2 of this series examines layering in detail, and shows an example implementation that achieves efficiency by compromising strict layering and passing pointers between layers.

The ISO protocol documents [2002a] and [2002b] describe ASN.1 in detail. Sun [RFC 1014] describes XDR, an example of what might be called a TCP/IP presentation protocol.

EXERCISES

10.1   Study the ISO layering model in more detail. How well does the model describe communication on a local area network like an Ethernet?

10.2   Build a case that TCP/IP is moving toward a six-layer protocol architecture that includes a presentation layer. (Hint: various programs use the XDR protocol, XML, and ASN.1.)

10.3   Do you think any single presentation protocol will eventually emerge that replaces all others? Why or why not?

10.4   Compare and contrast the tagged data format used by the ASN.1 presentation scheme with the untagged format used by XDR. Characterize situations in which one is better than the other.

10.5   Find out how a UNIX system uses the *mbuf* structure to make layered protocol software efficient.

10.6   Read about the System V UNIX *streams* mechanism. How does it help make protocol implementation easier? What is its chief disadvantage?

Chapter Contents

11

User Datagram Protocol (UDP)

11.1 Introduction

Previous chapters describe an abstract internet capable of transferring IP datagrams among host computers, where each datagram is forwarded through the internet based on the destination's IP address. At the internet layer, a destination address identifies a host computer; no further distinction is made regarding which user or which application program will receive the datagram. This chapter extends the TCP/IP protocol suite by adding a mechanism that distinguishes among destinations within a given host, allowing multiple application programs executing on a given computer to send and receive datagrams independently.

11.2 Identifying The Ultimate Destination

The operating systems in most computers support multiprogramming, which means they permit multiple application programs to execute simultaneously. Using operating system jargon, we refer to each executing program as a *process*, *task*, *application program*, or a *user level process*; the systems are called multitasking systems. It may seem natural to say that a process is the ultimate destination for a message. However, specifying that a particular process on a particular machine is the ultimate destination for a datagram is somewhat misleading. First, because processes are created and destroyed dynamically, senders seldom know enough to identify a process on another machine. Second, we would like to be able to replace processes that receive datagrams without informing all senders (e.g., rebooting a machine can change all the processes, but senders should not be required to know about the new processes). Third, it is desirable to identify a destination by the function it provides without knowing the process that implements the function (e.g., to allow a sender to contact an e-mail server without knowing which process on the destination machine implements the server function). More important, in systems that allow a single process to handle two or more functions, it is essential that we arrange a way for a process to decide exactly which function the sender desires.

Instead of thinking of a process as the ultimate destination, we will imagine that each machine contains a set of abstract destination points called *protocol ports*. Each protocol port is identified by a positive integer. The local operating system provides an interface mechanism that processes use to specify a port or access it.

Most operating systems provide synchronous access to ports. From a particular process's point of view, synchronous access means the computation stops during a port access operation. For example, if a process attempts to extract data from a port before any data arrives, the operating system temporarily stops (blocks) the process until data arrives. Once the data arrives, the operating system passes the data to the process and restarts it. In general, ports are *buffered*, so data that arrives before a process is ready to accept it will not be lost. To achieve buffering, the protocol software located inside the operating system places packets that arrive for a particular protocol port in a (finite) queue until a process extracts them.

To communicate with a foreign port, a sender needs to know both the IP address of the destination machine and the protocol port number of the destination within that machine. Each message must carry the number of the *destination port* on the machine to which the message is sent and the *source port* number on the source machine to which replies should be addressed. Thus, it is possible for any process that receives a message to reply to the sender.

11.3 The User Datagram Protocol

In the TCP/IP protocol suite, the *User Datagram Protocol* or *UDP* provides the primary mechanism that application programs use to send datagrams to other application programs. UDP provides protocol ports used to distinguish among multiple programs executing on a single machine. That is, in addition to the data sent, each UDP message contains both a destination port number and a source port number, making it possible for the UDP software at the destination to deliver the message to the correct recipient and for the recipient to send a reply.

UDP uses the underlying internet layer to transport a message from one machine to another, and provides the same unreliable, connectionless datagram delivery semantics as IP. It does not use acknowledgements to make sure messages arrive; it does not order incoming messages, nor does it provide feedback to control the rate at which information flows between the machines. Thus, UDP messages can be lost, duplicated, or arrive out of order. Furthermore, packets can arrive faster than the recipient can process them. We can summarize:

The User Datagram Protocol (UDP) provides an unreliable connectionless delivery service using IP to transport messages between machines. It uses IP to carry messages, but adds the ability to distinguish among multiple destinations within a given host computer.

An application program that uses UDP accepts full responsibility for handling the problem of reliability, including message loss, duplication, delay, out-of-order delivery, and loss of connectivity. Unfortunately, application programmers often ignore these problems when designing software. Furthermore, because programmers often test network software using highly reliable, low-delay local area networks, testing may not expose potential failures. Thus, many application programs that rely on UDP work well in a local environment, but fail in dramatic ways when used in the global Internet.

11.4 Format Of UDP Messages

Each UDP message is called a *user datagram*. Conceptually, a user datagram consists of two parts: a UDP header and a UDP data area. As Figure 11.1 shows, the header is divided into four 16-bit fields that specify the port from which the message was sent, the port to which the message is destined, the message length, and a UDP checksum.

0	16	31
UDP SOURCE PORT	UDP DESTINATION PORT	
UDP MESSAGE LENGTH	UDP CHECKSUM	
DATA		
. . .		

Figure 11.1   The format of fields in a UDP datagram.

The *SOURCE PORT* and *DESTINATION PORT* fields contain the 16-bit UDP protocol port numbers used to demultiplex datagrams among the processes waiting to receive them. The *SOURCE PORT* is optional. When used, it specifies the port to which replies should be sent; if not used, it should be zero.

The *LENGTH* field contains a count of octets in the UDP datagram, including the UDP header and the user data. Thus, the minimum value for *LENGTH* is eight, the length of the header alone.

The UDP checksum is optional and need not be used at all; a value of zero in the *CHECKSUM* field means that the checksum has not been computed. The designers chose to make the checksum optional to allow implementations to operate with little computational overhead when using UDP across a highly reliable local area network. Recall, however, that IP does not compute a checksum on the data portion of an IP datagram. Thus, the UDP checksum provides the only way to guarantee that data has arrived intact and should be used.

Beginners often wonder what happens to UDP messages for which the computed checksum is zero. A computed value of zero is possible because UDP uses the same checksum algorithm as IP: it divides the data into 16-bit quantities and computes the one's complement of their one's complement sum. Surprisingly, zero is not a problem because one's complement arithmetic has two representations for zero: all bits set to zero or all bits set to one. When the computed checksum is zero, UDP uses the representation with all bits set to one.

11.5 UDP Pseudo-Header

The UDP checksum covers more information than is present in the UDP datagram alone. To compute the checksum, UDP prepends a *pseudo-header* to the UDP datagram, appends an octet of zeros to pad the datagram to an exact multiple of 16 bits, and computes the checksum over the entire object. The octet used for padding and the pseudo-header are *not* transmitted with the UDP datagram, nor are they included in the length. To compute a checksum, the software first stores zero in the *CHECKSUM* field, then accumulates a 16-bit one's complement sum of the entire object, including the pseudo-header, UDP header, and user data.

The purpose of using a pseudo-header is to verify that the UDP datagram has reached its correct destination. The key to understanding the pseudo-header lies in realizing that the correct destination consists of a specific machine and a specific protocol port within that machine. The UDP header itself specifies only the protocol port number. Thus, to verify the destination, UDP on the sending machine computes a checksum that covers the destination IP address as well as the UDP datagram. At the ultimate destination, UDP software verifies the checksum using the destination IP address obtained from the header of the IP datagram that carried the UDP message. If the checksums agree, then it must be true that the datagram has reached the intended destination host as well as the correct protocol port within that host.

The pseudo-header used in the UDP checksum computation consists of 12 octets of data arranged as Figure 11.2 shows. The fields of the pseudo-header labeled *SOURCE IP ADDRESS* and *DESTINATION IP ADDRESS* contain the source and destination IP addresses that will be used when sending the UDP message. Field *PROTO* contains the IP protocol type code (*17* for UDP), and the field labeled *UDP LENGTH* contains the length of the UDP datagram (not including the pseudo-header). To verify the checksum, the receiver must extract these fields from the IP header, assemble them into the pseudo-header format, and recompute the checksum.

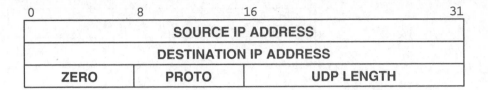

0	8	16	31
SOURCE IP ADDRESS			
DESTINATION IP ADDRESS			
ZERO	PROTO	UDP LENGTH	

Figure 11.2 The 12 octets of the pseudo-header used during UDP checksum computation.

11.6 UDP Encapsulation And Protocol Layering

UDP provides our first example of a transport protocol. In the layering model of Chapter 10, UDP lies in the layer above the internet layer. Conceptually, application programs access UDP, which uses IP to send and receive datagrams as Figure 11.3 shows.

Conceptual Layering

Application
User Datagram (UDP)
Internet (IP)
Network Interface

Figure 11.3 The conceptual layering of UDP between application programs and IP.

Layering UDP above IP means that a complete UDP message, including the UDP header and data, is encapsulated in an IP datagram as it travels across an internet as Figure 11.4 shows.

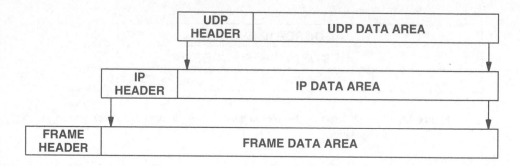

Figure 11.4 A UDP datagram encapsulated in an IP datagram for transmission across an internet. The datagram is further encapsulated in a frame each time it travels across a single network.

For the protocols we have examined, encapsulation means that UDP prepends a header to the data that a user sends and passes it to IP. The IP layer prepends a header to what it receives from UDP. Finally, the network interface layer embeds the datagram in a frame before sending it from one machine to another. The format of the frame depends on the underlying network technology. Usually, network frames include an additional header.

On input, a packet arrives at the lowest layer of network software and begins its ascent through successively higher layers. Each layer removes one header before passing the message on, so that by the time the highest level passes data to the receiving process, all headers have been removed. Thus, the outermost header corresponds to the lowest protocol layer, while the innermost header corresponds to the highest protocol layer. When considering how headers are inserted and removed, it is important to keep in mind the layering principle. In particular, observe that the layering principle applies to UDP, so the UDP datagram received from IP on the destination machine is identical to the datagram that UDP passed to IP on the source machine. Also, the data that UDP delivers to a user process on the receiving machine will be exactly the data that a user process passed to UDP on the sending machine.

The division of duties among various protocol layers is rigid and clear:

> *The IP layer is responsible only for transferring data between a pair of hosts on an internet, while the UDP layer is responsible only for differentiating among multiple sources or destinations within one host.*

Thus, only the IP header identifies the source and destination hosts; only the UDP layer identifies the source or destination ports within a host.

11.7 Layering And The UDP Checksum Computation

Observant readers will have noticed a seeming contradiction between the layering rules and the UDP checksum computation. Recall that the UDP checksum includes a pseudo-header that has fields for the source and destination IP addresses. It can be argued that the destination IP address must be known to the user when sending a UDP datagram, and the user must pass it to the UDP layer. Thus, the UDP layer can obtain the destination IP address without interacting with the IP layer. However, the source IP address depends on the route IP chooses for the datagram, because the IP source address identifies the network interface over which the datagram is transmitted. Thus, unless it interacts with the IP layer, UDP cannot know the IP source address.

We assume that UDP software asks the IP layer to compute the source and (possibly) destination IP addresses, uses them to construct a pseudo-header, computes the checksum, discards the pseudo-header, and then passes the UDP datagram to IP for transmission. An alternative approach that produces greater efficiency arranges to have the UDP layer encapsulate the UDP datagram in an IP datagram, obtain the source address from IP, store the source and destination addresses in the appropriate fields of the datagram header, compute the UDP checksum, and then pass the IP datagram to the IP layer, which only needs to fill in the remaining IP header fields.

Does the strong interaction between UDP and IP violate our basic premise that layering reflects separation of functionality? Yes. UDP has been tightly integrated with the IP protocol. It is clearly a compromise of the pure separation, made for entirely practical reasons. We are willing to overlook the layering violation because it is impossible to fully identify a destination application program without specifying the destination machine, and we want to make the mapping between addresses used by UDP and those used by IP efficient. One of the exercises examines this issue from a different point of view, asking the reader to consider whether UDP should be separated from IP.

11.8 UDP Multiplexing, Demultiplexing, And Ports

We have seen in Chapter 10 that software throughout the layers of a protocol hierarchy must multiplex or demultiplex among multiple objects at the next layer. UDP software provides another example of multiplexing and demultiplexing. It accepts UDP datagrams from many application programs and passes them to IP for transmission, and it accepts arriving UDP datagrams from IP and passes each to the appropriate application program.

Conceptually, all multiplexing and demultiplexing between UDP software and application programs occur through the port mechanism. In practice, each application program must negotiate with the operating system to obtain a protocol port and an associated port number before it can send a UDP datagram†. Once the port has been assigned, any datagram the application program sends through the port will have that port number in its UDP *SOURCE PORT* field.

---

†For now, we will describe ports abstractly; Chapter 21 provides an example of the operating system primitives used to create and use ports.

While processing input, UDP accepts incoming datagrams from the IP software and demultiplexes based on the UDP destination port, as Figure 11.5 shows.

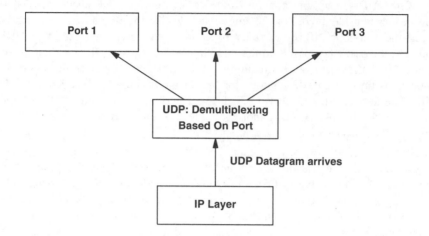

Figure 11.5 Example of demultiplexing one layer above IP. UDP uses the UDP destination port number to select an appropriate destination port for incoming datagrams.

The easiest way to think of a UDP port is as a queue. In most implementations, when an application program negotiates with the operating system to use a given port, the operating system creates an internal queue that can hold arriving messages. Often, the application can specify or change the queue size. When UDP receives a datagram, it checks to see that the destination port number matches one of the ports currently in use. If not, it sends an ICMP *port unreachable* error message and discards the datagram. If a match is found, UDP enqueues the new datagram at the port where an application program can access it. Of course, an error occurs if the port is full, and UDP discards the incoming datagram.

11.9 Reserved And Available UDP Port Numbers

How should protocol port numbers be assigned? The problem is important because two computers need to agree on port numbers before they can interoperate. For example, when computer *A* needs to obtain a file from computer *B*, it needs to know what port the file transfer program on computer *B* uses. There are two fundamental approaches to port assignment. The first approach uses a central authority. Everyone agrees to allow a central authority to assign port numbers as needed and to publish the list of all assignments. Then, all software is built according to the list. This approach is sometimes called *universal assignment*, and the port assignments specified by the authority are called *well-known port assignments*.

The second approach to port assignment uses dynamic binding. In the dynamic binding approach, ports are not globally known. Instead, whenever a program needs a port, the network software assigns one. To learn about the current port assignment on another computer, it is necessary to send a request that asks about the current port assignment (e.g., ''What port is the file transfer service using?''). The target machine replies by giving the correct port number to use.

The TCP/IP designers adopted a hybrid approach that assigns some port numbers a priori, but leaves many available for local sites or application programs to assign dynamically. The assigned port numbers begin at low values and extend upward, leaving large integer values available for dynamic assignment. The table in Figure 11.6 lists some of the currently assigned UDP port numbers. The second column contains Internet standard assigned keywords, while the third contains keywords used on most UNIX systems.

Decimal	Keyword	UNIX Keyword	Description
0	-	-	Reserved
7	ECHO	echo	Echo
9	DISCARD	discard	Discard
11	USERS	systat	Active Users
13	DAYTIME	daytime	Daytime
15	-	netstat	Network Status Program
17	QUOTE	qotd	Quote of the Day
19	CHARGEN	chargen	Character Generator
37	TIME	time	Time
42	NAMESERVER	name	Host Name Server
43	NICNAME	whois	Who Is
53	DOMAIN	nameserver	Domain Name Server
67	BOOTPS	bootps	BOOTP or DHCP Server
68	BOOTPC	bootpc	BOOTP or DHCP Client
69	TFTP	tftp	Trivial File Transfer
88	KERBEROS	kerberos	Kerberos Security Service
111	SUNRPC	sunrpc	Sun Remote Procedure Call
123	NTP	ntp	Network Time Protocol
161	-	snmp	Simple Network Management Protocol
162	-	snmp-trap	SNMP traps
512	-	biff	UNIX comsat
513	-	who	UNIX rwho Daemon
514	-	syslog	System Log
525	-	timed	Time Daemon

Figure 11.6 A sample of currently assigned UDP ports showing the standard Internet keyword and the UNIX equivalent; the list is not exhaustive. To the extent possible, other transport protocols that offer identical services use the same port numbers as UDP.

11.10 Summary

Most computer systems permit multiple application programs to execute simultane-ously. Using operating system jargon, we refer to each executing program as a *process*. The User Datagram Protocol, UDP, distinguishes among multiple processes within a given machine by allowing senders and receivers to add two 16-bit integers called pro-tocol port numbers to each UDP message. The port numbers identify the source and destination. Some UDP port numbers, called *well known*, are permanently assigned and honored throughout the Internet (e.g., port *69* is reserved for use by the Trivial File Transfer Protocol, *TFTP*, described in Chapter 25). Other port numbers are available for arbitrary application programs to use.

UDP is a thin protocol in the sense that it does not add significantly to the seman-tics of IP. It merely provides application programs with the ability to communicate us-ing IP's unreliable connectionless packet delivery service. Thus, UDP messages can be lost, duplicated, delayed, or delivered out of order; the application program using UDP must handle these problems. Many programs that use UDP do not work correctly across an internet because they fail to accommodate these conditions.

In the protocol layering scheme, UDP lies in the transport layer, above the internet layer and below the application layer. Conceptually, the transport layer is independent of the internet layer, but in practice they interact strongly. The UDP checksum includes IP source and destination addresses, meaning that UDP software must interact with IP software to find addresses before sending datagrams.

FOR FURTHER STUDY

The UDP protocol described here is a standard for TCP/IP, and is defined by Pos-tel [RFC 768].

EXERCISES

11.1   Try UDP in your local environment. Measure the average transfer speed with messages of 256, 512, 1024, 2048, 4096, and 8192 bytes. Can you explain the results (hint: what is your network MTU)?

11.2   Why is the UDP checksum separate from the IP checksum? Would you object to a pro-tocol that used a single checksum for the complete IP datagram including the UDP mes-sage?

11.3   Not using checksums can be dangerous. Explain how a single corrupted ARP packet broadcast by machine *P* can make it impossible to reach another machine, *Q*.

11.4   Should the notion of multiple destinations identified by protocol ports have been built into IP? Why, or why not?

11.5   *Name Registry.* Suppose you want to allow arbitrary pairs of application programs to establish communication with UDP, but you do not wish to assign them fixed UDP port numbers. Instead, you would like potential correspondents to be identified by a character string of 64 or fewer characters. Thus, a program on machine A might want to communicate with the "funny-special-long-id" program on machine B (you can assume that a process always knows the IP address of the host with which it wants to communicate). Meanwhile, a process on machine C wants to communicate with the "comer's-own-program-id" on machine A. Show that you only need to assign one UDP port to make such communication possible by designing software on each machine that allows (a) a local process to pick an unused UDP port ID over which it will communicate, (b) a local process to register the 64-character name to which it responds, and (c) a foreign process to use UDP to establish communication using only the 64-character name and destination internet address.

11.6   Implement the name registry software from the previous exercise.

11.7   What is the chief advantage of using preassigned UDP port numbers? The chief disadvantage?

11.8   What is the chief advantage of using protocol ports instead of process identifiers to specify the destination within a machine?

11.9   UDP provides unreliable datagram communication because it does not guarantee delivery of the message. Devise a reliable datagram protocol that uses timeouts and acknowledgements to guarantee delivery. How much network overhead and delay does reliability introduce?

11.10   Send UDP datagrams across a wide area network and measure the percentage lost and the percentage reordered. Does the result depend on the time of day? The network load?

Chapter Contents

12

Reliable Stream Transport Service (TCP)

12.1 Introduction

Previous chapters explore the unreliable connectionless packet delivery service that forms the basis for all Internet communication and the IP protocol that defines it. This chapter introduces the second most important and well-known network-level service, reliable stream delivery, and the *Transmission Control Protocol* (*TCP*) that defines it. We will see that TCP adds substantial functionality to the protocols already discussed, but that its implementation is also substantially more complex.

Although TCP is presented here as part of the TCP/IP Internet protocol suite, it is an independent, general purpose protocol that can be adapted for use with other delivery systems. For example, because TCP makes very few assumptions about the underlying network, it is possible to use it over a single network like an Ethernet, as well as over the global Internet.

12.2 The Need For Stream Delivery

At the lowest level, computer communication networks provide unreliable packet delivery. Packets can be lost or destroyed when transmission errors interfere with data, when network hardware fails, or when networks become too heavily loaded to accommodate the load presented. Packet switching systems change routes dynamically, deliver packets out of order, deliver them after a substantial delay, or deliver duplicates.

Furthermore, underlying network technologies may dictate an optimal packet size or pose other constraints needed to achieve efficient transfer rates.

At the highest level, application programs often need to send large volumes of data from one computer to another. Using an unreliable connectionless delivery system for large volume transfers becomes tedious and annoying, and it requires that programmers build error detection and recovery into each application program. Because it is difficult to design, understand, or modify software that correctly provides reliability, few application programmers have the necessary technical background. As a consequence, one goal of network protocol research has been to find general purpose solutions to the problems of providing reliable stream delivery, making it possible for experts to build a single instance of stream protocol software that all application programs use. Having a single general purpose protocol helps isolate application programs from the details of networking, and makes it possible to define a uniform interface for the stream transfer service.

12.3 Properties Of The Reliable Delivery Service

The interface between application programs and the TCP/IP reliable delivery service can be characterized by five features:

• *Stream Orientation*. When two application programs transfer large volumes of data, the data is viewed as a *stream* of bits, divided into 8-bit *octets* or *bytes*. The stream delivery service on the destination machine passes to the receiver exactly the same sequence of octets that the sender passes to it on the source machine.

• *Virtual Circuit Connection*. Making a stream transfer is analogous to placing a telephone call. Before transfer can start, both the sending and receiving application programs interact with their respective operating systems, informing them of the desire for a stream transfer. Conceptually, one application places a "call" which must be accepted by the other. Protocol software modules in the two operating systems communicate by sending messages across the underlying internet, verifying that the transfer is authorized, and that both sides are ready. Once all details have been settled, the protocol modules inform the application programs that a *connection* has been established and that transfer can begin. During transfer, protocol software on the two machines continue to communicate to verify that data is received correctly. If the communication fails for any reason (e.g., because network hardware along the path between the machines fails), both machines detect the failure and report it to the appropriate application programs. We use the term *virtual circuit* to describe such connections because although application programs view the connection as a dedicated hardware circuit, the reliability is an illusion provided by the stream delivery service.

• *Buffered Transfer*. Application programs send a data stream across the virtual circuit by repeatedly passing data octets to the protocol software. When transferring data, an application uses whatever size pieces it finds convenient, which can be as small as a single octet. At the receiving end, the protocol software delivers octets from the data stream in exactly the same order they were sent, making them available to the receiving application program as soon as they have been received and verified. The protocol software is free to divide the stream into packets independent of the pieces the application program transfers. To make transfer more efficient and to minimize network traffic, implementations usually collect enough data from a stream to fill a reasonably large datagram before transmitting it across an internet. Thus, even if the application program generates the stream one octet at a time, transfer across an internet may be quite efficient. Similarly, if the application program chooses to generate extremely large blocks of data, the protocol software can choose to divide each block into smaller pieces for transmission.

For those applications where data should be delivered without waiting to fill a buffer, the stream service provides a *push* mechanism that applications use to force immediate transfer. At the sending side, a push forces protocol software to transfer all data that has been generated without waiting to fill a buffer. When it reaches the receiving side, the push causes TCP to make the data available to the application without delay. The reader should note, however, that the push function only guarantees that all data will be transferred; it does not provide record boundaries. Thus, even when delivery is forced, the protocol software may choose to divide the stream in unexpected ways.

• *Unstructured Stream.* It is important to understand that the TCP/IP stream service does not honor structured data streams. For example, there is no way for a payroll application to have the stream service mark boundaries between employee records, or to identify the contents of the stream as being payroll data. Application programs using the stream service must understand stream content and agree on stream format before they initiate a connection.

• *Full Duplex Connection.* Connections provided by the TCP/IP stream service allow concurrent transfer in both directions. Such connections are called *full duplex*. From the point of view of an application process, a full duplex connection consists of two independent streams flowing in opposite directions, with no apparent interaction. The stream service allows an application process to terminate flow in one direction while data continues to flow in the other direction, making the connection *half duplex*. The advantage of a full duplex connection is that the underlying protocol software can send control information for one stream back to the source in datagrams carrying data in the opposite direction. Such *piggybacking* reduces network traffic.

12.4 Providing Reliability

We have said that the reliable stream delivery service guarantees to deliver a stream of data sent from one machine to another without duplication or data loss. The question arises: "How can protocol software provide reliable transfer if the underlying communication system offers only unreliable packet delivery?" The answer is complicated, but most reliable protocols use a single fundamental technique known as *positive acknowledgement with retransmission*. The technique requires a recipient to communicate with the source, sending back an *acknowledgement* (*ACK*) message as it receives data. The sender keeps a record of each packet it sends, and waits for an acknowledgement before sending the next packet. The sender also starts a timer when it sends a packet, and *retransmits* the packet if the timer expires before an acknowledgement arrives.

Figure 12.1 shows how the simplest positive acknowledgement protocol transfers data.

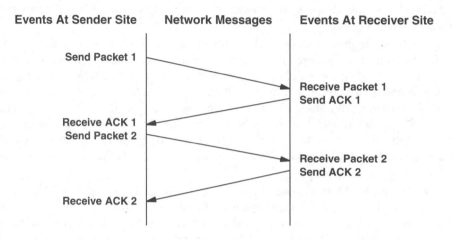

Figure 12.1 A protocol using positive acknowledgement with retransmission in which the sender awaits an acknowledgement for each packet sent. Vertical distance down the figure represents increasing time, and diagonal lines across the middle represent network packet transmission.

In the figure, events at the sender and receiver are shown on the left and right. Each diagonal line crossing the middle shows the transfer of one message across the network.

Figure 12.2 uses the same format diagram as Figure 12.1 to show what happens when a packet is lost or corrupted. The sender starts a timer after transmitting a packet. When the timer expires, the sender assumes the packet was lost and retransmits it.

The final reliability problem arises when an underlying packet delivery system duplicates packets. Duplicates can also arise when networks experience high delays that cause premature retransmission. Solving duplication requires careful thought because both packets and acknowledgements can be duplicated. Usually, reliable protocols detect duplicate packets by assigning each packet a sequence number and requiring the receiver to remember which sequence numbers it has received. To avoid confusion caused by delayed or duplicated acknowledgements, positive acknowledgement protocols send sequence numbers back in acknowledgements, so the receiver can correctly associate acknowledgements with packets.

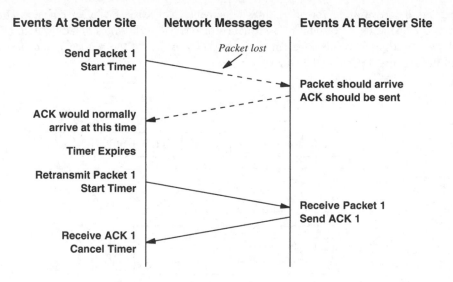

Figure 12.2 Timeout and retransmission that occurs when a packet is lost. The dotted lines show the time that would be taken by the transmission of a packet and its acknowledgement, if the packet was not lost.

12.5 The Idea Behind Sliding Windows

Before examining the TCP stream service, we need to explore an additional concept that underlies stream transmission. The concept, known as a *sliding window*, makes stream transmission efficient. To understand the motivation for sliding windows, recall the sequence of events that Figure 12.1 depicts. To achieve reliability, the sender transmits a packet and then waits for an acknowledgement before transmitting another. As Figure 12.1 shows, data only flows between the machines in one direction at any time, even if the network is capable of simultaneous communication in both directions. The network will remain completely idle during times that machines delay responses (e.g., while machines compute routes or checksums). If we imagine a network with high transmission delays, the problem becomes clear:

> *A simple positive acknowledgement protocol wastes a substantial amount of network bandwidth because it must delay sending a new packet until it receives an acknowledgement for the previous packet.*

The sliding window technique is a more complex form of positive acknowledgement and retransmission than the simple method discussed above. Sliding window protocols use network bandwidth better because they allow the sender to transmit multiple packets before waiting for an acknowledgement. The easiest way to envision sliding window operation is to think of a sequence of packets to be transmitted as Figure 12.3 shows. The protocol places a small, fixed-size *window* on the sequence and transmits all packets that lie inside the window.

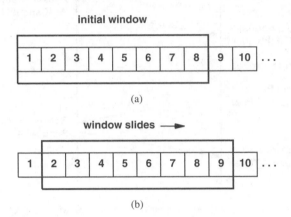

Figure 12.3 (a) A sliding window protocol with eight packets in the window, and (b) The window sliding so that packet *9* can be sent when an acknowledgement has been received for packet *1*. Only unacknowledged packets are retransmitted.

We say that a packet is *unacknowledged* if it has been transmitted but no acknowledgement has been received. Technically, the number of packets that can be unacknowledged at any given time is constrained by the *window size*, which is limited to a small, fixed number. For example, in a sliding window protocol with window size *8*, the sender is permitted to transmit *8* packets before it receives an acknowledgement.

As Figure 12.3 shows, once the sender receives an acknowledgement for the first packet inside the window, it ''slides'' the window along and sends the next packet. The window continues to slide as long as acknowledgements are received.

The performance of sliding window protocols depends on the window size and the speed at which the network accepts packets. Figure 12.4 shows an example of the operation of a sliding window protocol when sending three packets. Note that the sender transmits all three packets before receiving any acknowledgements.

With a window size of *1*, a sliding window protocol is exactly the same as our simple positive acknowledgement protocol. By increasing the window size, it is possible to eliminate network idle time completely. That is, in the steady state, the sender can transmit packets as fast as the network can transfer them. The main point is:

> *Because a well-tuned sliding window protocol keeps the network completely saturated with packets, it obtains substantially higher throughput than a simple positive acknowledgement protocol.*

Conceptually, a sliding window protocol always remembers which packets have been acknowledged and keeps a separate timer for each unacknowledged packet. If a packet is lost, the timer expires and the sender retransmits that packet. When the sender slides its window, it moves past all acknowledged packets. At the receiving end, the protocol software keeps an analogous window, accepting and acknowledging packets as they arrive. Thus, the window partitions the sequence of packets into three sets: those packets to the left of the window have been successfully transmitted, received, and acknowledged; those packets to the right have not yet been transmitted; and those packets that lie in the window are being transmitted. The lowest numbered packet in the window is the first packet in the sequence that has not been acknowledged.

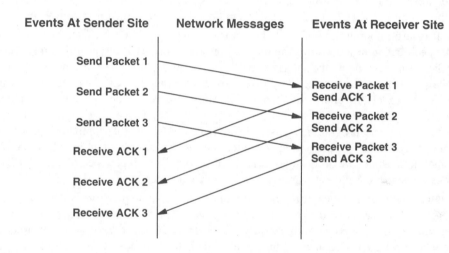

Figure 12.4 An example of three packets transmitted using a sliding window protocol. The key concept is that the sender can transmit all packets in the window without waiting for an acknowledgement.

12.6 The Transmission Control Protocol

Now that we understand the principle of sliding windows, we can examine the reliable stream service provided by the TCP/IP Internet protocol suite. The service is defined by the *Transmission Control Protocol*, or *TCP*. The reliable stream service is so significant that the entire protocol suite is referred to as TCP/IP. It is important to understand that:

TCP is a communication protocol, not a piece of software.

The difference between a protocol and the software that implements it is analogous to the difference between the definition of a programming language and a compiler. As in the programming language world, the distinction between definition and implementation sometimes becomes blurred. People encounter TCP software much more frequently than they encounter the protocol specification, so it is natural to think of a particular implementation as the standard. Nevertheless, the reader should try to distinguish between the two.

Exactly what does TCP provide? TCP is complex, so there is no simple answer. The protocol specifies the format of the data and acknowledgements that two computers exchange to achieve a reliable transfer, as well as the procedures the computers use to ensure that the data arrives correctly. It specifies how TCP software distinguishes among multiple destinations on a given machine, and how communicating machines recover from errors like lost or duplicated packets. The protocol also specifies how two computers initiate a TCP stream transfer and how they agree when it is complete.

It is also important to understand what the protocol does not include. Although the TCP specification describes how application programs use TCP in general terms, it does not dictate the details of the interface between an application program and TCP. That is, the protocol documentation only discusses the operations TCP supplies; it does not specify the exact procedures application programs invoke to access these operations. The reason for leaving the application program interface unspecified is flexibility. In particular, because programmers usually implement TCP in the computer's operating system, they need to employ whatever interface the operating system supplies. Allowing the implementor flexibility makes it possible to have a single specification for TCP that can be used to build software for a variety of machines.

Because TCP assumes little about the underlying communication system, TCP can be used with a variety of packet delivery systems. In particular, because it does not require the underlying system to be reliable or fast, TCP can run over a variety of hardware mechanisms such as a dialup telephone line, a local area network, a high-speed fiber optic network, a satellite connection, or a noisy wireless connection in which many packets are lost. The large variety of delivery systems TCP can use is one of its strengths.

12.7 Ports, Connections, And Endpoints

Like the User Datagram Protocol (UDP) presented in Chapter 11, TCP resides above IP in the protocol layering scheme. Figure 12.5 shows the conceptual organization. TCP allows multiple application programs on a given machine to communicate concurrently, and it demultiplexes incoming TCP traffic among application programs. Like the User Datagram Protocol, TCP uses *protocol port* numbers to identify the ultimate destination within a machine. Each port is assigned a small integer used to identify it†.

Conceptual Layering

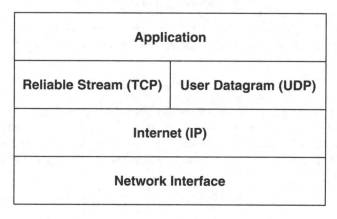

Figure 12.5 The conceptual layering of UDP and TCP above IP. TCP provides a reliable stream service, while UDP provides an unreliable datagram delivery service. Application programs use both.

When we discussed UDP ports, we said to think of each port as a queue into which protocol software places arriving datagrams. TCP ports are much more complex because a given port number does not correspond to a single object. Instead, TCP has been built on the *connection abstraction*, in which the objects to be identified are virtual circuit connections, not individual ports. Understanding that TCP uses the notion of connections is crucial because it helps explain the meaning and use of TCP port numbers:

> *TCP uses the connection, not the protocol port, as its fundamental abstraction; connections are identified by a pair of endpoints.*

Exactly what are the "endpoints" of a connection? We have said that a connection consists of a virtual circuit between two application programs, so it might be natural to assume that an application program serves as the connection "endpoint." It is not. Instead, TCP defines an *endpoint* to be a pair of integers (*host, port*), where *host* is the IP address for a host and *port* is a TCP port on that host. For example, the endpoint (*128.10.2.3, 25*) specifies TCP port *25* on the machine with IP address *128.10.2.3*.

---

†Although both TCP and UDP use integer port identifiers starting at *1* to identify ports, there is no confusion between them because an incoming IP datagram identifies the protocol being used as well as the port number.

Now that we have defined endpoints, it will be easy to understand connections. Recall that a connection is defined by its two endpoints. Thus, if there is a connection from machine (*18.26.0.36*) at MIT to machine (*128.10.2.3*) at Purdue University, it might be defined by the endpoints:

$$(18.26.0.36, 1069) \text{ and } (128.10.2.3, 25).$$

Meanwhile, another connection might be in progress from machine (*128.9.0.32*) at the Information Sciences Institute to the same machine at Purdue, identified by its endpoints:

$$(128.9.0.32, 1184) \text{ and } (128.10.2.3, 53).$$

So far, our examples of connections have been straightforward because the ports used at all endpoints have been unique. However, the connection abstraction allows multiple connections to share an endpoint. For example, we could add another connection to the two listed above from machine (*128.2.254.139*) at CMU to the machine at Purdue:

$$(128.2.254.139, 1184) \text{ and } (128.10.2.3, 53).$$

It might seem strange that two connections can use the TCP port *53* on machine 128.10.2.3 simultaneously, but there is no ambiguity. Because TCP associates incoming messages with a connection instead of a protocol port, it uses both endpoints to identify the appropriate connection. The important idea to remember is:

> *Because TCP identifies a connection by a pair of endpoints, a given TCP port number can be shared by multiple connections on the same machine.*

From a programmer's point of view, the connection abstraction is significant. It means a programmer can devise a program that provides concurrent service to multiple connections simultaneously without needing unique local port numbers for each connection. For example, most systems provide concurrent access to their electronic mail service, allowing multiple computers to send them electronic mail simultaneously. Because the program that accepts incoming mail uses TCP to communicate, it only needs to use one local TCP port even though it allows multiple connections to proceed concurrently.

12.8 Passive And Active Opens

Unlike UDP, TCP is a connection-oriented protocol that requires both endpoints to agree to participate. That is, before TCP traffic can pass across an internet, application programs at both ends of the connection must agree that the connection is desired. To do so, the application program on one end performs a *passive open* function by contacting its operating system and indicating that it will accept an incoming connection. At that time, the operating system assigns a TCP port number for its end of the connection. The application program at the other end must then contact its operating system using an *active open* request to establish a connection. The two TCP software modules communicate to establish and verify a connection. Once a connection has been created, application programs can begin to pass data; the TCP software modules at each end exchange messages that guarantee reliable delivery. We will return to the details of establishing connections after examining the TCP message format.

12.9 Segments, Streams, And Sequence Numbers

TCP views the data stream as a sequence of octets or bytes that it divides into *segments* for transmission. Usually, each segment travels across the underlying internet in a single IP datagram.

TCP uses a specialized sliding window mechanism to solve two important problems: efficient transmission and flow control. Like the sliding window protocol described earlier, the TCP window mechanism makes it possible to send multiple segments before an acknowledgement arrives. Doing so increases total throughput because it keeps the network busy. The TCP form of a sliding window protocol also solves the end-to-end *flow control* problem, by allowing the receiver to restrict transmission until it has sufficient buffer space to accommodate more data.

The TCP sliding window mechanism operates at the octet level, not at the segment or packet level. Octets of the data stream are numbered sequentially, and a sender keeps three pointers associated with every connection. The pointers define a sliding window as Figure 12.6 illustrates. The first pointer marks the left of the sliding window, separating octets that have been sent and acknowledged from octets yet to be acknowledged. A second pointer marks the right of the sliding window and defines the highest octet in the sequence that can be sent before more acknowledgements are received. The third pointer marks the boundary inside the window that separates those octets that have already been sent from those octets that have not been sent. The protocol software sends all octets in the window without delay, so the boundary inside the window usually moves from left to right quickly.

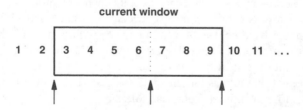

current window

1 2 | 3 4 5 6 7 8 9 | 10 11 . . .

Figure 12.6 An example of the TCP sliding window. Octets through 2 have been sent and acknowledged, octets 3 through 6 have been sent but not acknowledged, octets 7 though 9 have not been sent but will be sent without delay, and octets 10 and higher cannot be sent until the window moves.

We have described how the sender's TCP window slides along and mentioned that the receiver must maintain a similar window to piece the stream together again. It is important to understand, however, that because TCP connections are full duplex, two transfers proceed simultaneously over each connection, one in each direction. We think of the transfers as completely independent because at any time data can flow across the connection in one direction, or in both directions. Thus, TCP software at each end maintains two windows per connection (for a total of four), one slides along the data stream being sent, while the other slides along as data is received.

12.10 Variable Window Size And Flow Control

One difference between the TCP sliding window protocol and the simplified sliding window protocol presented earlier occurs because TCP allows the window size to vary over time. Each acknowledgement, which specifies how many octets have been received, contains a *window advertisement* that specifies how many additional octets of data the receiver is prepared to accept. We think of the window advertisement as specifying the receiver's current buffer size. In response to an increased window advertisement, the sender increases the size of its sliding window and proceeds to send octets that have not been acknowledged. In response to a decreased window advertisement, the sender decreases the size of its window and stops sending octets beyond the boundary. TCP software should not contradict previous advertisements by shrinking the window past previously acceptable positions in the octet stream. Instead, smaller advertisements accompany acknowledgements, so the window size changes at the time it slides forward.

The advantage of using a variable size window is that it provides flow control as well as reliable transfer. To avoid receiving more data than it can store, the receiver sends smaller window advertisements as its buffer fills. In the extreme case, the receiver advertises a window size of zero to stop all transmissions. Later, when buffer space becomes available, the receiver advertises a nonzero window size to trigger the flow of data again†.

Having a mechanism for flow control is essential in an environment where machines of various speeds and sizes communicate through networks and routers of various speeds and capacities. There are two independent problems. First, protocols need to provide end-to-end flow control between the source and ultimate destination. For example, when a hand-held PDA communicates with a fast PC, the PDA needs to regulate the influx of data, or protocol software would be overrun quickly. Thus, TCP must implement end-to-end flow control to guarantee reliable delivery. Second, a mechanism is needed that allows intermediate systems (i.e., routers) to control a source that sends more traffic than the machine can tolerate.

When intermediate machines become overloaded, the condition is called *congestion*, and mechanisms to solve the problem are called *congestion control* mechanisms. TCP uses its sliding window scheme to solve the end-to-end flow control problem. We

†There are two exceptions to transmission when the window size is zero. First, a sender is allowed to transmit a segment with the urgent bit set to inform the receiver that urgent data is available. Second, to avoid a potential deadlock that can arise if a nonzero advertisement is lost after the window size reaches zero, the sender probes a zero-sized window periodically.

will discuss congestion control later, but it should be noted that a well-designed proto-col can detect and recover from congestion, while a poorly-designed protocol will make congestion worse. In particular, a carefully chosen retransmission scheme can help avoid congestion, but a poorly chosen scheme can exacerbate it by aggressively re-transmitting.

12.11 TCP Segment Format

The unit of transfer between the TCP software on two machines is called a *seg-ment*. Segments are exchanged to establish connections, transfer data, send acknowl-edgements, advertise window sizes, and close connections. Because TCP uses piggy-backing, an acknowledgement traveling from machine *A* to machine *B* may travel in the same segment as data traveling from machine *A* to machine *B*, even though the ac-knowledgement refers to data sent from *B* to *A*†. Figure 12.7 shows the TCP segment format.

0	4	10	16	24	31
SOURCE PORT			DESTINATION PORT		
SEQUENCE NUMBER					
ACKNOWLEDGEMENT NUMBER					
HLEN	RESERVED	CODE BITS	WINDOW		
CHECKSUM			URGENT POINTER		
OPTIONS (IF ANY)				PADDING	
DATA					
. . .					

Figure 12.7 The format of a TCP segment with a TCP header followed by data. Segments are used to establish connections as well as to carry data and acknowledgements.

Each segment is divided into two parts, a header followed by data. The header, known as the *TCP header*, carries the expected identification and control information. Fields *SOURCE PORT* and *DESTINATION PORT* contain the TCP port numbers that identify the application programs at the ends of the connection. The *SEQUENCE NUMBER* field identifies the position in the sender's byte stream of the data in the seg-ment. The *ACKNOWLEDGEMENT NUMBER* field identifies the number of the octet that the source expects to receive next. Note that the sequence number refers to the stream flowing in the same direction as the segment, while the acknowledgement number refers to the stream flowing in the opposite direction from the segment.

---

†In practice, piggybacking does not usually occur because most applications do not send data in both directions simultaneously.

The *HLEN†* field contains an integer that specifies the length of the segment header measured in 32-bit multiples. It is needed because the *OPTIONS* field varies in length, depending on which options have been included. Thus, the size of the TCP header varies depending on the options selected. The 6-bit field marked *RESERVED* is reserved for future use (a later section describes a proposed use).

Some segments carry only an acknowledgement while some carry data. Others carry requests to establish or close a connection. TCP software uses the 6-bit field labeled *CODE BITS* to determine the purpose and contents of the segment. The six bits tell how to interpret other fields in the header according to the table in Figure 12.8.

Bit (left to right)	Meaning if bit set to 1
URG	Urgent pointer field is valid
ACK	Acknowledgement field is valid
PSH	This segment requests a push
RST	Reset the connection
SYN	Synchronize sequence numbers
FIN	Sender has reached end of its byte stream

Figure 12.8 Bits of the CODE BITS field in the TCP header.

TCP software advertises how much data it is willing to accept every time it sends a segment by specifying its buffer size in the *WINDOW* field. The field contains a 16-bit unsigned integer in network-standard byte order. Window advertisements provide another example of piggybacking because they accompany all segments, including those carrying data as well as those carrying only an acknowledgement.

12.12 Out Of Band Data

Although TCP is a stream-oriented protocol, it is sometimes important for the program at one end of a connection to send data *out of band*, without waiting for the program at the other end of the connection to consume octets already in the stream. For example, when TCP is used for a remote login session, the user may decide to send a keyboard sequence that *interrupts* or *aborts* the program at the other end. Such signals are most often needed when a program on the remote machine fails to operate correctly. The signals must be sent without waiting for the program to read octets already in the TCP stream (or one would not be able to abort programs that stop reading input).

To accommodate out of band signaling, TCP allows the sender to specify data as *urgent*, meaning that the receiving program should be notified of its arrival as quickly as possible, regardless of its position in the stream. The protocol specifies that when urgent data is found, the receiving TCP should notify the application program associat-

---

†The specification says the *HLEN* field is the *offset* of the data area within the segment.

ed with the connection to go into "urgent mode." After all urgent data has been consumed, TCP tells the application program to return to normal operation.

The exact details of how TCP informs the application program about urgent data depend on the computer's operating system. The mechanism used to mark urgent data when transmitting it in a segment consists of the URG code bit and the *URGENT POINTER* field. When the URG bit is set, the *URGENT POINTER* field specifies the position in the segment where urgent data ends.

12.13 TCP Options

As Figure 12.7 shows, a TCP segment can contain zero or more *options* in the header. Each option begins with a 1-octet field that specifies the option *type*† followed by a 1-octet length field that specifies the size of the option in octets. If the options do not occupy an exact multiple of 32 bits, *PADDING* is added to the end of the header.

12.13.1 Maximum Segment Size Option

A sender can choose the amount of data that is placed in each segment. However, both ends of a TCP connection need to agree on a maximum segment they will transfer. TCP uses a *maximum segment size (MSS)* option to allow a receiver to specify the maximum size segment that it is willing to receive. Thus, an embedded system that only has a few hundred bytes of buffer space can specify an MSS that restricts segments so they fit in the buffer. MSS negotiation is especially significant because it permits heterogeneous systems to communicate — a supercomputer can communicate with a small embedded system. To maximize throughput, when two computers attach to the same physical network, TCP usually computes a maximum segment size such that the resulting IP datagrams will match the network MTU. If the endpoints do not lie on the same physical network, they can attempt to discover the minimum MTU along the path between them, or choose a maximum segment size of *536* (the default size of an IP datagram, *576*, minus the standard size of IP and TCP headers).

In a general internet environment, choosing a good maximum segment size can be difficult because performance can be poor for either extremely large segment sizes or extremely small segment sizes. On one hand, when the segment size is small, network utilization remains low. To see why, recall that TCP segments travel encapsulated in IP datagrams which are encapsulated in physical network frames. Thus, each segment has at least 40 octets of TCP and IP headers in addition to the data. Therefore, datagrams carrying only one octet of data use at most 1/41 of the underlying network bandwidth for user data; in practice, minimum interpacket gaps and network hardware framing bits make the ratio even smaller.

On the other hand, extremely large segment sizes can also produce poor performance. Large segments result in large IP datagrams. When such datagrams travel across a network with small MTU, IP must fragment them. Unlike a TCP segment, a fragment cannot be acknowledged or retransmitted independently; all fragments must

---

†RFCs use the term *kind* rather than *type*.

arrive or the entire datagram must be retransmitted. Because the probability of losing a given fragment is nonzero, increasing segment size above the fragmentation threshold decreases the probability the datagram will arrive, which decreases throughput.

In theory, the optimum segment size, S, occurs when the IP datagrams carrying the segments are as large as possible without requiring fragmentation anywhere along the path from the source to the destination. In practice, finding S is difficult for several reasons. First, most implementations of TCP do not include a mechanism for doing so†. Second, because routers in an internet can change routes dynamically, the path datagrams follow between a pair of communicating computers can change dynamically and so can the size at which datagrams must be fragmented. Third, the optimum size depends on lower-level protocol headers (e.g., the segment size must be reduced to accommodate IP options).

12.13.2 Window Scaling Option

Because the *WINDOW* field in the TCP header is 16 bits long, the maximum size window is 64 Kbytes. Although the window was sufficient for early networks, a larger window size is needed to obtain high throughput on a network such as a satellite channel that has a large delay-bandwidth product (informally called a *long fat pipe*).

To accommodate larger window sizes, a *window scaling option* was proposed for TCP. The option consists of three octets: a type, a length, and a *shift* value, S. In essence, the shift value specifies a binary scaling factor to be applied to the window value. When window scaling is in effect, a receiver extracts the value from the *WINDOW* field, W, and shifts W left S bits to obtain the actual window size.

Several details complicate the design. The option can be negotiated when the connection is initially established, in which case all successive window advertisements are assumed to use the negotiated scale, or the option can be specified on each segment, in which case the scaling factor can vary from one segment to another. Furthermore, if either side of a connection implements window scaling but does not need to scale its window, the side sends the option set to zero, which makes the scaling factor 1.

12.13.3 Timestamp Option

The TCP *timestamp option* was invented to help TCP compute the delay on the underlying network, and it is also used to handle the case where TCP sequence numbers exceed 2^{32} (known as *Protect Against Wrapped Sequence* numbers, *PAWS*). In addition to the required type and length fields, a timestamp option includes two values: a timestamp value and an echo reply timestamp value. A sender places the time from its current clock in the timestamp field when sending a packet; a receiver copies the timestamp field into the echo reply field before returning an acknowledgement for the packet. Thus, when an acknowledgement arrives, the sender can accurately compute the total elapsed time since the segment was sent.

---

†To discover the path MTU, a sender probes the path by sending datagrams with the IP *do not fragment* bit set. It then decreases the size if ICMP error messages report that fragmentation was required.

12.14 TCP Checksum Computation

The *CHECKSUM* field in the TCP header contains a 16-bit integer checksum used to verify the integrity of the data as well as the TCP header. To compute the checksum, TCP software on the sending machine follows a procedure like the one described in Chapter 11 for UDP. It prepends a *pseudo header* to the segment, appends enough zero bits to make the segment a multiple of 16 bits, and computes the 16-bit checksum over the entire result. TCP does not count the pseudo header or padding in the segment length, nor does it transmit them. Also, it assumes the checksum field itself is zero for purposes of the checksum computation. As with other checksums, TCP uses 16-bit arithmetic and takes the one's complement of the one's complement sum. At the receiving site, TCP software performs the same computation to verify that the segment arrived intact.

The purpose of using a pseudo header is exactly the same as in UDP. It allows the receiver to verify that the segment has reached its correct destination, which includes both a host IP address as well as a protocol port number. Both the source and destination IP addresses are important to TCP because it must use them to identify the connection to which the segment belongs. Therefore, whenever a datagram arrives carrying a TCP segment, IP must pass to TCP the source and destination IP addresses from the datagram as well as the segment itself. Figure 12.9 shows the format of the pseudo header used in the checksum computation.

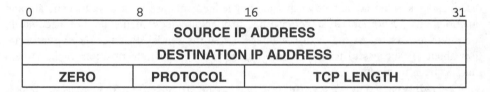

Figure 12.9 The format of the pseudo header used in TCP checksum computations. At the receiving site, this information is extracted from the IP datagram that carried the segment.

The sending TCP assigns field *PROTOCOL* the value that the underlying delivery system will use in its protocol type field. For IP datagrams carrying TCP, the value is *6*. The *TCP LENGTH* field specifies the total length of the TCP segment including the TCP header. At the receiving end, information used in the pseudo header is extracted from the IP datagram that carried the segment and included in the checksum computation to verify that the segment arrived at the correct destination intact.

12.15 Acknowledgements, Retransmission, And Timeouts

Because TCP sends data in variable length segments and because retransmitted segments can include more data than the original, acknowledgements cannot easily refer to datagrams or segments. Instead, they refer to a position in the stream using the stream sequence numbers. The receiver collects data octets from arriving segments and reconstructs an exact copy of the stream being sent. Because segments travel in IP datagrams, they can be lost or delivered out of order; the receiver uses the sequence numbers to reorder segments. At any time, the receiver will have reconstructed zero or more octets contiguously from the beginning of the stream, but may have additional pieces of the stream from datagrams that arrived out of order. The receiver always acknowledges the longest contiguous prefix of the stream that has been received correctly. Each acknowledgement specifies a sequence value one greater than the highest octet position in the contiguous prefix it received. Thus, the sender receives continuous feedback from the receiver as it progresses through the stream. We can summarize this important idea:

> *A TCP acknowledgement specifies the sequence number of the next octet that the receiver expects to receive.*

The TCP acknowledgement scheme is called *cumulative* because it reports how much of the stream has accumulated. Cumulative acknowledgements have both advantages and disadvantages. One advantage is that acknowledgements are both easy to generate and unambiguous. Another advantage is that lost acknowledgements do not necessarily force retransmission. A major disadvantage is that the sender does not receive information about all successful transmissions, but only about a single position in the stream that has been received.

To understand why lack of information about all successful transmissions makes cumulative acknowledgements less efficient, think of a window that spans *5000* octets starting at position *101* in the stream, and suppose the sender has transmitted all data in the window by sending five segments. Suppose further that the first segment is lost, but all others arrive intact. As each segment arrives, the receiver sends an acknowledgement, but each acknowledgement specifies octet *101*, the next highest contiguous octet it expects to receive. There is no way for the receiver to tell the sender that most of the data for the current window has arrived.

When a timeout occurs at the sender's side, the sender must choose between two potentially inefficient schemes. It may choose to retransmit one segment or all five segments. In this case retransmitting all five segments is inefficient. When the first segment arrives, the receiver will have all the data in the window, and will acknowledge *5101*. If the sender follows the accepted standard and retransmits only the first unacknowledged segment, it must wait for the acknowledgement before it can decide what and how much to send. Thus, it reverts to a simple positive acknowledgement protocol, and may lose the advantages of having a large window.

One of the most important and complex ideas in TCP is embedded in the way it handles timeout and retransmission. Like other reliable protocols, TCP expects the destination to send acknowledgements whenever it successfully receives new octets from the data stream. Every time it sends a segment, TCP starts a timer and waits for an acknowledgement. If the timer expires before data in the segment has been acknowledged, TCP assumes that the segment was lost or corrupted and retransmits it.

To understand why the TCP retransmission algorithm differs from the algorithm used in many network protocols, we need to remember that TCP is intended for use in an internet environment. In an internet, a segment traveling between a pair of machines may traverse a single, low-delay network (e.g., a high-speed LAN), or it may travel across multiple intermediate networks through multiple routers. Thus, it is impossible to know *a priori* how quickly acknowledgements will return to the source. Furthermore, the delay at each router depends on traffic, so the total time required for a segment to travel to the destination and an acknowledgement to return to the source varies dramatically from one instant to another. Figure 12.10, which shows measurements of round trip times across the global Internet for 100 consecutive packets, illustrates the problem. TCP software must accommodate both the vast differences in the time required to reach various destinations and the changes in time required to reach a given destination as traffic load varies.

TCP accommodates varying internet delays by using an *adaptive retransmission algorithm*. In essence, TCP monitors the performance of each connection and deduces reasonable values for timeouts. As the performance of a connection changes, TCP revises its timeout value (i.e., it adapts to the change).

To collect the data needed for an adaptive algorithm, TCP records the time at which each segment is sent and the time at which an acknowledgement arrives for the data in that segment. From the two times, TCP computes an elapsed time known as a *sample round trip time* or *round trip sample*. Whenever it obtains a new round trip sample, TCP adjusts its notion of the average round trip time for the connection. TCP computes an estimated round trip time *RTT*, as a weighted average and uses new round trip samples to change the average slowly. For example, when computing a new weighted average, the original averaging technique used a constant weighting factor, α, where $0 \leq \alpha < 1$, to weight the old average against the latest round trip sample:

$$RTT = (\alpha * Old\_RTT) + ((1-\alpha) * New\_Round\_Trip\_Sample)$$

Choosing a value for α close to *1* makes the weighted average immune to changes that last a short time (e.g., a single segment that encounters long delay). Choosing a value for α close to *0* makes the weighted average respond to changes in delay very quickly.

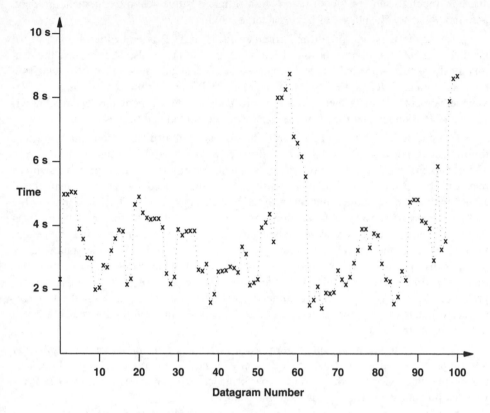

Figure 12.10 A plot of Internet round trip times as measured for 100 successive IP datagrams. Although the Internet now operates with
much lower delay, the delays still vary over time.

When it sends a segment, TCP computes a timeout value as a function of the
current round trip estimate. Early implementations of TCP used a constant weighting
factor, β ($\beta > 1$), and made the timeout greater than the current round trip estimate:

$$\text{Timeout} = \beta * \text{RTT}$$

The original specification recommended setting $\beta = 2$; more recent work described
below has produced better techniques for adjusting timeout.

We can summarize the ideas presented so far:

> *To accommodate the varying delays encountered in an internet environment, TCP uses an adaptive retransmission algorithm that monitors delays on each connection and adjusts its timeout parameter accordingly.*

12.16 Accurate Measurement Of Round Trip Samples

In theory, measuring a round trip sample is trivial — it consists of subtracting the time at which the segment is sent from the time at which the acknowledgement arrives. However, complications arise because TCP uses a cumulative acknowledgement scheme in which an acknowledgement refers to data received, and not to the instance of a specific datagram that carried the data. Consider a retransmission. TCP forms a segment, places it in a datagram and sends it, the timer expires, and TCP sends the segment again in a second datagram. Because both datagrams carry exactly the same data, the sender has no way of knowing whether an acknowledgement corresponds to the original or retransmitted datagram. This phenomenon has been called *acknowledgement ambiguity*, and TCP acknowledgements are said to be *ambiguous*.

Should TCP assume acknowledgements belong with the earliest (i.e., original) transmission or the latest (i.e., the most recent retransmission)? Surprisingly, neither assumption works. Associating the acknowledgement with the original transmission can make the estimated round trip time grow without bound in cases where an internet loses datagrams†. If an acknowledgement arrives after one or more retransmissions, TCP will measure the round trip sample from the original transmission, and compute a new RTT using the excessively long sample. Thus, RTT will grow slightly. The next time TCP sends a segment, the larger RTT will result in slightly longer timeouts, so if an acknowledgement arrives after one or more retransmissions, the next sample round trip time will be even larger, and so on.

Associating the acknowledgement with the most recent retransmission can also fail. Consider what happens when the end-to-end delay suddenly increases. When TCP sends a segment, it uses the old round trip estimate to compute a timeout, which is now too small. The segment arrives and an acknowledgement starts back, but the increase in delay means the timer expires before the acknowledgement arrives, and TCP retransmits the segment. Shortly after TCP retransmits, the first acknowledgement arrives and is associated with the retransmission. The round trip sample will be much too small and will result in a slight decrease of the estimated round trip time, RTT. Unfortunately, lowering the estimated round trip time guarantees that TCP will set the timeout too small for the next segment. Ultimately, the estimated round trip time can stabilize at a value, T, such that the correct round trip time is slightly longer than some multiple of T. Implementations of TCP that associate acknowledgements with the most recent retransmission have been observed in a stable state with RTT slightly less than one-half of the correct value (i.e., TCP sends each segment exactly twice even though no loss occurs).

---

†The estimate can only grow arbitrarily large if every segment is lost at least once.

12.17 Karn's Algorithm And Timer Backoff

If the original transmission and the most recent transmission both fail to provide accurate round trip times, what should TCP do? The accepted answer is simple: TCP should not update the round trip estimate for retransmitted segments. The idea, known as *Karn's Algorithm*, avoids the problem of ambiguous acknowledgements altogether by only adjusting the estimated round trip for unambiguous acknowledgements (acknowledgements that arrive for segments that have only been transmitted once).

Of course, a simplistic implementation of Karn's algorithm, one that merely ignores times from retransmitted segments, can lead to failure as well. Consider what happens when TCP sends a segment after a sharp increase in delay. TCP computes a timeout using the existing round trip estimate. The timeout will be too small for the new delay and will force retransmission. If TCP ignores acknowledgements from retransmitted segments, it will never update the estimate and the cycle will continue.

To accommodate such failures, Karn's algorithm requires the sender to combine retransmission timeouts with a *timer backoff* strategy. The backoff technique computes an initial timeout using a formula like the one shown above. However, if the timer expires and causes a retransmission, TCP increases the timeout. In fact, each time it must retransmit a segment, TCP increases the timeout (to keep timeouts from becoming ridiculously long, most implementations limit increases to an upper bound that is larger than the delay along any path in the internet).

Implementations use a variety of techniques to compute backoff. Most choose a multiplicative factor, γ, and set the new value to:

$$new\_timeout = \gamma * timeout$$

Typically, γ is 2. (It has been argued that values of γ less than 2 lead to instabilities.) Other implementations use a table of multiplicative factors, allowing arbitrary backoff at each step†.

Karn's algorithm combines the backoff technique with round trip estimation to solve the problem of never increasing round trip estimates:

> *Karn's algorithm: When computing the round trip estimate, ignore samples that correspond to retransmitted segments, but use a backoff strategy, and retain the timeout value from a retransmitted packet for subsequent packets until a valid sample is obtained.*

Generally speaking, when an internet misbehaves, Karn's algorithm separates computation of the timeout value from the current round trip estimate. It uses the round trip estimate to compute an initial timeout value, but then backs off the timeout on each retransmission until it can successfully transfer a segment. When it sends subsequent segments, it retains the timeout value that results from backoff. Finally, when an acknowledgement arrives corresponding to a segment that did not require retransmission, TCP

---

†Berkeley UNIX is the most notable system that used a table of factors, but values in the table were equivalent to using $\gamma=2$.

recomputes the round trip estimate and resets the timeout accordingly. Experience shows that Karn's algorithm works well even in networks with high packet loss†.

12.18 Responding To High Variance In Delay

Research into round trip estimation has shown that the computations described above do not adapt to a wide range of variation in delay. Queueing theory suggests that the round trip time increases proportional to $1/(1-L)$, where L is the current network load, $0 \le L \le 1$, and the variation in round trip time, σ, is proportional to $1/(1-L)^2$. If an internet is running at 50% of capacity, we expect the round trip delay to vary by a factor of *4* from the mean round trip time. When the load reaches 80%, we expect a variation by a factor of *25*. The original TCP standard specified the technique for estimating round trip time that we described earlier. Using that technique and limiting β to the suggested value of *2* means the round trip estimation can adapt to loads of at most 30%.

The 1989 specification for TCP requires implementations to estimate both the average round trip time and the variance, and to use the estimated variance in place of the constant β. As a result, new implementations of TCP can adapt to a wider range of variation in delay and yield substantially higher throughput. Fortunately, the approximations require little computation; extremely efficient programs can be derived from the following simple equations:

$$DIFF = SAMPLE - Old\_RTT$$

$$Smoothed\_RTT = Old\_RTT + \delta * DIFF$$

$$DEV = Old\_DEV + \rho (|DIFF| - Old\_DEV)$$

$$Timeout = Smoothed\_RTT + \eta * DEV$$

where *DEV* is the estimated mean deviation, δ is a fraction between *0* and *1* that controls how quickly the new sample affects the weighted average, ρ is a fraction between *0* and *1* that controls how quickly the new sample affects the mean deviation, and η is a factor that controls how much the deviation affects the round trip timeout. To make the computation efficient, TCP chooses δ and ρ to each be an inverse of a power of *2*, scales the computation by 2^n for an appropriate *n*, and uses integer arithmetic. Research suggests values of $\delta = 1/2^3$, $\rho = 1/2^2$, and $\eta = 3$ will work well. The original value for η in 4.3BSD UNIX was *2*; it was changed to *4* in 4.4 BSD UNIX.

Figure 12.11 uses a set of randomly generated values to illustrate how the computed timeout changes as the roundtrip time varies. Although the roundtrip times are artificial, they follow a pattern observed in practice: successive packets show small variations in delay as the overall average rises or falls.

---

†Phil Karn is an amateur radio enthusiast who developed this algorithm to allow TCP communication across a high-loss packet radio connection.

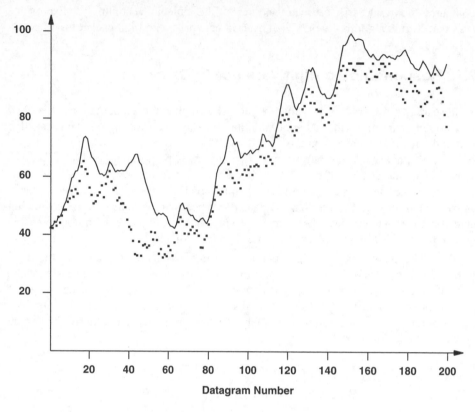

Figure 12.11 A set of 200 (randomly generated) roundtrip times shown as
dots, and the TCP retransmission timer shown as a solid line.
The timeout increases when delay varies.

Note that frequent change in the roundtrip time, including a cycle of increase and
decrease, can produce an increase in the retransmission timer. Furthermore, although
the timer tends to increase quickly when delay rises, it does not decrease as rapidly
when delay falls.

Figure 12.12 uses the data points from Figure 12.10 to show how TCP responds to
the extreme case of variance in delay. Recall that the goal is to have the retransmission
timer estimate the actual roundtrip time as closely as possible without underestimating.
The figure shows that although the timer responds quickly, it can underestimate. For
example, between the two successive datagrams marked with arrows, the delay doubles
from less than 4 seconds to more than 8. More important, the abrupt change follows a
period of relative stability in which the variation in delay is small, making it impossible
for any algorithm to anticipate the change. In the case of the TCP algorithm, because
the timeout (approximately 5) substantially underestimates the large delay, an unnecessary retransmission occurs. However, the estimate responds quickly to the increase in
delay, meaning that successive packets arrive without retransmission.

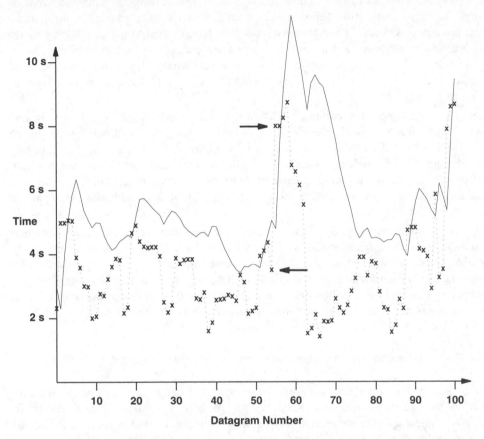

Figure 12.12 The value of TCP's retransmission timer for the data from Figure 12.10. Arrows mark two successive datagrams where the delay doubles.

12.19 Response To Congestion

It may seem that TCP software could be designed by considering the interaction between the two endpoints of a connection and the communication delays between those endpoints. In practice, however, TCP must also react to *congestion* in an internet. Congestion is a condition of severe delay caused by an overload of datagrams at one or more switching points (e.g., at routers). When congestion occurs, delays increase and the router begins to enqueue datagrams until it can forward them. We must remember that each router has finite storage capacity and that datagrams compete for that storage (i.e., in a datagram-based internet, there is no preallocation of resources to individual TCP connections). In the worst case, the total number of datagrams arriving at the congested router grows until the router reaches capacity and starts to drop datagrams.

Endpoints do not usually know the details of where congestion has occurred or why. To them, congestion simply means increased delay. Unfortunately, most transport protocols use timeout and retransmission, so they respond to increased delay by retransmitting datagrams. Retransmissions aggravate congestion instead of alleviating it. If unchecked, the increased traffic will produce increased delay, leading to increased traffic, and so on, until the network becomes useless. The condition is known as *congestion collapse*.

To avoid congestion collapse, TCP must reduce transmission rates when congestion occurs. Routers watch queue lengths and use techniques like ICMP source quench to inform hosts that congestion has occurred†, but transport protocols like TCP can help avoid congestion by reducing transmission rates automatically whenever delays occur. Of course, algorithms to avoid congestion must be constructed carefully because even under normal operating conditions an internet will exhibit wide variation in round trip delays.

To avoid congestion, the TCP standard now recommends using two techniques: *slow-start* and *multiplicative decrease*. They are related and can be implemented easily. We said that for each connection, TCP must remember the size of the receiver's window (i.e., the buffer size advertised in acknowledgements). To control congestion TCP maintains a second limit, called the *congestion window limit* or *congestion window*, that it uses to restrict data flow to less than the receiver's buffer size when congestion occurs. That is, at any time, TCP acts as if the window size is:

$$Allowed\_window = min(\,receiver\_advertisement,\; congestion\_window\,)$$

In the steady state on a non-congested connection, the congestion window is the same size as the receiver's window. Reducing the congestion window reduces the traffic TCP will inject into the connection. To estimate congestion window size, TCP assumes that most datagram loss comes from congestion and uses the following strategy:

> *Multiplicative Decrease Congestion Avoidance: Upon loss of a segment, reduce the congestion window by half (down to a minimum of at least one segment). For those segments that remain in the allowed window, backoff the retransmission timer exponentially.*

Because TCP reduces the congestion window by half for *every* loss, it decreases the window exponentially if loss continues. In other words, if congestion is likely, TCP reduces the volume of traffic exponentially and the rate of retransmission exponentially. If loss continues, TCP eventually limits transmission to a single datagram and continues to double timeout values before retransmitting. The idea is to provide quick and significant traffic reduction to allow routers enough time to clear the datagrams already in their queues.

How can TCP recover when congestion ends? You might suspect that TCP should reverse the multiplicative decrease and double the congestion window when traffic be-

---

†In a congested network, queue lengths grow exponentially for a significant time.

gins to flow again. However, doing so produces an unstable system that oscillates wildly between no traffic and congestion. Instead, TCP uses a technique called *slow-start†* to scale up transmission:

> *Slow-Start (Additive) Recovery: Whenever starting traffic on a new connection or increasing traffic after a period of congestion, start the congestion window at the size of a single segment and increase the congestion window by one segment each time an acknowledgement arrives.*

Slow-start avoids swamping the underlying internet with additional traffic immediately after congestion clears or when new connections suddenly start.

The term *slow-start* may be a misnomer because under ideal conditions, the start is not very slow. TCP initializes the congestion window to *1*, sends an initial segment, and waits. When the acknowledgement arrives, it increases the congestion window to *2*, sends two segments, and waits. When the two acknowledgements arrive they each increase the congestion window by *1*, so TCP can send *4* segments. Acknowledgements for those will increase the congestion window to *8*. Within four round-trip times, TCP can send *16* segments, often enough to reach the receiver's window limit. Even for extremely large windows, it takes only $\log_2 N$ round trips before TCP can send *N* segments.

To avoid increasing the window size too quickly and causing additional congestion, TCP adds one additional restriction. Once the congestion window reaches one half of its original size before congestion, TCP enters a *congestion avoidance* phase and slows down the rate of increment. During congestion avoidance, it increases the congestion window by *1* only if all segments in the window have been acknowledged. The overall approach is known as *Additive Increase Multiplicative Decrease (AIMD)*.

Taken together, slow-start, multiplicative decrease, additive increase, measurement of variation, and exponential timer backoff improve the performance of TCP dramatically without adding any significant computational overhead to the protocol software. Versions of TCP that use these techniques have improved the performance of previous versions by factors of *2* to *10*.

12.20 Fast Recovery And Other Modifications

The early version of TCP, sometimes referred to as *Tahoe*, used the retransmission scheme described above, waiting for a timer to expire before retransmitting. In 1990, the *Reno* version of TCP appeared that introduced several changes, including a heuristic known as *fast recovery* or *fast retransmit* that has higher throughput in cases where only occasional loss occurs.

---

†The term *slow-start* is attributed to John Nagle; the technique was originally called *soft-start*.

The trick used in fast recovery arises from TCP's cumulative acknowledgement scheme: loss of a single segment means that the arrival of subsequent segments will cause the receiver to generate an ACK for the point in the stream where the missing segment begins. From a sender's point of view, a series of acknowledgements arrive that each carry the same sequence number. The fast retransmit heuristic uses a series of three *duplicate acknowledgements* (i.e., an original plus three absolutely identical copies) to trigger a retransmission without waiting for the timer to expire.

In a case where only one segment is lost, waiting for the retransmitted segment to be acknowledged also reduces throughput. Therefore, to maintain higher throughput, the fast retransmit heuristic continues to send data from the window while awaiting acknowledgement of the retransmitted segment. Furthermore, the congestion window is artificially inflated: the congestion window is halved for the retransmission, but then the congestion window is increased by one maximum size segment for each duplicate ACK that previously arrived or arrives after the retransmission occurs. As a result, while fast retransmit occurs, TCP keeps many segments "in flight" between the sender and receiver.

A further optimization of the fast retransmit hueristic was incorporated in a later version of TCP known as the *NewReno* version. The optimization handles a case where two segments are lost within a single window. In essence, when fast retransmit occurs, NewReno records information about the current window and retransmits as described above. When the ACK arrives, for the retransmitted segment, there are two possibilities: the ACK specifies the sequence number at the end of the window (in which case the retransmitted segment was the only segment missing from the window), or the ACK specifies a sequence number higher than the missing segment, but less than the end of the window (in which case a second segment from the window has also been lost). In the latter case, NewReno proceeds to retransmit the second missing segment.

Minor modifications to the AIMD scheme have also been proposed and used in later versions of TCP. To understand, consider how AIMD† changes the sender's congestion window in response to segment loss or the arrival of an acknowledgement:

$$w \leftarrow w - aw \qquad \text{when loss is detected}$$

$$w \leftarrow w + \frac{b}{w} \qquad \text{when an ACK arrives}$$

In the original scheme, a is .5 and b is 1. In thinking about protocols like *STCP*, researchers have proposed setting a to 0.125 and b to 0.01 to prevent the congestion window from oscillating and increase throughput slightly. Other proposals for modifications (e.g. a protocol known as *HSTCP*) suggest making a and b functions of w (i.e. $a(w)$ and $b(w)$). Finally, proposals for TCP congestion control such as *Vegas* and *FAST* use increasing RTT as a measure of congestion instead of packet loss, and define the congestion window size to be a function of the measured RTT. Typically the modifications only lead to performance improvements in special cases (e.g., networks with high bandwidth and low loss rates); the original (Reno) AIMD congestion control is used for other cases.

---

†See Section 12.19.

A final proposal related to TCP congestion control concerns UDP. Observe that although TCP reduces transmission when congestion occurs, UDP does not, which means that as TCP flows continue to back off, UDP flows consume more of the bandwidth. A solution known as *TCP Friendly Rate Control* (*TFRC*) has been proposed. Because UDP does not use a sliding window, TFRC attempts to emulate TCP behavior by having a receiver report packet loss back to the sender and by having the sender use the reported loss data to compute a rate at which UDP should be sent.

12.21 Explicit Feedback Mechanisms (SACK and ECN)

Most versions of TCP use *implicit* techniques to detect loss and congestion. That is, TCP uses timeout and duplicate ACKs to detect loss, and changes in round-trip times to detect congestion. Researchers have observed that slight improvements are possible if TCP includes mechanisms that provided such information *explicitly*. The next two sections describe two explicit techniques that have been proposed.

12.21.1 Selective Acknowledgement (SACK)

The alternative to TCP's cumulative acknowledgement mechanism is known as a *selective acknowledgement* mechanism. In essence, selective acknowledgements allow a receiver to specify exactly which data has been received and which is still missing. The chief advantage of selective acknowledgements arises in situations where occasional loss occurs: selective acknowledgements allow a sender to know exactly which segments to retransmit.

The *Selective ACKnowledgement* (*SACK*) mechanism proposed for TCP does not completely replace the cumulative acknowledgement mechanism nor is it mandatory. Instead, TCP includes two options for SACK. The first option is used when the connection is established to allow a sender to specify that SACK is permitted. The second option is used by a receiver to include in each acknowledgement information about specific blocks of data that were received. The information for each block includes the first sequence number in a block (called the *left edge*) and the sequence number immediately beyond the block (called the *right edge*). Because the maximum size of a segment header is fixed, an acknowledgement can contain at most four SACK blocks. Interestingly, the SACK documents do not specify exactly how a sender responds to SACK; most implementations retransmit all missing blocks.

12.21.2 Explicit Congestion Notification

A second proposed technique to avoid implicit measurement is intended to handle congestion in the network. Known as *Explicit Congestion Notification* (*ECN*), the mechanism requires routers throughout an internet to notify TCP as congestion occurs. The mechanism is conceptually straightforward: as a TCP segment passes through the internet, routers along the path use a pair of bits in the IP header to record congestion.

Thus, when a segment arrives, the receiver knows whether the segment experienced congestion at any point. Unfortunately, the sender, not the receiver, needs to learn about congestion. Therefore, the receiver uses the next ACK to inform the sender that congestion occurred. The sender then responds by reducing its congestion window.

ECN uses two bits in the IP header to allow routers to record congestion, and uses two bits in the TCP header (taken from the reserved area) to allow the sending and receiving TCP to communicate. One of the TCP header bits is used by a receiver to send congestion information back to a sender; the other bit allows a sender to inform the receiver that the congestion notification has been received. Bits in the IP header are taken from the TYPE OF SERVICE field†. A router can choose to set either bit to specify that congestion occurred (two bits are used to make the mechanism more robust).

12.22 Congestion, Tail Drop, And TCP

We said that communication protocols are divided into layers to make it possible for designers to focus on a single problem at a time. The separation of functionality into layers is both necessary and useful — it means that one layer can be changed without affecting other layers, but it means that layers operate in isolation. For example, because it operates end-to-end, TCP remains unchanged when the path between the endpoints changes (e.g., routes change or additional networks routers are added). However, the isolation of layers restricts inter-layer communication. In particular, although TCP on the original source interacts with TCP on the ultimate destination, it cannot interact with lower-layer elements along the path. Thus, neither the sending nor receiving TCP receives reports about conditions in the network, nor does either end inform lower layers along the path before transferring data.

Researchers have observed that the lack of communication between layers means that the choice of policy or implementation at one layer can have a dramatic effect on the performance of higher layers. In the case of TCP, policies that routers use to handle datagrams can have a significant effect on both the performance of a single TCP connection and the aggregate throughput of all connections. For example, if a router delays some datagrams more than others‡, TCP will back off its retransmission timer. If the delay exceeds the retransmission timeout, TCP will assume congestion has occurred. Thus, although each layer is defined independently, researchers try to devise mechanisms and implementations that work well with protocols in other layers.

The most important interaction between IP implementation policies and TCP occurs when a router becomes overrun and drops datagrams. Because a router places each incoming datagram in a queue in memory until it can be processed, the policy focuses on queue management. When datagrams arrive faster than they can be forwarded, the queue grows; when datagrams arrive slower than they can be forwarded, the queue shrinks. However, because memory is finite, the queue cannot grow without bound. Early routers used a *tail-drop* policy to manage queue overflow:

---

†To make ECN compatible with DiffServ, ECN uses two bits not used by DiffServ.
‡Technically, variance in delay is referred to as *jitter*.

> *Tail-Drop Policy For Routers: if the input queue is filled when a datagram arrives, discard the datagram.*

The name *tail-drop* arises from the effect of the policy on an arriving sequence of datagrams. Once the queue fills, the router begins discarding all additional datagrams. That is, the router discards the ''tail'' of the sequence.

Tail-drop has an interesting effect on TCP. In the simple case where datagrams traveling through a router carry segments from a single TCP connection, the loss causes TCP to enter slow-start, which reduces throughput until TCP begins receiving ACKs and increases the congestion window. A more severe problem can occur, however, when the datagrams traveling through a router carry segments from many TCP connections because tail-drop can cause global synchronization. To see why, observe that datagrams are typically multiplexed, with successive datagrams each coming from a different source. Thus, a tail-drop policy makes it likely that the router will discard one segment from N connections rather than N segments from one connection. The simultaneous loss causes all N instances of TCP to enter slow-start at the same time†.

12.23 Random Early Detection (RED)

How can a router avoid global synchronization? The answer lies in a clever scheme that avoids tail-drop whenever possible. Known as *Random Early Detection*, *Random Early Drop*, or *Random Early Discard*, the scheme is more frequently referred to by its acronym, *RED*. A router that implements RED uses two threshold values to mark positions in the queue: T_{min} and T_{max}. The general operation of RED can be described by three rules that determine the disposition of each arriving datagram:

- If the queue currently contains fewer than T_{min} datagrams, add the new datagram to the queue.
- If the queue contains more than T_{max} datagrams, discard the new datagram.
- If the queue contains between T_{min} and T_{max} datagrams, randomly discard the datagram according to a probability, p.

The randomness of RED means that instead of waiting until the queue overflows and then driving many TCP connections into slow-start, a router slowly and randomly drops datagrams as congestion increases. We can summarize:

> *RED Policy For Routers: if the input queue is full when a datagram arrives, discard the datagram; if the input queue is not full but the size exceeds a minimum threshold, avoid synchronization by discarding the datagram with probability* p.

---

†Interestingly, global synchronization does not occur if the number of TCP connections sharing a link is sufficiently large (>500) and the RTTs vary.

The key to making RED work well lies in the choice of the thresholds T_{min} and T_{max}, and the discard probability p. T_{min} must be large enough to ensure that the output link has high utilization. Furthermore, because RED operates like tail-drop when the queue size exceeds T_{max}, the value must be greater than T_{min} by more than the typical increase in queue size during one TCP round trip time (e.g., set T_{max} at least twice as large as T_{min}). Otherwise, RED can cause the same global oscillations as tail-drop.

Computation of the discard probability, p, is the most complex aspect of RED. Instead of using a constant, a new value of p is computed for each datagram; the value depends on the relationship between the current queue size and the thresholds. To understand the scheme, observe that all RED processing can be viewed probabilistically. When the queue size is less than T_{min}, RED does not discard any datagrams, making the discard probability 0. Similarly, when the queue size is greater than T_{max}, RED discards all datagrams, making the discard probability 1. For intermediate values of queue size, (i.e., those between T_{min} and T_{max}), the probability can vary from 0 to 1 linearly.

Although the linear scheme forms the basis of RED's probability computation, a change must be made to avoid overreacting. The need for the change arises because network traffic is bursty, which results in rapid fluctuations of a router's queue. If RED used a simplistic linear scheme, later datagrams in each burst would be assigned high probability of being dropped (because they arrive when the queue has more entries). However, a router should not drop datagrams unnecessarily because doing so has a negative impact on TCP throughput. Thus, if a burst is short, it is unwise to drop datagrams because the queue will never overflow. Of course, RED cannot postpone discard indefinitely because a long-term burst will overflow the queue, resulting in a tail-drop policy which has the potential to cause global synchronization problems.

How can RED assign a higher discard probability as the queue fills without discarding datagrams from each burst? The answer lies in a technique borrowed from TCP: instead of using the actual queue size at any instant, RED computes a weighted average queue size, avg, and uses the average size to determine the probability. The value of avg is an exponential weighted average, updated each time a datagram arrives according to the equation:

$$avg = (1 - \gamma) * Old\_avg + \gamma * Current\_queue\_size$$

where γ denotes a value between 0 and 1. If γ is small enough, the average will track long term trends, but will remain immune to short bursts†

In addition to equations that determine γ, RED contains other details that we have glossed over. For example, RED computations can be made extremely efficient by choosing constants as powers of two and using integer arithmetic. Another important detail concerns the measurement of queue size, which affects both the RED computation and its overall effect on TCP. In particular, because the time required to forward a datagram is proportional to its size, it makes sense to measure the queue in octets rather than in datagrams; doing so requires only minor changes to the equations for p and γ. Measuring queue size in octets affects the type of traffic dropped because it makes the

---

†An example value suggested for γ is .002.

discard probability proportional to the amount of data a sender puts in the stream rather than the number of segments. Small datagrams (e.g., those that carry remote login traffic or requests to servers) have lower probability of being dropped than large datagrams (e.g., those that carry file transfer traffic). One positive consequence of using size is that when acknowledgements travel over a congested path, they have a lower probability of being dropped. As a result, if a (large) data segment does arrive, the sending TCP will receive the ACK and will avoid unnecessary retransmission.

Both analysis and simulations show that RED works well. It handles congestion, avoids the synchronization that results from tail drop, and allows short bursts without dropping datagrams unnecessarily. The IETF now recommends that routers implement RED.

12.24 Establishing A TCP Connection

To establish a connection, TCP uses a *three-way handshake*. In the simplest case, the handshake proceeds as Figure 12.13 shows.

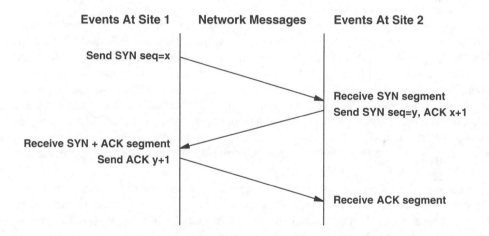

Figure 12.13 The sequence of messages in a three-way handshake. Time proceeds down the page; diagonal lines represent segments sent between sites. SYN segments carry initial sequence number information.

The first segment of a handshake can be identified because it has the SYN† bit set in the code field. The second message has both the SYN and ACK bits set, indicating that it acknowledges the first SYN segment as well as continuing the handshake. The final handshake message is only an acknowledgement and is merely used to inform the destination that both sides agree that a connection has been established.

---

†SYN stands for *synchronization*; it is pronounced "sin."

Usually, the TCP software on one machine waits passively for the handshake, and the TCP software on another machine initiates it. However, the handshake is carefully designed to work even if both machines attempt to initiate a connection simultaneously. Thus, a connection can be established from either end or from both ends simultaneously. Once the connection has been established, data can flow in both directions equally well. There is no master or slave.

The three-way handshake is both necessary and sufficient for correct synchronization between the two ends of the connection. To understand why, remember that TCP builds on an unreliable packet delivery service, so messages can be lost, delayed, duplicated, or delivered out of order. Thus, the protocol must use a timeout mechanism and retransmit lost requests. Trouble arises if retransmitted and original requests arrive while the connection is being established, or if retransmitted requests are delayed until after a connection has been established, used, and terminated. A three-way handshake (plus the rule that TCP ignores additional requests for connection after a connection has been established) solves these problems.

12.25 Initial Sequence Numbers

The three-way handshake accomplishes two important functions. It guarantees that both sides are ready to transfer data (and that they know they are both ready), and it allows both sides to agree on initial sequence numbers. Sequence numbers are sent and acknowledged during the handshake. Each machine must choose an initial sequence number at random that it will use to identify bytes in the stream it is sending. Sequence numbers cannot always start at the same value. In particular, TCP cannot merely choose sequence *1* every time it creates a connection (one of the exercises examines problems that can arise if it does). Of course, it is important that both sides agree on an initial number, so octet numbers used in acknowledgements agree with those used in data segments.

To see how machines can agree on sequence numbers for two streams after only three messages, recall that each segment contains both a sequence number field and an acknowledgement field. The machine that initiates a handshake, call it A, passes its initial sequence number, x, in the sequence field of the first SYN segment in the three-way handshake. The second machine, B, receives the SYN, records the sequence number, and replies by sending its initial sequence number in the sequence field as well as an acknowledgement that specifies B expects octet $x+1$. In the final message of the handshake, A "acknowledges" receiving from B all octets through y. In all cases, acknowledgements follow the convention of using the number of the *next* octet expected.

We have described how TCP usually carries out the three-way handshake by exchanging segments that contain a minimum amount of information. Because of the protocol design, it is possible to send data along with the initial sequence numbers in the handshake segments. In such cases, the TCP software must hold the data until the handshake completes. Once a connection has been established, the TCP software can release data being held and deliver it to a waiting application program quickly. The reader is referred to the protocol specification for the details.

12.26 Closing a TCP Connection

Two programs that use TCP to communicate can terminate the conversation gracefully using the *close* operation. Internally, TCP uses a modified three-way handshake to
close connections. Recall that TCP connections are full duplex and that we view them
as containing two independent stream transfers, one going in each direction. When an
application program tells TCP that it has no more data to send, TCP will close the connection *in one direction*. To close its half of a connection, the sending TCP finishes
transmitting the remaining data, waits for the receiver to acknowledge it, and then sends
a segment with the FIN bit set. The receiving TCP acknowledges the FIN segment and
informs the application program on its end that no more data is available (e.g., using the
operating system's end-of-file mechanism).

Once a connection has been closed in a given direction, TCP refuses to accept
more data for that direction. Meanwhile, data can continue to flow in the opposite
direction until the sender closes it. Of course, acknowledgements continue to flow back
to the sender even after a connection has been closed. When both directions have been
closed, the TCP software at each endpoint deletes its record of the connection.

The details of closing a connection are even more subtle than suggested above because TCP uses a modified three-way handshake to close a connection. Figure 12.14 illustrates the procedure.

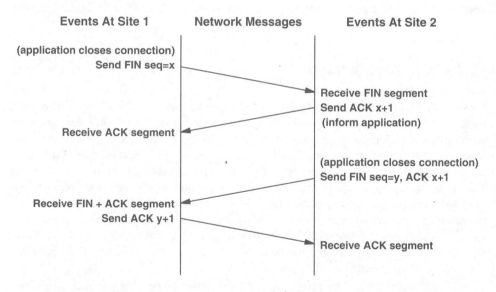

Figure 12.14 The modified three-way handshake used to close connections.
The site that receives the first FIN segment acknowledges it
immediately, and then delays before sending the second FIN
segment.

The difference between three-way handshakes used to establish and break connections occurs after a machine receives the initial FIN segment. Instead of generating a second FIN segment immediately, TCP sends an acknowledgement and then informs the application of the request to shut down. Informing the application program of the request and obtaining a response may take considerable time (e.g., it may involve human interaction). The acknowledgement prevents retransmission of the initial FIN segment during the wait. Finally, when the application program instructs TCP to shut down the connection completely, TCP sends the second FIN segment and the original site replies with the third message, an ACK.

12.27 TCP Connection Reset

Normally, an application program uses the *close* operation to shut down a connection when it finishes using it. Thus, closing connections is considered a normal part of use, analogous to closing files. Sometimes abnormal conditions arise that force an application program or the network software to break a connection. TCP provides a reset facility for such abnormal disconnections.

To reset a connection, one side initiates termination by sending a segment with the RST bit in the *CODE* field set. The other side responds to a reset segment immediately by aborting the connection. TCP also informs the application program that a reset occurred. A reset is an instantaneous abort that means that transfer in both directions ceases immediately and resources such as buffers are released.

12.28 TCP State Machine

Like most protocols, the operation of TCP can best be explained with a theoretical model called a *finite state machine*. Figure 12.15 shows the TCP finite state machine, with circles representing states and arrows representing transitions between them. The label on each transition shows what TCP receives to cause the transition and what it sends in response. For example, the TCP software at each endpoint begins in the *CLOSED* state. Application programs must issue either a *passive open* command (to wait for a connection from another machine), or an *active open* command (to initiate a connection). An active open command forces a transition from the *CLOSED* state to the *SYN SENT* state. When TCP follows the transition, it emits a SYN segment. When the other end returns a segment that contains a SYN plus ACK, TCP moves to the *ES-TABLISHED* state and begins data transfer.

The *TIMED WAIT* state reveals how TCP handles some of the problems incurred with unreliable delivery. TCP keeps a notion of *maximum segment lifetime* (*MSL*), the maximum time an old segment can remain alive in an internet. To avoid having segments from a previous connection interfere with a current one, TCP moves to the *TIMED WAIT* state after closing a connection. It remains in that state for twice the maximum segment lifetime before deleting its record of the connection. If any duplicate segments happen to arrive for the connection during the timeout interval, TCP will reject them. However, to handle cases where the last acknowledgement was lost, TCP acknowledges valid segments and restarts the timer. Because the timer allows TCP to distinguish old connections from new ones, it prevents TCP from responding with a *RST* (reset) if the other end retransmits a *FIN* request.

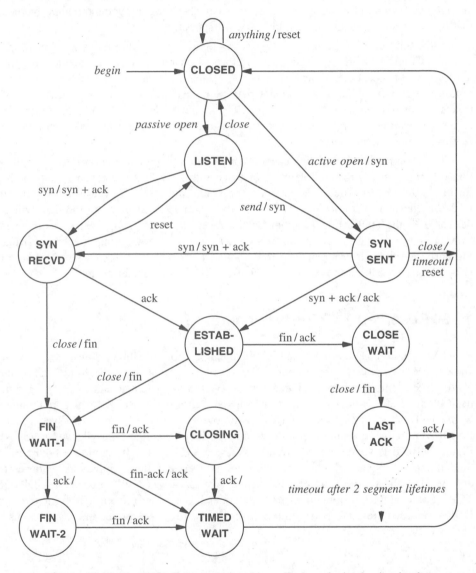

Figure 12.15 The TCP finite state machine. Each endpoint begins in the *closed* state. Labels on transitions show the input that caused the transition followed by the output if any.

12.29 Forcing Data Delivery

We have said that TCP is free to divide the stream of data into segments for transmission without regard to the size of transfer that application programs use. The chief advantage of allowing TCP to choose a division is efficiency. It can accumulate enough octets in a buffer to make segments reasonably long, reducing the high overhead that occurs when segments contain only a few data octets.

Although buffering improves network throughput, it can interfere with some applications. Consider using a TCP connection to pass characters from an interactive terminal to a remote machine. The user expects instant response to each keystroke. If the sending TCP buffers the data, response may be delayed, perhaps for hundreds of keystrokes. Similarly, because the receiving TCP may buffer data before making it available to the application program on its end, forcing the sender to transmit data may not be sufficient to guarantee delivery.

To accommodate interactive users, TCP provides a *push* operation that an application program can use to force delivery of octets currently in the stream without waiting for the buffer to fill. The *push* operation does more than force TCP to send a segment. It also requests TCP to set the *PSH* bit in the segment code field, so the data will be delivered to the application program on the receiving end. Thus, when sending data from an interactive terminal, the application uses the *push* function after each keystroke. Similarly, application programs can force output to be sent and displayed on the terminal promptly by calling the *push* function after writing a character or line.

12.30 Reserved TCP Port Numbers

Like UDP, TCP combines static and dynamic port binding, using a set of *well-known port assignments* for commonly invoked programs (e.g., electronic mail), but leaving most port numbers available for the operating system to allocate as programs need them. Many well-known ports now exist. Originally, well-known port numbers were small, but some ports above 1024 have now been assigned (in UNIX systems, the first 1023 ports are considered privileged and are only available to privileged programs). Figure 12.16 lists some of the currently assigned TCP ports. It should be pointed out that although TCP and UDP port numbers are independent, the designers have chosen to use the same integer port numbers for any service that is accessible from both UDP and TCP. For example, a domain name server can be accessed either with TCP or with UDP. In either protocol, port number *53* has been reserved for servers in the domain name system.

12.31 TCP Performance

As we have seen, TCP is a complex protocol that handles communication over a wide variety of underlying network technologies. Many people assume that because TCP tackles a much more complex task than other transport protocols, the code must be cumbersome and inefficient. Surprisingly, the generality we discussed does not seem to hinder TCP performance. Experiments at Berkeley have shown that the same TCP that operates efficiently over the global Internet can deliver 8 Mbps of sustained throughput of user data between two workstations on a 10 Mbps Ethernet†. At Cray Research, Inc., researchers have demonstrated TCP throughput approaching a gigabit per second.

Decimal	Keyword	Description
0		Reserved
7	ECHO	Echo
9	DISCARD	Discard
11	USERS	Active Users
13	DAYTIME	Daytime
15	netstat	Network Status program
17	QUOTE	Quote of the day
19	CHARGEN	Character Generator
20	FTP-DATA	File Transfer Protocol (data)
21	FTP	File Transfer Protocol
22	SSH	Secure Shell
23	TELNET	Terminal connection
25	SMTP	Simple Mail Transport Protocol
37	TIME	Time
53	DOMAIN	Domain name server
67	BOOTPS	BOOTP or DHCP Server
79	FINGER	Finger
80	WWW	World Wide Web server
88	KERBEROS	Kerberos security service
110	POP3	Post Office Protocol vers. 3
111	SUNRPC	SUN Remote Procedure Call
119	NNTP	USENET News Transfer Protocol
123	NTP	Network Time Protocol
143	IMAP	Internet Message Access Protocol
161	SNMP	Simple Network Management Protocol
443	HTTPS	Secure HTTP
465	SMTPS	SMTP over SSL (TLS)
515	SPOOLER	LPR spooler
873	RSYNC	Rsync protocol
993	IMAPS	Secure IMAP
995	POP3S	Secure POP3
1080	SOCKS	Proxy server protocol

Figure 12.16 Examples of currently assigned TCP port numbers. To the extent possible, UDP uses the same numbers.

---

†Ethernet, IP, and TCP headers and the required inter-packet gap account for the remaining bandwidth.

12.32 Silly Window Syndrome And Small Packets

Researchers who developed TCP observed a serious performance problem that can result when the sending and receiving applications operate at different speeds. To understand the problem, remember that TCP buffers incoming data, and consider what can happen if a receiving application chooses to read incoming data one octet at a time. When a connection is first established, the receiving TCP allocates a buffer of *K* bytes, and uses the *WINDOW* field in acknowledgement segments to advertise the available buffer size to the sender. If the sending application generates data quickly, the sending TCP will transmit segments with data for the entire window. Eventually, the sender will receive an acknowledgement that specifies the entire window has been filled and no additional space remains in the receiver's buffer.

When the receiving application reads an octet of data from a full buffer, one octet of space becomes available. We said that when space becomes available in its buffer, TCP on the receiving machine generates an acknowledgement that uses the *WINDOW* field to inform the sender. In the example, the receiver will advertise a window of *1* octet. When it learns that space is available, the sending TCP responds by transmitting a segment that contains one octet of data.

Although single-octet window advertisements work correctly to keep the receiver's buffer filled, they result in a series of small data segments. The sending TCP must compose a segment that contains one octet of data, place the segment in an IP datagram, and transmit the result. When the receiving application reads another octet, TCP generates another acknowledgement, which causes the sender to transmit another segment that contains one octet of data. The resulting interaction can reach a steady state in which TCP sends a separate segment for each octet of data.

Transferring small segments unnecessarily consumes network bandwidth and introduces computational overhead. The transmission of small segments consumes unnecessary network bandwidth because each datagram carries only one octet of data; the ratio of header to data is large. Computational overhead arises because TCP on both the sending and receiving computers must process each segment. The sending TCP software must allocate buffer space, form a segment header, and compute a checksum for the segment. Similarly, IP software on the sending machine must encapsulate the segment in a datagram, compute a header checksum, forward the datagram, and transfer it to the appropriate network interface. On the receiving machine, IP must verify the IP header checksum and pass the segment to TCP. TCP must verify the segment checksum, examine the sequence number, extract the data, and place it in a buffer.

Although we have described how small segments result when a receiver advertises a small available window, a sender can also cause each segment to contain a small amount of data. For example, imagine a TCP implementation that aggressively sends data whenever it is available, and consider what happens if a sending application generates data one octet at a time. After the application generates an octet of data, TCP creates and transmits a segment. TCP can also send a small segment if an application generates data in fixed-sized blocks of B octets, and the sending TCP extracts data from the buffer in maximum segment sized blocks, M, where $M \neq B$, because the last block in a buffer can be small.

Known as *silly window syndrome* (*SWS*), the problem plagued early TCP implementations. To summarize,

> *Early TCP implementations exhibited a problem known as* silly window syndrome *in which each acknowledgement advertises a small amount of space available and each segment carries a small amount of data.*

12.33 Avoiding Silly Window Syndrome

TCP specifications now include heuristics that prevent silly window syndrome. A heuristic used on the sending machine avoids transmitting a small amount of data in each segment. Another heuristic used on the receiving machine avoids sending small increments in window advertisements that can trigger small data packets. Although the heuristics work well together, having both the sender and receiver avoid silly window helps ensure good performance in the case that one end of a connection fails to correctly implement silly window avoidance.

In practice, TCP software must contain both sender and receiver silly window avoidance code. To understand why, recall that a TCP connection is full duplex — data can flow in either direction. Thus, an implementation of TCP includes code to send data as well as code to receive it.

12.33.1 Receive-Side Silly Window Avoidance

The heuristic a receiver uses to avoid silly window is straightforward and easier to understand. In general, a receiver maintains an internal record of the currently available window, but delays advertising an increase in window size to the sender until the window can advance a significant amount. The definition of "significant" depends on the receiver's buffer size and the maximum segment size. TCP defines it to be the minimum of one half of the receiver's buffer or the number of data octets in a maximum-sized segment.

Receive-side silly window prevents small window advertisements in the case where a receiving application extracts data octets slowly. For example, when a receiver's buffer fills completely, it sends an acknowledgement that contains a zero window advertisement. As the receiving application extracts octets from the buffer, the receiving TCP computes the newly available space in the buffer. Instead of sending a window advertisement immediately, however, the receiver waits until the available space reaches one half of the total buffer size or a maximum sized segment. Thus, the sender always receives large increments in the current window, allowing it to transfer large segments. The heuristic can be summarized as follows.

> *Receive-Side Silly Window Avoidance: Before sending an updated window advertisement after advertising a zero window, wait for space to become available that is either at least 50% of the total buffer size or equal to a maximum sized segment.*

12.33.2 Delayed Acknowledgements

Two approaches have been taken to implement silly window avoidance on the receive side. In the first approach, TCP acknowledges each segment that arrives, but does not advertise an increase in its window until the window reaches the limits specified by the silly window avoidance heuristic. In the second approach, TCP delays sending an acknowledgement when silly window avoidance specifies that the window is not sufficiently large to advertise. The standards recommend delaying acknowledgements.

Delayed acknowledgements have both advantages and disadvantages. The chief advantage arises because delayed acknowledgements can decrease traffic and thereby increase throughput. For example, if additional data arrives during the delay period, a single acknowledgement will acknowledge all data received. If the receiving application generates a response immediately after data arrives (e.g., character echo in a remote login session), a short delay may permit the acknowledgement to piggyback on a data segment. Furthermore, TCP cannot move its window until the receiving application extracts data from the buffer. In cases where the receiving application reads data as soon as it arrives, a short delay allows TCP to send a single segment that acknowledges the data and advertises an updated window. Without delayed acknowledgements, TCP will acknowledge the arrival of data immediately, and later send an additional acknowledgement to update the window size.

The disadvantages of delayed acknowledgements should be clear. Most important, if a receiver delays acknowledgements too long, the sending TCP will retransmit the segment. Unnecessary retransmissions lower throughput because they waste network bandwidth. In addition, retransmissions require computational overhead on the sending and receiving machines. Furthermore, TCP uses the arrival of acknowledgements to estimate round trip times; delaying acknowledgements can confuse the estimate and make retransmission times too long.

To avoid potential problems, the TCP standards place a limit on the time TCP delays an acknowledgement. Implementations cannot delay an acknowledgement for more than 500 milliseconds. Furthermore, to guarantee that TCP receives a sufficient number of round trip estimates, the standard recommends that a receiver should acknowledge at least every other data segment.

12.33.3 Send-Side Silly Window Avoidance

The heuristic a sending TCP uses to avoid silly window syndrome is both surprising and elegant. Recall that the goal is to avoid sending small segments. Also recall that a sending application can generate data in arbitrarily small blocks (e.g., one octet at a time). Thus, to achieve the goal, a sending TCP must allow the sending application to make multiple calls to *write*, and must collect the data transferred in each call before transmitting it in a single, large segment. That is, a sending TCP must delay sending a segment until it can accumulate a reasonable amount of data. The technique is known as *clumping*.

The question arises, "How long should TCP wait before transmitting data?" On one hand, if TCP waits too long, the application experiences large delays. More important, TCP cannot know whether to wait because it cannot know whether the application will generate more data in the near future. On the other hand, if TCP does not wait long enough, segments will be small and throughput will be low.

Protocols designed prior to TCP confronted the same problem and used techniques to clump data into larger packets. For example, to achieve efficient transfer across a network, early remote terminal protocols delayed transmitting each keystroke for a few hundred milliseconds to determine whether the user would continue to press keys. Because TCP is designed to be general, however, it can be used by a diverse set of applications. Characters may travel across a TCP connection because a user is typing on a keyboard or because a program is transferring a file. A fixed delay is not optimal for all applications.

Like the algorithm TCP uses for retransmission and the slow-start algorithm used to avoid congestion, the technique a sending TCP uses to avoid sending small packets is adaptive — the delay depends on the current performance of the underlying internet. Like slow-start, send-side silly window avoidance is called *self clocking* because it does not compute delays. Instead, TCP uses the arrival of an acknowledgement to trigger the transmission of additional packets. The heuristic can be summarized:

> *Send-Side Silly Window Avoidance: When a sending application generates additional data to be sent over a connection for which previous data has been transmitted but not acknowledged, place the new data in the output buffer as usual, but do not send additional segments until there is sufficient data to fill a maximum-sized segment. If still waiting to send when an acknowledgement arrives, send all data that has accumulated in the buffer. Apply the rule even when the user requests a* push *operation.*

If an application generates data one octet at a time, TCP will send the first octet immediately. However, until the ACK arrives, TCP will accumulate additional octets in its buffer. Thus, if the application is reasonably fast compared to the network (i.e., a file transfer), successive segments will each contain many octets. If the application is slow compared to the network (e.g., a user typing on a keyboard), small segments will be sent without long delay.

Known as the *Nagle algorithm* after its inventor, the technique is especially elegant because it requires little computational overhead. A host does not need to keep separate timers for each connection, nor does the host need to examine a clock when an application generates data. More important, although the technique adapts to arbitrary combinations of network delay, maximum segment size, and application speed, it does not lower throughput in conventional cases.

To understand why throughput remains high for conventional communication, observe that applications optimized for high throughput do not generate data one octet at a time (doing so would incur unnecessary operating system overhead). Instead, such applications write large blocks of data with each call. Thus, the outgoing TCP buffer begins with sufficient data for at least one maximum size segment. Furthermore, because the application produces data faster than TCP can transfer data, the sending buffer remains nearly full, and TCP does not delay transmission. As a result, TCP continues to send segments at whatever rate the underlying internet can tolerate, while the application continues to fill the buffer. To summarize:

> *TCP now requires the sender and receiver to implement heuristics that avoid the silly window syndrome. A receiver avoids advertising a small window, and a sender uses an adaptive scheme to delay transmission so it can clump data into large segments.*

12.34 Summary

The Transmission Control Protocol, TCP, defines a key service provided by an internet, namely, reliable stream delivery. TCP provides a full duplex connection between two machines, allowing them to exchange large volumes of data efficiently.

Because it uses a sliding window protocol, TCP can make efficient use of a network. Because it makes few assumptions about the underlying delivery system, TCP is flexible enough to operate over a large variety of delivery systems. Because it provides flow control, TCP allows systems of widely varying speeds to communicate.

The basic unit of transfer used by TCP is a segment. Segments are used to pass data or control information (e.g., to allow TCP software on two machines to establish connections or break them). The segment format permits a machine to piggyback acknowledgements for data flowing in one direction by including them in the segment headers of data flowing in the opposite direction.

TCP implements flow control by having the receiver advertise the amount of data it is willing to accept. It also supports out-of-band messages using an urgent data facility and forces delivery using a push mechanism.

The current TCP standard specifies exponential backoff for retransmission timers and congestion avoidance algorithms like slow-start, multiplicative decrease, and additive increase. In addition, TCP uses heuristics to avoid transferring small packets. Finally, the IETF recommends that routers use RED instead of tail-drop because doing so avoids TCP synchronization and improves throughput.

FOR FURTHER STUDY

The standard for TCP can be found in Postel [RFC 793]; Braden [RFC 1122] contains an update that clarifies several points. Clark [RFC 813] describes TCP window management, and Postel [RFC 879] reports on TCP maximum segment sizes. Nagle [RFC 896] comments on congestion in TCP/IP networks and explains the effect of self clocking for send-side silly window avoidance. Karn and Partridge [1987] discusses estimation of round-trip times, and presents Karn's algorithm. Jacobson [1988] gives the congestion control algorithms that are now a required part of the standard. Floyd and Jacobson [1993] presents the RED scheme, and Clark and Fang [1998] discusses an allocation framework that uses RED. Tomlinson [1975] considers the three-way handshake in more detail. Mills [RFC 889] reports measurements of Internet round-trip delays. Jain [1986] describes timer-based congestion control in a sliding window environment. Floyd et. al. [RFC 3782] describes the NewReno modifications for fast recovery. Handly et. al. [RFC 3448] discusses TCP Friendly Rate Control (TFRC). Mathis et. al. [RFC 2018] defines the SACK option, and Ramakrishnan et. al. [RFC 3168] defines the ECN option.

EXERCISES

12.1 TCP uses a finite field to contain stream sequence numbers. Study the protocol specification to find out how it allows an arbitrary length stream to pass from one machine to another.

12.2 The text notes that one of the TCP options permits a receiver to specify the maximum segment size it is willing to accept. Why does TCP support an option to specify maximum segment size when it also has a window advertisement mechanism?

12.3 Under what conditions of delay, bandwidth, load, and packet loss will TCP retransmit significant volumes of data unnecessarily?

12.4 A lost TCP acknowledgement does not necessarily force a retransmission. Explain why.

12.5 Experiment with local machines to determine how TCP handles machine restart. Establish a connection (e.g., a remote login) and leave it idle. Wait for the destination machine to crash and restart, and then force the local machine to send a TCP segment (e.g., by typing characters to the remote login).

12.6 Imagine an implementation of TCP that discards segments that arrive out of order, even if they fall in the current window. That is, the imagined version only accepts segments that extend the byte stream it has already received. Does it work? How does it compare to a standard TCP implementation?

12.7 Consider computation of a TCP checksum. Assume that although the checksum field in the segment has *not* been set to zero, the result of computing the checksum *is* zero. What can you conclude?

12.8 What are the arguments for and against automatically closing idle connections?

12.9 If two application programs use TCP to send data but only send one character per segment (e.g., by using the *push* operation), what is the maximum percent of the network bandwidth they will have for their data?

12.10 Suppose an implementation of TCP uses initial sequence number *1* when it creates a connection. Explain how a system crash and restart can confuse a remote system into believing that the old connection remained open.

12.11 Find out how implementations of TCP must solve the *overlapping segment problem*. The problem arises because the receiver must accept only one copy of all bytes from the data stream even if the sender transmits two segments that partially overlap one another (e.g., the first segment carries bytes 100 through 200 and the second carries bytes 150 through 250).

12.12 Trace the TCP finite state machine transitions for two sites that execute a passive and active open and step through the three-way handshake.

12.13 Read the TCP specification to find out the exact conditions under which TCP can make the transition from *FIN WAIT-1* to *TIMED WAIT*.

12.14 Trace the TCP state transitions for two machines that agree to close a connection gracefully.

12.15 Assume TCP is sending segments using a maximum window size of 64 Kbytes on a channel that has infinite bandwidth and an average roundtrip time of 20 milliseconds. What is the maximum throughput? How does throughput change if the roundtrip time increases to 40 milliseconds (while bandwidth remains infinite)?

12.16 Can you derive an equation that expresses the maximum possible TCP throughput as a function of the network bandwidth, the network delay, and the time to process a segment and generate an acknowledgement. Hint: consider the previous exercise.

12.17 Describe (abnormal) circumstances that can leave one end of a connection in state *FIN WAIT-2* indefinitely (hint: think of datagram loss and system crashes).

12.18 Show that when a router implements RED, the probability a packet will be discarded from a particular TCP connection is proportional to the percentage of traffic that the connection generates.

Chapter Contents

13

Routing Architecture: Cores, Peers, And Algorithms

13.1 Introduction

Previous chapters concentrate on the network level services TCP/IP offers and the details of the protocols in hosts and routers that provide the services. In the discussion, we assumed that routers always contain correct routes, and saw that a router can use the ICMP redirect mechanism to instruct a directly connected host to change a route.

This chapter considers two broad questions: "What values should each routing table contain?" and "How can those values be obtained?" To answer the first question, we will consider the relationship between internet architecture and routing. In particular, we will discuss internets structured around a backbone and those composed of multiple peer networks, and consider the consequences for routing. To answer the second question, we will consider the two basic types of route propagation algorithms and see how each supplies routing information automatically.

We begin by discussing forwarding in general. Later sections concentrate on internet architecture and describe the algorithms routers use to exchange routing information. Chapters 14 and 15 continue to expand our discussion of routing. They explore protocols that routers owned by two independent administrative groups use to exchange information, and protocols that a single group uses among all its routers.

13.2 The Origin Of Routing Tables

Recall from Chapter 3 that IP routers provide active interconnections among networks. Each router attaches to two or more physical networks and forwards IP datagrams among them, accepting datagrams that arrive over one network interface, and sending them out over another interface. Except for destinations on directly attached networks, hosts pass all IP traffic to routers which forward datagrams on toward their final destinations. A datagram travels from router to router until it reaches a router that attaches directly to the same network as the final destination. Thus, the router system forms the architectural basis of an internet and handles all traffic except for direct delivery from one host to another.

Chapter 7 describes the algorithm that hosts and routers follow to forward datagrams, and shows how the algorithm uses a table to make decisions. Each entry in the routing table specifies the network portion of a destination address and gives the address of the next machine along a path used to reach that network. In practice, each entry also specifies an interface used to reach the next hop.

We have not said how hosts or routers obtain the information for their routing tables. The issue has two aspects: *what* values should be placed in the tables, and *how* routers obtain the values. Both choices depend on the architectural complexity and size of the internet as well as administrative policies.

In general, establishing routes involves initialization and update. Each router must establish an initial set of routes when it starts, and it must update the table as routes change (e.g., when hardware in a particular network fails). Initialization depends on the operating system. In some systems, the router reads an initial routing table from secondary storage at startup, keeping it resident in high-speed memory. In others, the router begins with an empty table which must be filled in by executing explicit commands (e.g., commands found in a startup command script). Finally, some systems start by deducing an initial set of routes from the set of addresses for the local networks to which the machine attaches and contacting a neighboring machine to ask for additional routes.

Once an initial routing table has been built, a router must accommodate changes in routes. In small, slowly changing internets, managers can establish and modify routes by hand. In large, rapidly changing environments, however, manual update is impossibly slow and prone to human errors. Automated methods are needed. Before we can understand the automatic routing table update protocols used in IP routers, we need to review several underlying ideas. The next sections do so, providing the necessary conceptual foundation for routing.

13.3 Forwarding With Partial Information

The principal difference between routers and typical hosts is that hosts usually know little about the structure of the internet to which they connect. Hosts do not have complete knowledge of all possible destination addresses, or even of all possible destination networks. In fact, many hosts have only two entries in their routing table: a route for the local network and a default route for a nearby router. The host sends all nonlocal datagrams to the local router for delivery. The point is:

A host can forward datagrams successfully even if it only has partial forwarding information because it can rely on a router.

Can routers also forward datagrams with only partial information? Yes, but only under certain circumstances. To understand the criteria, imagine an internet to be a foreign country crisscrossed with dirt roads that have directional signs posted at intersections. Imagine that you have no map, cannot ask directions because you cannot speak the local language, have no ideas about visible landmarks, but you need to travel to a village named *Sussex*. You leave on your journey, following the only road out of town, and begin to look for directional signs. The first sign reads:

Norfolk to the left; Hammond to the right; others straight ahead.†

Because the destination you seek is not listed explicitly, you continue straight ahead. In routing jargon, we say you follow a *default route*. After several more signs, you finally find one that reads:

Essex to the left; Sussex to the right; others straight ahead.

You turn to the right, follow several more signs, and emerge on a road that leads to Sussex.

Our imagined travel is analogous to a datagram traversing an internet, and the road signs are analogous to routing tables in routers along the path. Without a map or other navigational aids, travel is completely dependent on road signs, just as datagram forwarding in an internet depends entirely on routing tables. Clearly, it is possible to navigate even though each road sign contains only partial information.

A central question concerns correctness. As a traveler, you might ask, "How can I be sure that following the signs will lead to my destination?" You also might ask, "How can I be sure that following the signs will lead me to my destination along a shortest path?" These questions may seem especially troublesome if you pass many signs without finding your destination listed explicitly. Of course, the answers depend on the topology of the road system and the contents of the signs, but the fundamental idea is that when taken as a whole, the information on the signs should be both consistent and complete. Looking at this another way, we see that it is not necessary for

---

†Fortunately, signs are printed in a language you can read.

each intersection to have a sign for every destination. The signs can list default paths as long as all explicit signs point along a shortest path, and the turns for shortest paths to all destinations are marked. A few examples will explain some ways that consistency can be achieved.

At one extreme, consider a simple star-shaped topology of roads in which each village has exactly one road leading to it, and all the roads meet at a central point. To guarantee consistency, the sign at the central intersection must contain information about all possible destinations. At the other extreme, imagine an arbitrary set of roads with signs at all intersections listing all possible destinations. To guarantee consistency, it must be true that at any intersection if the sign for destination D points to road R, no road other than R leads to a shorter path to D.

Neither of these architectural extremes works well for an internet router system. On one hand, the central intersection approach fails because no machine is fast enough to serve as a central switch through which all traffic passes. On the other hand, having information about all possible destinations in all routers is impractical because it requires propagating large volumes of information whenever a change occurs or whenever administrators need to check consistency. Thus, we seek a solution that allows groups to manage local routers autonomously, adding new network interconnections and routes without changing distant routers.

To understand the architecture described later, consider a third topology in which half the cities lie in the eastern part of the country and half lie in the western part. Suppose a single bridge spans the river that separates east from west. Assume that people living in the eastern part do not like westerners, so they are willing to allow road signs that list destinations in the east, but none in the west. Assume that people living in the west do the opposite. Routing will be consistent if every road sign in the east lists all eastern destinations explicitly and points the default path to the bridge, and every road sign in the west lists all western destinations explicitly and points the default path to the bridge.

13.4 Original Internet Architecture And Cores

Much of our knowledge of forwarding and route propagation protocols has been derived from experience with the Internet. When TCP/IP was first developed, participating research sites were connected to the ARPANET, which served as the Internet backbone. During initial experiments, each site managed routing tables and installed routes to other destinations by hand. As the fledgling Internet began to grow, it became apparent that manual maintenance of routes was impractical; automated mechanisms were needed.

The Internet designers selected a router architecture that consisted of a small, central set of routers that kept complete information about all possible destinations, and a larger set of outlying routers that kept partial information. In terms of our analogy, it is like designating a small set of centrally located intersections to have signs that list all destinations, and allowing the outlying intersections to list only local destinations. As long as the default route at each outlying intersection points to one of the central intersections, travelers will eventually reach their destination.

The central set of routers that maintained complete information was known as the *core* of the Internet, and is sometimes referred to as the *default-free zone*. The advantage of partitioning Internet routing into a two-tier system is that it permits local administrators to manage local changes in outlying routers without affecting other parts of the Internet. The disadvantage is that it introduces the potential for inconsistency. In the worst case, an error in an outlying router can make distant routes unreachable.

We can summarize the ideas:

> *The advantage of core routing architecture is that because noncore routers use partial information, an outlying site has autonomy in making local routing changes. The disadvantage is that a site can introduce inconsistencies that make some destinations unreachable.*

Inconsistencies among routing tables usually arise from errors in the algorithms that compute routing tables, incorrect data supplied to those algorithms, or from errors that occur while transmitting the results to other routers. Protocol designers look for ways to limit the impact of errors, with the objective being to keep all routes consistent at all times. If routes become inconsistent, the routing protocols should be robust enough to detect and correct the errors quickly. Most important, the protocols should be designed to constrain the effect of errors.

The early Internet architecture is easy to understand if one remembers that the Internet evolved with a wide-area backbone, the ARPANET, already in place. A major motivation for the core router system came from the desire to connect local networks to the ARPANET. Figure 13.1 illustrates the idea.

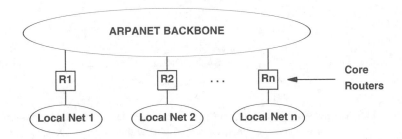

Figure 13.1 The early Internet core router system viewed as a set of routers that connect local area networks to the ARPANET. Hosts on the local networks pass all nonlocal traffic to the closest core router.

To understand why routers in Figure 13.1 cannot use partial information, consider the path a datagram follows if some routers use a default route. At the source site, the local router checks to see if it has an explicit route to the destination, and if not, sends the datagram along the path specified by its default route. All datagrams for which the router has no route follow the same default path regardless of their ultimate destination. The next router along the path diverts datagrams for which it has an explicit route, and sends the rest along its default route. To ensure global consistency, the chain of default routes must reach every router in a giant cycle. Thus, the architecture requires all local sites to coordinate their default routes. More important, even if the default routes are coordinated, forwarding is inefficient because a datagram may pass through all n routers when traveling from source to destination.

To avoid the inefficiencies default routes cause, the early Internet avoided default routes. Designers arranged routers to exchange routing information so that each had complete routes. Doing so was easy because all routers connected to a single backbone network.

13.5 Beyond The Core Architecture To Peer Backbones

The introduction of the NSFNET backbone into the Internet added new complexity to the routing structure and forced designers to invent a new routing architecture. In essence, the Internet evolved from single, central backbone to a set of *peer backbone networks* or simply *peers*. Figure 13.2 illustrates an Internet topology with two backbones.

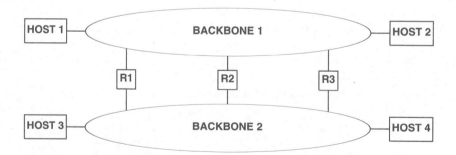

Figure 13.2 An example of two peer backbones interconnected by multiple routers. The Internet had such an architecture in 1989.

To understand the difficulties of IP routing among peer backbones, consider routes from host *3* to host *2* in Figure 13.2. Assume for the moment that the figure shows geographic orientation: host *3* is on the West Coast attached to backbone 2, while host *2* is on the East Coast attached to backbone 1. When establishing routes between hosts *3* and *2*, the managers must decide whether to (a) route the traffic from host *3* through the West Coast router, *R1*, and then across backbone 1, or (b) forward the traffic from host *3* across backbone 2, through the Midwest router, *R2*, and then across backbone 1 to host *2*, or (c) forward the traffic across backbone 2, through the East Coast router, *R3*, and then to host *2*. A more circuitous route is possible as well: traffic could flow from host *3* through the West Coast router, across backbone 1 to the Midwest router, back onto backbone 2 to the East Coast router, and finally across backbone 1 to host *2*. Such a route may or may not be advisable, depending on the policies for network use and the capacity of various routers and backbones.

For most peer backbone configurations, traffic between a pair of geographically close hosts should take a shortest path, independent of the routes chosen for cross-country traffic. For example, traffic from host *3* to host *1* should flow through the West Coast router because it minimizes distance on both backbones.

All the statements sound simple, but they are complex to implement for two reasons. First, although the standard IP forwarding algorithm uses the network portion of an IP address to choose a route, optimal forwarding in a peer backbone architecture requires individual routes for individual hosts. For our example above, the routing table in host *3* needs different routes for host *1* and host *2*, even though both hosts *1* and *2* attach to the ARPANET backbone. Second, managers of the two backbones must agree to keep routes consistent among all routers or *forwarding loops*† can develop (a forwarding loop occurs when routes in a set of routers point in a cycle).

13.6 Automatic Route Propagation

We said that the original Internet core system avoided default routes because it propagated complete information about all possible destinations to every core router. Many corporate internets now use a similar scheme — routers in the corporation run programs that communicate routing information. The next sections discuss two basic types of algorithms that compute and propagate routing information; later chapters discuss protocols that use the algorithms.

Routing protocols serve two important functions. First, they compute a set of shortest paths. Second, they respond to network failures or topology changes by continually updating the routing information. Thus, when we think about route propagation, it is important to consider the dynamic behavior of protocols and algorithms.

13.7 Distance Vector (Bellman-Ford) Routing

The term *distance-vector*‡ refers to a class of algorithms used to propagate routing information. The idea behind distance-vector algorithms is quite simple. Each router keeps a list of all known routes in a table. When it boots, a router initializes its routing table to contain an entry for each directly connected network. Each entry in the table

---

†A forwarding loop is also known as a *routing loop*.

‡The terms *vector-distance*, *Ford-Fulkerson*, *Bellman-Ford*, and *Bellman* are synonymous with *distance-vector*; the last three are taken from the names of researchers who published the idea.

identifies a destination network and gives the distance to that network, usually measured in hops (which will be defined more precisely later). For example, Figure 13.3 shows the initial contents of the table on a router that attaches to two networks.

Destination	Distance	Route
Net 1	0	direct
Net 2	0	direct

Figure 13.3 An initial distance-vector routing table with an entry for each directly connected network. Each entry contains the IP address of a network and an integer distance to that network.

Periodically, each router sends a copy of its routing table to any other router it can reach directly. When a report arrives at router K from router J, K examines the set of destinations reported and the distance to each. If J knows a shorter way to reach a destination, or if J lists a destination that K does not have in its table, or if K currently routes to a destination through J and J's distance to that destination changes, K replaces its table entry. For example, Figure 13.4 shows an existing table in a router, K, and an update message from another router, J.

Destination	Distance	Route		Destination	Distance
Net 1	0	direct		Net 1	2
Net 2	0	direct	→	Net 4	3
Net 4	8	Router L		Net 17	6
Net 17	5	Router M	→	Net 21	4
Net 24	6	Router J		Net 24	5
Net 30	2	Router Q		Net 30	10
Net 42	2	Router J	→	Net 42	3

(a)   (b)

Figure 13.4 (a) An existing route table for router K, and (b) an incoming routing update message from router J. The marked entries will be used to update existing entries or add new entries to K's table.

Note that if J reports distance N, an updated entry in K will have distance $N+1$ (the distance to reach the destination from J plus the distance to reach J). Of course, the routing table entries contain a third column that specifies a next hop. The next hop entry in each initial route is marked *direct delivery*. When router K adds or updates an entry in response to a message from router *J*, it assigns router *J* as the next hop for that entry.

The term *distance-vector* comes from the information sent in the periodic messages. A message contains a list of pairs *(D, V)*, where *V* identifies a destination (called the *vector*), and *D* is the distance to that destination. Note that distance-vector algorithms report routes in the first person (i.e., we think of a router advertising, "I can reach destination *V* at distance *D*"). In such a design, all routers must participate in the distance-vector exchange for the routes to be efficient and consistent.

Although distance-vector algorithms are easy to implement, they have disadvantages. In a completely static environment, distance-vector algorithms compute shortest paths and correctly propagate routes to all destinations. When routes change rapidly, however, the computations may not stabilize. When a route changes (i.e, a new connection appears or an old one fails), the information propagates slowly from one router to another. Meanwhile, some routers may have incorrect routing information.

13.8 Reliability And Routing Protocols

Most routing protocols use connectionless transport — early protocols encapsulated messages directly in IP; modern routing protocols usually encapsulate in UDP†. Unfortunately, IP and UDP offer the same semantics: messages can be lost, delayed, duplicated, corrupted, or delivered out of order. Thus, a routing protocol that uses them must compensate for failures.

Routing protocols use several techniques to handle delivery problems. Checksums are used to handle corruption. Loss is either handled by *soft state*‡ or through acknowledgement and retransmission. To handle delivery out of order and the corresponding reply that occurs when an old message arrives, routing protocols often used *sequence numbers*.

13.9 Link-State (SPF) Routing

The main disadvantage of the distance-vector algorithm is that it does not scale well. Besides the problem of slow response to change mentioned earlier, the algorithm requires the exchange of large messages — because each routing update contains an entry for every possible network, message size is proportional to the total number of networks in an internet. Furthermore, because a distance-vector protocol requires every router to participate, the volume of information exchanged can be enormous.

The primary alternative to distance-vector algorithms is a class of algorithms known as *link state*, *link status*, or *Shortest Path First*§ *(SPF)*. The SPF algorithm requires each participating router to be given or to compute topology information. The easiest way to think of topology information is to imagine that every router has a map

---

†The next chapter discusses an exception — a routing protocol that uses TCP.

‡Recall that soft state relies on timeouts to remove old information.

§The name "shortest path first" is a misnomer because all routing algorithms compute shortest paths.

that shows all other routers and the networks to which they connect. In abstract terms, the routers correspond to nodes in a graph and networks that connect routers correspond to edges. There is an edge (link) between two nodes if and only if the corresponding routers can communicate directly.

Instead of sending messages that contain lists of destinations, a router participating in an SPF algorithm performs two tasks. First, it actively tests the status of all neighbor routers. In terms of the graph, two routers are neighbors if they share a link; in network terms, two neighbors connect to a common network. Second, a router periodically propagates the link status information to all other routers.

To test the status of a directly connected neighbor, the two neighbors exchange short messages that verify that the neighbor is alive and reachable. If the neighbor replies, the link between them is said to be *up*. Otherwise, the link is said to be *down*†. To inform all other routers, each router periodically broadcasts a message that lists the status (state) of each of its links. A status message does not specify routes — it simply reports whether communication is possible between pairs of routers. Protocol software in the routers arranges to deliver a copy of each link status message to all participating routers (if the underlying networks do not support broadcast, delivery is done by forwarding individual copies of the message point-to-point).

Whenever a link status message arrives, a router uses the information to update its map of the internet, by marking links up or down. Whenever link status changes, the router recomputes routes by applying the well-known *Dijkstra shortest path algorithm* to the resulting graph‡. Dijkstra's algorithm computes the shortest paths to all destinations from a single source.

One of the chief advantages of SPF algorithms is that each router computes routes independently using the same original status data; they do not depend on the computation of intermediate routers. Because link status messages propagate unchanged, it is easy to debug problems. Because routers perform the route computation locally, the computation is guaranteed to converge. Finally, because link status messages only carry information about the direct connections from a single router, the size does not depend on the number of networks in the underlying internet. Thus, SPF algorithms scale better than distance-vector algorithms.

13.10 Summary

To ensure that all networks remain reachable with high reliability, an internet must provide globally consistent forwarding. Hosts and most routers contain only partial routing information; they depend on default routes to send datagrams to distant destinations. Originally, the global Internet solved the routing problem by using a core router architecture in which a set of core routers each contained complete information about all networks.

---

†In practice, to prevent oscillations between the up and down states, many protocols use a *k-out-of-n rule* to test liveness, meaning that the link remains up until a significant percentage of requests have no reply, and then it remains down until a significant percentage of messages receive a reply.

‡Dijkstra coined the phrase *shortest path first*.

When additional backbone networks were added to the Internet, a new routing architecture arose to match the extended topology. Currently, a set of separately managed peer backbone networks exist that interconnect at multiple places.

When routers exchange routing information they usually use one of two basic algorithms, distance-vector or SPF. The chief disadvantage of distance-vector algorithms is that they perform a distributed shortest path computation that may not converge if the status of network connections changes continually. Thus, for large internets or internets where the underlying topology changes quickly, SPF is superior.

FOR FURTHER STUDY

The definition of the core router system in this chapter comes from Hinden and Sheltzer [RFC 823]. Braden and Postel [RFC 1812] contains further specifications for Internet routers. Braun [RFC 1093] and Rekhter [RFC 1092] discuss routing in the NSFNET backbone. The use of SPF routing predates the Internet; one of the earliest examples of an SPF protocol comes from the ARPANET, which used a routing protocol internally to establish and maintain routes among packet switches. Clark [RFC 1102] and Braun [RFC 1104] both discuss policy-based routing.

EXERCISES

13.1   Suppose a router discovers it is about to forward an IP datagram back over the same network interface on which the datagram arrived. What should it do? Why?

13.2   After reading RFC 823 and RFC 1812, explain what an Internet core router (i.e., one with complete routing information) should do in the situation described in the previous question.

13.3   How can routers in a core system use default routes to send all illegal datagrams to a specific machine?

13.4   Imagine that a manager accidentally misconfigures a router to advertise that it has direct connections to six specific networks when it does not. How can other routers that receive the advertisement protect themselves from invalid advertisements while still accepting other updates from ''untrusted'' routers?

13.5   Which ICMP messages does a router generate?

13.6   Assume a router is using unreliable transport for delivery. How can the router determine whether a designated neighbor is ''up'' or ''down''? (Hint: consult RFC 823 to find out how the original core system solved the problem.)

13.7   Suppose two routers each advertise the same cost, k, to reach a given network, N. Describe the circumstances under which forwarding through one of them may take fewer total hops than forwarding through the other one.

13.8   How does a router know whether an incoming datagram carries a routing update message?

13.9   Consider the distance-vector update shown in Figure 13.4 carefully. For each item updated in the table, give the reason why the router will perform the update.

13.10   Consider the use of sequence numbers to ensure that two routers do not become confused when datagrams are duplicated, delayed, or delivered out of order. How should initial sequence numbers be selected? Why?

Chapter Contents

14

Routing Between Peers (BGP)

14.1 Introduction

The previous chapter introduces the idea of route propagation. This chapter extends our understanding of internet routing architectures. It discusses the concept of autonomous systems, and shows a protocol that a group of networks and routers operating under one administrative authority uses to propagate routing information about its networks to other groups.

14.2 Routing Update Protocol Scope

No routing update protocol can scale to allow all routers in the Internet to exchange routes. Instead, routers must be divided into groups. There are three reasons. First, even if each site consists of a single network, no routing protocol can accommodate an arbitrary number of sites because adding sites increases routing traffic — if the set of routers is sufficiently large, the routing traffic becomes overwhelming. Second, because they do not share a common network, Internet routers cannot communicate directly. Third, in a large internet, the networks and routers are not all managed by a single entity, nor are shortest paths always used. Instead, because networks are owned and managed by independent commercial groups, the groups may choose policies that differ. A routing architecture must provide a way for each group to independently control routing and access.

The consequences of limiting router interaction are significant. The idea provides the motivation for much of the routing architecture used in the Internet, and explains some of the mechanisms we will study. To summarize this important principle:

> *Although it is desirable for routers to exchange routing information, it is impractical for all routers in an arbitrarily large internet to participate in a single routing update protocol.*

14.3 Determining A Practical Limit On Group Size

The above statement leaves many questions open. For example, what internet size is considered "large"? If only a limited set of routers can participate in an exchange of routing information, what happens to routers that are excluded? Do they function correctly? Can a router that is not participating ever forward a datagram to a router that is participating? Can a participating router forward a datagram to a non-participating router?

The answer to the question of size involves understanding the algorithm being used and the capacity of the network that connects the routers as well as the details of the routing protocol. There are two issues: delay and overhead. Delay is easy to understand. For example, consider the maximum delay until all routers are informed about a change when they use a distance-vector protocol. Each router must receive the new information, update its routing table, and then forward the information to its neighbors. In an internet with N routers arranged in a linear topology, N steps are required. Thus, N must be limited to guarantee rapid distribution of information.

The issue of overhead is also easy to understand. Because each router that participates in a routing protocol must send messages, a larger set of participating routers means more routing traffic. Furthermore, if routing messages contain a list of possible destinations, the size of each message grows as the number of routers and networks increase. To ensure that routing traffic remains a small percentage of the total traffic on the underlying networks, the size of routing messages must be limited.

In fact, most network managers do not have sufficient information required to perform detailed analysis of the delay or overhead. Instead, they follow a simple heuristic guideline:

> *It is safe to allow up to a dozen routers to participate in a single routing information protocol across a wide area network; approximately five times as many can safely participate across a set of local area networks.*

Of course, the rule only gives general advice and there are many exceptions. For example, if the underlying networks have especially low delay and high capacity, the number of participating routers can be larger. Similarly, if the underlying networks have unusually low capacity or a high amount of traffic, the number of participating routers must be smaller to avoid overloading the networks with routing traffic.

Because an internet is not static, it can be difficult to estimate how much traffic routing protocols will generate or what percentage of the underlying bandwidth the routing traffic will consume. For example, as the number of hosts on a network grows over time, increases in the traffic generated consume more of the network capacity. In addition, increased traffic can arise from new applications. Therefore, network managers cannot rely solely on the guideline above when choosing a routing architecture. Instead, they usually implement a *traffic monitoring* scheme. In essence, a traffic monitor listens passively to a network and records statistics about the traffic. In particular, a monitor can compute both the network utilization (i.e., percentage of the underlying bandwidth being used) and the percentage of packets carrying routing protocol messages. A manager can observe traffic trends by taking measurements over long periods (e.g., weeks or months), and can use the output to determine whether too many routers are participating in a single routing protocol.

14.4 A Fundamental Idea: Extra Hops

Although the number of routers that participate in a single routing protocol must be limited, doing so has an important consequence because it means that some routers will be outside the group. It might seem that an ''outsider'' could merely make a member of the group a default. In the early Internet, as routers were added to sites, the core system functioned as a central routing mechanism to which noncore routers sent datagrams for delivery. The addition of noncore routers taught researchers an important lesson: if a router outside of a group uses a member of the group as a default route, routing will be suboptimal. More important, one does not need a large number of routers or a wide area network — the problem can occur whenever a nonparticipating router uses a participating router for delivery. To see why, consider the example in Figure 14.1.

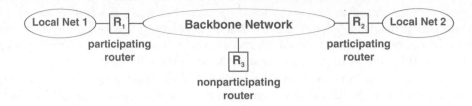

Figure 14.1 An architecture that can cause the extra hop problem. Nonoptimal routing occurs when a nonparticipating router connected to the backbone has a default route to a participating router.

In the figure, routers R_1 and R_2 connect to local area networks *1* and *2*, respectively. Because they participate in a routing protocol, they each know how to reach both networks. Suppose nonparticipating router R_3 chooses one of the participating routers, say R_1, as a default. That is, R_3 sends R_1 all datagrams destined for networks to which it has no direct connection. In particular, R_3 sends datagrams destined for network *2* across the backbone to its chosen participating router, R_1, which must then forward them back across the backbone to router R_2. The optimal route, of course, requires R_3 to transmit datagrams destined for network *2* directly to R_2. Notice that the choice of participating router makes no difference. Only destinations that lie beyond the chosen router have optimal routes; all paths that go through other backbone routers require the datagram to make a second, unnecessary trip across the backbone network. Also notice that the participating routers cannot use ICMP redirect messages to inform R_3 that it has nonoptimal routes because ICMP redirect messages can only be sent to the original source and not to intermediate routers.

We call the routing anomaly illustrated in Figure 14.1 the *extra hop problem*. The problem is insidious because everything appears to work correctly — datagrams do reach their destination. However, because routing is not optimal, the system is extremely inefficient. Each datagram that takes an extra hop consumes resources on the intermediate router as well as twice as much backbone bandwidth as it should. Solving the problem requires us to change our view of architecture:

> *Treating a group of routers that participate in a routing update protocol as a default delivery system can introduce an extra hop for datagram traffic; a mechanism is needed that allows nonparticipating routers to learn routes from participating routers so they can choose optimal routes.*

14.5 Autonomous System Concept

How should the Internet be divided into sets of routers that can each run a routing update protocol? The key to the answer lies in realizing that the Internet does not consist of independent networks. Instead, networks and routers are owned by organizations and individuals. Because the networks and routers owned by a given entity fall under a single administrative authority, the authority can guarantee that internal routes remain consistent and viable. Furthermore, the administrative authority can choose one of its routers to serve as the machine that will apprise the outside world of networks within the organization and learn about networks that are outside the organization.

For purposes of routing, a group of networks and routers controlled by a single administrative authority is called an *autonomous system* (*AS*). Routers within an autonomous system are free to choose their own mechanisms for discovering, propagating, validating, and checking the consistency of routes (the next chapter reviews some of the protocols that autonomous systems use to propagate routing information internally).

Although the definition of an autonomous system may seem vague, the boundaries between autonomous systems must be defined precisely to allow automated algorithms to make routing decisions. For example, an autonomous system may prefer to avoid routing packets through a competitor's autonomous system even if such a path exists. To make it possible for automated routing algorithms to distinguish among autonomous systems, each is assigned an *autonomous system number* by the central authority that is charged with assigning all Internet numbers. When routers in two autonomous systems exchange routing information, the protocol arranges for each router to learn the other's autonomous system number.

We can summarize the ideas:

> *The Internet is divided into autonomous systems that are each owned by a single administrative authority. An autonomous system is free to choose an internal routing architecture and protocols.*

In practice, although some large organizations have obtained autonomous system numbers to allow them to connect to multiple ISPs, we think of an autonomous system as corresponding to a large ISP. The point is:

> *In the current Internet, each large ISP is an autonomous system. During informal discussions, engineers often refer to routing among major ISPs when they mean routing among autonomous systems.*

14.6 Exterior Gateway Protocols And Reachability

Each autonomous system needs to configure one or more of its routers to communicate with other autonomous system(s). A router is configured to know or collect information about networks inside its autonomous system and pass the information out as well as to accept information about networks in other autonomous system(s) and disseminate the information inside. Technically, we say that the autonomous system advertises *network reachability* to the outside, and use the term *Exterior Gateway Protocol* (*EGP*)† to denote any protocol used to pass network reachability information between two autonomous systems. Strictly speaking, an EGP is not a routing protocol because advertising reachability is not the same as propagating routing information. In practice, however, most networking professionals do not make a distinction — one is likely to hear exterior gateway protocols referred to as routing protocols.

Currently, a single EGP is used to exchange reachability information in the Internet. Known as the *Border Gateway Protocol* (*BGP*), it has evolved through four (quite different) versions. Each version is numbered, which gives rise to the formal name of the current version: *BGP-4*. Following standard practice in the networking industry, we will use the term *BGP* in place of *BGP-4*.

When a pair of autonomous systems agree to exchange routing information, each must designate a router‡ that will speak BGP on its behalf; the two routers are said to become *BGP peers* of one another. Because a router speaking BGP must communicate with a peer in another autonomous system, it makes sense to select a machine that is near the "edge" of the autonomous system. Hence, BGP terminology calls the machine a *border gateway* or *border router*. Figure 14.2 illustrates the idea.

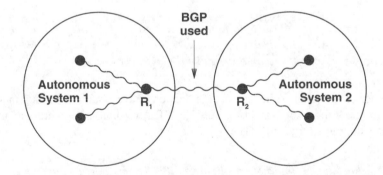

Figure 14.2 Conceptual illustration of two routers, R_1 and R_2, using BGP to advertise networks in their autonomous systems after collecting the information from other routers internally. An organization using BGP usually chooses a router that is close to the outer "edge" of the autonomous system.

---

†The term was coined at a time when *gateway* was used in place of *router*, and still persists.

‡An autonomous system usually runs BGP on each router that connects to another autonomous system.

In the figure, router R_1 gathers information about networks in autonomous system *1* and reports that information to router R_2 using BGP, while router R_2 reports information from autonomous system *2*.

14.7 BGP Characteristics

BGP is unusual in several ways. Most important, because it advertises reachability instead of routing information, BGP does not use either the distance-vector algorithm or the link state algorithm. Instead, BGP can be characterized by the following:

Inter-Autonomous System Communication. Because BGP is designed as an exterior gateway protocol, its primary role is to allow one autonomous system to communicate with another.

Coordination Among Multiple BGP Speakers. If an autonomous system has multiple routers each communicating with a peer in an outside autonomous system, a form of BGP known as *iBGP* can be used to coordinate among routers in the set to guarantee that they all propagate consistent information.

Propagation Of Reachability Information. BGP allows an autonomous system to advertise destinations that are reachable either in or through it, and to learn such information from another autonomous system.

Next-Hop Paradigm. Like distance-vector routing protocols, BGP supplies *next hop* information for each destination.

Policy Support. Unlike most distance-vector protocols that advertise exactly the routes in the local routing table, BGP can implement policies that the local administrator chooses. In particular, a router running BGP can be configured to distinguish between the set of destinations reachable by computers inside its autonomous system and the set of destinations advertised to other autonomous systems.

Reliable Transport. BGP is unusual among protocols that pass routing information because it assumes reliable transport. Thus, BGP uses TCP for all communication.

Path Information. Instead of specifying destinations that can be reached and a next hop for each, BGP advertisements specify path information that allows a receiver to learn a series of autonomous systems along a path to the destination and avoid cycles.

Incremental Updates. To conserve network bandwidth, BGP does not pass full information in each update message. Instead, full information is exchanged once, and then successive messages carry incremental changes called *deltas*.

Support For Classless Addressing. BGP supports CIDR addresses. That is, BGP sends a prefix length along with each address.

Route Aggregation. BGP conserves network bandwidth by allowing a sender to aggregate route information and send a single entry to represent multiple, related destinations.

Authentication. BGP allows a receiver to authenticate messages (i.e., verify the identity of a sender).

14.8 BGP Functionality And Message Types

BGP peers perform three basic functions. The first function consists of initial peer acquisition and authentication. The two peers establish a TCP connection and perform a message exchange that guarantees both sides have agreed to communicate. The second function forms the primary focus of the protocol — each side sends positive or negative reachability information. That is, a sender can advertise that one or more destinations are reachable by giving a next hop for each, or the sender can declare that one or more previously advertised destinations are no longer reachable. The third function provides ongoing verification that the peers and the network connections between them are functioning correctly.

To handle the three functions described above, BGP defines five basic message types. Figure 14.3 contains a summary.

Type Code	Message Type	Description
1	OPEN	Initialize communication
2	UPDATE	Advertise or withdraw routes
3	NOTIFICATION	Response to an incorrect message
4	KEEPALIVE	Actively test peer connectivity
5	REFRESH	Request readvertisement from peer

Figure 14.3 The five basic message types in BGP.

14.9 BGP Message Header

Each BGP message begins with a fixed header that identifies the message type. Figure 14.4 illustrates the header format. The 16-octet *MARKER* field contains a value that both sides agree to use to mark the beginning of a message. The 2-octet *LENGTH* field specifies the total message length measured in octets. The minimum message size is *19* octets (for a message type that has no data following the header), and the maximum allowable length is *4096* octets. Finally, the 1-octet *TYPE* field contains one of the five values for the message type listed in Figure 14.3.

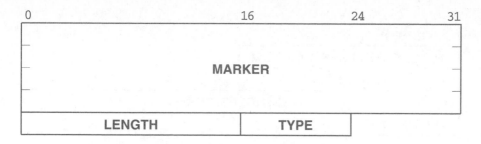

Figure 14.4 The format of the header that precedes every BGP message.

The *MARKER* may seem unusual. In the initial message, the marker consists of all 1s; if the peers agree to use an authentication mechanism, the marker can contain authentication information. In any case, both sides must agree on the value so it can be used for *synchronization*. To understand why synchronization is necessary, recall that all BGP messages are exchanged across a stream transport (i.e., TCP), which does not identify the boundary between one message and the next. In such an environment, a simple error on either side can have dramatic consequences. In particular, if either the sender or receiver miscounts the octets in a message, a *synchronization error* will occur. More important, because the transport protocol does not specify message boundaries, the transport protocol will not alert the receiver to the error. Thus, to ensure that the sender and receiver remain synchronized, BGP places a well-known sequence at the beginning of each message, and requires a receiver to verify that the value is intact before processing the message.

14.10 BGP OPEN Message

As soon as two BGP peers establish a TCP connection, they each send an *OPEN* message to declare their autonomous system number and establish other operating parameters. In addition to the standard header, an *OPEN* message contains a value for a *hold timer* that is used to specify the maximum number of seconds which may elapse between the receipt of two successive messages. Figure 14.5 illustrates the format.

Most fields are straightforward. The *VERSION* field identifies the protocol version used (this format is for version 4). Recall that each autonomous system is assigned a unique number. Field *AUTONOMOUS SYSTEMS NUM* gives the autonomous system number of the sender's system. The *HOLD TIME* field specifies a maximum time that the receiver should wait for a message from the sender. The receiver is required to implement a timer using this value. The timer is reset each time a message arrives; if the timer expires, the receiver assumes the sender is no longer available (and stops forwarding datagrams along routes learned from the sender).

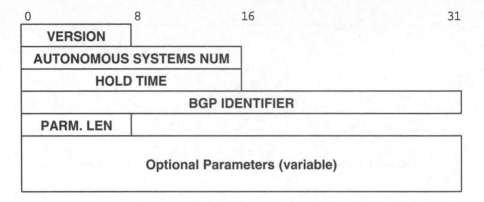

Figure 14.5 The format of the BGP OPEN message that is sent at startup.
These octets follow the standard message header.

Field *BGP IDENTIFIER* contains a 32-bit integer value that uniquely identifies the sender. If a machine has multiple peers (e.g., perhaps in multiple autonomous systems), the machine must use the same identifier in all communication. The protocol specifies that the identifier is an IP address. Thus, a router must choose one of its IP addresses to use with all BGP peers.

The last field of an *OPEN* message is optional. If present, field *PARM. LEN* specifies the length measured in octets, and the field labeled *Optional Parameters* contains a list of parameters. It has been labeled *variable* to indicate that the size varies from message to message. When parameters are present, each parameter in the list is preceded by a 2-octet header, with the first octet specifying the type of the parameter, and the second octet specifying the length. If there are no parameters, the value of *PARM. LEN* is zero and the message ends with no further data.

Parameters currently exist for authentication and capability negotiation; a parameter has been proposed to allow larger AS numbers†. The authentication parameter consists of a header that identifies the type of authentication followed by data appropriate for the type. The motivation for making authentication a parameter arises from a desire to allow BGP peers to choose an authentication mechanism without making the choice part of the BGP standard.

When it accepts an incoming *OPEN* message, a machine speaking BGP responds by sending a *KEEPALIVE* message (discussed below). Each side must send an *OPEN* and receive a *KEEPALIVE* message before they can exchange routing information. Thus, a *KEEPALIVE* message functions as the acknowledgement for an *OPEN*.

---

†Currently over 30,000 AS numbers have been assigned (approximately half of the available autonomous system numbers), so the proposal is to expand the size from 16 bits to 32.

14.11 BGP UPDATE Message

Once BGP peers have created a TCP connection, sent *OPEN* messages, and acknowledged them, the peers use *UPDATE* messages to advertise new destinations that are reachable or to withdraw previous advertisements when a destination has become unreachable. Figure 14.6 illustrates the format of *UPDATE* messages.

As the figure shows, each *UPDATE* message is divided into two parts: the first lists previously advertised destinations that are being withdrawn, and the second specifies new destinations being advertised. As usual, fields labeled *variable* do not have a fixed size; if the information is not needed for a particular *UPDATE*, the field can be omitted from the message. Field *WITHDRAWN LEN* is a 2-octet field that specifies the size of the *Withdrawn Destinations* field that follows. If no destinations are being withdrawn, *WITHDRAWN LEN* contains zero. Similarly, the *PATH ATTR LEN* field specifies the size of the *Path Attributes* that are associated with new destinations being advertised. If there are no new destinations, the *PATH LEN* field contains zero.

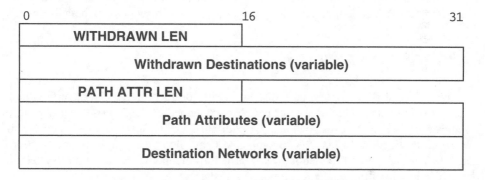

Figure 14.6 BGP UPDATE message format in which variable size areas of the message may be omitted. These octets follow the standard message header.

14.12 Compressed Mask-Address Pairs

Both the *Withdrawn Destinations* and the *Destination Networks* fields contain a list of IP network addresses. To accommodate classless addressing, BGP must send an address mask with each IP address. Instead of sending an address and a mask as separate 32-bit quantities, BGP uses a compressed representation to reduce message size. Figure 14.7 illustrates the format:

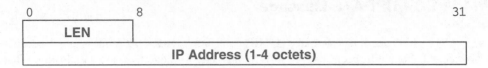

Figure 14.7 The compressed format BGP uses to store a destination address
and the associated mask.

The figure shows that BGP does not actually send a bit mask. Instead, it encodes
information about the mask into a single octet that precedes each address. The mask
octet contains a binary integer that specifies the number of bits in the mask (mask bits
are assumed to be contiguous). The address that follows the mask octet is also
compressed — only those octets covered by the mask are included. Thus, only one address octet follows a mask value of *8* or less, two follow a mask value of *9* to *16*, three
follow a mask value of *17* to *24*, and four follow a mask value of *25* to *32*. Interestingly, the standard also allows a mask octet to contain zero (in which case no address octets follow it). A zero length mask is useful because it corresponds to a default route.

14.13 BGP Path Attributes

We said that BGP is not a pure distance-vector protocol because it advertises more
than a next hop. The additional information is contained in the *Path Attributes* field of
an update message. A sender can use the path attributes to specify: a next hop for the
advertised destinations, a list of autonomous systems along the path to the destinations,
and whether the path information was learned from another autonomous system or
derived from within the sender's autonomous system.

It is important to note that the path attributes are factored to reduce the size of the
UPDATE message, meaning that the attributes apply to all destinations advertised in the
message. Thus, if different attributes apply to some destinations, they must be advertised in a separate UPDATE message.

Path attributes are important in BGP for three reasons. First, path information allows a receiver to check for forwarding loops. The sender can specify an exact path
through all autonomous systems to the destination. If the receiver's autonomous system
appears on the list, the advertisement must be rejected or there will be a forwarding
loop. Second, path information allows a receiver to implement policy constraints (e.g.,
reject a path that includes a competitor's autonomous system). Third, path information
allows a receiver to know the source of all routes. In addition to allowing a sender to
specify whether the information came from inside its autonomous system or from another system, the path attributes allow the sender to declare whether the information was
collected with an exterior gateway protocol such as BGP or an interior gateway proto-
col†. Thus, each receiver can decide whether to accept or reject routes that originate in
autonomous systems beyond the peer's.

---

†The next chapter describes interior gateway protocols.

Conceptually, the *Path Attributes* field contains a list of items, where each item consists of a triple:

(type, length, value)

Instead of fixed-size fields, the designers chose a flexible encoding scheme that minimizes the space each item occupies. As specified in Figure 14.8, the type information always requires two octets, but other fields vary in size.

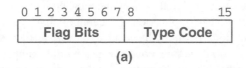

(a)

Flag Bits	Description
0	0 for required attribute, 1 if optional
1	1 for transitive, 0 for nontransitive
2	0 for complete, 1 for partial
3	0 if length field is one octet; 1 if two
5-7	unused (must be zero)

(b)

Figure 14.8 (a) The two-octet type field that appears before each BGP attribute path item, and (b) the meaning of each flag bit.

Each item in the *Path attributes* field can have one of eight possible type codes. Figure 14.9 summarizes the possibilities.

Type Code	Meaning
1	ID of the origin of the path information
2	List of autonomous systems on path to destination
3	Next hop to use for destination
4	Discriminator used for multiple AS exit points
5	Preference used within an autonomous system
6	Indication that routes have been aggregated
7	ID of autonomous system that aggregated routes
8	ID of community for advertised destinations

Figure 14.9 The BGP attribute type codes and the meaning of each.

For each item in the *Path Attributes* list, a length field follows the 2-octet type field, and may be either one or two octets long. As the figure shows, flag bit *3* specifies the size of the length field. A receiver uses the type field to determine the size of the length field, and then uses the contents of the length field to compute the size of the value field.

14.14 BGP KEEPALIVE Message

Two BGP peers periodically exchange *KEEPALIVE* messages to test network connectivity and to verify that both peers continue to function. A *KEEPALIVE* message consists of the standard message header with no additional data. Thus, the total message size is *19* octets (the minimum BGP message size).

There are two reasons why BGP uses *keepalive* messages. First, periodic message exchange is needed because BGP uses TCP for transport, and TCP does not include a mechanism to continually test whether a connection endpoint is reachable. However, TCP does report an error to an application if it cannot deliver data the application sends. Thus, as long as both sides periodically send a *keepalive*, they will know if the TCP connection fails. Second, *keepalives* conserve bandwidth compared to other messages. Many early routing protocols used periodic exchange of routing information to test connectivity. However, because routing information changes infrequently, the message content seldom changes. Furthermore, because routing messages are usually large, resending the same message wastes network bandwidth. To avoid the inefficiency, BGP separates the functionality of route update from connectivity testing, allowing BGP to send small *KEEPALIVE* messages frequently, and reserving larger *UPDATE* messages for situations when reachability information changes.

Recall that a BGP speaker specifies a *hold timer* when it opens a connection; the hold timer defines a maximum time that BGP is to wait without receiving a message. As a special case, the hold timer can be zero to specify that no *KEEPALIVE* messages are used. If the hold timer is greater than zero, the standard recommends setting the *KEEPALIVE* interval to one third of the hold timer. In no case can a BGP speaker make the *KEEPALIVE* interval less than one second (which agrees with the requirement that a nonzero hold timer cannot be less than three seconds).

14.15 Information From The Receiver's Perspective

Unlike most protocols that propagate routing information, an Exterior Gateway Protocol does not merely report the set of destinations it can reach. Instead, exterior protocols must provide information that is correct from the outsider's perspective. There are two issues: policies and optimal routes. The policy issue is obvious: a router inside an autonomous system may be allowed to reach a given destination, while outsiders are prohibited from reaching the same destination. The routing issue means that a router must advertise a next hop that is optimal from the outsider's perspective. Figure 14.10 illustrates the idea.

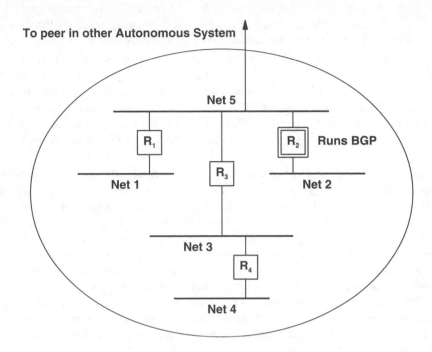

Figure 14.10 Example of an autonomous system. Router R_2 runs BGP and reports information from the outsider's perspective, not from its own routing table.

In the figure, router R_2 has been designated to speak BGP on behalf of the autonomous system. It must report reachability to networks *1* through *4*. However, when giving a next hop, it reports network *1* as reachable through router R_1, networks *3* and *4* as reachable through router R_3, and network *2* as reachable through R_2.

14.16 The Key Restriction Of Exterior Gateway Protocols

We have already seen that because exterior protocols follow policy restrictions, the networks they advertise may be a subset of the networks they can reach. However, there is a more fundamental limitation imposed on exterior routing:

> *An exterior gateway protocol does not communicate or interpret distance metrics, even if metrics are available.*

Protocols like BGP do allow a speaker to declare that a destination has become unreachable or to give a list of autonomous systems on the path to the destination, but they cannot transmit or compare the cost of two routes unless the routes come from within the same autonomous system. In essence, BGP can only specify whether a path exists to a given destination; it cannot transmit or compute the shorter of two paths.

We can see now why BGP is careful to label the origin of information it sends. The essential observation is this: when a router receives advertisements for a given destination from peers in two different autonomous systems, it cannot compare the costs. Thus, advertising reachability with BGP is equivalent to saying, "My autonomous system provides a path to this network." There is no way for the router to say, "My autonomous system provides a better path to this network than another autonomous system."

Looking at interpretation of distances allows us to realize that BGP cannot be used as a routing algorithm. In particular, even if a router learns about two paths to the same network, it cannot know which path is shorter because it cannot know the cost of routes across intermediate autonomous systems. For example, consider a router that uses BGP to communicate with two peers in autonomous systems p and f. If the peer in autonomous system p advertises a path to a given destination through autonomous systems p, q, and r, and the peer in f advertises a path to the same destination through autonomous systems f and g, the receiver has no way of comparing the lengths of the two paths. The path through three autonomous systems might involve one local area network in each system, while the path through two autonomous systems might require several hops in each. Because a receiver does not obtain full routing information, it cannot compare.

Because it does not include a distance metric, an autonomous system must be careful to advertise only routes that traffic should follow. Technically, we say that an Exterior Gateway Protocol is a *reachability protocol* rather than a routing protocol. We can summarize:

> *Because an Exterior Gateway Protocol like BGP only propagates reachability information, a receiver can implement policy constraints, but cannot choose a least cost route. A sender must only advertise paths that traffic should follow.*

The key point here is that any internet which uses BGP to provide exterior routing information must either rely on policies or assume that each autonomous system crossing is equally expensive. Although it may seem innocuous, the restriction has some surprising consequences:

1. Although BGP can advertise multiple paths to a given network, it does not provide for the simultaneous use of multiple paths. That is, at any given instant, all traffic routed from a computer in one autonomous system to a network in another will traverse one path, even if multiple physical connections are present. Also note that an outside autonomous system will only use one return path even if the

source system divides outgoing traffic among two or more paths. As a result, delay and throughput between a pair of machines can be asymmetric, making an internet difficult to monitor or debug.

2.   BGP does not support load sharing on routers between arbitrary autonomous systems. If two autonomous systems have multiple routers connecting them, one would like to balance the traffic equally among all routers. BGP allows autonomous systems to divide the load by network (e.g., to partition themselves into multiple subsets and have multiple routers advertise partitions), but it does not support more general load sharing.

3.   As a special case of point 2, BGP alone is inadequate for optimal routing in an architecture that has two or more wide area networks interconnected at multiple points. Instead, managers must manually configure which networks are advertised by each exterior router.

4.   To have rationalized routing, all autonomous systems in an internet must agree on a consistent scheme for advertising reachability. That is, BGP alone will not guarantee global consistency.

14.17 The Internet Routing Architecture

For an internet to operate flawlessly, routing information must be globally consistent. Individual protocols such as BGP that handle the exchange between a pair of routers, do not guarantee global consistency. Thus, further effort is needed to rationalize routing information globally. In the original Internet routing architecture, the core system guaranteed globally consistent routing information because at any time the core had exactly one path to each destination. However, the core system and its successor (called the routing arbiter system) have been removed. Ironically, no single mechanism has been devised as a replacement to handle the task of routing rationalization — the current Internet does not have a central mechanism to validate routes and guarantee global consistency.

To understand the current routing architecture, we need to examine the physical topology. A pair of ISPs can interconnect privately (e.g., by agreeing to lease a circuit between two routers), or can interconnect at *Internet Exchange Points* (*IXPs*), which are also known as *Network Access Points* (*NAPs*). We say that the ISPs engage in *private peering* or that they enter into a *peering agreement*. In terms of routing, a private peering represents the boundary between the two autonomous systems. The two ISPs define their relationship, which can be viewed as *upstream* (a large ISP agrees to take traffic from a smaller ISP), *downstream* (a large ISP passes traffic to a smaller ISP) or *transit* (an ISP agrees to accept and forward traffic to other ISPs).

To assist in assuring that routes are valid, ISPs use services known as *Routing Registries*. In essence, a Routing Registry maintains information about which ISPs own which blocks of addresses. Thus, if ISP *A* sends an advertisement to ISP *B* claiming to have reachability to network *N*, ISP *B* can use information from a Routing Registry to verify that address *N* has been assign to ISP *A*. Unfortunately, many Routing Registries exist, and there is no mechanism in place to validate the data in a registry. Thus, temporary routing problems occur such as *black holes* in which a given address is not reachable from all parts of the Internet. Of course, ISPs and most Routing Registries attempt to find and repair such problems quickly, but without a centralized, authoritative registry, Internet routing cannot be completely flawless.

14.18 BGP NOTIFICATION Message

In addition to the OPEN and UPDATE message types described above, BGP supports a *NOTIFICATION* message type used for control or when an error occurs. Errors are permanent — once it detects a problem, BGP sends a notification message and then closes the TCP connection. Figure 14.11 illustrates the message format.

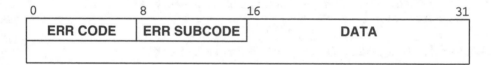

Figure 14.11 BGP NOTIFICATION message format. These octets follow the standard message header.

The 8-bit field labeled *ERR CODE* specifies one of the possible reasons listed in Figure 14.12.

ERR CODE	Meaning
1	Error in message header
2	Error in OPEN message
3	Error in UPDATE message
4	Hold timer expired
5	Finite state machine error
6	Cease (terminate connection)

Figure 14.12 The possible values of the *ERR CODE* field in a BGP NOTIFICATION message.

For each possible *ERR CODE*, the *ERR SUBCODE* field contains a further explanation. Figure 14.13 lists the possible values.

Subcodes For Message Header Errors

1   Connection not synchronized
2   Incorrect message length
3   Incorrect message type

Subcodes For OPEN Message Errors

1   Version number unsupported
2   Peer AS invalid
3   BGP identifier invalid
4   Unsupported optional parameter
5   Authentication failure
6   Hold time unacceptable

Subcodes For UPDATE Message Errors

1   Attribute list malformed
2   Unrecognized attribute
3   Missing attribute
4   Attribute flags error
5   Attribute length error
6   Invalid ORIGIN attribute
7   AS routing loop
8   Next hop invalid
9   Error in optional attribute
10   Invalid network field
11   Malformed AS path

Figure 14.13 The meaning of the *ERR SUBCODE* field in a BGP NOTIFI-
CATION message.

14.19 Summary

Routers must be partitioned into groups or the volume of routing traffic would be intolerable. The connected Internet is composed of a set of autonomous systems, where each autonomous system consists of routers and networks under one administrative authority. An autonomous system uses an Exterior Gateway Protocol to advertise routes to other autonomous systems. Specifically, an autonomous system must advertise reachability of its networks to another system before its networks are reachable from sources within the other system.

The Border Gateway Protocol, BGP, is the most widely used Exterior Gateway Protocol. We saw that BGP contains five message types that are used to initiate communication (OPEN), send reachability information (UPDATE), report an error condition (NOTIFICATION), revalidate information (REFRESH), and ensure peers remain in communication (KEEPALIVE). Each message starts with a standard header that includes (optional) authentication information. BGP uses TCP for communication.

In the global Internet, each large ISP is a separate autonomous system, and the boundary between autonomous systems consists of a peering agreement between two ISPs. Physically, peering can occur in an Internet Exchange Point or over a private leased circuit. An ISP uses BGP to communicate with its peer, both to advertise networks (i.e., address prefixes) that can be reached through it and to learn about networks that can be reached by forwarding to the peer. Although services known as Routing Registries exist that aid ISPs in validating advertisements, problems can occur because the Internet does not currently have an authoritative, centralized registry.

FOR FURTHER STUDY

Background on early Internet routing can be found in [RFCs 827, 888, 904, and 975]. Rekhter and Li [RFC 1771] describes version 4 of the Border Gateway Protocol *(BGP-4)*. BGP has been through three substantial revisions; earlier versions appear in [RFCs 1163, 1267, and 1654]. Traina [RFC 1773] reports experience with BGP-4, and Traina [RFC 1774] analyzes the volume of routing traffic generated. Finally, Villamizar et. al. [RFC 2439] considers the problem of route flapping (i.e., periodic changes in routes). Additional details related to BGP-4 can be found in [RFCs 1997, 2918,3392, 2796, and 3065].

EXERCISES

14.1   If your site runs an Exterior Gateway Protocol such as BGP, how many routes do you advertise? How many routes do you import from an ISP?

14.2   Some implementations of BGP use a ''hold down'' mechanism that causes the protocol to delay accepting an *OPEN* from a peer for a fixed time following the receipt of a *cease request* message from that neighbor. Find out what problem a hold down helps solve.

14.3   The formal specification of BGP includes a finite state machine that explains how BGP operates. Draw a diagram of the state machine and label transitions.

14.4   What happens if a router in an autonomous system sends BGP routing update messages to a router in another autonomous system, claiming to have reachability for every possible Internet destination?

14.5   Can two autonomous systems establish a forwarding loop by sending BGP update messages to one another? Why or why not?

14.6   Should a router that uses BGP to advertise routes treat the set of routes advertised differently than the set of routes in the local routing table? For example, should a router ever advertise reachability if it has not installed a route to that network in its routing table? Why or why not? Hint: read RFC 1771.

14.7   With regard to the previous question, examine the BGP-4 specification carefully. Is it legal to advertise reachability to a destination that is not listed in the local routing table?

14.8   If you work for a large corporation, find out whether it includes more than one autonomous system. If so, how do they exchange routing information?

14.9   What is the chief advantage of dividing a large, multi-national corporation into multiple autonomous systems? What is the chief disadvantage?

14.10   Corporations *A* and *B* use BGP to exchange routing information. To keep computers in *B* from reaching machines on one of its networks, *N*, the network administrator at corporation *A* configures BGP to omit *N* from advertisements sent to *B*. Is network *N* secure? Why or why not?

14.11   Because BGP uses a reliable transport protocol, KEEPALIVE messages cannot be lost. Does it make sense to specify a keepalive interval as one-third of the hold timer value? Why or why not?

14.12   Consult the RFCs for details of the *Path Attributes* field. What is the minimum size of a BGP UPDATE message?

Chapter Contents

15

Routing Within An Autonomous System (RIP, OSPF)

15.1 Introduction

The previous chapter introduces the autonomous system concept and examines BGP, an Exterior Gateway Protocol that a router uses to advertise networks within its system to other autonomous systems. This chapter completes our overview of internet routing by examining how a router in an autonomous system learns about other networks within its autonomous system.

15.2 Static Vs. Dynamic Interior Routes

Two routers within an autonomous system are said to be *interior* to one another. For example, two routers on a university campus are considered interior to one another as long as machines on the campus are collected into a single autonomous system.

How can routers in an autonomous system learn about networks within the autonomous system? In small, slowly changing internets, managers can establish and modify routes manually. The administrator keeps a table of networks and updates the table whenever a new network is added to, or deleted from, the autonomous system. For example, consider the small corporate internet shown in Figure 15.1.

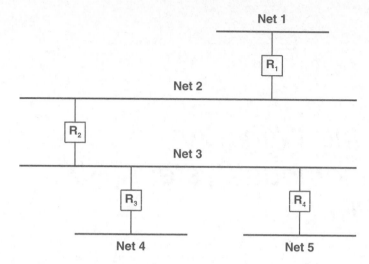

Figure 15.1 An example of a small internet consisting of 5 Ethernets and 4
routers at a single site. Only one possible route exists between
any two hosts in this internet.

Routing for the internet in the figure is trivial because only one path exists between
any two points. The manager can manually configure routes in all hosts and routers. If
the internet changes (e.g., a new network is added), the manager must reconfigure the
routes in all machines.

The disadvantages of a manual system are obvious: manual systems cannot accommodate rapid growth, and rely on humans to change routes whenever a network failure
occurs. In most internets, humans simply cannot respond to changes fast enough to
handle problems; automated methods must be used. To understand how automated
routing can increase reliability, consider what happens if we add one additional router to
the internet in Figure 15.1, producing the internet shown in Figure 15.2.

In the figure, multiple paths exist between some hosts. In such cases, a manager
usually chooses one path to be a *primary path* (i.e., the path that will be used for all
traffic). If a router or network along the primary path fails, routes must be changed to
send traffic along an alternate path. Automated route changes help in two ways. First,
because computers can respond to failures much faster than humans, automated route
changes are less time consuming. Second, because humans can make small errors when
entering network addresses, automated routing is less error-prone. Thus, even in small
internets, an automated system is used to change routes quickly and reliably.

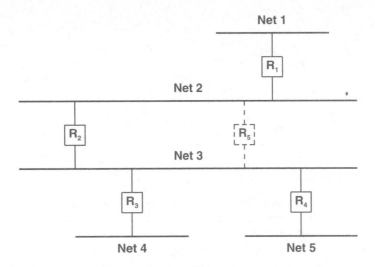

Figure 15.2 The addition of router R_5 introduces an alternate path between
networks *2* and *3*. Routing software can quickly adapt to a
failure and automatically switch routes to the alternate path.

To automate the task of keeping routing information accurate, interior routers periodically communicate with one another to exchange routing information. Unlike exterior router communication, for which BGP provides a widely accepted standard, no single protocol has emerged for use within an autonomous system or a site. Part of the reason for diversity comes from the varied topologies and technologies in use. Another part of the reason stems from the tradeoffs between simplicity and functionality — protocols that are easy to install and configure do not provide sophisticated functionality. As a result, a handful of protocols have become popular. Most small autonomous systems choose a single protocol, and use it exclusively to propagate routing information internally. Larger autonomous systems often choose a small set.

Because there is no single standard, we use the term *Interior Gateway Protocol (IGP)* as a generic description that refers to any protocol that interior routers use when they exchange routing information. Figure 15.3 illustrates the general idea: two autonomous systems each use a specific IGP to propagate routing information among interior routers, and then use BGP to communicate with outside autonomous systems.

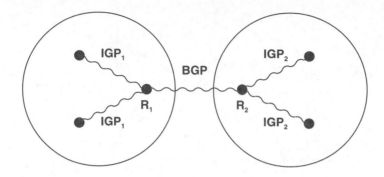

Figure 15.3 Conceptual view of two autonomous systems each using its own
IGP internally, but using BGP to communicate between an exterior router and the other system.

In the figure, IGP_1 refers to the interior router protocol used within autonomous
system *1*, and IGP_2 refers to the protocol used within autonomous system 2. The figure
also illustrates an important idea:

> *A single router may use two different routing protocols simultaneous-
> ly, one for communication outside its autonomous system and another
> for communication within its autonomous system.*

In particular, routers that run BGP to advertise reachability usually also need to run an
IGP to obtain information from within their autonomous system.

15.3 Routing Information Protocol (RIP)

15.3.1 History of RIP

One of the most widely used IGPs is the *Routing Information Protocol* (*RIP*),
which was originally known by the name of a program that implements it, *routed†*.
The *routed* software was originally designed at the University of California at Berkeley
to provide consistent routing information among machines on their local networks. It
relies on physical network broadcast to make routing exchanges quickly, and was not
designed to be used on large, wide area networks (although vendors now sell versions
of RIP adapted for use on WANs).

Based on earlier internetworking research done at Xerox Corporation's Palo Alto
Research Center (PARC), *routed* implemented a protocol derived from the Xerox *NS
Routing Information Protocol* (*RIP*), but generalized it to cover multiple families of net-
works.

---

†The name comes from the UNIX convention of attaching ''d'' to the names of daemon processes; it is
pronounced ''route-d''.

Despite minor improvements over its predecessors, the popularity of RIP as an IGP does not arise from its technical merits alone. Instead, it is the result of Berkeley distributing *routed* software along with their popular 4BSD UNIX systems. Thus, many early TCP/IP sites adopted and installed RIP without even considering its technical merits or limitations. Once installed and running, it became the basis for local routing, and vendors later began offering products compatible with RIP.

15.3.2 RIP Operation

The underlying RIP protocol is a straightforward implementation of distance-vector routing for local networks. It partitions participants into *active* and *passive* (i.e., *silent*) machines. Active participants advertise their routes to others; passive participants listen to RIP messages and use them to update their routing table, but do not advertise. Only a router can run RIP in active mode; if a host runs RIP, the host must use passive mode.

A router running RIP in active mode broadcasts a routing update message every 30 seconds. The update contains information taken from the router's current routing database. Each update contains a set of pairs, where each pair specifies an IP network address and an integer distance to that network. RIP uses a *hop count metric* to measure distances. In the RIP metric, a router is defined to be one hop from a directly connected network†, two hops from a network that is reachable through one other router, and so on. Thus, the *number of hops* or the *hop count* along a path from a given source to a given destination refers to the number of networks that a datagram encounters along that path. It should be obvious that using hop counts to calculate shortest paths does not always produce optimal results. For example, a path with hop count *3* that crosses three Ethernets may be substantially faster than a path with hop count *2* that crosses two satellite connections. To compensate for differences in technologies, many RIP implementations allow managers to configure artificially high hop counts when advertising connections to slow networks.

Both active and passive RIP participants listen to all broadcast messages, and update their tables according to the distance-vector algorithm described earlier. For example, in the internet of Figure 15.2, router R_1 will broadcast a message on network *2* that contains the pair $(1,1)$, meaning that it can reach network *1* at cost *1*. Routers R_2 and R_5 will receive the broadcast and install a route to network *1* through R_1 (at cost *2*). Later, routers R_2 and R_5 will include the pair $(1,2)$ when they broadcast their RIP messages on network *3*. Eventually, all routers and hosts will install a route to network *1*.

RIP specifies a few rules to improve performance and reliability. For example, once a router learns a route from another router, it must apply *hysteresis*, meaning that it does not replace the route with an equal cost route. In our example, if routers R_2 and R_5 both advertise network *1* at cost *2*, routers R_3 and R_4 will install a route through the one that happens to advertise first. We can summarize:

---

†Other routing protocols define a direct connection to be zero hops.

> *To prevent oscillation among equal cost paths, RIP specifies that existing routes should be retained until a new route has strictly lower cost.*

What happens if the first router to advertise a route fails (e.g., if it crashes)? RIP specifies that all listeners must timeout routes they learn via RIP. When a router installs a route in its table, it starts a timer for that route. The timer must be restarted whenever the router receives another RIP message advertising the route. The route becomes invalid if 180 seconds pass without the route being advertised again.

RIP must handle three kinds of errors caused by the underlying algorithm. First, because the algorithm does not explicitly detect forwarding loops, RIP must either assume participants can be trusted or take precautions to prevent such loops. Second, to prevent instabilities, RIP must use a low value for the maximum possible distance (RIP uses *16*). Thus, for internets in which legitimate hop counts approach *16*, managers must divide the internet into sections or use an alternative protocol†. Third, the distance-vector algorithm used by RIP can create a *slow convergence* or *count to infinity* problem, in which inconsistencies arise because routing update messages propagate slowly across the network. Choosing a small infinity (*16*) helps limit slow convergence, but does not eliminate it.

15.4 Slow Convergence Problem

Routing table inconsistencies and the slow convergence problem mentioned are not unique to RIP. They are fundamental problems that can occur with any distance-vector protocol in which update messages carry only pairs of destination network and distance to that network. To understand the problem consider the set of routers shown in Figure 15.4. The figure depicts routes to network *1* for the internet shown in Figure 15.2.

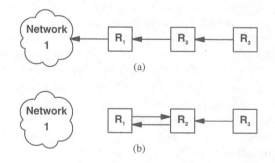

(a)

(b)

Figure 15.4 The slow convergence problem. In (a) three routers each have a route to network *1*. In (b) the connection to network *1* has vanished, but R_2 causes a loop by advertising it.

---

†Note that the hop count measures the span of the network — the longest distance between two routers — and not the number of routers. Most corporate internets have a small span.

As Figure 15.4a shows, router R_1 has a direct connection to network 1, so there is a route in its table with distance 1, which will be included in its periodic broadcasts. Router R_2 has learned the route from R_1, installed the route in its routing table, and advertises the route at distance 2. Finally, R_3 has learned the route from R_2 and advertises it at distance 3.

Now suppose that R_1's connection to network 1 fails. R_1 will update its routing table immediately to make the distance 16 (infinity). In the next broadcast, R_1 will report the higher cost route. However, unless the protocol includes extra mechanisms to prevent it, some other router could broadcast its routes before R_1. In particular, suppose R_2 happens to advertise routes just after R_1's connection fails. If so, R_1 will receive R_2's message and follow the usual distance-vector algorithm: it notices that R_2 has advertised a route to network 1 at lower cost, calculates that it now takes 3 hops to reach network 1 (2 for R_2 to reach network 1 plus 1 to reach R_2), *and installs a new route with R_2 listed as the next hop.* Figure 15.4b depicts the result. At this point, if either R_1 or R_2 receives a datagram destined for network 1, they will route the datagram back and forth until the datagram's time-to-live counter expires.

Subsequent RIP broadcasts by the two routers do not solve the problem quickly. In the next round of routing exchanges, R_1 broadcasts its routing table entries. When it learns that R_1's route to network 1 has distance 3, R_2 calculates a new distance for its route, making it 4. In the third round, R_1 receives a report from R_2 which includes the increased distance, and then increases the distance in its table to 5. The two routers continue counting to RIP infinity.

15.5 Solving The Slow Convergence Problem

For the example in Figure 15.4, it is possible to solve the slow convergence problem by using a technique known as *split horizon update*. When using split horizon, a router does not propagate information about a route back over the same interface from which the route arrived. In the example, split horizon prevents router R_2 from advertising a route to network 1 back to router R_1, so if R_1 loses connectivity to network 1, it must stop advertising a route. With split horizon, no forwarding loop appears in the example network. Instead, after a few rounds of routing updates, all routers will agree that the network is unreachable. However, the split horizon heuristic does not prevent forwarding loops in all possible topologies as one of the exercises suggests.

Another way to think of the slow convergence problem is in terms of information flow. If a router advertises a short route to some network, all receiving routers respond quickly to install that route. If a router stops advertising a route, the protocol must depend on a timeout mechanism before it considers the route unreachable. Once the timeout occurs, the router finds an alternative route, and starts propagating that information. Unfortunately, a router cannot know if the alternate route depended on the route that just disappeared. Thus, negative information does not always propagate quickly. A short epigram captures the idea and explains the phenomenon:

Good news travels quickly; bad news travels slowly.

Another technique used to solve the slow convergence problem employs *hold down*. Hold down forces a participating router to ignore information about a network for a fixed period of time following receipt of a message that claims the network is unreachable. Typically, the hold down period is set to 60 seconds. The idea is to wait long enough to ensure that all machines receive the bad news and not mistakenly accept a message that is out of date. It should be noted that all machines participating in a RIP exchange need to use identical notions of hold down, or forwarding loops can occur. The disadvantage of a hold down technique is that if forwarding loops occur, they will be preserved for the duration of the hold down period. More important, the hold down technique preserves all incorrect routes during the hold down period, even when alternatives exist.

A final technique for solving the slow convergence problem is called *poison reverse*. Once a connection disappears, the router advertising the connection retains the entry for several update periods, and includes an infinite cost in its broadcasts. To make poison reverse most effective, it must be combined with *triggered updates*. Triggered updates force a router to send an immediate broadcast when receiving bad news, instead of waiting for the next periodic broadcast. By sending an update immediately, a router minimizes the time it is vulnerable to believing good news.

Unfortunately, while triggered updates, poison reverse, hold down, and split horizon techniques all solve some problems, they introduce others. For example, consider what happens with triggered updates when many routers share a common network. A single broadcast may change all their routing tables, triggering a new round of broadcasts. If the second round of broadcasts changes tables, it will trigger even more broadcasts. A broadcast avalanche can result†.

The use of broadcast, potential for forwarding loops, and use of hold down to prevent slow convergence can make RIP extremely inefficient in a wide area network. Broadcasting always takes substantial bandwidth. Even if no avalanche problems occur, having all machines broadcast periodically means that the traffic increases as the number of routers increases. The potential for forwarding loops can also be deadly when line capacity is limited. Once lines become saturated by looping packets, it may be difficult or impossible for routers to exchange the routing messages needed to break the loops. Also, in a wide area network, hold down periods are so long that the timers used by higher-level protocols can expire and lead to broken connections.

15.6 RIP1 Message Format

RIP messages can be broadly classified into two types: routing information messages and messages used to request information. Both use the same format which consists of a fixed header followed by an optional list of network and distance pairs. Figure 15.5 shows the message format used with RIP version *1* (*RIP1*):

---

†To help avoid collisions on the underlying network, RIP requires each router to wait a small random time before sending a triggered update.

0	8	16	24	31

COMMAND (1-5)	VERSION (1)	MUST BE ZERO		
FAMILY OF NET 1		MUST BE ZERO		
IP ADDRESS OF NET 1				
MUST BE ZERO				
MUST BE ZERO				
DISTANCE TO NET 1				
FAMILY OF NET 2		MUST BE ZERO		
IP ADDRESS OF NET 2				
MUST BE ZERO				
MUST BE ZERO				
DISTANCE TO NET 2				
. . .				

Figure 15.5 The format of a version 1 RIP message. After the 32-bit header, the message contains a sequence of pairs, where each pair consists of a network IP address and an integer distance to that network.

In the figure, field *COMMAND* specifies an operation; only a few commands are used:

Command	Meaning
1	Request for partial or full routing information
2	Response containing network-distance pairs from sender's routing table
9	Update Request (used with demand circuits)
10	Update Response (used with demand circuits)
11	Update Acknowledge (used with demand circuits)

A router or host can ask another router for routing information by sending a *request* command. Routers can use the *response* command to reply to requests. In most cases, however, a router broadcasts unsolicited response messages periodically. Field *VERSION* contains the protocol version number (*1* in this case), and is used by the receiver to verify it will interpret the message correctly.

15.7 RIP2 Address Conventions

The generality of RIP is also evident in the way it transmits network addresses. The address format is not limited to use by TCP/IP; it can be used with multiple network protocol suites. As Figure 15.5 shows, each network address reported by RIP can have an address of up to 14 octets. Of course, IP addresses need only 4; RIP specifies that the remaining octets must be zero†. The field labeled *FAMILY OF NET i* identifies the protocol family under which the network address should be interpreted. RIP uses values assigned to address families under the 4BSD UNIX operating system (IP addresses are assigned value *2*).

In addition to normal IP addresses, RIP uses the convention that address *0.0.0.0* denotes a *default route*. RIP attaches a distance metric to every route it advertises, including default routes. Thus, it is possible to arrange for two routers to advertise a default route (e.g., a route to the rest of the internet) at different metrics, making one of them a primary path and the other a backup.

The final field of each entry in a RIP message, *DISTANCE TO NET i*, contains an integer count of the distance to the specified network. Distances are measured in router hops, but values are limited to the range *1* through *16*, with distance *16* used to signify infinity (i.e., no route exists).

15.8 RIP Route Interpretation And Aggregation

Because RIP was originally designed to be used with classful addresses, version 1 did not include any provision for a subnet mask. When subnet addressing was added to IP, version 1 of RIP was extended to permit routers to exchange subnetted addresses. However, because RIP1 update messages do not contain explicit mask information, an important restriction was added: a router can include host-specific or subnet-specific addresses in routing updates as long as all receivers can unambiguously interpret the addresses. In particular, subnet routes can only be included in updates sent across a network that is part of the subnetted prefix, and only if the subnet mask used with the network is the same as the subnet mask used with the address. In essence, the restriction means that RIP1 cannot be used to propagate variable-length subnet address or classless addresses. We can summarize:

Because it does not include explicit subnet information, RIP1 only permits a router to send subnet routes if receivers can unambiguously interpret the addresses according to the subnet mask they have available locally. As a consequence, RIP1 can only be used with classful or fixed-length subnet addresses.

---

†The designers chose to locate an IP address in the third through sixth octets of the address field to ensure 32-bit alignment.

What happens when a router running RIP1 connects to one or more networks that are subnets of a prefix N as well as to one or more networks that are not part of N? The router must prepare different update messages for the two types of interfaces. Updates sent over the interfaces that are subnets of N can include subnet routes, but updates sent over other interfaces cannot. Instead, when sending over other interfaces, the router is required to *aggregate* the subnet information and advertise a single route to network N.

15.9 RIP2 Extensions And Message Format

The restriction on address interpretation means that version 1 of RIP cannot be used to propagate either variable-length subnet addresses or the classless addresses used with CIDR. When version 2 of RIP (*RIP2*) was defined, the protocol was extended to include an explicit subnet mask along with each address, which means that version 2 can propagate arbitrary routing information. In addition, RIP2 updates include explicit next-hop information. That is, RIP2 reports the origin of each route, which means that RIP2 can prevent forwarding loops and the slow convergence problem from occurring.

To prevent RIP from increasing the CPU load of hosts unnecessarily, the designers allow RIP2 to multicast updates instead of broadcasting them. Furthermore, RIP2 is assigned a fixed multicast address, 224.0.0.9, which means that machines using RIP2 do not need to run IGMP†. Finally, the RIP2 multicast is restricted to a single network.

As a result of the features described above, the second version enhances the protocol significantly. It offers increased functionality, more efficient transport, and improved resistance to errors.

The message format used with RIP2 is an extension of the RIP1 format, with additional information occupying unused octets of the address field. In particular, each address includes an explicit next hop as well as an explicit subnet mask as Figure 15.6 illustrates.

RIP2 also attaches a 16-bit *ROUTE TAG* field to each entry. A router must send the same tag it receives when it transmits the route. Thus, the tag provides a way to propagate additional information such as the origin of the route. In particular, if RIP2 learns a route from another autonomous system, it can use the *ROUTE TAG* to propagate the autonomous system's number.

Because the version number in RIP2 occupies the same octet as in RIP1, both versions of the protocols can be used on a given router simultaneously without interference. Before processing an incoming message, RIP software examines the version number.

---

†Chapter 16 describes the *Internet Group Management Protocol*.

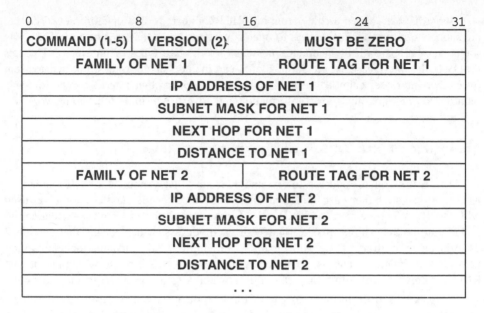

0	8	16	24	31
COMMAND (1-5)	VERSION (2)	MUST BE ZERO		
FAMILY OF NET 1		ROUTE TAG FOR NET 1		
IP ADDRESS OF NET 1				
SUBNET MASK FOR NET 1				
NEXT HOP FOR NET 1				
DISTANCE TO NET 1				
FAMILY OF NET 2		ROUTE TAG FOR NET 2		
IP ADDRESS OF NET 2				
SUBNET MASK FOR NET 2				
NEXT HOP FOR NET 2				
DISTANCE TO NET 2				
. . .				

Figure 15.6 The format of a RIP2 message. In addition to pairs of a network
IP address and an integer distance to that network, the message
contains a subnet mask for each address and explicit next-hop
information.

RIP messages do not contain an explicit length field or an explicit count of entries. Instead, RIP assumes that the underlying delivery mechanism will tell the receiver the length of an incoming message. In particular, when used with TCP/IP, RIP messages rely on UDP to tell the receiver the message length. RIP operates on UDP port *520*. Although a RIP request can originate at other UDP ports, the destination UDP port for requests is always *520*, as is the source port from which RIP broadcast messages originate.

15.10 The Disadvantage Of RIP Hop Counts

Using RIP as an interior router protocol limits routing in two ways. First, RIP restricts routing to a hop-count metric. Second, because it uses a small value of hop count for infinity, RIP restricts the size of any internet using it. In particular, RIP restricts the *span* of an internet (i.e., the maximum distance across) to 16. That is, an internet using RIP can have at most 15 routers between any two hosts.

Note that the limit on network span is neither a limit on the total number of routers nor a limit on density. In fact, most campus networks have a small span even if they have many routers because the topology is arranged as a *hierarchy*. Consider, for example, a typical corporate intranet. Most use a hierarchy that consists of a high-speed backbone network with multiple routers each connecting the backbone to a workgroup, where each workgroup occupies a single LAN. Although the corporation can include dozens of workgroups, the span of the entire intranet is only 2. Even if each workgroup is extended to include a router that connects one or more additional LANs, the maximum span only increases to 4. Similarly, extending the hierarchy one more level only increases the span to 6. Thus, the limit that RIP imposes affects large autonomous systems or autonomous systems that do not have a hierarchical organization.

Even in the best cases, however, hop counts provide only a crude measure of network capacity or responsiveness. Thus, using hop counts does not always yield routes with least delay or highest capacity. Furthermore, computing routes on the basis of minimum hop counts has the severe disadvantage that it makes routing relatively static because routes cannot respond to changes in network load. The next sections consider an alternative metric, and explain why hop count metrics remain popular despite their limitations.

15.11 Delay Metric (HELLO)

Although now obsolete, the HELLO protocol provides an example of an IGP that was once deployed in the Internet and uses a routing metric other than hop count. HELLO provided two functions: it synchronized the clocks among a set of routers, and it allowed each machine to compute shortest delay paths to destinations. Thus, each HELLO message carried timestamp information as well as routing information.

The basic idea behind HELLO is simple: use a distance-vector algorithm to propagate routing information. Instead of having routers report a hop count, however, HELLO reports an estimate of the delay to the destination. Having synchronized clocks allows a router to estimate delay for each arriving packet: before sending a packet, the sender places the current clock value in the packet, and the receiver subtracts the value from the current clock.

HELLO uses the standard distance-vector approach for update. When a message arrives from machine X, the receiver examines each entry in the message and changes the next hop to X if the route through X is less expensive than the current route (i.e., the delay to X plus the delay from X to the destination is less than the current delay to the destination).

15.12 Delay Metrics And Oscillation

It may seem that using delay as a routing metric would produce better routes than using a hop count. In fact, HELLO worked well in the early Internet backbone. However, there is an important reason why delay is not used as a metric in most protocols: instability.

Even if two paths have identical characteristics, any protocol that changes routes quickly can become unstable. Instability arises because delay, unlike hop counts, is not fixed. Minor variations in delay measurements occur because of hardware clock drift, CPU load during measurement, or bit delays caused by link-level synchronization. Thus, if a routing protocol reacts quickly to slight differences in delay, it can produce a two-stage oscillation effect in which traffic switches back and forth between the alternate paths. In the first stage, the router finds the delay on path *1* slightly less and abruptly switches traffic onto it. In the next round, the router finds that path *B* has slightly less delay and switches traffic back.

To help avoid oscillation, protocols that use delay implement several heuristics. First, they employ the *hold down* technique discussed previously to prevent routes from changing rapidly. Second, instead of measuring as accurately as possible and comparing the values directly, the protocols round measurements to large multiples or implement a minimum *threshold* by ignoring differences less than the threshold. Third, instead of comparing each individual delay measurement, they keep a running *average* of recent values or alternatively apply a *K-out-of-N* rule that requires at least *K* of the most recent *N* delay measurements be less than the current delay before the route can be changed.

Even with heuristics, protocols that use delay can become unstable when comparing delays on paths that do not have identical characteristics. To understand why, it is necessary to know that traffic can have a dramatic effect on delay. With no traffic, the network delay is simply the time required for the hardware to transfer bits from one point to another. As the traffic load imposed on the network increases, however, delays begin to rise because routers in the system need to enqueue packets that are waiting for transmission. If the load is even slightly more than 100% of the network capacity, the queue becomes unbounded, meaning that the effective delay becomes infinite. To summarize:

> *The effective delay across a network depends on traffic; as the load increases to 100% of the network capacity, delay grows rapidly.*

Because delays are extremely sensitive to changes in load, protocols that use delay as a metric can easily fall into a *positive feedback cycle*. The cycle is triggered by a small external change in load (e.g., one computer injecting a burst of additional traffic). The increased traffic raises the delay, which causes the protocol to change routes. However, because a route change affects the load, it can produce an even larger change in delays, which means the protocol will again recompute routes. As a result, protocols that use delay must contain mechanisms to dampen oscillation.

We described heuristics that can solve simple cases of route oscillation when paths have identical throughput characteristics and the load is not excessive. The heuristics can become ineffective, however, when alternative paths have different delay and throughput characteristics. As an example consider the delay on two paths: one over a satellite and the other over a low-capacity serial line (e.g., a 9600 baud serial line). In the first stage of the protocol when both paths are idle, the serial line will appear to have significantly lower delay than the satellite, and will be chosen for traffic. Because the serial line has low capacity, it will quickly become overloaded, and the delay will rise sharply. In the second stage, the delay on the serial line will be much greater than that of the satellite, so the protocol will switch traffic away from the overloaded path. Because the satellite path has large capacity, traffic which overloaded the serial line does not impose a significant load on the satellite, meaning that the delay on the satellite path does not change with traffic. In the next round, the delay on the unloaded serial line will once again appear to be much smaller than the delay on the satellite path. The protocol will reverse the routing, and the cycle will continue. Such oscillations do, in fact, occur in practice. As the example shows, they are difficult to manage because traffic which has little effect on one network can overload another.

15.13 Combining RIP, Hello, And BGP

We have already observed that a single router may use both an Interior Gateway Protocol to gather routing information within its autonomous system and an Exterior Gateway Protocol to advertise routes to other autonomous systems. In principle, it should be easy to construct a single piece of software that combines the two protocols, making it possible to gather routes and advertise them without human intervention. In practice, technical and political obstacles make doing so complex.

Technically, IGP protocols, like RIP and Hello, are routing protocols. A router uses such protocols to update its routing table based on information it acquires from other routers inside its autonomous system. Thus, *routed*, the UNIX program that implements RIP, advertises information from the local routing table and changes the local routing table when it receives updates. RIP trusts routers within the same autonomous system to pass correct data.

In contrast, exterior protocols such as BGP do not trust routers in other autonomous systems. Consequently, exterior protocols do not advertise all possible routes from the local routing table. Instead, such protocols keep a database of network reachability, and apply policy constraints when sending or receiving information. Ignoring such policy constraints can affect routing in a larger sense — some parts of the Internet can be become unreachable. For example, if a router in an autonomous system that is running RIP happens to propagate a low-cost route to a network at Purdue University when it has no such route, other routers running RIP will accept and install the route. They will then pass Purdue traffic to the router that made the error. As a result, it may be impossible for hosts in that autonomous system to reach Purdue. The problem becomes more serious if Exterior Gateway Protocols do not implement policy constraints. For example, if a border router in the autonomous system uses BGP to propagate the illegal route to other autonomous systems, the network at Purdue may become unreachable from some parts of the Internet.

15.14 Gated: Inter-Autonomous System Communication

A mechanism has been created to provide an interface between autonomous systems. Known as *gated*†, the mechanism understands multiple protocols (both IGPs and BGP), and ensures that policy constraints are honored. For example, *gated* can accept RIP messages and modify the local computer's routing table just like the *routed* program. It can also advertise routes from within its autonomous system using BGP. The rules *gated* follows allow a system administrator to specify exactly which networks *gated* may and may not advertise and how to report distances to those networks. Thus, although *gated* is not an IGP, it plays an important role in routing because it demonstrates that it is feasible to build an automated mechanism linking an IGP with BGP without sacrificing protection.

Gated has an interesting history. It was originally created by Mark Fedor at Cornell, and was adopted by MERIT for use with the NSFNET backbone. Academic researchers contributed new ideas, an industry consortium was formed, and eventually, MERIT sold *gated* to Nexthop.

Gated performs another useful task by implementing metric transformations. Thus, it is possible and convenient to use *gated* between two autonomous systems as well as on the boundary between two groups of routers that each participate in an IGP.

15.15 The Open SPF Protocol (OSPF)

In Chapter 13, we said that a link state routing algorithm, which uses SPF to compute shortest paths, scales better than a distance-vector algorithm. To encourage the adoption of link state technology, a working group of the IETF designed an interior gateway protocol that uses the link state algorithm. Called *Open SPF (OSPF)*, the protocol tackles several ambitious goals.

• As the name implies, the specification is available in the published literature. Making it an open standard that anyone can implement without paying license fees has encouraged many vendors to support OSPF. Consequently, it has become a popular replacement for proprietary protocols.

• OSPF includes *type of service routing*. Managers can install multiple routes to a given destination, one for each priority or type of service. When routing a datagram, a router running OSPF uses both the destination address and type of service field in an IP header to choose a route. OSPF is among the first TCP/IP protocols to offer type of service routing.

• OSPF provides *load balancing*. If a manager specifies multiple routes to a given destination at the same cost, OSPF distributes traffic over all routes equally. Again, OSPF is among the first open IGPs to offer load balancing; protocols like RIP compute a single route to each destination.

---

†The name *gated* is pronounced "gate d" from "gate daemon."

• To permit growth and make the networks at a site easier to manage, OSPF allows a site to partition its networks and routers into subsets called *areas*. Each area is self-contained; knowledge of an area's topology remains hidden from other areas. Thus, multiple groups within a given site can cooperate in the use of OSPF for routing even though each group retains the ability to change its internal network topology independently.

• The OSPF protocol specifies that all exchanges between routers can be *authenticated*. OSPF allows a variety of authentication schemes, and even allows one area to choose a different scheme than another area. The idea behind authentication is to guarantee that only trusted routers propagate routing information. To understand why this could be a problem, consider what can happen when using RIP1, which has no authentication. If a malicious person uses a personal computer to propagate RIP messages advertising low-cost routes, other routers and hosts running RIP will change their routes and start sending datagrams to the personal computer.

• OSPF includes support for host-specific, subnet-specific, and classless routes as well as classful network-specific routes. All types may be needed in a large internet.

• To accommodate multi-access networks like Ethernet, OSPF extends the SPF algorithm described in Chapter 13. We described the algorithm using a point-to-point graph and said that each router running SPF would periodically broadcast link status messages about each reachable neighbor. If K routers attach to an Ethernet, they will broadcast K^2 reachability messages. OSPF reduces broadcasting by allowing a more complex graph topology in which each node represents either a router or a network. Consequently, OSPF allows every multi-access network to have a *designated gateway* (i.e., a *designated router*) that sends link status messages on behalf of all routers attached to the network; the messages report the status of all links from the network to routers attached to the network.

• To reduce the load on nonparticipating systems, OSPF uses hardware multicast capabilities, where they exist, to deliver link status messages. Interestingly, OSPF sends messages via IP multicast, and allows the IP multicast mechanism to map the multicast into the underlying network. Furthermore, to eliminate the need for IGMP, two IP multicast addresses are preassigned: 224.0.0.5 for all routers and 224.0.0.6 for all designated routers. To avoid OSPF messages traveling beyond the local network, routers are configured to prohibit forwarding of datagrams sent to either address.

• To permit maximum flexibility, OSPF allows managers to describe a virtual network topology that abstracts away from the details of physical connections. For example, a manager can configure a virtual link between two routers in the routing graph even if the physical connection between the two routers requires communication across a transit network.

• OSPF allows routers to exchange routing information learned from other (external) sites. Basically, one or more routers with connections to other sites learn information about the sites and include it when sending update messages. The message format distinguishes between information acquired from external sources and information acquired from routers interior to the site, so there is no ambiguity about the source or reliability of routes.

15.15.1 OSPF Message Format

Each OSPF message begins with a fixed, 24-octet header as Figure 15.7 shows:

0	8	16	24	31
VERSION	TYPE	MESSAGE LENGTH		
SOURCE ROUTER IP ADDRESS				
AREA ID				
CHECKSUM		AUTHENTICATION TYPE		
AUTHENTICATION (octets 0-3)				
AUTHENTICATION (octets 4-7)				

Figure 15.7 The fixed 24-octet OSPF message header.

Field *VERSION* specifies the version of the protocol. Field *TYPE* identifies the message type as one of:

Type	Meaning
1	Hello (used to test reachability)
2	Database description (topology)
3	Link status request
4	Link status update
5	Link status acknowledgement

The field labeled *SOURCE ROUTER IP ADDRESS* gives the address of the sender, and the field labeled *AREA ID* gives the 32-bit identification number of the area.

Because each message can include authentication, field *AUTHENTICATION TYPE* specifies which authentication scheme is used (currently, *0* means no authentication and *1* means a simple password is used).

15.15.2 OSPF Hello Message Format

OSPF sends *hello* messages on each link periodically to establish and test neighbor reachability. Figure 15.8 shows the format. Field *NETWORK MASK* contains a mask for the network over which the message has been sent (see Chapter 9 for details about masks). Field *ROUTER DEAD INTERVAL* gives a time in seconds after which a non-responding neighbor is considered dead. Field *HELLO INTERVAL* is the normal period, in seconds, between hello messages. Field *GWAY PRIO* is the integer priority of this router, and is used in selecting a backup designated router. The fields labeled *DESIGNATED ROUTER* and *BACKUP DESIGNATED ROUTER* contain IP addresses that give the sender's view of the designated router and backup designated router for the network over which the message is sent. Finally, fields labeled *NEIGHBOR$_i$ IP ADDRESS* give the IP addresses of all neighbors from which the sender has recently received hello messages.

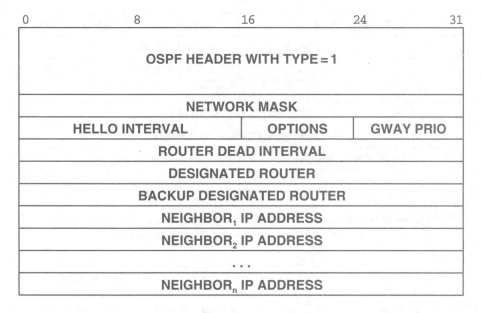

Figure 15.8 OSPF *hello* message format. A pair of neighbor routers exchanges these messages periodically to test reachability.

15.15.3 OSPF Database Description Message Format

Routers exchange OSPF *database description* messages to initialize their network topology database. In the exchange, one router serves as a master, while the other is a slave. The slave acknowledges each database description message with a response. Figure 15.9 shows the format.

Because it can be large, the topology database may be divided into several messages using the *I* and *M* bits. Bit *I* is set to 1 in the initial message; bit *M* is set to 1 if additional messages follow. Bit *S* indicates whether a message was sent by a master (1) or by a slave (0). Field *DATABASE SEQUENCE NUMBER* numbers messages sequentially so the receiver can tell if one is missing. The initial message contains a random integer *R*; subsequent messages contain sequential integers starting at *R*.

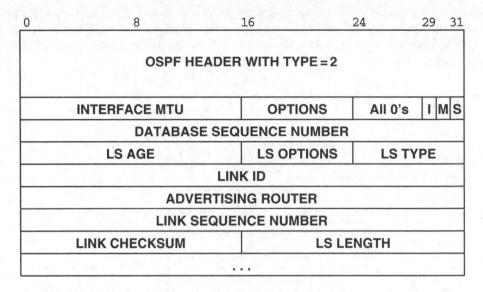

Figure 15.9 OSPF *database description* message format. The fields starting at *LS AGE* are repeated for each link being specified.

Field *INTERFACE MTU* gives the size of the largest IP datagram that can be transmitted over the interface without fragmentation. The fields from *LS AGE* through *LS LENGTH* describe one link in the network topology; they are repeated for each link. The *LS TYPE* describes a link according to the following table.

LS Type	Meaning
1	Router link
2	Network link
3	Summary link (IP network)
4	Summary link (link to border router)
5	External link (link to another site)

Field *LINK ID* gives an identification for the link (which can be the IP address of a router or a network, depending on the link type).

Field *LS AGE* helps order messages — it gives the time in seconds since the link was established. Field *ADVERTISING ROUTER* specifies the address of the router advertising this link, and *LINK SEQUENCE NUMBER* contains an integer generated by that router to ensure that messages are not missed or received out of order. Field *LINK CHECKSUM* provides further assurance that the link information has not been corrupted.

15.15.4 OSPF Link Status Request Message Format

After exchanging database description messages with a neighbor, a router may discover that parts of its database are out of date. To request that the neighbor supply updated information, the router sends a *link status request* message. The message lists specific links as shown in Figure 15.10. The neighbor responds with the most current information it has about those links. The three fields shown are repeated for each link about which status is requested. More than one request message may be needed if the list of requests is long.

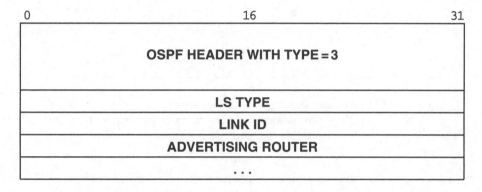

Figure 15.10 OSPF *link status request* message format. A router sends this message to a neighbor to request current information about a specific set of links.

15.15.5 OSPF Link Status Update Message Format

Routers broadcast the status of links with a *link status update* message. Each update consists of a list of advertisements, as Figure 15.11 shows.

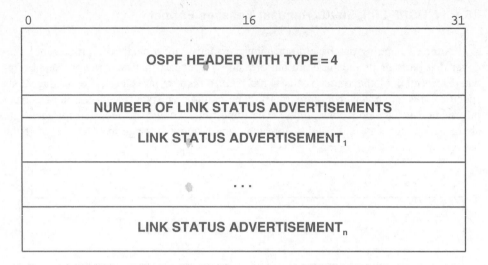

0   16   31

| OSPF HEADER WITH TYPE = 4 |
| NUMBER OF LINK STATUS ADVERTISEMENTS |
| LINK STATUS ADVERTISEMENT$_1$ |
| . . . |
| LINK STATUS ADVERTISEMENT$_n$ |

Figure 15.11 OSPF *link status update* message format. A router sends such a message to broadcast information about its directly connected links to all other routers.

Each link status advertisement has a header format as shown in Figure 15.12. The values used in each field are the same as in the database description message.

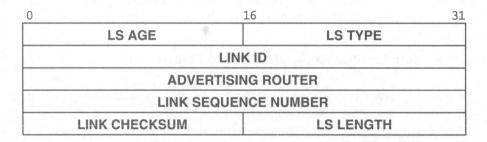

0   16   31

LS AGE	LS TYPE
LINK ID	
ADVERTISING ROUTER	
LINK SEQUENCE NUMBER	
LINK CHECKSUM	LS LENGTH

Figure 15.12 The format of the header used for all link status advertisements.

Following the link status header comes one of four possible formats to describe the links from a router to a given area, the links from a router to a specific network, the links from a router to the physical networks that constitute a single, subnetted IP network (see Chapter 9), or the links from a router to networks at other sites. In all cases, the *LS TYPE* field in the link status header specifies which of the formats has been used. Thus, a router that receives a link status update message knows exactly which of the described destinations lie inside the site and which are external.

15.16 Routing With Partial Information

We began our discussion of internet router architecture and routing by discussing the concept of partial information. Hosts can route with only partial information because they rely on routers. It should be clear now that not all routers have complete information. Most autonomous systems have a single router that connects the autonomous system to other autonomous systems. For example, if the site connects to the global Internet, at least one router must have a connection that leads from the site to an ISP. Routers within the autonomous system know about destinations within that autonomous system, but they use a default route to send all other traffic to the ISP.

How to do routing with partial information becomes obvious if we examine a router's routing tables. Routers at the center of the Internet have a complete set of routes to all possible destinations; such routers do not use default routing. Routers beyond those in ISPs at the center of the Internet do not usually have a complete set of routes; they rely on a default route to handle network addresses they do not understand.

Using default routes for most routers has two consequences. First, it means that local routing errors can go undetected. For example, if a machine in an autonomous system incorrectly routes a packet to an external autonomous system instead of to a local router, the external system will route it back (perhaps to a different entry point). Thus, connectivity may appear to be preserved even if routing is incorrect. The problem may not seem severe for small autonomous systems that have high-speed local area networks, but in a wide area network, incorrect routes can be disastrous. Second, on the positive side, using default routes whenever possible means that the routing update messages exchanged by most routers will be much smaller than they would be if complete information were included.

15.17 Summary

Managers must choose how to pass routing information among the local routers within an autonomous system. Manual maintenance of routing information suffices only for small, slowly changing internets that have minimal interconnection; most require automated procedures that discover and update routes automatically. Two routers under the control of a single manager run an Interior Gateway Protocol, IGP, to exchange routing information.

An IGP implements either the distance-vector algorithm or the link state algorithm, which is known by the name Shortest Path First (SPF). We examined three specific IGPs: RIP, HELLO, and OSPF. RIP, a distance-vector protocol implemented by the UNIX program *routed*, is among the most popular. It uses split horizon, hold-down, and poison reverse techniques to help eliminate forwarding loops and the problem of counting to infinity. Although it is obsolete, Hello is interesting because it illustrates a distance-vector protocol that uses delay instead of hop counts as a distance metric. We discussed the disadvantages of using delay as a routing metric, and pointed out that although heuristics can prevent instabilities from arising when paths have equal throughput characteristics, long-term instabilities arise when paths have different characteristics. Finally, OSPF is a protocol that implements the link status algorithm.

We saw that the *gated* program provides a platform for the development of an interface between an Interior Gateway Protocol like RIP and the Exterior Gateway Protocol, BGP, automating the process of gathering routes from within an autonomous system and advertising them to another autonomous system.

FOR FURTHER STUDY

Hedrick [RFC 1058] discusses algorithms for exchanging routing information in general and contains the standard specification for RIP1. Malkin [RFC 2453] gives the standard for RIP2. The HELLO protocol is documented in Mills [RFC 891]. Mills and Braun [1987] considers the problems of converting between delay and hop-count metrics. Moy [RFC 1583] contains the lengthy specification of OSPF as well as a discussion of the motivation behind it; Moy [RFC 2328] documents OSPF version 2. Fedor [June 1988] describes *gated*.

EXERCISES

15.1   What network families does RIP support? Hint: read the networking section of the 4.3 BSD UNIX Programmer's Manual.

15.2   Consider a large autonomous system using an interior router protocol like HELLO that bases routes on delay. What difficulty does this autonomous system have if a subgroup decides to use RIP on its routers?

15.3   Within a RIP message, each IP address is aligned on a 32-bit boundary. Will such addresses be aligned on a 32-bit boundary if the IP datagram carrying the message starts on a 32-bit boundary?

15.4   An autonomous system can be as small as a single local area network or as large as multiple long haul networks. Why does the variation in size make it difficult to find a standard IGP?

15.5   Characterize the circumstances under which the split horizon technique will prevent slow convergence.

15.6   Consider an internet composed of many local area networks running RIP as an IGP. Find an example that shows how a forwarding loop can result even if the code uses ''hold down'' after receiving information that a network is unreachable.

15.7   Should a host ever run RIP in active mode? Why or why not?

15.8   Under what circumstances will a hop count metric produce better routes than a metric that uses delay?

15.9 Can you imagine a situation in which an autonomous system chooses *not* to advertise all its networks? Hint: think of a university.

15.10 In broad terms, we could say that RIP distributes the local routing table, while BGP distributes a table of networks and routers used to reach them (i.e., a router can send a BGP advertisement that does not exactly match items in its own routing table). What are the advantages of each approach?

15.11 Consider a function used to convert between delay and hop-count metrics. Can you find properties of such functions that are sufficient to prevent forwarding loops. Are your properties necessary as well? (Hint: look at Mills and Braun [1987].)

15.12 Are there circumstances under which an SPF protocol can form forwarding loops? Hint: think of best-effort delivery.

15.13 Build an application program that sends a request to a router running RIP and displays the routes returned.

15.14 Read the RIP specification carefully. Can routes reported in a response to a query differ from the routes reported by a routing update message? If so how?

15.15 Consider a site that uses variable length subnets. Show that RIP2 is needed for correct propagation of routes (i.e., find a case where RIP2 works, but RIP1 fails to work correctly).

15.16 Read the OSPF specification carefully. How can a manager use the virtual link facility?

15.17 OSPF allows managers to assign many of their own identifiers, possibly leading to duplication of values at multiple sites. Which identifier(s) may need to change if two sites running OSPF decide to merge?

15.18 Compare the version of OSPF available under 4BSD UNIX to the version of RIP for the same system. What are the differences in source code size? Object code size? Data storage size? What can you conclude?

15.19 Can you use ICMP redirect messages to pass routing information among *interior* routers? Why or why not?

15.20 Write a program that takes as input a description of your organization's internet, uses RIP queries to obtain routes from the routers, and reports any inconsistencies.

15.21 If your organization runs software such as *Zebra* that manages multiple TCP/IP routing protocols, obtain a copy of the configuration files and explain the meaning of each item.

Chapter Contents

16

Internet Multicasting

16.1 Introduction

Earlier chapters define the mechanisms IP uses to deliver unicast datagrams. This chapter explores another feature of IP: multipoint delivery of datagrams. We begin with a brief review of the underlying hardware support. Later sections describe IP addressing for multipoint delivery and protocols that routers use to propagate the necessary routing information.

16.2 Hardware Broadcast

Many hardware technologies contain mechanisms to send packets to multiple destinations simultaneously (or nearly simultaneously). Chapter 2 reviews several technologies and discusses the most common form of multipoint delivery: *broadcasting*. Broadcast delivery means that the network delivers one copy of a packet to each destination. On bus technologies like Ethernet, broadcast delivery can be accomplished with a single packet transmission. On networks composed of switches with point-to-point connections, software must implement broadcasting by forwarding copies of the packet across individual connections until all switches have received a copy.

With most hardware technologies, a computer specifies broadcast delivery by sending a packet to a special, reserved destination address called the *broadcast address*. For example, Ethernet hardware addresses consist of 48-bit identifiers, with the all 1s address used to denote broadcast. Hardware on each machine recognizes the machine's hardware address as well as the broadcast address, and accepts incoming packets that have either address as their destination.

The chief disadvantage of broadcasting arises from its demand on resources — in addition to using network bandwidth, each broadcast consumes computational resources on all machines. For example, it would be possible to design an alternative internet protocol suite that used broadcast to deliver datagrams on a local network and relied on IP software to discard datagrams not intended for the local machine. However, such a scheme would be extremely inefficient because all computers on the network would receive and process every datagram, even though a machine would discard most of the datagrams that arrived. Thus, the designers of TCP/IP used unicast addressing and address binding mechanisms like ARP to eliminate broadcast delivery.

16.3 Hardware Origins Of Multicast

Some hardware technologies support a second, less common form of multi-point delivery called *multicasting*. Unlike broadcasting, multicasting allows each system to choose whether it wants to participate in a given multicast. Typically, a hardware technology reserves a large set of addresses for use with multicast. When a group of machines want to communicate, they choose one particular *multicast address* to use for communication. After configuring their network interface hardware to recognize the selected multicast address, all machines in the group will receive a copy of any packet sent to that multicast address.

At a conceptual level, multicast addressing can be viewed as a generalization of all other address forms. For example, we can think of a conventional *unicast address* as a form of multicast addressing in which there is exactly one computer in the multicast group. Similarly, we can think of directed broadcast addressing as a form of multicasting in which all computers on a particular network are members of the multicast group. Other multicast addresses can correspond to arbitrary sets of machines.

Despite its apparent generality, multicasting cannot replace conventional forms of addressing because there is a fundamental difference in the underlying mechanisms that implement forwarding and delivery. Unicast and broadcast addresses identify a computer or a set of computers attached to one physical segment, so forwarding depends on the network topology. A multicast address identifies an arbitrary set of listeners, so the forwarding mechanism must propagate the packet to all segments. For example, consider two LAN segments connected by an adaptive bridge that has learned host addresses. If a host on segment *1* sends a unicast frame to another host on segment *1*, the bridge will not forward the frame to segment *2*. If a host uses a multicast address, however, the bridge will forward the frame. Thus, we can conclude:

> *Although it may help us to think of multicast addressing as a generalization that subsumes unicast and broadcast addresses, the underlying forwarding and delivery mechanisms can make multicast less efficient.*

16.4 Ethernet Multicast

Ethernet provides a good example of hardware multicasting. One-half of the Ethernet addresses are reserved for multicast — the low-order bit of the high-order octet distinguishes conventional unicast addresses (*0*) from multicast addresses (*1*). In dashed hexadecimal notation†, the multicast bit is given by:

$$01\text{-}00\text{-}00\text{-}00\text{-}00\text{-}00_{16}$$

When an Ethernet interface board is initialized, it begins accepting packets destined for either the computer's hardware address or the Ethernet broadcast address. However, device driver software can reconfigure the device to allow it to also recognize one or more multicast addresses. For example, suppose the driver configures the Ethernet multicast address:

$$01\text{-}5E\text{-}00\text{-}00\text{-}00\text{-}01_{16}$$

After the configuration, an interface will accept any packet sent to the computer's unicast address, the broadcast address, or that one multicast address (the hardware will continue to ignore packets sent to other multicast addresses). The next sections explain both how IP uses basic multicast hardware and the special meaning of the multicast address

16.5 IP Multicast

IP multicasting is the internet abstraction of hardware multicasting. It follows the paradigm of allowing transmission to a subset of host computers, but generalizes the concept to allow the subset to spread across arbitrary physical networks throughout an internet. In IP terminology, a given subset is known as a *multicast group*. IP multicasting has the following general characteristics:

- *Group Address.* Each multicast group is a unique class *D* address. A few IP multicast addresses are permanently assigned by the Internet authority, and correspond to groups that always exist even if they have no current members. Other addresses are temporary, and are available for private use.

- *Number Of Groups.* IP provides addresses for up to 2^{28} simultaneous multicast groups. Thus, the number of groups is limited by practical constraints on routing table size rather than addressing.

- *Dynamic Group Membership.* A host can join or leave an IP multicast group at any time. Furthermore, a host may be a member of an arbitrary number of multicast groups.

---

†Dashed hexadecimal notation represents each octet as two hexadecimal digits with octets separated by a dash; the subscript *16* can be omitted only when the context is unambiguous.

- *Use Of Hardware.* If the underlying network hardware supports multicast, IP uses hardware multicast to send IP multicast. If the hardware does not support multicast, IP uses broadcast or unicast to deliver IP multicast.

- *Inter-network Forwarding.* Because members of an IP multicast group can attach to multiple physical networks, special *multicast routers* are required to forward IP multicast; the capability is usually added to conventional routers.

- *Delivery Semantics.* IP multicast uses the same best-effort delivery semantics as other IP datagram delivery, meaning that multicast datagrams can be lost, delayed, duplicated, or delivered out of order.

- *Membership And Transmission.* An arbitrary host may send datagrams to any multicast group; group membership is only used to determine whether the host receives datagrams sent to the group.

16.6 The Conceptual Pieces

Three conceptual pieces are required for a general purpose internet multicasting system:

1. A multicast addressing scheme
2. An effective notification and delivery mechanism
3. An efficient internetwork forwarding facility

Many goals, details, and constraints present challenges for an overall design. For example, in addition to providing sufficient addresses for many groups, the multicast *addressing scheme* must accommodate two conflicting goals: allow local autonomy in assigning addresses, while defining addresses that have meaning globally. Similarly, hosts need a *notification mechanism* to inform routers about multicast groups in which they are participating, and routers need a *delivery mechanism* to transfer multicast packets to hosts. Again there are two possibilities: we desire a system that makes effective use of hardware multicast when it is available, but also allows IP multicast delivery over networks that do not have hardware support for multicast. Finally a multicast *forwarding facility* presents the biggest design challenge of the three: our goal is a scheme that is both efficient and dynamic — it should forward multicast packets along the shortest paths, should not send a copy of a datagram along a path if the path does not lead to a member of the group, and should allow hosts to join and leave groups at any time.

IP multicasting includes all three aspects. It defines IP multicast addressing, specifies how hosts send and receive multicast datagrams, and describes the protocol routers use to determine multicast group membership on a network. The remainder of the chapter considers each aspect in more detail, beginning with addressing.

16.7 IP Multicast Addresses

We said that IP multicast addresses are divided into two types: those that are permanently assigned and those that are available for temporary use. Permanent addresses are called *well-known*; they are used for major services on the global Internet as well as for infrastructure maintenance (e.g., multicast routing protocols). Other multicast addresses correspond to *transient multicast groups* that are created when needed and discarded when the count of group members reaches zero.

Like hardware multicasting, IP multicasting uses the datagram's destination address to specify that a particular datagram must be delivered via multicast. IP reserves class *D* addresses for multicast; they have the form shown in Figure 16.1.

Figure 16.1 The format of class D IP addresses used for multicasting. Bits *4* through *31* identify a particular multicast group.

The first *4* bits contain *1110* and identify the address as a multicast. The remaining *28* bits specify a particular multicast group. There is no further structure in the group bits. In particular, the group field is not partitioned into bits that identify the origin or owner of the group, nor does it contain administrative information such as whether all members of the group are on one physical network.

When expressed in dotted decimal notation, multicast addresses range from

224.0.0.0   through   239.255.255.255

Many parts of the address space have been assigned special meaning. For example, the lowest address, 224.0.0.0, is reserved; it cannot be assigned to any group. Address 224.0.0.1 is permanently assigned to the *all systems group*, and address 224.0.0.2 is permanently assigned to the *all routers group*. The *all systems* group includes all hosts and routers on a network that are participating in IP multicast, whereas the *all routers* group includes only the routers that are participating. Both of these groups are used for control protocols, and must be on the same local network as the sender; there are no IP multicast addresses that refer to all systems in the Internet or all routers in the Internet. Furthermore, the remaining addresses up through 224.0.0.255 are restricted to a single network (i.e., a router is prohibited from forwarding a datagram sent to any address in the range, and a sender is supposed to set the TTL to 1). Typically, multicast routing protocols use such addresses. Figure 16.2 shows a few examples of permanently assigned addresses†.

---

†In addition to the examples, it has also been proposed that multicast addresses in 233.0.0.0/8 be reserved for intra-autonomous system multicast.

Address	Meaning
224.0.0.0	Base Address (Reserved)
224.0.0.1	All Systems on this Subnet
224.0.0.2	All Routers on this Subnet
224.0.0.3	Unassigned
224.0.0.4	DVMRP Routers
224.0.0.5	OSPFIGP All Routers
224.0.0.6	OSPFIGP Designated Routers
224.0.0.7	ST Routers
224.0.0.8	ST Hosts
224.0.0.9	RIP2 Routers
224.0.0.10	IGRP Routers
224.0.0.11	Mobile-Agents
224.0.0.12	DHCP Server / Relay Agent
224.0.0.13	All PIM Routers
224.0.0.14	RSVP-Encapsulation
224.0.0.15	All-CBT-Routers
224.0.0.16	Designated-Sbm
224.0.0.17	All-Sbms
224.0.0.18 through 224.0.0.255	VRRP Other Link Local Addresses
224.0.1.0 through 238.255.255.255	Globally Scoped Addresses
239.0.0.0 through 239.255.255.255	Scope restricted to one organization

Figure 16.2 Examples of a few permanent IP multicast address assignments. Many other addresses have specific meanings.

16.8 Multicast Address Semantics

IP treats multicast addresses differently than unicast addresses. For example, a multicast address can only be used as a destination address. Thus, a multicast address can never appear in the source address field of a datagram, nor can it appear in a source route or record route option. Furthermore, no ICMP error messages can be generated about multicast datagrams (e.g., destination unreachable, source quench, echo reply, or time exceeded). Thus, a ping sent to a multicast address will go unanswered.

The rule prohibiting ICMP errors is somewhat surprising because IP routers do honor the time-to-live field in the header of a multicast datagram. As usual, each router decrements the count, and discards the datagram (without sending an ICMP message) if the count reaches zero. We will see that some protocols use the time-to-live count as a way to limit datagram propagation.

16.9 Mapping IP Multicast To Ethernet Multicast

Although the IP multicast standard does not cover all types of network hardware, it does specify how to map an IP multicast address to an Ethernet multicast address. The mapping is efficient and easy to understand:

> *To map an IP multicast address to the corresponding Ethernet multicast address, place the low-order 23 bits of the IP multicast address into the low-order 23 bits of the special Ethernet multicast address $01\text{-}00\text{-}5E\text{-}00\text{-}00\text{-}00_{16}$.*

For example, IP multicast address 224.0.0.2 becomes Ethernet multicast address $01\text{-}00\text{-}5E\text{-}00\text{-}00\text{-}02_{16}$.

Interestingly, the mapping is not unique. Because IP multicast addresses have 28 significant bits that identify the multicast group, more than one multicast group may map onto the same Ethernet multicast address at the same time. The designers chose this scheme as a compromise. On one hand, using 23 of the 28 bits for a hardware address means most of the multicast address is included. The set of addresses is large enough so the chances of two groups choosing addresses with all low-order 23 bits identical is small. On the other hand, arranging for IP to use a fixed part of the Ethernet multicast address space makes debugging much easier and eliminates interference between IP and other protocols that share an Ethernet. The consequence of this design is that some multicast datagrams may be received at a host that are not destined for that host. Thus, the IP software must carefully check addresses on all incoming datagrams, and discard any unwanted multicast datagrams.

16.10 Hosts And Multicast Delivery

We said that IP multicasting can be used on a single physical network or throughout an internet. In the former case, a host can send directly to a destination host merely by placing the datagram in a frame and using a hardware multicast address to which the receiver is listening. In the latter case, special *multicast routers* forward multicast datagrams among networks, so a host must send the datagram to a multicast router. Surprisingly, a host does not need to install a route to a multicast router, nor does the host's default route need to specify one. Instead, the technique a host uses to forward a multicast datagram to a router is unlike the routing lookup used for unicast and broadcast datagrams — the host merely uses the local network hardware's multicast capability to transmit the datagram. Multicast routers listen for all IP multicast transmissions; if a multicast router is present on the network, it will receive the datagram and forward it on to another network if necessary. Thus, the primary difference between local and nonlocal multicast lies in multicast routers, not in hosts.

16.11 Multicast Scope

The *scope* of a multicast group refers to the range of group members. If all members are on the same physical network, we say that the group's scope is restricted to one network. Similarly, if all members of a group lie within a single organization, we say that the group has a scope limited to one organization.

In addition to the group's scope, each multicast datagram has a scope which is defined to be the set of networks over which a given multicast datagram will be propagated. Informally, a datagram's scope is referred to as its *range*.

IP uses two techniques to control multicast scope. The first technique relies on the datagram's *time-to-live* (*TTL*) field to control its range. By setting the TTL to a small value, a host can limit the distance the datagram will be forwarded. For example, the standard specifies that control messages, which are used for communication between a host and a router on the same network, must have a TTL of 1. As a consequence, a router never forwards any datagram carrying control information because the TTL expires causing the router to discard the datagram. Similarly, if two applications running on a single host want to use IP multicast for interprocess communication (e.g., for testing software), they can choose a TTL value of 0 to prevent the datagram from leaving the host. It is possible to use successively larger values of the TTL field to further extend the notion of scope. For example, some router vendors suggest configuring routers at a site to restrict multicast datagrams from leaving the site unless the datagram has a TTL greater than 15. We conclude that it is possible to use the TTL field in a datagram header to provide coarse-grain control over the datagram's scope.

Known as *administrative scoping*, the second technique used to control scope consists of reserving parts of the address space for groups that are local to a given site or local to a given organization. According to the standard, routers in the Internet are forbidden from forwarding any datagram that has an address chosen from the restricted space. Thus, to prevent multicast communication among group members from accidentally reaching outsiders, an organization can assign the group an address that has local scope.

16.12 Extending Host Software To Handle Multicasting

A host can participate in IP multicast at one of three levels as Figure 16.3 shows:

Level	Meaning
0	Host can neither send nor receive IP multicast
1	Host can send but not receive IP multicast
2	Host can both send and receive IP multicast

Figure 16.3 The three levels of host participation in IP multicast.

Modifications that allow a host to send IP multicast are not difficult; extending host software to receive IP multicast datagrams is more complex. To send a multicast datagram, an application must be able to supply a multicast address as a destination. To receive multicast, an application must be able to declare that it wants to join or leave a particular multicast group, and protocol software must forward a copy of an arriving datagram to each application that joined the group. Furthermore, as we will see in later sections, the host must run a protocol that informs the local multicast routers of its group membership status. Much of the complexity comes from a basic idea:

> *Hosts join specific IP multicast groups on specific networks.*

That is, a host with multiple network connections may join a particular multicast group on one network and not on another. To understand the reason for keeping group membership associated with networks, remember that it is possible to use IP multicasting among local sets of machines. The host may want to use a multicast application to interact with machines on one physical net, but not with machines on another.

Because group membership is associated with particular networks, the software must keep separate lists of multicast addresses for each network to which the machine attaches. Furthermore, an application program must specify a particular network when it asks to join or leave a multicast group.

16.13 Internet Group Management Protocol

To participate in IP multicast on a local network, a host must have software that allows it to send and receive multicast datagrams. To participate in a multicast that spans multiple networks, the host must inform local multicast routers. The local routers contact other multicast routers, passing on the membership information and establishing routes. We will see later that the concept is similar to conventional route propagation among internet routers.

Before a multicast router can propagate multicast membership information, it must determine that one or more hosts on the local network have decided to join a multicast group. To do so, multicast routers and hosts that implement multicast must use the *Internet Group Management Protocol* (*IGMP*) to communicate group membership information. Because the current version is *3*, the protocol described here is officially known as *IGMPv3*.

IGMP is analogous to ICMP†. Like ICMP, it uses IP datagrams to carry messages. Also like ICMP, it provides a service used by IP. Therefore,

Although IGMP uses IP datagrams to carry messages, we think of it as an integral part of IP, not a separate protocol.

Furthermore, IGMP is a standard for TCP/IP; it is required on all machines that receive IP multicast (i.e., all hosts and routers that participate at level *2*).

Conceptually, IGMP has two phases. Phase 1: When a host joins a new multicast group, it sends an IGMP message to the group's multicast address declaring its membership. Local multicast routers receive the message, and establish necessary routing by propagating the group membership information to other multicast routers throughout the internet. Phase 2: Because membership is dynamic, local multicast routers periodically poll hosts on the local network to determine whether any hosts still remain members of each group. If any host responds for a given group, the router keeps the group active. If no host reports membership in a group after several polls, the multicast router assumes that none of the hosts on the network remain in the group, and stops advertising group membership to other multicast routers.

To further complicate group membership, IGMP permits an application on a host to install a *source address filter* that specifies whether the host should include or exclude multicast traffic from a given source address. Thus, it is possible to join a multicast group, but to exclude datagrams sent to the group by a given source. The presence of filters is important because IGMP allows a host to pass the set of filter specifications to the local router along with group membership information. In the case where two applications disagree (i.e., one application excludes a given source and another includes the source), software on the host must rationalize the two specifications and then handle the decision about which applications receive a given datagram locally.

16.14 IGMP Implementation

IGMP is carefully designed to avoid adding overhead that can congest networks. In particular, because a given network can include multiple multicast routers as well as hosts that all participate in multicasting, IGMP must avoid having participants generate unnecessary control traffic. There are several ways IGMP minimizes its effect on the network:

---

†Chapter 8 discusses ICMP, the Internet Control Message Protocol.

First, all communication between hosts and multicast routers uses IP multicast. That is, when IGMP messages are encapsulated in an IP datagram for transmission, the IP destination address is a multicast address — routers send general IGMP queries to the all systems address, hosts send some IGMP messages to the all routers address, and both hosts and routers send IGMP messages that are specific to a group to the group's address. Thus, datagrams carrying IGMP messages are transmitted using hardware multicast if it is available. As a result, on networks that support hardware multicast, hosts not participating in IP multicast never receive IGMP messages.

Second, when polling to determine group membership, a multicast router sends a single query to request information about all groups instead of sending a separate message to each†. The default polling rate is 125 seconds, which means that IGMP does not generate much traffic.

Third, if multiple multicast routers attach to the same network, they quickly and efficiently choose a single router to poll host membership. Thus, the amount of IGMP traffic on a network does not increase as additional multicast routers are attached to the net.

Fourth, hosts do not respond to a router's IGMP query at the same time. Instead, each query contains a value, N, that specifies a maximum response time (the default is 10 seconds). When a query arrives, a host chooses a random delay between 0 and N which it waits before sending a response. In fact, if a given host is a member of multiple groups, the host chooses a different random number for each. Thus, a host's response to a router's query will be spaced randomly over 10 seconds.

Fifth, reports for multiple group memberships can be sent in a single packet to minimize bandwidth.

The previous version of IGMP, *IGMPv2*, used an alternative approach to network bandwidth minimization. In IGMPv2, hosts on a network listened to reports, and once one host on a network reported membership in a group, other hosts on the network suppressed their reports (which were unnecessary because routers on the network already knew the group had a member). In IGMPv3, instead of sending one report per packet, a host places many reports in a single packet. Because we only expect a host to be a member of a few groups at one time, it is likely that all reports from the host will fit into a single packet. So, instead of mandating suppression, IGMPv3 mandates transmission, which means routers must keep track of each host's group membership and filters.

---

†The protocol does include a message type that allows a router to query a specific group.

16.15 Group Membership State Transitions

On a host, IGMP must remember the status of each multicast group to which the host belongs along with the source filters associated with each group†. We think of a host as keeping a table in which it records group membership information. Initially, all entries in the table are unused. Whenever an application program on the host joins a new group, IGMP software allocates an entry and fills in information about the group, including address filters that the application has specified. When an application leaves a group, the corresponding entry is removed from the system. When forming a report, the software consults the table, rationalizes all filters for a group, and forms a single report.

The actions IGMP software takes in response to various events can best be explained by the state transition diagram in Figure 16.4.

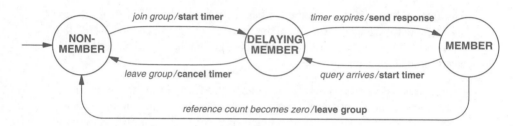

Figure 16.4 The three possible states of an entry in a host's multicast group table and transitions among them, where each transition is labeled with an event and an action. The state transitions do not show messages sent when joining and leaving a group.

A host maintains an independent table entry for each group of which it is currently a member. As the figure shows, when a host first joins the group or when a query arrives from a multicast router, the host moves the entry to the *DELAYING MEMBER* state and chooses a random delay. If another host in the group responds to the router's query before the timer expires, the host cancels its timer and moves to the *MEMBER* state. If the timer expires, the host sends a response message before moving to the *MEMBER* state. Because a router only generates a query every 125 seconds, one expects a host to remain in the *MEMBER* state most of the time.

The diagram in Figure 16.4 omits a few details. For example, if a query arrives while the host is in the *DELAYING MEMBER* state, the protocol requires the host to reset its timer. More important, to maintain backward compatibility with IGMPv1 and IGMPv2, version *3* also handles version *1* and version *2* messages, making it possible to use versions 1, 2, and 3 of IGMP on the same network concurrently.

---

†The *all systems group*, 224.0.0.1, is an exception — a host never reports membership in that group.

16.16 IGMP Membership Query Message Format

IGMPv3 defines two message types: a *membership query* message that a router sends to probe for group members, and a *membership report* message that a host generates to report the groups that applications on the host are currently using. Figure 16.5 illustrates the membership query message format.

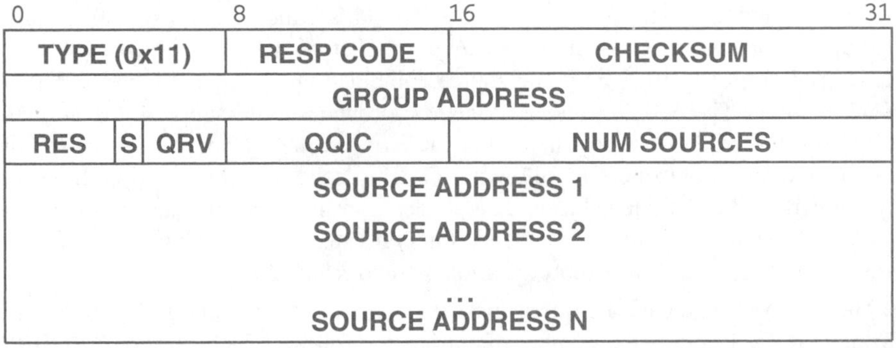

Figure 16.5 The format of an IGMP *membership query* message.

As the figure shows, a membership query message begins with a fixed-size header of twelve octets. Field *TYPE* identifies the type of message, with the types for various versions of IGMP listed in Figure 16.6.

Type	Protocol Vers.	Meaning
0x11	3	Membership query
0x22	3	Membership report
0x12	1	Membership report
0x16	2	Membership report
0x17	2	Leave group

Figure 16.6 IGMP message types. To accommodate backward compatibility, a version 3 implementation must recognize version 1 and 2 message types.

When a router polls for group membership, the field labeled *RESP CODE* specifies a maximum interval for the random delay that group members compute. If the field starts with a 0 bit, the value is taken to be an integer measured in tenths of seconds; if the field begins with a 1, the value is a floating point number with three bits of exponent and four bits of mantissa. Each host in the group delays a random time between zero and the specified value before responding. As we said, the default is 10 seconds, which means all hosts in a group choose a random value between 0 and 10. IGMP allows routers to set a maximum value in each query message to give managers control over IGMP traffic. If a network contains many hosts, a higher delay value further spreads out response times, and thereby lowers the probability of having more than one host respond to the query. The *CHECKSUM* field contains a checksum for the message (IGMP checksums are computed over the IGMP message only, and use the same algorithm as TCP and IP). The *GROUP ADDRESS* field is either used to specify a particular group or contains zero for a general query. That is, when it sends a query to a specific group or a specific group and source combination, a router fills in the *GROUP ADDRESS* field. The *S* field indicates whether a router should suppress the normal timer updates that are performed when an update arrives; the bit does not apply to hosts. Field *QRV* controls robustness by allowing IGMP to send a packet multiple times on a lossy network. The default value is 2; a sender transmits the message *QRV–1* times. Field *QQIC* specifies the Querier's Query Interval (i.e., the time between membership queries). *QQIC* uses the same representation as field *RESP CODE*.

The last part of an IGMP query message consists of zero or more sources; field *NUM SOURCES* specifies the number of entries that follow. Each *SOURCE ADDRESS* consists of a 32-bit IP address. The number of sources is zero in a *general query* (i.e., a request from a router for information about all multicast groups in use on the network) and in a *group specific query* (i.e., a request from a router for information about a specified multicast group). For a *group and source specific query*, the message contains a list of one or more sources; a router uses such a message to request reception status for a combination of the multicast group and any of the specified sources.

16.17 IGMP Membership Report Message Format

The second type of message used with IGMPv3 is a *membership report* that hosts use to pass participation status to a router. Figure 16.7 illustrates the format.

As the figure shows, a membership report message consists of an 8-octet header that specifies the message type and an integer count of group records, *K*, followed by *K* group records. Figure 16.8 illustrates the format of each group record. The format is straightforward. The initial field, labeled *REC TYPE* allows the sender to specify whether the list of sources in the record corresponds to an *inclusive filter*, an *exclusive filter*, or a change in a previous report (e.g., an additional source to be included or excluded). The field labeled *MULTICAST ADDRESS* specifies the multicast address to which the group record refers, and the field labeled *NUM OF SOURCES* specifies the number of source addresses contained in the group record.

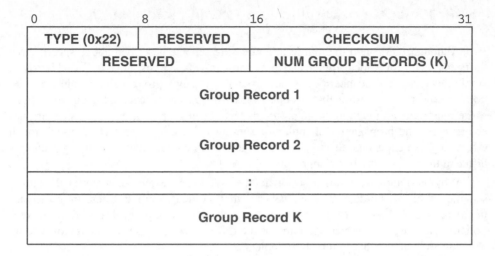

Figure 16.7 The format of an IGMP *membership report* message.

0	8	16	31
REC TYPE	ZEROES	NUM OF SOURCES	
MULTICAST ADDRESS			
SOURCE ADDRESS 1			
SOURCE ADDRESS 2			
⋮			
SOURCE ADDRESS N			

Figure 16.8 The format of each *group record* within an IGMP *membership report* message.

It is important to note that IGMP does not provide all possible messages or facilities. For example, IGMP does not include a mechanism that allows a host to discover the IP address of a group — application software must know the group address before it can use IGMP to join the group. Thus, some applications use permanently assigned group addresses, some allow a manager to configure the address when the software is installed, and others obtain the address dynamically (e.g., from a server). Similarly, version 3 does not provide explicit messages a host can issue to leave a group or to listen for all communication on a group. Instead, to leave a group, a host sends a membership report message that specifies an inclusive filter with an empty IP source address list, and to listen to all sources, a host sends a membership report message that specifies an exclusive filter with an empty IP source address list.

16.18 Multicast Forwarding And Routing Information

Although IGMP and the multicast addressing scheme described above specify how hosts interact with a local router and how multicast datagrams are transferred across a single network, they do not specify how routers exchange group membership information or how routers ensure that a copy of each datagram reaches all group members. More important, although multiple protocols have been proposed, no single standard has emerged for the propagation of multicast routing information. In fact, although much effort has been expended, there is no agreement on an overall plan — existing protocols differ in their goals and basic approach.

Why is multicast routing so difficult? Why not extend conventional routing schemes to handle multicast? The answer is that multicast routing differs from conventional routing in fundamental ways because multicast forwarding differs from conventional forwarding. To appreciate some of the differences, consider multicast forwarding over the architecture that Figure 16.9 depicts.

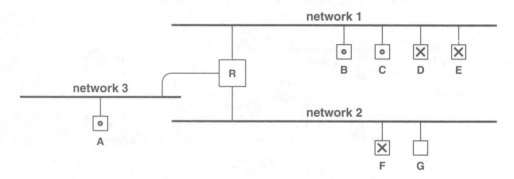

Figure 16.9 A simple internet with three networks connected by a router that illustrates multicast forwarding. Hosts marked with a dot participate in one multicast group, while those marked with an ''x'' participate in another.

16.18.1 Need For Dynamic Forwarding

Even for the simple topology shown in Figure 16.9, multicast forwarding differs from unicast forwarding. For example, the figure shows two multicast groups: the group denoted by a dot has members A, B, and C, and the group denoted by a cross has members D, E, and F. The dotted group has no members on network 2. To avoid wasting bandwidth unnecessarily, the router should never send packets intended for the dotted group across network 2. However, a host can join any group at any time — if the host is the first on its network to join the group, multicast forwarding must be changed to include the network. Thus, we come to an important difference between conventional route propagation and multicast route propagation:

> *Unlike unicast forwarding in which routes change only when the topology changes or equipment fails, multicast routes can change simply because an application program joins or leaves a multicast group.*

16.18.2 Insufficiency Of Destination Forwarding

The example in Figure 16.9 illustrates another aspect of multicast forwarding. If host *F* and host *E* each send a datagram to the cross group, router *R* will receive and forward them. Because both datagrams are directed at the same group, they have the same destination address. However, the correct forwarding actions differ: *R* sends the datagram from *E* to net *2*, and sends the datagram from *F* to net *1*. Interestingly, when it receives a datagram destinated for the cross group sent by host *A*, the router uses a third action: it forwards two copies, one to net *1* and the other to net *2*. Thus, we see the second major difference between conventional forwarding and multicast forwarding:

> *Multicast forwarding requires a router to examine more than the destination address.*

16.18.3 Arbitrary Senders

The final feature of multicast forwarding illustrated by Figure 16.9 arises because IP allows an arbitrary host, one that is not necessarily a member of the group, to send a datagram to the group. In the figure, host *G* can send a datagram to the dotted group even though *G* is not a member of any group and there are no members of the dotted group on *G's* network. More important, as it travels through the internet, the datagram may pass across other networks that have no group members attached. Thus, we can summarize:

> *A multicast datagram may originate on a computer that is not part of the multicast group, and may be forwarded across networks that do not have any group members attached.*

16.19 Basic Multicast Forwarding Paradigms

We know from the example above that multicast routers must use more than a destination address when processing a datagram. So, the question arises: "Exactly what information does a multicast router use when deciding how to forward a datagram?" The answer lies in understanding that because a multicast destination represents a set of computers, an optimal forwarding system will reach all members of the set without sending a datagram across a given network twice. Although a single multicast router such as the one in Figure 16.9 can simply avoid sending a datagram back over the interface on which it arrives, using the interface alone will not prevent a datagram from being forwarded among a set of routers that are arranged in a cycle. To avoid such forwarding loops, multicast routers rely on the datagram's source address.

One of the first ideas to emerge for multicast forwarding was a form of broadcasting described earlier. Known as *Reverse Path Forwarding (RPF)*,† the scheme uses a datagram's source address to prevent the datagram from traveling around a loop repeatedly. To use RPF, a multicast router must have a conventional routing table with shortest paths to all destinations. When a datagram arrives, the router extracts the source address, looks it up in the local routing table, and finds *I*, the interface that leads to the source. If the datagram arrived over interface *I*, the router forwards a copy to each of the other interfaces; otherwise, the router discards the copy.

Because it ensures that a copy of each multicast datagram is sent across every network in an internet, the basic RPF scheme guarantees that every host in a multicast group will receive a copy of each datagram sent to the group. However, RPF alone is not used for multicast forwarding because it wastes bandwidth by transmitting multicast datagrams over networks that neither have group members nor lead to group members.

To avoid propagating multicast datagrams where they are not needed, a modified form of RPF was invented. Known as *Truncated Reverse Path Forwarding* (*TRPF*) or *Truncated Reverse Path Broadcasting* (*TRPB*), the scheme follows the RPF algorithm, but further restricts propagation by avoiding paths that do not lead to group members. To use TRPF, a multicast router needs two pieces of information: a conventional routing table and a list of multicast groups reachable through each network interface. When a multicast datagram arrives, the router first applies the RPF rule. If RPF specifies discarding the copy, the router does so. However, if RPF specifies transmitting the datagram over a particular interface, the router first makes an additional check to verify that one or more members of the group designated in the datagram's destination address are reachable over the interface. If no group members are reachable over the interface, the router skips that interface, and continues examining the next one. In fact, we can now understand the origin of the term *truncated* — a router truncates forwarding when no group members lie along the path.

We can summarize:

> *When making a forwarding decision, a multicast router uses both the datagram's source and destination addresses. The basic mechanism is known as Truncated Reverse Path Forwarding.*

---

†Reverse path forwarding is sometimes called *Reverse Path Broadcasting* (*RPB*).

16.20 Consequences Of TRPF

Although TRPF guarantees that each member of a multicast group receives a copy of each datagram sent to the group, it has two surprising consequences. First, because it relies on RPF to prevent loops, TRPF delivers an extra copy of datagrams to some networks just like conventional RPF. Figure 16.10 illustrates how duplicates arise.

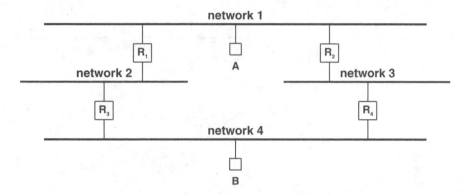

Figure 16.10 A topology that causes an RPF scheme to deliver multiple copies of a datagram to some destinations.

In the figure, when host A sends a datagram, routers R_1 and R_2 each receive a copy. Because the datagram arrives over the interface that lies along the shortest path to A, R_1 forwards a copy to network 2, and R_2 forwards a copy to network 3. When it receives a copy from network 2 (the shortest path to A), R_3 forwards the copy to network 4. Unfortunately, R_4 also forwards a copy to network 4. Thus, although RPF allows R_3 and R_4 to prevent a loop by discarding the copy that arrives over network 4, host B receives two copies of the datagram.

A second surprising consequence arises because TRPF uses both source and destination addresses when forwarding datagrams: delivery depends on a datagram's source. For example, Figure 16.11 shows how multicast routers forward datagrams from two different sources across a fixed topology.

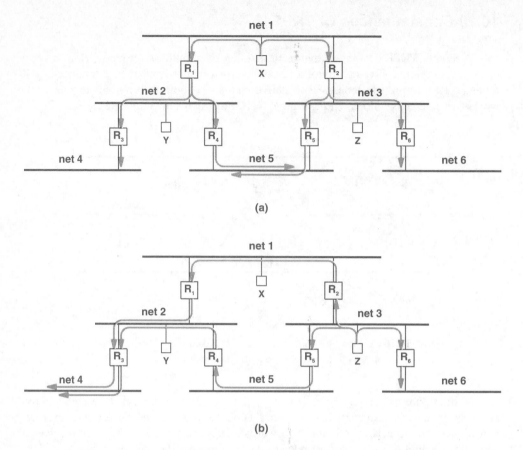

(a)

(b)

Figure 16.11 Examples of paths a multicast datagram follows under TRPF assuming the source is (a) host X, and (b) host Z, and the group has a member on each of the networks. The number of copies received depends on the source.

As the figure shows, the source affects both the path a datagram follows to reach a given network as well as the delivery details. For example, in part (a) of the figure, a transmission by host X causes TRPF to deliver two copies of the datagram to network 5. In part (b), only one copy of a transmission by host Z reaches network 5, but two copies reach networks 2 and 4.

16.21 Multicast Trees

Researchers use graph theory terminology to describe the set of paths from a given source to all members of a multicast group: they say that the paths define a graph-theoretic *tree*†, which is sometimes called a *forwarding tree* or a *delivery tree*. Each multicast router corresponds to a *node* in the tree, and a network that connects two routers corresponds to an *edge* in the tree. The source of a datagram is the *root* or *root node* of the tree. Finally, the last router along each of the paths from the source is called a *leaf* router. The terminology is sometimes applied to networks as well — researchers call a network hanging off a leaf router a *leaf network*.

As an example of the terminology, consider Figure 16.11. Part *a* shows a tree with root X, and leaves R_3, R_4, R_5, and R_6. Technically, part *b* does not show a tree because router R_3 lies along two paths. Informally, researchers often overlook the details and refer to such graphs as trees.

The graph terminology allows us to express an important principle:

> *A multicast forwarding tree is defined as a set of paths through multicast routers from a source to all members of a multicast group. For a given multicast group, each possible source of datagrams can determine a different forwarding tree.*

One of the immediate consequences of the principle concerns the size of tables used to forward multicast. Unlike conventional routing tables, each entry in a multicast table is identified by a pair:

(multicast group, source)

Conceptually, *source* identifies a single host that can send datagrams to the group (i.e., any host in the internet). In practice, keeping a separate entry for each host is unwise because the forwarding trees defined by all hosts on a single network are identical. Thus, to save space, forwarding protocols use a network prefix as a *source*. That is, each router defines one forwarding entry that is used for all hosts on the same physical network.

Aggregating entries by network prefix instead of by host address reduces the table size dramatically. However, multicast routing tables can grow much larger than conventional routing tables. Unlike a conventional table in which the size is proportional to the number of networks in the underlying internet, a multicast table has size proportional to the product of the number of networks in the internet and the number of multicast groups.

---

†A graph is a tree if it does not contain any cycles (i.e., a router does not appear on more than one path).

16.22 The Essence Of Multicast Route Propagation

Observant readers may have noticed an inconsistency between the features of IP multicasting and TRPF. We said that TRPF is used instead of conventional RPF to avoid unnecessary traffic: TRPF does not forward a datagram to a network unless that network leads to at least one member of the group. Consequently, a multicast router must have knowledge of group membership. We also said that IP allows any host to join or leave a multicast group at any time, which results in rapid membership changes. More important, membership does not follow local scope — a host that joins may be far from some router that is forwarding datagrams to the group. So, group membership information must be propagated across the underlying internet.

The issue of membership is central to routing; all multicast routing schemes provide a mechanism for propagating membership information as well as a way to use the information when forwarding datagrams. In general, because membership can change rapidly, the information available at a given router is imperfect, so route updates may lag changes. Therefore, a multicast design represents a tradeoff between the overhead of extra routing traffic and inefficient data transmission. On one hand, if group membership information is not propagated rapidly, multicast routers will not make optimal decisions (i.e., they either forward datagrams across some networks unnecessarily or fail to send datagrams to all group members). On the other hand, a multicast routing scheme that communicates every membership change to every router is doomed because the resulting traffic can overwhelm an internet. Each design chooses a compromise between the two extremes.

16.23 Reverse Path Multicasting

One of the earliest forms of multicast routing was derived from TRPF. Known as *Reverse Path Multicast* (*RPM*), the scheme extends TRPF to make it more dynamic. Three assumptions underlie the design. First, it is more important to ensure that a multicast datagram reaches each member of the group to which it is sent than to eliminate unnecessary transmission. Second, multicast routers each contain a conventional routing table that has correct information. Third, multicast routing should improve efficiency when possible (i.e. eliminate needless transmission).

RPM uses a two step process. When it begins, RPM uses the RPF broadcast scheme to send a copy of each datagram across all networks in the internet. Doing so ensures that all group members receive a copy. Simultaneously, RPM proceeds to have multicast routers inform one another about paths that do not lead to group members. Once it learns that no group members lie along a given path, a router stops forwarding along that path.

How do routers learn about the location of group members? As in most multicast routing schemes, RPM propagates membership information bottom-up. The information starts with hosts that choose to join or leave groups. Hosts communicate membership information with their local router by using IGMP. Thus, although a multicast router does not know about distant group members, it does know about local members (i.e. members on each of its directly-attached networks). As a consequence, routers attached to leaf networks can decide whether to forward over the leaf network — if a leaf network contains no members for a given group, the router connecting that network to the rest of the internet does not forward on the network. In addition to taking local action, the leaf router informs the next router along the path back to the source. Once it learns that no group members lie beyond a given network interface, the next router stops forwarding datagrams for the group across the network. When a router finds that no group members lie beyond it, the router informs the next router along the path to the root.

Using graph-theoretic terminology, we say that when a router learns that a group has no members along a path and stops forwarding, it has *pruned* (i.e., removed) the path from the forwarding tree. In fact, RPM is called a *broadcast and prune* strategy because a router broadcasts (using RPF) until it receives information that allows it to prune a path. Researchers also use another term for the RPM algorithm: they say that the system is *data-driven* because a router does not send group membership information to any other routers until datagrams arrive for that group.

In the data-driven model, a router must also handle the case where a host decides to join a particular group after the router has pruned the path for that group. RPM handles joins bottom-up: when a host informs a local router that it has joined a group, the router consults its record of the group and obtains the address of the router to which it had previously sent a prune request. The router sends a new message that undoes the effect of the previous prune and causes datagrams to flow again. Such messages are known as *graft requests*, and the algorithm is said to graft the previously pruned branch back onto the tree.

16.24 Multicast Routing Protocols

The IETF has investigated many multicast protocols, including *Distance Vector Multicast Routing Protocol (DVMRP)*, *Core Based Trees (CBT)*, *Protocol Independent Multicast (PIM)*, and *Multicast extensions to OSPF (MOSPF)*. Each uses a slightly different paradigm. Although the protocols have been implemented and vendors have offered some support, none of them is a required standard. The next sections describe each of the protocols.

16.24.1 Distance Vector Multicast Routing Protocol And Tunneling

An early protocol, known as *Distance Vector Multicast Routing Protocol (DVMRP)*, allows multicast routers to pass group membership and routing information among themselves. DVMRP resembles the RIP protocol described in Chapter 15, but has been extended for multicast. In essence, the protocol passes information about current multicast group membership and the cost to transfer datagrams between routers. For each possible (group, source) pair, the routers impose a forwarding tree on top of the physical interconnections. When a router receives a datagram destined for an IP multicast group, it sends a copy of the datagram out over the network links that correspond to branches in the forwarding tree†. DVMPR is implemented by a Unix program named *mrouted* that uses a special *multicast kernel*.

Mrouted uses multicast tunneling to allow sites to forward multicast across the Internet. At each site, a manager configures an *mrouted tunnel* to other sites. The tunnel uses IP-in-IP encapsulation to send multicast. That is, when it receives a multicast datagram generated by a local host, *mrouted* encapsulates the datagram in a conventional unicast datagram, and forwards a copy to *mrouted* at each of the other sites. When it receives a unicast datagram through one of its tunnels, *mrouted* extracts the multicast datagram, and then forwards according to its multicast routing table.

16.24.2 Core Based Trees (CBT)

CBT avoids broadcasting and allows all sources to share the same forwarding tree whenever possible. To avoid broadcasting, CBT does not forward multicasts along a path until one or more hosts along that path join the multicast group. Thus, CBT reverses the flood-and-prune approach used by DVMRP — instead of forwarding datagrams until negative information has been propagated, CBT does not forward along a path until positive information has been received. We say that instead of using the data-driven paradigm, CBT uses a *demand-driven* paradigm.

The demand-driven paradigm in CBT means that when a host uses IGMP to join a particular group, the local router must then inform other routers before datagrams will be forwarded. Which router or routers should be informed? The question is critical in all demand-driven multicast routing schemes. Recall that in a data-driven scheme, a router uses the arrival of data traffic to know where to send routing messages (it propagates routing messages back over networks from which the traffic arrives). However, in a demand-driven scheme, no traffic will arrive for a group until the membership information has been propagated.

CBT uses a combination of static and dynamic algorithms to build a multicast forwarding tree. To make the scheme scalable, CBT divides the underlying internet into *regions*, where the size of a region is determined by network administrators. Within each region, one of the routers is designated as a *core router*, and other routers in the region must either be configured to know the core router for their region, or to use a dynamic *discovery mechanism* to find the core router when they boot.

Knowledge of a core router is important because it allows multicast routers in a region to form a *shared tree* for the region. As soon as a host joins a multicast group, a local router, *L*, receives the host request. Router *L* generates a CBT *join request* which it sends to the core router using conventional unicast forwarding. Each intermediate router along the path to the core router examines the request. As soon as the request reaches a router *R* that is already part of the CBT shared tree, *R* returns an ack-

---

†DVMRP changed substantially between version *2* and *3* when it incorporated the RPM algorithm described above.

nowledgement, passes the group membership information on to its parent, and begins forwarding traffic for the group. As the acknowledgement passes back to the leaf router, intermediate routers examine the message, and configure their multicast routing table to forward datagrams for the group. Thus, router L is linked into the forwarding tree at router R.

We can summarize:

> *Because CBT uses a demand-driven paradigm, it divides an internet into regions and designates a* core router *for each region; other routers in the region dynamically build a forwarding tree by sending* join requests *to the core.*

16.24.3 Protocol Independent Multicast (PIM)

In reality, PIM consists of two independent protocols that share little beyond the name and basic message header formats: *PIM - Dense Mode* (*PIM-DM*) and *PIM - Sparse Mode* (*PIM-SM*). The distinction arises because no single protocol works well in all situations. In particular, PIM's dense mode is designed for a LAN environment in which all, or nearly all, networks have hosts listening to each multicast group; whereas, PIM's sparse mode is designed to accommodate a wide area environment in which the members of a given multicast group occupy a small subset of all possible networks.

The term *protocol independence* arises because PIM assumes a traditional unicast routing table that contains a shortest path to each destination. Because PIM does not specify how such a table should be built, an arbitrary routing protocol can be used. Thus, PIM operates "independently" from the unicast routing protocol(s) that a router employs.

To accommodate many listeners, PIM-DM uses a broadcast-and-prune approach in which datagrams are forwarded to all routers using RPF until a router sends an explicit request. By contrast, PIM's sparse mode can be viewed as an extension of basic concepts from CBT. Sparse mode designates a router, called a *Rendezvous Point* (*RP*), that is the functional equivalent of a CBT core router.

16.24.4 Multicast Extensions To OSPF (MOSPF)

In addition to multicast routing protocols like PIM that use information from a unicast routing table, researchers have investigated a broader question: "How can multicast routing protocols benefit from additional information that is gathered by conventional routing protocols?" In particular, a link state protocol such as OSPF provides each router with a copy of the topology of the underlying internet. More specifically, OSPF provides a router with the topology of its OSPF *area*.

When such information is available, multicast protocols can indeed use it to compute a forwarding tree. The idea has been demonstrated in a protocol known as *Multicast extensions to OSPF* (*MOSPF*), which uses OSPF's topology database to form a forwarding tree for each source. MOSPF has the advantage of being *demand-driven*, meaning that the traffic for a particular group is not propagated until it is needed (i.e., because a host joins or leaves the group). The disadvantage of a demand-driven scheme arises from the cost of propagating routing information — all routers in an area must maintain membership information about every group. Furthermore, the information must be synchronized to ensure that every router has exactly the same database. As a consequence, MOSPF sends less data traffic, but sends more routing information than data-driven protocols.

16.25 Reliable Multicast And ACK Implosions

The term *reliable multicast* refers to any system that uses multicast delivery, but also guarantees that all group members receive data in order without any loss, duplication, or corruption. In theory, reliable multicast combines the advantage of a forwarding scheme that is more efficient than broadcast with the advantage of having all data arrive intact. Thus, reliable multicast has great potential benefit and applicability (e.g., a stock exchange could use reliable multicast to deliver stock prices to many destinations).

In practice, reliable multicast is not as general or straightforward as it sounds. First, if a multicast group has multiple senders, the notion of delivering datagrams "in sequence" becomes meaningless. Second, we have seen that widely used multicast forwarding schemes such as RPF can produce duplication even on small internets. Third, in addition to guarantees that all data will eventually arrive, applications like audio or video expect reliable systems to bound the delay and jitter. Fourth, because reliability requires acknowledgements and a multicast group can have an arbitrary number of members, traditional reliable protocols require a sender to handle an arbitrary number of acknowledgements. Unfortunately, no computer has enough processing power to do so. We refer to the problem as an *ACK implosion*; the problem has become the focus of much research.

To overcome the ACK implosion problem, reliable multicast protocols take a hierarchical approach in which multicasting is restricted to a single source†. Before data is sent, a forwarding tree is established from the source to all group members and *acknowledgement points* must be identified.

An acknowledgement point, which is also known as an *acknowledgement aggregator* or *designated router* (*DR*), consists of a router in the forwarding tree that agrees to cache copies of the data and process acknowledgements from routers or hosts further down the tree. If a retransmission is required, the acknowledgement point obtains a copy from its cache.

---

†Note that a single source does not limit functionality because the source can agree to forward any message it receives via unicast. Thus, an arbitrary host can send a packet to the source, which then multicasts the packet to the group.

Most reliable multicast schemes use negative rather than positive acknowledgements — the host does not respond unless a datagram is lost. To allow a host to detect loss, each datagram must be assigned a unique sequence number. When it detects loss, a host sends a *NACK* to request retransmission. The NACK propagates along the forwarding tree toward the source until it reaches an acknowledgement point. The acknowledgement point processes the NACK, and retransmits a copy of the lost datagram along the forwarding tree.

How does an acknowledgement point ensure that it has a copy of all datagrams in the sequence? It uses the same scheme as a host. When a datagram arrives, the acknowledgement point checks the sequence number, places a copy in its memory, and then proceeds to propagate the datagram down the forwarding tree. If it finds that a datagram is missing, the acknowledgement point sends a NACK up the tree toward the source. The NACK either reaches another acknowledgement point that has a copy of the datagram (in which case the acknowledgement point transmits a second copy), or the NACK reaches the source (which retransmits the missing datagram).

The choice of a branching topology and acknowledgement points is crucial to the success of a reliable multicast scheme. Without sufficient acknowledgement points, a missing datagram can cause an ACK implosion. In particular, if a given router has many descendants, a lost datagram can cause that router to be overrun with retransmission requests. Unfortunately, automating selection of acknowledgement points has not turned out to be simple. Consequently, many reliable multicast protocols require manual configuration. Thus, multicast is best suited to: services that tend to persist over long periods of time, topologies that do not change rapidly, and situations where intermediate routers agree to serve as acknowledgement points.

Is there an alternative approach to reliability? Some researchers are experimenting with protocols that incorporate redundant information to reduce or eliminate retransmission. One scheme sends redundant datagrams. Instead of sending a single copy of each datagram, the source sends N copies (typically *2* or *3*). Redundant datagrams work especially well when routers implement a *Random Early Discard* (*RED*) strategy because the probability of more than one copy being discarded is extremely small.

Another approach to redundancy involves *forward error-correcting codes*. Analogous to the error-correcting codes used with audio CDs, the scheme requires a sender to incorporate error-correction information into each datagram in a data stream. If one datagram is lost, the error correcting code contains sufficient redundant information to allow a receiver to reconstruct the missing datagram without requesting a retransmission.

16.26 Summary

IP multicasting is an abstraction of hardware multicasting. It allows delivery of a datagram to multiple destinations. IP uses class D addresses to specify multicast delivery; actual transmission uses hardware multicast, if it is available.

IP multicast groups are dynamic: a host can join or leave a group at any time. For local multicast, hosts only need the ability to send and receive multicast datagrams. However, IP multicasting is not limited to a single physical network – multicast routers propagate group membership information and arrange routing so that each member of a multicast group receives a copy of every datagram sent to the group.

Hosts communicate their group membership to multicast routers using IGMP. IGMP has been designed to be efficient and to avoid using network resources.

A variety of protocols have been designed to propagate multicast routing information across an internet. The two basic approaches are data-driven and demand-driven. In either case, the amount of information in a multicast forwarding table is much larger than in a unicast routing table because multicasting requires entries for each (group, source) pair.

Not all routers in the global Internet propagate multicast routes or forward multicast traffic. Groups at two or more sites, separated by an internet that does not support multicast routing, can use an IP tunnel to transfer multicast datagrams. When using a tunnel, a program encapsulates a multicast datagram in a conventional unicast datagram. The receiver must extract and handle the multicast datagram.

Reliable multicast refers to a scheme that uses multicast forwarding but offers reliable delivery semantics. To avoid the ACK implosion problem, reliable multicast schemes either use a hierarchy of acknowledgement points or send redundant information.

FOR FURTHER STUDY

Cain et. al. [RFC 3376] specifies the standard for IP multicasting described in this chapter, which includes Version 3 of IGMP. Waitzman, Partridge, and Deering [RFC 1075] describes DVMRP, Estrin et. al. [RFC 2362] describes PIM sparse mode, Ballardie [RFCs 2189 2201] describes CBT, and Moy [RFC 1585] describes MOSPF.

Eriksson [1994] explains the multicast backbone. Casner and Deering [July 1992] reports on the first multicast of an IETF meeting.

EXERCISES

16.1   The standard suggests using 23 bits of an IP multicast address to form a hardware multicast address. In such a scheme, how many IP multicast addresses map to a single hardware multicast address?

16.2   Argue that IP multicast addresses should use only 23 of the 28 possible bits. Hint: what are the practical limits on the number of groups to which a host can belong and the number of hosts on a single network?

16.3   IP must always check the destination addresses on incoming multicast datagrams and discard datagrams if the host is not in the specified multicast group. Explain how the host might receive a multicast destined for a group to which that host is not a member.

16.4   Multicast routers need to know whether a group has members on a given network. Is there any advantage to routers knowing the exact set of hosts on a network that belong to a given multicast group?

16.5   Find three applications in your environment that can benefit from IP multicast.

16.6   The standard says that IP software must arrange to deliver a copy of any outgoing multicast datagram to application programs on the host that belong to the specified multicast group. Does this design make programming easier or more difficult? Explain.

16.7   When the underlying hardware does not support multicast, IP multicast uses hardware broadcast for delivery. How can doing so cause problems? Is there any advantage to using IP multicast over such networks?

16.8   DVMRP was derived from RIP. Read RFC 1075 on DVMRP and compare the two protocols. How much more complex is DVMRP than RIP?

16.9   Version 3 of IGMP includes a measure of robustness that is intended to accommodate packet loss by allowing transmission of multiple copies of a message. How does the protocol arrive at an estimate of the robustness value needed on a given network?

16.10 Explain why a multi-homed host may need to join a multicast group on one network, but not on another. (Hint: consider an audio teleconference.)

16.11 Estimate the size of the multicast forwarding table needed to handle multicast of audio from 100 radio stations, if each station has a total of ten million listeners at random locations around the world.

16.12 Argue that only two types of multicast are practical in the Internet: statically configured commercial services that multicast to large numbers of subscribers and dynamically configured services that include a few participants (e.g., family members in three households participating in a single IP phone call).

16.13 Consider reliable multicast achieved through redundant transmission. If a given link has high probability of corruption, is it better to send redundant copies of a datagram or to send one copy that uses forward error-correcting codes? Explain.

16.14 The data-driven multicast routing paradigm works best on local networks that have low delay and excess capacity, while the demand-driven paradigm works best in a wide area environment that has limited capacity and higher delay. Does it make sense to devise a single protocol that combines the two schemes? Why or why not? (Hint: investigate MOSPF.)

16.15 Devise a quantitative measure that can be used to decide when PIM-SM should switch from a shared tree to a shortest path tree.

16.16 Read the protocol specification to find out the notion of ''sparse'' used in PIM-SM. Find an example of an internet in which the population of group members is sparse, but for which DVMRP is a better multicast routing protocol.

Chapter Contents

17

IP Switching And MPLS

17.1 Introduction

Earlier chapters describe IP addressing and give algorithms for datagram forwarding that use a routing table and longest-prefix matching to look up a next hop. This chapter considers an alternative approach that avoids the overhead of longest prefix matching. The chapter explains the basic technology, and describes its use for traffic engineering.

17.2 Switching Technology

In the 1980s, as the Internet grew in popularity, researchers began to explore ways to increase the performance of packet processing systems. An idea emerged that was eventually adopted by commercial vendors: replace IP's connectionless packet switching approach that requires longest-prefix table lookup with a connection-oriented approach that accommodates a faster lookup algorithm. The general concept, which is known as *switching*, is often associated with *Asynchronous Transfer Mode* (*ATM*) hardware because the two emerged at the same time. As we will see, however, it is possible to implement switching on a conventional router, without relying on connection-oriented hardware. At the heart of switching lies a basic idea about lookup algorithms: a typical processor can index into an array in constant time, but requires log_2N to search a set of N items. Furthermore, indexing only requires calculation, but searching usually involves multiple memory references.

Switching technologies exploit indexing to achieve high speed. To do so, each packet carries a small integer known as a *label*. When a packet arrives at a switch, the switch extracts the label and uses the value as an index into the table that specifies the appropriate action. Figure 17.1 illustrates the concept.

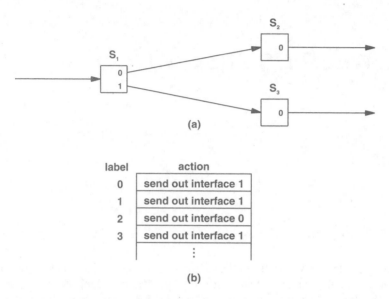

(a)

label	action
0	send out interface 1
1	send out interface 1
2	send out interface 0
3	send out interface 1
	⋮

(b)

Figure 17.1 Illustration of basic switching with (a) a network of three inter-connected switches, and (b) a table from switch S_1.

In the figure, the table entries specify how switch S_1 forwards packets with labels in the range 0 through 3. According to the table, a packet with label 2 will be forwarded out interface 0, which leads to switch S_2; a packet with a label of 0, 1, or 3 will be forwarded over interface 1, which leads to switch S_3.

17.3 Large Networks, Label Swapping, And Paths

The chief drawback of the basic switching scheme described above arises because each label consists of a small integer. How can the scheme be extended to a network that has many destinations? There are two answers. First, because a label is only needed when a *flow* is active and the number of flows active at a given time is small, switching uses a *connection-oriented* approach in which labels are only assigned to active flows and are recovered once a flow is terminated. Second, to avoid requiring global agreements on the use of labels, switching systems employ a concept of *label swapping* or *label switching*. Label swapping means the label on a packet can change as the packet passes from switch to switch. That is, the action a switch performs can include rewriting the label. Figure 17.2 illustrates the concept.

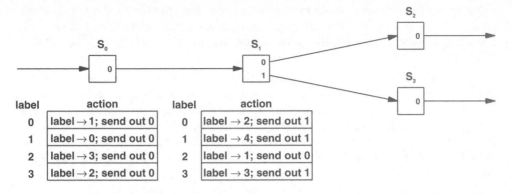

label	action	label	action
0	label → 1; send out 0	0	label → 2; send out 1
1	label → 0; send out 0	1	label → 4; send out 1
2	label → 3; send out 0	2	label → 1; send out 0
3	label → 2; send out 0	3	label → 3; send out 1

Figure 17.2 Illustration of label swapping in which the label in a packet can be rewritten by each switch.

In the figure, a packet that enters S_0 with label *0* has the label rewritten before being forwarded. Thus, when switch S_1 receives the packet, the label will be *1*. Similarly, S_1 replaces label *1* with *4* before sending the packet to S_3. Label swapping makes it easier to configure a switched network because it allows a manager to define a path through the network without forcing the same label to be used at each point along the path. In fact, a label only needs to be valid across one hop — the two switches that share the physical connection need to agree on the label to be assigned to each flow that crosses the connection.

The point is:

> *Switching uses a connection-oriented approach. To avoid the need for global agreement on the use of labels, the technology allows a manager to define a path of switches without requiring that the same label be used across the entire path.*

17.4 Using Switching With IP

Although the connection-oriented paradigms used with switching appear to conflict with IP's connectionless paradigm, the two have been combined. There are three motivations:

- Faster forwarding
- Aggregated route information
- Ability to manage aggregate flows

Faster Forwarding. The point is easy to understand: adopting a connection-oriented approach allows routers to perform forwarding faster because the router can use

indexing in place of routing table lookup. Of course, the additional speed is only needed for routers that have both high-speed connections (e.g., OC-192) and high traffic
rates. Such routers are typically found in the core of the Internet (e.g., owned by a
large ISP).

Aggregated Route Information. Large ISPs at the center of the Internet use switching as a way to avoid having complete routing tables in each of their routers. Instead,
IP routing table lookup is performed once (e.g., when a packet first arrives at the ISP),
the packet is assigned a label, and routers in the ISP use the label to forward the packet.
Furthermore, because the label only needs to specify the next ISP to which the packet
should be sent and not the ultimate destination, many packets can be assigned the same
label.

Ability To Manage Aggregate Flows. We said that large ISPs often write *Service
Level Agreements* (*SLAs*) regarding traffic that can be sent across a peering point. Usually, such SLAs refer to aggregate traffic (e.g., all traffic forwarded between the two
ISPs or all VoIP traffic). Having a label assigned to each aggregate makes it easier to
implement mechanisms that measure or enforce the SLA.

17.5 IP Switching Technologies And MPLS

So far, we have described switching as a general-purpose, connection-oriented network technology. Ipsilon Corporation was one of the first companies to produce products that combined IP and hardware switches; they used ATM switches, called their
technology *IP switching*, and called the devices they produced *IP switches*. Since Ipsilon, other companies have produced a series of designs and names, including *tag
switching*, *layer 3 switching*, and *label switching*. Several of the ideas have been folded
into a standard endorsed by the IETF known as *Multi-Protocol Label Switching*
(*MPLS*)†.

How does MPLS work? The general idea is straightforward: routers that connect
to user's computer systems use conventional forwarding, while routers at the center of
the network understand MPLS and use switching instead of conventional IP routing
table lookup. For example, a large corporation with multiple sites might choose to use
conventional forwarding within each building and MPLS on networks that interconnect
buildings.

Before it can cross from a conventional network to an *MPLS core* (i.e., a contiguous set of routers using MPLS), a datagram must be assigned a label. Each router in
the MPLS core uses the label to determine how to forward the datagram. Eventually,
the datagram either reaches the edge of the MPLS core, in which case the label is removed, or the datagram passes directly to the MPLS core in another company (e.g.,
from the MPLS core in a large ISP to the MPLS core in another large ISP). Of course,
before datagrams can pass from one MPLS core to another, managers at the two ISPs
must agree on the assignment and meaning of each label.

---

†Despite having "multi-protocol" in the name, MPLS is focused almost exclusively on IP.

17.6 Classification, Flows, And Higher Layer Switching

When a datagram first arrives at an MPLS core, the datagram must be assigned an initial label (i.e., must be mapped onto a flow). We use the term *classification* to refer to the process of assigning a label, and the term *classifier* to refer to the hardware or software that performs classification. One can think of the mapping mathematically as a function:

$$l = c\,(\,datagram\,)$$

where l is a label that identifies a particular flow.

In practice, function c does not examine the entire datagram. Instead, only header fields are used. Strict *layer 3 classification* only uses fields in the IP header such as the source and destination IP addresses and type of service. Most vendors implement *layer 4 classification*†, and some offer *layer 5 classification*. In addition to examining fields in the IP header, layer 4 classification schemes also examine protocol port numbers in the TCP or UDP header. Layer 5 classification looks further into the datagram and considers the payload.

17.7 Hierarchical Use Of MPLS

The above describes the use of MPLS in an organization that is organized into a 2-level hierarchy: an outer region that uses conventional IP forwarding and an inner region that uses MPLS. As we will see, the protocol makes additional levels of hierarchy possible. For example, suppose a corporation has three campuses, with multiple buildings on each campus. The corporation can use conventional forwarding within a building, one level of MPLS to interconnect the buildings within a campus, and a second level of MPLS to interconnect sites. Two levels of hierarchy allows the corporation to choose policies for traffic between sites separately from the policies used between buildings (e.g., the path that traffic travels between buildings is determined by the type of traffic, but all traffic between a pair of sites follows the same path).

To provide for a multi-level hierarchy, MPLS incorporates a *label stack*. That is, instead of attaching a single label to a packet, MPLS allows multiple labels to be attached. At any time, only the top label is used; once the top label has been removed, processing continues with the next label.

In the case of our example corporation, it is possible to arrange two MPLS areas — one for traffic traveling between buildings and one for traffic traveling between two sites. Thus, when a datagram travels between two buildings at a given site, the datagram will have one label attached (the label will be removed when the datagram reaches the correct building). If a datagram must travel between sites and then to the correct building at the destination site, the datagram will have two labels attached. The top label will be used to move the datagram between the sites, and will be removed

---

†Some vendors use the term *layer 4 switching* to characterize products that implement layer 4 classification.

once the datagram reaches the correct site. When the top label is removed, the second label is used to forward the datagram to the correct building.

17.8 MPLS Encapsulation

MPLS does not require the use of a connection-oriented network technology — the physical connection between a pair of MPLS routers can consist of a dedicated circuit, such as an OC-48 line, or a conventional network, such as an Ethernet. However, conventional networks do not provide a way to pass a label along with a packet, and an IPv4 datagram header does not provide space to store a label. So, the question arises: "How can an MPLS label travel with a datagram?" The answer lies in an encapsulation technique: when encapsulating a datagram, an MPLS header is inserted before the datagram. Figure 17.3 illustrates the encapsulation used with Ethernet.

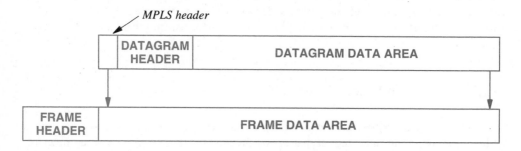

Figure 17.3 Illustration of the encapsulation MPLS uses to send an IP datagram across an Ethernet. An MPLS header consists of one or more entries, each 32 bits long.

When sending a frame that uses MPLS encapsulation, the Ethernet type field is set to 8847_{16} for unicast or type 8848_{16} for MPLS multicast†. Thus, there is no ambiguity about the contents of a frame — a receiver can use the frame type to determine whether the frame carries MPLS or a conventional datagram.

An MPLS header consists of one or more entries, each of which is 32 bits long and specifies a label plus information used to control label processing. Figure 17.4 illustrates the format of an entry in the header.

Figure 17.4 Illustration of the fields in an MPLS header entry. An MPLS header consists of one or more of these entries; there is no field to specify the overall header size.

---

†Although a type has been assigned, MPLS does not handle multicast well.

An entry begins with a *LABEL*; when the entry reaches the top of the stack (i.e., is the first entry in the header), MPLS uses the label to forward the packet†. The field labeled *EXP* is reserved for experimental use. The *S* bit is set to 1 to denote the bottom of the stack (i.e., the last entry in the header); in other entries, the *S* bit is 0. Finally, the *TTL* field (*Time To Live*) is analogous to the TTL field in an IP datagram header: each switch along the path that uses the label to forward the packet decrements the TTL value. If the TTL reaches zero, MPLS discards the packet. Thus, MPLS prevents a packet from cycling forever, even if a manager misconfigures switches and accidentally creates a forwarding loop.

Note that an MPLS label is 20 bits wide. In theory, an MPLS configuration can use all 20 bits of the label to accommodate up to 2^{20} simultaneous flows (i.e., 1,048,576 flows). In practice, however, few MPLS installations use a large number of flows because a manager is usually required to authorize and configure each switched path.

17.9 Label Switching Router

A router that implements MPLS is known as a *Label Switching Router* (*LSR*). Typically, an LSR consists of a conventional router that has been augmented to handle MPLS. Thus, in addition to switching MPLS traffic, an LSR can usually serve as the interface between a non-MPLS internet and an MPLS core. That is, an LSR can accept a datagram from a conventional network and classify the datagram to assign an initial MPLS label, and can terminate an MPLS path by removing the label and forwarding datagrams over a conventional network. The functions are known as *MPLS ingress* and *MPLS egress*.

The table inside an LSR that specifies an action for each label is known as a *Next Hop Label Forwarding Table*, and each entry in the table is called a *Next Hop Label Forwarding Entry* (*NHLFE*). Each NHLFE specifies two items, and may specify three more:

1. Next hop information (e.g., the outgoing interface).

2. The operation to be performed.

3. The encapsulation to use (optional).

4. How to encode the label (optional).

5. Other information needed to handle the packet (optional).

The operation in an NHLFE specifies whether the packet is crossing a transition to or from another level of MPLS hierarchy or merely being switched along a path within a single level. The possibilities are:

---

†Although it is common, MPLS does not require that each label correspond to an array index — it is possible to add one level of indirection that maps a label to an index.

1. Replace the label at the top of the stack with a specified new label, and continue to forward at the current level.

2. Pop the label stack to exit one level of MPLS hierarchy. Either use the next label on the stack to forward the datagram, or use conventional forwarding if no labels remain on the stack.

3. Replace the label on the top of the stack with a specified new label, and then push one or more new labels on the stack to increase the level(s) of MPLS hierarchy.

17.10 Control Processing And Label Distribution

The discussion above has focused on *data path* processing (i.e., forwarding packets). In addition, engineers who defined MPLS considered mechanisms for a *control path*. Control path processing refers to configuration and management — control path protocols make it easy for a manager to create or manage a *label switched path* (*LSP*).

The primary functionality provided by a control path protocol is automatic selection of labels. That is, the protocols allow a manager to establish an MPLS path without manually configuring each LSR along the path. The protocols allow pairs of LSRs along the path to choose an unused label for the link between a pair, and fill in NHLFE information for the flow so the labels can be swapped at each hop.

The process of choosing labels along a path is known as *label distribution*. Two protocols have been created to perform label distribution for MPLS: the *Label Distribution Protocol* (*LDP*), which is sometimes referred to as *MPLS-LDP*, and the *Constraint-based Routing LDP* (*CR-LDP*). In addition, existing protocols such as *OSPF*, *BGP* and *RSVP* have been extended to provide label distribution. Although it recognized the need for a label distribution protocol, the IETF working group that developed MPLS did not specify any of the protocols as the required standard.

17.11 MPLS And Fragmentation

MPLS and IP fragmentation interact in two ways. First, we said that when it sends a datagram over an LSP, MPLS adds a header of four or more octets. Doing so can have an interesting consequence when all underlying networks have the same maximum frame size. For example, consider an ingress LSR that connects multiple Ethernets. If a datagram arrives over a non-MPLS path with size exactly equal to the Ethernet MTU, adding a 32-bit MPLS header will make the resulting payload exceed the Ethernet MTU. As a result, the ingress LSR must fragment the original datagram, add the MPLS header to each fragment, and transmit two packets instead of one.

A second interaction between MPLS and fragmentation occurs when an ingress LSR receives IP fragments instead of a complete datagram. In most cases, the classification examines TCP or UDP port numbers as well as addresses in the IP header (i.e., most MPLS systems perform classification at layer 4 or higher). Unfortunately, only the first fragment of a datagram contains the transport protocol header. Thus, an ingress LSR must either collect fragments and reassemble the datagram or use conventional IP forwarding to handle fragments. In cases where the core of the network only permits MPLS traffic, an ingress LSR that does not reassemble datagrams must discard fragments.

17.12 Mesh Topology And Traffic Engineering

Interestingly, many ISPs who use MPLS follow a straightforward approach: they define a *full mesh* of MPLS paths. That is, if the ISP has K sites and peers with J other ISPs, the ISP defines an MPLS path for each possible pair of points. As a result, traffic moving between any pair of sites travels over a single MPLS path between the sites. A beneficial side effect of defining separate paths arises from the ability to measure (or control) the traffic traveling from one site to another. For example, by watching a single MPLS connection, an ISP can determine how much traffic travels from one of its sites across a peering connection to another ISP.

Some sites extend the idea of a full mesh by defining multiple paths between each pair of sites to accommodate various types of service. For example, an MPLS path with minimum hops might be reserved for voice traffic, which needs minimum delay, while a longer path might be used for other traffic such as e-mail and web traffic. As an alternative, MPLS allows an ISP to balance traffic between two disjoint paths. MPLS classification makes it possible to use a variety of measures to choose a path for data, including the IP source address as well as the transport protocol port numbers. The point is:

> *Because MPLS classification can use arbitrary fields in a datagram, including the IP source address, the service a datagram receives can depend on the customer sending the datagram as well as the type of data being carried.*

We use the term *traffic engineering* to characterize the process of creating MPLS paths and assigning datagrams to each path. In addition to defining the set of LSRs for each path, traffic engineering allows managers to use *Quality of Service (QoS)* techniques defined in Chapter 28 to control the rate of traffic on each path. Thus, it is possible to define two MPLS flows over a single physical connection, and use QoS techniques to guarantee that if each flow has traffic to send, 75% of the underlying bandwidth is devoted to one flow and the other flow receives 25%.

17.13 Summary

To achieve high speed, switching technologies use indexing rather than longest-prefix lookup. As a consequence, switching follows a connection-oriented paradigm. Because switches along a path can rewrite labels, the label assigned to a flow can change along the path.

The standard for switching IP datagrams, which is known as MPLS, was created by the IETF. When sending a datagram along an LSP, MPLS prepends a header, creating a stack of one or more labels; subsequent LSRs along the path use the labels to forward the datagram without performing routing table lookups. An ingress LSR classifies each datagram that arrives from a non-MPLS host or router, and an egress LSR can pass datagrams from an MPLS path to a non-MPLS host or router.

FOR FURTHER STUDY

Many RFCs contain proposals for MPLS, consider how to extend routing protocols to handle label distribution, or specify how to use MPLS with specific network technologies such as ATM and Frame Relay. Rosen et. al. [RFC 3031] specifies the overall architecture, and Rosen et. al. [RFC 3032] gives the details of MPLS headers and label stacking. Andersson et. al. [RFC 3036] specifies LDP, and Jamoussi [RFC 3212] specifies Constraint-Based LDP. Finally, Awduche et. al. [RFC 2702] discusses traffic engineering over MPLS.

EXERCISES

17.1   Look at the definition of IPv6 described in Chapter 31. What new mechanism relates directly to switched technologies?

17.2   Read about MPLS. Should MPLS accommodate layer 2 forwarding (i.e., bridging) as well as optimized IP forwarding? Why or why not?

17.3   If all traffic from host X will traverse a two-level MPLS hierarchy, what action could be taken to ensure that no fragmentation will occur?

17.4   Read more about Constraint-Based LDP. What are the possible constraints being considered?

17.5   If a router at your site supports MPLS, enable MPLS switching and measure the performance improvement over conventional routing table lookup. (Hint: be sure to measure many packets to a given destination to avoid having measurements affected by the cost of handling the initial packet).

17.6   Is it possible to conduct an experiment to determine whether your ISP uses MPLS? (assume it is possible to transmit arbitrary packets.)

17.7 Cisco Systems, Inc. offers a switching technology known as *Multi-Layer Switching* (*MLS*). Read about MLS. In what ways does MLS differ from MPLS?

17.8 If your site has a VLAN switch that offers MLS service, enable the service and test what happens if one sends a valid Ethernet frame that contains an incorrect IP datagram. Should a layer 2 switch examine IP headers? Why or why not?

Chapter Contents

18

Mobile IP

18.1 Introduction

Previous chapters describe the IP addressing and forwarding schemes used with stationary computers. This chapter considers an extension of IP designed to allow portable computers to move from one network to another.

18.2 Mobility, Routing, and Addressing

In the broadest sense, the term *mobile computing* refers to a system that allows computers to move from one location to another. Mobility is often associated with wireless technologies that allow movement easily. The IP addressing scheme, which was designed and optimized for a stationary environment, makes mobility difficult because the prefix of a host address identifies the network to which the host attaches. As a result, moving a host to a new network means either:

- The host's address must change.
- Routers must propagate a host-specific route across the entire Internet.

Neither alternative works well. On one hand, changing an address breaks all existing transport-layer connections, and may require restarting some network services. In addition, if the host contacts a server that uses reverse DNS lookup to authenticate, an additional change to DNS may be required. On the other hand, a host-specific routing approach cannot scale because communicating and storing a route for each host requires excessive bandwidth and memory.

18.3 Mobile IP Characteristics

The IETF devised a technology to permit IP mobility. Officially named *IP mobility support*, it is popularly called *mobile IP*. The general characteristics include:

Transparency. Mobility is transparent to applications and transport layer protocols as well as to routers not involved in the change — a TCP connection can survive a change in location provided the connection is not used during the transition.

Interoperability With IPv4. A host using mobile IP can interoperate with stationary hosts that run conventional IPv4 software as well as with other mobile hosts. Furthermore, conventional IP addresses are assigned to mobile hosts.

Scalability. The solution permits mobility across the Internet.

Security. Mobile IP provides security facilities that can be used to ensure all messages are authenticated (i.e., to prevent an arbitrary computer from impersonating a mobile host).

Macro Mobility. Rather than attempting to handle rapid ongoing movement, mobile IP focuses on the problem of long-duration moves (e.g., a user who takes a portable computer on a business trip).

18.4 Overview Of Mobile IP Operation

The biggest challenge for mobility lies in allowing a host to retain its address without requiring routers to learn host-specific routes. Mobile IP solves the problem by allowing a single computer to hold two addresses simultaneously: a permanent and fixed *primary address* that applications use, and a *secondary address* that is temporary. The temporary address is only valid while the computer visits a given location.

A mobile host's primary address is assigned on the host's *home* network. After it moves to a *foreign* network and obtains a secondary address, the mobile host must send the secondary address to a *home agent*, usually a router located on the home network. The agent agrees to intercept datagrams sent to the mobile's primary address, and uses *IP-in-IP* encapsulation to *tunnel* each datagram to the secondary address.

If the mobile moves again, it obtains a new secondary address and informs the home agent of its new location. When the mobile returns home, it contacts the home agent to *deregister*, meaning that the agent will stop intercepting datagrams. Similarly, a mobile can choose to deregister at any time (e.g., when leaving a remote location).

We said that mobile IP is designed for macroscopic mobility rather than continuous, high-speed movement. The reason should be clear: overhead. In particular, after it moves, a mobile must detect that it has moved, communicate across the foreign network to obtain a secondary address, and then communicate across the Internet to its agent at home to arrange forwarding. The point is:

> *Because it requires considerable overhead after each move, mobile IP is intended for situations in which a host moves infrequently and remains at a given location for a relatively long period of time (e.g., hours or days).*

18.5 Mobile Addressing Details

A mobile's primary or *home address* is a conventional IP address that is assigned and administered as usual. The secondary address obtained while visiting a foreign network, known as a *care-of address*, is only used by IP software on the mobile and agents on the home or foreign networks; applications only use the primary address.

In practice, there are two types of care-of addresses; the type available on a given foreign network is determined by the network's administrator. The two types differ in the method by which the address is obtained and in the entity responsible for forwarding. The first form, known as a *co-located care-of address*, requires a mobile computer to handle all forwarding and tunneling itself. In essence, a mobile obtains a local address (e.g., through DHCP discussed in Chapter 22), and then handles the details of contacting a home agent to register and accepting datagrams sent to the temporary address.

The chief advantage of a co-located address is portability — because the host handles all communication, the foreign network does not need any special facilities. The chief disadvantage arises from the extra software required on a mobile.

The second form of mobile IP, which is known as a *foreign agent care-of address*, requires an active participant on the remote network called a *foreign agent*. When a mobile arrives at a foreign network, the mobile must first discover the identity of an agent, and then communicate with the agent to obtain a care-of address. Surprisingly, a foreign agent does not need to assign the mobile a unique address. Instead, the agent can assign its own IP address to all visiting mobiles.

18.6 Foreign Agent Discovery

The process of *foreign agent discovery* uses the ICMP *router discovery* mechanism in which each router periodically sends an ICMP *router advertisement* message, and allows a host to send an ICMP *router solicitation* to prompt for an advertisement†. If it also acts as a foreign agent, a router appends a *mobility agent extension‡*. Mobility extensions do not use a separate ICMP message type. Instead, a mobile extension is present if the datagram length specified in the IP header is greater than the length specified in the ICMP router discovery message. Figure 18.1 illustrates the extension format.

---

†A mobile can also multicast to the *all agents group* (*224.0.0.11*).

‡A mobility agent also appends a *prefix extension* to each message; the extension specifies the network prefix, which a mobile uses to determine that it has moved to a new network.

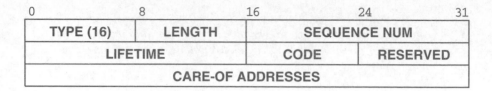

Figure 18.1 The format of a *mobility agent advertisement extension* message. This extension is appended to an ICMP router advertisement.

Each extension message begins with a 1-octet *TYPE* field followed by a 1-octet *LENGTH* field. The *LENGTH* field specifies the size of the extension message in octets, excluding the *TYPE* and *LENGTH* octets. The *LIFETIME* field specifies the maximum amount of time in seconds that the agent is willing to accept registration requests, with all 1s indicating *infinity*. Field *SEQUENCE NUM* specifies a sequence number for the message to allow a recipient to determine when a message is lost. Each bit in the *CODE* field defines a specific feature of the agent as listed in Figure 18.2.

Bit	Meaning
7	Registration with an agent is required even when using a co-located care-of address
6	The agent is busy and is not accepting registrations
5	Agent functions as a home agent
4	Agent functions as a foreign agent
3	Agent uses minimal encapsulation†
2	Agent uses GRE-style encapsulation‡
1	Unused (must be zero)
0	Agent supports reversed tunneling

Figure 18.2 Bits of the CODE field of a mobility agent advertisement, with bit 0 being the least-significant bit of the octet.

18.7 Agent Registration

Before it can receive datagrams at a foreign location, a mobile host must register. The *registration* procedure allows a host to:

- Register with an agent on the foreign network.
- Register directly with its home agent to request forwarding.
- Renew a registration that is due to expire.
- Deregister after returning home.

---

†*Minimal encapsulation* is a standard for IP-in-IP tunneling that abbreviates fields from the original header to save space.

‡*Generic Route Encapsulation* (*GRE*) is a standard that allows an arbitrary protocol to be encapsulated; IP-in-IP is one particular case.

If it obtains a co-located care-of address, a mobile performs registration directly; the mobile uses the care-of address to communicate with its home agent. If it obtains a care-of address from a foreign agent, a mobile allows the foreign agent to register on its behalf.

18.8 Registration Message Format

All registration messages are sent via UDP; agents use port 434. A registration message begins with a set of fixed-size fields followed by variable-length *extensions*. Each request is required to contain a *mobile-home authentication extension* that allows the home agent to verify the mobile's identity. Figure 18.3 illustrates the message format.

0	8	16	31
TYPE (1 or 3)	FLAGS/CODE	LIFETIME	
HOME ADDRESS			
HOME AGENT			
CARE-OF-ADDRESS (request only)			
IDENTIFICATION			
EXTENSIONS . . .			

Figure 18.3 The format of a mobile IP *registration request* or *reply* message.

The *TYPE* field specifies whether the message is a registration request (*1*) or a registration reply (*3*). The *LIFETIME* field specifies the number of seconds the registration is valid (a zero requests immediate deregistration, and all 1s specifies an infinite lifetime). The *HOME ADDRESS*, *HOME AGENT*, and *CARE-OF ADDRESS* fields specify the two IP addresses of the mobile and the address of its home agent, and the *IDENTIFICATION* field contains a 64-bit number generated by the mobile that is used to match requests with incoming replies and to prevent the mobile from accepting old messages. Bits of the *FLAGS/CODE* field are used as a result code in a registration reply message and to specify forwarding details in a registration request such as whether the registration corresponds to an additional (i.e., new) address request and the encapsulation that the agent should use when forwarding datagrams to the mobile.

In the case of a co-located care-of address, a mobile sends a registration request directly to its home agent. Otherwise, the mobile sends the request to a foreign agent, which then forwards the request to the home agent. If a foreign agent is used, both foreign and home agents must approve.

18.9 Communication With A Foreign Agent

We said that a foreign agent can assign one of its IP addresses for use as a care-of address. The consequence is that the mobile will not have a unique address on the foreign network. The question becomes: how can a foreign agent and a mobile host communicate over a network if the mobile does not have a valid IP address on the network? Communication requires relaxing the rules for IP addressing and using an alternative scheme for address binding: when a mobile host sends to a foreign agent, the mobile is allowed to use its home address as an IP source address, and when a foreign agent sends a datagram to a mobile, the agent is allowed to use the mobile's home address as an IP destination address. To avoid sending an invalid ARP request, a foreign agent records the mobile's hardware address when the first request arrives, and uses the hardware address to send a reply. Thus, although it does not use ARP, the agent can send datagrams to a mobile via hardware unicast. We can summarize:

> *If a mobile does not have a unique foreign address, a foreign agent must use the mobile's home address for communication. Instead of relying on ARP for address binding, the agent records the mobile's hardware address when a request arrives and uses the recorded information to supply the necessary binding.*

18.10 Datagram Transmission And Reception

Once it has registered, a mobile host on a foreign network can communicate with an arbitrary computer. To do so, the mobile creates a datagram that has the computer's address in the destination field and the mobile's home address in the source field†. The datagram follows the shortest path from the foreign network to the destination. However, a reply will not follow the shortest path directly to the mobile. Instead, the reply will travel to the mobile's home network. The home agent, which has learned the mobile's location from the registration, intercepts the datagram and uses *IP-in-IP* encapsulation to tunnel the datagram to the care-of address. To summarize:

> *Because a mobile uses its home address as a source address when communicating with an arbitrary destination, each reply is forwarded to the mobile's home network, where an agent intercepts the datagram, encapsulates it in another datagram, and forwards it either directly to the mobile or to the foreign agent the mobile is using.*

---

†The foreign network and the ISP that connects it to the rest of the Internet must agree to transmit datagrams with an arbitrary source address.

18.11 The Two-Crossing Problem

The description above highlights the major disadvantage of mobile IP: inefficient forwarding. Because a mobile uses its home address, a datagram sent to the mobile will be forwarded to the mobile's home network first and then to the mobile. The problem is especially severe because computer communication often exhibits *spatial locality of reference*, which means that a mobile visiting a foreign network will tend to communicate with computers on that network. To understand why mobile IP handles spatial locality poorly, consider Figure 18.4.

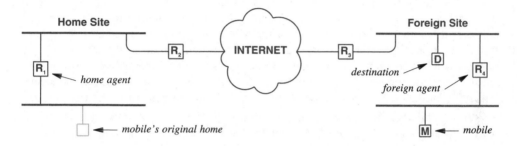

Figure 18.4 A topology in which mobile IP routing is inefficient. When mobile *M* communicates with local destination *D*, datagrams from *D* travel across the Internet to the mobile's home agent and then back to the mobile.

In the figure, mobile *M* has moved from its original home to a foreign network. We assume the mobile has registered with its home agent, router R_1, and the home agent has agreed to forward datagrams. Now consider communication between the mobile and destination *D*, which is located at the same site as the mobile. Datagrams from *M* to *D* travel through router R_4 and are then delivered to *D*. However, because datagrams sent from *D* to *M* contain *M*'s home address, they follow a path through R_3 and across the Internet to the mobile's home network. When the datagrams reach R_1 (the mobile's home agent), they are tunneled back across the Internet to the foreign site (either directly to *M* or to a foreign agent). Because crossing the Internet is much more expensive than local delivery, the situation described above is known as the *two-crossing problem*, and is sometimes called the *2X problem*†.

If a site expects a visiting mobile to interact heavily with local computers, the site can optimize forwarding by propagating a host-specific route for the mobile throughout the site. The host-specific route must then be deleted when the mobile leaves. Of course, the 2X problem remains for destinations outside the foreign site.

We can summarize:

---

†If destination *D* is not close to the mobile, a slightly less severe version of the problem occurs which is known as *triangle forwarding* or *dog-leg forwarding*.

Mobile IP introduces a routing inefficiency known as the 2X problem that occurs when a visiting mobile communicates with a computer at or near the foreign site. Each datagram sent to the mobile travels across the Internet to the mobile's home agent which then forwards the datagram back to the foreign site. Eliminating the inefficiency requires propagation of a host-specific route.

18.12 Communication With Computers On the Home Network

We said that when a mobile is visiting a foreign network, the mobile's home agent must intercept all datagrams sent to the mobile. Because it usually runs on a router that connects the home site to the Internet, a home agent can easily intercept all datagrams that arrive from the outside. A special case arises when a host on the mobile's home network sends a datagram to a mobile. Because IP specifies direct delivery over the local network, the sender will not forward the datagram to a router. Instead, the sender will ARP for the mobile's hardware address, encapsulate the datagram, and transmit it.

If a mobile has moved to a foreign network, the home agent must arrange to forward all datagrams, including those sent by local hosts. Thus, a home agent uses a form of *proxy ARP* to handle local transmission: whenever a host on the home network ARPs for the mobile, the home agent answers the request and supplies its own hardware address. That is, local hosts are tricked into forwarding any datagram destined for the mobile to the home agent, which then forwards the datagram to the mobile.

18.13 Summary

Mobile IP allows a computer to move from one network to another without changing its IP address and without requiring all routers to propagate a host-specific route. When it moves from its original home network to a foreign network, a mobile computer must obtain an additional, temporary address known as a care-of address. Applications use the mobile's original, home address; the care-of address is only used by underlying network software to enable forwarding and delivery across the foreign network.

Once it detects that it has moved, a mobile either obtains a co-located care-of address or discovers a foreign mobility agent and requests the agent to assign a care-of address. After obtaining a care-of address, the mobile registers with its home agent (either directly or indirectly through the foreign agent), and requests the agent to forward datagrams.

Once registration is complete, a mobile can communicate with an arbitrary computer on the Internet. Datagrams sent by the mobile are forwarded directly to the specified destination. However, each datagram sent back to the mobile follows a route to the mobile's home network where it is intercepted by the home agent, encapsulated in IP, and then tunneled to the mobile.

FOR FURTHER STUDY

Perkins [RFC 3344] describes IP Mobility Support and defines the details of messages. Perkins [RFC 2003], Perkins [RFC 2004], and Hanks et. al. [RFC 1701] describe the details of three IP-in-IP encapsulation schemes. Montenegro [RFC 3024] describes a reverse tunneling scheme for mobile IP. Finally, Johnson et. al. [RFC 3775] considers mobility support for IPv6.

EXERCISES

18.1   Compare the encapsulation schemes in RFCs 2003 and 2004. What are the advantages and disadvantages of each?

18.2   Read the mobile IP specification carefully. How frequently must a router send a mobility agent advertisement? Why?

18.3   Consult the mobile IP specification. When a foreign agent forwards a registration request to a mobile's home agent, which protocol ports are used? Why?

18.4   The specification for mobile IP allows a single router to function as both a home agent for a network and a foreign agent that supports visitors on the network. What are the advantages and disadvantages of using a single router for both functions?

18.5   The mobile IP specification defines three conceptually separate forms of authentication: mobile to home agent, mobile to foreign agent, and foreign agent to home agent. What are the advantages of separating them? The disadvantages?

18.6   Read the mobile IP specification to determine how a mobile host joins a multicast group. How are multicast datagrams routed to the mobile? What is the optimal scheme?

Chapter Contents

19

Private Network Interconnection (NAT, VPN)

19.1 Introduction

Previous chapters describe an internet as a single-level abstraction that consists of networks interconnected by routers. This chapter considers an alternative — a two-level internet architecture in which each organization has a private internet and a central internet interconnects them.

The chapter examines technologies used with a two-level architecture. One solves the pragmatic problem of limited address space, and the other offers increased functionality in the form of *privacy* that prevents outsiders from viewing the data.

19.2 Private And Hybrid Networks

One of the major drawbacks of a single-level internet architecture is the lack of privacy. If an organization comprises multiple sites, the contents of datagrams that travel across the Internet between the sites can be viewed by outsiders because they pass across networks owned by outsiders (i.e., ISPs). A two-level architecture distinguishes between *internal* and *external* datagrams (i.e., datagrams sent between two computers within an organization and datagrams sent between a computer in the organization and a computer in another organization). The goal is to keep internal datagrams *private*, while still allowing external communication.

The easiest way to guarantee privacy among an organization's computers consists of building a completely isolated *private internet*, which is usually referred to as a *private network* or *private intranet*. Because private networks use leased digital circuits to interconnect sites, and because the phone companies guarantee that no outsiders have access to such circuits, all data remains private.

A completely isolated intranet is not always desirable for two reasons. First, most organizations need access to the Internet to contact customers and suppliers. Second, a leased circuit is expensive. Consequently, many organizations seek alternatives that offer lower cost. For example, a common carrier may charge less for a Frame Relay connection than for a leased circuit that has equivalent capacity. Another way to lower costs involves using fewer circuits to connect sites and relying on intermediate sites to forward datagrams.

The lowest cost alternative consists of using the Internet as an interconnection among sites. The question becomes:

> *How can an organization that uses the Internet to connect its sites keep its data private?*

The answer lies in a technology that allows an organization to configure a *Virtual Private Network (VPN)*†. A VPN is *private* because technology guarantees that communication between any pair of computers remains concealed from outsiders, and *virtual* because it does not require leased circuits to interconnect sites.

Two basic techniques make a VPN possible: *tunneling* and *encryption*. We have already encountered tunneling in Chapters 16 and 18. VPNs use the same basic idea — a VPN defines a tunnel across the Internet between a router at one site and a router at another, and uses *IP-in-IP* encapsulation to forward datagrams across the tunnel.

Despite using the same basic concept, a VPN tunnel differs dramatically from the tunnels described previously. In particular, to guarantee privacy, a VPN encrypts each outgoing datagram before encapsulating it in another datagram for transmission‡. Figure 19.1 illustrates the concept.

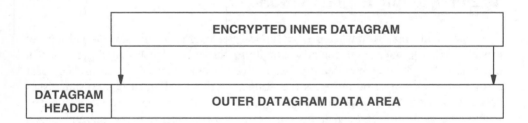

Figure 19.1 Illustration of IP-in-IP encapsulation used with a VPN. To ensure privacy, the inner datagram is encrypted before being sent.

---

†The name is a slight misnomer because the technology actually provides a virtual private intranet.
‡Chapter 30 considers IP security, and discusses the encapsulation used with IPsec.

As the figure shows, the entire inner datagram, including the header, is encrypted before being encapsulated. When a datagram arrives over a tunnel, the receiving router decrypts the data area to reproduce the inner datagram, which it then forwards. Although the outer datagram traverses arbitrary networks as it passes across the tunnel, outsiders cannot decode the contents because they do not have the encryption key. Furthermore, even the identity of the original source and destination are hidden because the header of the inner datagram is encrypted as well. Thus, only addresses in the outer datagram header are visible: the source address is the IP address of the router at one end of a tunnel, and the destination address is the IP address of the router at the other end of the tunnel.

To summarize:

> *A Virtual Private Network sends data across the Internet, but encrypts intersite transmissions to guarantee privacy.*

19.3 VPN Addressing And Routing

The easiest way to understand VPN addressing and routing is to think of each VPN tunnel as a replacement for a leased circuit in a private network. As in the private network case, a router contains explicit routes for destinations within the organization. However, instead of routing data across a leased line, a VPN routes the data through a tunnel. For example, Figure 19.2 shows a VPN with the routing table for a router that handles tunneling.

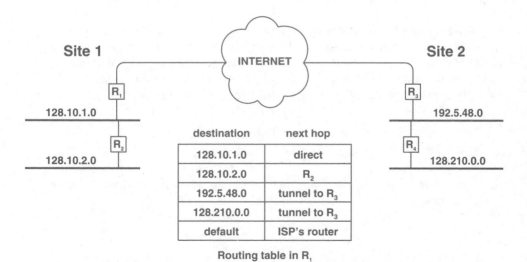

Figure 19.2 A VPN that spans two sites and R_1's routing table. The tunnel from R_1 to R_3 is configured like a point-to-point leased circuit.

As an example of forwarding in a VPN, consider a datagram sent from a computer on network *128.10.2.0* to a computer on network *128.210.0.0*. The sending host forwards the datagram to R_2, which forwards it to R_1. According to the routing table in R_1, the datagram must be sent across the tunnel to R_3. Therefore, R_1 encrypts the datagram, encapsulates it in the data area of an outer datagram with destination R_3. R_1 then forwards the outer datagram through the local ISP and across the Internet. The datagram arrives at R_3, which recognizes it as tunneled from R_1. R_3 decrypts the data area to produce the original datagram, looks up the destination in its routing table, and forwards the datagram to R_4 for delivery.

19.4 Extending VPN Technology To Individual Hosts

The same technology that provides low-cost, confidential communication among an organization's sites can easily be extended to handle individual host computers. In particular, many corporations provide employees with VPN software that gives each employee secure access to the corporate network over a conventional Internet connection. In essence, VPN software reconfigures the protocol stack in the computer so the only communication that can occur is with a VPN router at the corporation. Outgoing datagrams are encrypted and sent to the corporation for processing, and incoming datagrams from the corporation are accepted and decrypted. Thus, in all our descriptions of VPNs, the reader should keep in mind that a single computer can be used in place of a site.

19.5 A VPN With Private Addresses

A VPN offers an organization the same addressing options as a private network. If hosts in the VPN do not need general Internet connectivity, the VPN can be configured to use arbitrary IP addresses; if hosts need Internet access, a hybrid addressing scheme can be used. A minor difference is that when private addressing is used, one globally valid IP address is needed at each site for tunneling. Figure 19.3 illustrates the concept.

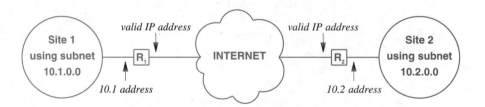

Figure 19.3 Illustration of addressing for a VPN that interconnects two completely private sites over the global Internet. Computers at each site use private addresses.

As the figure shows, site 1 uses subnet 10.1.0.0/16, while site 2 uses subnet 10.2.0.0/16. Only two globally valid IP addresses are needed. One is assigned to the connection from router R_1 to the Internet, and the other is assigned to the connection from R_2 to the Internet. Routing tables at the sites specify routes for private addresses; only the VPN tunneling software needs to know about or use the globally valid IP addresses.

VPNs use the same addressing structure as a private network. Hosts in a completely isolated VPN can use arbitrary addresses, but a hybrid architecture with valid IP addresses must be employed to provide hosts with access to the global Internet. The question remains: "How can a site provide access to the global Internet without assigning each host a valid IP address?" There are two general solutions.

Known as an *application gateway* approach, the first solution offers hosts access to Internet services without offering IP-level access. Each site has a multi-homed host connected to both the global Internet (with a globally valid IP address) and the internal network (using a private IP address). The multi-homed host runs a set of application programs, known as *application gateways*, that each handle one service. Hosts at the site do not send datagrams to the global Internet. Instead, they send each request to the appropriate application gateway on the multi-homed host, which accesses the service on the Internet and then relays the information back across the internal network. For example, Chapter 26 describes an e-mail forwarder that can relay e-mail messages between external hosts and internal hosts.

The chief advantage of the application gateway approach lies in its ability to work without changes to the underlying infrastructure or addressing. The chief disadvantage arises from the lack of generality, which can be summarized:

> *Each application gateway handles only one specific service; multiple gateways are required for multiple services.*

Consequently, although they are useful in special circumstances, application gateways do not solve the problem in a general way. Thus, a second solution was invented.

19.6 Network Address Translation (NAT)

A technology has been created that solves the general problem of providing IP-level access between hosts at a site and the rest of the Internet, without requiring each host at the site to have a globally valid IP address. Known as *Network Address Translation (NAT)*, the technology requires a site to have a single connection to the global Internet and at least one globally valid IP address, G. Address G is assigned to a computer (a multi-homed host or a router) that connects the site to the Internet and runs NAT software. Informally, we refer to a computer that runs NAT software as a *NAT box*; all datagrams pass through the NAT box as they travel from the site out to the Internet or from the Internet into the site.

NAT translates the addresses in both outgoing and incoming datagrams by replacing the source address in each outgoing datagram with *G* and replacing the destination address in each incoming datagram with the private address of the correct host. Thus, from the view of an external host, all datagrams come from the NAT box and all responses return to the NAT box. From the view of internal hosts, the NAT box appears to be a router that can reach the global Internet.

The chief advantage of NAT arises from its combination of generality and transparency. NAT is more general than application gateways because it allows an arbitrary internal host to access an arbitrary service on a computer in the global Internet. NAT is transparent because it allows an internal host to send and receive datagrams using a private (i.e., nonroutable) address.

To summarize:

> *Network Address Translation technology provides transparent IP-level access to the Internet from a host with a private address.*

19.7 NAT Translation Table Creation

Our overview of NAT omits an important detail because it does not specify how NAT knows which internal host should receive a datagram that arrives from the Internet. In fact, NAT maintains a translation table that it uses to perform the mapping. Each entry in the table specifies two items: the IP address of a host on the Internet and the internal IP address of a host at the site. When an incoming datagram arrives from the Internet, NAT looks up the datagram's destination address in the translation table, extracts the corresponding address of an internal host, replaces the datagram's destination address with the host's address, and forwards the datagram across the local network to the host†.

The NAT translation table must be in place before a datagram arrives from the Internet. Otherwise, NAT has no way to identify the correct internal host to which the datagram should be forwarded. How and when is the table initialized? There are several possibilities:

- *Manual Initialization.* A manager configures the translation table manually before any communication occurs.

- *Outgoing Datagrams.* The table is built as a side-effect of an internal host sending a datagram. NAT uses the outgoing datagram to create a translation table entry that records the source and destination addresses.

- *Incoming Name Lookups.* The table is built as a side-effect of handling domain name lookups. When a host on the Internet looks up the domain name of an internal host‡, the DNS software sends address *G* as the answer, and then creates an entry in the NAT translation table to forward incoming datagrams to the correct internal host.

---

†Whenever it replaces an address in a datagram header, NAT must recompute the header checksum.
‡Chapter 23 describes how the *Domain Name System* (*DNS*) operates.

Each initialization technique has advantages and disadvantages. Manual initialization provides permanent mappings and allows IP datagrams to be sent in either direction at any time. Using an outgoing datagram to initialize the table has the advantage of being automatic, but does not allow communication to be initiated from the outside. Using incoming domain name lookups requires modifying domain name software. It accommodates communication initiated from outside the site, but only works if the sender performs a domain name lookup before sending datagrams.

Most implementations of NAT use outgoing datagrams to initialize the table; the strategy is especially popular among ISPs. To understand why, consider a small ISP that serves dialup customers. Figure 19.4 illustrates the architecture.

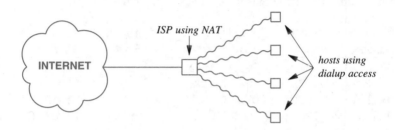

Figure 19.4 The use of NAT by a small ISP that serves dialup customers. NAT translation allows the ISP to assign a private address to each dialup customer.

The ISP must assign an IP address to a customer whenever the customer dials in. NAT permits the ISP to assign private addresses (e.g., the first customer is assigned *10.0.0.1*, the second *10.0.0.2*, and so on). When a customer sends a datagram to a destination on the Internet, NAT uses the outgoing datagram to initialize its translation table.

19.8 Multi-Address NAT

So far, we have described a simplistic implementation of NAT that performs a 1-to-1 address mapping between an external address and an internal address. That is, a 1-to-1 mapping permits at most one computer at the site to access a given machine on the global Internet at any time. In practice, more complex forms of NAT are used that allow multiple hosts at a site to access a given external address concurrently.

One variation of NAT permits concurrency by retaining the 1-to-1 mapping, but allowing the NAT box to hold multiple Internet addresses. Known as *multi-address NAT*, the scheme assigns the NAT box a set of K globally valid addresses, G_1, G_2,... G_k. When the first internal host accesses a given destination, the NAT box chooses address G_1, adds an entry to the translation table, and sends the datagram. If another host initiates contact with the same destination, the NAT box chooses address G_2, and so on.

Thus, multi-address NAT allows up to K internal hosts to access a given destination concurrently.

19.9 Port-Mapped NAT

Another popular variant of NAT provides concurrency by translating TCP or UDP protocol port numbers as well as addresses. Sometimes called *Network Address Port Translation (NAPT)*, the scheme expands the NAT translation table to include additional fields. Besides a pair of source and destination IP addresses, the table contains a pair of source and destination protocol port numbers and a protocol port number used by the NAT box. Figure 19.5 illustrates the contents of the table.

Private Address	Private Port	External Address	External Port	NAT Port	Protocol Used
10.0.0.5	21023	128.10.19.20	80	14003	tcp
10.0.0.1	386	128.10.19.20	80	14010	tcp
10.0.2.6	26600	207.200.75.200	21	14012	tcp
10.0.0.3	1274	128.210.1.5	80	14007	tcp

Figure 19.5 An example of a translation table used by NAPT. The table includes port numbers as well as IP addresses.

The table in the figure has entries for four internal computers that are currently accessing destinations on the global Internet. All communication is using TCP. Interestingly, the table shows two internal hosts, *10.0.0.5* and *10.0.0.1*, both accessing protocol port *80* (a Web server) on computer *128.10.19.20*. In this case, it happens that the two source ports being used for the two connections differ. However, source port uniqueness cannot be guaranteed — it could turn out that two internal hosts happen to choose the same source port number. Thus, to avoid potential conflicts, NAT assigns a unique port number to each communication that is used on the Internet. Recall that TCP identifies each connection with a 4-tuple that represents the IP address and protocol port number of each endpoint. The first two items in the table correspond to TCP connections that the two internal hosts identify with the 4-tuples:

$$(10.0.0.5, \ 21023, \ 128.10.19.20, \ 80)$$
$$(10.0.0.1, \ \ \ \ 386, \ 128.10.19.20, \ 80)$$

However, the computer in the Internet that receives datagrams after NAPT performs the translation identifies the same two connections with the 4-tuples:

$$(G, \ 14003, \ 128.10.19.20, \ 80)$$
$$(G, \ 14010, \ 128.10.19.20, \ 80)$$

where G is the globally valid address of the NAT box.

The primary advantage of NAPT lies in the generality it achieves with a single globally valid IP address; the primary disadvantage arises because it restricts communication to TCP or UDP. As long as all communication uses TCP or UDP, NAPT allows an internal computer to access multiple external computers, and multiple internal computers to access the same external computer without interference. A port space of 16 bits allows up to 2^{16} pairs of applications to communicate at the same time. To summarize:

> *Several variants of NAT exist, including the popular NAPT form that translates protocol port numbers as well as IP addresses.*

19.10 Interaction Between NAT And ICMP

Even straightforward changes to an IP address can cause unexpected side-effects in higher layer protocols. In particular, to maintain the illusion of transparency, NAT must handle ICMP. For example, suppose an internal host uses *ping* to test reachability of a destination on the Internet. The host expects to receive an ICMP *echo reply* for each ICMP *echo request* message it sends. Thus, NAT must forward incoming echo replies to the correct host. However, NAT does not forward all ICMP messages that arrive from the Internet. If routes in the NAT box are incorrect, for example, an ICMP *redirect* message must be processed locally. Thus, when an ICMP message arrives from the Internet, NAT must first determine whether the message should be handled locally or sent to an internal host. Before forwarding to an internal host, NAT translates the ICMP message.

To understand the need for ICMP translation, consider an ICMP *destination unreachable* message. The message contains the header from a datagram, D, that caused the error. Unfortunately, NAT translated addresses before sending D, so the source address is not the address the internal host used. Thus, before forwarding the message, NAT must open the ICMP message and translate the addresses in D so they appear in exactly the form that the internal host used. After making the change, NAT must recompute the checksum in D, the checksum in the ICMP header, and the checksum in the outer datagram header.

19.11 Interaction Between NAT And Applications

Although ICMP makes NAT complex, application protocols have a more serious effect. In general, NAT will not work with any application that sends IP addresses or protocol ports as data. For example, when two programs use the *File Transfer Protocol* (*FTP*) described in Chapter 25, they have a TCP connection between them. As part of the protocol, one program obtains a protocol port on the local machine, converts the number to ASCII, and sends the result across a TCP connection to another program. If the connection between the programs passes through NAPT from an internal host to a host on the Internet, the port number in the data stream must be changed to agree with the port number NAPT has selected instead of the port the internal host is using. In fact, if NAT fails to open the data stream and change the number, the protocol will fail. Implementations of NAT have been created that recognize popular protocols such as FTP and make the necessary change in the data stream, and variants of applications have been created that avoid forming connections in the reverse direction†. However, it is possible to define an application that will not operate across NAT. To summarize:

> *NAT affects ICMP and higher layer protocols; except for a few standard applications like FTP, an application protocol that passes IP addresses or protocol port numbers as data will not operate correctly across NAT.*

Changing items in a data stream increases the complexity of NAPT in two ways. First, it means that NAPT must have detailed knowledge of each application that transfers such information. Second, if the port numbers are represented in ASCII, as is the case with FTP, changing the value can change the number of octets transferred. Inserting even one additional octet into a TCP connection is difficult because each octet in the stream has a sequence number. Because a sender does not know that additional data has been inserted, it continues to assign sequence numbers without the additional data. When it receives additional data, the receiver will generate acknowledgements that account for the data. Thus, after it inserts additional data, NAT must translate the sequence numbers in each outgoing segment and each incoming acknowledgement.

19.12 NAT In The Presence Of Fragmentation

The description of NAT above has made an important assumption about IP: a NAT system receives complete IP datagrams and not fragments. What happens if a datagram is fragmented? There are two situations. For basic NAT, fragmentation does not pose a problem because each fragment carries the IP source and destination addresses. In the case of NAPT (the most widely used variant of NAT), however, the table lookup uses protocol port numbers from the transport header as well as IP addresses from the IP header. Unfortunately, only the first fragment of a datagram carries the transport proto-

---

†The version of FTP that does not require the server to connect back to the client is known as *passive FTP*.

col header. Thus, before it can perform the lookup, a NAPT system must receive and examine the first fragment of the datagram.

Consequently, a NAPT system can follow one of two designs: the system can save the fragments and attempt to reassemble the datagram, or the system can discard fragments and only process complete datagrams. Neither option is desirable. Reassembly requires state information, which means the system cannot scale to high speed or high numbers of flows. Discarding fragments means the system will not process arbitrary traffic. In practice, only those NAPT systems that are designed for slow-speed networks choose to reassemble; many systems reject fragmented datagrams.

19.13 Conceptual Address Domains

We have described NAT as a technology that can be used to connect a private network to the global Internet. In fact, NAT can be used to interconnect any two *address domains*. Thus, NAT can be used between two corporations that each have a private network using address 10.0.0.0. More important, NAT can be used at two levels: between a customer's private and an ISP's private address domains as well as between the ISP's address domain and the global Internet. Finally, NAT can be combined with VPN technology to form a hybrid architecture in which private addresses are used within the organization, and NAT is used to provide connectivity between each site and the global Internet.

As an example of multiple levels of NAT, consider an individual who works at home from several computers which are connected to a LAN. The individual can assign private addresses to the computers at home, and use NAT between the home network and the corporate intranet. The corporation can also assign private addresses and use NAT between its intranet and the global Internet.

19.14 Slirp And Iptables

Two implementations of Network Address Translation have been especially popular at various times; both were designed for the Unix operating system. The *slirp* program, derived from 4.4 BSD, was designed for use in a dialup architecture like the one shown in Figure 19.4†. *Slirp* combines PPP and NAT into a single program. It runs on a computer that has: a valid IP address, a permanent Internet connection, and one or more dialup modems. The chief advantage of *slirp* is that it can use an ordinary user account on a Unix system for general-purpose Internet access. A computer that has a private address dials in and runs *slirp*. Once *slirp* begins, the dialup line switches from ASCII commands to PPP. The dialup computer starts PPP and obtains access to the Internet (e.g., to access a Web site).

Slirp implements NAPT — it uses protocol port numbers to demultiplex connections, and can rewrite protocol port numbers as well as IP addresses. It is possible to

---

†Figure 19.4 can be found on page 355.

have multiple computers (e.g., computers on a LAN) accessing the Internet at the same time through a single occurrence of *slirp* running on a UNIX system.

Another popular implementation of NAT has been designed for the Linux operating system. Known as *iptables*, the software is a combination of tools and kernel support for packet rewriting and firewalling. Because *iptables* provides stateful packet inspection, NAT or NAPT can be formed using specific sets of *iptables* rules.

19.15 Summary

Although a private network guarantees privacy, the cost can be high. Virtual Private Network (VPN) technology offers a lower-cost alternative that allows an organization to use the global Internet to interconnect multiple sites and use encryption to guarantee that intersite traffic remains private. Like a traditional private network, a VPN can either be completely isolated (in which case hosts are assigned private addresses) or a hybrid architecture that allows hosts to communicate with destinations on the global Internet.

Two technologies exist that provide communication between hosts in different address domains: application gateways and Network Address Translation (NAT). An application gateway acts like a proxy by receiving a request from a host in one domain, sending the request to a destination in another, and then returning the result to the original host. A separate application gateway must be installed for each service.

Network Address Translation provides transparent IP-level access to the global Internet from a host that has a private address. NAT is especially popular among ISPs because it allows customers to access arbitrary Internet services while using a private IP address. Applications that pass address or port information in the data stream will not work with NAT until NAT has been programmed to recognize the application and make the necessary changes in the data; most implementations of NAT only recognize a few (standard) services.

Several variants of NAT exist. Most NAT implementations perform Network Address and Port Translation (NAPT). In addition to rewriting IP addresses, NAPT rewrites transport-level protocol port numbers, which provides complete generality and permits arbitrary applications running on a computer in an organization to access arbitrary services on the Internet simultaneously.

FOR FURTHER STUDY

Many router and software vendors sell Virtual Private Network technologies, usually with a choice of encryption schemes and addressing architecture. Consult the vendors' literature for more information.

Several versions of NAT are also available commercially, including dedicated hardware devices that combine NAT and security firewalling into a single box. Srisuresh and Holdrege [RFC 2663] and Srisuresh and Egevang [RFC 3022] define NAT terminology, including NAPT.

More details about the *iptables* tools can be found in the Linux documentation. A resource page can be found at URL:

http://www.netfilter.org

More information on *slirp* can be found in the program documentation; a resource page for *slirp* can be found at:

http://slirp.sourceforge.net

EXERCISES

19.1   Under what circumstances will a VPN transfer substantially more packets than conventional IP when sending the same data across the Internet? Hint: think about encapsulation.

19.2   Read the *slirp* document to find out about *port redirection*. Why is it needed?

19.3   What are the potential problems when three address domains are connected by two NAT boxes?

19.4   In the previous question, how many times will a destination address be translated? A source address?

19.5   Consider an ICMP host unreachable message sent through two NAT boxes that interconnect three address domains. How many address translations will occur? How many translations of protocol port numbers will occur?

19.6   Imagine that we decide to create a new Internet parallel to the existing Internet that allocates addresses from the same address space. Can NAT technology be used to connect the two arbitrarily large Internets that use the same address space? If so, explain how. If not, explain why not.

19.7   Is NAT completely transparent to a host? To answer the question, try to find a sequence of packets that a host can transmit to determine whether it is located behind a NAT box.

19.8   What are the advantages of combining NAT technology with VPN technology? The disadvantages?

19.9   Obtain a copy of *slirp* and instrument it to measure performance. Does *slirp* processing overhead ever delay datagrams? Why or why not?

19.10   Configure NAT on a Linux system between a private address domain and the Internet. Which well-known services work correctly and which do not?

19.11   Read about a variant of NAT called *twice NAT* that allows communication to be initiated from either side of the NAT box at any time. How does twice NAT ensure that translations are consistent? If two instances of twice NAT are used to interconnect three address domains, is the result completely transparent to all hosts?

Chapter Contents

20

Client-Server Model Of Interaction

20.1 Introduction

Early chapters present the details of TCP/IP technology, including the protocols that provide basic services and the router architecture that provides necessary routing information. Now that we understand the basic technology, we can examine application programs that profit from the cooperative use of a TCP/IP internet. While the example applications are both practical and interesting, they do not form the main emphasis. Instead, focus rests on the patterns of interaction among the communicating application programs. The primary pattern of interaction among cooperating applications is known as the *client-server* paradigm†. Client-server interaction forms the basis of network communication, and provides the foundation for application services. This chapter considers the basic model; later chapters describe its use in specific applications

20.2 The Client-Server Model

A *server* is a computer program that offers a service over a network. A server accepts an incoming request, forms a response, and returns the result to the requester. For the simplest services, each request arrives in a single datagram and the server returns a response in another datagram.

---

†Although recent media stories claim that client-server computing has been replaced by *peer-to-peer* (*P2P*), the underlying software still follows the client-server paradigm described here.

An executing program becomes a *client* when it sends a request to a server and waits for a response. Because the client-server model is a convenient and natural extension of interprocess communication used on a single machine, it is easy for programmers to build programs that use the model to interact.

Servers can perform simple or complex tasks. For example, a *time-of-day server* merely returns the current time whenever a client sends the server a packet. A *web server* receives requests from a browser to fetch a copy of a Web page; the server returns the requested page to the browser.

Usually, servers are implemented as application programs†. The advantage of implementing servers as application programs is that they can execute on any computing system that supports TCP/IP communication. For example, if the load on a server increases, the server can be moved to a faster CPU. Technologies exist that allow a server to be replicated on multiple physical computers to increase reliability or performance. If a computer's primary purpose is support of a particular server program, the term "server" may be applied to the computer as well as to the server program. Thus, one hears statements such as "machine *A* is our web server."

20.3 A Simple Example: UDP Echo Server

The simplest form of client-server interaction uses datagram delivery to convey messages from a client to a server and back. For example, Figure 20.1 illustrates the interaction in a *UDP echo server*. A UDP *echo server* is started first. The server specifies that it will use the port reserved for the UDP *echo* service, port 7. The server then enters an infinite loop that has three steps: (1) wait for a datagram to arrive at the echo port, (2) reverse the source and destination addresses‡ (including source and destination IP addresses as well as UDP port ids), and (3) return the datagram to its original sender. At some other site, a program becomes a UDP *echo client* when it allocates an unused UDP protocol port, sends a UDP message to the UDP echo server, and awaits the reply. The client expects to receive back exactly the same data as it sent.

The UDP echo service illustrates two important points that are generally true about client-server interaction. The first concerns the difference between the lifetime of servers and clients:

> *A server starts execution before interaction begins and continues to accept requests and send responses without ever terminating. A client is any program that makes a request and awaits a response; it (usually) terminates after using a server a finite number of times.*

---

†Many operating systems refer to a running application program as a *process*, a *user process*, or a *task*.
‡One of the exercises suggests considering this step in more detail.

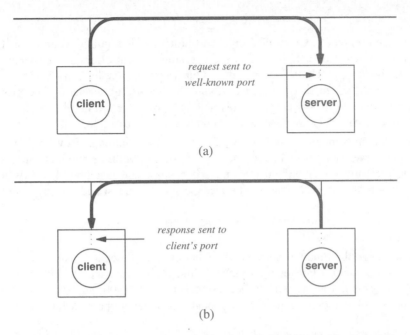

(a)

(b)

Figure 20.1 UDP echo as an example of the client-server model. In (a) the
client sends a request to the server at a known IP address and at
a well-known UDP port, and in (b) the server returns a response.
Clients use any UDP port that is available.

The second point, which is more technical, concerns the use of reserved and non-reserved port identifiers:

> *A server waits for requests at a well-known port that has been
> reserved for the service it offers. A client allocates an arbitrary,
> unused, nonreserved port for its communication.*

In a client-server interaction, only one of the two ports needs to be reserved. Assigning a unique port identifier to each service makes it easy to build both clients and servers.

Who would use an echo service? It is not a service that the average user finds interesting. However, programmers who design, implement, measure, or modify network protocol software, or network managers who test routes and debug communication problems, often use echo servers in testing. For example, an echo service can be used to determine if it is possible to reach a remote machine.

20.4 Time And Date Service

The echo server is extremely simple, and little code is required to implement either the server or client side (provided that the operating system offers a reasonable way to access the underlying UDP/IP protocols). Our second example, a time server, shows that even simple client-server interaction can provide useful services. The problem a time server solves is that of automatically setting a computer's time-of-day clock. Once set, the time of day clock keeps time as accurately as a wristwatch.

Most laptop computers use a battery to keep a clock running. However, interaction with a time server can be used to set the clock to the correct time automatically, without requiring the battery to maintain the time. If at least one machine on every network runs a time-of-day server, a laptop only needs to send a request and obtain the time.

20.4.1 Representation for the Date and Time

How should the time be represented? One useful representation stores the time and date in a single (large) integer by giving a count of seconds since an epoch date. The TCP/IP protocols define the epoch date to be January 1, 1900, and store the time in a 32-bit integer. The representation accommodates all dates in the near future.

20.4.2 Time Server Interaction

The interaction between a client and a server that offers time service works much like an echo service. The server application begins first, and waits to be contacted. The server assumes that each arriving datagram is a request for the current time, and responds by sending a UDP message that contains the current time in a 32-bit integer. We can summarize:

> *Sending a datagram to a time server is equivalent to making a request for the current time; the server responds by returning a UDP message that contains the current time.*

20.5 The Complexity of Servers

The examples above illustrate basic sequential servers (i.e., a server that processes one request at a time). After accepting a request, a sequential server sends a reply before going back to see if another request has arrived. Protocol software in the operating system must queue requests that arrive for a server while it is busy.

In practice, servers are usually much more difficult to build than clients because production servers are *concurrent*, which means the server can handle multiple requests at the same time. To understand why concurrency is important, imagine a web server sending a large image to a user over a dialup connection. The server must respond to other requests while the slow transfer continues. To do so, a server takes the following steps:

Open port
> The server opens the well-known port at which it can be reached.

Wait for client
> The server waits for a client to send a request.

Start copy
> The master starts an independent, concurrent copy of itself to handle the request (i.e., a process or thread). The copy handles one request and then terminates.

Continue
> The original server returns to the *wait* step, and continues accepting new requests while the newly created copy handles the previous request concurrently.

Figure 20.2 The steps a concurrent server takes that allow the server to handle multiple requests at the same time.

The chief advantage of a concurrent server is speed: requests that arrive later do not need to wait for requests that started earlier. The chief disadvantage is complexity: a concurrent server is more difficult to construct.

In addition to the complexity that results because servers handle concurrent requests, complexity also arises because servers must enforce authorization and protection rules. Server programs usually need to execute with highest privilege because they must read system files, keep logs, and access protected data. The operating system will not restrict a server program if it attempts to access users' files. Thus, servers cannot blindly honor requests from other sites. Instead, each server takes responsibility for enforcing the system access and protection policies.

Finally, servers must protect themselves against malformed requests or against requests that will cause the server program itself to abort. Often, it is difficult to foresee potential problems. For example, one project at Purdue University designed a file server that allowed student operating systems to access files on a UNIX timesharing system. Students discovered that requesting the server to open a file named */dev/tty* caused the server to abort because in UNIX the name refers to the control terminal a program is using; because it was launched at startup, the server had no such terminal.

We can summarize our discussion of servers:

Servers are usually more difficult to build than clients because, although they can be implemented with application programs, servers must enforce all the access and protection policies of the computer system on which they run, and must protect themselves against all possible errors.

20.6 Broadcasting A Request

So far, all our examples of client-server interaction require the client to know the complete server address. In some cases, however, a client does not know the server's address. For example, when it boots, a computer can use DHCP to obtain an address, but the client does not know the address of a server†. Instead, the client broadcasts its request.

The point is:

For protocols where the client does not know the location of a server, the client-server paradigm permits client programs to broadcast requests.

20.7 Alternatives To The Client-Server Model

Are there any alternatives to client-server interaction? One special case is particularly significant. We said that an application becomes a client when it needs information. However, it is sometimes important to lower the latency. The ARP protocol from Chapter 5 uses one modification of client-server interaction: caching. A computer that runs ARP must keep a cache of address bindings to improve the efficiency of later queries. Caching improves the performance of client-server interaction in cases where the recent history of queries is a good indicator of future use.

Although caching improves performance, it does not change the essence of client-server interaction. The essence lies in our assumption that processing must be driven by demand. We have assumed that a program executes until it needs information and then acts as a client to obtain the needed information. Taking a demand-driven view of the world is natural and arises from experience. Caching helps alleviate the cost of obtaining information by lowering the retrieval cost for all except the first process that makes a request.

How can we lower the cost of information retrieval for the first request? In a distributed system, it may be possible to have concurrent background activities that collect and propagate information *before* any particular program requests it, making retrieval costs low even for the initial request. More important, precollecting information can al-

---

†Chapter 22 examines DHCP.

low a given system to continue executing even though other machines or the networks connecting them fail.

An early Unix program named *ruptime* illustrates the idea. When invoked, *ruptime* reports the CPU load and time since system startup for each computer on the local network. The report occurs instantly because a background program running on each computer uses UDP to broadcast information periodically and collects incoming information sent by other computers. Thus, the information is always available locally without delay (i.e., without requiring network communication).

Precollection has one major disadvantage: it uses processor time and network bandwidth even when no one cares about the data being collected. For example, the *ruptime* broadcast and collection continues running throughout the night, even if no one is logged in to read the information. If only a few machines connect to a given network, precollection cost is insignificant. For networks with many hosts, however, the large volume of broadcast traffic generated by precollection makes it too expensive. Thus, precollection is not among the most popular alternatives to client-server.

20.8 Summary

Distributed programs require network communication. Such programs often fall into a pattern of use known as client-server interaction. A server process awaits a request, and performs actions based on the request. The action usually includes sending a response. A client program formulates a request, sends it to a server, and then awaits a reply.

We have seen examples of clients and servers and found that some clients send requests directly, while others broadcast requests. Broadcast is especially useful on a local network when a machine does not know the address of a server.

We also noted that if servers use Internet protocols like UDP, they can accept and respond to requests across an internet. If they communicate using physical frames and physical hardware addresses, they are restricted to a single physical network.

Finally, we considered an alternative to the client-server paradigm that uses precollection of information to avoid delays. An example of precollection came from a machine status service.

FOR FURTHER STUDY

UDP echo service is defined in Postel [RFC 862]. The *UNIX Programmer's Manual* describes the *ruptime* command (also see the related description of *rwho*). Various RFCs specify many server protocols not discussed here, including discard, character generation, day and time, active users, and quote of the day. The next chapters consider others.

EXERCISES

20.1 Build a UDP echo client that sends a datagram to a specified echo server, awaits a reply, and compares it to the original message.

20.2 Carefully consider the manipulation of IP addresses in a UDP echo server. Under what conditions is it incorrect to create new IP addresses by reversing the source and destination IP addresses?

20.3 As we have seen, servers can be implemented by separate application programs or by building server code into the protocol software in an operating system. What are the advantages and disadvantages of having an application program (user process) per server?

20.4 Suppose you do not know the IP address of a local machine running a UDP echo server, but you know that it responds to requests sent to port 7. Is there an IP address you can use to reach it?

20.5 Build a client for the UDP time service.

20.6 Characterize situations in which a server can be located on a separate physical network from its client. Why or why not?

20.7 What is the chief disadvantage of having all machines broadcast their status periodically?

20.8 Examine the format of data broadcast by the servers that implement the 4BSD UNIX *ruptime* command. What information is available to the client in addition to machine status?

20.9 What servers are running on computers at your site? If you do not have access to system configuration files that list the servers started for a given computer, see if your system has a command that prints a list of open TCP and UDP ports (e.g., the UNIX *netstat* command).

20.10 Some servers allow a manager to gracefully shut them down or restart them. What is the advantage of graceful server shutdown?

Chapter Contents

21

The Socket Interface

21.1 Introduction

Previous chapters discuss the principles and concepts that underlie the TCP/IP protocols without specifying the interface between the application programs and the protocol software. This chapter reviews an *Application Program Interface (API)* that has become a de facto standard, and describes the paradigm application programs use to access the protocols.

There are two reasons for postponing the discussion of APIs. First, in principle, we must distinguish between the interface and protocols because the protocol standards do not specify an exact interface. Second, in practice, the exact details of an interface depend on a specific operating system and programming language.

We will examine the *socket* API. Sockets were originally created as part of the BSD UNIX operating system, and later appeared in Linux and more recent BSD systems; Microsoft adapted a version known as *Windows Sockets†* for their systems. The reader should remember that the operations listed here are not part of the TCP/IP standards.

21.2 The UNIX I/O Paradigm And Network I/O

Developed in the late 1960s and early 1970s, UNIX was originally designed as a timesharing system for single processor computers. It is a process-oriented operating system in which each application program executes as a user level process. An application program interacts with the operating system by making *system calls*. From the programmer's point of view, system calls look and behave exactly like other procedure

---

†Programmers often use the term *WINSOCK* as a replacement for Windows Sockets.

calls. They take arguments and return one or more results. Arguments can be values (e.g., an integer count) or pointers to objects in the application program (e.g., a buffer to be filled with characters).

Derived from those in Multics and earlier systems, the UNIX input and output (I/O) primitives follow a paradigm sometimes referred to as *open-read-write-close*. Before a user process can perform I/O operations, it calls *open* to specify the file or device to be used and obtains permission. The call to *open* returns a small integer *file descriptor*† that the process uses when performing I/O operations on the opened file or device. Once an object has been opened, the user process invokes *read* or *write* operations to transfer data. *Read* transfers data into the user process; *write* transfers data from the user process to the file or device. Both *read* and *write* take three arguments that specify the file descriptor to use, the address of a buffer, and the number of bytes to transfer. After all transfer operations are complete, the user process calls *close* to inform the operating system that it has finished using the object (the operating system automatically closes all open descriptors if a process terminates without calling *close*).

21.3 Adding Network I/O to UNIX

The group adding network protocols to BSD UNIX decided that because network protocols are more complex than conventional I/O devices, interaction between user processes and network protocols must be more complex than interactions between user processes and conventional I/O facilities. In particular, the protocol interface must allow programmers to create both server code that awaits connections passively as well as client code that forms connections actively. Furthermore, application programs sending datagrams may wish to specify the destination address along with each datagram instead of binding destinations at the time they call *open*. To handle all these cases, the designers chose to abandon the traditional UNIX open-read-write-close paradigm, and added several new operating system calls as well as new library routines. Adding network protocols to UNIX increased the complexity of the I/O interface substantially.

Further complexity arises in the UNIX protocol interface because designers attempted to build a general mechanism to accommodate many protocols. For example, the generality makes it possible for the operating system to include software for other protocol suites as well as TCP/IP, and to allow an application program to use one or more of them at a time. As a consequence, the application program cannot merely supply a 32-bit address and expect the operating system to interpret it correctly. The application must explicitly specify that the 32-bit number represents an IP address.

---

†The term ''file descriptor'' arises because in UNIX devices are mapped into the file system.

21.4 The Socket Abstraction

The basis for network I/O in the socket API centers on an abstraction known as the *socket*†. We think of a socket as a mechanism that provides an endpoint for communication. An application program requests that a socket be created when one is needed, and the system returns a small integer that the application program uses to reference the socket. If it corresponds to a TCP connection, both endpoints of the connection must be specified. If a socket is used for UDP, the remote endpoint can be left unspecified, in which case the remote endpoint must be passed as an argument each time a message is sent.

21.5 Creating A Socket

The *socket* function creates sockets on demand. It takes three integer arguments and returns an integer result:

$$result = socket(pf, type, protocol)$$

Argument *pf* specifies the protocol family to be used with the socket (i.e., it specifies how to interpret addresses). Current families include IP version 4 (PF_INET), IP version 6 (PF_INET6), Xerox Corporation PUP internet (PF_PUP), Apple Computer Incorporated AppleTalk network (PF_APPLETALK), and UNIX file system (PF_UNIX)‡.

Argument *type* specifies the type of communication desired. Possible types include reliable stream delivery service (SOCK_STREAM) and connectionless datagram delivery service (SOCK_DGRAM), as well as a raw type (SOCK_RAW) that allows privileged programs to access low-level protocols or network interfaces.

Because a single protocol family can have multiple protocols that provide the same type of communication, the *socket* call has a third argument that can be used to select a specific protocol; if the protocol family only contains one protocol of a given *type* (e.g., only TCP supplies a SOCK_STREAM service for IPv4), the third argument can be set to 0.

21.6 Socket Inheritance And Termination

Operating systems provide mechanisms that can be used to create new processes or threads. For example, UNIX systems use the *fork* and *exec* system calls to create a process running a specific application program. In most systems, when a new process is created, the newly created process inherits access to open sockets. We will see that a server uses socket inheritance to allow concurrent copies of the server to handle multiple requests. Internally, the operating system keeps a reference count associated with each socket, so it knows how many application programs (processes) have access to it.

---

†For now, it is sufficient to think of sockets as part of the operating system kernel. However, it is also possible to provide a socket API with library procedures.

‡To make programs readable, programmers use symbolic constants like *PF_INET* in place of numeric values; the socket API defines a numeric value for each constant.

Both the old and the new process share access rights to existing descriptors, and both can access the sockets. Thus, it is the responsibility of the programmer to ensure that the two processes use the shared socket meaningfully.

When a process finishes using a socket it calls *close*. *Close* has the form:

$$close(socket)$$

where argument *socket* specifies the descriptor of a socket to close. When a process terminates for any reason, the system closes all sockets that remain open. Internally, a call to *close* decrements the reference count for a socket and destroys the socket if the count reaches zero.

21.7 Specifying A Local Address

Initially, a socket is created without any association to local or destination addresses. For the TCP/IP protocols, this means that a new socket does not begin with local or remote IP addresses or protocol port numbers. Client programs do not care about the local address they use, and are willing to allow the protocol software to fill in the computer's IP address and choose a port number. However, server processes that operate at a well-known port must be able to specify that port to the system. Once a socket has been created, a server uses the *bind* function to establish a local address for it†. *Bind* has the following form:

$$bind(socket, localaddr, addrlen)$$

Argument *socket* is the integer descriptor of the socket to be bound. Argument *localaddr* is a structure that specifies the local address to which the socket should be bound, and argument *addrlen* is an integer that specifies the length of the structure measured in bytes. Instead of giving the address merely as a sequence of bytes, the designers chose to use a structure for addresses as Figure 21.1 illustrates.

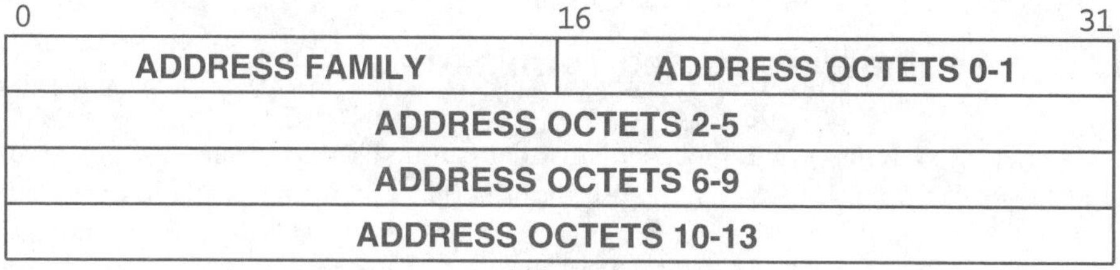

```
0                          16                          31
+----------------------------+----------------------------+
|       ADDRESS FAMILY       |    ADDRESS OCTETS 0-1      |
+----------------------------+----------------------------+
|               ADDRESS OCTETS 2-5                        |
+---------------------------------------------------------+
|               ADDRESS OCTETS 6-9                        |
+---------------------------------------------------------+
|               ADDRESS OCTETS 10-13                      |
+---------------------------------------------------------+
```

Figure 21.1 The *sockaddr* structure used when passing a TCP/IP address to the socket interface.

---

†If a client does not call *bind*, the operating system assigns a port number automatically; typically, port numbers are assigned sequentially.

The structure, generically named *sockaddr*, begins with a 16-bit *ADDRESS FAMI-LY* field that identifies the protocol suite to which the address belongs. It is followed by an address of up to *14* octets. Note that when a specific address structure is passed as an argument to a socket function, the structure must be cast to the generic structure *sockaddr*.

The value in the *ADDRESS FAMILY* field determines the format of the remaining address octets. For example, the value *2* in the *ADDRESS FAMILY* field means the remaining address octets contain a TCP/IP address. Each protocol family defines how it will use octets in the address field. For TCP/IP addresses, the socket address is known as *sockaddr_in*. It includes both an IP address and a protocol port number (i.e., an internet socket address structure can contain both an IP address and a protocol port at that address). Figure 21.2 shows the exact format of a TCP/IP socket address.

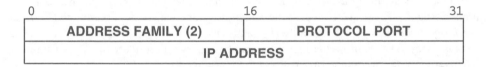

Figure 21.2 The format of a socket address structure (*sockaddr_in*) used with a TCP/IP address. The structure includes both an IP address and a protocol port at that address.

Although it is possible to specify arbitrary values in the address structure when calling *bind*, not all possible bindings are valid. For example, the caller might request a local protocol port that is already in use by another program, or it might request an invalid IP address. In such cases, the *bind* call fails and returns an error code.

21.8 Connecting Sockets To Destination Addresses

Initially, a socket is created in the *unconnected state*, which means that the socket is not associated with any remote destination. The function *connect* binds a permanent destination to a socket, placing it in the *connected state*. An application program must call *connect* to establish a connection before it can transfer data through a reliable stream socket. Sockets used with connectionless datagram services need not be connected before they are used, but doing so makes it possible to transfer data without specifying the destination each time.

The *connect* function has the form:

                    connect(socket, destaddr, addrlen)

Argument *socket* is the integer descriptor of the socket to connect. Argument *destaddr* is a socket address structure that specifies the destination address to which the socket should be bound. Argument *addrlen* specifies the length of the destination address measured in bytes.

The semantics of *connect* depend on the underlying protocols. Selecting the reliable stream delivery service in the PF_INET family means choosing TCP. In such cases, *connect* builds a TCP connection with the destination and returns an error if it cannot. In the case of connectionless service, *connect* does nothing more than store the destination address locally.

21.9 Sending Data Through A Socket

Once an application program has established a socket, it can use the socket to transmit data. There are five possible functions from which to choose: *send*, *sendto*, *sendmsg*, *write*, and *writev*. *Send*, *write*, and *writev* only work with connected sockets because they do not allow the caller to specify a destination address. The differences between the three are minor. *Write* takes three arguments:

write(socket, buffer, length)

Argument *socket* contains an integer socket descriptor (*write* can also be used with other types of descriptors). Argument *buffer* contains the address of the data to be sent, and argument *length* specifies the number of bytes to send. The call to *write* blocks until the data can be transferred (e.g., it blocks if internal system buffers for the socket are full). Like most system calls, *write* returns an error code to the application calling it, allowing the programmer to know if the operation succeeded.

The system call *writev* works like *write* except that it uses a "gather write" form, making it possible for the application program to write a message without copying the message into contiguous bytes of memory. *Writev* has the form:

writev(socket, iovector, vectorlen)

Argument *iovector* gives the address of an array of type *iovec* that contains a sequence of pointers to the blocks of bytes that form the message. As Figure 21.3 shows, a length accompanies each pointer. Argument *vectorlen* specifies the number of entries in *iovector*.

0   31

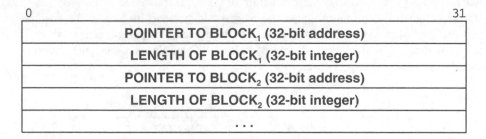

| POINTER TO BLOCK₁ (32-bit address) |
| LENGTH OF BLOCK₁ (32-bit integer) |
| POINTER TO BLOCK₂ (32-bit address) |
| LENGTH OF BLOCK₂ (32-bit integer) |
| . . . |

Figure 21.3 The format of an iovector of type *iovec* used with *writev* and *readv*.

The *send* function has the form:

send(socket, message, length, flags)

where argument *socket* specifies the socket to use, argument *message* gives the address of the data to be sent, argument *length* specifies the number of bytes to be sent, and argument *flags* controls the transmission. One value for *flags* allows the sender to specify that the message should be sent out-of-band on sockets that support such a notion. For example, recall from Chapter 12 that out-of-band messages correspond to TCP's notion of urgent data. Another value for *flags* allows the caller to request that the message be sent without using local routing tables. The intention is to allow the caller to take control of routing, making it possible to write network debugging software. Of course, not all sockets support all requests from arbitrary programs. Some requests require the program to have special privileges; others are simply not supported on all sockets.

Functions *sendto* and *sendmsg* allow the caller to send a message through an unconnected socket because they both require the caller to specify a destination. *Sendto*, which takes the destination address as an argument, has the form:

sendto(socket, message, length, flags, destaddr, addrlen)

The first four arguments are exactly the same as those used with the *send* function. The final two arguments specify a destination address and give the length of that address. Argument *destaddr* specifies the destination address using the *sockaddr_in* structure as defined in Figure 21.2.

A programmer may choose to use function *sendmsg* in cases where the long list of arguments required for *sendto* makes the program inefficient or difficult to read. *Sendmsg* has the form:

sendmsg(socket, messagestruct, flags)

where argument *messagestruct* is a structure of the form illustrated in Figure 21.4. The structure contains information about the message to be sent, its length, the destination address, and the address length. This call is especially useful because there is a corresponding input operation (described below) that produces a message structure in exactly the same format.

0   31

| POINTER TO SOCKETADDR |
| SIZE OF SOCKETADDR |
| POINTER TO IOVEC LIST |
| LENGTH OF IOVEC LIST |
| POINTER TO ACCESS RIGHTS LIST |
| LENGTH OF ACCESS RIGHTS LIST |
| RECEIVE FLAGS |

Figure 21.4 The format of message structure *messagestruct* used by *sendmsg*.

21.10 Receiving Data Through A Socket

Analogous to the five different output operations, the socket API offers five functions that a process can use to receive data through a socket: *read*, *readv*, *recv*, *recvfrom*, and *recvmsg*. The conventional input operation, *read*, can only be used when the socket is connected. It has the form:

read(descriptor, buffer, length)

where *descriptor* gives the integer descriptor of a socket or file descriptor from which to read data, *buffer* specifies the address in memory at which to store the data, and *length* specifies the maximum number of bytes to read.

An alternative form, *readv*, allows the caller to use a "scatter read" style of interface that places the incoming data in noncontiguous locations. *Readv* has the form:

readv(descriptor, iovector, vectorlen)

Argument *iovector* gives the address of a structure of type *iovec* (see Figure 21.3) that contains a sequence of pointers to blocks of memory into which the incoming data should be stored. Argument *vectorlen* specifies the number of entries in *iovector*.

In addition to the conventional input operations, there are three additional functions for network message input. Processes call *recv* to receive data from a connected socket. It has the form:

recv(socket, buffer, length, flags)

Argument *socket* specifies a socket descriptor from which data should be received. Argument *buffer* specifies the address in memory into which the message should be placed, and argument *length* specifies the length of the buffer area. Finally, argument *flags* allows the caller to control the reception. Among the possible values for the *flags* argument is one that allows the caller to look ahead by extracting a copy of the next incoming message without removing the message from the socket.

The function *recvfrom* allows the caller to specify input from an unconnected socket. It includes additional arguments that allow the caller to specify where to record the sender's address. The form is:

recvfrom(socket, buffer, length, flags, fromaddr, addrlen)

The two additional arguments, *fromaddr* and *addrlen*, are pointers to a socket address structure and an integer. The operating system uses *fromaddr* to record the address of the message sender and uses *fromlen* to record the length of the sender's address. Notice that the output operation *sendto*, discussed above, takes an address in exactly the same form as *recvfrom* generates. Thus, sending replies is easy.

The final function used for input, *recvmsg*, is analogous to the *sendmsg* output operation. *Recvmsg* operates like *recvfrom*, but requires fewer arguments. Its form is:

recvmsg(socket, messagestruct, flags)

where argument *messagestruct* gives the address of a structure that holds the address for an incoming message as well as locations for the sender's address. The structure produced by *recvmsg* is exactly the same as the structure used by *sendmsg*, making them operate well as a pair.

21.11 Obtaining Local And Remote Socket Addresses

We said that newly created processes inherit the set of open sockets from the process that created them. Sometimes, a newly created process needs to determine the destination address to which a socket connects. A process may also wish to determine the local address of a socket. Two functions provide such information: *getpeername* and *getsockname* (despite their names, both deal with what we think of as "addresses").

A process calls *getpeername* to determine the address of the peer (i.e., the remote end) to which a socket connects. It has the form:

getpeername(socket, destaddr, addrlen)

Argument *socket* specifies the socket for which the address is desired. Argument *destaddr* is a pointer to a structure of type *sockaddr* (see Figure 21.1) that will receive the socket address. Finally, argument *addrlen* is a pointer to an integer that will receive the length of the address. *Getpeername* only works with connected sockets.

Function *getsockname* returns the local address associated with a socket. It has the form:

getsockname(socket, localaddr, addrlen)

As expected, argument *socket* specifies the socket for which the local address is desired. Argument *localaddr* is a pointer to a structure of type *sockaddr* that will contain the address, and argument *addrlen* is a pointer to an integer that will contain the length of the address.

21.12 Obtaining And Setting Socket Options

In addition to binding a socket to a local address or connecting it to a destination address, the need arises for a mechanism that permits application programs to control the socket. For example, when using protocols that use timeout and retransmission, the application program may want to obtain or set the timeout parameters. It may also want to control the allocation of buffer space, determine if the socket allows transmission of broadcast, or control processing of out-of-band data. Rather than add new functions for each new control operation, the designers decided to build a single mechanism. The mechanism has two operations: *getsockopt* and *setsockopt*.

Function *getsockopt* allows the application to request information about the socket. A caller specifies the socket, the option of interest, and a location at which to store the requested information. The operating system examines its internal data structures for the socket, and passes the requested information to the caller. The call has the form:

getsockopt(socket, level, optionid, optionval, length)

Argument *socket* specifies the socket for which information is needed. Argument *level* identifies whether the operation applies to the socket itself or to the underlying protocols being used. Argument *optionid* specifies a single option to which the request applies. The pair of arguments *optionval* and *length* specify two pointers. The first gives the address of a buffer into which the system places the requested value, and the second gives the address of an integer into which the system places the length of the option value.

Function *setsockopt* allows an application program to set a socket option using the set of values obtained with *getsockopt*. The caller specifies a socket for which the option should be set, the option to be changed, and a value for the option. The call to *setsockopt* has the form:

setsockopt(socket, level, optionid, optionval, length)

where the arguments are like those for *getsockopt*, except that the *length* argument contains the length of the option being passed to the system. The caller must supply a legal value for the option as well as a correct length for that value. Of course, not all options apply to all sockets. The correctness and semantics of individual requests depend on the current state of the socket and the underlying protocols being used.

21.13 Specifying A Queue Length For A Server

One of the options that applies to sockets is used so frequently, a separate function has been dedicated to it. To understand how it arises, consider a server. The server creates a socket, binds it to a well-known protocol port, and waits for requests. If the server uses a reliable stream delivery, or if computing a response takes nontrivial amounts of time, it may happen that a new request arrives before the server finishes responding to an old request. To avoid having protocols reject or discard incoming requests, a server must tell the underlying protocol software that it wishes to have such requests enqueued until it has time to process them.

The function *listen* allows servers to prepare a socket for incoming connections. In terms of the underlying protocols, *listen* puts the socket in a passive mode ready to accept connections. When the server invokes *listen*, it also informs the operating system that the protocol software should enqueue multiple simultaneous requests that arrive at the socket. The form is:

listen(socket, qlength)

Argument *socket* gives the descriptor of a socket that should be prepared for use by a server, and argument *qlength* specifies the length of the request queue for that socket. After the call, the system will enqueue up to *qlength* requests for connections. If the queue is full when a request arrives, the operating system will refuse the connection by discarding the request. *Listen* applies only to sockets that have selected reliable stream delivery service.

21.14 How A Server Accepts Connections

As we have seen, a server process uses the functions *socket*, *bind*, and *listen* to create a socket, bind it to a well-known protocol port, and specify a queue length for connection requests. Note that the call to *bind* associates the socket with a well-known protocol port, but that the socket is not connected to a specific foreign destination. In fact, the foreign destination must specify a *wildcard*, allowing the socket to receive connection requests from an arbitrary client.

Once a socket has been established, the server needs to wait for a connection. To do so, it uses function *accept*. A call to *accept* blocks until a connection request arrives. It has the form:

$$newsock = accept(socket, addr, addrlen)$$

Argument *socket* specifies the descriptor of the socket on which to wait. Argument *addr* is a pointer to a structure of type *sockaddr*, and *addrlen* is a pointer to an integer. When a request arrives, the system fills in argument *addr* with the address of the client that has placed the request and sets *addrlen* to the length of the address. Finally, the system creates a new socket that has its destination connected to the requesting client, and returns the new socket descriptor to the caller. The original socket still has a wildcard foreign destination, and it still remains open. Thus, the master server can continue to accept additional requests at the original socket.

When a connection request arrives, the call to *accept* returns. The server can either handle requests iteratively or concurrently. In the iterative approach, the server handles the request itself, closes the new socket, and then calls *accept* to obtain the next connection request. In the concurrent approach, after the call to *accept* returns, the master server creates a slave to handle the request (in UNIX terminology, it forks a child process to handle the request). The slave process inherits a copy of the new socket, so it can proceed to service the request. When it finishes, the slave closes the socket and terminates. The original (master) server process closes its copy of the new socket after starting the slave. It then calls *accept* to obtain the next connection request.

The concurrent design for servers may seem confusing because multiple processes will be using the same local protocol port number. The key to understanding the mechanism lies in the way underlying protocols treat protocol ports. Recall that in TCP, a pair of endpoints define a connection. Thus, it does not matter how many processes use a given local protocol port number as long as they connect to different destinations. In the case of a concurrent server, there is one process per client and one additional process that accepts connections. The socket the master server process uses has a wildcard for the foreign destination, allowing it to connect with an arbitrary foreign site. Each remaining process has a specific foreign destination. When a TCP segment arrives, it will be sent to the socket connected to the segment's source. If no such socket exists, the segment will be sent to the socket that has a wildcard for its foreign destination. Furthermore, because the socket with a wildcard foreign destination does not have an open connection, it will only honor TCP segments that request a new connection.

21.15 Servers That Handle Multiple Services

The socket API provides another interesting possibility for server design because it allows a single process to wait for connections on multiple sockets. The system call that makes the design possible is called *select*, and it applies to I/O in general, not just to communication over sockets†. *Select* has the form:

$$nready = select(ndesc, indesc, outdesc, excdesc, timeout)$$

---

†The version of *select* in Windows Sockets applies only to socket descriptors.

In general, a call to *select* blocks waiting for one of a set of file descriptors to become ready. Argument *ndesc* specifies how many descriptors should be examined (the descriptors checked are always *0* through *ndesc*-1). Argument *indesc* is a pointer to a bit mask that specifies the file descriptors to check for input, argument *outdesc* is a pointer to a bit mask that specifies the file descriptors to check for output, and argument *excdesc* is a pointer to a bit mask that specifies the file descriptors to check for exception conditions. Finally, if argument *timeout* is nonzero, it is the address of an integer that specifies how long to wait for a connection before returning to the caller. A zero value for timeout forces the call to block until a descriptor becomes ready. Because the *timeout* argument contains the address of the timeout integer and not the integer itself, a process can request zero delay by passing the address of an integer that contains zero (i.e., a process can poll to see if I/O is ready).

A call to *select* returns the number of descriptors from the specified set that are ready for I/O. It also changes the bit masks specified by *indesc*, *outdesc*, and *excdesc* to inform the application which of the selected file descriptors are ready. Thus, before calling *select*, the caller must turn on those bits that correspond to descriptors to be checked. Following the call, all bits that remain set to *1* correspond to a ready file descriptor.

To communicate over more than one socket at a time, a process first creates all the sockets it needs and then uses *select* to determine which of them becomes ready for I/O first. Once it finds a socket has become ready, the process uses the input or output procedures defined above to communicate.

21.16 Obtaining And Setting Host Names

Most operating systems maintain an internal host name. For machines on the Internet, the internal name is usually chosen to be the domain name for the machine's main network interface. The *gethostname* function allows user processes to access the host name, and the *sethostname* function allows privileged processes to set the host name. *Gethostname* has the form:

gethostname(name, length)

Argument *name* gives the address of an array of bytes where the name is to be stored, and argument *length* is an integer that specifies the length of the *name* array. To set the host name, a privileged process makes a call of the form:

sethostname(name, length)

Argument *name* gives the address of an array where the name is stored, and argument *length* is an integer that gives the length of the name array.

21.17 Obtaining And Setting The Internal Host Domain

The operating system maintains a string that specifies the name domain to which a machine belongs. When a site obtains authority for part of the domain name space, it invents a string that identifies its piece of the space and uses the string as the name of the domain. For example, machines in the domain

cs.purdue.edu

have names taken from the Arthurian legend. Thus, one finds machines named *merlin*, *arthur*, *guenevere*, and *lancelot*. The domain itself has been named *camelot*, so the operating system on each host in the group must be informed that it resides in the *camelot* domain. To do so, a privileged process uses function *setdomainname*, which has the form:

setdomainname(name, length)

Argument *name* gives the address of an array of bytes that contains the name of a domain, and argument *length* is an integer that gives the length of the name.

User processes call *getdomainname* to retrieve the name of the domain from the system. It has the form:

getdomainname(name, length)

where argument *name* specifies the address of an array where the name should be stored, and argument *length* is an integer that specifies the length of the array.

21.18 Socket Library Calls

In addition to the functions described above, the socket API offers a set of library routines that perform useful functions related to networking. Figure 21.5 illustrates the difference between system calls and library routines. System calls pass control to the computer's operating system, while library routines are like other procedures that the programmer binds into a program.

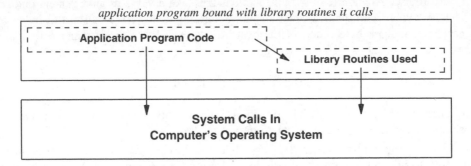

application program bound with library routines it calls

Application Program Code

Library Routines Used

System Calls In
Computer's Operating System

Figure 21.5 The difference between library routines, which are bound into an application program, and system calls, which are part of the operating system. A program can call either; library routines can call other library routines·or system calls.

Many of the socket library routines provide database services that allow a process to determine the names of machines and network services, protocol port numbers, and other related information. For example, one set of library routines provides access to the database of network services. We think of entries in the services database as 3-tuples, where each 3-tuple contains the (human readable) name of a network service, the protocol that supports the service, and a protocol port number for the service. Library routines exist that allow a process to obtain information from an entry given any piece.

The next sections examine groups of library routines, explaining their purposes and providing information about how they can be used. As we will see, the sets of library routines that provide access to a sequential database follow a pattern. Each set allows the application to: establish communication with the database (which can be a file on the local computer or a remote server), obtain entries one at a time, and terminate use. The routines used for the three operations are named *setXent*, *getXent*, and *endXent*, where *X* is the name of the database. For example, the library routines for the host database are named *sethostent*, *gethostent*, and *endhostent*. The sections that describe the routines summarize the calls without repeating the details of their use.

21.19 Network Byte Order Conversion Routines

Recall that machines differ in the way they store integer quantities and that the TCP/IP protocols define a machine independent standard for byte order. The socket API provides four macros that convert between the local machine byte order and the network standard byte order. To make programs portable, they must be written to call the conversion routines every time they copy an integer value from the local machine to a network packet, or when they copy a value from a network packet to the local machine.

All four conversion routines are functions that take a value as an argument and return a new value with the bytes rearranged. For example, to convert a short (2-byte) integer from network byte order to the local host byte order, a programmer calls *ntohs* (network to host short). The format is:

$$localshort = ntohs(netshort)$$

Argument *netshort* is a 2-byte (16-bit) integer in network standard byte order and the result, *localshort*, is in local host byte order.

The C programming language calls 4 byte (32 bit) integers *longs*. Function *ntohl* (network to host long) converts 4-byte longs from network standard byte order to local host byte order. Programs invoke *ntohl* as a function, supplying a long integer in network byte order as an argument:

$$locallong = ntohl(netlong)$$

Two analogous functions allow the programmer to convert from local host byte order to network byte order. Function *htons* converts a 2-byte (short) integer in the host's local byte order to a 2-byte integer in network standard byte order. Programs invoke *htons* as a function:

$$netshort = htons(localshort)$$

The final conversion routine, *htonl*, converts long integers to network standard byte order. Like the others, *htonl* is a function:

$$netlong = htonl(locallong)$$

It should be obvious that the conversion routines preserve the following mathematical relationships:

$$netshort = htons(\ ntohs(netshort)\ )$$

and

$$localshort = ntohs(\ htons(localshort)\ )$$

Similar relationships hold for the long integer conversion routines.

21.20 IP Address Manipulation Routines

Because many programs translate between 32-bit IP addresses and the corresponding dotted decimal notation, the socket library includes utility routines that perform the translation. Procedures *inet_aton* and *inet_network* both translate from dotted decimal format to a 32-bit IP address in network byte order. *Inet_aton* forms a 32-bit host IP address; *inet_network* forms the network address with zeroes for the host part†. They have the form:

error_code = inet_aton(string, address)

and

address = inet_network(string)

where argument *string* gives the address of an ASCII string that contains the number expressed in dotted decimal format, and *address* is a pointer to a long integer into which the binary value is placed. The dotted decimal form can have one to four segments of digits separated by periods (dots). If all four appear, each corresponds to a single byte of the resulting 32-bit integer. If less than four appear, the last segment is expanded to fill remaining bytes.

Procedure *inet_ntoa* performs the inverse of *inet_aton* by mapping a 32-bit integer to an ASCII string in dotted decimal format. It has the form:

str = inet_ntoa(internetaddr)

where argument *internetaddr* is a 32-bit IP address in network byte order, and *str* is the address of the resulting ASCII version.

Often programs that manipulate IP addresses must combine a network address with the local address of a host on that network. Procedure *inet_makeaddr* performs such a combination. It has the form:

internetaddr = inet_makeaddr(net, local)

Argument *net* is a 32-bit network IP address in host byte order, and argument *local* is the integer representing a local host address on that network, also in local host byte order.

Procedures *inet_netof* and *inet_lnaof* provide the inverse of *inet_makeaddr* by separating the network and local portions of an IP address. They have the form:

net = inet_netof(internetaddr)

and

local = inet_lnaof(internetaddr)

where argument *internetaddr* is a 32-bit IP address in network byte order, and the results are returned in host byte order.

---

†Because they assume classful addressing, functions such as *inet_network* and *inet_lnaof* do not handle CIDR addresses.

21.21 Accessing The Domain Name System†

A set of five library procedures constitute the interface to the TCP/IP domain name system. Application programs that call these routines become clients of one domain name system, sending one or more domain name servers requests and receiving responses.

The general idea is that a program makes a query, sends it to a server, and awaits an answer. Because many options exist, the routines have only a few basic parameters and use a global structure, *res*, to hold others. For example, one field in *res* enables debugging messages, while another controls whether the code uses UDP or TCP for queries. Most fields in *res* begin with reasonable defaults, so the routines can be used without changing *res*.

A program calls *res_init* before using other procedures. The call takes no arguments:

res_init()

Res_init reads a file that contains information like the name of the machine that runs the domain name server and stores the results in global structure *res*.

Procedure *res_mkquery* forms a domain name query and places it in a buffer in memory. The form of the call is:

res_mkquery(op, dname, class, type, data, datalen, newrr, buffer, buflen)

The first seven arguments correspond directly to the fields of a domain name query. Argument *op* specifies the requested operation, *dname* gives the address of a character array that contains a domain name, *class* is an integer that gives the class of the query, *type* is an integer that gives the type of the query, *data* gives the address of an array of data to be included in the query, and *datalen* is an integer that gives the length of the data. In addition to the library procedures, the socket API provides application programs with definitions of symbolic constants for important values. Thus, programmers can use the domain name system without understanding the details of the protocol. The last two arguments, *buffer* and *buflen*, specify the address of an area into which the query should be placed and the integer length of the buffer area, respectively. Finally, in the current implementation, argument *newrr* is unused.

Once a program has formed a query, it calls *res_send* to send it to a name server and obtain a response. The form is:

res_send(buffer, buflen, answer, anslen)

Argument *buffer* is a pointer to memory that holds the message to be sent (presumably, the application called procedure *res_mkquery* to form the message). Argument *buflen* is an integer that specifies the length. Argument *answer* gives the address in memory into which a response should be written, and integer argument *anslen* specifies the length of the answer area.

---

†Chapter 23 considers the domain name system in detail.

In addition to routines that make and send queries, the socket library contains two routines that translate domain names between conventional ASCII and the compressed format used in queries. Procedure *dn_expand* expands a compressed domain name into a full ASCII version. It has the form:

dn_expand(msg, eom, compressed, full, fullen)

Argument *msg* gives the address of a domain name message that contains the name to be expanded, with *eom* specifying the end-of-message limit beyond which the expansion cannot go. Argument *compressed* is a pointer to the first byte of the compressed name. Argument *full* is a pointer to an array into which the expanded name should be written, and argument *fullen* is an integer that specifies the length of the array.

Generating a compressed name is more complex than expanding a compressed name because compression involves eliminating common suffixes. When compressing names, the client must keep a record of suffixes that have appeared previously. Procedure *dn_comp* compresses a full domain name by comparing suffixes to a list of previously used suffixes and eliminating the longest possible suffix. A call has the form:

dn_comp(full, compressed, cmprlen, prevptrs, lastptr)

Argument *full* gives the address of a full domain name. Argument *compressed* points to an array of bytes that will hold the compressed name, with argument *cmprlen* specifying the length of the array. The argument *prevptrs* is the address of an array of pointers to previously compressed suffixes in the current message, with *lastptr* pointing to the end of the array. Normally, *dn_comp* compresses the name and updates *prevptrs* if a new suffix has been used.

Procedure *dn_comp* can also be used to translate a domain name from ASCII to the internal form without compression (i.e., without removing suffixes). To do so, a process invokes *dn_comp* with the *prevptrs* argument set to *NULL* (i.e., zero).

21.22 Obtaining Information About Hosts

Library procedures exist that allow a process to retrieve information about a host given either its domain name or its IP address. When used on a machine that has access to a domain name server, the library procedures make the process a client of the domain name system by sending a request to a server and waiting for a response. When used on systems that do not have access to the domain name system (e.g., a host not on the Internet), the routines obtain the desired information from a database kept on secondary storage.

Function *gethostbyname* takes a domain name and returns a pointer to a structure of information for that host. A call takes the form:

ptr = gethostbyname(namestr)

Argument *namestr* is a pointer to a character string that contains a domain name for the host. The value returned, *ptr*, points to a structure that contains the following information: the official host name, a list of aliases that have been registered for the host, the host address type (i.e., whether the address is an IP address), the address length, and a list of one or more addresses for the host. More details can be found in the UNIX Programmer's Manual.

Function *gethostbyaddr* produces the same information as *gethostbyname*. The difference between the two is that *gethostbyaddr* accepts a host address as an argument:

ptr = gethostbyaddr(addr, len, type)

Argument *addr* is a pointer to a sequence of bytes that contain a host address. Argument *len* is an integer that gives the length of the address, and argument *type* is an integer that specifies the type of the address (e.g., that it is an IP address).

As mentioned earlier, procedures *sethostent*, *gethostent*, and *endhostent* provide sequential access to the host database.

21.23 Obtaining Information About Networks

Hosts either use the domain name system or keep a simple database of networks in their internet. The socket library routines include five routines that allow a process to access the network database. Procedure *getnetbyname* obtains and formats the contents of an entry from the database given the domain name of a network. A call has the form:

ptr = getnetbyname(name)

where argument *name* is a pointer to a string that contains the name of the network for which information is desired. The value returned is a pointer to a structure that contains fields for the official name of the network, a list of registered aliases, an integer address type, and a 32-bit network address (i.e., an IP address with the host portion set to zero).

A process calls library routine *getnetbyaddr* when it needs to search for information about a network given its address. The call has the form:

ptr = getnetbyaddr(netaddr, addrtype)

Argument *netaddr* is a 32-bit network address, and argument *addrtype* is an integer that specifies the type of *netaddr*. Procedures *setnetent*, *getnetent*, and *endnetent* provide sequential access to the network database.

21.24 Obtaining Information About Protocols

Five library routines provide access to the database of protocols available on a machine. Each protocol has an official name, registered aliases, and an official protocol number. Procedure *getprotobyname* allows a caller to obtain information about a protocol given its name:

$$ptr = getprotobyname(name)$$

Argument *name* is a pointer to an ASCII string that contains the name of the protocol for which information is desired. The function returns a pointer to a structure that has fields for the official protocol name, a list of aliases, and a unique integer value assigned to the protocol.

Procedure *getprotobynumber* allows a process to search for protocol information using the protocol number as a key:

$$ptr = getprotobynumber(number)$$

Finally, procedures *getprotoent*, *setprotoent*, and *endprotoent* provide sequential access to the protocol database.

21.25 Obtaining Information About Network Services

Recall from Chapters 11 and 12 that some UDP and TCP protocol port numbers are reserved for well-known services. For example, TCP port *43* is reserved for the *whois* service. *Whois* allows a client on one machine to contact a server on another and obtain information about a user that has an account on the server's machine. The entry for *whois* in the services database specifies the service name, *whois*, the protocol, *TCP*, and the protocol port number *43*. Five library routines exist that obtain information about services and the protocol ports they use.

Procedure *getservbyname* maps a named service onto a port number:

$$ptr = getservbyname(name, proto)$$

Argument *name* specifies the address of a string that contains the name of the desired service, and argument *proto* is a string that gives the name of the protocol with which the service is to be used. Typically, protocols are limited to TCP and UDP. The value returned is a pointer to a structure that contains fields for the name of the service, a list of aliases, an identification of the protocol with which the service is used, and an integer protocol port number assigned for that service.

Procedure *getservbyport* allows the caller to obtain an entry from the services database given the port number assigned to it. A call has the form:

$$ptr = getservbyport(port, proto)$$

Argument *port* is the integer protocol port number assigned to the service, and argument *proto* specifies the protocol for which the service is desired. As with other databases, a process can access the services database sequentially using *setservent*, *getservent*, and *endservent*.

21.26 An Example Client

The following example C program illustrates how a program uses the socket API to access TCP/IP protocols. It is a simple implementation of a *whois* client and server. As defined in RFC 3912, the *whois* service allows a client on one machine to obtain information about a user on a remote system. In this implementation, the client is an application program that a user invokes with two arguments: the name of a remote machine and the name of a user on that machine about whom information is desired. The client calls *gethostbyname* to map the remote machine name into an IP address and calls *getservbyname* to find the well-known port for the *whois* service. Once it has mapped the host and service names, the client creates a socket, specifying that the socket will use reliable stream delivery (i.e., TCP). The client then connects the socket to the *whois* protocol port on the specified destination machine.

```
/* whoisclient.c - main */

#include <stdio.h>
#include <sys/types.h>
#include <sys/socket.h>
#include <netinet/in.h>
#include <netdb.h>


/*------------------------------------------------------------------------
 * Program:      whoisclient
 *
 * Purpose:      UNIX application program that becomes a client for the
 *               Internet "whois" service.
 *
 * Use:          whois hostname username
 *
 * Author:       Barry Shein, Boston University
 *
 * Date:         Long ago in a universe far, far away
 *
 *------------------------------------------------------------------------
 */
main(argc, argv)
```

```
int argc;                       /* standard UNIX argument declarations */
char *argv[];
{
    int s;                      /* socket descriptor                   */
    int len;                    /* length of received data             */
    struct sockaddr_in sa;      /* Internet socket addr. structure     */
    struct hostent *hp;         /* result of host name lookup          */
    struct servent *sp;         /* result of service lookup            */
    char buf[BUFSIZ+1];         /* buffer to read whois information     */
    char *myname;               /* pointer to name of this program     */
    char *host;                 /* pointer to remote host name         */
    char *user;                 /* pointer to remote user name         */

    myname = argv[0];
    /*
     * Check that there are two command line arguments
     */
    if(argc != 3) {
            fprintf(stderr, "Usage: %s host username\n", myname);
            exit(1);
    }
    host = argv[1];
    user = argv[2];
    /*
     * Look up the specified hostname
     */
    if((hp = gethostbyname(host)) == NULL) {
            fprintf(stderr,"%s: %s: no such host?\n", myname, host);
            exit(1);
    }
    /*
     * Put host's address and address type into socket structure
     */
    bcopy((char *)hp->h_addr, (char *)&sa.sin_addr, hp->h_length);
    sa.sin_family = hp->h_addrtype;
    /*
     * Look up the socket number for the WHOIS service
     */
    if((sp = getservbyname("whois","tcp")) == NULL) {
            fprintf(stderr,"%s: No whois service on this host\n", myname);
            exit(1);
    }
    /*
     * Put the whois socket number into the socket structure.
```

```
   */
  sa.sin_port = sp->s_port;
  /*
   * Allocate an open socket
   */
  if((s = socket(hp->h_addrtype, SOCK_STREAM, 0)) < 0) {
        perror("socket");
        exit(1);
  }
  /*
   * Connect to the remote server
   */
  if(connect(s, &sa, sizeof sa) < 0) {
        perror("connect");
        exit(1);
  }
  /*
   * Send the request
   */
  if(write(s, user, strlen(user)) != strlen(user)) {
        fprintf(stderr, "%s: write error\n", myname);
        exit(1);
  }
  /*
   * Read the reply and put to user's output
   */
  while( (len = read(s, buf, BUFSIZ)) > 0)
        write(1, buf, len);
  close(s);
  exit(0);
}
```

21.27 An Example Server

The example server is only slightly more complex than the client. The server is
iterative: it listens on the well-known ''whois'' port, repeatedly accepts the next request,
uses the UNIX *getpwnam* function to lookup the name in the UNIX password file, and
returns the requested information to the client.

```
/* whoisserver.c - main */

#include <stdio.h>
#include <sys/types.h>
```

```
#include <sys/socket.h>
#include <netinet/in.h>
#include <netdb.h>
#include <pwd.h>


/*--------------------------------------------------------------------
 * Program:     whoisserver
 *
 * Purpose:     UNIX application program that acts as a server for
 *              the "whois" service on the local machine.  It listens
 *              on well-known WHOIS port (43) and answers queries from
 *              clients.  This program requires super-user privilege to
 *              run.
 *
 * Use:         whois hostname username
 *
 * Author:      Barry Shein, Boston University
 *
 * Date:        Long ago in a universe far, far away
 *
 *--------------------------------------------------------------------
 */

#define BACKLOG        5       /* # of requests we're willing to queue */
#define MAXHOSTNAME    32      /* maximum host name length we tolerate */

main(argc, argv)
int argc;                      /* standard UNIX argument declarations  */
char *argv[];
{
  int s, t;                    /* socket descriptors                   */
  int i;                       /* general purpose integer              */
  struct sockaddr_in sa, isa;  /* Internet socket address structure    */
  struct hostent *hp;          /* result of host name lookup           */
  char *myname;                /* pointer to name of this program      */
  struct servent *sp;          /* result of service lookup             */
  char localhost[MAXHOSTNAME+1];/* local host name as character string */

  myname = argv[0];
  /*
   * Look up the WHOIS service entry
   */
  if((sp = getservbyname("whois","tcp")) == NULL) {
        fprintf(stderr, "%s: No whois service on this host\n", myname);
```

```
        exit(1);
}
/*
 * Get our own host information
 */
gethostname(localhost, MAXHOSTNAME);
if((hp = gethostbyname(localhost)) == NULL) {
        fprintf(stderr, "%s: cannot get local host info?\n", myname);
        exit(1);
}
/*
 * Put the WHOIS socket number and our address info
 * into the socket structure
 */
sa.sin_port = sp->s_port;
bcopy((char *)hp->h_addr, (char *)&sa.sin_addr, hp->h_length);
sa.sin_family = hp->h_addrtype;
/*
 * Allocate an open socket for incoming connections
 */
if((s = socket(hp->h_addrtype, SOCK_STREAM, 0)) < 0) {
        perror("socket");
        exit(1);
}
/*
 * Bind the socket to the service port
 * so we hear incoming connections
 */
if(bind(s, &sa, sizeof sa) < 0) {
        perror("bind");
        exit(1);
}
/*
 * Set maximum connections we will fall behind
 */
listen(s, BACKLOG);
/*
 * Go into an infinite loop waiting for new connections
 */
while(1) {
        i = sizeof isa;
        /*
         * We hang in accept() while waiting for new customers
         */
```

```
        if((t = accept(s, &isa, &i)) < 0) {
          perror("accept");
          exit(1);
        }
        whois(t);              /* perform the actual WHOIS service */
        close(t);
    }
}
/*
 * Get the WHOIS request from remote host and format a reply.
 */
whois(sock)
int sock;
{
  struct passwd *p;
  char buf[BUFSIZ+1];
  int i;

  /*
   * Get one line request
   */
  if( (i = read(sock, buf, BUFSIZ)) <= 0)
        return;
  buf[i] = '\0';          /* Null terminate */
  /*
   * Look up the requested user and format reply
   */
  if((p = getpwnam(buf)) == NULL)
        strcpy(buf,"User not found\n");
  else
        sprintf(buf, "%s: %s\n", p->pw_name, p->pw_gecos);
  /*
   * Return reply
   */
  write(sock, buf, strlen(buf));
  return;
}
```

21.28 Summary

Because TCP/IP protocol software resides inside an operating system, the exact interface between an application program and TCP/IP protocols depends on the details of
the operating system; it is not specified by the TCP/IP protocol standard. We examined

the socket API, which was originally designed for BSD UNIX, but has become a de facto standard used by vendors such as Microsoft. We saw that sockets adopted the UNIX open-read-write-close paradigm. To use TCP, a program must create a socket, bind addresses to it, accept incoming connections, and then communicate. Finally, when finished using a socket, the program must close it. In addition to the socket abstraction and system calls that operate on sockets, BSD UNIX includes library routines that help programmers create and manipulate IP addresses, convert integers between the local machine format and network standard byte order, and search for information such as network addresses.

The socket API has become popular and is widely supported by many vendors. Vendors who do not offer socket facilities in their operating systems often provide a socket library that makes it possible for programmers to write applications using socket calls even though the underlying operating system uses a different set of system calls.

FOR FURTHER STUDY

Detailed information on the socket functions can be found in the *UNIX Programmer's Manual*, where Section 2 contains a description of each UNIX system call and Section 3 contains a description of each library procedure. UNIX also supplies on-line copies of the manual pages via the *man* command. McKusick, Bostic, Karels, and Quarterman [1996] explores the UNIX system in more detail. Hall et. al. [1993] contains the original standard for Windows Sockets.

Operating system vendors often provide libraries of procedures that emulate sockets on their systems. Consult vendors' programming manuals for details. Gilligan et. al. [RFC 3493] considers socket extensions for IPv6.

Volume 3 of this series describes how client and server programs are structured; there are four versions of the text that each use a different API: a BSD sockets version, a Windows sockets version (for Microsoft Windows), a Linux/POSIX version, and a version that uses the *Transport Layer Interface*, defined for AT&T System V UNIX and available in Solaris.

EXERCISES

21.1   Try running the sample *whois* client and server on your local system.

21.2   Build a simple server that accepts multiple concurrent connections (to test it, have the process that handles a connection print a short message, delay a random time, print another message, and exit).

21.3   When is the *listen* call important?

21.4   What procedures does your local system provide to access the domain name system?

21.5   Devise a server that uses a single Linux process (i.e., a single thread of execution), but handles multiple concurrent TCP connections. Hint: think of *select*.

21.6   Read about alternatives to the socket interface, such as the *Transport Library Interface* (*TLI*), and compare them to sockets. What are the major conceptual differences?

21.7   Each operating system limits the number of sockets a given program can use at any time. How many sockets can a program create on your local system?

21.8   The socket/file descriptor mechanism and associated *read* and *write* operations can be considered a form of object-oriented design. Explain why.

21.9   Consider an alternative interface design that provides an interface for every layer of protocol software (e.g., the system allows an application program to send and receive raw packets without using IP, or to send and receive IP datagrams without using UDP or TCP). What are the advantages of having such an interface? The disadvantages?

21.10 A client and server can both run on the same computer and use a TCP socket to communicate. Explain how it is possible to build a client and server that can communicate on a single machine without learning the host's IP address.

21.11 Experiment with the sample server in this chapter to see if you can generate TCP connections sufficiently fast to exceed the backlog the server specifies. Do you expect incoming connection requests to exceed the backlog faster if the server operates on a computer that has one processor than on a computer that has five processors? Explain.

Chapter Contents

22

Bootstrap And Autoconfiguration (DHCP)

22.1 Introduction

This chapter shows how the client-server paradigm is used for bootstrapping. Each computer attached to a TCP/IP internet needs to obtain an IP address and the associated address mask for the network as well as other information including the addresses of a router and a name server. This chapter describes a protocol that allows a host to determine the information automatically at startup. Such automatic initialization is important because it permits a user to connect a computer to the Internet without understanding the details of addresses, masks, routers, or how to configure protocol software.

The bootstrapping procedure described here is surprising because it uses UDP to transfer messages. It might seem impossible to use UDP to find an IP address because each UDP message is sent in an IP datagram. We will see, however, that the special IP addresses mentioned in Chapter 3 make it possible.

22.2 History Of Bootstrapping

As Chapter 5 describes, the RARP protocol was initially developed to permit a computer to obtain an IP address. A more general protocol named *BOOTstrap Protocol* (*BOOTP*) later replaced RARP. Finally, the *Dynamic Host Configuration Protocol* (*DHCP*) was developed as a successor to BOOTP. Because DHCP is a successor to BOOTP, the description in this chapter generally applies to both. To simplify the text, however, we will refer to DHCP.

403

Because it uses UDP and IP, DHCP can be implemented by an application program. Like other application protocols, DHCP follows the client-server paradigm; the protocol requires only a single packet exchange in which a computer sends a packet to request bootstrap information and a server responds by sending a single packet that specifies items needed at startup, including the computer's IP address, the address of a router, and the address of a name server. DHCP also includes an *options* field in the reply that allows vendors to send additional information used only for their computers†.

22.3 Using IP To Determine An IP Address

We said that DHCP uses UDP to carry messages and that UDP messages are encapsulated in IP datagrams for delivery. To understand how a computer can send DHCP in an IP datagram before the computer learns its IP address, recall from Chapter 3 that there are several special-case IP addresses. In particular, when used as a destination address, the IP address consisting of all *1*s (255.255.255.255) specifies limited broadcast. IP software can accept and broadcast datagrams that specify the limited broadcast address even before the software has discovered its local IP address information. The point is that:

> *An application program can use the limited broadcast IP address to force IP to broadcast a datagram on the local network before IP has discovered the IP address of the local network or the machine's IP address.*

Suppose client machine *A* wants to use DHCP to find bootstrap information (including its IP address) and suppose *B* is the server on the same physical net that will answer the request. Because *A* does not know *B*'s IP address or the IP address of the network, it must broadcast its initial DHCP request using the IP limited broadcast address. What about the reply? Can *B* send a directed reply? No, it cannot, even though it knows *A*'s IP address. To see why, consider what happens if an application program on *B* attempts to send a datagram using *A*'s IP address. After routing the datagram, IP software on *B* will pass the datagram to the network interface software. The interface software must map the next hop IP address to a corresponding hardware address, presumably using ARP as described in Chapter 5. However, because *A* has not yet received the DHCP reply, it does not recognize its IP address, so it cannot answer *B*'s ARP request. Therefore, *B* has only two alternatives: either broadcast the reply or use information from the request packet to manually add an entry to its ARP cache. On systems that do not allow application programs to modify the ARP cache, broadcasting is the only solution.

---

†As we will see, the term "options" is somewhat misleading because the specification recommends using an options field for general purpose information such as subnet masks.

22.4 The DHCP Retransmission Policy

DHCP places all responsibility for reliable communication on the client. We know that because UDP uses IP for delivery, messages can be delayed, lost, delivered out of order, or duplicated. Furthermore, because IP does not provide a checksum for data, the UDP datagram could arrive with some bits corrupted. To guard against corruption, DHCP requires that UDP use checksums. It also specifies that requests and replies should be sent with the *do not fragment* bit set to accommodate clients that have too little memory to reassemble datagrams. DHCP is also constructed to allow multiple replies; it accepts and processes the first.

To handle datagram loss, DHCP uses the conventional technique of *timeout and retransmission*. When the client transmits a request, it starts a timer. If no reply arrives before the timer expires, the client must retransmit the request. Of course, after a power failure all machines on a network will reboot simultaneously, possibly overrunning the DHCP server(s) with requests. If all clients use exactly the same retransmission timeout, many or all of them will attempt to retransmit simultaneously. To avoid the resulting collisions, the DHCP specification recommends using a random delay. In addition, the specification recommends starting with a random timeout value between *0* and *4* seconds, and doubling the timer after each retransmission. After the timer reaches a large value, *60* seconds, the client does not increase the timer, but continues to use randomization. Doubling the timeout after each retransmission keeps DHCP from adding excessive traffic to a congested network; the randomization helps avoid simultaneous transmissions.

22.5 The DHCP Message Format

To keep an implementation as simple as possible, DHCP messages have fixed-length fields, and replies have the same format as requests. Although we said that clients and servers are programs, the DHCP protocol uses the terms loosely, referring to the machine that sends a DHCP request as the *client* and any machine that sends a reply as a *server*. Figure 22.1 shows the DHCP message format.

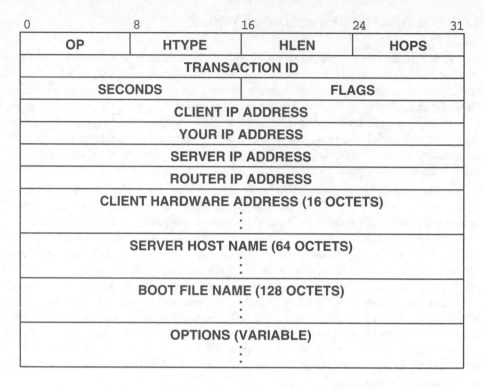

Figure 22.1 The format of a DHCP message. To keep implementations small enough to fit in ROM, fields except for options have fixed length.

Field *OP* specifies whether the message is a request (*1*) or a reply (*2*). As in ARP, fields *HTYPE* and *HLEN* specify the network hardware type and length of the hardware address (e.g., Ethernet has type *1* and address length *6*)†. The client places *0* in the *HOPS* field. If it receives the request and decides to pass the request on to another machine (e.g., to allow bootstrapping across multiple routers), the DHCP server increments the *HOPS* count. The *TRANSACTION ID* field contains an integer that clients use to match responses with requests. The *SECONDS* field reports the number of seconds since the client started to boot.

The *CLIENT IP ADDRESS* field and all fields following it contain the most important information. To allow the greatest flexibility, clients fill in as much information as they know and leave remaining fields set to zero. For example, if a client knows the name or address of a specific server from which it wants information, it can fill in the *SERVER IP ADDRESS* or *SERVER HOST NAME* fields. If these fields are nonzero, only the server with matching name/address will answer the request; if they are zero, any server that receives the request will reply.

---

†Values for the *HTYPE* field can be found in the latest Assigned Numbers RFC.

DHCP can be used from a client that already knows its IP address (i.e., to obtain other information). A client that knows its IP address places it in the *CLIENT IP AD-DRESS* field; other clients use zero. If the client's IP address is zero in the request, a server returns the client's IP address in the *YOUR IP ADDRESS* field.

The 16-bit *FLAGS* field allows control of the request and response. As Figure 22.2 shows, only the high-order bit of the *FLAGS* field has been assigned a meaning.

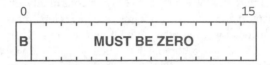

Figure 22.2 The format of the 16-bit *FLAGS* field in a DHCP message. The leftmost bit is interpreted as a broadcast request; all others bits must be set to zero.

A client uses the high-order bit in the *FLAGS* field to control whether the server sends the response via unicast or broadcast. To understand why a client might choose a broadcast response, recall that while it communicates with a DHCP server, a client does not yet have an IP address, which means the client cannot answer ARP queries. Thus, to ensure that the client can receive messages sent by a DHCP server, a client can request that the server send responses using IP broadcast, which corresponds to hardware broadcast. The rules for datagram processing allow IP to discard any datagram that arrives via hardware unicast if the destination address does not match the computer's address. However, IP is required to accept and handle any datagram sent to the IP broadcast address.

Interestingly, DHCP does not provide space in the message to download a specific memory image for an embedded system. Instead, DHCP provides a *BOOT FILE NAME* field that a small diskless system can use. The client can use the field to supply a generic name like "unix," which means, "I want to boot the UNIX operating system for this machine." The DHCP server consults its configuration database to map the generic name into a specific file name that contains the memory image appropriate for the client hardware, and returns the fully qualified file name in its reply. Of course, the configuration database also allows completely automatic bootstrapping in which the client places zeros in the *BOOT FILE NAME* field, and DHCP selects a memory image for the machine. The client then uses a standard file transfer protocol such as TFTP to obtain the image. The advantage of the approach is that a diskless client can use a generic name without encoding a specific file, and the network manager can change the location of a boot image without changing the ROM in embedded systems.

Items in the *OPTIONS* area all use a *Type-Length-Value (TLV)* style encoding — each item contains a *type* octet, a *length* octet, and ends with a *value* of the specified length.

22.6 The Need For Dynamic Configuration

Early bootstrap protocols operated in a relatively static environment in which each host had a permanent network connection. A manager created a configuration file that specified a set of parameters for each host, including an IP address. The file did not change frequently because the configuration usually remained stable. Typically, a configuration continued unchanged for weeks.

In the modern Internet, however, ISPs have a continually changing set of customers, and portable laptop computers with wireless connections make it possible to move a computer from one location to another quickly and easily. To handle automated address assignment, DHCP allows a computer to obtain an IP address quickly and dynamically. That is, when configuring a DHCP server, a manager supplies a set of IP addresses. Whenever a new computer connects to the network, the new computer contacts the server and requests an address. The server chooses one of the addresses from the set that the manager specified, and allocates the address to the computer.

To be completely general, DHCP allows three types of address assignment; a manager chooses how DHCP will respond for each network or for each host. Like its predecessor BOOTP, DHCP allows *manual configuration* in which a manager configures a specific address for a specific computer. DHCP also permits a form of *automatic configuration* or *autoconfiguration* in which a manager allows a DHCP server to assign a permanent address when a computer first attaches to the network. Finally, DHCP permits completely *dynamic configuration* in which a server ''loans'' an address to a computer for a limited time. Dynamic address assignment is the most powerful and novel aspect of DHCP.

DHCP uses the identity of the client and the server configuration files to decide how to proceed. When a client contacts a DHCP server, the client sends an identifier, usually the client's hardware address. The server uses the client's identifier and the network to which the client has connected to determine how to assign the client and IP address. Thus, a manager has complete control over how addresses are assigned. A server can be configured to allocate addresses to specific computers statically, while allowing other computers to obtain permanent or temporary addresses dynamically. To summarize:

> *DHCP permits a computer to obtain information needed to operate on a given network, including an IP address, without manual intervention and without a priori configuration. Dynamic assignment is subject to administrative constraints.*

22.7 DHCP Lease Concept

Dynamic address assignment is temporary. We say that a DHCP server *leases* an address to a client for a finite period of time. The server specifies the lease period when it allocates the address. During the lease period, the server will not lease the same address to another client. At the end of the lease period, however, the client must renew the lease or stop using the address.

How long should a DHCP lease last? The optimal time for a lease depends on the particular network and the needs of a particular host. For example, to guarantee that addresses can be recycled quickly, computers on a network used by students in a university laboratory might have a short lease period (e.g., one hour). By contrast, a corporate network might use a lease period of one day or one week. An ISP might make the duration of a lease depend on a customer's contract. To accommodate all possible environments, DHCP does not specify a fixed constant for the lease period. Instead, the protocol allows a client to request a specific lease period, and allows a server to inform the client of the lease period it grants. Thus, a manager can decide how long each server should allocate an address to a client. In the extreme, DHCP reserves a value for *infinity* to permit a lease to last arbitrarily long (i.e., to make a permanent address assignment).

22.8 Multiple Addresses And Relays

A multi-homed computer connects to more than one network. When such a computer boots, it may need to obtain configuration information for each of its interfaces. However, a DHCP message only provides information about one interface. A computer with multiple interfaces must handle each interface separately. Thus, although we will describe DHCP as if a computer needs only one address, the reader must remember that each interface of a multi-homed computer may be at a different point in the protocol.

DHCP uses the notion of *relay agent* to permit a computer to contact a server on a nonlocal network. When a relay agent, typically a router, receives a broadcast request from a client, it forwards the request to a server and then returns the reply from the server to the host. Relay agents can complicate multi-homed configuration because a server may receive multiple requests from the same computer. However, although DHCP use the term *client identifier*, we assume that a multi-homed client sends a value that identifies a particular interface (e.g., a unique hardware address). Thus, a server will always be able to distinguish among requests from a multi-homed host, even when the server receives such requests via a relay agent.

22.9 Address Acquisition States

When it uses DHCP to obtain an IP address, a client is in one of six states. The state transition diagram in Figure 22.3 shows events and messages that cause a client to change state.

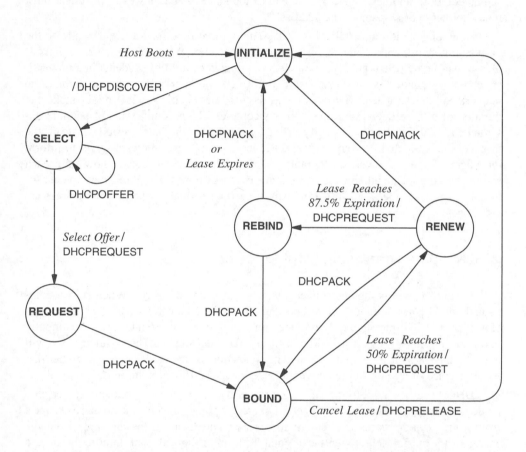

Figure 22.3 The six main states of a DHCP client and transitions among them. Each label on a transition lists the incoming message or event that causes the transmission, followed by a slash and the message the client sends.

When a client first boots, it enters the *INITIALIZE* state. To start acquiring an IP address, the client first contacts all DHCP servers in the local net. To do so, the client broadcasts a *DHCPDISCOVER* message and moves to the state labeled *SELECT*. Because the protocol is an extension of BOOTP, the client sends the *DHCPDISCOVER* message in a UDP datagram with the destination port set to the BOOTP port (i.e., port

67). All DHCP servers on the local net receive the message, and those servers that have been programmed to respond to the particular client send a *DHCPOFFER* message. Thus, a client may receive zero or more responses.

While in state *SELECT*, the client collects *DHCPOFFER* responses from DHCP servers. Each offer contains configuration information for the client along with an IP address that the server is offering to lease to the client. The client must choose one of the responses (e.g., the first to arrive), and negotiate with the server for a lease. To do so, the client sends the server a *DHCPREQUEST* message and enters the *REQUEST* state. To acknowledge receipt of the request and start the lease, the server responds by sending a *DHCPACK*. Arrival of the acknowledgement causes the client to move to the *BOUND* state, where the client proceeds to use the address. To summarize:

> *To use DHCP, a host becomes a client by broadcasting a message to all servers on the local network. The host then collects offers from servers, selects one of the offers, and verifies acceptance with the server.*

22.10 Early Lease Termination

We think of the *BOUND* state as the normal state of operation; a client typically remains in the *BOUND* state while it uses the IP address it has acquired. If a client has secondary storage (e.g., a local disk), the client can store the IP address it was assigned, and request the same address when it restarts again. In some cases, however, a client in the *BOUND* state may discover it no longer needs an IP address. For example, suppose a user attaches a laptop computer to a network, uses DHCP to acquire an IP address, and then uses the computer to read electronic mail. The protocol specifies that a lease must last a minimum of one hour, which may be longer than the user needs.

In any case, when an address is no longer needed, DHCP allows a client to terminate the lease early without waiting for the lease to expire. Early termination is especially important if the number of IP addresses a server has available is much smaller than the number of computers that attach to the network. If each client terminates its lease as soon as the IP address is no longer needed, the server will be able to assign the address to another client.

To terminate a lease early, a client sends a *DHCPRELEASE* message to the server. Releasing an address is a final action that prevents the client from using the address further. Thus, after transmitting the release message, the client must not send any other datagrams that use the address. In terms of the state transition diagram of Figure 22.3, a host that sends a *DHCPRELEASE* leaves the *BOUND* state, and must start at the *INITIALIZE* state again before it can use IP.

22.11 Lease Renewal States

We said that when it acquires an address, a DHCP client moves to the *BOUND* state. Upon entering the *BOUND* state, the client sets three timers that control lease renewal, rebinding, and expiration. A DHCP server can specify explicit values for the timers when it allocates an address to the client; if the server does not specify timer values, the client uses defaults. The default value for the first timer is one-half of the total lease time. When the first timer expires, the client must attempt to renew its lease. To request a renewal, the client sends a *DHCPREQUEST* message to the server from which the lease was obtained. The client then moves to the *RENEW* state to await a response. The *DHCPREQUEST* contains the IP address the client is currently using, and asks the server to extend the lease on the address. As in the initial lease negotiation, a client can request a period for the extension, but the server ultimately controls the renewal. A server can respond to a client's renewal request in one of two ways: it can instruct the client to stop using the address or it can approve continued use. If it approves, the server sends a *DHCPACK*, which causes the client to return to the *BOUND* state and continue using the address. The *DHCPACK* can also contain new values for the client's timers. If a server disapproves of continued use, the server sends a *DHCPNACK* (negative acknowledgement), which causes the client to stop using the address immediately and return to the *INITIALIZE* state.

After sending a *DHCPREQUEST* message that requests an extension on its lease, a client remains in state *RENEW* awaiting a response. If no response arrives, the server that granted the lease is either down or unreachable. To handle the situation, DHCP relies on a second timer, which was set when the client entered the *BOUND* state. The second timer expires after *87.5%* of the lease period, and causes the client to move from state *RENEW* to state *REBIND*. When making the transition, the client assumes the old DHCP server is unavailable, and begins broadcasting a *DHCPREQUEST* message to any server on the local net. Any server configured to provide service to the client can respond positively (i.e., to extend the lease), or negatively (i.e. to deny further use of the IP address). If it receives a positive response, the client returns to the *BOUND* state, and resets the two timers. If it receives a negative response, the client must move to the *INITIALIZE* state, must immediately stop using the IP address, and must acquire a new IP address before it can continue to use IP.

After moving to the *REBIND* state, a client will have asked the original server plus all servers on the local net for a lease extension. In the rare case that a client does not receive a response from any server before its third timer expires, the lease expires. The client must stop using the IP address, must move back to the *INITIALIZE* state, and begin acquiring a new address.

22.12 DHCP Options And Message Type

Surprisingly, DHCP does not allocate fixed fields in the message for lease information. Instead, DHCP kept the message BOOTP format, and uses the *OPTIONS* field to identify the message as DHCP. Figure 22.4 illustrates the *DHCP message type* option used to specify which DHCP message is being sent.

0	8	16	23
CODE (53)	LENGTH (1)	TYPE (1 - 7)	

TYPE FIELD	Corresponding DHCP Message Type
1	DHCPDISCOVER
2	DHCPOFFER
3	DHCPREQUEST
4	DHCPDECLINE
5	DHCPACK
6	DHCPNACK
7	DHCPRELEASE
8	DHCPINFORM

Figure 22.4 The format of a DHCP option used to specify the DHCP message type with a list of the possible values for the third octet.

The *OPTIONS* in a DHCP reply each have a type and length field that together determine the size of the option. Figure 22.5 lists some of the possible options.

Item Type	Item Code	Length Octet	Contents of Value
Routers	3	N	IP addresses of N/4 routers
Time Server	4	N	IP addresses of N/4 time servers
IEN116 Server	5	N	IP addresses of N/4 IEN116 servers
Domain Server	6	N	IP addresses of N/4 DNS servers
Log Server	7	N	IP addresses of N/4 log servers
Quote Server	8	N	IP addresses of N/4 quote servers
Lpr Servers	9	N	IP addresses of N/4 lpr servers
Impress	10	N	IP addresses of N/4 Impress servers
RLP Server	11	N	IP addresses of N/4 RLP servers
Hostname	12	N	N bytes of client host name
Boot Size	13	2	2-octet integer size of boot file
RESERVED	128-254	-	Reserved for site specific use

Figure 22.5 Types and contents of items in the *OPTIONS* of a DHCP reply that have variable lengths.

22.13 Option Overload

Fields *SERVER HOST NAME* and *BOOT FILE NAME* in the DHCP message header each occupy many octets. If a given message does not contain information in either of those fields, the space is wasted. To allow a DHCP server to use the two fields for other options, DHCP defines an *Option Overload* option. When present, the overload option tells a receiver to ignore the usual meaning of the *SERVER HOST NAME* and *BOOT FILE NAME* fields, and look for options in the fields instead.

22.14 DHCP And Domain Names†

Although it can allocate an IP address to a computer on demand, DHCP does not completely automate all the procedures required to attach a permanent host to an internet. In particular, the DHCP protocol does not specify any interaction with the domain name system. Thus, unless an additional mechanism is used, the binding between a host name and the IP address DHCP assigns the host will remain independent.

Despite the lack of a standard, some implementations of DHCP do indeed interact with DNS. For example, Unix systems such as Linux or BSD arrange for DHCP to coordinate with the DNS software, which is known as *named bind*‡ or simply *bind*. Similarly, the Microsoft DHCP software coordinates with the Microsoft DNS software to ensure a host that is assigned a DHCP address also has a domain name. The coordination mechanisms also work in reverse to ensure that when a DHCP lease is revoked, DNS is notified to revoke the corresponding name.

22.15 Summary

The Dynamic Host Configuration Protocol allows a computer to obtain information at startup, including the address of a default router, the address of a domain name server, and an IP address. DHCP permits a server to allocate IP addresses automatically or dynamically. Dynamic allocation is necessary for environments such as a wireless network where computers can attach and detach quickly.

To use DHCP, a computer becomes a client. The computer broadcasts a request for DHCP servers, selects one of the offers it receives, and exchanges messages with the server to obtain a lease on the advertised IP address. A relay agent can forward DHCP requests on behalf of the client, which means a site can have a single DHCP server handle address assignment for multiple subnets.

When a client obtains an IP address, the client starts three timers. After the first timer expires, the client attempts to renew its lease. If a second timer expires before renewal completes, the client attempts to rebind its address from any server. If the final

---

†Chapter 23 considers the domain name system in detail.

‡The term *named* is short for *name daemon*.

timer expires before a lease has been renewed, the client stops using the IP address and returns to the initial state to acquire a new address. A finite state machine explains lease acquisition and renewal.

FOR FURTHER STUDY

Details about BOOTP can be found in Croft and Gilmore [RFC 951], which compares BOOTP to RARP and serves as the official standard. Droms [RFC 2131] and Lemon and Cheshire [RFC 3396] contain the specification for DHCP, including a description of state transitions. Alexander and Droms [RFCs 2132] and Lemon et. al. [RFC 3442] specify the encoding of DHCP options. Finally, Droms [RFC 1534] discusses the interoperability of BOOTP and DHCP.

EXERCISES

22.1   DHCP does not contain an explicit field for returning the time of day from the server to the client, but makes it part of the (optional) vendor-specific information. Should the time be included in the required fields? Why or why not?

22.2   Argue that separation of configuration and storage of memory images is *not* good. (See RFC 951 for hints.)

22.3   The DHCP message format is inconsistent because it has two fields for client IP address and one for the name of the boot image. If the client leaves its IP address field empty, the server returns the client's IP address in the second field. If the client leaves the boot file name field empty, the server *replaces* it with an explicit name. Why?

22.4   Read the standard to find out how clients and servers use the *HOPS* field.

22.5   When a DHCP client receives a reply via hardware broadcast, how does it know whether the reply is intended for another DHCP client on the same physical net?

22.6   When a machine obtains its subnet mask with DHCP instead of ICMP, it places less load on *other* host computers. Explain.

22.7   Read the standard to find out how a DHCP client and server can agree on a lease duration without having synchronized clocks.

22.8   Consider a host that has a disk and uses DHCP to obtain an IP address. If the host stores its address on disk along with the date the lease expires and then reboots within the lease period, can it use the address? Why or why not?

22.9   DHCP mandates a minimum address lease of one hour. Can you imagine a situation in which DHCP's minimum lease causes inconvenience? Explain.

22.10 Read the RFC to find out how DHCP specifies renewal and rebinding timers. Should a server ever set one without the other? Why or why not?

22.11 The state transition diagram does not show retransmission. Read the standard to find out how many times a client should retransmit a request.

22.12   Can DHCP guarantee that a client is not "spoofing" (i.e., can DHCP guarantee that it will not send configuration information for host *A* to host *B*)? Does the answer differ for BOOTP? Why or why not?

22.13   DHCP specifies that a client must be prepared to handle at least *312* octets of options. How did the number *312* arise?

22.14   Can a computer that uses DHCP to obtain an IP address operate a server? If so, how does a client reach the server?

Chapter Contents

23

The Domain Name System (DNS)

23.1 Introduction

The protocols described in earlier chapters use 32-bit integers called Internet Protocol addresses (IP addresses) to identify machines. Although such addresses provide a convenient, compact representation for specifying the source and destination in datagrams sent across an internet, users prefer to assign machines pronounceable, easily remembered names.

This chapter considers a scheme for assigning meaningful high-level names to a large set of machines, and discusses a mechanism that maps between high-level machine names and IP addresses. It considers both the translation from high-level names to IP addresses and the translation from IP addresses to high-level machine names. The naming scheme is interesting for two reasons. First, it has been used to assign machine names throughout the Internet. Second, because it uses a geographically distributed set of servers to map names to addresses, the implementation of the name mapping mechanism provides a large scale example of the client-server paradigm described in Chapter 20.

23.2 Names For Machines

The earliest computer systems forced users to understand numeric addresses for objects like system tables and peripheral devices. Timesharing systems advanced computing by allowing users to invent meaningful symbolic names for both physical objects (e.g., peripheral devices) and abstract objects (e.g., files). A similar pattern has emerged in computer networking. Early systems supported point-to-point connections between computers and used low-level hardware addresses to specify machines. Internetworking introduced universal addressing as well as protocol software to map universal addresses into low-level hardware addresses. Because most computing environments contain multiple machines, users need meaningful, symbolic names to identify them.

Early machine names reflected the small environment in which they were chosen. It was quite common for a site with a handful of machines to choose names based on the machines' purposes. For example, machines often had names like *accounting*, *development*, and *production*. Users find such names preferable to cumbersome hardware addresses.

Although the distinction between *address* and *name* is intuitively appealing, it is artificial. Any *name* is merely an identifier that consists of a sequence of characters chosen from a finite alphabet. Names are only useful if the system can efficiently map them to the object they denote. Thus, we think of an IP address as a *low-level name*, and we say that users prefer *high-level names* for machines.

The form of high-level names is important because it determines how names are translated to low-level names or bound to objects, as well as how name assignments are authorized. With only a few machines, choosing names is easy — each administrator can choose an arbitrary name and verify that the name is not in use. For example, when its main departmental computer was connected to the Internet in 1980, the Computer Science Department at Purdue University chose the name *purdue* to identify the connected machine. The list of potential conflicts contained only a few dozen names. By mid 1986, the official list of hosts on the Internet contained 3100 officially registered names and 6500 official aliases. Although the list was growing rapidly in the 1980s, most sites had additional machines (e.g., personal computers) that were not registered. In the current Internet, with hundreds of millions of machines, choosing symbolic names is much more difficult.

23.3 Flat Namespace

The original set of machine names used throughout the Internet formed a *flat namespace* in which each name consisted of a sequence of characters without any further structure. In the original scheme, a central site, the Network Information Center (*NIC*), administered the namespace and determined whether a new name was appropriate (i.e., it prohibited obscene names or new names that conflicted with existing names).

The chief advantage of a flat namespace is that names are convenient and short; the chief disadvantage is that a flat namespace cannot generalize to large sets of machines for both technical and administrative reasons. First, because names are drawn from a single set of identifiers, the potential for conflict increases as the number of sites increases. Second, because authority for adding new names must rest at a single site, the administrative workload at that central site also increases with the number of sites. To understand the severity of the problem, imagine a rapidly growing internet with thousands of sites, each of which has hundreds of individual personal computers and workstations. Every time someone acquires and connects a new personal computer, its name must be approved by the central authority. Third, because the name-to-address bindings change frequently, the cost of maintaining correct copies of the entire list at each site is high and increases as the number of sites increases. Alternatively, if the name database resides at a single site, network traffic to that site increases with the number of sites.

23.4 Hierarchical Names

How can a naming system accommodate a large, rapidly expanding set of names without requiring a central site to administer it? The answer lies in decentralizing the naming mechanism by delegating authority for parts of the namespace and distributing responsibility for the mapping between names and addresses. The Internet uses such a scheme. Before examining the details, we will consider the motivation and intuition behind it.

The partitioning of a namespace must be defined in a way that supports efficient name mapping and guarantees autonomous control of name assignment. Optimizing only for efficient mapping can lead to solutions that retain a flat namespace and reduce traffic by dividing the names among multiple mapping machines. Optimizing only for administrative ease can lead to solutions that make delegation of authority easy but name mapping expensive or complex.

To understand how the namespace should be divided, consider the internal structure of large organizations. At the top, a chief executive has overall responsibility. Because the chief executive cannot oversee everything, the organization may be partitioned into divisions, with an executive in charge of each division. The chief executive grants each division autonomy within specified limits. More to the point, the executive in charge of a particular division can hire or fire employees, assign offices, and delegate authority, without obtaining direct permission from the chief executive.

Besides making it easy to delegate authority, the hierarchy of a large organization introduces autonomous operation. For example, when an office worker needs information like the telephone number of a new employee, he or she begins by asking local clerical workers (who may contact clerical workers in other divisions). The point is that although authority always passes down the corporate hierarchy, information can flow across the hierarchy from one office to another.

23.5 Delegation Of Authority For Names

A hierarchical naming scheme works like the management of a large organization. The namespace is *partitioned* at the top level, and authority for names in subdivisions is passed to designated agents. For example, one might choose to partition the namespace based on *site name* and to delegate to each site responsibility for maintaining names within its partition. The topmost level of the hierarchy divides the namespace and delegates authority for each division; it need not be bothered by changes within a division.

The syntax of hierarchically assigned names often reflects the hierarchical delegation of authority used to assign them. As an example, consider a namespace with names of the form:

$$local . site$$

where *site* is the site name authorized by the central authority, *local* is the part of a name controlled by the site, and the period† (".") is a delimiter used to separate them. When the topmost authority approves adding a new site, *X*, it adds *X* to the list of valid sites and delegates to site *X* authority for all names that end in "*.X*".

23.6 Subset Authority

In a hierarchical namespace, authority may be further subdivided at each level. In our example of partition by sites, the site itself may consist of several administrative groups, and the site authority may choose to subdivide its namespace among the groups. The idea is to keep subdividing the namespace until each subdivision is small enough to be manageable.

Syntactically, subdividing the namespace introduces another partition of the name. For example, adding a *group* subdivision to names already partitioned by site produces the following name syntax:

$$local . group . site$$

Because the topmost level delegates authority, group names do not have to agree among all sites. A university site might choose group names like *engineering*, *science*, and *arts*, while a corporate site might choose group names like *production*, *accounting*, and *personnel*.

The U.S. telephone system provides another example of a hierarchical naming syntax. The 10 digits of a phone number have been partitioned into a 3-digit *area code*, 3-digit *exchange*, and 4-digit *subscriber number* within the exchange. Each exchange has authority for assigning subscriber numbers within its piece of the namespace. Although it is possible to group arbitrary subscribers into exchanges and to group arbitrary exchanges into area codes, the assignment of telephone numbers is not capricious; they are carefully chosen to make it easy to route phone calls across the telephone network.

---

†In domain names, the period delimiter is pronounced "dot."

The telephone example is important because it illustrates a key distinction between the hierarchical naming scheme used in a TCP/IP internet and other hierarchies: partitioning the set of machines owned by an organization along lines of authority does not necessarily imply partitioning by physical location. For example, it could be that at some university, a single building houses the mathematics department as well as the computer science department. It might even turn out that although the machines from these two groups fall under completely separate administrative domains, they connect to the same physical network. It also may happen that a single group owns machines on several physical networks. For these reasons, the TCP/IP naming scheme allows arbitrary delegation of authority for the hierarchical namespace without regard to physical connections. The concept can be summarized:

> *In the Internet, hierarchical machine names are assigned according to the structure of organizations that obtain authority for parts of the namespace, not necessarily according to the structure of the physical network interconnections.*

Of course, at many sites the organizational hierarchy corresponds with the structure of physical network interconnections. For example, suppose the computers in a given department all connect to the same network. If the department is also assigned part of the naming hierarchy, all machines with names in that part of the hierarchy will also connect to a single physical network.

23.7 Internet Domain Names

The *Domain Name System* (*DNS*) is the system that provides name to address mapping for the Internet. DNS has two, conceptually independent aspects. The first is abstract: it specifies the name syntax and rules for delegating authority over names. The second is concrete: it specifies the implementation of a distributed computing system that efficiently maps names to addresses. This section considers the name syntax, and later sections examine the implementation.

The domain name system uses a hierarchical naming scheme known as *domain names*. As in our earlier examples, a domain name consists of a sequence of subnames separated by a delimiter character, the period. In our examples we said that individual sections of the name might represent sites or groups, but the domain name system simply calls each section a *label*. Thus, the domain name

cs.purdue.edu

contains three labels: *cs, purdue*, and *edu*. Any suffix of a label in a domain name is also called a *domain*. In the above example, the lowest-level domain is *cs.purdue.edu*, (the domain name for the Computer Science Department at Purdue University), the second level domain is *purdue.edu* (the domain name for Purdue University), and the top-level domain is *edu* (the domain name for educational institutions). As the example shows, domain names are written with the local label first and the top domain last. As we will see, writing them in this order makes it possible to compress messages that contain multiple domain names.

23.8 Top-Level Domains

Figure 23.1 lists the top-level domain names.

Domain Name	Meaning
aero	Air transport industry
arpa	Infrastructure domain
biz	Businesses
com	Commercial organization
coop	Cooperative associations
edu	Educational institution (4-year)
gov	United States government
info	Information
int	International treaty organizations
mil	United States military
museum	Museums
name	Individuals
net	Major network support centers
org	Organizations other than those above
pro	Credentialed professionals
country code	Each country (geographic scheme)

Figure 23.1 The top-level Internet domains and their meanings. Although labels are shown in lower case, domain name system comparisons are insensitive to case, so *COM* is equivalent to *com*.

Conceptually, the top-level names permit two completely different naming hierarchies: geographic and organizational. The geographic scheme divides the universe of machines by country. Machines in the United States fall under the top-level domain *us*; when a foreign country wants to register machines in the domain name system, the central authority assigns the country a new top-level domain with the country's international standard 2-letter identifier as its label. The authority for the US domain has chosen to divide it into one second-level domain per state. For example, the domain for the state of Virginia is

va.us

As an alternative to the geographic hierarchy, the top-level domains also allow organizations to be grouped by organizational type. When an organization wants to participate in the domain naming system, it chooses how it wishes to be registered and requests approval. A *domain name registrar* reviews the application and assigns the organization a subdomain† under one of the existing top-level domains. The owner of a given top-level domain can decide what to allow and how to further partition the namespace. For example, in the United Kingdom, which has the two-letter country code *uk*, universities and other academic institutions are registered under domain *ac.uk*.

An example may help clarify the relationship between the naming hierarchy and authority for names. A machine named *xinu* in the Computer Science Department at Purdue University has the official domain name

xinu.cs.purdue.edu

The machine name was approved and registered by the local network manager in the Computer Science Department. The department manager had previously obtained authority for the subdomain *cs.purdue.edu* from a university network authority, who had obtained permission to manage the subdomain *purdue.edu* from the Internet authority. The Internet authority retains control of the *edu* domain, so new universities can only be added with its permission. Similarly, the university network manager at Purdue University retains authority for the *purdue.edu* subdomain, so new third-level domains may only be added with the manager's permission.

Figure 23.2 illustrates a small part of the Internet domain name hierarchy. As the figure shows, IBM corporation, a commercial organization, registered as *ibm.com*, Purdue University registered as *purdue.edu*, and the National Science Foundation, a government agency, registered as *nsf.gov*. In contrast, the Corporation for National Research Initiatives chose to register under the geographic hierarchy as *cnri.reston.va.us*.

---

†The standard does not define the term ''subdomain.'' We have chosen to use it because its analogy to ''subset'' helps clarify the relationship among domains.

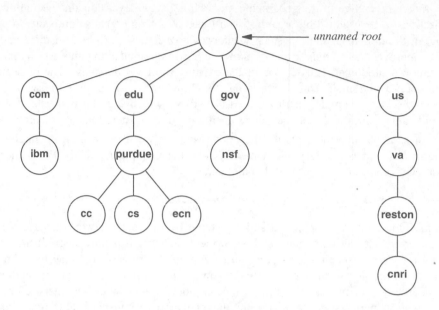

Figure 23.2 A small part of the Internet domain name hierarchy (tree). In practice, the tree is broad and flat; most host entries appear by the fifth level.

23.9 Name Syntax And Type

The domain name system is quite general because it allows multiple naming hierarchies to be embedded in one system. To allow clients to distinguish among multiple types of entries, each named item stored in the system is assigned a *type* that specifies whether it is the address of a machine, a mailbox, a user, and so on. When a client asks the domain system to resolve a name, it must specify the type of answer desired. For example, when an electronic mail application uses the domain system to resolve a name, it specifies that the answer should be the address of a *mail exchanger*. A remote login application specifies that it seeks a machine's IP address. It is important to understand the following:

> *A given name may map to more than one item in the domain system.*
> *The client specifies the type of object desired when resolving a name,*
> *and the server returns objects of that type.*

In addition to specifying the type of answer sought, the domain system allows the client to specify the protocol family to use. The domain system partitions the entire set of names by *class*, allowing a single database to store mappings for multiple protocol suites†.

---

†In practice, few domain servers use multiple protocol suites.

The syntax of a name does not determine what type of object it names or the class of protocol suite. In particular, the number of labels in a name does not determine whether the name refers to an individual object (machine) or a domain. Thus, in our example, it is possible to have a machine named

gwen.purdue.edu

even though

cs.purdue.edu

names a subdomain. We can summarize this important point:

> *One cannot distinguish the names of subdomains from the names of individual objects or the type of an object using only the domain name syntax.*

23.10 Mapping Domain Names To Addresses

In addition to the rules for name syntax and delegation of authority, the domain name scheme includes an efficient, reliable, general purpose, distributed system for mapping names to addresses. The system is distributed in the technical sense, meaning that a set of servers operating at multiple sites cooperatively solve the mapping problem. It is efficient in the sense that most names can be mapped locally; only a few require internet traffic. It is general purpose because it is not restricted to machine names (although we will use that example for now). Finally, it is reliable in that no single machine failure will prevent the system from operating correctly.

The domain mechanism for mapping names to addresses consists of independent, cooperative systems called *name servers*. A name server is a server program that supplies name-to-address translation, mapping from domain names to IP addresses. Often, server software executes on a dedicated processor, and the machine itself is called the name server. The client software, called a *name resolver*, uses one or more name servers when translating a name.

The easiest way to understand how domain servers work is to imagine them arranged in a tree structure that corresponds to the naming hierarchy, as Figure 23.3 illustrates. The root of the tree is a server that recognizes the top-level domains and knows which server resolves each domain. Given a name to resolve, the root can choose the correct server for that name. At the next level, a set of name servers each provide answers for one top-level domain (e.g., *edu*). A server at this level knows which servers can resolve each of the subdomains under its domain. At the third level of the tree, name servers provide answers for subdomains (e.g., *purdue* under *edu*). The conceptual tree continues with one server at each level for which a subdomain has been defined.

Links in the conceptual tree do not indicate physical network connections. Instead, they show which other name servers a given server knows and contacts. The servers themselves may be located at arbitrary locations on an internet. Thus, the tree of servers is an abstraction that uses an internet for communication.

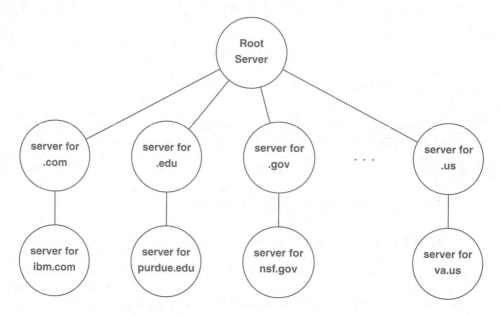

Figure 23.3 The conceptual arrangement of domain name servers in a tree that corresponds to the naming hierarchy. In theory, each server knows the addresses of all lower-level servers for all subdomains within the domain it handles.

If servers in the domain system worked exactly as our simplistic model suggests, the relationship between connectivity and authorization would be quite simple. When authority was granted for a subdomain, the organization requesting it would need to establish a domain name server for that subdomain and link it into the tree.

In practice, the relationship between the naming hierarchy and the tree of servers is not as simple as our model implies. The tree of servers has few levels because a single physical server can contain all of the information for large parts of the naming hierarchy. In particular, organizations often collect information from all of their subdomains into a single server. Figure 23.4 shows a more realistic organization of servers for the naming hierarchy of Figure 23.2.

A root server contains information about the root and top-level domains, and each organization uses a single server for its names. Because the tree of servers is shallow, at most two servers need to be contacted to resolve a name like *xinu.cs.purdue.edu*:

the root server and the server for domain *purdue.edu* (i.e., the root server knows which server handles *purdue.edu*, and the entire domain information for Purdue resides in one server).

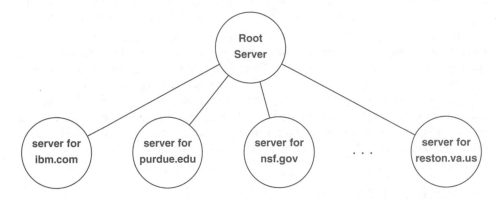

Figure 23.4 A realistic organization of servers for the naming hierarchy of Figure 23.2. Because the tree is broad and flat, few servers need to be contacted when resolving a name.

23.11 Domain Name Resolution

Although the conceptual tree makes understanding the relationship between servers easy, it hides several subtle details. Looking at the name resolution algorithm will help explain them. Conceptually, domain name resolution proceeds top-down, starting with the root name server and proceeding to servers located at the leaves of the tree. There are two ways to use the domain name system: by contacting name servers one at a time or asking the name server system to perform the complete translation. In either case, the client software forms a domain name query that contains the name to be resolved, a declaration of the class of the name, the type of answer desired, and a code that specifies whether the name server should translate the name completely. It sends the query to a name server for resolution.

When a domain name server receives a query, it checks to see if the name lies in the subdomain for which it is an authority. If so, it translates the name to an address according to its database, and appends an answer to the query before sending it back to the client. If the name server cannot resolve the name completely, it checks to see what type of interaction the client specified. If the client requested complete translation (*recursive resolution*, in domain name terminology), the server contacts a domain name server that can resolve the name and returns the answer to the client. If the client requested non-recursive resolution (*iterative resolution*), the name server cannot supply an answer. It generates a reply that specifies the name server the client should contact next to resolve the name.

How does a client find a name server at which to begin the search? How does a name server find other name servers that can answer questions when it cannot? The answers are simple. A client must know how to contact at least one name server. To ensure that a domain name server can reach others, the domain system requires that each server know the address of at least one root server†. In addition, a server may know the address of a server for the domain immediately above it (called the *parent*).

Domain name servers use a well-known protocol port for all communication, so clients know how to communicate with a server once they know the IP address of the machine in which the server executes. There is no standard way for hosts to locate a machine in the local environment on which a name server runs; that is left to whoever designs the client software. In some systems, the address of the machine that supplies domain name service is bound into application programs at compile time, while in others, the address is stored in a file on secondary storage. Many systems obtain the address of a domain server automatically as part of the bootstrap process‡.

23.12 Efficient Translation

Although it may seem natural to resolve queries by working down the tree of name servers, doing so can lead to inefficiencies for three reasons. First, most name resolution refers to local names, those found within the same subdivision of the namespace as the machine from which the request originates. Tracing a path through the hierarchy to contact the local authority would be inefficient. Second, if each name resolution always started by contacting the topmost level of the hierarchy, the machine at that point would become overloaded. Third, failure of machines at the topmost levels of the hierarchy would prevent name resolution, even if the local authority could resolve the name. The telephone number hierarchy mentioned earlier helps explain. Although telephone numbers are assigned hierarchically, they are resolved in a bottom-up fashion. Because the majority of telephone calls are local, they can be resolved by the local exchange without searching the hierarchy. Furthermore, calls within a given area code can be resolved without contacting sites outside the area code. When applied to domain names, these ideas lead to a two-step name resolution mechanism that preserves the administrative hierarchy but permits efficient translation.

We have said that most queries to name servers refer to local names. In the two-step name resolution process, resolution begins with the local name server. If the local server cannot resolve a name, the query must then be sent to another server in the domain system.

---

†For reliability, there are multiple servers for each node in the domain server tree; the root server is further replicated to provide load balancing.

‡See DHCP in Chapter 22 for details.

23.13 Caching: The Key To Efficiency

The cost of lookup for nonlocal names can be extremely high if resolvers send each query to the root server. Even if queries could go directly to the server that has authority for the name, name lookup can present a heavy load to an internet. Thus, to improve the overall performance of a name server system, it is necessary to lower the cost of lookup for nonlocal names.

Internet name servers use *caching* to optimize search costs. Each server maintains a cache of recently used names as well as a record of where the mapping information for that name was obtained. When a client asks the server to resolve a name, the server first checks to see if it has authority for the name according to the standard procedure. If not, the server checks its cache to see if the name has been resolved recently. Servers report cached information to clients, but mark it as a *nonauthoritative* binding, and give the domain name of the server, S, from which they obtained the binding. The local server also sends along additional information that tells the client the binding between S and an IP address. Therefore, clients receive answers quickly, but the information may be out-of-date. If efficiency is important, the client will choose to accept the nonauthoritative answer and proceed. If accuracy is important, the client will choose to contact the authority and verify that the binding between name and address is still valid.

Caching works well in the domain name system because name to address bindings change infrequently. However, they do change. If servers cached information the first time it was requested and never updated it, entries in the cache could become *stale* (i.e., incorrect). To keep the cache correct, servers time each entry and dispose of entries that exceed a reasonable time. When a server is asked for the information after it has removed the entry from its cache, the server must go back to the authoritative source and obtain the binding again. More important, servers do not apply a single fixed timeout to all entries, but allow the authority for an entry to configure its timeout. Whenever an authority responds to a request, it includes a *Time To Live* (TTL) value in the response that specifies how long it guarantees the binding to remain valid. Thus, authorities can reduce network overhead by specifying long timeouts for entries that they expect to remain unchanged, while improving correctness by specifying short timeouts for entries that they expect to change frequently.

Caching is important in hosts as well as in local domain name servers. Most resolver software caches DNS entries in the host. Thus, if a user looks up the same name repeatedly, subsequent lookups can be resolved from the local cache without using the network.

23.14 Domain Name System Message Format

Looking at the details of messages exchanged between clients and domain name servers will help clarify how the system operates from the view of a typical application program. We assume that a user invokes an application program and supplies the name

of a machine with which the application must communicate. Before it can use protocols like TCP or UDP to communicate with the specified machine, the application program must find the machine's IP address. It passes the domain name to a local resolver
and requests an IP address. The local resolver checks its cache and returns the answer
if one is present. If the local resolver does not have an answer, it formats a message
and sends it to the server (i.e., it becomes a client). Although our example only involves one name, the message format allows a client to ask multiple questions in a single message. Each question consists of a domain name for which the client seeks an IP
address, a specification of the query class (i.e., *internet*), and the type of object desired
(e.g., *address*). The server responds by returning a similar message that contains
answers to the questions for which the server has bindings. If the server cannot answer
all questions, the response will contain information about other name servers that the
client can contact to obtain the answers.

Responses also contain information about the servers that are authorities for the replies and the IP addresses of those servers. Figure 23.5 shows the message format.

0	16	31
IDENTIFICATION	PARAMETER	
NUMBER OF QUESTIONS	NUMBER OF ANSWERS	
NUMBER OF AUTHORITY	NUMBER OF ADDITIONAL	
QUESTION SECTION . . .		
ANSWER SECTION . . .		
AUTHORITY SECTION . . .		
ADDITIONAL INFORMATION SECTION . . .		

Figure 23.5 Domain name server message format. The *QUESTION*,
ANSWER, *AUTHORITY*, and *ADDITIONAL INFORMATION*
sections are variable length.

As the figure shows, each message begins with a fixed header. The header contains a unique *IDENTIFICATION* field that the client uses to match responses to
queries, and a *PARAMETER* field that specifies the operation requested and a response
code. Figure 23.6 gives the interpretation of bits in the *PARAMETER* field.

Bit of PARAMETER field	Meaning

0	Operation:
	   0 Query
	   1 Response

1-4	Query Type:
	   0 Standard
	   1 Inverse
	   2 Server status request
	   4 Notify
	   5 Update

5	Set if answer authoritative
6	Set if message truncated
7	Set if recursion desired
8	Set if recursion available
9	Set if data is authenticated
10	Set if checking is disabled
11	Reserved

12-15	Response Type:
	   0 No error
	   1 Format error in query
	   2 Server failure
	   3 Name does not exist
	   5 Refused
	   6 Name exists when it should not
	   7 RR set exists
	   8 RR set that should exist does not
	   9 Server not authoritative for the zone
	   10 Name not contained in zone

Figure 23.6 The meaning of bits of the *PARAMETER* field in a domain name
server message. Bits are numbered left to right starting at 0.

The fields labeled *NUMBER OF* each give a count of entries in the corresponding
sections that occur later in the message. For example, the field labeled *NUMBER OF
QUESTIONS* gives the count of entries that appear in the *QUESTION SECTION* of the
message.

The *QUESTION SECTION* contains queries for which answers are desired. The
client fills in only the question section; the server returns the questions and answers in
its response. Each question consists of a *QUERY DOMAIN NAME* followed by *QUERY
TYPE* and *QUERY CLASS* fields, as Figure 23.7 shows.

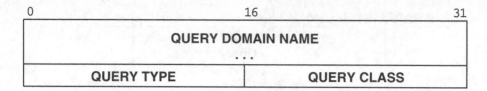

Figure 23.7 The format of entries in the *QUESTION SECTION* of a domain
name server message. The domain name is variable length.
Clients fill in the questions; servers return them along with
answers.

Although the *QUERY DOMAIN NAME* field has variable length, we will see in the next
section that the internal representation of domain names makes it possible for the receiver to know the exact length. The *QUERY TYPE* encodes the type of the question
(e.g., whether the question refers to a machine name or a mail address). The *QUERY
CLASS* field allows domain names to be used for arbitrary objects because official Internet names are only one possible class. It should be noted that, although the diagram in
Figure 23.5 follows our convention of showing formats in 32-bit multiples, the *QUERY
DOMAIN NAME* field may contain an arbitrary number of octets. No padding is used.
Therefore, messages to or from domain name servers may contain an odd number of oc-
tets.

In a domain name server message, each of the *ANSWER SECTION*, *AUTHORITY
SECTION*, and *ADDITIONAL INFORMATION SECTION* consists of a set of *resource
records* that describe domain names and mappings. Each resource record describes one
name. Figure 23.8 shows the format.

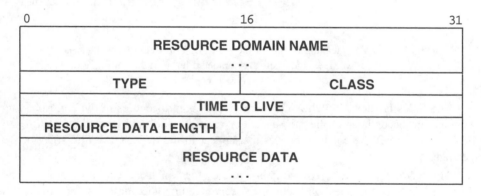

Figure 23.8 The format of resource records used in later sections of messages
returned by domain name servers.

The *RESOURCE DOMAIN NAME* field contains the domain name to which this resource record refers. It may be an arbitrary length. The *TYPE* field specifies the type of the data included in the resource record; the *CLASS* field specifies the data's class. The *TIME TO LIVE* field contains a 32-bit integer that specifies the number of seconds information in this resource record can be cached. It is used by clients who have requested a name binding and may want to cache the results. The last two fields contain the results of the binding, with the *RESOURCE DATA LENGTH* field specifying the count of octets in the *RESOURCE DATA* field.

23.15 Compressed Name Format

When represented in a message, domain names are stored as a sequence of labels. Each label begins with an octet that specifies its length. Thus, the receiver reconstructs a domain name by repeatedly reading a 1-octet length, n, and then reading a label n octets long. A length octet containing zero marks the end of the name.

Domain name servers often return multiple answers to a query and, in many cases, suffixes of the domain overlap. To conserve space in the reply packet, the name servers compress names by storing only one copy of each domain name. When extracting a domain name from a message, the client software must check each segment of the name to see whether it consists of a literal string (in the format of a 1-octet count followed by the characters that make up the name) or a pointer to a literal string. When it encounters a pointer, the client must follow the pointer to a new place in the message to find the remainder of the name.

Pointers always occur at the beginning of segments and are encoded in the count byte. If the top two bits of the 8-bit segment count field are 1s, the client must take the next 14 bits as an integer pointer. If the top two bits are zero, the next 6 bits specify the number of characters in the label that follow the count octet.

23.16 Abbreviation Of Domain Names

The telephone number hierarchy illustrates another useful feature of local resolution, *name abbreviation*. Abbreviation provides a method of shortening names when the resolving process can supply part of the name automatically. Normally, a subscriber omits the area code when dialing a local telephone number. The resulting digits form an abbreviated name assumed to lie within the same area code as the subscriber's phone. Abbreviation also works well for machine names. Given a name like *xyz*, the resolving process can assume it lies in the same local authority as the machine on which it is being resolved. Thus, the resolver can supply missing parts of the name automatically. For example, within the Computer Science Department at Purdue, the abbreviated name

xinu

is equivalent to the full domain name

xinu.cs.purdue.edu

Most client software implements abbreviations with a *domain name suffix list*. The local network manager configures a list of possible suffixes to be appended to names during lookup. When a resolver encounters a name, it steps through the list, appending each suffix and trying to look up the resulting name. For example, the suffix list for the Computer Science Department at Purdue includes:

<code>.cs.purdue.edu</code>
<code>.cc.purdue.edu</code>
<code>.purdue.edu</code>
null

Thus, local resolvers first append *cs.purdue.edu* onto the name *xinu*. If that lookup fails, they append *cc.purdue.edu* onto the name and look that up. The last suffix in the example list is the null string, meaning that if all other lookups fail, the resolver will attempt to look up the name with no suffix. Managers can use the suffix list to make abbreviation convenient or to restrict application programs to local names.

We said that the client takes responsibility for the expansion of such abbreviations, but it should be emphasized that such abbreviations are not part of the domain name system itself. The domain system only allows lookup of a fully specified domain name. As a consequence, programs that depend on abbreviations may not work correctly outside the environment in which they were built. We can summarize:

> *The domain name system only maps full domain names into addresses; abbreviations are not part of the domain name system itself, but are introduced by client software to make local names convenient for users.*

23.17 Inverse Mappings

We said that the domain name system can provide mappings other than machine name to IP address. *Inverse queries* allow the client to ask a server to map "backwards" by taking an answer and generating the question that would produce that answer. Of course, not all answers have a unique question. Even when they do, a server may not be able to provide it. Although inverse queries have been part of the domain system since it was first specified, they are generally not used because there is often no way to find the server that can resolve the query without searching the entire set of servers.

23.18 Pointer Queries

One form of inverse mapping is used as an authentication mechanism that a server uses to verify that a client is authorized to access the service: the server maps the client's IP address to a domain name. For example, a server at corporation *example.com* might be configured to only provide the service to clients from the same corporation. When a client contacts the server, the server maps the client's IP address to an equivalent domain name and verifies that the name ends in *example.com* before granting access. Reverse lookup is so important that the domain system supports a special domain and a special form of question called a *pointer query* to provide it. In a pointer query, the question presented to a domain name server specifies an IP address encoded as a printable string in the form of a domain name (i.e., a textual representation of digits separated by periods). A pointer query requests the name server to return the correct domain name for the machine with the specified IP address.

Pointer queries are not difficult to generate. If we think of an IP address written in dotted-decimal form, it has the following format:

$$aaa.bbb.ccc.ddd$$

To form a pointer query, the client rearranges the dotted decimal representation of the address into a string of the form:

$$ddd.ccc.bbb.aaa.in\text{-}addr.arpa$$

The new form is a name in the special *in-addr.arpa* domain†. Because the local name server may not be the authority for either the *arpa* domain or the *in-addr.arpa* domain, it may need to contact other name servers to complete the resolution. To make the resolution of pointer queries efficient, the Internet root domain servers maintain a database of valid IP addresses along with information about domain name servers that can resolve each address group.

23.19 Object Types And Resource Record Contents

We have mentioned that the domain name system can be used for translating a domain name to a mail exchanger address as well as for translating a host name to an IP address. The domain system is quite general in that it can be used for arbitrary hierarchical names. For example, one might decide to store the names of available computational services along with a mapping from each name to the telephone number to call to find out about the corresponding service. Or one might store names of protocol products along with a mapping to the names and addresses of vendors that offer such products.

---

†The octets of the IP address must be reversed when forming a domain name because IP addresses have the most significant octets first while domain names have the least-significant octets first.

Recall that the system accommodates a variety of mappings by including a *type* in each resource record. When sending a request, a client must specify the type in its query†; servers specify the data type in all resource records they return. The type determines the contents of the resource record according to the table in Figure 23.9

Type	Meaning	Contents
A	Host Address	32-bit IP address
CNAME	Canonical Name	Canonical domain name for an alias
HINFO	CPU & OS	Name of CPU and operating system
MINFO	Mailbox info	Information about a mailbox or mail list
MX	Mail Exchanger	16-bit preference and name of host that acts as mail exchanger for the domain
NS	Name Server	Name of authoritative server for domain
PTR	Pointer	Domain name (like a symbolic link)
SOA	Start of Authority	Multiple fields that specify which parts of the naming hierarchy a server implements
TXT	Arbitrary text	Uninterpreted string of ASCII text

Figure 23.9 A few examples of domain name system resource record types. More than fifty types have been defined.

Most data is of type *A*, meaning that it consists of the name of a host attached to the Internet along with the host's IP address. The second most useful domain type, *MX*, is assigned to names used for electronic mail exchangers. It allows a site to specify multiple hosts that are each capable of accepting mail. When sending electronic mail, the user specifies an electronic mail address in the form *user@domain-part*. The mail system uses the domain name system to resolve *domain-part* with query type *MX*. The domain system returns a set of resource records that each contain a preference field and a host's domain name. The mail system steps through the set from highest preference to lowest (lower numbers mean higher preference). For each *MX* resource record, the mailer extracts the domain name and uses a type *A* query to resolve that name to an IP address. It then tries to contact the host and deliver mail. If the host is unavailable, the mailer will continue trying other hosts on the list.

To make lookup efficient, a server always returns additional bindings that it knows in the *ADDITIONAL INFORMATION SECTION* of a response. In the case of *MX* records, a domain server can use the *ADDITIONAL INFORMATION SECTION* to return type *A* resource records for domain names reported in the *ANSWER SECTION*. Doing so substantially reduces the number of queries a mailer sends to its domain server.

---

†Queries can specify a few additional types (e.g., there is a query type that requests all resource records).

23.20 Obtaining Authority For A Subdomain

Before an institution is granted authority for an official second-level domain, it must agree to operate a domain name server that meets Internet standards. Of course, a domain name server must obey the protocol standards that specify message formats and the rules for responding to requests. The server must also know the addresses of servers that handle each subdomain (if any exist) as well as the address of at least one root server.

In practice, the domain system is much more complex than we have outlined. In most cases, a single physical server can handle more than one part of the naming hierarchy. For example, a single name server at Purdue University handles both the second-level domain *purdue.edu* as well as the geographic domain *laf.in.us*. A subtree of names managed by a given name server forms a *zone of authority*. Another practical complication arises because servers must be able to handle many requests, even though some requests take a long time to resolve. Usually, servers support concurrent activity, allowing work to proceed on later requests while earlier ones are being processed. Handling requests concurrently is especially important when the server receives a recursive request that forces it to send the request on to another server for resolution.

Server implementation is also complicated because the Internet authority requires that the information in every domain name server be replicated. Information must appear in at least two servers that do not operate on the same computer. In practice, the requirements are quite stringent: the servers must have no single common point of failure. Avoiding common points of failure means that the two name servers cannot both attach to the same network; they cannot even obtain electrical power from the same source. Thus, to meet the requirements, a site must find at least one other site that agrees to operate a backup name server. Of course, at any point in the tree of servers, a server must know how to locate both the primary and backup name servers for subdomains, and it must direct queries to a backup name server if the primary server is unavailable.

23.21 Dynamic DNS Update And Notification

Our discussions of NAT in Chapter 19 and DHCP in Chapter 22 both mention the need for interaction with DNS. In the case of a NAT box that obtains a dynamic address from an ISP, a server can only be placed behind the NAT box if the domain name server and the NAT system coordinate. In the case of DHCP, when a host obtains a dynamic address, the DNS server for the host must be updated with the host's current address. To handle the situations described above and to permit multiple parties to share administration (e.g., to allow multiple registrars to jointly manage a top-level domain), the IETF developed a technology known as *Dynamic DNS*.

There are two aspects of Dynamic DNS: *update* and *notification*. As the name implies, Dynamic DNS update permits changes to be made dynamically to the information that a server stores. Thus, when it assigns an IP address to a host, a DHCP server can use the dynamic update mechanism to inform the DNS server about the assignment. Notification messages solve the problem of propagating changes. In particular, observe that because DNS uses backup servers, changes made in the primary server must be propagated to each backup. When a dynamic change occurs, the primary server sends a notification to the backup servers, which allows each backup to request an update of the zone information. Because it avoids sending copies unnecessarily, notification takes less bandwidth than merely using a small timeout for updates.

23.22 DNS Security Extensions (DNSSEC)

Because it is among the most important aspects of Internet infrastructure, the domain name system is often cited as a critical mechanism that should be protected. In particular, if a host is giving incorrect answers to DNS queries, application software or users can be fooled into believing imposter web sites or revealing confidential information. To help protect DNS, the IETF has invented a technology known as *DNS Security* (*DNSSEC*).

The primary services provided by DNSSEC include *authentication* of the message origin and *integrity* of the data. That is, when it uses DNSSEC, a host can verify a DNS message did indeed originate at an authoritative DNS server (i.e., the server responsible for the name in the query) and that the data in the message arrived without being changed. Furthermore, DNSSEC can authenticate negative answers — a host can obtain an authenticated message that states a particular domain name does not exist.

Despite offering authentication and integrity, DNSSEC does not solve all problems. In particular, DNSSEC does not provide confidentiality, nor does it fend off denial-of-service attacks. The former means that even if a host uses DNSSEC, an outside observer snooping on a network will be able to know which names the host looks up (i.e., the observer may be able to guess why a given business is being contacted). The inability to fend off denial-of-service attacks means that even if a host and server both use DNSSEC, there is no guarantee that messages sent between them will be received.

To provide authentication and data integrity, DNSSEC uses a digital signature mechanism — in addition to the requested information, a reply from a DNSSEC server contains a digital signature that allows the receiver to verify that the contents of the message were not changed. One of the most interesting aspects of DNSSEC arises from the way the digital signature mechanism is administered. Like many security mechanisms, the DNSSEC mechanism uses *public key encryption* technology. The interesting twist is that to distribute public keys, DNSSEC uses the DNS. That is, a server contains the public keys for zones further down the hierarchy (e.g., the server for *.com* contains the public key for *example.com*). To guarantee security for the entire system, the public key for the top level of the hierarchy (i.e., the key for a root server) must be manually configured into a resolver.

23.23 Summary

Hierarchical naming systems allow delegation of authority for names, making it possible to accommodate an arbitrarily large set of names without overwhelming a central site with administrative duties. Although name resolution is separate from delegation of authority, it is possible to create hierarchical naming systems in which resolution is an efficient process that starts at the local server even though delegation of authority always flows from the top of the hierarchy downward.

We examined the Internet domain name system (DNS) and saw that it offers a hierarchical naming scheme. DNS uses distributed lookup in which domain name servers map each domain name to an IP address or mail exchanger address. Clients begin by trying to resolve names locally. When the local server cannot resolve the name, the client must choose to work through the tree of name servers iteratively or request the local name server to do it recursively. Finally, we saw that the domain name system supports a variety of bindings including bindings from IP addresses to high-level names.

DNSSEC provides a mechanism that can be used to secure DNS; it authenticates replies and guarantees the integrity of the answers. DNSSEC uses public-key encryption, and arranges to use DNS to distribute the set of public keys.

FOR FURTHER STUDY

Many RFCs focus on DNS and proposed extensions. Mockapetris [RFC 1034] discusses Internet domain naming in general, giving the overall philosophy, while Mockapetris [RFC 1035] provides a protocol standard for the domain name system. Mockapetris [RFC 1101] discusses using the domain name system to encode network names and proposes extensions useful for other mappings. Postel and Reynolds [RFC 920] states the requirements that an Internet domain name server must meet. Stahl [RFC 1032] gives administrative guidelines for establishing a domain, Lottor [RFC 1033] provides guidelines for operating a domain name server, and Eastlake et. al [RFC 2929] discusses IANA considerations. Vixie [RFC 1996] defines notification and Vixie et. al. [RFC 2136] defines dynamic updates. Eastlake [RFC 2535] presents security extensions. Klensin [RFC 2821] relates domain naming to electronic mail addressing. Wellington [RFC 3008] proposes DNSSEC, and RFCs 3658, 3755, 3757, and 3845 update details.

EXERCISES

23.1   Machine names should not be bound into the operating system at compile time. Explain why.

23.2   Would you prefer to use a machine that obtained its name from a remote file or from a name server? Why?

23.3   Why should each name server know the IP address of its parent instead of the domain name of its parent?

23.4   Devise a naming scheme that tolerates changes to the naming hierarchy. As an example, consider two large companies that each have an independent naming hierarchy, and suppose the companies merge. Can you arrange to have all previous names still work correctly?

23.5   Read the standard and find out how the domain name system uses *SOA* records.

23.6   The Internet domain name system can also accommodate mailbox names. Find out how.

23.7   The standard suggests that when a program needs to find the domain name associated with an IP address, it should send an inverse query to the local server first and use domain *in-addr.arpa* only if that fails. Why?

23.8   How would you accommodate abbreviations in a domain naming scheme? As an example, show two sites that are both registered under *.edu* and a top level server. Explain how each site would treat each type of abbreviation.

23.9   Obtain the official description of the domain name system and build a client program. Look up the name *merlin.cs.purdue.edu*.

23.10   Extend the exercise above to include a pointer query. Try looking up the domain name for address *128.10.2.3*.

23.11   Find a copy of the program *dig*, and use it to look up the names in the two previous exercises.

23.12   If we extended the domain name syntax to include a dot after the top-level domain, names and abbreviations would be unambiguous. What are the advantages and disadvantages of the extension?

23.13   Read the RFCs on the domain name system. What are the maximum and minimum possible values a DNS server can store in the *TIME-TO-LIVE* field of a resource record?

23.14   Should the domain name system permit partial match queries (i.e. a wildcard as part of a name)? Why or why not?

23.15   The Computer Science Department at Purdue University chose to place the following type *A* resource record entry in its domain name server:

```
localhost.cs.purdue.edu     127.0.0.1
```

Explain what will happen if a remote site tries to *ping* a machine with domain name *localhost.cs.purdue.edu*.

Chapter Contents

24

Remote Login And Desktop (TELNET, SSH)

24.1 Introduction

This chapter and the next five continue our exploration of internetworking by examining application-level Internet services and the protocols that support them. These services form an integral part of TCP/IP. They determine how users perceive an internet and demonstrate the power of the technology. We will see that application-level services provide increased communication functionality, and allow users and programs to interact with automated services on remote machines and with remote users. We will understand that high-level protocols are implemented with application programs, and will learn how they depend on the network level services described in previous chapters. This chapter begins by examining remote access.

24.2 Remote Interactive Computing

We have already seen how the client–server model can provide specific computational services like a time-of-day service to multiple machines. Reliable stream protocols like TCP make possible interactive use of remote machines as well. For example, imagine building a server that provides a remote word processing service. To implement such a service, we need a server that accepts requests and a client to make such requests. To invoke the remote word processor, a user executes a client program that establishes a TCP connection to the server, and then begins sending keystrokes to the server and displaying output that the server sends back.

How can our imagined remote word processing service be generalized? The problem with using one server for each computational service is that machines quickly become swamped with server processes. We can eliminate most specialized servers and provide more generality by creating a mechanism that allows a user to establish a session on the remote machine and then run arbitrary applications. On text-based computing systems, such a session is known as a *remote login* facility; on a windowing system, such a session is known as a *remote desktop* facility.

Of course, providing remote login may not be simple. Computer systems are designed to handle keystrokes, track the mouse, and control the display locally. For example, an operating system may assign special meaning to some keystrokes (e.g., CONTROL-ALT-DELETE on a Windows machine or CONTROL–C on a Linux machine). If the client passes all keystrokes to the remote server, it may be impossible to abort or control the local client process.

24.3 TELNET Protocol

The TCP/IP protocol suite includes a simple textual remote terminal protocol called *TELNET* that allows a user to log into a computer across an internet. TELNET establishes a TCP connection, and then passes keystrokes from the user's keyboard directly to the remote computer as if they had been typed on a keyboard attached to the remote machine. TELNET also carries textual output from the remote machine back to the user's screen. The service is called *transparent* because it gives the appearance that the user's keyboard and display attach directly to the remote machine.

TELNET offers three basic services. First, it defines a *network virtual terminal* that provides a standard interface to remote systems. Client programs do not have to understand the details of all possible remote systems; they are built to use the standard interface. Second, TELNET includes a mechanism that allows the client and server to negotiate options, and it provides a set of standard options (e.g., one of the options controls whether data passed across the connection uses the standard 7-bit ASCII character set or an 8-bit character set). Finally, TELNET treats both ends of the connection symmetrically. In particular, TELNET does not force client input to come from a keyboard, nor does it force the client to display output on a screen. Thus, TELNET allows an arbitrary program to become a client. Furthermore, either end can negotiate options.

Figure 24.1 illustrates how application programs are used to implement a TELNET client and a TELNET server.

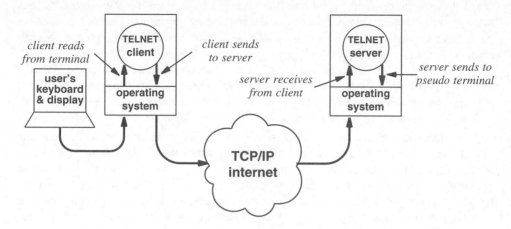

Figure 24.1 The path of data in a TELNET remote terminal session as it travels from the user's keyboard to the remote operating system.

As the figure shows, when a user invokes TELNET, an application program on the user's machine becomes the client. The client establishes a TCP connection to the server over which they will communicate. Once the connection has been established, the client accepts keystrokes from the user's keyboard and sends them to the server, while it concurrently accepts characters that the server sends back and displays them on the user's screen. The client also checks for an *escape character* that a user can type to control the client. The server accepts a TCP connection from the client, and then relays data between the TCP connection and the local operating system.

In practice, the server is more complex than the figure shows because it must handle multiple, concurrent connections. Usually, a master server process waits for new connections and creates a new slave copy to handle each connection. Thus, the 'TELNET server', shown in Figure 24.1, represents the slave that handles one particular connection. The figure does not show the master server that listens for new requests, nor does it show the slaves handling other connections.

We use the term *pseudo terminal*† to describe the operating system entry point that allows a running program like the TELNET server to transfer characters to the operating system as if they came from a keyboard. It is impossible to build a TELNET server unless the operating system supplies such a facility. If the system supports a pseudo terminal abstraction, the TELNET server can be implemented with application programs. Each slave server connects a TCP stream from one client to a particular pseudo terminal.

Arranging for the TELNET server to be an application-level program has advantages and disadvantages. The most obvious advantage is that it makes modification and control of the server easier than if the code were embedded in the operating system. The obvious disadvantage is inefficiency. Each keystroke travels from the user's key-

---

†UNIX calls the system entry point a *pseudo tty* because character-oriented devices are called *tty*s.

board through the operating system to the client program, from the client program back through the operating system and across the underlying internet to the server machine. After reaching the destination machine, the data must travel up through the server's operating system to the server application program, and from the server application program back into the server's operating system at a pseudo terminal entry point. Finally, the remote operating system delivers the character to the application program the user is running. Meanwhile, output (including remote character echo if that option has been selected) travels back from the server to the client over the same path.

Readers who understand operating systems will appreciate that for the implementation shown in Figure 24.1, every keystroke requires computers to switch process context several times. In most systems, an additional context switch is required because the operating system on the server's machine must pass characters from the pseudo terminal back to another application program (e.g., a command interpreter). Although context switching is expensive, the scheme is practical because users do not type at high speed.

24.4 Accommodating Heterogeneity

To make TELNET interoperate between as many systems as possible, it must accommodate the details of heterogeneous computers and operating systems. For example, some systems require lines of text to be terminated by the ASCII *carriage control* character (*CR*). Others require the ASCII *linefeed* (*LF*) character. Still others require the two-character sequence of *CR* followed by *LF*†. In addition, most interactive systems provide a way for a user to enter a key that interrupts a running program. However, the specific keystroke used to interrupt a program varies from system to system (e.g., some systems use Control–C, while others use ESCAPE).

To accommodate heterogeneity, TELNET defines how data and command sequences are sent across the Internet. The definition is known as the *network virtual terminal* (*NVT*). As Figure 24.2 illustrates, the client software translates keystrokes and command sequences from the user's terminal into NVT format and sends them to the server. Server software translates incoming data and commands from NVT format into the format the remote system requires. For data returning, the remote server translates from the remote machine's format to NVT, and the local client translates from NVT to the local machine's format.

The definition of NVT format is straightforward. All communication involves 8-bit bytes. At startup, NVT uses the standard 7-bit USASCII representation for data and reserves bytes with the high order bit set for command sequences. All characters that represent printable values are assigned the same meaning as in the standard USASCII character set. The NVT standard defines interpretations for control characters as shown in Figure 24.3‡.

---

†The sequence *CR* followed by *LF* is often written *crlf*, and is pronounced "curl-if".
‡The NVT interpretation of control characters follows the usual ASCII interpretation.

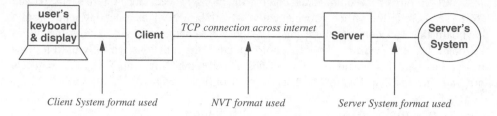

Figure 24.2 Use of the Network Virtual Terminal (NVT) format by TELNET.

ASCII Control Code	Decimal Value	Assigned Meaning
NUL	0	No operation (has no effect on output)
BEL	7	Sound audible/visible signal (no motion)
BS	8	Move left one character position
HT	9	Move right to the next horizontal tab stop
LF	10	Move down (vertically) to the next line
VT	11	Move down to the next vertical tab stop
FF	12	Move to the top of the next page
CR	13	Move to the left margin on the current line
other control	–	No operation (has no effect on output)

Figure 24.3 The TELNET NVT interpretation of USASCII control characters.
TELNET does not specify the locations of tab stops.

In addition to the control character interpretation in Figure 24.3, NVT defines the standard line termination to be a two-character sequence *CR-LF*. When a user presses the key that corresponds to end-of-line on the local terminal (e.g., *ENTER* or *RETURN*), the TELNET client must map it into *CR-LF* for transmission. The TELNET server translates *CR-LF* into the appropriate end-of-line character sequence for the remote machine.

24.5 Passing Commands That Control The Remote Side

We said that most systems provide a mechanism that allows users to terminate a running program. Usually, the local operating system binds such mechanisms to a particular key or keystroke sequence. For example, unless the user specifies otherwise, many UNIX systems reserve the character generated by *CONTROL-C* as the interrupt key. Depressing *CONTROL-C* causes UNIX to terminate the executing program; the program does not receive *CONTROL-C* as input. The system may reserve other characters or character sequences for other control functions.

TELNET NVT accommodates control functions by defining how they are passed from the client to the server. Conceptually, we think of NVT as accepting input from a keyboard that can generate more than 128 possible characters. We assume the user's keyboard has extra (virtual) keys that correspond to the functions typically used to control processing. For example, NVT defines a conceptual ''interrupt'' key that requests program termination. Figure 24.4 lists the control functions that NVT allows.

Signal	Meaning
IP	Interrupt Process (terminate running program)
AO	Abort Output (discard any buffered output)
AYT	Are You There (test if server is responding)
EC	Erase Character (delete the previous character)
EL	Erase Line (delete the entire current line)
SYNCH	Synchronize (clear data path until TCP urgent data point, but do interpret commands)
BRK	Break (break key or attention signal)

Figure 24.4 The control functions TELNET NVT recognizes. Conceptually, the client receives control functions from a user in addition to normal data, and passes them to the server's system where they must be interpreted.

To pass control functions across the TCP connection, TELNET encodes them using an *escape sequence*. An escape sequence uses a reserved octet to indicate that a control code octet follows. In TELNET, the reserved octet that starts an escape sequence is known as the *interpret as command* (*IAC*) octet. Figure 24.5 lists the possible commands and the decimal encoding used for each.

As the figure shows, the signals generated by conceptual keys on an NVT keyboard each have a corresponding command. For example, to request that the server interrupt the executing program, the client must send the 2-octet sequence *IAC IP* (255 followed by 244). Additional commands allow the client and server to negotiate which options they will use and to synchronize communication.

24.6 Forcing The Server To Read A Control Function

Sending control functions along with normal data is not always sufficient to guarantee the desired results. To see why, consider the situation under which a user sends *interrupt process* to the server. Usually, such control is only needed when the program executing on the remote machine is misbehaving and the user wants the server to terminate the program. Unfortunately, if the application at the server's site stops reading input, operating system buffers will eventually fill and the server will block attempting to write data to the pseudo terminal. The server stops reading data from the

TCP connection, and then its buffers fill, TCP on the server machine will begin advertising a zero window size, preventing data from flowing across the connection.

Command	Decimal Encoding	Meaning
IAC	255	Interpret next octet as command (when the IAC octet appears as data, the sender doubles it and sends the 2-octet sequence IAC-IAC)
DON'T	254	Denial of request to perform specified option
DO	253	Approval to allow specified option
WON'T	252	Refusal to perform specified option
WILL	251	Agreement to perform specified option
SB	250	Start of option subnegotiation
GA	249	The "go ahead" signal
EL	248	The "erase line" signal
EC	247	The "erase character" signal
AYT	246	The "are you there" signal
AO	245	The "abort output" signal
IP	244	The "interrupt process" signal
BRK	243	The "break" signal
DMARK	242	The data stream portion of a SYNCH (always accompanied by TCP Urgent notification)
NOP	241	No operation
SE	240	End of option subnegotiation
EOR	239	End of record

Figure 24.5 TELNET commands and encoding for each. The codes only have meaning if preceded by an *IAC* character. When *IAC* occurs in the data, it is sent twice.

If the user generates an interrupt control function when buffers are filled, the control function will never reach the server. That is, the client can form the command sequence *IAC IP* and write it to the TCP connection, but because TCP has stopped sending to the server's machine, the server will not read the control sequence. The point is:

> *TELNET cannot rely on the conventional data stream alone to carry control sequences between client and server because a misbehaving application that needs to be controlled might inadvertently block the data stream.*

To solve the problem, TELNET uses an *out of band* signal. TCP implements out of band signaling with the *urgent data* mechanism. Whenever it places a control function in the data stream, TELNET also sends a *SYNCH* command. TELNET then appends a reserved octet called the *data mark*, and causes TCP to signal the server by sending a segment with the URGENT DATA bit set. Segments carrying urgent data bypass flow control and reach the server immediately. In response to an urgent signal, the server reads and discards all data until it finds the data mark. The server returns to normal processing when it encounters the data mark.

24.7 TELNET Options

Our simple description of TELNET omits one of the most complex aspects: options. In TELNET, options are negotiable, making it possible for the client and server to reconfigure their connection. For example, we said that usually the data stream passes 7-bit data and uses octets with the eighth bit set to pass control information like the *Interrupt Process* command. However, TELNET also provides an option that allows the client and server to pass 8-bit data (when passing 8-bit data, the reserved octet *IAC* must still be doubled if it appears in the data). The client and server must negotiate, and both must agree to pass 8-bit data before such transfers are possible.

The range of TELNET options is wide: some extend the capabilities in major ways, while others deal with minor details. For example, the original protocol was designed for a half-duplex environment where it was necessary to tell the other end to ''go ahead'' before it would send more data. One of the options controls whether TELNET operates in half- or full-duplex mode. Another option allows the server on a remote machine to determine the user's terminal type. The terminal type is important for software that generates cursor positioning sequences (e.g., a full screen editor executing on a remote machine). Figure 24.6 lists examples of TELNET options.

24.8 TELNET Option Negotiation

The way TELNET negotiates options is interesting. Because it sometimes makes sense for the server to initiate a particular option, the protocol is designed to allow either end to make a request. Thus, the protocol is said to be *symmetric* with respect to option processing. The receiving end either responds to a request with a positive acceptance or a rejection. In TELNET terminology, the request is *WILL X*, meaning *will you agree to let me use option X*; and the response is either *DO X* or *DON'T X*, meaning *I do agree to let you use option X* or *I don't agree to let you use option X*. The symmetry arises because *DO X* requests that the receiving party begin using option *X*, and *WILL X* or *WON'T X* means *I will start using option X* or *I won't start using it*†.

---

†To eliminate potential loops that arise when two sides each think the other's acknowledgement is a request, the protocol specifies that no acknowledgement be given to a request for an option that is already in use.

Name	Code	RFC	Meaning
Transmit Binary	0	856	Change transmission to 8-bit binary
Echo	1	857	Allow one side to echo data it receives
Suppress-GA	3	858	Suppress (no longer send) Go-ahead signal after data
Status	5	859	Request for status of a TELNET option from remote site
Timing-Mark	6	860	Request timing mark be inserted in return stream to synchronize two ends of a connection
Terminal-Type	24	884	Exchange information about the make and model of a terminal being used (allows programs to tailor output like cursor positioning sequences for the user's terminal)
End-of-Record	25	885	Terminate data sent with EOR code
Linemode	34	1116	Use local editing and send complete lines instead of individual characters

Figure 24.6 A few of the many TELNET options.

We can summarize:

TELNET uses a symmetric option negotiation mechanism to allow clients and servers to reconfigure the parameters controlling their interaction. Because all TELNET software understands a basic NVT protocol, clients and servers can interoperate even if one understands options another does not.

24.9 Secure Shell (SSH)

A technology known as *secure shell* (*SSH*) has become a popular alternative to TELNET. Like TELNET, SSH uses TCP to establish a connection to a remote computer and allows remote login. However, SSH provides two significant enhancements that TELNET does not. First, SSH provides secure communication. Second, SSH provides users with the ability to perform additional, independent data transfers over the same connection that is used for remote login. Although it originated commercially, SSH is now a proposed IETF standard.

SSH offers three mechanisms that form the basis of the services it provides.

- A *transport layer protocol* that provides server authentication, data confidentiality, and data integrity with perfect forward secrecy (i.e., if a key is compromised during one session, the knowledge does not affect the security of earlier sessions). Thus, even if a third party obtains a copy of packets sent over an SSH connection, the data being sent remains confidential.

- A *user authentication protocol* that authenticates the user to the server. Thus, a server can tell exactly which user is attempting to form a connection.

- A *connection protocol* that multiplexes multiple logical communication channels over a single underlying SSH connection.

To provide maximal flexibility, SSH does not mandate that a specific cryptographic protocol be used for all aspects of communication. Instead, SSH uses public key cryptography for server authentication, and allows the use of either iterative passwords or public key cryptography for user authentication. In addition, SSH allows the choice among several shared secret cryptographic protocols for the communication that occurs following the authentication phase. The secret key, also known as a session key, is negotiated by the client and the server before any application data transfer occurs. Thus, SSH can avoid the overhead of public key encryption except during connection startup when a session key is chosen.

Note that although we think of SSH as a secure remote login service, SSH provides a general-purpose secure connection. and facilities for multiplexing multiple services over the connection. Thus, remote login is simply a service that is multiplexed over an SSH connection. In the next chapter, for example, we will see that it is possible to multiplex file transfer over a secure SSH connection.

Port Forwarding. One of the most powerful aspects of the SSH multiplexing mechanism is known as *Port Forwarding*. There are two types: local and remote. The idea of forwarding is straightforward: an SSH connection can be used as a secure tunnel between two computers, and a user can configure SSH to automatically splice an incoming TCP connection to a new connection across the tunnel. Splicing that occurs when a connection is made to the client side of the tunnel is known as *local* port forwarding, and splicing that occurs when a connection is made to the server side is known as *remote* port forwarding. For example, suppose computer C_1 at site 1 (client side) forms an SSH connection to computer C_2 at site 2, and specifies that incoming TCP connection for port 2000 be automatically forwarded across the tunnel to C_2 and then spliced to a connection to port 80 on computer C_3, also at site 2. Once the SSH connection has been established and forwarding enabled, whenever a computer at site 1 forms a connection to port 2000 on C_1, SSH will automatically arrange to forward the data to port 80 on C_3. Furthermore, both ends of the communication appear to be local: the client at site 1 sees a TCP connection to local computer C_1, and the server on C_3 sees a TCP connection coming from C_2.

The chief advantage of Port Forwarding arises because it allows arbitrary applications to pass data between two sites — instead of having separate client and server software implement encryption for each application, SSH can be configured to allow all of a user's applications to communicate over a single SSH connection.

24.10 Other Remote Access Technologies

Although TELNET and SSH are part of the TCP/IP protocols, many other remote access protocols have been devised. A few examples illustrate some of the diversity.

Rlogin. One of the earliest alternatives to TELNET, devised as part of the BSD Unix operating system, was known as *rlogin*. Rlogin pioneered an idea that has been used with subsequent services, including SSH: *trusted hosts*. In essence, the mechanism allows system administrators to choose a set of machines over which login names and file access protections are shared and to establish equivalences among user logins. Users can control access to their personal accounts by authorizing remote login based on remote host and remote user names. Thus, it is possible for a user to have login name X on one machine and Y on another, and still be able to remotely login from one of the machines to the other without typing a password each time†.

Virtual Network Computing (VNC). Unlike TELNET, rlogin, or SSH, VNC provides a *remote desktop* capability instead of a textual interface. That is, VNC allows a user on one computer to see an exact copy of the desktop on another computer and to use the keyboard and mouse to interact with the remote computer — the user can see the windows, icons, and other graphics. More important, VNC software runs across multiple platforms. As a result, the client can run on a computer that uses Linux, even if the server runs on a computer that uses Windows.

Remote Desktop Protocol (RDP). Microsoft Corporation has defined a remote desktop protocol for use with their operating system. Like other remote desktop systems, RDP allows a remote computer to see an exact copy of the desktop and to run applications. Also like other remote desktop technologies, RDP can be used across platforms (e.g., a Linux client exists).

24.11 Summary

Much of the rich functionality associated with TCP/IP results from a variety of application-level protocols. The services usually follow the client-server model in which servers operate at known protocol ports so clients know how to contact them.

---

†Using an IP address or user name for authentication is no longer considered sufficiently secure; additional mechanisms such as encryption are required.

We reviewed a remote access system, TELNET, which is part of the TCP/IP standards. TELNET uses a TCP connection to allow a client to pass commands such as *interrupt process* as well as data to a server. It also permits a client and server to negotiate options.

The Secure Shell, SSH, provides an authenticated, confidential remote login facility. Because the SSH remote login facility is built on top of a general-purpose, secure multiplexing mechanism, other services can be forwarded over a single SSH connection. The Port Forwarding mechanism allows a user to configure SSH so that arbitrary applications can share a single SSH connection.

Other remote access systems have been devised that use TCP/IP protocols to provide connectivity between a client and server that provide remote access. Examples include rlogin, VNC, and RDP. VNC and RDP provide a remote desktop capability instead of textual interaction.

FOR FURTHER STUDY

Many high-level protocols have been proposed. Edge [1979] compares end-to-end protocols with the hop-by-hop approach. Saltzer, Reed, and Clark [1984] argues for having the highest-level protocols perform end-to-end acknowledgement and error detection.

Postel [RFC 854] contains the TELNET remote login protocol specification. It was preceded by over three dozen RFCs that discuss TELNET options, weaknesses, experiments, and proposed changes, including Postel [RFC 764] that contains an earlier standard. Postel and Reynolds [RFC 855] gives a specification for options and considers subnegotiation. A lengthy set of options can be found in RFCs 856, 857, 858, 859, 860, 861, 884, 885, 1041, 1091, 1096, 1097, 1184, 1372, 1416, and 1572.

For information on SSH, see the IETF repository at:

http://www.ietf.org/html.charters/secsh-charter.html

Information about the UK company *RealVNC* that maintains VNC is available on the web site:

http://www.realvnc.com

EXERCISES

24.1   Read about TELNET and *SSH*. What are the noticeable differences in functionality?

24.2   What is a remote procedure call?

24.3   Folklore says that operating systems come and go while protocols last forever. Test this axiom by surveying your local computing site to see whether operating systems or communication protocols have changed more frequently.

24.4   Build TELNET client software.

24.5   Use a TELNET client to connect your keyboard and display to the TCP protocol port for *echo* or *chargen* on your local system to see what happens.

24.6   TELNET uses TCP's *urgent data* mechanism to force the remote operating system to respond to control functions quickly. Read the standard to find out which commands the remote server honors while scanning the input stream.

24.7   How can the symmetric DO / DON'T — WILL / WON'T option negotiation produce an endless loop of responses if the other party *always* acknowledges a request?

24.8   RFC 854 (the TELNET protocol specification) contains exactly 854 lines of text. Do you think there is cosmic significance in this?

24.9   Download VNC software and experiment with a client and server running under heterogeneous operating systems. Can you find any functions that are not available to a remote user?

24.10   Can SSH be used to achieve all the functionality provided by rlogin? Explain.

24.11   If your home site offers SSH access, design a port forwarding scheme that allows you to use an SSH tunnel to read and send e-mail messages from a remote site (e.g., while you are traveling). Hint: assume your local e-mail software accesses IMAP and SMTP servers.

Chapter Contents

25

File Transfer And Access
(FTP, TFTP, NFS)

25.1 Introduction

This chapter continues our exploration of application protocols by examining file access and transfer protocols that are part of the TCP/IP protocol suite. The chapter describes the design and capabilities. We will learn that the most widely used file transfer protocol builds on TCP, covered in Chapter 12, and TELNET, described in the previous chapter.

25.2 Remote File Access, Transfer, And Storage Networks

Many network systems provide computers with the ability to access files on remote machines. Designers have explored a variety of approaches to remote file access, with each approach optimized for a particular set of goals. For example, some designs use remote file access to lower overall cost. In such architectures, a single, centralized *file server* provides secondary storage for a set of inexpensive computers that have little or no local disk storage. The diskless machines do not need to be conventional computers — they can be portable, hand-held scanning devices used for chores such as inventory, and they can communicate with a file server over a wireless network.

Some designs use remote storage to archive data. In such designs, users have conventional computers with local storage facilities and operate them as usual. Periodically, each computer sends copies of files (or copies of entire disks) across the network to an archival facility, where they are stored in case of accidental loss.

Finally, some designs emphasize the ability to share data across multiple programs, multiple users, or multiple sites. For example, an organization might choose to have a single on-line database of outstanding orders shared by all groups in the organization. Such facilities are known as *Storage Area Network* (*SAN*) systems.

25.3 On-line Shared Access

File sharing takes two distinct forms: *on-line access* and *whole-file copying*. On-line access means allowing multiple programs to access a single file concurrently. Changes to the file take effect immediately and are available to all programs that access the file. Whole-file copying means that whenever a program wants to access a file, the program obtains a local copy. Copying is often used for read-only data, but if the file must be modified, the program must make changes to the local copy and then transfer a copy of the modified file back to the original site.

Many users think that on-line data sharing can only be provided by a distributed database system that allows users (clients) to make transactions (i.e., access or modify items in the database) from remote sites. However, file sharing mechanisms exist that are more general. For example, if an operating system makes files available via a shared, on-line access protocol, remote operating systems can run software that accesses the files without requiring users to invoke a special application such as a database client. Instead, a user can run an arbitrary application and access the remote files as if they were local. We say that the remote file is *integrated* into the local file system, and that the entire file system provides *transparent access* to shared files.

The advantage of transparent access should be obvious: remote file access occurs with no visible changes to application programs. Users can access both local and remote files, allowing them to perform arbitrary computations on shared data. The disadvantages are less obvious. Users may be surprised by the results. For example, consider an application program that uses both local and remote files. If the network or the remote machine is down, the application program may not work even though the user's machine is operating. Even if the remote machine is operating, it may be overloaded or the network may be congested, causing the application program to run slowly, or causing communication protocols to report timeout conditions that the user does not expect. The application program seems less reliable.

Despite its advantages, implementing integrated, transparent file access can be difficult. In a heterogeneous environment, file names available on one computer may be impossible to map into the file namespace of another. Similarly, a remote file access mechanism must handle notions of ownership, authorization, and access protection, which do not transcend computer system boundaries. Finally, because file representations and allowed operations vary from machine to machine, it may be difficult or impossible to implement all operations on all files.

25.4 Sharing By File Transfer

The alternative to integrated, transparent on-line access is a *file transfer mechanism*. Accessing remote data with a transfer mechanism is a two-step process: the user first obtains a local copy of a file and then operates on the copy. Most transfer mechanisms operate outside the local file system (i.e., they are not integrated). A user must invoke a special-purpose client program to transfer files. The client contacts a server on the remote machine and requests a copy of the file. Once the transfer is complete, the user terminates the client and uses an application program on the local system to read or modify the local copy. One advantage of whole-file copying lies in the efficiency of operations — once a local copy of a remote file has been made, application programs can operate on the local copy at high speed.

As with on-line sharing, whole-file transfer between heterogeneous machines can be difficult. The client and server must agree on authorization, notions of file ownership and access protections, and data formats. Data formats are especially important because translation may change the file slightly (e.g., may modify line termination). As a consequence, if a file is transferred from machine *A* to B and then back to *A*, the result can differ from the original.

25.5 FTP: The Major TCP/IP File Transfer Protocol

File transfer is among the most frequently used TCP/IP applications, and still accounts for a nontrivial amount of Internet traffic. Standard file transfer protocols existed for the ARPANET before TCP/IP became operational. These early versions of file transfer software evolved into a current standard known as the *File Transfer Protocol* (*FTP*).

25.6 FTP Features

Given a reliable end-to-end transport protocol like TCP, file transfer might seem trivial. However, as the previous sections pointed out, the details of authorization, naming, and representation among heterogeneous machines make the protocol complex. In addition, FTP offers many facilities beyond the transfer function itself.

• *Interactive Access*. Although FTP is designed to be used by programs, most implementations also provide an interactive interface that allows humans to interact with remote servers.

• *Format Specification*. FTP allows the client to specify the type and representation of stored data. For example, the user can specify whether a file contains text or binary data and whether text files use the ASCII or EBCDIC character sets.

• *Authentication Control.* FTP requires clients to authorize themselves by sending a login name and password to the server before requesting file transfers. The server refuses access to clients that cannot supply a valid login and password.

25.7 FTP Process Model

Like other servers, most FTP server implementations allow concurrent access by multiple clients. Clients use TCP to connect to a server. As described in Chapter 20, a single master server process awaits connections and creates a slave process to handle each connection. Unlike most servers, however, the FTP slave process does not perform all necessary computation. Instead, the slave accepts and handles a *control connection* from the client, but uses an additional process and an additional TCP connection to handle each *data transfer* operation. The control connection carries commands that tell the server which file to transfer. A new TCP connection and a new process on both the client and server side is created for each data transfer operation (i.e., each file transfer). While the exact details of the process architecture depend on the operating systems used, Figure 25.1 illustrates the concept:

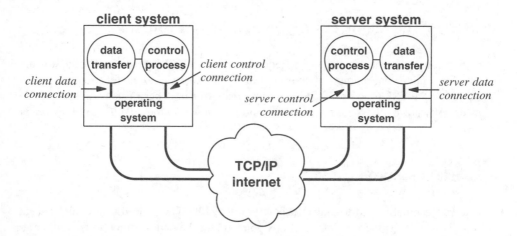

Figure 25.1 An FTP client and server with a TCP control connection between them and a separate TCP connection between their associated data transfer processes.

As the figure shows, the client control process connects to the server control process using one TCP connection, while the associated data transfer processes use their own TCP connection. In general, the control processes and the control connection remain alive as long as the user keeps the FTP session active, and a data transfer connection persists for one file transfer. The idea can be summarized:

Data transfer connections and the data transfer processes that use them are created dynamically when needed, but the control connection persists throughout a session. Once the control connection disappears, the session is terminated and the software at both ends terminates all data transfer processes.

25.8 TCP Port Numbers And Data Connections

When a client forms an initial connection to a server, the client uses a random, locally assigned, protocol port number, and contacts the server at a well-known port (*21*). As Chapter 20 points out, a server that uses only one protocol port can accept connections from many clients because TCP uses both endpoints to identify a connection. The question arises, "When the control processes create a new TCP connection for a given data transfer, what protocol port numbers do they use?" Obviously, they cannot use the same pair of port numbers used in the control connection. Instead, the client obtains an unused port on its machine, sends the port number across the control connection, and waits for the server to form a TCP connection to the specified port. That is, when forming a data connection, the FTP client becomes a server, and the FTP server becomes a client! Interestingly, when it forms a data connection, the FTP server uses a well-known port: the port reserved for FTP data transfer (*20*).

We can see why the protocol uses two connections — the client control process obtains a local port to be used in the file transfer, creates a transfer process on the client machine to listen at that port, communicates the port number to the server over the control connection, and then waits for the server to establish a TCP connection to the port. In general:

In addition to passing user commands to the server, FTP uses the control connection to allow client and server control processes to coordinate their use of dynamically assigned TCP protocol ports and the creation of data transfer processes that use those ports.

Because the original FTP design does not work well with security firewalls and NAT systems, an extension has been added. Known as *passive FTP*, the extension allows a client to initiate each data transfer connection, which means FTP can be used across a firewall or NAT system without being a special case. Most FTP servers and clients support the passive FTP extension.

What format should FTP use for data passing across the control connection? Although they could have invented a new specification, the designers of FTP did not. Instead, they allow FTP to use the TELNET network virtual terminal protocol described in Chapter 24. Unlike the full TELNET protocol, FTP does not allow option negotiation. Instead, FTP only uses the basic NVT definition, which makes management of an

FTP control connection much simpler than management of a TELNET connection. Despite its limitations, using the TELNET definition instead of inventing a new one helps simplify FTP considerably.

25.9 The User's View Of FTP

Although FTP was originally implemented with an interactive application program, few users now invoke FTP directly. Instead, most users access FTP through a web browser as Chapter 27 explains. For example, suppose someone has placed an on-line copy of a textbook in a file named *tcpbook.tar* in directory† */pub/comer* on computer *ftp.cs.purdue.edu*. To obtain a copy, a user can launch a browser and enter the following URL:

ftp://ftp.cs.purdue.edu/pub/comer/tcpbook.tar

The browser will retrieve a copy of the file. Furthermore, if the user enters a URL that corresponds to a directory, the browser will display a list of files in the directory:

ftp://ftp.cs.purdue.edu/pub/comer

25.10 Anonymous FTP

Although FTP's authorization mechanism can help keep sensitive files from being accessed, requiring a login and password prohibits users from accessing public files until the user obtains an account. To provide access to public files, most TCP/IP sites allow *anonymous FTP*. Anonymous FTP access means a client does not need an account or password. Instead, the user specifies login name *anonymous* and a password equal to the user's e-mail address or the password *guest*. A server that allows anonymous logins restricts access to publicly available files.

25.11 Secure File Transfer (SSL-FTP, Scp, Sftp)

Although the original version of FTP includes a password mechanism to allow a server to distinguish among users, the password is sent unencrypted. Furthermore, data sent via FTP is also unencrypted. Thus, if someone wiretaps a connection, it is possible to obtain either a copy of the data being transferred or a user's login and password. Several mechanisms have been created to provide additional security for file transfers.

Secure Sockets Layer FTP (SSL-FTP). One FTP extension uses the secure sockets layer technology, a de facto standard used by applications, such as the web, to add encryption to FTP. When using SSL-FTP, all transfers are confidential, including passwords as well as the data being transferred. Furthermore, because basic SSL follows

---

†Some operating systems use the term *folder* instead of *directory*.

the socket API, only minor modifications are required for FTP client and server software to use the extension.

Secure File Transfer Program (*sftp*). The secure file transfer program, *sftp* was created as an alternative to FTP (i.e., the *sftp* protocol has almost nothing in common with FTP). Although it performs arbitrary file transfer, *sftp* is built to use an SSH tunnel rather than to stand alone. Thus, *sftp* transfers are multiplexed over the single SSH connection that is used to provide security for other applications.

Secure Copy (scp). The secure copy program (*scp*) is another alternative to FTP — a derivative of the Unix *remote copy* program (*rcp*) that uses encryption to provide secure transfer. Like *sftp*, *scp* uses an SSH channel for transfers, and relies on the SSH server for file access on the remote computer. Unlike *sftp*, however, *scp* uses the same syntax as the Unix file copy command, *cp*. Thus, *scp* can be used in a script as well as from a command line.

25.12 TFTP

Although FTP is the most general file transfer protocol in the TCP/IP suite, it is also the most complex and difficult to program. Many applications do not need the full functionality FTP offers, nor can they afford the complexity. For example, FTP requires clients and servers to manage multiple concurrent TCP connections, something that may be difficult or impossible on embedded computers that do not have sophisticated operating systems.

The TCP/IP suite contains a second file transfer protocol that provides inexpensive, unsophisticated service. Known as the *Trivial File Transfer Protocol*, or (*TFTP*), it is intended for applications that do not need complex interactions between the client and server. TFTP restricts operations to simple file transfers and does not provide authentication. Because it is more restrictive, TFTP software is much smaller than FTP.

Small size is important in many applications. For example, manufacturers of embedded systems can encode TFTP in read-only memory (ROM) and use it to obtain an initial memory image when the machine is powered on. The program in ROM is called the system *bootstrap*†. The advantage of using TFTP is that it allows bootstrapping code to use the same underlying TCP/IP protocols that the operating system uses once it begins execution. Thus, it is possible for a computer to bootstrap from a server on another physical network.

Unlike FTP, TFTP does not need a reliable stream transport service. It runs on top of UDP or any other unreliable packet delivery system, using timeout and retransmission to ensure that data arrives. The sending side transmits a file in fixed size (*512* byte) blocks and awaits an acknowledgement for each block before sending the next. The receiver acknowledges each block upon receipt.

The rules for TFTP are simple. The first packet sent requests a file transfer and establishes the interaction between client and server — the packet specifies a file name and whether the file will be read (transferred to the client) or written (transferred to the

---

†Chapter 22 discusses the details of bootstrapping with DHCP.

server). Blocks of the file are numbered consecutively starting at *1*. Each data packet contains a header that specifies the number of the block it carries, and each acknowledgement contains the number of the block being acknowledged. A block of less than *512* bytes signals the end of file. It is possible to send an error message either in the place of data or an acknowledgement; errors terminate the transfer.

Figure 25.2 shows the format of the five TFTP packet types. The initial packet must use operation codes *1* or *2* to specify either a *read request* or a *write request*, the *FILENAME* field to specify the name of a file, and the *MODE* field to specify whether the client will *read* the file, *write* the file, or both.

2-octet opcode	n octets	1 octet	n octets	1 octet
READ REQ. (1)	FILENAME	0	MODE	0

2-octet opcode	n octets	1 octet	n octets	1 octet
WRITE REQ. (2)	FILENAME	0	MODE	0

2-octet opcode	2 octets	up to 512 octets
DATA (3)	BLOCK #	DATA OCTETS...

2-octet opcode	2 octets
ACK (4)	BLOCK #

2-octet opcode	2 octets	n octets	1 octet
ERROR (5)	ERROR CODE	ERROR MESSAGE	0

Figure 25.2 The five TFTP message types. Fields are not shown to scale because some are variable length; an initial 2-octet operation code identifies the message format.

Once a *read* or *write* request has been made, the server uses the IP address and UDP protocol port number of the client to identify subsequent operations. Thus, neither *data* messages (the messages that carry blocks from the file) nor *ack* messages (the messages that acknowledge data blocks) need to specify the file name. The final message type illustrated in Figure 25.2 is used to report errors. Lost messages can be retransmitted after a timeout, but most other errors simply cause termination of the interaction.

TFTP retransmission is unusual because it is symmetric — each side implements a timeout and retransmission. If the side sending data times out, it retransmits the last data block. If the side responsible for acknowledgements times out, it retransmits the last acknowledgement. Having both sides participate in retransmission helps ensure that transfer will not fail after a single packet loss.

While symmetric retransmission guarantees robustness, it can lead to excessive retransmissions. The problem, known as the *Sorcerer's Apprentice Bug*, arises when an acknowledgement for data packet k is delayed, but not lost. The sender retransmits the data packet, which the receiver acknowledges. Both acknowledgements eventually arrive, and each triggers a transmission of data packet $k+1$. The receiver will acknowledge both copies of data packet k+1, and the two acknowledgements will each cause the sender to transmit data packet $k+2$. The Sorcerer's Apprentice Bug can also start if the underlying internet duplicates packets. Once started, the cycle continues indefinitely with each data packet being transmitted exactly twice. A fix for the Sorcerer's Apprentice Bug appears in the latest version of TFTP.

25.13 NFS

Initially developed by Sun Microsystems Incorporated, the *Network File System* (*NFS*) has been published as an IETF standard for transparent and integrated shared file access. Figure 25.3 illustrates how NFS is embedded in an operating system.

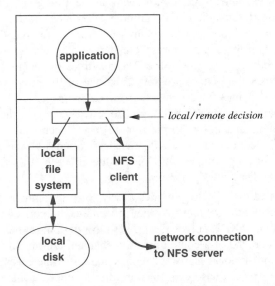

Figure 25.3 Implementation of NFS in an operating system. When an application requests a file operation, the operating system must pass the request to the local file system or to the NFS client software.

When an application program executes, it calls the operating system to *open* a file, to *read* data from a file, or to *write* data into a file. The file access mechanism accepts the request, and automatically passes it to either the local file system software or to the NFS client, depending on whether the file is on the local disk or on a remote machine. When it receives a request, the client software uses the NFS protocol to contact the appropriate server on a remote machine and perform the requested operation. When the remote server replies, the client software returns the results to the application program.

25.14 Implementation Of NFS (RPC And XDR)

Instead of defining the NFS protocol from scratch, the designers chose to build three independent pieces: the NFS protocol itself, a general-purpose *Remote Procedure Call* (*RPC*) mechanism, and a general-purpose *eXternal Data Representation* (*XDR*). Their intent was to separate the three to make it possible to use RPC and XDR in other software, including application programs as well as other protocols.

From the programmer's point of view, NFS itself provides no new procedures that a program can call. Instead, once a manager has configured NFS, programs access remote files using exactly the same operations as they use for local files. However, both RPC and XDR provide mechanisms that programmers can use to build distributed programs. For example, a programmer can divide a program into a client side and a server side that use RPC as the chief communication mechanism. On the client side, the programmer designates some procedures as *remote*, forcing the compiler to incorporate RPC code into those procedures. On the server side, the programmer implements the desired procedures and uses other RPC facilities to declare them to be part of a server. When the executing client program calls one of the remote procedures, RPC automatically collects values for arguments, forms a message, sends the message to the remote server, awaits a response, and stores returned values in the designated arguments. In essence, communication with the remote server occurs automatically as a side-effect of a remote procedure call. The RPC mechanism hides all the details of protocols, making it possible for programmers who know little about the underlying communication protocols to write distributed programs.

A related tool, XDR, provides a way for programmers to pass data among heterogeneous machines without writing procedures to convert among the hardware data representations. XDR solves the problem by defining a machine-independent representation. At one end of a communication channel, a program invokes XDR procedures to convert from the local hardware representation to the machine-independent representation. Once the data has been transferred to another machine, the receiving program invokes XDR routines to convert from the machine-independent representation to the machine's local representation.

25.15 Summary

Access to data on remote files takes two forms: whole-file copying and shared on-line access. The File Transfer Protocol, FTP, is the major file transfer protocol in the TCP/IP suite. FTP uses whole-file copying and provides the ability to list directories on the remote machine as well as transfer files in either direction. The Trivial File Transfer Protocol, TFTP, provides a small, simple alternative to FTP for applications that need only file transfer. Because it is small enough to be contained in ROM, TFTP can be used for bootstrapping embedded systems.

The Network File System (NFS) designed by Sun Microsystems Incorporated provides on-line shared file access. NFS uses UDP for message transport and Sun's Remote Procedure Call (RPC) and eXternal Data Representation (XDR) mechanisms.

FOR FURTHER STUDY

Postel [RFC 959] contains the FTP protocol standard; Horowitz and Lunt [RFC 2228], Allman and Ostermann [RFC 2577], and Housley and Hoffman [RFC 2585] discuss security extensions. Over three dozen RFCs comment on FTP, propose modifications, or define new versions of the protocol. Among them, Lottor [RFC 913] describes a Simple File Transfer Protocol. DeSchon and Braden [RFC 1068] shows how to use FTP third-party transfer for background file transfer. Allman et. al. [RFC 2428] considers FTP with IPv6 and NATs. The Trivial File Transfer Protocol described in this chapter comes from Sollins [RFC 1350]; Finlayson [RFC 906] describes TFTP's use in bootstrapping computer systems, and Malkin and Harkin [RFCs 2347, 2348, and 2349] discuss options.

Sun Microsystems has published three RFCs that define the Network File System and related protocols. RFC 1094 contains the standard for NFS, RFC 1057 defines RPC, and RFC 1014 specifies XDR. More details about RPC and NFS can be found in Volume 3 of this series.

EXERCISES

25.1   Why should file transport protocols compute a checksum on the file data they receive, even when using a reliable end-to-end stream transfer protocol like TCP?

25.2   Find out whether FTP computes a checksum for files it transfers.

25.3   What happens in FTP if the TCP connection being used for data transfer breaks, but the control connection does not?

25.4   What is the chief advantage of using separate TCP connections for control and data transfer? (Hint: think of abnormal conditions.)

25.5   Outline a method that uses TFTP to bootstrap a diskless machine. Be careful. Exactly what IP addresses does it use at each step?

25.6   Implement a TFTP client.

25.7   Experiment with FTP or an equivalent protocol to see how fast you can transfer a file between two reasonably large systems across a local area network. Try the experiment when the network is busy and when it is idle. Explain the result.

25.8   Try FTP from a machine to itself and then from the machine to another machine on the same local area network. Do the data transfer rates surprise you?

25.9   Compare the rates of transfer for FTP and NFS on a local area network. Can you explain the difference?

25.10   Examine the RPC definition. Does it handle datagram loss? duplication? delay? corruption?

25.11   Extend the previous question and consider NFS running over RPC. Will NFS work well across the global Internet? Why or why not?

25.12   Under what circumstances is the XDR scheme inefficient?

25.13   Consider translating floating point numbers from an internal form to an external form and back to an internal form. What are the tradeoffs in the choice of exponent and mantissa sizes in the external form?

25.14   FTP defaults to using *ASCII mode* (i.e. text mode) to transfer files. Is the default wise? Argue that the ASCII mode default can be considered ''harmful''.

Chapter Contents

26

Electronic Mail (SMTP, POP, IMAP, MIME)

26.1 Introduction

This chapter continues our exploration of internetworking by considering electronic mail service and the protocols that support it. The chapter describes how a mail system is organized, explains alias expansion, and shows how mail system software uses the client-server paradigm to transfer each message.

26.2 Electronic Mail

An *electronic mail* (*e-mail*) facility allows users to send memos across the Internet. E-mail is one of the most widely used application services because it offers a fast, convenient method of transferring information, accommodates small notes or large voluminous memos, and allows communication between individuals or among a group.

E-mail differs fundamentally from most other uses of networks because a mail system must provide for instances when the remote destination is temporarily unreachable. To handle delayed delivery, mail systems use a technique known as *spooling*. When the user sends a mail message, the system places a copy in its private storage (called a spool†) along with identification of the sender, recipient, destination machine, and time of deposit. The system then initiates the transfer to the remote machine as a background activity, allowing the sender to proceed with other computational activities. Figure 26.1 illustrates the concept.

---

†A mail spool area is sometimes called a *mail queue* even though the term is technically inaccurate.

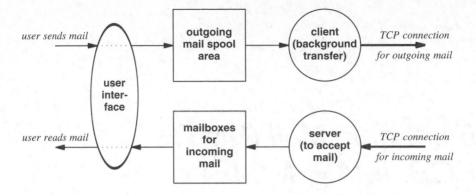

Figure 26.1 Conceptual components of an electronic mail system. The user invokes a mail interface application to deposit or retrieve mail; all transfers occur in the background.

The background mail transfer process becomes a client that uses the domain name system to map the destination machine name to an IP address and then attempts to form a TCP connection to the mail server on the destination machine. If it succeeds, the transfer process passes a copy of the message to the remote server, which stores the copy in the remote system's spool area. Once the client and server agree that the copy has been accepted and stored, the client removes the local copy. If it cannot form a TCP connection or if the connection fails, the transfer process records the time delivery was attempted and terminates. The background transfer process sweeps through the spool area periodically, typically once every 30 minutes, checking for undelivered mail. Whenever it finds a message or whenever a user deposits new outgoing mail, the background process attempts delivery. If it finds that a mail message cannot be delivered after a few hours, the mail software informs the sender; after an extended time (e.g., 3 days), the mail software returns the message to the sender.

26.3 Mailbox Names And Aliases

There are three important ideas hidden in our simplistic description of mail delivery. First, users specify each recipient by giving a text string that contains two items separated by an at-sign:

local-part @ *domain-name*

where *domain-name* is the domain name of a mail destination† to which the mail should be delivered, and *local-part* is the address of a mailbox on that machine. For example, the author's electronic mail address is:

comer @ *purdue*.*edu*

---

†Technically, the domain name specifies a *mail exchanger*, not a machine name.

Second, the names used in such specifications are independent of other names assigned to machines. Typically, a mailbox is the same as a user's login id, and a computer's domain name is used as the mail destination. However, many other designs are possible. For example, a mailbox can designate a position such as *department-head*. Because the domain name system includes a separate query type for mail destinations, it is possible to decouple mail destination names from the usual domain names assigned to machines. Thus, mail sent to a user at *example.com* may go to a different machine than a ping request sent to the same name. Third, our simplistic diagram fails to account for *mail forwarding*, in which some mail that arrives on a given machine is forwarded to another machine.

26.4 Alias Expansion And Mail Forwarding

Most e-mail servers provide *mail forwarding* software that includes a *mail alias expansion* mechanism. A mail forwarder allows copies of an incoming message to be sent to one or more destinations. Typically, the server consults a small database of mail aliases to map an incoming recipient address into a set of addresses, A, and then forwards a copy to each address in A.

Because they can be many-to-one or one-to-many, alias mappings increase mail system functionality and convenience substantially. A single user can have multiple mail identifiers, or a group can have a single mail alias. In the latter case, the set of recipients associated with an identifier is called an *electronic mailing list*. Figure 26.2 illustrates the components of a mail system that supports mail aliases and list expansion.

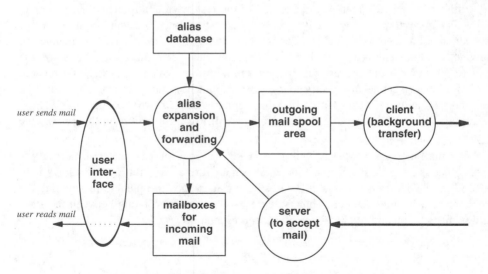

Figure 26.2 An extension of the mail system in Figure 26.1 that supports mail aliases and forwarding. Both incoming and outgoing mail passes through the alias expansion mechanism.

As the figure shows, incoming and outgoing mail passes through the mail forwarder that expands aliases. Thus, if the alias database specifies that mail address x maps to replacement y, alias expansion will rewrite destination address x, changing it to y. The alias expansion program then determines whether y specifies a local or remote address, so it knows whether to place the message in the incoming mail queue or outgoing mail queue.

Mail alias expansion can be dangerous. Suppose two sites establish conflicting aliases. For example, assume site A maps mail address x into mail address y at site B, while site B maps mail address y into address x at site A. A mail message sent to address x at site A could bounce forever between the two sites†.

26.5 TCP/IP Standards For Electronic Mail Service

Recall that the goal of the TCP/IP protocol effort is to provide for interoperability across the widest range of computer systems and networks. To extend the interoperability of electronic mail, TCP/IP divides its mail standards into two sets. One standard, given in RFC 2822, specifies the syntactic format used for mail messages‡; the other standard specifies the details of electronic mail exchange between two computers.

According to RFC 2822, a mail message is represented in textual form and is divided into two parts: a header and a body, which are separated by a blank line. The standard for mail messages specifies the exact format of mail headers as well as the semantic interpretation of each header field; it leaves the format of the body up to the sender. In particular, the standard specifies that headers contain readable text, divided into lines that consist of a keyword followed by a colon followed by a value. Some keywords are required, others are optional, and the rest are uninterpreted. For example, the header must contain a line that specifies the destination. The line begins with *To:* and contains the electronic mail address of the intended recipient on the remainder of the line. A line that begins with *From:* contains the electronic mail address of the sender. Optionally, the sender may specify an address to which replies should be sent (i.e., to allow the sender to specify that replies should be sent to an address other than the sender's mailbox). If present, a line that begins with *Reply-to:* specifies the address for replies. If no such line exists, the recipient will use information on the *From:* line as the return address.

The mail message format is chosen to make it easy to process and transport across heterogeneous machines. Keeping the mail header format straightforward allows it to be used on a wide range of systems. Restricting messages to readable text avoids the problems of selecting a standard binary representation and translating between the standard representation and the local machine's representation.

---

†In practice, most mail forwarders terminate messages after the number of exchanges reaches a predetermined threshold.

‡The original standard was specified in RFC 822; the IETF delayed issuing the replacement until RFC 2822 to make the numbers match.

26.6 Simple Mail Transfer Protocol (SMTP)

In addition to message formats, the TCP/IP protocol suite specifies a standard for the exchange of mail between machines. That is, the standard specifies the exact format of messages a client on one machine uses to transfer mail to a server on another. The standard transfer protocol is known as the *Simple Mail Transfer Protocol* (*SMTP*). As you might guess, SMTP is simpler than the earlier *Mail Transfer Protocol*, (*MTP*). The SMTP protocol focuses specifically on how the underlying mail delivery system passes messages across an internet from one machine to another. It does not specify how the mail system accepts mail from a user or how the user interface presents the user with incoming mail. Also, SMTP does not specify how mail is stored or how frequently the mail system attempts to send messages.

SMTP is surprisingly straightforward. Communication between a client and server consists of readable ASCII text. As with other application protocols, programs read the abbreviated commands and 3-digit numbers at the beginning of lines; the remaining text is intended to help humans debug mail software. Although SMTP rigidly defines the command format, humans can easily read a transcript of interactions between a client and server because each command appears on a separate line. Initially, the client establishes a reliable stream connection to the server and waits for the server to send a *220 READY FOR MAIL* message. (If the server is overloaded, it may delay sending the *220* message temporarily.) Upon receipt of the *220* message, the client sends a *HELO*† command (if the client supports extensions from RFC 2821, the client sends an *EHLO* command). The end of a line marks the end of a command. The server responds by identifying itself. Once communication has been established, the sender can transmit one or more mail messages and then terminate the connection. The receiver must acknowledge each command. It can also abort the entire connection or abort the current message transfer.

Mail transactions begin with a *MAIL* command that gives the sender identification as well as a *FROM:* field that contains the address to which errors should be reported. A recipient prepares its data structures to receive a new mail message, and replies to a *MAIL* command by sending the response *250*. Response *250* means that all is well. The full response consists of the text *250 OK*.

After a successful *MAIL* command, the sender issues a series of *RCPT* commands that identify recipients of the mail message. The receiver must acknowledge each *RCPT* command by sending *250 OK* or by sending the error message *550 No such user here.*

After all *RCPT* commands have been acknowledged, the sender issues a *DATA* command. In essence, a *DATA* command informs the receiver that the sender is ready to transfer a complete mail message. The receiver responds with message *354 Start mail input,* and specifies the sequence of characters used to terminate the mail message. The termination sequence consists of 5 characters: carriage return, line feed, period, carriage return, and line feed‡.

---

†*HELO* is an abbreviation for "hello."

‡SMTP uses *CR-LF* to terminate a line, and forbids the body of a mail message to have a period on a line by itself.

An example will clarify the SMTP exchange. Suppose user *Smith* at host *Alpha.edu* sends a message to users *Jones*, *Green*, and *Brown* at host *Beta.gov*. The SMTP client software on host *Alpha.edu* contacts the SMTP server software on host *Beta.gov* and begins the exchange shown in Figure 26.3.

```
S: 220 Beta.gov Simple Mail Transfer Service Ready
C: HELO Alpha.edu
S: 250 Beta.gov

C: MAIL FROM:<Smith@Alpha.edu>
S: 250 OK

C: RCPT TO:<Jones@Beta.gov>
S: 250 OK

C: RCPT TO:<Green@Beta.gov>
S: 550 No such user here

C: RCPT TO:<Brown@Beta.gov>
S: 250 OK

C: DATA
S: 354 Start mail input; end with <CR><LF>.<CR><LF>
C: ...sends body of mail message...
C: ...continues for as many lines as message contains
C: <CR><LF>.<CR><LF>
S: 250 OK

C: QUIT
S: 221 Beta.gov Service closing transmission channel
```

Figure 26.3 Example of SMTP transfer from Alpha.edu to Beta.gov during which recipient Green is not recognized. Lines that begin with ''C:'' are transmitted by the client (Alpha), and lines that begin ''S:'' are transmitted by the server.

In the example, the server rejects recipient *Green* because it does not recognize the name as a valid mail destination (i.e., it is neither a user nor a mailing list). The SMTP protocol does not specify the details of how a client handles such errors — the client must decide. Although clients can abort the delivery completely if an error occurs, most clients do not. Instead, they continue delivery to all valid recipients and then report problems to the original sender. Usually, the client reports errors using electronic mail. The error message contains a summary of the error as well as the header of the mail message that caused the problem.

Once it has finished sending all the mail messages, a client issues a *QUIT* command. The other side responds with command *221*, which means it agrees to terminate. Both sides then close the TCP connection gracefully.

SMTP is much more complex than we have outlined here. For example, if a user has moved, the server may know the user's new mailbox address. SMTP allows the server to inform the client about the new address so the client can use it in the future. When informing the client about a new address, the server may choose to forward the mail that triggered the message, or it may request that the client take the responsibility for forwarding. In addition, SMTP includes *Transport Layer Security* (*TLS*) extensions that allow an SMTP session to be encrypted.

26.7 Mail Retrieval And Mailbox Manipulation Protocols

The SMTP transfer scheme described above implies that a server must remain ready to accept e-mail at all times. The scenario works well if the server runs on a computer that has a permanent Internet connection, but it does not work well for a computer that has intermittent connectivity (e.g., a laptop computer that is disconnected when being moved). It makes no sense for such a computer to run an e-mail server because the server will only be available while the user's computer is connected — all other attempts to contact the server will fail, and e-mail sent to the user will remain undelivered. The question arises, "How can a user without a permanent connection receive e-mail?"

The answer to the question lies in a two-stage delivery process. In the first stage, each user is assigned a mailbox on a computer that is always on and has a permanent Internet connection. The computer runs a conventional SMTP server, which always remains ready to accept e-mail. In the second stage, the user connects to the Internet and then runs a protocol that retrieves messages from the permanent mailbox. The protocol transfers the messages to the user's computer where they can be read.

Two protocols exist that allow a remote user to access mail in a permanent mailbox. Although they have similar functionality, the protocols take opposite approaches: one allows the user to download a copy of messages, and the other allows a user to view and manipulate messages on the server. The next two sections describe the two protocols.

26.7.1 Post Office Protocol

The most popular protocol used to transfer e-mail messages from a permanent mailbox to a local computer is known as version 3 of the *Post Office Protocol* (*POP3*); a secure version of the protocol is known as *POP3S*. The user invokes a POP3 client, which creates a TCP connection to a POP3 server on the mailbox computer. The user first sends a *login* and a *password* to authenticate the session. Once authentication has been accepted, the client sends commands to retrieve a copy of one or more messages and to delete the message from the permanent mailbox. The messages are stored and transferred as text files in 2822 standard format.

Note that the computer with the permanent mailbox must run two servers — an SMTP server accepts mail sent to a user and adds each incoming message to the user's permanent mailbox, and a POP3 server allows a user to extract messages from the mailbox and delete them. To ensure correct operation, the two servers must coordinate use of the mailbox so that if a message arrives via SMTP while a user is extracting messages via POP3, the mailbox is left in a valid state.

26.7.2 Internet Message Access Protocol

Version 4 of the *Internet Message Access Protocol* (*IMAP4*) is an alternative to POP3 that allows users to view and manipulate messages; a secure version of IMAP has been defined, and is known as *IMAPS*. Like POP3, IMAP4 defines an abstraction known as a *mailbox*; mailboxes are located on the same computer as a server. Also like POP3, a user runs an IMAP4 client that contacts the server to manipulate messages. Unlike POP3, however, IMAP4 allows a user to access mail messages from multiple locations (e.g., from work and from home), and ensures that all copies are synchronized and consistent.

IMAP4 also provides extended functionality for message retrieval and processing. A user can obtain information about a message or examine header fields without retrieving the entire message. In addition, a user can search for a specified string and retrieve portions of a message. Partial retrieval is especially useful for slow-speed dialup connections because it means a user does not need to download useless information.

26.8 The MIME Extensions For Non-ASCII Data

The *Multipurpose Internet Mail Extensions* (*MIME*) were defined to allow transmission of non-ASCII data through e-mail. MIME does not change or replace protocols such as SMTP, POP3, and IMAP4. Instead, MIME allows arbitrary data to be encoded in ASCII and then transmitted in a standard e-mail message. To accommodate arbitrary data types and representations, each MIME message includes information that tells the recipient the type of the data and the encoding used. MIME information resides in the 2822 mail header — the MIME header lines specify the MIME version, the data type, and the encoding that was used to convert the data to ASCII. For example, Figure 26.4 illustrates a MIME message that contains a photograph in standard *JPEG†* representation. The JPEG image has been converted to a 7-bit ASCII representation using the *base64* encoding.

In the figure, the header line *MIME-Version:* declares that the message was composed using version *1.0* of the MIME protocol. The *Content-Type:* declaration specifies that the data is a JPEG image, and the *Content-Transfer-Encoding:* header declares that *base64* encoding was used to convert the image to ASCII.

---

†JPEG is the *Joint Picture Encoding Group* standard used for digital pictures.

```
From: bill@acollege.edu
To: john@example.com
MIME-Version: 1.0
Content-Type: image/jpeg
Content-Transfer-Encoding: base64

...data for the image...
```

Figure 26.4 An example MIME message. Lines in the header identify the type of the data as well as the encoding used.

To view the image in a figure, a receiver's mail system must first convert from *base64* encoding back to binary, and then run an application that displays a JPEG image on the user's screen. Base64 was chosen to provide sixty-four ASCII characters that have the same representation across various versions of ISO English character sets†. Thus, a receiver can be guaranteed that the image extracted from the encoded data is exactly the same as the original image.

The MIME standard specifies that a *Content-Type* declaration must contain two identifiers, a *content type* and a *subtype*, separated by a slash. In the example, *image* is the content type, and *jpeg* is the subtype.

The standard defines seven basic content types, the valid subtypes for each, and transfer encodings. For example, although an *image* must be of subtype *jpeg* or *gif*, *text* cannot use either subtype. In addition to the standard types and subtypes, MIME permits a sender and receiver to define private content types‡. Figure 26.5 lists the seven basic content types.

Content Type	Used When Data In the Message Is
text	Textual (e.g. a document).
image	A still photograph or computer-generated image
audio	A sound recording
video	A video recording that includes motion
application	Raw data for a program
multipart	Multiple messages that each have a separate content type and encoding
message	An entire e-mail message (e.g., a memo that has been forwarded) or an external reference to a message (e.g., an FTP server and file name)

Figure 26.5 The seven basic types that can appear in a MIME *Content-Type* declaration and their meanings.

---

†The characters consist of 26 uppercase letters, 26 lowercase letters, ten digits, the plus sign, and the slash character.

‡To avoid potential name conflicts, the standard requires that names chosen for private content types each begin with the string *X-*.

26.9 MIME Multipart Messages

The MIME multipart content type is useful because it adds considerable flexibility. The standard defines four possible subtypes for a multipart message; each provides important functionality. Subtype *mixed* allows a single message to contain multiple, independent submessages that each can have an independent type and encoding. Mixed multipart messages make it possible to include text, graphics, and audio in a single message, or to send a memo with additional data segments attached, similar to *enclosures* included with a business letter. Subtype *alternative* allows a single message to include multiple representations of the same data. Alternative multipart messages are useful when sending a memo to many recipients who do not all use the same hardware and software system. For example, one can send a document as both plain ASCII text and in formatted form, allowing recipients who have computers with graphic capabilities to select the formatted form for viewing†. Subtype *parallel* permits a single message to include subparts that should be viewed together (e.g., video and audio subparts that must be played simultaneously). Finally, subtype *digest* permits a single message to contain a set of other messages (e.g., a collection of the e-mail messages from a discussion).

Figure 26.6 illustrates one of the prime uses for multipart messages: an e-mail message can contain both a short text that explains the purpose of the message and other parts that contain nontextual information. In the figure, a note in the first part of the message explains that the second part contains a photographic image.

```
From: bill@acollege.edu
To: john@example.com
MIME-Version: 1.0
Content-Type: Multipart/Mixed; Boundary=StartOfNextPart

--StartOfNextPart
Content-Type: text/plain
Content-Transfer-Encoding: 7bit
John,
    Here is the photo of our research lab that I promised
to send you.  You can see the equipment you donated.

Thanks again,
Bill

--StartOfNextPart
Content-Type: image/gif
Content-Transfer-Encoding: base64
      ...data for the image...
```

Figure 26.6 An example of a MIME mixed multipart message. Each part of the message can have an independent content type.

---

†One widespread e-mail system uses the alternative MIME option to send a message in both ASCII and HTML formats.

The figure also illustrates a few details of MIME. For example, each header line can contain parameters of the form $X = Y$ after basic declarations. The keyword *Boundary=* following the multipart content type declaration in the header defines the string used to separate parts of the message. In the example, the sender has selected the string *StartOfNextPart* to serve as the boundary. Declarations of the content type and transfer encoding for a submessage, if included, immediately follow the boundary line. In the example, the second submessage is declared to be a *GIF* image.

26.10 Summary

Electronic mail is among the most widely available application services. Like most TCP/IP services, it follows the client-server paradigm. A mail system buffers outgoing and incoming messages, allowing a transfer from client and server to occur in background.

The TCP/IP protocol suite provides separate standards for mail message format and mail transfer. The mail message format, called *2822*, uses a blank line to separate a message header and the body. The Simple Mail Transfer Protocol (SMTP) defines how a mail system on one machine transfers mail to a server on another. Version 3 of the Post Office Protocol (POP3) and version 4 of the Internet Message Access Protocol (IMAP4) specify how a user can retrieve the contents of a mailbox; they allow a user to have a permanent mailbox on a computer with continuous Internet connectivity and to access the contents from a computer with intermittent connectivity.

The Multipurpose Internet Mail Extensions (MIME) provides a mechanism that allows arbitrary data to be transferred using SMTP. MIME adds lines to the header of an e-mail message to define the type of the data and the encoding used. MIME's mixed multipart type permits a single message to contain multiple data types.

FOR FURTHER STUDY

The protocols described in this chapter are all specified in Internet RFCs. Klensin [RFC 2821] describes the Simple Mail Transfer Protocol and gives many examples. The exact format of mail messages is given by Resnick [RFC 2822]; many RFCs specify additions and changes. Freed and Borenstein [RFCs 2045, 2046, 2047, 2048 and 2049] specify the standard for MIME, including the syntax of header declarations, the procedure for creating new content types, the interpretation of content types, and the *base64* encoding mentioned in this chapter. Dierks and Allen [RFC 2246] defines the Transport Layer Security extensions used with SMTP.

EXERCISES

26.1   Some mail systems force the user to specify a sequence of machines through which the message should travel to reach its destination. The mail protocol in each machine merely passes the message on to the next machine. List three disadvantages of such a scheme.

26.2   Find out if your computing system allows you to invoke SMTP directly.

26.3   Build an SMTP client and use it to transfer a mail message.

26.4   See if you can send mail through a mail forwarder and back to yourself.

26.5   Make a list of mail address forms that your site handles, and write a set of rules for parsing them.

26.6   Find out how a Linux system can be configured to act as a mail forwarder.

26.7   Find out how often your local mail system attempts delivery and how long it will continue before giving up.

26.8   Many mail systems allow users to direct incoming mail to a program instead of storing it in a mailbox. Build a program that accepts your incoming mail, places your mail in a file, and then sends a reply to tell the sender you are on vacation.

26.9   Read the SMTP standard carefully. Then use TELNET to connect to the SMTP port on a remote machine and ask the remote SMTP server to expand a mail alias.

26.10 A user receives mail in which the *To* field specifies the string *important-people*. The mail was sent from a computer on which the alias *important-people* includes no valid mailbox identifiers. Read the SMTP specification carefully to see how such a situation is possible.

26.11 POP3 separates message retrieval and deletion by allowing a user to retrieve and view a message without deleting it from the permanent mailbox. What are the advantages and disadvantages of such separation?

26.12 Read about POP3. How does the *TOP* command operate, and why is it useful?

26.13 Read about IMAP4. How does IMAP4 guarantee consistency when multiple concurrent clients access a given mailbox at the same time?

26.14 Read the MIME RFCs carefully. What servers can be specified in a MIME external reference?

Chapter Contents

27

World Wide Web (HTTP)

27.1 Introduction

This chapter continues the discussion of applications that use TCP/IP technology by focusing on the application that has had the most impact: the *World Wide Web* (*WWW*). After a brief overview of concepts, the chapter examines the primary protocol used to transfer a web page from a server to a web browser. The discussion covers caching as well as the basic transfer mechanism.

27.2 Importance Of The Web

During the early history of the Internet, FTP data transfers accounted for approximately one third of Internet traffic, more than any other application. From its inception in the early 1990s, however, the web had a much higher growth rate. By 1995, web traffic overtook FTP to become the largest consumer of Internet backbone bandwidth, and has remained the leader.

The impact of the web cannot be understood from traffic statistics alone. More people know about and use the web than any other Internet application. In fact, for many users, the Internet and the web are indistinguishable.

27.3 Architectural Components

Conceptually, the web consists of a large set of documents, called *web pages*, that are accessible over the Internet. Each web page is classified as a *hypermedia* document. The suffix *media* is used to indicate that a document can contain items other than text (e.g., graphics images); the prefix *hyper* is used because a document can contain *selectable links* that refer to other related documents.

Two main building blocks are used to implement the web on top of the global Internet. A *web browser* consists of an application program that a user invokes to access and display a web page. A browser becomes a client that contacts the appropriate *web server* to obtain a copy of the specified page. Because a given server can manage more than one web page, a browser must specify the exact page when making a request.

The data representation standard used for a web page depends on its contents. For example, standard graphics representations such as *Graphics Interchange Format* (*GIF*) or *Joint Picture Encoding Group* (*JPEG*) can be used for a page that contains a single graphics image. Pages that contain a mixture of text and other items are represented using *HyperText Markup Language* (*HTML*). An HTML document consists of a file that contains text along with embedded commands, called *tags*, that give guidelines for display. A tag is enclosed in less-than and greater-than symbols; some tags come in pairs that apply to all items between the pair. For example, the two commands *<CENTER>* and *</CENTER>* cause items between them to be centered in the browser's window.

27.4 Uniform Resource Locators

Each web page is assigned a unique name that is used to identify it. The name, which is called a *Uniform Resource Locator* (*URL*)†, begins with a specification of the *scheme* used to access the item. In effect, the scheme specifies the transfer protocol; the format of the remainder of the URL depends on the scheme. For example, a URL that follows the *http scheme* has the following form‡:

http: // *hostname* [: *port*] / *path* [; *parameters*] [? *query*]

where italic denotes an item to be supplied, and brackets denote an optional item. For now, it is sufficient to understand that the *hostname* string specifies the domain name or dotted decimal IP address of the computer on which the server for the item operates, *:port* is an optional protocol port number needed only in cases where the server does not use the well-known port (*80*), *path* is a string that identifies one particular document on the server, *;parameters* is an optional string that specifies additional parameters supplied by the client, and *?query* is an optional string used when the browser sends a question. A user is unlikely to ever see or use the optional parts directly. Instead, URLs that a user enters contain only a *hostname* and *path*. For example, the URL:

---

†A URL is a specific type of the more general *Uniform Resource Identifier* (*URI*).

‡Some of the literature refers to the initial string, *http:*, as a *pragma*.

http://www.cs.purdue.edu/people/comer/

specifies the author's web page at Purdue University. The server operates on computer *www.cs.purdue.edu*, and the document is named */people/comer/*.

The protocol standards distinguish between the *absolute* form of a URL, illustrated above, and a *relative* form. A relative URL, which is seldom seen by a user, is only meaningful when the server has already been determined. Relative URLs are useful once communication has been established with a specific server. For example, when communicating with server *www.cs.purdue.edu*, only the string */people/comer/* is needed to specify the document named by the absolute URL above. We can summarize.

> *Each web page is assigned a unique identifier known as a Uniform Resource Locator (URL). The absolute form of a URL contains a full specification; a relative form that omits the address of the server is only useful when the server is implicitly known.*

27.5 An Example Document

An example will illustrate how a URL is produced from a *selectable link* in a document. For each such link, a document contains a pair of values: an item to be displayed on the screen and a URL to follow if the user selects the item. In HTML, a pair of tags *<A>* and *</A>*, which are known as an *anchor*, define a link; a URL is added to the first tag, and items to be displayed are placed between the two tags. For example, the following HTML document contains a selectable link:

```
<HTML>
   The author of this text is
   <A HREF="http://www.cs.purdue.edu/people/comer">
   Douglas Comer.</A>
</HTML>
```

When the document is displayed, a single line of text appears on the screen:

The author of this text is <u>Douglas Comer.</u>

The browser underlines the phrase *Douglas Comer* to indicate that it corresponds to a selectable link. Internally, the browser stores the URL from the *<A>* tag, which it follows when the user selects the link.

27.6 Hypertext Transfer Protocol

The protocol used for communication between a browser and a web server or between intermediate machines and web servers is known as the *HyperText Transfer Protocol* (*HTTP*). HTTP has the following set of characteristics:

Application Level. HTTP operates at the application level. It assumes a reliable, connection-oriented transport protocol such as TCP, but does not provide reliability or retransmission itself.

Request/Response. Once a transport session has been established, one side (usually a browser) must send an HTTP request to which the other side responds.

Stateless. Each HTTP request is self-contained; the server does not keep a history of previous requests or previous sessions.

Bi-Directional Transfer. In most cases, a browser requests a web page, and the server transfers a copy to the browser. HTTP also allows transfer from a browser to a server (e.g., when a user submits a so-called "form").

Capability Negotiation. HTTP allows browsers and servers to negotiate details such as the character set to be used during transfers. A sender can specify the capabilities it offers, and a receiver can specify the capabilities it accepts.

Support For Caching. To improve response time, a browser caches a copy of each web page it retrieves. If a user requests a page again, HTTP allows the browser to interrogate the server to determine whether the contents of the page has changed since the copy was cached.

Support For Intermediaries. HTTP allows a machine along the path between a browser and a server to act as a *proxy server* that caches web pages and answers a browser's request from its cache.

27.7 HTTP GET Request

In the simplest case, a browser contacts a web server directly to obtain a page. The browser begins with a URL, extracts the hostname section, uses DNS to map the name into an equivalent IP address, and uses the IP address to form a TCP connection to the server. Once the TCP connection is in place, the browser and web server use HTTP to communicate; the browser sends a request to retrieve a specific page, and the server responds by sending a copy of the page.

A browser sends an HTTP *GET* command to request a web page from a server†. The request consists of a single line of text that begins with the keyword *GET* and is followed by a URL and an HTTP version number. For example, to retrieve the web page in the example above from server *www.cs.purdue.edu*, a browser can send the following request:

GET http://www.cs.purdue.edu/people/comer/ HTTP/1.1

Once a TCP connection is in place, there is no need to send an absolute URL — the following relative URL will retrieve the same page:

GET /people/comer/ HTTP/1.1

To summarize:

> *The Hypertext Transfer Protocol (HTTP) is used between a browser and a web server. The browser sends a GET request to which a server responds by sending the requested item.*

27.8 Error Messages

How should a web server respond when it receives an illegal request? In most cases, the request has been sent by a browser, and the browser will attempt to display whatever the server returns. Consequently, servers usually generate error messages in valid HTML. For example, one server generates the following error message:

```
<HTML>
  <HEAD> <TITLE>400 Bad Request</TITLE>
  </HEAD>
  <BODY>
    <H1>Bad Request</H1> Your browser sent a request
    that this server could not understand.
  </BODY>
</HTML>
```

The browser uses the "head" of the document (i.e., the items between <HEAD> and </HEAD>) internally, and only shows the "body" to the user. The pair of tags <H1> and </H1> causes the browser to display *Bad Request* as a heading (i.e., large and bold), resulting in two lines of output on the user's screen:

Bad Request

Your browser sent a request that this server could not understand.

---

†The standard uses the object-oriented term *method* instead of *command*.

27.9 Persistent Connections And Lengths

The first version of HTTP follows the same paradigm as FTP by using one TCP connection per data transfer. A client opens a TCP connection and sends a *GET* request, and the server closes the connection after transmitting a copy of the requested item. Thus, the client reads until an *end of file* condition is encountered, and then closes its end of the connection.

Version 1.1, of HTTP changed the basic paradigm in a fundamental way: instead of using a TCP connection per transfer, version 1.1 adopts a *persistent connection* approach as the default. That is, once a client opens a TCP connection to a particular server, the client leaves the connection in place during multiple requests and responses. When either a client or server is ready to close the connection, it informs the other side, and the connection is closed.

The chief advantage of persistent connections lies in reduced overhead — fewer TCP connections means lower response latency, less overhead on the underlying networks, less memory used for buffers, and less CPU time is used. A browser using a persistent connection can further optimize by *pipelining* requests (i.e., send requests back-to-back without waiting for a response). Pipelining is especially attractive in situations where multiple images must be retrieved for a given page, and the underlying internet has both high throughput and long delay.

The chief disadvantage of using a persistent connection lies in the need to identify the beginning and end of each item sent over the connection. There are two possible techniques to handle the situation: either send a length followed by the item, or send a *sentinel value* after the item to mark the end. HTTP cannot reserve a sentinel value because the items transmitted include graphics images that can contain arbitrary sequences of octets. Thus, to avoid ambiguity between sentinel values and data, HTTP uses the approach of sending a length followed by an item of that size.

27.10 Data Length And Program Output

It may not be convenient or even possible for a server to know the length of an item before sending. To understand why, one must know that some web pages are generated upon request. That is, the server uses a technology such as the *Common Gateway Interface* (*CGI*) that allows a computer program running on the server machine to create a web page. When a request arrives that corresponds to a CGI-generated page, the server runs the appropriate CGI program, and sends the output from the program back to the client as a response. Dynamic web page generation allows the creation of information that is current (e.g., a list of the current scores in sporting events), but means that the server may not know the exact data size in advance. Furthermore, saving the data to a file before sending it is undesirable for two reasons: it uses resources at the server and delays transmission. Thus, to provide for dynamic web pages, the HTTP standard specifies that if the server does not know the length of an item *a priori*, the server can inform the browser that it will close the connection after transmitting the item. To summarize:

> *To allow a TCP connection to persist through multiple requests and responses, HTTP sends a length before each response. If it does not know the length, a server informs the client, sends the response, and then closes the connection.*

27.11 Length Encoding And Headers

What representation should a server use to send length information? Interestingly, HTTP borrows the basic format from e-mail, using the 2822 format and MIME Extensions†. Like a standard 2822 message, each HTTP transmission contains a header, a blank line, and the item being sent. Furthermore, each line in the header contains a keyword, a colon, and information. Figure 27.1 lists a few of the possible headers and their meaning.

Header	Meaning
Content-Length	Size of item in octets
Content-Type	Type of the item
Content-Encoding	Encoding used for item
Content-Language	Language(s) used in item

Figure 27.1 Examples of items that can appear in the header sent before an item. The *Content-Type* and *Content-Encoding* are taken directly from MIME.

As an example, consider Figure 27.2 which shows a few of the headers that are used when an HTML document is transferred across a persistent TCP connection.

```
Content-Length:   34
Content-Language: en
Content-Encoding: ascii

<HTML> A trivial example. </HTML>
```

Figure 27.2 An illustration of an HTTP transfer with header lines used to specify attributes, a blank line, and the document itself. A *Content-Length* header is required if the connection is persistent.

In addition to the examples shown in the figure, HTTP includes a wide variety of headers that allow a browser and server to exchange meta information. For example,

---

†See Chapter 26 for a discussion of e-mail, 2822 format, and MIME.

we said that if a server does not know the length of an item, the server closes the connection after sending the item. However, the server does not act without warning — the server informs the browser to expect a close. To do so, the server includes a *Connection* header before the item in place of a *Content-Length* header:

Connection: close

When it receives a connection header, the browser knows that the server intends to close the connection after the transfer; the browser is forbidden from sending further requests. The next sections describe the purposes of other headers.

27.12 Negotiation

In addition to specifying details about an item being sent, HTTP uses headers to permit a client and server to *negotiate* capabilities. The set of negotiable capabilities includes a wide variety of characteristics about the connection (e.g., whether access is authenticated), representation (e.g., whether graphics images in jpeg format are acceptable or which types of compression can be used), content (e.g., whether text files must be in English), and control (e.g., the length of time a page remains valid).

There are two basic types of negotiation: *server-driven* and *agent-driven* (i.e., browser-driven). Server-driven negotiation begins with a request from a browser. The request specifies a list of preferences along with the URL of the desired item. The server selects, from among the available representations, one that satisfies the browser's preferences. If multiple items satisfy the preferences, the server makes a ''best guess.'' For example, if a document is stored in multiple languages and a request specifies a preference for English, the server will send the English version.

Agent-driven negotiation means that a browser uses a two-step process to perform the selection. First, the browser sends a request to the server to ask what is available. The server returns a list of possibilities. The browser selects one of the possibilities, and sends a second request to obtain the item. The disadvantage of agent-driven negotiation is that it requires two server interactions; the advantage is that a browser retains complete control over the choice.

A browser uses an HTTP *Accept* header to specify which media or representations are acceptable. The header lists names of formats with a preference value assigned to each. For example,

`Accept: text/html, text/plain; q=0.5, text/x-dvi; q=0.8`

specifies that the browser is willing to accept the *text/html* media type, but if that does not exist, the browser will accept *text/x-dvi*, and, if that does not exist, *text/plain*. The numeric values associated with the second and third entry can be thought of as a *preference level*, where no value is equivalent to $q=1$, and a value of $q=0$ means the type is unacceptable. For media types where "quality" is meaningful (e.g., audio), the value of q can be interpreted as a willingness to accept a given media type if it is the best available after other forms are reduced in quality by q percent.

A variety of *Accept* headers exist that correspond to the *Content* headers described earlier. For example, a browser can send any of the following:

```
Accept-Encoding:
Accept-Charset:
Accept-Language:
```

to specify which encodings, character sets, and languages the browser is willing to accept.

To summarize:

> *HTTP uses MIME-like headers to carry meta information. Both browsers and servers send headers that allow them to negotiate agreement on the document representation and encoding to be used.*

27.13 Conditional Requests

HTTP allows a sender to make a request *conditional*. That is, when a browser sends a request, it includes a header that qualifies conditions under which the request should be honored. If the specified condition is not met, the server does not return the requested item. Conditional requests allow a browser to optimize retrieval by avoiding unnecessary transfers. The *If-Modified-Since* request specifies one of the most straightforward conditionals — it allows a browser to avoid transferring an item unless the item has been updated since a specified date. For example, a browser can include the header:

> If-Modified-Since: Fri, 01 Apr 2005 05:00:01 GMT

with a *GET* request to avoid a transfer if the item is older than April 1, 2005.

27.14 Proxy Servers And Caching

Proxy servers are an important part of the web architecture because they provide an optimization that can decrease latency and reduce the load on servers. Two forms of proxy servers exist: *nontransparent* and *transparent*. As the name implies, a *nontransparent* server is visible to a user — the user configures a browser to contact the proxy instead of the original source. A *transparent* proxy does not require any changes to a browser's configuration. Instead, a transparent proxy examines all TCP connections that pass through the proxy, and intercepts any connection to port 80. In either case, a proxy caches web pages and answers subsequent requests for a page from the cache.

HTTP includes explicit support for proxy servers. The protocol specifies exactly how a proxy handles each request, how headers should be interpreted by proxies, how a browser negotiates with a proxy, and how a proxy negotiates with a server. Furthermore, several HTTP headers have been designed specifically for use by proxies. For example, one header allows a proxy to authenticate itself to a server, and another allows each proxy that handles an item to record its identity so the ultimate recipient receives a list of all intermediate proxies. Finally, HTTP allows a server to control how proxies handle each web page. For example, a server can include the *Max-Forwards* header in a response to limit the number of proxies that handle an item before it is delivered to a browser. If the server specifies a count of one, as in:

Max-Forwards: 1

at most one proxy can handle the item along the path from the server to the browser. A count of zero prohibits any proxy from handling the item.

27.15 Caching

The goal of caching is improved efficiency: a cache reduces both latency and network traffic by eliminating unnecessary transfers. The most obvious aspect of caching is storage: when a web page is initially accessed, a copy is stored on disk, either by the browser, an intermediate proxy, or both. Subsequent requests for the same page can short-circuit the lookup process and retrieve a copy of the page from the cache instead of the server.

The central question in all caching schemes concerns timing: "How long should an item be kept in a cache?" On one hand, keeping a cached copy too long results in the copy becoming *stale*, which means that changes to the original are not reflected in the cached copy. On the other hand, if the cached copy is not kept long enough, inefficiency results because the next request must go back to the server.

HTTP allows a server to control caching in two ways. First, when it answers a request for a page, a server can specify caching details, including whether the page can be cached at all, whether a proxy can cache the page, the community with which a cached copy can be shared, the time at which the cached copy must expire, and limits on transformations that can be applied to the copy. Second, HTTP allows a browser to force *revalidation* of a page. To do so, the browser sends a request for the page, and uses a header to specify that the maximum "age" (i.e., the time since a copy of the page was stored) cannot be greater than zero. No copy of the page in a cache can be used to satisfy the request because the copy will have a nonzero age. Thus, only the original server will answer the request. Intermediate proxies along the way will receive a fresh copy for their cache as will the browser that issued the request.

To summarize:

> *Caching is key to the efficient operation of the web. HTTP allows servers to control whether and how a page can be cached as well as its lifetime; a browser can force a request for a page to bypass caches and obtain a fresh copy from the server that owns the page.*

27.16 Other HTTP Functionality

Our description of HTTP has focused exclusively on retrieval in which a client, typically a browser, issues a *GET* request to retrieve a copy of a web page from a server. However, HTTP includes facilities that allow more complex interactions between a client and server. In particular, HTTP offers *PUT* and *POST* methods that allow a client to send data to a server. Thus, it is possible to build a script that prompts a user for an ID and password and then transfers the results to the server.

Surprisingly, although it permits transfer in either direction, the underlying HTTP protocol remains stateless (i.e., does not require a persistent transport-layer connection to remain in place during an interaction). Thus, additional information is often used to coordinate a series of transfers. For example, in response to an ID and password, a server might send an identifying integer known as a *cookie* that the client returns in successive transfers.

27.17 HTTP, Security, And E-Commerce

Although it defines a mechanism that can be used to access web pages, HTTP does not provide security. Thus, before they make web purchases that require the transfer of information such as a credit card number, users need assurance that the transaction is safe. There are two issues: confidentiality of the data being transferred and authentication of the web site offering items for sale. As we will see in Chapter 30, encryption is used to ensure confidentiality. In addition, a certificate mechanism can be used to authenticate the merchant.

A security technology has been devised for use with web transactions. Known as *HTTP over SSL* (*HTTPS*), the technology runs HTTP over the Secure Socket Layer (*SSL*) protocol. HTTPS solves both problems related to e-commerce: because they are encrypted, data transfers are confidential, and because SSL uses a certificate tree, a merchant is authenticated.

27.18 Summary

The World Wide Web consists of hypermedia documents stored on a set of web servers and accessed by browsers. Each document is assigned a URL that uniquely identifies it; the URL specifies the protocol used to retrieve the document, the location of the server, and the path to the document on that server.

The HyperText Markup Language, HTML, allows a document to contain text along with embedded commands that control formatting. HTML also allows a document to contain links to other documents.

A browser and server use the HyperText Transfer Protocol, HTTP, to communicate. HTTP is an application-level protocol with explicit support for negotiation, proxy servers, caching, and persistent connections. A related technology known as HTTPS uses SSL to provide secure HTTP communication.

FOR FURTHER STUDY

Berners-Lee [RFC 1630] and Berners-Lee, et. al. [RFC 1738] define URLs. A variety of RFCs contain proposals for extensions. Mealling [RFC 3401, 3402, 3403, and 3404] considers how to store URLs in the domain name system.

Connolly and Masinter [RFC 2854] contains the standard for the current version of HTML.

Fielding et. al. [RFC 2616] specifies version 1.1 of HTTP, which adds many features, including additional support for persistence and caching, to the previous version. Franks et. al. [RFC 2617] considers access authentication in HTTP.

A group of vendors known as the *World Wide Web consortium* now controls many of the protocol standards related to the web, including markup languages other than HTML. Information can be found at:

www.w3c.org

EXERCISES

27.1   Read the standard for URLs. What does a pound sign (#) followed by a string mean at the end of a URL?

27.2   Extend the previous exercise. Is it legal to send the pound sign suffix on a URL to a web server? Why or why not?

27.3   How does a browser distinguish between a document that contains HTML and a document that contains arbitrary text? To find out, experiment by using a browser to read from a file. Does the browser use the name of the file or the contents to decide how to interpret the file?

27.4   What is the purpose of an HTTP *TRACE* command?

27.5   What is the difference between an HTTP *PUT* command and an HTTP *POST* command? When is each useful?

27.6   When is an HTTP *Keep-Alive* header used?

27.7   Can an arbitrary web server function as a proxy? To find out, choose an arbitrary web server and configure your browser to use it as a proxy. Do the results surprise you?

27.8   Download and install the Squid transparent proxy cache. What networking facilities in the OS does Squid use to cache web pages?

27.9   Read about HTTP's *must-revalidate* cache control directive. Give an example of a web page that would use such a directive.

27.10 If a browser does not send an HTTP *Content-Length* header before a request, how does a server respond?

27.11 Read more about HTTPS and explain the impact of HTTPS on caching. Under what circumstances can a proxy cache web pages when using HTTPS?

Chapter Contents

28

Voice And Video Over IP (RTP, RSVP, QoS)

28.1 Introduction

This chapter focuses on the transfer of real-time data such as voice and video over an IP network. In addition to discussing the protocols used to transport such data, the chapter considers two broader issues. First, it examines protocols and technologies needed for commercial IP telephone service. Second, it examines the question of how routers in an IP network can guarantee sufficient quality of service to provide high-quality video and audio reproduction.

28.2 Digitizing And Encoding

Before voice or video can be sent over a packet network, hardware known as a *coder/decoder* (*codec*) must be used to convert the analog signal to digital form. The most common type of codec, a *waveform coder*, measures the amplitude of the input signal at regular intervals and converts each sample into a digital value (i.e., an integer)†. At the receiving side, a codec accepts a sequence of integers as input and re-creates a continuous analog signal that matches the digital values.

Several digital encoding standards exist, with the main tradeoff being between quality of reproduction and the size of digital representation. For example, the conventional telephone system uses the *Pulse Code Modulation* (*PCM*) standard that specifies taking an 8-bit sample every 125 μ seconds (i.e., 8000 times per second). As a result, a digitized telephone call produces data at a rate of 64 Kbps. The PCM encoding pro-

---

†An alternative known as a *voice coder/decoder* (*vocodec*) recognizes and encodes human speech rather than general waveforms.

duces a surprising amount of output — storing a 128 second audio clip requires one megabyte of memory.

There are three ways to reduce the amount of data generated by digital encoding: take fewer samples per second, use fewer bits to encode each sample, or use a digital compression scheme to reduce the size of the resulting output. Various systems exist that use one or more of the techniques, making it possible to find products that produce encoded audio at a rate of only 2.2 Kbps. However, each technique has disadvantages. The chief disadvantage of taking fewer samples or using fewer bits to encode a sample is lower quality audio — the system cannot reproduce as large a range of sounds. The chief disadvantage of compression is delay — digitized output must be held while it is compressed. Furthermore, because greater reduction in size requires more processing, the best compression either requires a fast CPU or introduces longer delay. Thus, compression is most useful when delay is unimportant (e.g., when the output from a codec is being stored in a file).

28.3 Audio And Video Transmission And Reproduction

Many audio and video applications are classified as *real-time* because they require timely transmission and delivery†. For example, an interactive telephone call is a real-time exchange because audio must be delivered without significant delay or users find the system unsatisfactory. Timely transfer means more than low delay because the resulting signal is unintelligible unless it is presented in exactly the same order as the original, and with exactly the same timing. Thus, if a sender takes a sample every 125 μ seconds, the receiver must convert digital values to analog at exactly the same rate.

How can a network guarantee that the stream is delivered at exactly the same rate that the sender used? The conventional telephone system introduced one answer: an *isochronous* architecture. Isochronous design means that the entire system, including the digital circuits, must be engineered to deliver output with exactly the same timing as was used to generate input. Thus, an isochronous system that has multiple paths between any two points must be engineered so all paths have exactly the same delay.

An IP internet is not isochronous. We have already seen that datagrams can be duplicated, delayed, or arrive out of order. Variance in delay, known as *jitter*, is especially pervasive in IP networks. To allow meaningful transmission and reproduction of digitized signals across a network with IP semantics, additional protocol support is required. To handle datagram duplication and out-of-order delivery, each transmission must contain a sequence number. To handle jitter, each transmission must contain a *timestamp* that tells the receiver at which time the data in the packet should be played back. Separating sequence and timing information allows a receiver to reconstruct the signal accurately independent of how the packets arrive. Such timing information is especially critical when a datagram is lost or if the sender stops encoding during periods of silence; it allows the receiver to pause during playback the amount of time specified by the timestamps. To summarize:

---

†Timeliness is more important than reliability; missing data is merely skipped.

Because an IP internet is not isochronous, additional protocol support is required when sending digitized real-time data. In addition to basic sequence information that allows detection of duplicate or reordered packets, each packet must carry a separate timestamp that tells the receiver the exact time at which the data in the packet should be played.

28.4 Jitter And Playback Delay

How can a receiver recreate a signal accurately if the network introduces jitter? The receiver must implement a *playback buffer*† as Figure 28.1 illustrates.

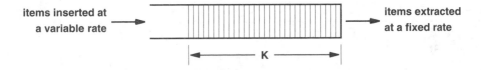

Figure 28.1 The conceptual organization of a playback buffer that compensates for jitter. The buffer holds *K* time units of data.

When a session begins, the receiver delays playback and places incoming data in the buffer. When data in the buffer reaches a predetermined threshold, known as the *playback point*, output begins. The playback point, labeled *K* in the figure, is measured in time units of data to be played. Thus, playback begins when a receiver has accumulated *K* time unit's worth of data.

As playback proceeds, datagrams continue to arrive. If there is no jitter, new data will arrive at exactly the same rate old data is being extracted and played, meaning the buffer will always contain exactly *K* time units of unplayed data. If a datagram experiences a small delay, playback is unaffected. The buffer size decreases steadily as data is extracted, and playback continues uninterrupted for *K* time units. When a delayed datagram arrives, the buffer is refilled.

Of course, a playback buffer cannot compensate for datagram loss. In such cases, playback eventually reaches an unfilled position in the buffer, and output pauses for a time period corresponding to the missing data. Furthermore, the choice of *K* is a compromise between loss and delay‡. If *K* is too small, a small amount of jitter causes the system to exhaust the playback buffer before the needed data arrives. If *K* is too large, the system remains immune to jitter, but the extra delay, when added to the transmission delay in the underlying network, may be noticeable to users. Despite the disadvantages, most applications that send real-time data across an IP internet depend on playback buffering as the primary solution for jitter.

---

†A playback buffer is also called a *jitter buffer.*

‡Although network delay and jitter can be used to determine a value for *K* dynamically, many playback buffering schemes use a constant.

28.5 Real-time Transport Protocol (RTP)

The protocol used to transmit digitized audio or video signals over an IP internet is known as the *Real-time Transport Protocol* (*RTP*). Interestingly, RTP does not contain mechanisms that ensure timely delivery; such guarantees must be made by the underlying system. Instead, RTP provides two key facilities: a sequence number in each packet that allows a receiver to detect out-of-order delivery or loss, and a timestamp that allows a receiver to control playback.

Because RTP is designed to carry a wide variety of real-time data, including both audio and video, RTP does not enforce a uniform interpretation of semantics. Instead, each packet begins with a fixed header; fields in the header specify how to interpret remaining header fields and how to interpret the payload. Figure 28.2 illustrates the format of RTP's fixed header.

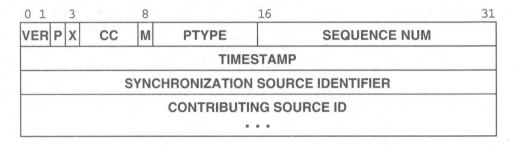

Figure 28.2 Illustration of the fixed header used with RTP. Each message begins with this header; the exact interpretation and additional header fields depend on the payload type, *PTYPE*.

As the figure shows, each packet begins with a two-bit RTP version number in field *VER*; the current version is *2*. The sixteen-bit *SEQUENCE NUM* field contains a sequence number for the packet. The first sequence number in a particular session is chosen at random. Some applications define an optional header extension to be placed between the fixed header and the payload. If the application type allows an extension, the *X* bit is used to specify whether the extension is present in the packet. The interpretation of most of the remaining fields in the header depends on the seven-bit *PTYPE* field that specifies the payload type. The *P* bit specifies whether zero padding follows the payload; it is used with encryption that requires data to be allocated in fixed-size blocks. Interpretation of the *M* (''marker'') bit also depends on the application; it is used by applications that need to mark points in the data stream (e.g., the beginning of each frame when sending video).

The payload type also affects the interpretation of the *TIMESTAMP* field. A *timestamp* is a 32-bit value that gives the time at which the first octet of digitized data was

sampled, with the initial timestamp for a session chosen at random. The standard specifies that the timestamp is incremented continuously, even during periods when no signal
is detected and no values are sent, but it does not specify the exact granularity. Instead,
the granularity is determined by the payload type, which means that each application
can choose a clock granularity that allows a receiver to position items in the output with
accuracy appropriate to the application. For example, if a stream of audio data is being
transmitted over RTP, a logical timestamp granularity of one clock tick per sample is
appropriate†. However, if video data is being transmitted, the timestamp granularity
needs to be higher than one tick per frame to achieve smooth playback. In any case, the
standard allows the timestamps in two packets to be identical, if the data in the two
packets was sampled at the same time.

28.6 Streams, Mixing, And Multicasting

A key part of RTP is its support for *translation* (i.e., changing the encoding of a
stream at an intermediate station) or *mixing* (i.e., receiving streams of data from multiple sources, combining them into a single stream, and sending the result). To understand the need for mixing, imagine that individuals at multiple sites participate in a
conference call using IP. To minimize the number of RTP streams, the group can
designate a *mixer*, and arrange for each site to establish an RTP session to the mixer.
The mixer combines the audio streams (possibly by converting them back to analog and
resampling the resulting signal), and sends the result as a single digital stream.

Fields in the RTP header identify the sender and indicate whether mixing occurred.
The field labeled *SYNCHRONIZATION SOURCE IDENTIFIER* specifies the source of a
stream. Each source must choose a unique 32-bit identifier; the protocol includes a
mechanism for resolving conflicts if they arise. When a mixer combines multiple
streams, the mixer becomes the synchronization source for the new stream. Information
about the original sources is not lost, however, because the mixer uses the variable-size
CONTRIBUTING SOURCE ID field to provide the synchronization IDs of streams that
were mixed together. The four-bit *CC* field gives a count of contributing sources; a
maximum of 15 sources can be listed.

RTP is designed to work with IP multicasting, and mixing is especially attractive
in a multicast environment. To understand why, imagine a teleconference that includes
many participants. Unicasting requires a station to send a copy of each outgoing RTP
packet to each participant. With multicasting, however, a station only needs to send
one copy of the packet, which will be delivered to all participants. Furthermore, if mixing is used, all sources can unicast to a mixer, which combines them into a single
stream before multicasting. Thus, the combination of mixing and multicast results in
substantially fewer datagrams being delivered to each participating host.

---

†The *TIMESTAMP* is sometimes referred to as a *MEDIA TIMESTAMP* to emphasize that its granularity
depends on the type of signal being measured.

28.7 RTP Encapsulation

Its name implies that RTP is a transport-level protocol. Indeed, if it functioned like a conventional transport protocol, RTP would require each message to be encapsulated directly in an IP datagram. In fact, RTP does not function like a transport protocol; although it is allowed, direct encapsulation in IP does not occur in practice. Instead, RTP runs over UDP, meaning that each RTP message is encapsulated in a UDP datagram. The chief advantage of using UDP is concurrency — a single computer can have multiple applications using RTP without interference.

Unlike many of the application protocols we have seen, RTP does not use a reserved UDP port number. Instead, a port is allocated for use with each session, and the remote application must be informed about the port number. By convention, RTP chooses an even numbered UDP port; the following section explains that a companion protocol, RTCP, uses the next port number.

28.8 RTP Control Protocol (RTCP)

So far, our description of real-time transmission has focused on the protocol mechanisms that allow a receiver to reproduce content. However, another aspect of real-time transmission is equally important: monitoring of the underlying network during the session and providing *out of band* communication between the endpoints. Such a mechanism is especially important in cases where adaptive schemes are used. For example, an application might choose a lower-bandwidth encoding when the underlying network becomes congested, or a receiver might vary the size of its playback buffer when network delay or jitter changes. Finally, an out-of-band mechanism can be used to send information in parallel with the real-time data (e.g., captions to accompany a video stream).

A companion protocol and integral part of RTP, known as the *RTP Control Protocol* (*RTCP*), provides the needed control functionality. RTCP allows senders and receivers to transmit a series of reports to one another that contain additional information about the data being transferred and the performance of the network. RTCP messages are encapsulated in UDP for transmission†, and are sent using a port number one greater than the port number of the RTP stream to which they pertain.

28.9 RTCP Operation

Figure 28.3 lists the five basic message types RTCP uses to allow senders and receivers to exchange information about a session. A sender transmits a *bye* message when shutting down a stream, and an *application specific* message to define a new message type. For example, to send closed caption information along with a video stream, an application might choose to define a new RTCP message.

---

†Because some messages are short, the standard allows multiple RTCP messages to be combined into a single UDP datagram for transmission.

Type	Meaning
200	Sender report
201	Receiver report
202	Source description message
203	Bye message
204	Application specific message

Figure 28.3 The five RTCP message types. Each message begins with a fixed header that identifies the type.

Receivers periodically transmit *receiver report* messages that inform the source about conditions of reception. Receiver reports are important for two reasons. First, they allow all receivers participating in a session as well as a sender to learn about reception conditions of other receivers. Second, they allow receivers to adapt their rate of reporting to avoid using excessive bandwidth and overwhelming the sender. The adaptive scheme guarantees that the total control traffic will remain less than 5% of the real-time data traffic and that receiver reports generate less than 75% of the control traffic. Each receiver report identifies one or more synchronization sources, and contains a separate section for each. A section specifies the highest sequence number packet received from the source, the cumulative and percentage packet loss experienced, time since the last RTCP report arrived from the source, and the interarrival jitter.

Senders periodically transmit a *sender report* message that provides an absolute timestamp. To understand the need for a timestamp, recall that RTP allows each stream to choose a granularity for its timestamp and that the first timestamp is chosen at random. The absolute timestamp in a sender report is essential because it provides the only mechanism a receiver has to *synchronize* multiple streams. In particular, because RTP requires a separate stream for each media type, the transmission of video and accompanying audio requires two streams. The absolute timestamp information allows a receiver to play the two streams simultaneously.

In addition to the periodic sender report messages, senders also transmit *source description* messages which provide general information about the user who owns or controls the source. Each message contains one section for each outgoing RTP stream; the contents are intended for humans to read. For example, the only required field consists of a *canonical name* for the stream owner, a character string in the form:

user @ host

where *host* is either the domain name of the computer or its IP address in dotted decimal form, and *user* is a login name. Optional fields in the source description contain further details such as the user's e-mail address (which may differ from the canonical name), telephone number, the geographic location of the site, the application program or tool used to create the stream, or other textual notes about the source.

28.10 IP Telephony And Signaling

One aspect of real-time transmission stands out as especially important: the use of IP as the foundation for telephone service. Known as *IP telephony* or *voice over IP*, the idea is endorsed by many telephone companies. The question arises, ''What additional technologies are needed before IP can be used in place of the existing isochronous telephone system?'' Although no simple answer exists, researchers are investigating three components. First, we have seen that a protocol like RTP is needed to transfer a digitized signal across an IP internet correctly. Second, a mechanism is needed to establish and terminate telephone calls. Third, researchers are exploring ways an IP internet can be made to function like an isochronous network.

The telephone industry uses the term *signaling* to refer to the process of establishing a telephone call. Specifically, the signaling mechanism used in the conventional *Public Switched Telephone Network* (*PSTN*) is *Signaling System 7* (*SS7*). SS7 performs call routing before any audio is sent. Given a phone number, it forms a circuit through the network, rings the designated telephone, and connects the circuit when the phone is answered. SS7 also handles details such as call forwarding and error conditions such as the destination phone being busy.

Before IP can be used to make phone calls, signaling functionality must be available. Furthermore, to enable adoption by the phone companies, IP telephony must be compatible with extant telephone standards — it must be possible for the IP telephony system to interoperate with the conventional phone system at all levels. Thus, it must be possible to translate between the signaling used with IP and SS7 just as it must be possible to translate between the voice encoding used with IP and standard PCM encoding. As a consequence, the two signaling mechanisms will have equivalent functionality.

The general approach to interoperability uses a *gateway* between the IP phone system and the conventional phone system. A call can be initiated on either side of the gateway. When a signaling request arrives, the gateway translates and forwards the request; the gateway must also translate and forward the response. Finally, after signaling is complete and a call has been established, the gateway must forward voice in both directions, translating from the encoding used on one side to the encoding used on the other.

Two groups have proposed standards for IP telephony. The ITU has defined a suite of protocols known as *H.323*, and the IETF has proposed a signaling protocol known as the *Session Initiation Protocol* (*SIP*). The next sections summarize the two approaches.

28.10.1 H.323 Standards

The ITU originally created H.323 to allow the transmission of voice over local area network technologies. The standard has been extended to allow transmission of voice over IP internets, and telephone companies are expected to adopt it. H.323 is not a single protocol. Instead, it specifies how multiple protocols can be combined to form a functional IP telephony system. For example, in addition to gateways, H.323 defines devices known as *gatekeepers* that each provide a contact point for telephones using IP. To obtain permission to place outgoing calls and enable the phone system to direct incoming calls to the correct destination, each IP telephone must register with a gatekeeper; H.323 includes the necessary protocols.

In addition to specifying a protocol for the transmission of real-time voice and video, the H.323 framework allows participants to transfer data. Thus, a pair of users engaged in an audio-video conference can also share an on-screen whiteboard, send still images, or exchange copies of documents.

H.323 relies on the four major protocols listed in Figure 28.4.

Protocol	Purpose
H.225.0	Signaling used to establish a call
H.245	Control and feedback during the call
RTP	Real-time data transfer (sequence and timing)
T.120	Exchange of data associated with a call

Figure 28.4 The protocols used by H.323 for IP telephony.

Together, the suite of protocols covers all aspects of IP telephony, including phone registration, signaling, real-time data encoding and transfer (both voice and video), and control.

Figure 28.5 illustrates relationships among the protocols that constitute H.323. As the figure shows, the entire suite ultimately depends on UDP and TCP running over IP.

audio / video applications		signaling and control				data applications
video codec	audio codec	RTCP	H.225 Registr.	H.225 Signaling	H.245 Control	T.120 Data
RTP						
UDP				TCP		
IP						

Figure 28.5 Relationship among some of the protocols that constitute the ITU's H.323 IP telephony standard. Protocols that are omitted handle details such as security and FAX transmission.

28.10.2 Session Initiation Protocol (SIP)

The IETF has proposed an alternative to H.323, called the *Session Initiation Protocol* (*SIP*), that only covers signaling; it does not recommend specific codecs nor does it require the use of RTP for real-time transfer. Thus, SIP does not supply all of H.323 functionality.

SIP uses client-server interaction, with servers being divided into two types. A *user agent server* runs in a SIP telephone. It is assigned an identifier (e.g., *user @ site*), and can receive incoming calls. The second type of server is intermediate (i.e., between two SIP telephones) and handles tasks such as call set up and call forwarding. An intermediate server functions as a *proxy server* that can forward an incoming call request to the next proxy server along the path to the called phone, or as a *redirect server* that tells a caller how to reach the destination.

To provide information about a call, SIP relies on a companion protocol, the *Session Description Protocol* (*SDP*). SDP is especially important in a conference call because participants join and leave the call dynamically. SDP specifies details such as the media encoding, protocol port numbers, and multicast address.

28.11 Quality Of Service Controversy

The term *Quality of Service* (*QoS*) refers to statistical performance guarantees that a network system can make regarding loss, delay, throughput, and jitter. An isochronous network that is engineered to meet strict performance bounds is said to provide QoS guarantees, while a packet switched network that uses best effort delivery is said to provide no QoS guarantee. Is guaranteed QoS needed for real-time transfer of voice and video over IP? If so, how should it be implemented? A major controversy surrounds the two questions. On one hand, engineers who designed the telephone system insist that toll-quality voice reproduction requires the underlying system to provide QoS guarantees about delay and loss for each phone call. On the other hand, engineers who designed IP insist that the Internet works reasonably well without QoS guarantees and that adding per-flow QoS is infeasible because routers will make the system both expensive and slow.

The QoS controversy has produced many proposals, implementations, and experiments. Although it operates without QoS, the Internet is already used to send audio. Technologies like ATM that were derived from the telephone system model provide QoS guarantees for each individual connection or *flow*. After an effort known as *Integrated Services* (*IntServ*) that investigated defining per-flow quality of service, the IETF adopted a conservative *Differentiated Services* (*DiffServ*) approach that divides traffic into separate classes. The differentiated services scheme, which sacrifices fine grain control for less complex forwarding, is sometimes called a *Class of Service* (*CoS*) approach.

28.12 QoS, Utilization, And Capacity

The debate over QoS is reminiscent of earlier debates on resource allocation such as those waged over operating system policies for memory allocation and processor scheduling. The central issue is utilization: when a network has sufficient resources for all traffic, QoS constraints are unnecessary; when traffic exceeds network capacity, no QoS system can satisfy all users' demands. That is, a network with 1% utilization does not need QoS, and a network with 101% utilization will fail under any QoS. In effect, proponents who argue for QoS mechanisms assert that complex QoS mechanisms achieve two goals. First, by dividing the existing resources among more users, they make the system more "fair". Second, by shaping the traffic from each user, they allow the network to run at higher utilization without danger of collapse.

One of the major arguments against complicated QoS mechanisms arises from improvements in the performance of underlying networks. Network capacity has increased dramatically. As long as rapid increases in capacity continue, QoS mechanisms merely represent unnecessary overhead. However, if demand rises more rapidly than capacity, QoS may become an economic issue — by associating higher prices with higher levels of service, ISPs can use cost to ration capacity.

28.13 IntServ Resource Reservation (RSVP)

If QoS is needed, how can an IP network provide it? As it explored IntServ, the IETF developed two protocols to provide QoS: the *Resource ReSerVation Protocol* (*RSVP*) and the *Common Open Policy Services* (*COPS*) protocol. Both protocols require changes to the basic infrastructure — all routers must agree to reserve resources (e.g., bandwidth) for each flow between a pair of endpoints. There are two aspects. First, before data is sent, the endpoints must send a request that specifies the resources needed, and all routers along the path must agree to supply the resources; the procedure can be viewed as a form of *signaling*. Second, as datagrams traverse the flow, routers need to monitor and control traffic forwarding. Monitoring, sometimes called *traffic policing*, is needed to ensure that the traffic sent on a flow does not exceed the specified bounds. Control of queueing and forwarding is needed for two reasons. The router must implement a queueing policy that meets the guaranteed bounds on delay, and the router must smooth packet bursts. The latter is sometimes referred to as *traffic shaping*, and is necessary because network traffic is often *bursty*. For example, a flow that specifies an average throughput of 1 Mbps may have 2 Mbps of traffic for a millisecond followed by no traffic for a millisecond. A router can reshape the burst by temporarily queueing incoming datagrams and sending them at a steady rate of 1 Mbps.

RSVP handles reservation requests and replies. It is not a route propagation protocol, nor does it enforce policies once a flow has been established. Instead, RSVP operates before any data is sent. To initiate an end-to-end flow, an endpoint first sends an RSVP *path* message to determine the path to the destination; the datagram carrying the message uses the *router alert* option to guarantee that routers examine the message.

After it receives a reply to its path message, the endpoint sends a *request* message to reserve resources for the flow. The request specifies QoS bounds desired; each router that forwards the request along to the destination must agree to reserve the resources the request specifies. If any router along the path denies the request, the router uses RSVP to send a negative reply back to the source. If all systems along the path agree to honor the request, RSVP returns a positive reply.

Each RSVP flow is *simplex* (i.e., unidirectional). If an application requires QoS guarantees in two directions, each endpoint must use RSVP to request a flow. Because RSVP uses existing forwarding, there is no guarantee that the two flows will pass through the same routers, nor does approval of a flow in one direction imply approval in the other. We can summarize:

> *An endpoint uses RSVP to request a simplex flow through an IP inter-net with specified QoS bounds. If routers along the path agree to honor the request, they approve it; otherwise, they deny it. If an application needs QoS in two directions, each endpoint must use RSVP to request a separate flow.*

28.14 IntServ Enforcement (COPS)

When an RSVP request arrives, a router must consider two aspects: feasibility (i.e., whether the router has the resources necessary to satisfy the request) and policy (i.e., whether the request lies within policy constraints). Feasibility is a local decision — a router can decide how to manage the bandwidth, memory, and processing power that is available locally. However, policy enforcement requires global cooperation — all routers must agree to the same set of policies.

To implement global policies, the IETF architecture uses a two-level model, with client-server interaction between the levels. When a router receives an RSVP request, it becomes a client that consults a server known as a *Policy Decision Point* (*PDP*) to determine whether the request meets policy constraints. The PDP does not handle traf-fic; it merely evaluates requests to see if they satisfy global policies. If a PDP approves a request, the router must operate as a *Policy Enforcement Point* (*PEP*) to ensure traffic does not exceed the approved policy.

The COPS protocol defines the client-server interaction between a router and a PDP (or between a router and a local PDP if the organization has multiple levels of pol-icy servers). Although COPS defines its own message header, the underlying format shares many details with RSVP. In particular, COPS uses the same format as RSVP for individual items in a request message. Thus, when a router receives an RSVP request, it can extract items related to policy, place them in a COPS message, and send the result to a PDP.

28.15 DiffServ And Per-Hop Behavior

DiffServ, which is described in Chapter 6, differs from IntServ in two significant ways. First, instead of individual flows, DiffServ allocates service to a class (i.e., a group of flows). Second, unlike the RSVP scheme in which a reservation is made end-to-end, DiffServ allows each node along the path to define the service that a given class will receive. For example, a router can choose to divide bandwidth so that the DiffServ class known as *Expedited Forwarding* (*EF*) receives 50% of the bandwidth and the remaining 50% is divided among the classes that are known as *Assured Forwarding* (*AF*). However, the next router along the path can choose to give class EF 90% of the bandwidth and divide the AF classes among the remaining 10%. We use the phrase *per-hop behavior* to describe the approach and to point out that DiffServ does not provide end-to-end guarantees.

28.16 Traffic Scheduling

To implement any form of QoS, a router needs to assign priorities to outgoing traffic and choose which packet to send at a given time. The process of selecting from among a set of packets is known as *traffic scheduling*, and the mechanism is called a *traffic scheduler*. There are four aspects to consider when constructing a scheduler:

- *Fairness.* The scheduler should ensure that the resources (i.e., bandwidth) consumed by a flow falls within the amount assigned to the flow†.

- *Delay.* Packets on a given flow should not be delayed excessively.

- *Adaptability.* If a given flow does not have packets to send, the scheduler should divide the extra bandwidth among other flows proportional to their assigned resources.

- *Computational Overhead.* Because it operates in the fast path, a scheduler must not incur much computational overhead. In particular, theoretical algorithms such as *Generalized Processor Scheduling* (*GPS*) cannot be used.

The most straightforward practical traffic scheduling scheme is named *Weighted Round Robin* (*WRR*) because it assigns each flow a weight and attempts to send data from the flow according to the flow's weight. For example, we can imagine three flows, *A*, *B*, and *C*, with weights 2, 2, and 4, respectively. If all three flows have packets waiting to be sent, the scheduler should send twice as much from flow *C* (weight 4) as from *A* or *B* (each with weight 2).

It may seem that a WRR scheduler could achieve the desired weights by selecting from flows in the following order:

---

†Throughout this section we will discuss scheduling among *flows*. However, the reader should understand that when DiffServ is used, scheduling is among classes.

C C A B

That is, the scheduler repeatedly makes selections:

C C A B C C A B C C A B ...

The pattern appears to achieve the desired weights because one half of the selections come from flow C, one quarter come from B, and one quarter come from A. Furthermore, the pattern services each queue at regular intervals throughout the sequence, which means that no flow is delayed unnecessarily (i.e., the rate at which packets are sent from a given flow is constant).

Although the sequence above does make the packet rate match the assigned weights, the WRR approach does not achieve the goal of making the data rates match the weights because datagrams are not uniform size. For example, if the average datagram size on flow C is half of the average datagram size on flow A, selecting flow C twice as often as flow A will make the data rate of the two flows equal.

To solve the problem, a modified algorithm was invented that accommodates variable-size packets. Known as *Deficit Round Robin* (*DRR*), the algorithm computes weights in terms of total bytes sent rather than number of packets. Initially, the algorithm allocates a number of bytes to each flow proportional to the bandwidth the flow should receive. When a flow is selected, DRR transmits as many packets as possible without exceeding the allotted number of bytes. The algorithm then computes the remainder (i.e., the difference between the number of bytes that was allocated and the size of the packets actually sent), and adds the remainder to the amount that will be sent in the next round. Thus, DRR keeps a running total of the "deficit" that each flow should receive. Even if the deficit gained on a given round is small, the value will grow through multiple rounds until it is large enough to accommodate an extra packet. Thus, over time the proportion of data that DRR sends from a given flow approaches the weighted value for the flow.

Round-robin scheduling algorithms such as WRR and DRR have advantages and disadvantages. The chief advantage and the reason for their popularity arises from efficiency: once weights have been assigned, little computation is required to make a packet selection. In fact, if all packets are the same size and weights are selected as multiples, the weighted selection can be achieved through the use of an array rather than through computation.

Despite their popularity, round-robin algorithms do have drawbacks. First, the delay that a given flow experiences depends on the number of other flows that have traffic to send. In the worst case, a given flow may need to wait while the scheduler sends one or more packets from each of the other flows. Second, because they send a burst of packets from a given queue and then delay while servicing other queues, round robin algorithms can introduce jitter.

28.17 Traffic Policing

A system that implements traffic scheduling also needs a *traffic policer* that can verify that arriving traffic does not exceed a stated statistical profile. To see why such a mechanism is needed, consider a system in which a scheduler allocates 25% of the outgoing bandwidth to a DiffServ class, Q. If three incoming flows all map to class Q, the flows will compete for the bandwidth allocated to Q. Thus, the system must police each incoming flow to ensure that none of the flows receives more than its fair share.

Several mechanisms have been proposed for traffic policing. An early mechanism, based on the *leaky bucket* approach, uses a counter to control the packet rate. Periodically, the algorithm increments the counter; each time a packet arrives, the algorithm decrements the counter. If the counter becomes negative, the incoming flow has exceeded its allocated packet rate.

As was pointed out, using a fixed packet rate does not make sense in the Internet because datagrams vary in size. Thus, more sophisticated policing schemes have been proposed to accommodate variable-size packets. For example, a *token bucket* mechanism extends the approach outlined above by making the counter correspond to bits rather than packets. The counter is incremented periodically in accordance with the desired data rate, and decremented by the size of each arriving packet.

In practice, the policing mechanisms described do not require a timer to periodically update a counter. Instead, each time a packet arrives, the policer examines the clock to determine how much time has elapsed since the flow was processed last, and uses the amount of time to compute an increment for the counter.

28.18 Summary

A hardware unit known as a codec encodes analog data such as audio in digital form. The telephone standard for digital audio encoding, Pulse Code Modulation (PCM), produces digital values at 64 Kbps; other encodings sacrifice some fidelity to achieve lower bit rates.

RTP is used to transfer real-time data across an IP network. Each RTP message contains two key pieces of information: a sequence number that a receiver uses to place messages in order and detect lost datagrams and a media timestamp that a receiver uses to determine when to play the encoded values. An associated control protocol, RTCP, is used to supply information about sources and to allow a mixer to combine several streams.

A debate continues over whether Quality of Service (QoS) guarantees are needed to provide real-time. Before announcing a Differentiated Services approach, the IETF devised an Integrated Services model and designed a pair of protocols that can be used to provide per-flow QoS. Endpoints use RSVP to request a flow with specific QoS; intermediate routers either approve or deny the request. When an RSVP request arrives, a router uses the COPS protocol to contact a Policy Decision Point and verify that the request meets policy constraints.

Implementation of QoS requires a traffic scheduling mechanism to select packets from outgoing queues and traffic policing to monitor incoming flows. Because they are computationally efficient and handle variable-size packets, the Deficit Round Robin algorithm is popular for traffic scheduling and the leaky bucket algorithm is popular for traffic policing.

FOR FURTHER STUDY

Schulzrinne et. al. [RFC 3550] gives the standard for RTP and RTCP. Perkins et. al. [RFC 2198] specifies the transmission of redundant audio data over RTP, and Schulzrinne [RFC 3551] specifies the use of RTP with an audio-video conference. Schulzrinne, Rao, and Lanphier [RFC 2326] describes a related protocol used for streaming of real-time traffic.

Braden et. al. [RFC 1633] describes IntServ, and Zhang et. al. [RFC 2205] contains the specification for RSVP. Durham et. al. [RFC 2748] specifies COPS, and Herzog et. al. [RFC 2749] describes the use of COPS with RSVP. Blake et. al. [RFC 2475] specifies DiffServ, and Heinanen et. al. [RFC 2597] discusses assured forwarding per-hop behavior; Davie et. al. [RFC 3246] discusses expedited forwarding. Parekh and Gallager [1993 and 1994] document Generalized Processor Sharing, and Shreedhar and Varghese [1995] discusses Deficit Round Robin scheduling.

EXERCISES

28.1   Read about the Real-Time Streaming Protocol, RTSP. What are the major differences between RTSP and RTP?

28.2   Argue that although bandwidth is often cited as an example of the facilities a QoS mechanism can guarantee, delay is a more fundamental resource. (Hint: which constraint can be eased with sufficient money?)

28.3   If an RTP message arrives with a sequence number far greater than the sequence expected, what does the protocol do? Why?

28.4   Are sequence numbers necessary in RTP, or can a timestamp be used instead? Explain.

28.5   Would you prefer an Internet where QoS was required for all traffic? Why or why not?

28.6   Measure the utilization on your connection to the Internet. If all traffic required QoS reservation, would service be better or worse? Explain.

Chapter Contents

29

Network Management (SNMP)

29.1 Introduction

In addition to protocols that provide network level services and application programs that use those services, a subsystem is needed that allows a manager to debug problems, control routing, and find computers that violate protocol standards. We refer to such activities as *network management*. This chapter considers the ideas behind TCP/IP network management, and describes a protocol used for network management.

29.2 The Level Of Management Protocols

Originally, many wide area networks included management protocols as part of their link level protocols. If a packet switch began misbehaving, the network manager could instruct a neighboring packet switch to send it a special *control packet*. Control packets caused the receiver to suspend normal operation and respond to commands from the manager. The manager could interrogate the packet switch to identify problems, examine or change routes, test one of the communication interfaces, or reboot the switch. Once the problem was repaired, the manager could instruct the switch to resume normal operations. Because management tools were part of the lowest-level protocol, managers were often able to control switches even if higher-level protocols failed.

Unlike a homogeneous wide area network, the Internet does not have a single link level protocol. Instead, the Internet consists of multiple physical network types and devices from multiple vendors. As a result, the Internet requires a new network

519

management paradigm that offers three important capabilities. First, a single manager can control heterogeneous devices, including IP routers, bridges, modems, workstations, and printers. Second, the controlled entities need not share a common link level protocol. Third, the set of machines a manager controls may lie at arbitrary points in the Internet. In particular, a manager may need to control one or more machines that do not attach to the same physical network as the manager's computer. Thus, it may not be possible for a manager to communicate with machines being controlled unless the management software uses protocols that provide end-to-end connectivity across the Internet. As a consequence, the network management protocol used with TCP/IP operates above the transport level:

> *In a TCP/IP internet, a manager needs to examine and control routers and other network devices. Because such devices attach to arbitrary networks, protocols for network management operate at the application layer and communicate using TCP/IP transport-layer protocols.*

Designing network management software to operate at the application level has several advantages. Because the protocols can be designed without regard to the underlying network hardware, one set of protocols can be used for all networks. Because the protocols can be designed without regard to the hardware on the managed machine, the same protocols can be used for all managed devices. From a manager's point of view, having a single set of management protocols means uniformity — all routers respond to exactly the same set of commands. Furthermore, because the management software uses IP for communication, a manager can control the routers across an entire TCP/IP internet without having direct attachment to every physical network or router.

Of course, building management software at the application level also has disadvantages. Unless the operating system, IP software, and transport protocol software work correctly, the manager may not be able to contact a router that needs managing. For example, if a router's routing table becomes damaged, it may be impossible to correct the table or reboot the machine from a remote site. If the operating system on a router crashes, it will be impossible to reach the application program that implements the internet management protocols even if the router can still process hardware interrupts and forward packets.

29.3 Architectural Model

Despite the potential disadvantages, having TCP/IP management software operate at the application level has worked well in practice. The most significant advantage of placing network management protocols at a high level becomes apparent when one considers a large internet, where a manager's computer does not need to attach directly to all physical networks that contain managed entities. Figure 29.1 shows an example of the architecture.

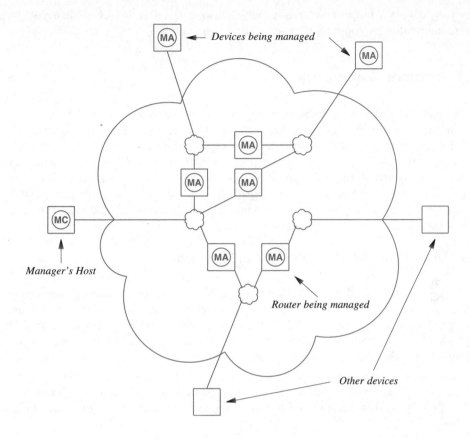

Figure 29.1 Example of network management. A manager invokes management client (MC) software that can contact management agent
(MA) software that runs on devices throughout an internet.

As the figure shows, client software usually runs on the manager's workstation.
Each participating network system runs a server program†. Technically, the server
software is called a *management agent* or merely an *agent*. A manager invokes client
software on the local host computer and specifies an agent with which it communicates.
After the client contacts the agent, it sends queries to obtain information or it sends
commands to change conditions in the router. Of course, not all devices in a large internet fall under a single manager. Most managers only control devices at their local
sites; a large site may have multiple managers.

Network management software uses an authentication mechanism to ensure only
authorized managers can access or control a particular device. Some management protocols support multiple levels of authorization, allowing a manager specific privileges
on each device. For example, a specific router could be configured to allow several

---

†We use the term *network system* to include conventional devices such as routers and desktop computers
as well as devices such as printers and sensors.

managers to obtain information, while only allowing a select subset of managers to change information or control the router.

29.4 Protocol Framework

TCP/IP network management protocols divide the management problem into two parts and specify separate standards for each part. The first part concerns communication of information. A protocol specifies how client software running on a manager's host communicates with an agent. The protocol defines the format and meaning of messages clients and servers exchange as well as the form of names and addresses. The second part concerns the data being managed. A protocol specifies which data items a managed device must keep as well as the name of each data item and the syntax used to express the name.

29.4.1 A Standard Network Management Protocol

The TCP/IP standard for network management is the *Simple Network Management Protocol* (*SNMP*). The protocol has evolved through three generations. Consequently, the current version is known as *SNMPv3*, and the predecessors are known as *SNMPv1* and *SNMPv2*. The changes have been minor — all three versions use the same general framework, and many features are backward compatible.

In addition to specifying details such as the message format and the use of transport protocols, the SNMP standard defines the set of operations and the meaning of each. We will see that the approach is minimalistic; a few operations provide all functionality.

29.4.2 A Standard For Managed Information

A device being managed must keep control and status information that the manager can access. For example, a router keeps statistics on the status of its network interfaces, incoming and outgoing packet traffic, dropped datagrams, and error messages generated; a modem keeps statistics about the number of bits (or characters) sent and received. Although it allows a manager to access statistics, SNMP does not specify exactly which data can be accessed on which devices. Instead, a separate standard specifies the details for each type of device. Known as a *Management Information Base* (*MIB*), the standard specifies the data items a managed device must keep, the operations allowed on each, and the meanings. For example, the MIB for IP specifies that the software must keep a count of all octets that arrive over each network interface and that network management software can only read the count.

The MIB for TCP/IP divides management information into many categories. The choice of categories is important because identifiers used to specify items include a code for the category. Figure 29.2 lists a few examples.

MIB category	Includes Information About
system	The host or router operating system
interfaces	Individual network interfaces
at	Address translation (e.g., ARP mappings)
ip	Internet Protocol software
icmp	Internet Control Message Protocol software
tcp	Transmission Control Protocol software
udp	User Datagram Protocol software
ospf	Open Shortest Path First software
bgp	Border Gateway Protocol software
rmon	Remote network monitoring
rip-2	Routing Information Protocol software
dns	Domain name system software

Figure 29.2 Example categories of MIB information. The category is encoded in the identifier used to specify an object.

Keeping the MIB definition independent of the network management protocol has advantages for both vendors and users. A vendor can include SNMP agent software in a product such as a router, with the guarantee that the software will continue to adhere to the standard after new MIB items are defined. A customer can use the same network management client software to manage multiple devices that have slightly different versions of a MIB. Of course, a device that does not have new MIB items cannot provide the information in those items. However, because all managed devices use the same language for communication, they can all parse a query and either provide the requested information or send an error message explaining the requested item is not available.

29.5 Examples of MIB Variables

Early versions of SNMP collected variables together in a single large MIB, with the entire set documented in a single RFC. To avoid having the MIB specification become unwieldy, the IETF decided to allow the publication of many individual MIB documents that each specify the variables for a specific type of device. As a result, more than 100 separate MIBs have been defined as part of the standards process; they specify more than 10,000 individual variables. For example, separate RFCs now exist that specify the MIB variables associated with devices such as: a hardware bridge, an uninterruptible power supply, an Ethernet switch, and a DSL modem. In addition, many vendors have defined MIB variables for their specific hardware or software products.

Examining a few of the MIB data items associated with TCP/IP protocols will help clarify the contents. Figure 29.3 lists example MIB variables along with their categories.

MIB Variable	Category	Meaning
sysUpTime	system	Time since last reboot
ifNumber	interfaces	Number of network interfaces
ifMtu	interfaces	MTU for a particular interface
ipDefaultTTL	ip	Value IP uses in time-to-live field
ipInReceives	ip	Number of datagrams received
ipForwDatagrams	ip	Number of datagrams forwarded
ipOutNoRoutes	ip	Number of routing failures
ipReasmOKs	ip	Number of datagrams reassembled
ipFragOKs	ip	Number of datagrams fragmented
ipRoutingTable	ip	IP Routing table
icmpInEchos	icmp	Number of ICMP Echo Requests received
tcpRtoMin	tcp	Minimum retransmission time TCP allows
tcpMaxConn	tcp	Maximum TCP connections allowed
tcpInSegs	tcp	Number of segments TCP has received
udpInDatagrams	udp	Number of UDP datagrams received

Figure 29.3 Examples of MIB variables along with their categories.

Most of the items listed in Figure 29.3 are numeric — each value can be stored in a single integer. However, the MIB also defines more complex structures. For example, the MIB variable *ipRoutingTable* refers to an entire routing table. Additional MIB variables define the contents of a routing table entry, and allow the network management protocols to reference an individual entry in the table, including the prefix, address mask, and next hop fields. Of course, MIB variables present only a logical definition of each data item — the internal data structures a router uses may differ from the MIB definition. When a query arrives, software in the agent on the router is responsible for mapping between the MIB variable and the data structure the router uses to store the information.

29.6 The Structure Of Management Information

In addition to the standards that specify MIB variables and their meanings, a separate standard specifies a set of rules used to define and identify MIB variables. The rules are known as the *Structure of Management Information* (*SMI*) specification. To keep network management protocols simple, the SMI places restrictions on the types of variables allowed in the MIB, specifies the rules for naming those variables, and creates rules for defining variable types. For example, the SMI standard includes definitions of terms like *IpAddress* (defining it to be a 4-octet string) and *Counter* (defining it to be an integer in the range of 0 to $2^{32} - 1$), and specifies that they are terms used to define MIB variables. More important, the rules in the SMI describe how the MIB refers to tables of values (e.g., the IP routing table).

29.7 Formal Definitions Using ASN.1

The SMI standard specifies that all MIB variables must be defined and referenced using ISO's *Abstract Syntax Notation 1 (ASN.1†)*. ASN.1 is a formal language that has two main features: a notation used in documents that humans read and a compact encoded representation of the same information used in communication protocols. In both cases, the precise, formal notation removes any possible ambiguities from both the representation and meaning. For example, instead of saying that a variable contains an integer value, a protocol designer who uses ASN.1 must state the exact form and range of each numeric value. Such precision is especially important when implementations include heterogeneous computers that do not all use the same representations for data items.

In addition to specifying the name and contents of each item, ASN.1 defines a set of *Basic Encoding Rules (BER)* that specify precisely how to encode both names and data items in a message. Thus, once the documentation of a MIB has been expressed using ASN.1, variables can be translated directly and mechanically into the encoded form used in messages. In summary:

> *The TCP/IP network management protocols use a formal notation called ASN.1 to define names and types for variables in the management information base. The precise notation makes the form and contents of variables unambiguous.*

29.8 Structure And Representation Of MIB Object Names

We said that ASN.1 specifies how to represent both data items and names. However, understanding the names used for MIB variables requires us to know about the underlying namespace. Names used for MIB variables are taken from the *object identifier* namespace administered by ISO and ITU. The key idea behind the object identifier namespace is that it provides a namespace in which all possible objects can be designated. The namespace is not restricted to variables used in network management — it includes names for arbitrary objects (e.g., each international protocol standard document has a name).

The object identifier namespace is *absolute (global)*, meaning that names are structured to make them globally unique. Like most namespaces that are large and absolute, the object identifier namespace is hierarchical. Authority for parts of the namespace is subdivided at each level, allowing individual groups to obtain authority to assign some of the names without consulting a central authority for each assignment‡.

The root of the object identifier hierarchy is unnamed, but has three direct descendants managed by: ISO, ITU, and jointly by ISO and ITU. The descendants are assigned both short text strings and integers that identify them (the text strings are used by humans to understand object names; computer software uses the integers to form compact, encoded representations of the names). ISO has allocated one subtree for use

---

†ASN.1 is usually pronounced by reading the dot: "A-S-N dot 1".

‡Readers should recall from the domain name system discussion in Chapter 23 how authority for a hierarchical namespace is subdivided.

by other national or international standards organizations (including U.S. standards organizations), and the U.S. National Institute for Standards and Technology† has allocated a subtree for the U.S. Department of Defense. Finally, the IAB has petitioned the
Department of Defense to allocate an Internet subtree in the namespace. Figure 29.4 illustrates pertinent parts of the object identifier hierarchy and shows the position of the
node used by TCP/IP network management protocols.

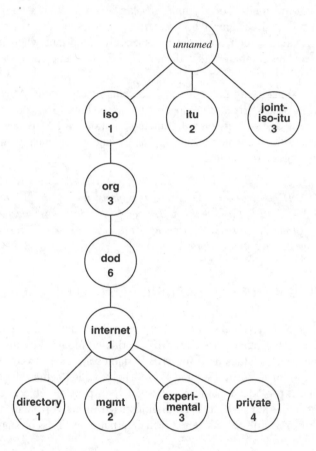

Figure 29.4 Part of the hierarchical object identifier namespace used to name
MIB variables. An object's name consists of the numeric labels
along a path from the root to the object.

The name of an object in the hierarchy is the sequence of numeric labels on the
nodes along a path from the root to the object. The sequence is written with periods
separating the individual components. For example, the name *1.3.6.1.2* denotes the
node labeled *mgmt*, the *Internet management* subtree. The MIB has been assigned a
node under the *mgmt* subtree with label *mib* and numeric value *1*. Because all MIB

---

†NIST was formerly the National Bureau of Standards.

variables fall under that node, they all have names beginning with the prefix *1.3.6.1.2.1.*

Earlier we said that the MIB groups variables into categories. The exact meaning of the categories can now be explained: they are the subtrees of the *mib* node of the object identifier namespace. Figure 29.5 illustrates the idea by showing part of the naming subtree under the *mib* node.

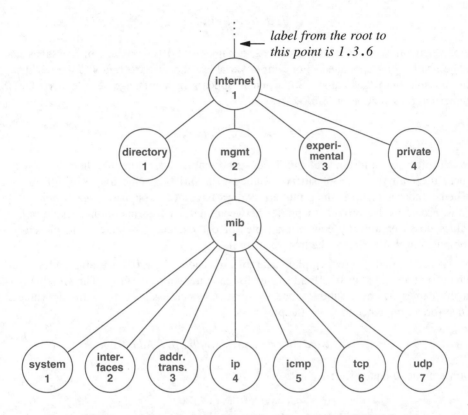

Figure 29.5 Part of the object identifier namespace under the IAB *mib* node. Each subtree corresponds to one of the categories of MIB variables.

Two examples will make the naming syntax clear. Figure 29.5 shows that the category labeled *ip* has been assigned the numeric value *4*. Thus, the names of all MIB variables corresponding to IP have an identifier that begins with the prefix *1.3.6.1.2.1.4*. If one wanted to write out the textual labels instead of the numeric representation, the name would be:

iso.org.dod.internet.mgmt.mib.ip

A MIB variable named *ipInReceives* has been assigned numeric identifier *3* under the *ip* node in the namespace, so its name is:

$$iso.org.dod.internet.mgmt.mib.ip.ipInReceives$$

and the corresponding numeric representation is:

$$1.3.6.1.2.1.4.3$$

When network management protocols use names of MIB variables in messages, each name has a suffix appended. For simple variables, the suffix *0* refers to the instance of the variable with that name. So, when it appears in a message sent to a router, the numeric representation of *ipInReceives* is:

$$1.3.6.1.2.1.4.3.0$$

which refers to the instance of *ipInReceives* on that router. Note that there is no way to guess the numeric value or suffix assigned to a variable. One must consult the published standards to find which numeric values have been assigned to each object type. Thus, programs that provide mappings between the textual form and underlying numeric values do so entirely by consulting tables of equivalences — there is no closed-form computation that performs the transformation.

As a second, more complex example, consider the MIB variable *ipAddrTable*, which contains a list of the IP addresses for each network interface. The variable exists in the namespace as a subtree under *ip*, and has been assigned the numeric value *20*. Therefore, a reference to it has the prefix:

$$iso.org.dod.internet.mgmt.mib.ip.ipAddrTable$$

with a numeric equivalent:

$$1.3.6.1.2.1.4.20$$

In programming language terms, we think of the IP address table as a one-dimensional array, where each element of the array consists of a structure (record) that contains five items: an IP address, the integer index of an interface corresponding to the entry, an IP subnet mask, an IP broadcast address, and an integer that specifies the maximum datagram size that the router will reassemble. Of course, it is unlikely that a router has such an array in memory. The router may keep this information in many variables or may need to follow pointers to find it. However, the MIB provides a name for the array as if it existed, and allows network management software on individual routers to map table references into appropriate internal variables. The point is:

Although they appear to specify details about data structures, MIB standards do not dictate the implementation. Instead, MIB definitions provide a uniform, virtual interface that managers use to access data; an agent must translate between the virtual items in a MIB and the internal implementation.

Using ASN.1 style notation, we can define *ipAddrTable*:

ipAddrTable ::= SEQUENCE OF IpAddrEntry

where *SEQUENCE* and *OF* are keywords that define an ipAddrTable to be a one-dimensional array of *IpAddrEntry*s. Each entry in the array is defined to consist of five fields (the definition assumes that *IpAddress* has already been defined).

```
IpAddrEntry ::= SEQUENCE {
    ipAdEntAddr
            IpAddress,
    ipAdEntIfIndex
            INTEGER,
    ipAdEntNetMask
            IpAddress,
    ipAdEntBcastAddr
            IpAddress,
    ipAdEntReasmMaxSize
            INTEGER (0..65535)
}
```

Further definitions must be given to assign numeric values to *ipAddrEntry* and to each item in the *IpAddrEntry* sequence. For example, the definition:

ipAddrEntry { ipAddrTable 1 }

specifies that *ipAddrEntry* falls under *ipAddrTable* and has numeric value *1*. Similarly, the definition:

ipAdEntNetMask { ipAddrEntry 3 }

assigns *ipAdEntNetMask* numeric value *3* under *ipAddrEntry*.

We said that *ipAddrTable* is like a one-dimensional array. However, there is a significant difference in the way programmers use arrays and the way network management software uses tables in the MIB. Programmers think of an array as a set of elements that have an index used to select a specific element. For example, the programmer might write *xyz[3]* to select the third element from array *xyz*. ASN.1 syntax does not use integer indices. Instead, MIB tables append a suffix onto the name to select a specific element in the table. For our example of an IP address table, the standard specifies that the suffix used to select an item consists of an IP address. Syntactically, the IP address (in dotted decimal notation) is concatenated onto the end of the object name to form the reference. Thus, to specify the network mask field in the IP address table entry corresponding to address 128.10.2.3, one uses the name:

iso.org.dod.internet.mgmt.mib.ip.ipAddrTable.ipAddrEntry.ipAdEntNetMask.128.10.2.3

which, in numeric form, becomes:

$$1.3.6.1.2.1.4.20.1.3.128.10.2.3$$

Although concatenating an index to the end of a name may seem awkward, it provides a powerful tool that allows clients to search tables without knowing the number of items or the type of data used as an index. The next section shows how network management protocols use this feature to step through a table one element at a time.

29.9 Simple Network Management Protocol

Network management protocols specify communication between the network management client program a manager invokes and a network management server program executing on a host or router. In addition to defining the form and meaning of messages exchanged and the representation of names and values in those messages, network management protocols also define administrative relationships among routers being managed. That is, they provide for authentication of managers.

One might expect network management protocols to contain a large number of commands. Some early protocols, for example, supported commands that allowed the manager to: *reboot* the system, *add* or *delete* routes, *disable* or *enable* a particular network interface, or *remove* cached address bindings. The main disadvantage of building management protocols around commands arises from the resulting complexity. The protocol requires a separate command for each operation on a data item. For example, the command to delete a routing table entry differs from the command to disable an interface. As a result, the protocol must change to accommodate new data items.

SNMP takes an interesting alternative approach to network management. Instead of defining a large set of commands, SNMP casts all operations in a *fetch-store paradigm*†. Conceptually, SNMP contains only two commands that allow a manager to fetch a value from a data item or store a value into a data item. All other operations are defined as side-effects of these two operations. For example, although SNMP does not have an explicit *reboot* operation, an equivalent operation can be defined by declaring a data item that gives the time until the next reboot and allowing the manager to assign the item a value (including zero).

---

†The fetch-store paradigm is derived from a management protocol system known as HEMS. See Partridge and Trewitt [RFCs 1021, 1022, 1023, and 1024] for details.

The chief advantages of using a fetch-store paradigm are stability, simplicity, and flexibility. SNMP is especially stable because its definition remains fixed, even though new data items are added to the MIB and new operations are defined as side-effects of storing into those items. SNMP is simple to implement, understand, and debug because it avoids the complexity of having special cases for each command. Finally, SNMP is especially flexible because it can accommodate arbitrary commands in an elegant framework.

From a manager's point of view, of course, SNMP remains hidden. The user interface to network management software can phrase operations as imperative commands (e.g., *reboot*). Thus, there is little visible difference between the way a manager uses SNMP and other network management protocols. In fact, vendors sell network management software that offers a graphical user interface. Such software displays diagrams of network connectivity, and uses a point-and-click style of interaction.

As Figure 29.6 shows, SNMP offers more than the two operations we have described.

Command	Meaning
get-request	Fetch a value from a specific variable
get-next-request	Fetch a value without knowing its exact name
get-bulk-request	Fetch a large volume of data (e.g., a table)
response	A response to any of the above requests
set-request	Store a value in a specific variable
inform-request	Reference to third-part data (e.g., for a proxy)
snmpv2-trap	Reply triggered by an event
report	Undefined at present

Figure 29.6 The set of possible SNMP operations. *Get-next-request* allows the manager to iterate through a table of items.

Operations *get-request* and *set-request* provide the basic fetch and store operations; *response* provides the reply. SNMP specifies that operations must be *atomic*, meaning that if a single SNMP message specifies operations on multiple variables, the server either performs all operations or none of them. In particular, no assignments will be made if any of them are in error. The *trap* operation allows managers to program servers to send information when an event occurs. For example, an SNMP server can be programmed to send a manager a *trap* message whenever one of the attached networks becomes unusable (i.e., an interface goes down).

29.9.1 Searching Tables Using Names

We said that ASN.1 does not provide mechanisms for declaring arrays or indexing them in the usual sense. However, it is possible to denote individual elements of a table by appending a suffix to the object identifier for the table. Unfortunately, a client program may wish to examine entries in a table for which it does not know all valid suffixes. The *get-next-request* operation allows a client to iterate through a table without knowing how many items the table contains. The rules are quite simple. When sending a *get-next-request*, the client supplies a prefix of a valid object identifier, *P*. The agent examines the set of object identifiers for all variables it controls, and sends a response for the variable that occurs next in lexicographic order. That is, the agent must know the ASN.1 names of all variables and be able to select the first variable with object identifier greater than *P*. Because the MIB uses suffixes to index a table, a client can send the prefix of an object identifier corresponding to a table and receive the first element in the table. The client can send the name of the first element in a table and receive the second, and so on.

Consider an example search. Recall that the *ipAddrTable* uses IP addresses to identify entries in the table. A client that does not know which IP addresses are in the table on a given router cannot form a complete object identifier. However, the client can still use the *get-next-request* operation to search the table by sending the prefix:

iso . org . dod . internet . mgmt . mib . ip . ipAddrTable . ipAddrEntry . ipAdEntNetMask

which, in numeric form, is:

$$1 . 3 . 6 . 1 . 2 . 1 . 4 . 20 . 1 . 3$$

The server returns the network mask field of the first entry in *ipAddrTable*. The client uses the full object identifier returned by the server to request the next item in the table.

29.10 SNMP Message Format

Unlike most TCP/IP protocols, SNMP messages do not have fixed fields. Instead, they use the standard ASN.1 encoding. Thus, a message can be difficult for humans to decode and understand. After examining the SNMP message definition in ASN.1 notation, we will review the ASN.1 encoding scheme briefly, and see an example of an encoded SNMP message.

Figure 29.7 shows how an SNMP message can be described with an ASN.1-style grammar. In general, each item in the grammar consists of a descriptive name followed by a declaration of the item's type. For example, an item such as

msgVersion INTEGER (0..2147483647)

declares the name *msgVersion* to be a nonnegative integer less than or equal to 2147483647.

```
SNMPv3Message ::=
    SEQUENCE {
        msgVersion  INTEGER (0..2147483647),
            -- note: version number 3 is used for SNMPv3
        msgGlobalData  HeaderData,
        msgSecurityParameters  OCTET STRING,
        msgData  ScopedPduData
    }
```

Figure 29.7 The SNMP message format in ASN.1-style notation. Text following two consecutive dashes is a comment.

As the figure shows, each SNMP message consists of four main parts: an integer that identifies the protocol *version*, additional header data, a set of security parameters, and a data area that carries the payload. A precise definition must be supplied for each of the terms used. For example, Figure 29.8 illustrates how the contents of the *HeaderData* section can be specified.

```
HeaderData ::= SEQUENCE {
    msgID  INTEGER (0..2147483647),
        -- used to match responses with requests
    msgMaxSize  INTEGER (484..2147483647),
        -- maximum size reply the sender can accept
    msgFlags  OCTET STRING (SIZE(1)),
        -- Individual flag bits specify message characteristics
        -- bit 7 authorization used
        -- bit 6 privacy used
        -- bit 5 reportability (i.e., a response needed)
    msgSecurityModel  INTEGER (1..2147483647)
        -- determines exact format of security parameters that follow
}
```

Figure 29.8 The definition of the *HeaderData* area in an SNMP message.

The data area in an SNMP message is divided into *Protocol Data Units* (*PDU*s). Each PDU consists of a request (sent by client) or a response (sent by an agent). SNMPv3 allows each PDU to be sent as plain text or to be encrypted for privacy. Thus, the grammar specifies a *CHOICE*. In programming language terminology, the concept is known as a *discriminated union*.

```
ScopedPduData ::= CHOICE {
    plaintext  ScopedPDU,
    encryptedPDU  OCTET STRING  -- encrypted ScopedPDU value
}
```

An encrypted PDU begins with an identifier of the *engine*† that produced it. The engine ID is followed by the name of the context and the octets of the encrypted message.

```
ScopedPDU ::= SEQUENCE {
    contextEngineID  OCTET STRING,
    contextName  OCTET STRING,
    data  ANY              -- e.g., a PDU as defined below
}
```

The item labeled *data* in the *ScopedPDU* definition has a type *ANY* because field *contextName* defines the exact details of the item. The SNMPv3 Message Processing Model (*v3MP*) specifies that the data must consist of one of the SNMP PDUs as Figure 29.9 illustrates:

```
PDU ::=
    CHOICE {
        get-request
            GetRequest-PDU,
        get-next-request
            GetNextRequest-PDU,
        get-bulk-request
            GetBulkRequest-PDU,
        response
            Response-PDU,
        set-request
            SetRequest-PDU,
        inform-request
            InformRequest-PDU,
        snmpV2-trap
            SNMPv2-Trap-PDU,
        report
            Report-PDU,
    }
```

Figure 29.9 The ASN.1 definitions of an SNMP PDU. The syntax for each request type must be specified further.

The definition specifies that each protocol data unit consists of one of eight types. To complete the definition of an SNMP message, we must further specify the syntax of the eight individual types. For example, Figure 29.10 shows the definition of a *get-request*.

---

†SNMPv3 distinguishes between an *application* that uses the service SNMP supplies and an *engine*, which is the underlying software that transmits requests and receives responses.

GetRequest-PDU ::= [0]
        IMPLICIT SEQUENCE {
          request-id
             Integer32,
          error-status
             INTEGER (0..18),
          error-index
             INTEGER (0..max-bindings),
          variable-bindings
             VarBindList
    }

Figure 29.10 The ASN.1 definition of a *get-request* message. Formally, the message is defined to be a *GetRequest-PDU*.

Further definitions in the standard specify the remaining undefined terms. Both *error-status* and *error-index* are single octet integers which contain the value zero in a request. If an error occurs, the values sent in a response identify the cause of the error. Finally, *VarBindList* contains a list of object identifiers for which the client seeks values. In ASN.1 terms, the definitions specify that *VarBindList* is a sequence of pairs of object name and value. ASN.1 represents the pairs as a sequence of two items. Thus, in the simplest possible request, *VarBindList* is a sequence of two items: a name and a *null*.

29.11 An Example Encoded SNMP Message

The encoded form of ASN.1 uses variable-length fields to represent items. In general, each field begins with a header that specifies the type of object and its length in bytes. For example, each *SEQUENCE* begins with an octet containing 30 (hexadecimal); the next octet specifies the number of following octets that constitute the sequence.

Figure 29.11 contains an example SNMP message that illustrates how values are encoded into octets. The message is a *get-request* that specifies data item *sysDescr* (numeric object identifier *1.3.6.1.2.1.1.1.0*). Because the example shows an actual message, it includes many details. In particular, the message contains a *msgSecurityParameters* section which has not been discussed above. This particular message uses the *UsmSecurityParameters* form of security parameters. It should be possible, however, to correlate other sections of the message with the definitions above.

```
   30      67      02      01      03
SEQUENCE len=103 INTEGER  len=1   vers=3


   30      0D      02      01      2A
SEQUENCE len=13 INTEGER   len=1   msgID=42


   02      02      08      00
INTEGER  len=2   maxmsgsize=2048


   04      01      04
 string  len=1  msgFlags=0x04 (bits mean noAuth, noPriv, reportable)


   02      01      03
INTEGER  len=1  used-based security


   04      25      30      23
 string  len=37 SEQUENCE len=35 UsmSecurityParameters


   04      0C      00      00      00      63      00      00      00
 string  len=12  msgAuthoritativeEngineID ...
   A1      C0      93      8E      23
engine is at IP address 192.147.142.35, port 161


   02      01      00
INTEGER  len=1  msgAuthoritativeEngineBoots=0


   02      01      00
INTEGER  len=1  msgAuthoritativeEngineTime=0


   04      09      43      6F      6D      65      72      42      6F
 string  len=9      -----msgUserName value is "ComerBook"-------------
   6F      6B
--------------


   04      00
 string  len=0   msgAuthenticationParameters (none)


   04      00
 string  len=0   msgPrivacyParameters (none)


   30      2C
SEQUENCE len=44  ScopedPDU


   04      0C      00      00      00      63      00      00
 string  len=12      -------------------contextEngineID-------
   00      A1      c0      93      8E      23
   ------------------------------------------------


   04      00
 string  len=0  contextName = "" (default)
```

```
CONTEXT [0] IMPLICIT SEQUENCE

   A0       1A
getreq. len=26

   02       02        4D       C6
INTEGER len=2     request-id = 19910

   02       01        00
INTEGER len=1 error-status = noError(0)

   02       01        00
INTEGER len=1 error-index=0

   30       0E
SEQUENCE   len=14 VarBindList

   30       0C
SEQUENCE   len=12 VarBind

   06                        08
OBJECT IDENTIFIER name    len=8

   2B       06       01       02       01       01       01       00
   1.3  .   6    .   1    .   2    .   1    .   1    .   1    .   0 (sysDescr.0)

   05       00
null    len=0 (no value specified)
```

Figure 29.11 The encoded form of an SNMPv3 *get-request* for data item *sys-Descr* with octets shown in hexadecimal and a comment explaining their meaning below. Related octets have been grouped onto lines; they are contiguous in the message.

As Figure 29.11 shows, the message starts with a code for *SEQUENCE* which has a length of 103 octets†. The first item in the sequence is a 1-octet integer that specifies the protocol *version*; the value *3* indicates that this is an SNMPv3 message. Successive fields define a message ID and the maximum message size the sender can accept in a reply. Security information, including the name of the user (*ComerBook*) follows the message header.

The *GetRequest-PDU* occupies the tail of the message. The sequence labeled *ScopedPDU* specifies a context in which to interpret the remainder of the message. The octet *A0* specifies the operation as a *get-Request*. Bit five of *A0* indicates a nonprimitive data type, and the high-order bit means the interpretation of the octet is *context specific*. That is, the hexadecimal value *A0* only specifies a *GetRequest-PDU* when used in context; it is not a universally reserved value. Following the request octet, the

---

†Sequence items occur frequently in an SNMP message because SNMP uses *SEQUENCE* instead of conventional programming language constructs like *array* or *struct*.

length octet specifies the request is *26* octets long. The request ID is *2* octets, but each of the error-status and error-index are one octet. Finally, the sequence of pairs contains one binding, a single object identifier bound to a *null* value. The identifier is encoded as expected except that the first two numeric labels are combined into a single octet.

29.12 New Features In SNMPv3

Version 3 of SNMP represents an evolution that follows and extends the basic framework of earlier versions. The primary changes arise in the areas of security and administration. The goals are twofold. First, SNMPv3 is designed to have both general and flexible security policies, making it possible for the interactions between a manager and managed devices to adhere to the security policies an organization specifies. Second, the system is designed to make administration of security easy.

To achieve generality and flexibility, SNMPv3 includes facilities for several aspects of security, and allows each to be configured independently. For example, v3 supports *message authentication* to ensure that instructions originate from a valid manager, *privacy* to ensure that no one can read messages as they pass between a manager's station and a managed device, and *authorization* and *view-based access control* to ensure that only authorized managers access particular items. To make the security system easy to configure or change, v3 allows *remote configuration*, meaning that an authorized manager can change the configuration of the security items listed above without being physically present at the device.

29.13 Summary

Network management protocols allow a manager to monitor and control routers and hosts. A network management client program executing on the manager's workstation contacts one or more servers, called agents, running on the devices to be controlled. Because an internet consists of heterogeneous machines and networks, TCP/IP management software executes as application programs and uses TCP/IP transport protocols (e.g., UDP) for communication between clients and servers.

The standard TCP/IP network management protocol is SNMP, the Simple Network Management Protocol. SNMP defines a low-level management protocol that provides two conceptual operations: fetch a value from a variable or store a value into a variable. In SNMP, other operations occur as side-effects of changing values in variables. SNMP defines the format of messages that travel between a manager's computer and a managed entity.

A set of companion standards to SNMP define the set of variables that a managed entity maintains. The set of variables constitute a Management Information Base (*MIB*). MIB variables are described using ASN.1, a formal language that provides a concise encoded form as well as a precise human-readable notation for names and objects. ASN.1 uses a hierarchical namespace to guarantee that all MIB names are globally unique while still allowing subgroups to assign parts of the namespace.

FOR FURTHER STUDY

Case et. al. [RFC 3410] presents an overview of SNMPv3, gives background and motivation, and discusses changes among the various versions. It also contains a summary of RFCs related to v3, and explains which v2 standards still apply. Many other RFCs discuss individual aspects of the protocol. For example, Wijnen et. al. [RFC 3415] presents the view-based access control model, and Case et. al. [RFC 3412] discusses message handling.

ISO standards 8824 and 8825 contain the specification for ASN.1 and specify the encoding. McCloghrie et. al. [RFCs 2578, 2579, 2580] define the language used for MIB modules and provide definitions of data types. Presuhn [RFC 3418] defines version 3 of the MIB.

EXERCISES

29.1   Capture an SNMP packet with a network analyzer and decode the fields.

29.2   Read the standard to find out how ASN.1 encodes the first two numeric values from an object identifier in a single octet. Why does it do so?

29.3   Read the two standards and compare SNMPv2 to SNMPv3. Under what circumstances are the v2 security features valid? Invalid?

29.4   Suppose the MIB designers need to define a variable that corresponds to a two-dimensional array. How can ASN.1 notation accommodate references to such a variable?

29.5   What are the advantages and disadvantages of defining globally unique ASN.1 names for MIB variables?

29.6   Consult the standards and match each item in Figure 29.11 with a corresponding definition.

29.7   If you have SNMP client code available, try using it to read MIB variables in a local router. What is the advantage of allowing arbitrary managers to read variables in all routers? The disadvantage?

29.8   Read the MIB specification to find the definition of variable *ipRoutingTable* that corresponds to an IP routing table. Design a program that will use SNMP to contact multiple routers and see if any entries in their routing tables cause a forwarding loop. Exactly what ASN.1 names should such a program generate?

29.9   Consider the implementation of an SNMP agent. Does it make sense to arrange MIB variables in memory exactly the way SNMP describes them? Why or why not?

29.10   Argue that SNMP is a misnomer because SNMP is not ''simple.''

29.11 Read about the IPsec security standard described in Chapter 30. If an organization uses IPsec, is the security in SNMPv3 also necessary? Why or why not?

29.12 Does it make sense to use SNMP to manage all devices? Why or why not? (Hint: consider a simple hardware device such as a dialup modem.)

Chapter Contents

30

Internet Security And Firewall Design (IPsec, SSL)

30.1 Introduction

Like the locks used to help keep tangible property secure, computers and data networks have provisions that help keep information secure. Security in an internet environment is both important and difficult. It is important because information has significant value — information can be bought and sold directly or used indirectly to create valuable artifacts. Security in an internet is difficult because security involves understanding when and how participating users, computers, services, and networks can trust one another as well as understanding the technical details of network hardware and protocols. A single weakness can compromise the security of an entire network. More important, because TCP/IP supports a wide diversity of users, services, and networks and because an internet can span many political and organizational boundaries, participating individuals and organizations may not agree on a level of trust or policies for handling data.

This chapter considers two fundamental techniques that form the basis for internet security: perimeter security and encryption. Perimeter security allows an organization to determine the services and networks it will make available to outsiders and the extent to which outsiders can use resources. Encryption handles most other aspects of security. We begin by reviewing a few basic concepts and terminology.

543

30.2 Protecting Resources

The terms *network security* and *information security* refer in a broad sense to confidence that information and services available on a network cannot be accessed by unauthorized users. Security implies safety, including assurance of data integrity, freedom from unauthorized access of computational resources, freedom from snooping or wiretapping, and freedom from disruption of service. Of course, just as no physical property is absolutely secure against crime, no network is completely secure. Organizations make an effort to secure networks for the same reason they make an effort to secure buildings and offices: basic security measures can discourage crime by making it significantly more difficult.

Providing security for information requires protecting both physical and abstract resources. Physical resources include passive storage devices such as disks and CD-ROMs as well as active devices such as users' computers. In a network environment, physical security extends to the cables, bridges, and routers that form the network infrastructure. Indeed, although physical security is seldom mentioned, it often plays an important role in an overall security plan. Obviously, physical security can prevent wiretapping. Good physical security can also eliminate sabotage (e.g., disabling a router to cause packets to be forwarded through an alternative, less secure path).

Protecting an abstract resource such as information is usually more difficult than providing physical security because information is elusive. Information security encompasses many aspects of protection:

- *Data Integrity.* A secure system must protect information from unauthorized change.

- *Data Availability.* The system must guarantee that outsiders cannot prevent legitimate access to data (e.g., any outsider should not be able to block customers from accessing a Web site).

- *Privacy Or Confidentiality.* The system must prevent outsiders from making copies of data as it passes across a network or understanding the contents if copies are made.

- *Authorization.* Although physical security often classifies people and resources into broad categories, (e.g., all nonemployees are forbidden from using a particular hallway), security for information usually needs to be more restrictive (e.g., some parts of an employee's record are available only to the personnel office, others are available only to the employee's boss, and others are available to the payroll office).

- *Authentication.* The system must allow two communicating entities to validate each other's identity.

- *Replay Avoidance.* To prevent outsiders from capturing copies of packets and using them later, the system must prevent a retransmitted copy of a packet from being accepted.

30.3 Information Policy

Before an organization can enforce network security, the organization must assess risks and develop a clear policy regarding information access and protection. The policy specifies who will be granted access to each piece of information, the rules an individual must follow in disseminating the information to others, and a statement of how the organization will react to violations.

An information policy begins with people because:

> *Humans are usually the most susceptible point in any security scheme. A worker who is malicious, careless, or unaware of an organization's information policy can compromise the best security.*

30.4 Internet Security

Internet security is difficult because datagrams traveling from source to destination often pass across many intermediate networks and through routers that are not owned or controlled by either the sender or the recipient. Thus, because datagrams can be intercepted or compromised, the contents cannot be trusted. As an example, consider a server that attempts to use *source authentication* to verify that requests originated from valid customers. Source authentication requires the server to examine the source IP address on each incoming datagram, and only accept requests from computers on an authorized list. Source authentication is *weak* because it can be broken easily. In particular, an intermediate router can watch traffic traveling to and from the server, and record the IP address of a valid customer. Later the intermediate router can manufacture a request that has the same source address (and intercept the reply). The point is:

> *An authorization scheme that uses a remote machine's IP address to authenticate its identity does not suffice in an unsecure internet. An imposter who gains control of an intermediate router can obtain access by impersonating an authorized client.*

Stronger authentication requires *encryption*. Careful choices of an encryption algorithm can make it virtually impossible for intermediate machines to decode messages or manufacture messages that are valid.

30.5 IP Security (IPsec)

The IETF has devised a set of protocols that provide secure Internet communication. Collectively known as *IPsec* (short for *IP security*), the protocols offer authentication and privacy services at the IP layer, and can be used with both IPv4 and IPv6†. More important, instead of completely specifying the functionality or the encryption algorithm to be used, the IETF chose to make the system both flexible and extensible. For example, an application that employs IPsec can choose whether to use an authentication facility that validates the sender or to use an encryption facility that also ensures the payload will remain confidential; the choices can be asymmetric (e.g., authentication in one direction, but not the other). Furthermore, IPsec does not restrict the user to a specific encryption or authentication algorithm. Instead, IPsec provides a general framework that allows each pair of communicating endpoints to choose algorithms and parameters (e.g., key size). To guarantee interoperability, IPsec does include a set of encryption algorithms that all implementations must recognize. The point is:

> *IPsec is not a single security protocol. Instead, IPsec provides a set of security algorithms plus a general framework that allows a pair of communicating entities to use whichever algorithms provide security appropriate for the communication.*

30.6 IPsec Authentication Header

Instead of changing the basic datagram header or creating an IP option, IPsec uses a separate *Authentication Header* (*AH*) to carry authentication information. Figure 30.1 illustrates the most straightforward use of an authentication header with IPv4.

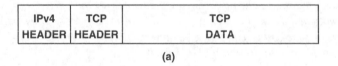

(a)

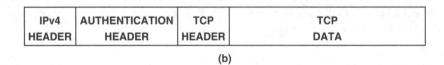

(b)

Figure 30.1 Illustration of (a) an IPv4 datagram, and (b) the same datagram after an IPsec authentication header has been added. The new header is inserted immediately after the IP header.

---

†The examples in this chapter focus on IPv4; Chapter 31 describes IPv6 in detail and illustrates how IPsec headers appear in IPv6 datagrams.

As the figure shows, IPsec inserts the authentication header immediately after the original IP header, but before the transport header. Furthermore, the *PROTOCOL* field in the IP header is changed to value *51* to indicate the presence of an authentication header.

If IPsec modifies the *PROTOCOL* field in the IP header, how does a receiver determine the type of information carried in the datagram? The authentication header has a *NEXT HEADER* field that specifies the type — IPsec records the original *PROTOCOL* value in the *NEXT HEADER* field. When a datagram arrives, the receiver uses security information from the authentication header to verify the sender, and uses the *NEXT HEADER* value to further demultiplex the datagram. Figure 30.2 illustrates the header format.

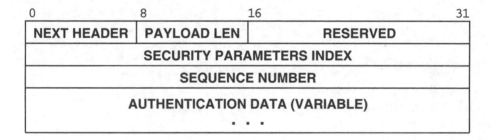

Figure 30.2 The IPsec authentication header format. The field labeled *NEXT HEADER* records the original value of the IP *PROTOCOL* field.

Interestingly, the *PAYLOAD LEN* field does not specify the size of the data area in the datagram. Instead, it specifies the length of the authentication header. Remaining fields are used to ensure security. Field *SEQUENCE NUMBER* contains a unique sequence number for each packet sent; the number starts at zero when a particular security algorithm is selected and increases monotonically. The *SECURITY PARAMETERS INDEX* field specifies the security scheme used, and the *AUTHENTICATION DATA* field contains data for the selected security scheme.

30.7 Security Association

To understand the reason for using a security parameters index, observe that a security scheme defines details that provide many possible variations. For example, the security scheme includes an authentication algorithm, a key (or keys) that the algorithm uses, a lifetime over which the key will remain valid, a lifetime over which the destination agrees to use the algorithm, and a list of source addresses that are authorized to use the scheme. Further observe that the information cannot fit into the header.

To save space in the header, IPsec arranges for each receiver to collect all the details about a security scheme into an abstraction known as a *security association* (*SA*).

Each SA is given a number, known as a *security parameters index*, through which it is identified. Before a sender can use IPsec to communicate with a receiver, the sender must know the index value for a particular SA. The sender then places the value in the field *SECURITY PARAMETERS INDEX* of each outgoing datagram.

Index values are not globally specified. Instead, each destination creates as many SAs as it needs, and assigns an index value to each. The destination can specify a lifetime for each SA, and can reuse index values once an SA becomes invalid. Consequently, the index cannot be interpreted without consulting the destination (e.g., the index *1* can have entirely different meanings to two destinations). To summarize:

> *A destination uses the security parameters index to identify the security association for a packet. The values are not global; a combination of destination address and security parameters index is needed to identify an SA.*

30.8 IPsec Encapsulating Security Payload

To handle privacy as well as authentication, IPsec uses an *Encapsulating Security Payload* (*ESP*), which is more complex than an authentication header. A value *50* in the *PROTOCOL* field of the datagram informs a receiver that the datagram carries ESP. Figure 30.3 illustrates the conceptual organization.

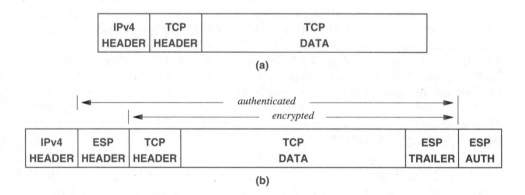

Figure 30.3 (a) A datagram, and (b) the same datagram using IPsec Encapsulating Security Payload. In practice, encryption means that fields are not easily identifiable.

As the figure shows, ESP adds three additional areas to the datagram. The *ESP HEADER* immediately follows the IP header and precedes the encrypted payload. The *ESP TRAILER* is encrypted along with the payload; a variable-size *ESP AUTH* field follows the encrypted section.

ESP uses many of the same items found in the authentication header, but rearranges their order. For example, the *ESP HEADER* consists of 8 octets that identify the security parameters index and a sequence number.

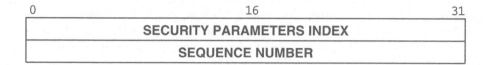

0	16	31
SECURITY PARAMETERS INDEX		
SEQUENCE NUMBER		

The *ESP TRAILER* consists of optional padding, a padding length field, *PAD LENGTH*, and a *NEXT HEADER* field that is followed by a variable amount of authentication data.

0	16	24	31
0 - 255 OCTETS OF PADDING	PAD LENGTH	NEXT HEADER	
ESP AUTHENTICATION DATA (VARIABLE)			

Padding is optional; it may be present for three reasons. First, some decryption algorithms require zeroes following an encrypted message. Second, note that the *NEXT HEADER* field is shown right-justified within a 4-octet field. The alignment is important because IPsec requires the authentication data that follows the trailer to be aligned at the start of a 4-octet boundary. Thus, padding may be needed to ensure alignment. Third, some sites may choose to add random amounts of padding to each datagram so eavesdroppers at intermediate points along the path cannot use the size of a datagram to guess its purpose.

30.9 Authentication And Mutable Header Fields

The IPsec authentication mechanism is designed to ensure that an arriving datagram is identical to the datagram sent by the source. However, such a guarantee is impossible to make. To understand why, recall that IP is a machine-to-machine layer, meaning that the layering principle only applies across one hop. In particular, each intermediate router decrements the time-to-live field and recomputes the checksum.

IPsec uses the term *mutable fields* to refer to IP header fields that are changed in transit. To prevent such changes causing authentication errors, IPsec specifically omits such fields from the authentication computation. Thus, when a datagram arrives, IPsec only authenticates immutable fields (e.g., the source address and protocol type).

30.10 IPsec Tunneling

Recall from Chapter 19 that VPN technology uses encryption along with IP-in-IP tunneling to keep inter-site transfers private. IPsec is specifically designed to accommodate an encrypted tunnel. In particular, the standard defines tunneled versions of both the authentication header and the encapsulating security payload. Figure 30.4 illustrates the layout of datagrams in tunneling mode.

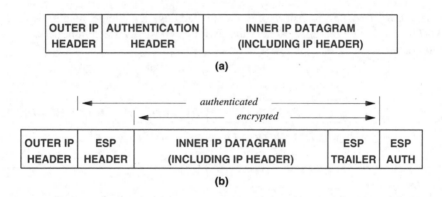

Figure 30.4 Illustration of IPsec tunneling mode for (a) authentication and (b) encapsulating security payload. The entire inner datagram is protected.

30.11 Required Security Algorithms

IPsec defines a minimal set of algorithms that are mandatory (i.e., that all implementations must supply). In each case, the standard defines specific uses. Figure 30.5 lists the required algorithms.

Authentication

HMAC with MD5	RFC 2403
HMAC with SHA-1	RFC 2404

Encapsulating Security Payload

DES in CBC mode	RFC 2405
HMAC with MD5	RFC 2403
HMAC with SHA-1	RFC 2404
Null Authentication	
Null Encryption	

Figure 30.5 The security algorithms that are mandatory for IPsec.

30.12 Secure Sockets (SSL and TLS)

By the mid 1990s when it became evident that security was important for Internet commerce, several groups proposed security mechanisms for use with the Web. Although not formally adopted by the IETF, one of the proposals has become a de facto standard.

Known as the *Secure Sockets Layer* (*SSL*), the technology was originally developed by Netscape, Inc. As the name implies, SSL resides at the same layer as the socket API. When a client uses SSL to contact a server, the SSL protocol allows each side to authenticate itself to the other. The two sides then negotiate to select an encryption algorithm that they both support. Finally, SSL allows the two sides to establish an encrypted connection (i.e., a connection that uses the chosen encryption algorithm to guarantee privacy). The IETF used SSL as the basis for a protocol known as *Transport Layer Security* (*TLS*). SSL and TLS are so closely related that they both use the same well-known port and most implementations of SSL support TLS.

30.13 Firewalls And Internet Access

Mechanisms that control *internet access* handle the problem of screening a particular network or an organization from unwanted communication. Such mechanisms can help prevent outsiders from: obtaining information, changing information, or disrupting communication on an organization's intranet. Successful access control requires a careful combination of restrictions on network topology, intermediate information staging, and packet filters.

A single technique, known as an *internet firewall†*, has emerged as the basis for internet access control. An organization places a firewall at its connection to external networks (e.g., the global Internet). A firewall partitions an internet into two regions, referred to informally as the *inside* and *outside*.

---

†The term *firewall* is derived from building architecture in which a firewall is a thick, fireproof partition that makes a section of a building impenetrable to fire.

30.14 Multiple Connections And Weakest Links

Although the concept seems simple, details complicate firewall construction. First, an organization's intranet can have multiple external connections. The organization must form a *security perimeter* by installing a firewall at each external connection. To guarantee that the perimeter is effective, all firewalls must be configured to use exactly the same access restrictions. Otherwise, it may be possible to circumvent the restrictions imposed by one firewall by entering the organization's internet through another†.

We can summarize:

> *An organization that has multiple external connections must install a firewall on each external connection and must coordinate all firewalls. Failure to restrict access identically on all firewalls can leave the organization vulnerable.*

30.15 Firewall Implementation And Packet Filters

How should a firewall be implemented? In theory, a firewall simply blocks all unauthorized communication between computers in the organization and computers outside the organization. In practice, the details depend on the network technology, the capacity of the connection, the traffic load, and the organization's policies. No single solution works for all organizations — firewall systems are designed to be configurable. Informally called a *packet filter*, the mechanism requires the manager to specify how the router should dispose of each datagram. For example, the manager might choose to *filter* (i.e. block) all datagrams that come from one source and allow those from another, or a manager might choose to block all datagrams destined for some TCP ports and allow datagrams destined for others.

To operate at network speeds, a packet filter needs hardware and software optimized for the task. Many commercial routers include separate hardware for high-speed packet filtering (e.g., a board in the router). Once a manager configures it, the filter operates at wire speed without delaying packets.

Because TCP/IP does not dictate a standard for packet filters, each router vendor is free to choose the capabilities of their packet filter as well as the interface a manager uses to configure the filter. Some routers permit a manager to configure separate filter actions for each interface, while others have a single configuration for all interfaces. Usually, a packet filter allows a manager to specify arbitrary combinations of source IP address, destination IP address, protocol, source protocol port number, and destination protocol port number. For example, Figure 30.6 illustrates a filter specification.

In the example, the manager has chosen to block incoming datagrams destined for FTP (TCP port *21*), TELNET (TCP port *23*), WHOIS (UDP port *43*), TFTP (UDP port *69*), or FINGER (TCP port *79*), and blocks outgoing datagrams that originate from any

---

†The well-known idea that security is only as strong as the weakest point has been termed the *weakest link axiom* in reference to the adage that a chain is only as strong as its weakest link.

host address matching the 16-bit prefix of *128.5.0.0* that are destined for a remote e-mail server (TCP port *25*).

ARRIVES ON INTERFACE	IP SOURCE	IP DEST.	PROTOCOL	SOURCE PORT	DEST. PORT
2	*	*	TCP	*	21
2	*	*	TCP	*	23
1	128.5.0.0 / 16	*	TCP	*	25
2	*	*	UDP	*	43
2	*	*	UDP	*	69
2	*	*	TCP	*	79

Figure 30.6 A router with two interfaces and an example datagram filter specification. A router that includes a packet filter forms the basic building block of a firewall.

30.16 Security And Packet Filter Specification

Although the example filter configuration in Figure 30.6 specifies a small list of services to be blocked, such an approach does not work well for an effective firewall. There are three reasons. First, the number of well-known ports is large and growing rapidly. Thus, listing each service requires a manager to update the list continually; an error of omission can leave the firewall vulnerable. Second, much of the traffic on an internet does not travel to or from a well-known port. In addition to programmers who can choose port numbers for their private client-server applications, services like *Remote Procedure Call* (*RPC*) assign ports dynamically. Third, listing ports of well-known services leaves the firewall vulnerable to *tunneling*. Tunneling can circumvent security if a host or router on the inside agrees to accept encapsulated datagrams from an outsider, remove one layer of encapsulation, and forward the datagram on to the service that would otherwise be restricted by the firewall.

How can a firewall use a packet filter effectively? The answer lies in reversing the idea of a filter: instead of specifying the datagrams that should be filtered, a firewall should be configured to block all datagrams except those destined for specific networks, hosts, and protocol ports for which external communication has been approved. Thus, a manager begins with the assumption that communication is not allowed, and then must examine the organization's information policy carefully before enabling any port. In fact, many packet filters allow a manager to specify a set of datagrams to admit instead of a set of datagrams to block. We can summarize:

> *To be effective, a firewall that uses datagram filtering should restrict access to all IP sources, IP destinations, protocols, and protocol ports except those computers, networks, and services the organization explicitly decides to make available externally. A packet filter that allows a manager to specify which datagrams to admit instead of which datagrams to block can make such restrictions easy to specify.*

30.17 The Consequence Of Restricted Access For Clients

A blanket prohibition on datagrams arriving for an unknown protocol port seems to solve many potential security problems by preventing outsiders from accessing arbitrary servers in the organization. Such a firewall has an interesting consequence: it also prevents an arbitrary computer inside the firewall from becoming a client that accesses a service outside the firewall. To understand why, recall that although each server operates at a well-known port, a client does not. When a client program begins execution, it requests the operating system to select a protocol port number that is neither among the well-known ports nor currently in use on the client's computer. When it attempts to communicate with a server outside the organization, a client will generate one or more datagrams and send them to the server. Each outgoing datagram has the client's protocol port as the source port and the server's well-known protocol port as the destination port. The firewall will not block such datagrams as they leave. When it generates a response, the server reverses the protocol ports. The client's port becomes the destination port and the server's port becomes the source port. When the datagram carrying the response reaches the firewall, however, it will be blocked because the destination port is not approved. Thus, we can see an important idea:

> *If an organization's firewall restricts incoming datagrams except for ports that correspond to services the organization makes available externally, an arbitrary application inside the organization cannot become a client of a server outside the organization.*

30.18 Stateful Firewalls

How can arbitrary clients within the organization be allowed to access services on the Internet without admitting incoming datagrams that are destined to arbitrary protocol ports? The answer lies in a technique known as a *stateful firewall*. In essence, the firewall watches outgoing connections and adapts the filter rules accordingly to accommodate reply packets.

As an example of a stateful firewall, suppose a client on the inside of an organization forms a TCP connection to a web server. If the client has source IP address I_1 and source TCP port P_1 and connects to a web server at port 80 with IP address I_2, the outgoing SYN segment that initiates the connection will pass through the firewall, which records the tuple:

$$(I_1, P_1, I_2, 80)$$

When the server returns a SYN+ACK, the firewall will match the two endpoints to the tuple that was stored, and the incoming segment will be admitted.

Interestingly, a stateful firewall does not permit clients inside the organization to initiate connections to arbitrary destinations. Instead, all actions in the stateful firewall are driven by a set of packet filter rules. Thus, a firewall administrator can still choose whether to permit or deny transit for a given packet. In the case of a packet that is allowed to pass through the firewall, the filter rule can further specify whether to record state information that will permit a reply to be returned.

How should state be managed in a stateful firewall? There are two broad approaches: a firewall can use *soft state* by setting a timer that removes inactive state information after a timeout period, and *connection monitoring* in which the firewall watches packets on the flow and removes state information when the flow terminates (e.g., when a FIN is received on a TCP connection). Even if a stateful firewall attempts to monitor connections, soft state is usually a backup to handle cases such as a UDP flow that does not have explicit termination.

30.19 Content Protection And Proxies

The mechanisms described above focus on access. Another aspect of security focuses on content. We know, for example, that an imported file or e-mail message can contain a virus. In general, such problems can only be eliminated by a system that examines incoming content.

Inspection of content at the packet level is impractical because packets can arrive out of order and content can be divided among many packets. Thus, the only practical way to examine content consists of extracting the content from a connection and then examining the result before allowing it to pass into the organization.

A mechanism that examines content must act as an *application proxy*. For example, an organization can run a file transfer proxy that intercepts each outgoing FTP request, fetches a copy of the requested file, scans the copy for viruses, and if the copy is found to be clean, completes transfer of the copy to the client. Similarly, an organization can run a web proxy. Note that an application proxy can be *transparent* (i.e., except for a delay, the client does not realize a proxy has intercepted a request) or *non-transparent* (i.e., the client must be configured to use a specific proxy).

Although many organizations use a stateful firewall to protect the organization against random probes from the outside, fewer check content. Thus, it is typical to find an organization that is immune to arbitrary attacks from the outside, but is still plagued with e-mail viruses and trojan horse problems when an unsuspecting employee imports a program that can breach a firewall by forming an outgoing connection.

30.20 Monitoring And Logging

Monitoring is one of the most important aspects of a firewall design. The network manager responsible for a firewall needs to be aware of attempts to bypass security. Unless a firewall reports incidents, a manager may be unaware of problems.

Monitoring can be *active* or *passive*. In active monitoring, a firewall notifies a manager whenever an incident occurs. The chief advantage of active monitoring is speed — a manager finds out about a potential problem immediately. The chief disadvantage is that active monitors often produce so much information that a manager cannot comprehend it or notice problems. Thus, most managers prefer passive monitoring, or a combination of passive monitoring with a few high-risk incidents also reported by an active monitor.

In passive monitoring, a firewall logs a record of each incident in a file on disk. A passive monitor usually records information about normal traffic (e.g., simple statistics) as well as datagrams that are filtered. A manager can access the log at any time; most managers use a computer program. The chief advantage of passive monitoring arises from its record of events — a manager can consult the log to observe trends and when a security problem does occur, review the history of events that led to the problem. More important, a manager can analyze the log periodically (e.g., daily) to determine whether attempts to access the organization increase or decrease over time.

30.21 Summary

Security problems arise because an internet can connect organizations that do not have mutual trust. Several technologies are available to help ensure that information remains secure when being sent across an internet. The Secure Sockets Layer (SSL) protocol adds encryption and authentication to the socket API. IPsec allows a user to choose between two basic schemes: one that provides authentication of the datagram and one that provides authentication plus privacy. IPsec modifies a datagram either by inserting an Authentication Header or by using an Encapsulating Security Payload, which inserts a header and trailer and encrypts the data being sent. IPsec provides a general framework that allows each pair of communicating entities to choose an encryption algorithm. Because security is often used with tunneling (e.g., in a VPN), IPsec defines a secure tunnel mode.

The firewall mechanism is used to control internet access. An organization places a firewall at each external connection to guarantee that the organization's intranet remains free from unauthorized traffic. A firewall contains a packet filter that an administrator must configure to specify which packets can pass in each direction. A stateful firewall can be configured so the firewall automatically allows reply packets once an outgoing connection has been established.

Although it provides access protection, a firewall does not examine or control the content. Thus, using a firewall to restrict access does not protect the site against all problems. To protect against vulnerabilities such as viruses and other unwanted content, an organization must use application proxies that examine content before admitting the data.

FOR FURTHER STUDY

In the mid 1990s, the IETF announced a major emphasis on security, and required each working group to consider the security implications of its designs. Consequently, many RFCs address issues of internet security and propose policies, procedures, and mechanisms. Dierks and Allen [RFC 2246] defines version 1 of TLS. Kent and Atkinson [RFC 2401] defines the IPsec architecture. Kent and Atkinson [RFC 2402] specifies the IPsec authentication header, and [RFC 2406] specifies the encapsulating security payload.

Many RFCs describe security for particular application protocols. For example, Wijnen et. al. [RFC 3415] presents the view-based security model, and Blumenthal and Wijnen [RFC 3414] presents a user-based security model. Both models are intended for use with SNMPv3.

Cheswick et. al. [2003] discusses firewalls and other topics related to the secure operation of TCP/IP internets. Kohl and Neuman [RFC 1510] describes the *kerberos* authentication service, and Borman [RFC 1411] discusses how *kerberos* can be used to authenticate TELNET.

EXERCISES

30.1   Read the description of a packet filter for a commercially available router. What features does it offer?

30.2   Collect a log of all traffic entering your site. Analyze the log to determine the percentage of traffic that arrives from or is destined to a well-known protocol port. Do the results surprise you?

30.3   If encryption software is available on your computer, measure the time required to encrypt a 10 Mbyte file, transfer it to another computer, and decrypt it. Compare the result to the time required for the transfer if no encryption is used.

30.4   Survey users at your site to determine if they send sensitive information in e-mail. Are users aware that SMTP transfers messages in ASCII, and that anyone watching network traffic can see the contents of an e-mail message?

30.5   Interview IT personnel at your site to see if they have configured SMTP servers to use SSL or other encryption technology automatically whenever possible (e.g., for all internal transfers).

30.6   Survey employees at your site to find out how many use modems and personal computers to import or export information. Ask if they understand the organization's information policy.

30.7   Can a firewall be used with other protocol suites such as AppleTalk or Netware? Why or why not?

30.8   Can a firewall be combined with NAT? What are the consequences?

30.9   The military only releases information to those who "need to know." Will such a scheme work for all information in your organization? Why or why not?

30.10   Give two reasons why the group of people who administer an organization's security policies should be separate from the group of people who administer the organization's computer and network systems.

30.11   Some organizations use firewalls to isolate groups of users internally. Give examples of ways that internal firewalls can improve network performance and examples of ways internal firewalls can degrade network performance.

30.12   If your organization uses IPsec, find out which algorithms are being used. What is the key size?

Chapter Contents

31

A Next Generation IP (IPv6)

31.1 Introduction

Evolution of TCP/IP technology has always been intertwined with evolution of the global Internet. With hundreds of millions of users at sites around the world depending on the global Internet as part of their daily work environment, it might appear that we have passed the early stages of development and now have a completely stable production facility. Despite appearances, however, neither the Internet nor the TCP/IP protocol suite is static. Researchers and engineers discover new ways to use the technology and improve the underlying mechanisms.

The purpose of this chapter is to consider the ongoing evolutionary process and examine one of the most significant engineering efforts: a proposed revision of IP. If the proposal is adopted by vendors, it will have a major impact on the protocols and the global Internet.

31.2 Why Change?

In the early 1990s, researchers argued that the current Internet was insufficient for new applications such as voice and video. They further argued that growth of the Internet, which was doubling in size every nine months or faster, would quickly exhaust the set of available addresses. Since then, two things have become apparent. First, applications such as telephony work well over the existing Internet. Second, CIDR addressing and NAT have provided the needed address extensions; current projections suggest that we will have enough addresses until 2022 (2028 if unused addresses are reclaimed).

31.3 Beyond IPv4

Version *4* of the Internet Protocol (*IPv4*) was the first working version; it has remained almost unchanged since its inception in the late 1970s. The longevity of version *4* shows that the design is flexible and powerful. Since the time IPv4 was designed, processor performance has increased over three orders of magnitude, typical memory sizes have increased by over a factor of 400, bandwidth of the highest-speed links in the Internet has risen by a factor of 150,000. LAN technologies have emerged, and the number of hosts on the Internet has risen from a handful to hundreds of millions.

Chapter 9 describes the main motivation for updating IP: the eventual address space limitations. When IP was designed, a 32-bit address space was more than sufficient. Only a handful of organizations used a LAN, and none had a PC. Now, however, even small corporations have LANs and multiple computers. If each cell phone is assigned an IP address, addresses will be exhausted quickly.

31.4 The Road To A New Version Of IP

It took several years for the IETF to formulate a new version of IP. Because the IETF produces *open* standards, it invited representatives from the many communities to participate in the process. Computer manufacturers, hardware and software vendors, users, managers, programmers, telephone companies, and the cable television industry all specified their requirements for the next version of IP, and all commented on specific proposals.

Many designs were proposed to serve a particular purpose or a particular community. In the end, a design known as *SIP†* (*Simple IP*) became the basis for an extended proposal that included ideas from other proposals. The extended version was named *Simple IP Plus* (*SIPP*), and eventually emerged as the design selected as a basis for the next IP.

31.5 The Name Of The Next IP

The IETF decided to assign the revision of IP version number *6*, and to name it *IPv6* (it was originally known as ''IP — The Next Generation,'' (*IPng*). Version number *5* was skipped after a series of mistakes and misunderstandings. Choosing to number the new version *6* eliminated confusion and ambiguity.

---

†The acronym *SIP* now refers to the *Session Initiation Protocol*.

31.6 Features Of IPv6

The proposed IPv6 protocol retains many of the features that contributed to the success of IPv4. In fact, the designers have characterized IPv6 as being basically the same as IPv4 with only minor modifications. For example, IPv6 still supports connectionless delivery (i.e., each datagram is routed independently), allows the sender to choose the size of a datagram, and requires the sender to specify the maximum number of hops a datagram can make before being terminated. As we will see, IPv6 also retains most of the concepts provided by IPv4 options, including facilities for fragmentation and source routing.

Despite many conceptual similarities, IPv6 changes most of the protocol details. For example, IPv6 uses larger addresses, and adds a few new features. More important, IPv6 completely revises the datagram format by replacing IPv4's variable-length options field by a series of fixed-format headers. We will examine details after considering major changes and the underlying motivation for each.

The changes introduced by IPv6 can be grouped into seven categories:

- *Larger Addresses.* The new address size is the most noticeable change. IPv6 quadruples the size of an IPv4 address from 32 bits to 128 bits.

- *Extended Address Hierarchy.* IPv6 uses the larger address space to create additional levels of addressing hierarchy (e.g., to allow an ISP to allocate blocks of addresses to each customer).

- *Flexible Header Format.* IPv6 uses an entirely new and incompatible datagram format that includes a set of optional headers.

- *Improved Options.* IPv6 allows a datagram to include optional control information; IPv6 options provide additional facilities not available in IPv4.

- *Provision For Protocol Extension.* Instead of specifying all details, the IPv6 extension capability allows the IETF to adapt the protocol to new network hardware and new applications.

- *Support For Autoconfiguration And Renumbering.* IPv6 allows computers on an isolated network to assign local addresses automatically; the design also allows a manager to renumber networks at a site dynamically.

- *Support For Resource Allocation.* IPv6 includes a flow abstraction and bits for differentiated service (DiffServ) specification. The latter is identical to IPv4 DiffServ.

31.7 General Form Of An IPv6 Datagram

IPv6 completely changes the datagram format. As Figure 31.1 shows, an IPv6 datagram has a fixed-size *base header* followed by zero or more *extension headers*, followed by data.

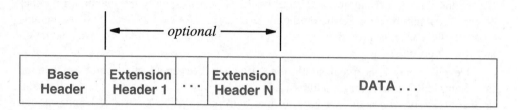

Figure 31.1 The general form of an IPv6 datagram with multiple headers. Only the base header is required; extension headers are optional.

31.8 IPv6 Base Header Format

Although it must accommodate larger addresses, an IPv6 base header contains less information than an IPv4 datagram header. Options and some of the fixed fields that appear in an IPv4 datagram header have been moved to extension headers in IPv6. In general, the changes in the datagram header reflect changes in the protocol:

- Alignment has been changed from 32-bit to 64-bit multiples.

- The header length field has been eliminated, and the datagram length field has been replaced by a *PAYLOAD LENGTH* field.

- The size of source and destination address fields has been increased to 16 octets each.

- Fragmentation information has been moved out of fixed fields in the base header into an extension header.

- The *TIME-TO-LIVE* field has been replaced by a *HOP LIMIT* field.

- The *SERVICE TYPE* is renamed to be a *TRAFFIC CLASS* field, and extended with a *FLOW LABEL* field.

- The *PROTOCOL* field has been replaced by a field that specifies the type of the next header.

Figure 31.2 shows the contents and format of an IPv6 base header. Several fields in an IPv6 base header correspond directly to fields in an IPv4 header. As in IPv4, the initial 4-bit *VERS* field specifies the version of the protocol; *VERS* always contains 6 in an IPv6 datagram. As in IPv4, the *SOURCE ADDRESS* and *DESTINATION ADDRESS* fields specify the addresses of the sender and intended recipient. In IPv6, however, each address requires 16 octets. The *HOP LIMIT* field corresponds to the IPv4 *TIME-TO-LIVE* field. Unlike IPv4, which interprets a time-to-live as a combination of hop-count and maximum time, IPv6 interprets the value as giving a strict bound on the maximum number of hops a datagram can make before being discarded.

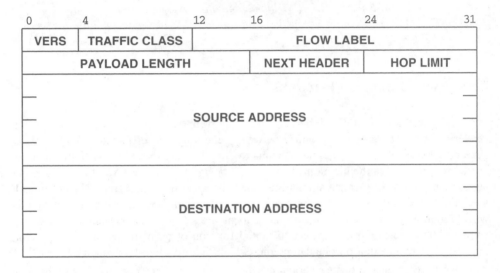

Figure 31.2 The format of the 40-octet IPv6 base header. Each IPv6 datagram begins with a base header.

IPv6 handles datagram length specifications in a new way. First, because the size of the base header is fixed at 40 octets, the base header does not include a field for the header length. Second, IPv6 replaces IPv4's datagram length field by a 16-bit *PAY-LOAD LENGTH* field that specifies the number of octets carried in the datagram excluding the header itself. Thus, an IPv6 datagram can contain 64K octets of data.

Two fields in the base header are used in making forwarding decisions. The IPv4 *SERVICE CLASS* field has been renamed *TRAFFIC CLASS*. In addition, a new mechanism in IPv6 supports resource reservation and allows a router to associate each datagram with a given resource allocation. The underlying abstraction, a *flow*, consists of a path through an internet along which intermediate routers guarantee a specific quality of service. Field *FLOW LABEL* in the base header contains information that routers use to associate a datagram with a specific flow and priority. For example, two applications that need to send video can establish a flow on which the delay and bandwidth is guaranteed. Alternatively, a network provider may require a subscriber to specify the quality of service desired, and then use a flow to limit the traffic a specific computer or a specific application sends. Note that flows can also be used within a given organization to manage network resources and ensure that all applications receive a fair share. A router uses the combination of datagram source address and flow identifier when associating a datagram with a specific flow. To summarize:

> *Each IPv6 datagram begins with a 40-octet base header that includes fields for the source and destination addresses, the maximum hop limit, the traffic class, the flow label, and the type of the next header. Thus, an IPv6 datagram must contain at least 40 octets in addition to the data.*

31.9 IPv6 Extension Headers

The paradigm of a fixed base header followed by a set of optional extension headers was chosen as a compromise between generality and efficiency. To be totally general, IPv6 needs to include mechanisms to support functions such as fragmentation, source routing, and authentication. However, choosing to allocate fixed fields in the datagram header for all mechanisms is inefficient because most datagrams do not use all mechanisms; the large IPv6 address size exacerbates the inefficiency. For example, when sending a datagram across a single local area network, a header that contains empty address fields can occupy a substantial fraction of each frame. More important, the designers realize that no one can predict which facilities will be needed.

The IPv6 extension header paradigm works similar to IPv4 options — a sender can choose which extension headers to include in a given datagram and which to omit. Thus, extension headers provide maximum flexibility. We can summarize:

> *IPv6 extension headers are similar to IPv4 options. Each datagram includes extension headers for only those facilities that the datagram uses.*

31.10 Parsing An IPv6 Datagram

Each of the base and extension headers contains a *NEXT HEADER* field that intermediate routers and the final destination use to parse the datagram. Processing is sequential — the *NEXT HEADER* field in each header tells what follows. For example, Figure 31.3 shows the *NEXT HEADER* fields of three datagrams that contain zero, one, and two extension headers.

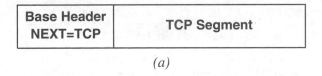

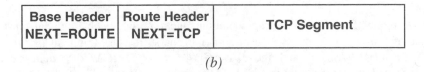

Figure 31.3 Three datagrams with (a) only a base header, (b) a base header and one extension, and (c) a base header plus two extensions. The *NEXT HEADER* field in each header specifies the type of the following header.

To speed processing, IPv6 requires that extension headers used by intermediate routers be placed before extension headers used by the final destination. IPv6 uses the term *hop-by-hop header* to refer to an extension header that an intermediate router must process. Thus, hop-by-hop headers precede end-to-end headers.

31.11 IPv6 Fragmentation And Reassembly

Fragmentation of IPv6 datagrams is allowed; an extension header is used to specify that a datagram is a fragment. As in IPv4, IPv6 arranges for the ultimate destination to perform datagram reassembly. However, the designers chose to make changes that avoid fragmentation by routers. Recall that IPv4 requires an intermediate router to fragment any datagram that is too large for the MTU of the network over which it must travel. In IPv6, fragmentation is end-to-end; no fragmentation occurs in intermediate routers. The source, which is responsible for fragmentation, has two choices: it can either use the *guaranteed minimum MTU* of *1280* octets or perform *Path MTU Discovery* to identify the minimum MTU along the path to the destination. In either case, the source fragments the datagram so that each fragment is less than the expected path MTU. Figure 31.4 shows the contents of a *Fragment Extension Header*.

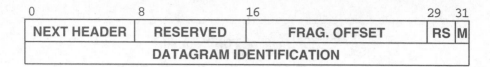

Figure 31.4 The format of a Fragment Extension Header.

IPv6 retains the basic IPv4 fragmentation functionality. Each fragment must be a multiple of *8* octets, the single bit in the *M* field marks the last fragment like the IPv4 *MORE FRAGMENTS* bit, and the *DATAGRAM IDENTIFICATION* field carries a unique ID that the receiver uses to group fragments†. Finally, field *RS* is currently reserved; the two bits are set to zero on transmission and ignored by the receiver.

31.12 The Consequence Of End-To-End Fragmentation

The motivation for using end-to-end fragmentation lies in its ability to reduce overhead in routers and permit each router to handle more datagrams per unit time. Indeed, the CPU overhead required for IPv4 fragmentation can be significant — in a conventional router, the CPU can reach 100% utilization if the router fragments all datagrams it receives. However, end-to-end fragmentation has an important consequence: it alters the fundamental IPv4 assumption that routes change dynamically.

To understand the consequence of end-to-end fragmentation, recall that IPv4 is designed to permit routes to change at any time. For example, if a network or router fails, traffic can be routed along a different path. The chief advantage of such a system is flexibility — traffic can be routed along an alternate path without disrupting service and without informing the source or destination. In IPv6, however, routes cannot be changed as easily because a change in a route can also change the path MTU. If the path MTU along a new route is less than the path MTU along the original route, either an intermediate router must fragment the datagram or the original source must be informed. The problem can be summarized:

> An internet protocol that uses end-to-end fragmentation requires a sender to discover the path MTU to each destination, and to fragment any outgoing datagram that is larger than the path MTU. End-to-end fragmentation does not accommodate route changes.

To solve the problem of route changes that affect the path MTU, IPv6 includes a new ICMP error message. When a router discovers that fragmentation is needed, it sends the message back to the source. When it receives such a message, the source performs another path MTU discovery to determine the new minimum MTU, and then fragments datagrams according to the new value.

---

†IPv6 expands the IPv4 *IDENTIFICATION* field to 32 bits to accommodate higher-speed networks.

31.13 IPv6 Source Routing

IPv6 retains the ability for a sender to specify a loose source route. Unlike IPv4, in which source routing is provided by options, IPv6 uses a separate extension header. As Figure 31.5 shows, the first four fields of the Routing Header are fixed. Field *ROUTING TYPE* specifies the type of routing information; the only type that has been defined, type *0*, corresponds to loose source routing. The *TYPE-SPECIFIC DATA* field contains a list of addresses of routers through which the datagram must pass. Field *SEG LEFT* specifies the total number of addresses in the list. Finally field *HDR EXT LEN* specifies the size of the Routing Header.

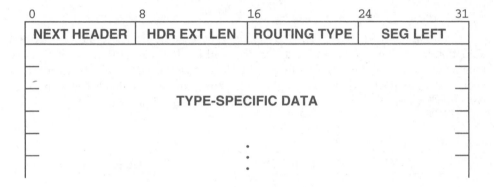

Figure 31.5 The format of an IPv6 Routing Header. Only type 0 (loose source route) is currently defined.

31.14 IPv6 Options

It may seem that IPv6 extension headers completely replace IPv4 options. However, the designers propose two additional IPv6 extension headers to accommodate miscellaneous information not included in other extension headers. The additional headers are a *hop by hop extension header* and an *end to end extension header*. As the names imply, the two headers separate the set of options that should be examined at each hop from the set that are only interpreted at the destination.

Although each of the two option headers has a unique type code, both headers use the format illustrated in Figure 31.6.

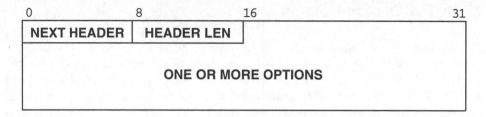

Figure 31.6 The format of an IPv6 option extension header. Both the *hop-by-hop* and *end-to-end* option headers use the same format; the *NEXT HEADER* field of the previous header distinguishes between the two types.

As usual, field *NEXT HEADER* gives the type of the header that follows. Because an option header does not have fixed size, the field labeled *HEADER LEN* specifies the total length of the header. The area labeled *ONE OR MORE OPTIONS* represents a sequence of individual options. Figure 31.7 illustrates how each individual option is encoded with a type, length, and value†; options are not aligned or padded.

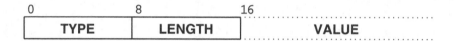

Figure 31.7 Encoding of an individual option in an IPv6 option extension header. Each option consists of a one-octet type and a one-octet length followed by zero or more octets of data for the option.

As the figure shows, IPv6 options follow the same form as IPv4 options. Each option begins with a one-octet *TYPE* field, followed by a one-octet *LENGTH* field. If the option requires additional data, octets that constitute the *VALUE* follow the *LENGTH*.

The two high-order bits of each option *TYPE* field specify how a host or router should dispose of a datagram if it does not understand the option:

Bits In Type	Meaning
00	Skip this option
01	Discard datagram; do not send ICMP message
10	Discard datagram; send ICMP message to source
11	Discard datagram; send ICMP if non-multicast

In addition, the third bit in the *TYPE* field specifies whether the option can change in transit. Having such information is important for authentication — the contents of an option that can change in transit are treated as zeroes for purposes of authentication.

---

†In the literature, an encoding of type, length, and value is sometimes called a *TLV encoding*.

31.15 Size Of The IPv6 Address Space

In IPv6, each address occupies 16 octets, four times the size of an IPv4 address. The large address space guarantees that IPv6 can tolerate any reasonable address assignment scheme. In fact, if the designers decide to change the addressing scheme later, the address space is sufficiently large to accommodate a reassignment.

It is difficult to comprehend the size of the IPv6 address space. One way to look at it relates the magnitude to the size of the population: the address space is so large that every person on the planet can have sufficient addresses to have their own internet as large as the current Internet. A second way to think of IPv6 addressing relates it to the physical space available: the earth's surface has approximately 5.1×10^8 square kilometers, meaning that there are over 10^{24} addresses per square meter of the earth's surface. Another way to understand the size relates it to address exhaustion. For example, consider how long it would take to assign all possible addresses. A 16-octet integer can hold 2^{128} values. Thus, the address space is greater than 3.4×10^{38}. If addresses are assigned at the rate of one million addresses every microsecond, it would take over 10^{20} years to assign all possible addresses.

31.16 IPv6 Colon Hexadecimal Notation

Although it solves the problem of having insufficient capacity, the large address size poses an interesting new problem: humans who maintain internets must read, enter, and manipulate such addresses. Obviously, binary notation is untenable. However, the dotted decimal notation used for IPv4 does not make such addresses sufficiently compact either. To understand why, consider an example 128-bit number expressed in dotted decimal notation:

```
104.230.140.100.255.255.255.255.0.0.17.128.150.10.255.255
```

To help make addresses slightly more compact and easier to enter, the IPv6 designers propose using *colon hexadecimal notation* (abbreviated *colon hex*) in which the value of each 16-bit quantity is represented in hexadecimal separated by colons. For example, when the value shown above in dotted decimal notation has been translated to colon hex notation and printed using the same spacing, it becomes:

```
68E6:8C64:FFFF:FFFF:0:1180:96A:FFFF
```

Colon hex notation has the obvious advantage of requiring fewer digits and fewer separator characters than dotted decimal. In addition, colon hex notation includes two techniques that make it extremely useful. First, colon hex notation allows *zero compression* in which a string of repeated zeros is replaced by a pair of colons. For example, the address:

```
FF05:0:0:0:0:0:0:B3
```

can be written:

```
FF05::B3
```

To ensure that zero compression produces an unambiguous interpretation, the proposal specifies that it can be applied only once in any address. Zero compression is especially useful when used with the proposed address assignment scheme because many addresses will contain contiguous strings of zeros. Second, colon hex notation incorporates dotted decimal suffixes; we will see that such combinations are intended to be used during the transition from IPv4 to IPv6. For example, the following string is a valid colon hex notation:

```
0:0:0:0:0:0:128.10.2.1
```

Note that although the numbers separated by colons each specify the value of a 16-bit quantity, numbers in the dotted decimal portion each specify the value of one octet. Of course, zero compression can be used with the number above to produce an equivalent colon hex string that looks quite similar to an IPv4 address:

```
::128.10.2.1
```

Finally, IPv6 extends CIDR-like notation by allowing an address to be followed by a slash and an integer that specifies a number of bits. For example,

```
12AB::CD30:0:0:0:0 / 60
```

specifies the first 60 bits of the address or 12AB00000000CD3 in hexadecimal.

31.17 Three Basic IPv6 Address Types

Like IPv4, IPv6 associates an address with a specific network connection, not with a specific computer. Thus, address assignments are similar to IPv4: an IPv6 router has two or more addresses, and an IPv6 host with one network connection needs only one address. IPv6 also retains (and extends) the IPv4 address hierarchy in which a physical network is assigned a prefix. However, to make address assignment and modification easier, IPv6 permits multiple prefixes to be assigned to a given network, and allows a computer to have multiple, simultaneous addresses assigned to a given interface.

In addition to permitting multiple, simultaneous addresses per network connection, IPv6 expands, and in some cases unifies, IPv4 special addresses. In general, a destination address on a datagram falls into one of three categories:

Unicast   The destination address specifies a single computer (host or router); the datagram should be routed to the destination along a shortest path.

Anycast   The destination is a set of computers, possibly at different locations, that all share a single address; the datagram should be routed along a shortest path and delivered to exactly one member of the group (i.e., the closest member)†.

Multicast   The destination is a set of computers, possibly at multiple locations. One copy of the datagram will be delivered to each member of the group using hardware multicast or broadcast if viable.

31.18 The Duality Of Broadcast And Multicast

IPv6 does not use the terms *broadcast* or *directed broadcast* to refer to delivery to all computers on a physical network or to a logical IP subnet. Instead, it uses the term *multicast*, and treats broadcast as a special form of multicast. The choice may seem odd to anyone who understands network hardware because more hardware technologies support broadcast than support multicast. In fact, a hardware engineer is likely to view multicasting as a restricted form of broadcasting — the hardware sends a multicast packet to all computers on the network exactly like a broadcast packet, and the interface hardware on each computer filters all multicast packets except those that software has instructed the interface hardware to accept.

In theory, the choice between multicast and limited forms of broadcast is irrelevant because one can be simulated with the other. That is, broadcasting and multicasting are duals of one another that provide the same functionality. To understand why, consider how to simulate one with the other. If broadcast is available, a packet can be delivered to a group by sending it to all machines and arranging for software on each computer to decide whether to accept or discard the incoming packet. If multicast is available, a packet can be delivered to all machines by arranging for all machines to listen to one multicast group similar to the *all systems* group discussed in Chapter 16.

31.19 An Engineering Choice And Simulated Broadcast

Knowing that broadcasting and multicasting are theoretical duals of one another does not help choose between them. To see why the designers of IPv6 chose multicasting as the central abstraction instead of broadcasting, consider applications instead of looking at the underlying hardware. An application either needs to communicate with a single application or with a group of applications. Direct communication is handled best via unicast; group communication is handled best by multicast or broadcast. To provide the most flexibility, group membership should not be determined by network

---

†Anycast addresses were formerly known as *cluster* addresses.

connections, because group members can reside at arbitrary locations. Using broadcast for all group communication does not scale to handle an internet as large as the global Internet.

Not surprisingly, the designers pre-define multicast addresses that can be used in place of an IPv4 network broadcast address. Thus, in addition to its own unicast address, each router is required to accept packets addressed to the *All Routers* multicast groups for its local environment.

31.20 Proposed IPv6 Address Space Assignment

The question of how to partition the IPv6 address space has generated much discussion. There are two central issues: how to manage address assignment and how to map an address to a route. The first issue focuses on the practical problem of devising a hierarchy of authority. Unlike the current Internet, which uses a two-level hierarchy of network prefix (assigned by an ISP) and host suffix (assigned by an organization), the large address space in IPv6 permits a multi-level hierarchy or multiple hierarchies. The second issue focuses on computational efficiency. Independent of the hierarchy of authority that assigns addresses, a router must examine each datagram and choose a path to the destination. To keep the cost of high-speed routers low, the processing time required to choose a path must be kept small.

As Figure 31.8 shows, the designers of IPv6 propose assigning blocks of addresses in a way similar to the scheme used for IPv4. Although the first 8 bits of an address are sufficient to identify its type, the address space is not partitioned into sections of equal size.

As the figure shows, only 15% of the address space has been assigned at present. The IETF will use the remaining portions as demand grows. Despite the sparse assignment, addresses have been chosen to make processing more efficient. For example, the high-order octet of an address distinguishes between multicast (all 1 bits) and unicast (a mixture of 0's and 1's).

31.21 Embedded IPv4 Addresses And Transition

Although the prefix *0000 0000* is labeled *Reserved* in the figure, the designers plan to use a small fraction of addresses in that section to encode IPv4 addresses. In particular, any address that begins with 80 zero bits followed by 16 bits of all ones or 16 bits of all zeros contains an IPv4 address in the low-order 32 bits. The value of the 16-bit field indicates whether the node also has a conventional IPv6 unicast address. Figure 31.9 illustrates the two forms.

Binary Prefix	Type Of Address	Part Of Address Space
0000 0000	Reserved (IPv4 compatibility)	1/256
0000 0001	Unassigned	1/256
0000 001	NSAP Addresses	1/128
0000 01	Unassigned	1/64
0000 1	Unassigned	1/32
0001	Unassigned	1/16
001	Global Unicast	1/8
010	Unassigned	1/8
011	Unassigned	1/8
100	Unassigned	1/8
101	Unassigned	1/8
110	Unassigned	1/8
1110	Unassigned	1/16
1111 0	Unassigned	1/32
1111 10	Unassigned	1/64
1111 110	Unassigned	1/128
1111 1110 0	Unassigned	1/512
1111 1110 10	Link-Local Unicast Addresses	1/1024
1111 1110 11	IANA - Reserved	1/1024
1111 1111	Multicast Addresses	1/256

Figure 31.8 The proposed division of IPv6 addresses into types, which are analogous to IPv4 classes. As in IPv4, the prefix of an address determines its address type.

◄─────── 80 zero bits ───────►	16 bits	◄─ 32 bits ─►
0000 0000	0000	IPv4 Address
0000 0000	FFFF	IPv4 Address

Figure 31.9 The encoding of an IPv4 address in an IPv6 address. The 16-bit field contains *0000* if the node also has a conventional IPv6 address, and *FFFF* if it does not.

The encoding will be needed during a transition from IPv4 to IPv6 for two reasons. First, a computer may choose to upgrade from IPv4 to IPv6 software before it has been assigned a valid IPv6 address. Second, a computer running IPv6 software may need to communicate with a computer that runs only IPv4 software.

Having a way to encode an IPv4 address in an IPv6 address does not solve the problem of making the two versions interoperate. In addition to address encoding, translation is needed. To use a translator, an IPv6 computer generates a datagram that contains the IPv6 encoding of the IPv4 destination address. The IPv6 computer sends the datagram to a translator, which uses IPv4 to communicate with the destination. When the translator receives a reply from the destination, it translates the IPv4 datagram to IPv6 and sends it back to the IPv6 source.

It may seem that translating protocol addresses could fail because higher layer protocols verify address integrity. In particular, TCP and UDP use a *pseudo header* in their checksum computation. The pseudo header includes both the source and destination protocol addresses, so changing such addresses could affect the computation. However, the designers planned carefully to allow TCP or UDP on an IPv4 machine to communicate with the corresponding transport protocol on an IPv6 machine. To avoid checksum mismatch, the IPv6 encoding of an IPv4 address has been chosen so that the 16-bit 1's complement checksum for both an IPv4 address and the IPv6 encoding of the address are identical. The point is:

> *In addition to choosing technical details of a new Internet Protocol, the IETF work on IPv6 has focused on finding a way to transition from the current protocol to the new protocol. In particular, the current proposal for IPv6 allows one to encode an IPv4 address inside an IPv6 address such that address translation does not change the pseudo header checksum.*

31.22 Unspecified And Loopback Addresses

As in IPv4, a few IPv6 addresses have been assigned special meaning. For example, the all 0's address:

$$0:0:0:0:0:0:0:0$$

is an *unspecified address* which cannot be assigned to any computer or used as a destination. It is only used as a source address during bootstrap by a computer that has not yet learned its address.

Like IPv4, IPv6 also has a *loopback address* that is used for testing software. The IPv6 loopback address is:

$$0:0:0:0:0:0:0:1$$

Any datagram sent to the loopback address will be delivered to the local machine; it must never be used as a destination address on an outgoing datagram.

31.23 Unicast Address Structure

The latest version of the IPv6 unicast addressing structure resembles the IPv4 subnet addressing scheme in which each address is divided into three conceptual parts. In IPv6, the three parts correspond to: a globally unique prefix used to route the datagram, a subnet ID used to distinguish among multiple physical networks at a given site, and an interface ID used to identify a particular connection to the subnet. Figure 31.10 illustrates how an IPv6 address is partitioned into parts.

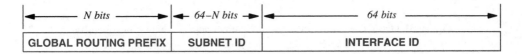

← N bits →	← 64–N bits →	← 64 bits →
GLOBAL ROUTING PREFIX	SUBNET ID	INTERFACE ID

Figure 31.10 The division of an IPv6 unicast address into three conceptual parts. The interface ID always occupies 64 bits.

31.24 Interface Identifiers

As Figure 31.10 shows, the low-order 64 bits of an IPv6 unicast address identifies a specific network interface. Unlike IPv4, however, the IPv6 suffix was chosen to be large enough to accommodate a direct encoding of the interface hardware address. Encoding a hardware address in an IP address has two consequences. First, IPv6 does not use ARP to resolve an IP address to a hardware address. Instead, IPv6 uses a *neighbor discovery protocol* available with a new version of ICMP (*ICMPv6*) to allow a node to determine which computers are its directly connected neighbors. Second, to guarantee interoperability, all computers must use the same encoding for a hardware address. Consequently, the IPv6 standards specify exactly how to encode various forms of hardware address. In the simplest case, the hardware address is placed directly in the IPv6 address; some formats use more complex transformations.

Two example encodings will help clarify the concept. For example, IEEE defines a standard 64-bit globally unique address format known as *EUI-64*. The only change needed when encoding an EUI-64 address in an IPv6 address consists of inverting bit 6 in the high-order octet of the address, which indicates whether the address is known to be globally unique.

A more complex change is required for a conventional 48-bit Ethernet address. Figure 31.11 illustrates the encoding. As the figure shows, bits from the original address are not contiguous in the encoded form. Instead, 16 bits with hexadecimal value $FFFE_{16}$ are inserted in the middle. In addition, bit *6*, which indicates whether the address has global scope, is changed from *0* to *1*. Remaining bits of the address, including the group bit (labeled *g*), the ID of the company that manufactured the interface (labeled *c*), and the manufacturer's extension are copied as shown.

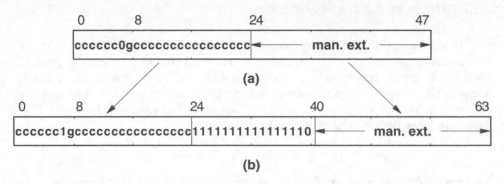

Figure 31.11 (a) The format of a 48-bit Ethernet address, with *c* bits identifying the company and *man. ext.* specifying the manufacturer's
extension, and (b) the encoding of the address in the low-order
64 bits of an IPv6 unicast address.

31.25 Local Addresses

In addition to the global unicast addresses described above, IPv6 includes prefixes
for unicast addresses that have local scope. As Figure 31.8 shows, the standard defines
link-local addresses which are each restricted to a single network. Other forms of restricted addresses have also been proposed. Routers honor the scoping rules in the following sense: a router never forwards a datagram that contains a locally-scoped address
outside the specified scope (i.e. off the local network).

Link-local addresses provide communication across a single physical network
without danger of the datagram being forwarded across the Internet. For example, when
it performs neighbor discovery, an IPv6 node uses a link-local address. The scope rules
specify that only computers on the same physical network as the sender will receive
neighbor discovery messages. Similarly, computers connected to an *isolated network*
(i.e., a network that does not have routers attached) can use link-local addresses to communicate.

31.26 Autoconfiguration And Renumbering

IPv6 is designed to support *serverless autoconfiguration*† that allows computers to
communicate without requiring a manager to specify an address. Two facilities discussed above make autoconfiguration possible and efficient: link-local addressing and
embedded interface identifiers. To begin autoconfiguration, a computer generates a
link-local address by combining the link-local prefix:

$$1111\ 1110\ 10$$

with 54 zero bits and its 64-bit interface identifier.

---

†Serverless autoconfiguration is also called *stateless autoconfiguration.*

Once it verifies that the link-local address is unique, a computer uses the address to send a *router solicitation* that requests additional information from a router. If a router is present on the network, the router responds by sending a *router advertisement* to inform the computer about prefixes that can be used for global addresses. When a router advertisement arrives, the computer makes the sender its default router. Finally, a flag in the advertisement tells the computer whether to rely on autoconfiguration or to use a conventional *managed configuration* (i.e., DHCP).

To facilitate network *renumbering*, IPv6 allows routers to limit the time that a computer can retain a prefix. To do so, a router advertisement specifies two time values for each prefix: a valid lifetime and a preferred lifetime. A host must listen for additional router advertisements. When the preferred lifetime of a prefix expires, the prefix remains valid, but the host must use another prefix for all communication when possible. When the valid lifetime expires, the host must stop using the prefix, even if existing communication is in progress.

The idea behind renumbering is straightforward: advertise a new (i.e., additional) prefix, wait for a short time, and disable use of the old prefix. In practice, however, such transitions are difficult. Long-lived transport connections will break when change occurs; a server that binds to an existing address will not receive contact at the new address; and routing must be changed. During the transition, each interface will have multiple addresses, and the address lifetimes must be coordinated with DNS to prevent cached copies of resource records for old addresses from being used. Thus, renumbering is not straightforward in a practical sense.

31.27 Summary

The IETF has defined a next generation of the Internet Protocol which is known as IPv6 because it has been assigned version number *6*. IPv6 retains many of the basic concepts from the current protocol, IPv4, but changes most details. Like IPv4, IPv6 provides a connectionless, best-effort datagram delivery service. However, the IPv6 datagram format differs from the IPv4 format, and IPv6 provides new features such as authentication and support for flow-labeling.

IPv6 organizes each datagram as a series of headers followed by data. A datagram always begins with a 40-octet base header, which contains source and destination addresses, a traffic class, and a flow identifier. The base header may be followed by zero or more extension headers, followed by data. Extension headers are optional — IPv6 uses them to hold much of the information IPv4 encodes in options.

An IPv6 address is 128 bits long, making the address space so large that the space cannot be exhausted in the foreseeable future. IPv6 uses address prefixes to determine the location and interpretation of remaining address fields. In addition to traditional unicast and multicast addresses, IPv6 also defines anycast addresses. A single anycast address can be assigned to a set of computers; a datagram sent to the address is delivered to exactly one computer in the set (i.e., the computer closest to the source).

IPv6 supports autoconfiguration and renumbering. Each host on an isolated network generates a unique link-local address which it uses for communication. The host also uses the link-local address to discover routers and global prefix information. To facilitate renumbering, all prefixes are assigned a lifetime; a host must use a new prefix if the lifetime on an existing prefix expires.

FOR FURTHER STUDY

Many RFCs have appeared that contain information pertinent to IPv6. Deering and Hinden [RFC 2460] specifies the basic protocol. Thomson and Narten [RFC 2462] describes stateless address autoconfiguration. Narten, Nordmark, and Simpson [RFC 2461] discusses neighbor discovery. Conta and Deering [RFC 2463] specifies ICMPv6 as a companion to IPv6. Crawford [RFC 2464] describes encapsulation of IPv6 for transmission over Ethernet networks.

Many RFCs focus on IPv6 addressing. Hinden and Deering [RFC 3513] describes the basic addressing architecture including the meanings of prefixes. Hinden, O'Dell, and Deering [RFC 3587] considers the aggregatable global unicast address format. Hinden and Deering [RFC 2375] specifies multicast address assignments. Johnson and Deering [RFC 2526] describes reserved anycast addresses. Information about the 64-bit EUI format can be found in:

http://standards.ieee.org/regauth/oui/tutorials/EUI64.html

EXERCISES

31.1   The current standard for IPv6 has no header checksum. What are the advantages and disadvantages of this approach?

31.2   How should extension headers be ordered to minimize processing time?

31.3   Although IPv6 addresses are assigned hierarchically, a router does not need to parse an address completely to select a route. Devise an algorithm and data structure for efficient routing. (Hint: consider a longest-match approach.)

31.4   Argue that 128-bit addresses are larger than needed, and that 96 bits provides sufficient capacity.

31.5   Assume your organization intends to adopt IPv6. Devise an address scheme the organization will use to assign each host an address. Did you choose a hierarchical assignment within your organization? Why or why not?

31.6   What is the chief advantage of encoding an Ethernet address in an IPv6 address? The chief disadvantage?

31.7   Consider a host that forms a link-local address by encoding its 48-bit Ethernet address with the standard link-local prefix. Is the resulting address guaranteed to be unique on the network? Why or why not?

31.8   Read about the IPv6 Neighbor Discovery Protocol. In the previous exercise, does the standard specify that the host must use Neighbor Discovery to verify that the address is unique? Why or why not?

31.9   If you were asked to choose sizes for the top-level, next-level, and site ID fields of an IPv6 unicast address, how large would you make each? Why?

31.10   Read about the IPv6 authentication and security headers. Why are two headers proposed?

31.11   How does the IPv6 minimum MTU of 1280 affect its flexibility?

Appendix 1

A Look At RFCs

Introduction

Most of the written information about TCP/IP and the connected Internet, including its architecture, protocols, and history, can be found in a series of reports known as *Request For Comments* or *RFCs*. An informal, loosely coordinated set of notes, RFCs are unusually rich in information and color. Before we consider the more serious aspects of RFCs, it is fitting that we take a few minutes to pay attention to the colorful side. A good place to begin is with Cerf's poem, *'Twas the Night Before Start-up* (RFC 968), a humorous parody that describes some of the problems encountered when starting a new network. Knowing not to take itself too seriously has pervaded the Internet effort. Anyone who can remember both their first Internet meeting, filled with networking jargon, and Lewis Carroll's *Jabberwocky*, filled with strangely twisted English, will know exactly why D. L. Covill put them together in *ARPAWOCKY* (RFC 527).

Other RFCs seem equally frivolous. Interspersed amid the descriptions of ideas that would turn out to dramatically change networking, we find notes like RFC 416, written in early November, 1972: *The ARC System will be Unavailable for Use During Thanksgiving Week*. It says exactly what you think it says. Or consider Crispin's tongue-in-cheek humor found in RFC 748, which describes the *TELNET Randomly-Lose Option* (a proposed option for TELNET that makes it randomly drop characters). In fact, any RFC dated April 1 should be considered a joke. If such items do not seem insignificant, think about the seventy-five RFCs listed as *never issued*. All were assigned a number and had an author, but none ever saw the light of day. The holes in the numbering scheme remain, preserved as little reminders of ideas that vaporized or work that remains incomplete.

Even after the silly, lighthearted, and useless RFCs have been removed, the remaining documents do not conform to most standards for scientific writing. Unlike scholarly scientific journals that concentrate on identifying papers of important archival interest, screening them carefully, and filing them for posterity, RFCs provide a record of ongoing conversations among the principals involved in designing, building, measuring, and using the global Internet. The reader understands at once that RFCs include the thoughts of researchers on the leading edge of technological innovation, not the studied opinions of scholars who have completely mastered a subject. The authors are not always sure of the consequences of their proposals, or even of the contents, but they clearly realize the issues are too complex to understand without community discussion. For example, RFC 1173 purports to document the "oral traditions" (which is an oxymoron because it became part of the written tradition once the RFC was published).

Despite the inconsistencies in RFCs that sometimes make them difficult for beginners to understand, the RFC mechanism has evolved and now works extremely well. Because RFCs are available electronically, information is propagated to the community quickly. Because they span a broad range of interests, practitioners as well as designers contribute. Because they record informal conversations, RFCs capture discussions and not merely final conclusions. Even the disagreements and contradictory proposals are useful in showing what the designers considered before settling on a given protocol (and readers interested in the history of a particular idea or protocol can use RFCs to follow it from its inception to its current state).

Importance Of Host And Gateway Requirements Documents

Unlike most RFCs, which concentrate on a single idea or protocol, three special RFCs cover a broad range of protocols. The special documents are entitled *Requirements for Internet Routers* and *Requirements for Internet Hosts* (parts 1 and 2).

The requirements documents, published after many years of experience with the TCP/IP protocols, are considered a major revision to the protocol standards. In essence, requirement documents each review many protocols. They point out known weaknesses or ambiguities in the RFCs that define the protocols, state conventions that have been adopted by vendors, document problems that occur in practice, and list solutions to those problems that have been accumulated through experience. The RFCs for individual protocols have *not* been updated to include changes and updates from the requirements documents. Thus, readers must be careful to always consult the requirements documents when studying a particular protocol.

RFC Numerology

RFCs cover a surprisingly large range of sizes, with the average size being 47842.7 bytes. The largest, RFC 3261 (Internet numbers), contains 647976 bytes, while the smallest consists of a 27-byte text file:

> This RFC was never issued.

A few interesting coincidences have occurred. For example, the ASCII text file for RFC 41 contains exactly 41 lines of text, and the ASCII text file for RFC 854, exactly 854 lines. RFC 1996 has a number that matches the year in which it was published. However, the number for no other RFC will match the year of publication.

The quantity of RFCs published per year varies widely. Figure A1.1 illustrates how the rate has changed over time. The surge of work in the 1970s represents an initial period of building; the high rate of publication in the 1990s and 2004 has resulted from commercialization.

Browsing Through RFCs

There are several indexes that can help one browse through RFCs. ISI publishes an index of all RFCs in chronological order. Readers often need to know which RFC contains the latest version of an official Internet protocol or which protocols are official and which are unofficial. To accommodate such needs, the IAB periodically publishes an RFC entitled *INTERNET OFFICIAL PROTOCOL STANDARDS*, which provides a list of all protocols that have been adopted as TCP/IP standards, along with the number of the most recent RFC or RFCs describing each protocol. RFC 1602, *The Internet Standards Process – Revision 2*, describes the Internet standardization process and defines the meaning of the terms *proposed standard*, *draft standard*, *Internet standard*, *required*, *recommended*, and *historic*.

Despite the available indexes, browsing through RFCs can be difficult, especially when the reader is searching for information pertinent to a given topic, which may be spread across RFCs published in many years. Browsing is particularly difficult because titles do not provide sufficient identification of the content. (How could one guess from the title *Leaving Well Enough Alone* that the RFC pertains to FTP?) Finally, having multiple RFCs with a single title (e.g., Internet Numbers) can be confusing because the reader cannot easily tell whether a document is out-of-date without checking the archive.

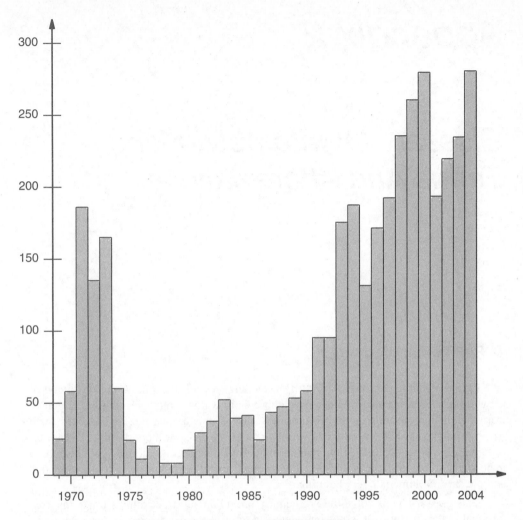

Figure A1.1 The number of RFCs published per year.

How To Obtain An RFC Over The Internet

RFCs are available electronically from many repositories around the world. Check with your local network administrator to find the site nearest you, or begin with the following URL:

http://www.rfc-editor.org

Appendix 2

Glossary Of Internetworking Terms And Abbreviations

TCP/IP Terminology

Like most large enterprises, TCP/IP has a language all its own. A curious blend of networking jargon, protocol names, and abbreviations, the language is both difficult to learn and difficult to remember. To outsiders, discussions among the cognoscenti sound like meaningless babble laced with acronyms at every possible opportunity. Even after a moderate amount of exposure, readers may find that specific terms are difficult to understand. The problem is compounded because some terminology is loosely defined and the sheer volume is overwhelming.

This glossary helps solve the problem by providing short definitions for terms used throughout the Internet. It is not intended as a tutorial for beginners. Instead, we focus on providing a concise reference to make it easy for those who are generally knowledgeable about networking to look up the meaning of specific terms or acronyms quickly. Readers will find it substantially more useful as a reference after they have studied the text than before.

A Glossary of Terms and Abbreviations
In Alphabetical Order

10/100/1000 hardware
Applied to Ethernet hardware that negotiates whether to operate at 10 Mbps, 100 Mbps, or 1 Gbps.

10Base-T
The technical name for twisted pair Ethernet operating at 10 Mbps.

100Base-T
The technical name for twisted pair Ethernet operating at 100 Mbps. The term *100Base-TX* is more specific.

1000Base-T
The technical name for twisted pair Ethernet operating at 1000 Mbps. See GigE.

127.0.0.1
The IP *loopback* address used for testing. Packets sent to this address are processed by the local protocol software without ever being sent across a network.

5-layer reference model
The protocol layering model used by TCP/IP. See *7-layer reference model*.

576 (MTU)
The minimum datagram size all IPv4 hosts and routers must handle.

7-layer reference model
An older protocol layering model created by ISO. See *5-layer reference model*.

802.3
The IEEE standard for Ethernet.

802.11
A prefix for IEEE standards that specify wireless networking. Specific standards include 802.11a, 802.11b, 802.11g, 802.11i, and 802.11n.

1280 (MTU)
The minimum datagram size all IPv6 hosts and routers must handle.

2822 mail

The standard format for electronic mail messages. The name is taken from the RFC that contains the specification (formerly 822).

3-way handshake

The technique used in TCP to start or terminate a connection reliably.

AAL

(*ATM Adaptation Layer*) An ATM standard for encapsulation; AAL5 is used for data.

ABR

Either *Available Bit Rate*, an ATM designation for service that does not guarantee a rate, or *Area Border Router*, an OSPF designation for a router that communicates with another area.

ACK

Abbreviation for *acknowledgement*.

acknowledgement

A response sent by a receiver to indicate successful reception. Typically, an acknowledgement is sent when a packet arrives.

active open

The operation that a client performs to establish a TCP connection with a server at a known address.

adaptive retransmission

The scheme TCP uses to make the retransmission timer track changes in the round-trip time.

address

An integer value used to identify a particular computer. Each packet sent to the computer contains the address.

address binding

Synonym for address resolution.

address mask

A 32-bit value with 1 bits indicating the network prefix and 0 bits indicating the host suffix. An address mask is used for either IP subnetting or CIDR.

address resolution

Conversion of a protocol address into a corresponding physical address (e.g., conversion of an IP address into an Ethernet address). See ARP.

ADSL

(*Asymmetric Digital Subscriber Line*) A popular technology for simultaneously sending data over the same wires used for telephone service.

AFRINIC

See *registry*.

agent

In network management, an agent is the server software that runs on a host or router being managed.

AH

(*Authentication Header*) A header used by IPsec to guarantee the authenticity of a datagram's source.

AIMD

(*Additive Increase Multiplicative Decrease*) A reference to TCP's congestion control mechanism in which the congestion window decreases rapidly and increases slowly.

all routers group

The well-known IP multicast group that includes all routers on the local network.

all systems group

The well-known IP multicast group that includes all hosts and routers on the local network.

anonymous FTP

An FTP session that uses login name *anonymous* to access public files. A server that permits anonymous FTP often allows the password *guest*.

anonymous network

A synonym for *unnumbered network*.

ANSI

(*American National Standards Institute*) An organization that defines U.S. standards for the information processing industry.

anycast

An address form introduced with IPv6 in which a datagram sent to the address can be routed to any of a set of computers. An *anycast address* was originally called a *cluster address*.

API

(*Application Program Interface*) The specification of the interface an application uses. The socket API is the most popular for Internet communication.

APNIC
See *registry*.

area
In OSPF, a group of routers that exchange routing information.

area manager
A person in charge of an IETF area. The set of area managers form the IESG.

ARIN
See *registry*.

ARP
(*Address Resolution Protocol*) The TCP/IP protocol used to dynamically bind a high-level IP Address to a low-level physical hardware address. ARP is used across a single physical network and is limited to networks that support hardware broadcast.

ARPA
(*Advanced Research Projects Agency*) The government agency that funded the AR-PANET, and later, the global Internet. ARPA is also known as *DARPA*.

ARPANET
A pioneering long haul network funded by ARPA and built by BBN. It served from 1969 through 1990 as the basis for early networking research and as a central backbone during development of the Internet. The ARPANET consisted of individual packet switching nodes interconnected by leased lines.

AS
(*Autonomous System*) A collection of routers and networks that fall under one administrative entity and cooperate closely to propagate network reachability (and routing) information among themselves using an interior gateway protocol of their choice. Routers within an autonomous system have a high degree of trust. Before two autonomous systems can communicate, one router in each system sends reachability information to a router in the other.

ASN.1
(*Abstract Syntax Notation.1*) The ISO presentation standard protocol used by SNMP to represent messages.

ATM
(*Asynchronous Transfer Mode*) A connection-oriented network technology that uses small, fixed-size cells at the lowest layer.

ATM Adaptation Layer (AAL)

An ATM standard that specifies how an application sends and receives information over an ATM network. Data transmissions use AAL5.

authority zone

A part of the domain name hierarchy in which a single name server is the authority.

autonomous system

See *AS*.

base64

An encoding used with MIME to send non-textual data such as a binary file through e-mail.

base header

The required header found at the beginning of each IPv6 datagram.

baseband

Characteristic of any network technology like Ethernet in which all stations share access to the medium. Compare to *broadband*.

BCP

(*Best Current Practice*) A label given to a subset of RFCs that contain recommendations from the IETF about the use, configuration, or deployment of internet technologies.

Bellman-Ford

A synonym for *distance-vector*.

best-effort delivery

Characteristic of network technologies that do not provide reliability at link levels. IP works well over best-effort delivery hardware because IP does not assume that the underlying network provides reliability. The UDP protocol provides best-effort delivery service to application programs.

BGP

(*Border Gateway Protocol*) The major exterior gateway protocol used in the Internet. Four major versions of BGP have appeared, with BGP-4 being the current.

big endian

A format for storage or transmission of binary data in which the most-significant byte (bit) comes first. The TCP/IP standard network byte order is big endian. Compare to *little endian*.

binary exponential backoff

A technique used to control network contention or congestion quickly. A sender doubles the amount of time it waits between each successive retransmission.

bps

(*bits per second*) A measure of the rate of data transmission.

bridge

A device that connects two or more networks and forwards frames among them. Bridges differ from routers because bridges use physical addresses, while routers use IP addresses.

broadband

Characteristic of a network technology that multiplexes multiple, independent network carriers onto a single cable (usually using frequency division multiplexing). Compare to *baseband*.

broadcast

A packet delivery system that delivers a copy of a given packet to all hosts that attach to it is said to broadcast the packet. Broadcast can be implemented with hardware (e.g., as in Ethernet) or software (e.g., IP broadcasting in the presence of subnets).

broadcast and prune

A technique used in data-driven multicast forwarding in which routers forward each datagram to each network until they learn that the network has no group members.

BSD UNIX

(*Berkeley Software Distribution UNIX*) A version of the UNIX operating system modified at U.C. Berkeley to contain TCP/IP protocols.

care-of address

A temporary IP address used by a mobile while visiting a foreign network.

category 5 cable

The standard for wiring used with twisted pair Ethernet. Variants include *Cat5*, *Cat5e*, and *Cat6*, which each provide more speed than the previous category.

CBT

(*Core Based Trees*) A demand-driven multicast routing protocol that builds shared forwarding trees.

CCITT

(*Consultative Committee on International Telephony and Telegraphy*) The former name of the ITU.

cell

A small, fixed-size packet. An ATM cell contains 48 octets of data and 5 octets of header.

CGI

(*Common Gateway Interface*) A technology a server uses to create a Web page dynamically when the request arrives.

checksum

A small integer value sent with a packet and used to detect errors that can result when a packet is transmitted from one machine to another.

CIDR

(*Classless Inter-Domain Routing*) The standard that specifies the details of both classless addressing and an associated routing scheme.

CL network

See *connectionless service*.

class of address

In classful addressing, the class of an address determined the location of the boundary between network prefix and host suffix.

classful addressing

The original IPv4 addressing scheme in which host addresses were divided into three classes: A, B, and C.

classless addressing

An extension of the original IPv4 addressing scheme that ignores the original class boundaries to make better use of the address space.

client-server

The model of interaction in a distributed system in which a client program on one computer sends a request to a server program on another computer and awaits a response.

closed window

A situation in TCP where a receiver has sent a window advertisement of size zero because no additional buffer space is available. When space becomes available, the receiver opens the window again.

CO

See *connection-oriented service*.

codec

(*coder/decoder*) A hardware device used to convert between an analog audio signal and a stream of digital values.

congestion

A situation in which traffic (temporarily) exceeds the capacity of networks or routers.

connection

An abstraction provided by protocol software. TCP provides a connection from one application program to another.

connection-oriented service

Characteristic of the service offered by any networking technology in which communicating parties first establish communication and then send data. TCP provides connection-oriented service as does ATM hardware.

connectionless service

Characteristic of the service offered by any networking technology in which each message or packet identifies the destination and is handled independently. Both IP and UDP provide connectionless service.

COPS

(*Common Open Policy Service*) A protocol used with RSVP to verify whether a request meets policy constraints.

count to infinity

An informal name for the *slow convergence* problem.

CR-LF

(*Carriage Return - Line Feed*) The two-character sequence used to terminate each line of text in application-layer protocols such as TELNET and SMTP.

CRC

(*Cyclic Redundancy Code*) A small, integer value sent with a packet that is used to detect transmission errors. Also see *checksum*.

CSMA/CA

(*Carrier Sense Multiple Access with Collision Avoidance*) A characteristic of network hardware that operates by allowing multiple stations to contend for access to a transmission medium by listening to see if the medium is idle, and by sending a short reservation message to inform other stations before transmitting data. 802.11 wireless networks use CSMA/CA.

CSMA/CD

(*Carrier Sense Multiple Access with Collision Detection*) A characteristic of network hardware that operates by allowing multiple stations to contend for access to a transmission medium by listening to see if the medium is idle, and a mechanism that allows the hardware to detect when two stations simultaneously attempt transmission. Ethernet uses CSMA/CD.

CSU/DSU

(*Channel Service Unit / Data Service Unit*) An electronic device that connects a computer or router to a digital circuit leased by the telephone company. Although the device fills two rolls, it usually consists of a single physical piece of hardware.

cumulative acknowledgement

The acknowledgement scheme used by TCP in which an acknowledgement reports the point in a stream at which data has been received successfully. See *SACK*.

DARPA

(*Defense Advanced Research Projects Agency*) The government agency that funded the ARPANET, and later, the global Internet. DARPA is also known as *ARPA*.

datagram

See *IP datagram*.

DCE

(*Data Communications Equipment*) Equipment in the network as opposed to user's equipment that attaches to the network. Also see *DTE*.

default route

A single entry in a list of routes that covers all destinations which are not included explicitly. The routing tables in most routers and hosts contain an entry for a default route.

delay

One of the two primary measures of a network. Delay refers to the difference between the time a bit of data is injected into a network and the time the bit exits.

delayed acknowledgement

A heuristic employed by a receiving TCP to avoid silly window syndrome.

demultiplex

To separate from a common input into several outputs. Demultiplexing occurs at each layer of the protocol stack. See *multiplex*.

DHCP

(*Dynamic Host Configuration Protocol*) A protocol that a host uses to obtain configuration information including an IP address, the address of a router, and the address of a domain name server.

DiffServ

(*Differentiated Services*) The definition now used for type-of-service in an IP datagram. DiffServ uses six bits in the IP header.

dig

An application program used by network managers to query the domain name system.

directed broadcast address

An IPv4 address that specifies "all hosts" on a specific network. Use of directed broadcast is discouraged.

distance-vector

A class of routing update protocols in which each participating router sends its neighbors a list of networks it can reach and the distance to each network. See *link state*.

DNS

(*Domain Name System*) The system used to map human-readable machine names into IP addresses. DNS uses a hierarchy of servers.

DNSSEC

(*Domain Name System SECurity*) A set of security extensions for the domain name system.

domain name

A name consisting of a sequence of labels separated by periods (dots). Each computer in the Internet is assigned a unique domain name.

dotted decimal notation

A syntactic form used to represent 32-bit binary integers. Four 8-bit values are written in base 10 with periods (dots) separating them.

dotted hex notation

A syntactic form used to represent binary values that consists of hexadecimal values for each 8-bit quantity with dots separating them.

dotted quad notation

A syntactic form used to represent binary values that consists of hexadecimal values for each 16-bit quantity with dots separating them.

DSL

(Digital Subscriber Line) A set of technologies used to provide high-speed data service over the copper wires that connect between telephone offices, local residences or businesses.

DTE

(Data Terminal Equipment) Equipment that attaches to a network as opposed to equipment that forms the network. Also see *DCE*.

DVMRP

(Distance Vector Multicast Routing Protocol) A protocol used to propagate multicast routes.

E.164

An address format specified by ITU and used with ATM.

echo request and reply

A type of message that is used to test network connectivity. The ping program uses ICMP echo request and reply messages.

EGP

(Exterior Gateway Protocol) A term applied to any protocol used by a router in one autonomous system to advertise network reachability to a router in another autonomous system. BGP-4 is currently the most widely used exterior gateway protocol.

encapsulation

The technique used by layered protocols in which a lower-level protocol accepts a message from a higher-level protocol and places it in the data portion of the low-level packet.

end-to-end

Characteristic of any mechanism that provides communication from the original source to the final destination. Protocols like TCP are classified as end-to-end.

epoch date

A point in history chosen as the date from which time is measured. TCP/IP uses January 1, 1900, Universal Time (formerly called Greenwich Mean Time) as its epoch date.

ESP

(Encapsulating Security Payload) A packet format used by IPsec to send encrypted information.

Ethernet

A popular local area network technology originally invented at the Xerox Corporation's Palo Alto Research Center. Ethernet is a best-effort delivery system that uses CSMA/CD technology.

EUI-64

A 64-bit IEEE layer-2 addressing standard.

exponential backoff

See *binary exponential backoff*.

extension header

Any of the optional IPv6 headers that follows the base header.

eXternal Data Representation

See *XDR*.

extra hop problem

An error condition in which communication is possible, but each datagram takes an extra, unnecessary trip across a network.

fair queueing

A well-known technique for traffic scheduling that is used in routers. See *WRR*.

Fast Ethernet

A popular term for 100 Mbps Ethernet.

FDM

(*Frequency Division Multiplexing*) The method of passing multiple, independent signals across a single medium by assigning each a unique carrier frequency. Hardware to combine signals is called a multiplexor; hardware to separate them is called a demultiplexor. Also see *TDM*.

file server

An application program that provides remote clients with access to files. The term is also used informally for the computer that runs the file server application.

FIN

A type of TCP segment. To close a connection, each side must send a FIN.

firewall

A mechanism placed between an organization's internal intranet and the Internet to provide security.

fixed-length subnetting

A subnet address assignment scheme in which all physical nets in an organization use the same mask. The alternative is *variable-length subnetting*.

flat namespace

Characteristic of any naming scheme in which object names are selected from a single set of strings (e.g., street names in a typical city).

flow

A term used to characterize a sequence of packets sent from a source to a destination. Some networking technologies define a separate flow for each pair of communicating applications, while others define a single flow to include all packets between a pair of hosts.

flow control

Control exerted by a receiver, typically in a transport protocol, to limit the rate at which a sender transfers data.

Ford-Fulkerson algorithm

A synonym for the distance-vector algorithm that refers to the researchers who discovered it.

forwarding

The process of accepting an incoming packet, looking up a next hop in a routing table, and sending the packet on to the next hop.

forwarding loop

An error condition in which a cycle of routers each has the next router in the cycle as the shortest path to a given destination. Also known as a *routing loop*.

fragment extension header

An optional header used by IPv6 to mark a datagram as a fragment.

fragmentation

The process of dividing an IP datagram into smaller pieces. A router fragments a datagram when the network MTU is smaller than the datagram; the ultimate destination reassembles fragments.

frame

A term for a layer 2 packet derived from early protocols that added special start-of-frame and end-of-frame markers when transmitting a packet.

Frame Relay

The name of an older connection-oriented network technology offered by telephone companies.

FTP
(*File Transfer Protocol*) A TCP/IP application-layer protocol that uses TCP to transfer files from one computer to another.

full duplex
Characteristic of a technology that allows simultaneous transfer of data in two directions.

FYI
(*For Your Information*) A subset of the RFCs that contain tutorials or general information about topics related to TCP/IP or the connected Internet.

gated
(*gateway daemon*) A program that runs on a router and interconnects multiple routing protocols, often an IGP and an EGP.

gateway
Any mechanism that connects two or more heterogeneous systems and translates among them. Originally, researchers used the term *IP gateway*; vendors adopted *IP router*.

gateway requirements
See *router requirements*.

Gbps
(*Giga bits per second*) A measure of the rate of data transmission equal to 10^9 bits per second. Also see *Kbps* and *Mbps*.

GigE
(*Gigabit Ethernet*) An Ethernet technology that operates at 1 Gbps.

graceful shutdown
A protocol mechanism that allows two communicating parties to agree to terminate communication without confusion even if underlying packets are lost, delayed, or duplicated. TCP uses a 3-way handshake to guarantee graceful shutdown.

GRE
(*Generic Routing Encapsulation*) A scheme for encapsulating information in IP that includes IP-in-IP as one possibility.

H.323
An ITU recommendation for a suite of protocols used for IP telephony.

half duplex

Characteristic of a technology that only permits data transmission in one direction at a time. Compare to *full duplex*.

hardware address

An address used by a physical network (e.g., Ethernet uses a 48-bit hardware address). Synonyms include *physical address* and *MAC address*.

header

Information at the beginning of a packet or message that describes the contents and specifies a destination.

HELLO

A protocol used on the original NSFNET backbone. Although obsolete, Hello is interesting because it uses delay as the routing metric and chooses a path with minimum delay.

HELO

The command on the initial exchange of the SMTP protocol.

hierarchical addressing

An addressing scheme in which an address can be subdivided into parts that each identify successively finer granularity. IPv4 addresses use a two-level hierarchy in which the first part of the address identifies a network and the second part identifies a particular host on that network; subnetting introduced an additional level of addressing hierarchy.

historic

An IETF classification used to discourage the use of a protocol. In essence, a protocol that is declared historic is obsolete.

hold down

A short fixed time period following a change to a routing table during which no further changes are accepted. Hold down helps avoid forwarding loops.

hop count

A measure of distance between two points in the Internet. A hop count of n means that n networks separate the source and destination.

hop limit

The IPv6 name for the datagram header field that IPv4 calls *time to live*. The hop limit prevents datagrams from following a forwarding loop forever.

host

The TCP/IP term for an end-user computer system. In addition to desktop systems, hosts include devices such as printers, laptops, and small embedded systems. Compare to *IP router*.

host requirements

Two RFC documents that specify revisions and updates of many TCP/IP protocols. See *router requirements*.

host-specific route

An entry in a routing table that refers to a single host computer as opposed to routes that refer to a network, an IP subnet, or a default.

HTML

(*HyperText Markup Language*) The standard document format used for Web pages.

HTTP

(*HyperText Transfer Protocol*) The protocol used to transfer Web documents from a server to a browser.

IAB

(*Internet Architecture Board*) A small group of people who set policy and direction for TCP/IP and the global Internet. The IAB was formerly known as the *Internet Activities Board*. See *IETF*.

ICANN

(*Internet Corporation For Assigned Names and Numbers*) A group responsible for setting policy and coordinating registries that assign IP addresses.

ICMP

(*Internet Control Message Protocol*) An integral part of the Internet Protocol (IP) that handles error and control messages (e.g., *ping*). Routers and hosts use ICMP to send reports of problems about datagrams back to the original source that sent the datagram.

ICMPv6

(*Internet Control Message Protocol version 6*) The version of ICMP that has been defined for use with IPv6.

IESG

(*Internet Engineering Steering Group*) A committee consisting of the IETF chairperson and the area managers that charters working groups and approves RFCs.

IETF

(*Internet Engineering Task Force*) A group of people under the IAB who work on the design and engineering of TCP/IP and the global Internet. The IETF is divided into areas, which are further subdivided into working groups.

IGMP

(*Internet Group Management Protocol*) A protocol that hosts use to keep local routers apprised of their membership in multicast groups.

IGP

(*Interior Gateway Protocol*) The generic term applied to any protocol used to propagate network reachability and routing information within an autonomous system.

IMAP

(*Internet Message Access Protocol*) A protocol used to transfer e-mail messages between a user's mailbox and an agent that the user runs to read e-mail. See SMTP.

inter-autonomous system routing

A synonym for exterior routing. See *BGP*.

International Organization for Standardization

See *ISO*.

International Telecommunications Union

See *ITU*.

Internet

A collection of data networks around the world that are interconnected by routers and use TCP/IP protocols to function as a single, large, virtual network.

Internet address

See *IP address*.

Internet draft

A draft document generated by the IETF; if approved, the document will become an RFC.

Internet Protocol

See IP.

interoperability

The ability of software and hardware on multiple machines from multiple vendors to communicate efficiently, reliably, and meaningfully.

intranet

A private corporate network consisting of hosts, routers, and networks that use TCP/IP technology. Most corporate intranets connect to the Internet.

IP

(*Internet Protocol*) The protocol in the TCP/IP suite that defines the connectionless, best-effort packet delivery service that forms the basis for the Internet.

IP address

A 32-bit address assigned to each host in the Internet.

IP datagram

The basic unit of information passed across a TCP/IP internet analogous to a hardware packet. Each datagram contains the addresses of the original sender and ultimate destination.

IP gateway

A synonym for *IP router*.

IP-in-IP

The encapsulation of one IP datagram inside another for transmission through a tunnel. IP-in-IP is used with VPNs.

IP multicast

An addressing and forwarding scheme that allows transmission of IP datagrams to a subset of hosts. The Internet currently does not have extensive facilities to handle IP multicast.

IP router

A special purpose network system that connects two or more (possibly heterogeneous) networks and passes IP traffic between them.

IP switching

Originally a high-speed IP forwarding technology developed by Ipsilon Corporation, now generally used in reference to any of several similar technologies.

IP telephony

A telephone system that uses IP to transport digitized voice. See *VoIP*.

IPng

(*Internet Protocol — the Next Generation*) An older term used for *IPv6*.

IPsec

(*IP security*) A security standard used with either IPv4 or IPv6 to allow a sender to authenticate or encrypt a datagram.

IPv4

(*Internet Protocol version 4*). A reference to the current version of IP.

IPv6

(*Internet Protocol version 6*). A reference to the next version of IP.

IRTF

(*Internet Research Task Force*) A relatively inactive group parallel to the IETF.

ISO

(*International Organization for Standardization*) An international body that drafts, discusses, proposes, and specifies standards for network protocols. ISO is best know for its 7-layer reference model that describes the conceptual organization of protocols.

isochronous

Characteristic of a network system that does not introduce jitter. The conventional telephone system is isochronous.

ISP

(*Internet Service Provider*) Any organization that sells Internet access, either permanent connectivity or dialup access.

ITU

(*International Telecommunication Union*) An international organization that sets standards for interconnection of telephone equipment.

IXP

(*Internet eXchange Point*) A physical location at which ISPs connect. See *NAP* and *peering agreement*.

jitter

A term used to describe unwanted variance in delay caused when one packet in a sequence must be delayed more than another. Jitter can result when routers in a packet switching network experience congestion.

Karn's Algorithm

An algorithm that allows transport protocols to distinguish between valid and invalid round-trip time samples and thus, improve round-trip estimations.

Kbps

(*Kilo bits per second*) A measure of the rate of data transmission equal to 10^3 bits per second. Also see *Gbps* and *Mbps*.

keepalive

A small message sent periodically between two communicating entities to ensure that network connectivity remains intact and that both sides are still responding.

LAN

(*Local Area Network*) Any physical network technology designed to span short distances (up to a few thousand meters). See *WAN*.

LATNIC

See *registry*.

layer 1

A reference to the lowest layer in a layering model. Layer 1 includes physical connections and voltages on wires.

layer 2

A reference to the second lowest layer in a layering model. Layer 2 includes frame format and addressing.

layer 3

A reference to the IP layer that provides Internetworking.

layer 4

A reference to the transport layer that includes TCP and UDP.

link-local address

An address used with IPv6 that has significance only on a single network.

link state

A class of routing update protocols in which each participating router broadcasts status messages and each router uses Dijkstra's SPF algorithm to compute shortest routes to each destination. See *distance-vector*.

link status

A synonym for *link state*.

LIS

(*Logical IP Subnet*) A term used when IP runs over ATM to describe a virtual network that has a single IP prefix.

little endian

A format for storage or transmission of binary data in which the least-significant byte (bit) comes first. See *big endian*.

logical subnet
See *LIS*.

long haul network
Older term for *WAN*.

longest-prefix match
See *LPM*.

loopback address
A network address used for testing that causes outgoing packets to be delivered to the local machine. IP uses 127.0.0.0 as the loopback prefix.

LPM
(*Longest-Prefix Match*) The technique used when searching a routing table that chooses an entry with the largest prefix that matches the target address.

LSP
(*Label Switched Path*) A path through a series of LSRs that run MPLS.

LSR
(*Loose Source Route* also *Label Switching Router*) Loose Source Route is an IP option that contains a list of router addresses that the datagram must visit in order. The datagram may also be forwarded to additional intermediate stops A Label Switching Router is a router that has facilities to forward MPLS traffic. Usually, such a router also handles conventional IP forwarding, and can be configured to transfer packets between MPLS and conventional IP.

MABR
(*Multicast Area Border Router*) The MOSPF term for a multicast router that exchanges routing information with another area.

MAC
(*Media Access Control*) A general reference to the low-level hardware protocols used to access a particular network. The term *MAC address* is often used as a synonym for *physical address*.

mail exchanger
A computer that accepts e-mail. DNS has a separate lookup type for mail exchangers.

Management Information Base
See *MIB*.

mask

See *address mask*.

maximum transfer unit

See *MTU*.

MBONE

(*Multicast BackBONE*) A cooperative agreement among sites to forward multicast datagrams across the Internet by use of IP tunneling.

Mbps

(*Millions of bits per second*) A measure of the rate of data transmission equal to 10^6 bits per second. Also see *Gbps* and *Kbps*.

MIB

(*Management Information Base*) The set of variables (database) that a system running an SNMP agent maintains. Managers can fetch or store into MIB variables.

MIME

(*Multipurpose Internet Mail Extensions*) A standard used to encode data such as images as printable ASCII text for transmission through e-mail.

MLS

(Multi-Layer Switching) An IP switching technology offered by Cisco Systems.

mobile IP

A technology developed by the IETF to permit a computer to travel to a new site while retaining its original IP address.

MOSPF

(*Multicast Open Shortest Path First*) Multicast extensions to the OSPF routing protocol.

MPLS

(*Multi-Protocol Label Switching*) A technology that uses high-speed switching hardware to carry IP datagrams. MPLS is derived from IP switching.

mrouted

(*multicast route daemon*) A program used with a protocol stack that supports IP multicast to establish multicast forwarding.

MSL

(*Maximum Segment Lifetime*) The longest time a datagram can survive in the Internet. Protocols use the MSL to guarantee a bound on the time duplicate packets can survive.

MSS

(*Maximum Segment Size*) A value negotiated when using TCP that specifies the largest amount of data that can be transmitted in one segment.

MTU

(*Maximum Transmission Unit*) The largest amount of data that can be transferred across a given physical network in a single packet.

multi-homed host

A TCP/IP host that has connections to two or more physical networks.

multicast

A technique that allows copies of a single packet to be passed to a selected subset of all possible destinations. Some hardware (e.g., Ethernet) supports multicast.

multiplex

To combine data from several sources into a single stream in such a way that it can be separated again later. See *demultiplex*.

multiplicative decrease

A technique used by TCP to reduce transmission when congestion occurs. The size of the effective window is reduced by half each time a segment is lost.

MX record

(*Mail eXchanger record*) A type of DNS record used to store the address of a mail server for a given domain.

Nagle algorithm

A self-clocking heuristic that clumps outgoing data to improve throughput and avoid silly window syndrome.

name resolution

The process of mapping a name into a corresponding address. The domain name system provides a mechanism for naming computers in which programs use remote name servers to resolve a machine name into an IP address.

NAP

(*Network Access Point*) A physical location where ISPs interconnect networks. Also see IXP.

NAPT

(*Network Address and Port Translation*) The most popular form of NAT in which protocol port numbers and IP addresses are used in the translation.

NAT

(*Network Address Translation*) A technology that allows hosts using private addresses to communicate with an arbitrary destination on the Internet.

net 10 address

A general reference to a nonroutable address (i.e., one that is reserved for use in an intranet and not used on the Internet).

network byte order

The TCP/IP standard for transmission of integers that specifies the most significant byte appears first (big endian).

network management

See *MIB* and *SNMP*.

Next Header

A field used in IPv6 to specify the type of the item that follows.

NFS

(*Network File System*) A protocol that uses UDP to allow a set of cooperating computers to access each other's file systems.

NIC

(*Network Interface Card*) A hardware device that plugs into the bus on a computer and connects the computer to a network.

NOC

(*Network Operations Center*) Originally, the organization at BBN that monitored and controlled several networks that formed part of the Internet. Now, used for any organization that manages a network.

nonroutable address

Any address using a prefix reserved for use in intranets. Routers in the Internet will not forward datagrams that contain a nonroutable address. See *net 10 address*.

NVT

(*Network Virtual Terminal*) The character-oriented protocol used by TELNET.

OC series standards

A series of standards for the transmission of data over optical fiber. For example, OC-48 has a bit rate of approximately 2.5 gigabits per second.

octet

An 8-bit unit of data. Although engineers frequently use the term *byte* as a synonym for octet, a byte can be smaller or larger than 8 bits.

one-armed router

An IP router that understands two addressing domains, but only has one physical network connection. Also called a *one-armed firewall*.

OSPF

(*Open Shortest Path First*) A link state routing protocol designed by the IETF.

OUI

(*Organizationally Unique Identifier*) Part of an address assigned to an organization that manufactures network hardware; the organization assigns a unique address to each device by using its OUI plus a suffix number.

out of band data

Data sent outside the normal delivery path, often used to carry abnormal or error indicators (e.g., TCP's *urgent data*).

packet

A small unit of data sent across a packet switching network.

packet filter

A mechanism in a router that can be configured to reject some types of packets and admit others. Packet filters are used to create a security firewall.

path MTU

The minimum MTU along a path from the source to destination (i.e., the size of the largest datagram that can be sent along the path without fragmentation).

PCM

(*Pulse Code Modulation*) A standard for voice encoding used in digital telephony that produces 8000 8-bit samples per second.

PDU

(*Packet Data Unit*) An ISO term for packet.

peering agreement

A cooperative agreement between two ISPs to exchange both reachability information and data packets. In addition to peering at IXPs, large ISPs often have private peering agreements.

perimeter security

A network security mechanism that places a firewall at each connection between a site and outside networks.

physical address

A synonym for *MAC address* or *hardware address*.

PIM-DM

(*Protocol Independent Multicast Dense Mode*) A multicast routing protocol similar to DVMRP.

PIM-SM

(*Protocol Independent Multicast Sparse Mode*) A multicast routing protocol that uses an approach similar to CBT.

PING

(*Packet InterNet Groper*) The name of a program used with TCP/IP internets to test reachability of destinations by sending them an ICMP echo request and waiting for a reply. The term is now used like a verb as in, ''please ping host *A* to see if it is alive.''

playback point

The minimum amount of data required in a jitter buffer before playback can begin.

PoE

(*Power over Ethernet*) A technology used with IP telephones to supply power over the same cable used for an Ethernet connection.

point-to-point network

Any network technology that connects exactly two machines (e.g., a leased circuit or dialup connection).

poison reverse

A heuristic used by distance-vector protocols such as RIP to avoid forwarding loops.

POP

(*Post Office Protocol*) A protocol used to access and extract e-mail from a mailbox. The current version is POP3, and a secure version named POP3S also exists.

port

See *protocol port*.

positive acknowledgement

Synonym for *acknowledgement*.

POTS

(*Plain Old Telephone Service*) A reference to the standard voice telephone system.

PPP

(*Point to Point Protocol*) A protocol for framing when sending IP datagrams across a serial line.

PPPoE
A version of the Point to Point Protocol used over Ethernet.

promiscuous mode
A feature of network interface hardware that allows a computer to receive all packets on the network.

protocol
A formal description of message formats and the rules two or more machines must follow to exchange those messages.

protocol port
The abstraction that TCP/IP transport protocols use to distinguish among multiple destinations within a given host computer. TCP and UDP use small integers as port numbers.

provider prefix
An addressing scheme in which an ISP owns a network prefix and assigns each customer addresses that begin with the prefix.

provisioned service
A service that is configured manually.

proxy
Any device or system that acts in place of another (e.g., a proxy Web server acts in place of another Web server).

proxy ARP
The technique in which one machine, usually a router, answers ARP requests intended for another by supplying its own physical address. Proxy ARP allows multiple networks to share a single IP prefix.

pseudo header
Additional information used in a TCP or UDP checksum computation, but not present in the UDP datagram or TCP segment. A pseudo header includes source and destination IP addresses.

PSTN
(*Public Switched Telephone Network*) The standard voice telephone system.

public key encryption
An encryption technique that generates encryption keys in pairs. One of the pair must be kept secret, and one is published.

push

The operation an application performs on a TCP connection to force data to be sent immediately. A bit in the segment header marks pushed data.

PVC

(*Permanent Virtual Circuit*) The type of ATM virtual circuit established by an administrator rather than by software in a computer. See *SVC*.

QoS

(*Quality of Service*) Bounds on the loss, delay, jitter, and minimum throughput that a network guarantees to deliver.

RDP

(*Remote Desktop Protocol*) A protocol defined by Microsoft that provides a remote desktop capability for their operating systems.

reachability

A destination is "reachable" from a given source if a route exists from the source to the destination.

reassembly

The process of collecting all the fragments of an IP datagram and using them to create a copy of the original datagram. The ultimate destination performs reassembly.

RED

(*Random Early Detection*) A technique routers use instead of tail-drop to manage buffers when memory begins to fill.

redirect

An ICMP message sent from a router to a host on a local network to instruct the host to change a route.

reference model

A description of how layered protocols fit together. TCP/IP uses a 5-layer reference model; earlier protocols used the ISO 7-layer reference model.

registry

An organization authorized to assign blocks of IP addresses. The registries include: AFRINIC, APNIC, ARIN, LATNIC, and RIPE.

reliable transfer

Characteristic of a mechanism that guarantees to deliver data without loss, without corruption, without duplication, and in the same order as it was sent, or to inform the sender that delivery is impossible.

replay

An error situation in which packets from a previous session are erroneously accepted as part of a later session.

reserved address

A synonym for *nonroutable address*.

reset

A segment sent by TCP in response to an error condition such as a malformed incoming segment or an incoming segment for which the receiver has no record of a connection.

resolution

See *address resolution*

RFC

(*Request For Comments*) The name of a series of documents that contain surveys, measurements, ideas, techniques, and observations, as well as proposed and accepted TCP/IP protocol standards. RFCs are available on-line.

RIP

(*Routing Information Protocol*) A protocol used to propagate routing information inside an autonomous system.

RIPE

See *registry*.

round trip time

See *RTT*.

route

The path that network traffic takes from source to destination.

route aggregation

The technique used by routing protocols to combine multiple destinations that have the same next hop into a single entry.

routed

(*route daemon*) A UNIX program that implements the RIP protocol. Pronounced ''route-d.''

router

See *IP router*.

router requirements

A document that contains updates to TCP/IP protocols used in routers. See *host requirements*.

routing loop

An error condition in which a cycle of routers each has the next router in the cycle as the shortest path to a given destination. Also known as a *forwarding loop*.

RPC

(*Remote Procedure Call*) A technology in which a program invokes services across a network by making modified procedure calls.

RPF

(*Reverse Path Forwarding*) A technique used to propagate broadcast packets that ensures there are no forwarding loops. IP uses reverse path forwarding to propagate subnet broadcast and multicast datagrams.

RPM

(*Reverse Path Multicast*) A general approach to multicasting that uses the TRPB algorithm.

RST

(*ReSeT*) An abbreviation for a TCP *reset* segment.

RSVP

(*Resource ReserVation Protocol*) The protocol that allows an endpoint to request a flow with specific QoS; routers along the path to the destination must agree before they approve the request.

RTCP

(*RTP Control Protocol*) The companion protocol to RTP used to control a session.

RTO

(*Round-trip Time-Out*) The time a protocol waits before retransmitting a packet. See *RTT*.

RTP

(*Real-time Transport Protocol*) The primary protocol used to transfer real-time data such as voice and video over the Internet.

RTT

(*Round Trip Time*) The total time taken for a single packet or datagram to leave one computer, reach another, and return.

SA

(*Security Association*) Used with IPsec to denote a binding between a set of security parameters and an identifier carried in a datagram header. A host chooses SA bindings; they are not globally standardized. See *SPI*.

SACK

(*Selective ACKnowledgement*) An optional addition to the TCP acknowledgement mechanism that allows a receiver to specify which segments have been received. Compare with *cumulative acknowledgement*.

SAR

(*Segmentation And Reassembly*) The process of dividing a message into cells, sending them across an ATM network, and reforming the original message. AAL5 performs SAR when sending IP across an ATM network.

scp

(secure copy program) A program that operates like the Unix copy command *cp*, except that *scp* can transfer files from one computer to another and uses encryption to keep the transfer secure.

segment

The unit of transfer used by TCP.

selective acknowledgement

See SACK.

self clocking

Characteristic of any system that operates periodically without requiring an external clock (e.g., uses the arrival of a packet to trigger an action).

server

An application program that supplies service to clients over a network.

SFTP

(*Secure File Transfer Protocol*) A protocol that offers the same interface as FTP, but multiplexes transfers over an ssh channel to keep them secure.

shortest path first

See *SPF*.

signaling

A telephony term that refers to protocols which establish a circuit.

silly window syndrome

A condition that can arise in TCP in which the receiver repeatedly advertises a small window and the sender repeatedly sends a small segment to fill it.

SIP

(*Session Initiation Protocol*) A protocol devised by the IETF for signaling in IP telephony.

sliding window

Characteristic of a protocol that allows a sender to transmit more than one packet of data before receiving an acknowledgement. The number of outstanding packets or bytes is known as the window size; increasing the window size improves throughput.

slow-start

A congestion avoidance scheme in TCP in which TCP increases its window size as ACKs arrive.

slow convergence

A problem in distance-vector protocols in which two or more routers form a forwarding loop that persists until the routing protocols increment the distance to infinity.

SMTP

(*Simple Mail Transfer Protocol*) The TCP/IP standard protocol for transferring electronic mail messages from one machine to another.

SNAP

(*SubNetwork Attachment Point*) An IEEE standard for a small header placed in the data area of a frame to specify the data type.

SNMP

(*Simple Network Management Protocol*) A protocol used to manage devices such as hosts, routers, and printers. Also see *MIB*.

SOA

(*Start Of Authority*) A keyword used with DNS to denote the beginning of the records for which a particular server is the authority.

socket API

The definition of an interface between application programs and TCP/IP software.

soft state

A technique in which a receiver times out information rather than depending on the sender to maintain it.

source quench

An ICMP message sent back to the source when datagrams overrun a router.

source route

A route that is determined by the source and specified as a list of specific intermediate routers the packet should visit. See *LSR* and *SSR*.

SPF

(*Shortest Path First*) A class of routing update protocols that uses Dijkstra's algorithm to compute shortest paths. See *link state*.

SPI

(*Security Parameters Index*) The identifier IPsec uses to specify the Security Association that should be used to process a datagram.

split horizon

A heuristic used by distance-vector protocols such as RIP to avoid forwarding loops.

SS7

(*Signaling System 7*) The conventional telephone system standard used for signaling.

ssh

(*secure shell*) An alternative to TELNET that uses encryption to keep sessions confidential.

SSL

(*Secure Sockets Layer*) A de facto standard for secure communication originally created by Netscape, Inc.

SSL-FTP

(*Secure Sockets Layer File Transfer Protocol*) A variant of FTP that uses SSL to ensure transfers are secure.

SSR

(*Strict Source Route*) An IP option that contains a list of router addresses that the datagram must visit in order. See *LSR*.

standard byte order

See *network byte order*.

STD

(*STanDard*) The designation used to classify a particular RFC as describing a standard protocol.

store-and-forward

The paradigm used by packet switching systems in which an incoming packet is stored in memory until it can be forwarded on toward its destination.

subnet addressing

An extension of the IP addressing scheme that allows a site to use a single IP network address for multiple physical networks.

subnet mask

See address mask.

SubNetwork Attachment Point

See *SNAP*.

supernet addressing

Another name for *CIDR*.

SVC

(*Switched Virtual Circuit*) The type of ATM virtual circuit established when needed by software rather than by an administrator.

SWS

See *silly window syndrome*.

SYN

(*SYNchronizing segment*) The first segment sent by the TCP protocol, it is used to synchronize the two ends of a connection in preparation for opening a connection.

tail drop

A policy routers use to manage buffers by discarding all packets that arrive after memory is full. See *RED*.

TCP

(*Transmission Control Protocol*) The TCP/IP standard transport-layer protocol that provides the reliable, full duplex, stream service on which many application protocols depend.

TCP/IP Internet Protocol Suite

The official name of the TCP/IP protocols.

TDM

(*Time Division Multiplexing*) A technique used to multiplex multiple signals onto a single hardware transmission channel by allowing each signal to use the channel for a short time before going on to the next one. See *FDM*.

TELNET

The TCP/IP standard protocol for remote terminal access.

TFTP

(*Trivial File Transfer Protocol*) A TCP/IP standard protocol for file transfer with minimal capability and minimal overhead.

three-way handshake

The 3-segment exchange TCP uses to reliably start or gracefully terminate a connection.

TLV encoding

Any representation format that encodes each item with three fields: a type, a length, and a value.

TOS

(*Type Of Service*) A reference to the original interpretation of the field in an IPv4 header that allows the sender to specify the type of service desired. Now replaced by *DiffServ*.

traceroute

A program that uses successively larger TTL values and ICMP error messages to determine intermediate hops along the path to a destination.

traffic class

A reference to a set of services available in the *DiffServ* interpretation.

traffic policing

Checking to ensure that incoming traffic adheres to preestablished bounds.

traffic shaping

Ensuring that outgoing traffic adheres to a specified rate.

triggered updates

A heuristic used with distance-vector protocols such as RIP to send an update as soon as routes change without waiting for the next update cycle.

TRPB

(*Truncated Reverse Path Broadcast*) A technique used in data-driven multicasting to forward multicast datagrams.

TRPF

(*Truncated Reverse Path Forwarding*) A synonym for *TRPB*.

TTL

(*Time To Live*) A value in the IP header used to ensure that a datagram does not remain in the Internet forever, even if routes are incorrectly configured.

tunneling

A technique in which a packet is encapsulated in a high-level protocol for transmission. Tunneling is used for VPNs. See *IP-in-IP*.

twisted pair Ethernet

Ethernet wiring scheme that uses twisted pair cable. See *GigE* and *Category 5 cable*.

type of service routing

A routing scheme in which the choice of path depends on the characteristics of the network needed by the flow as well as the shortest path to the destination.

UDP

(*User Datagram Protocol*) A transport protocol that allows an application program on one machine to send a datagram to an application program on another.

unicast

An address that specifies forwarding a packet to a single destination. See *broadcast* and *multicast*.

unnumbered network

A technique for conserving IP network prefixes in which a point to point connection between two routers is not assigned a prefix.

unreliable delivery

Characteristic of a mechanism that does not guarantee to deliver data without loss, corruption, duplication, or in the same order as it was sent. See *best-effort delivery*.

urgent data

A facility that TCP uses to send data out of band.

URL

(*Uniform Resource Locator*) A syntactic form that specifies an item and a protocol used to access the item.

variable-length subnetting

A subnet address assignment scheme in which each physical net in an organization can have a different mask. See *fixed-length subnetting*.

VC

(*Virtual Circuit*) A path through a network from one application to another that is used to send data.

vector-distance

Now called *distance-vector*.

VLSM

(*Variable Length Subnet Mask*) The mask used with *variable-length subnetting*.

VoIP

(*Voice over IP*) Technology that allows voice telephone calls to be carried over the Internet. See *IP telephony*.

VPI / VCI

(*Virtual Path Identifier* plus *Virtual Circuit Identifier*) A connection identifier used by ATM.

VPN

(*Virtual Private Network*) A technology that connects two or more separate sites over the Internet, but allows them to function as if they were a single, private network.

WAN

(*Wide Area Network*) Any physical network technology that spans large geographic distances. See *LAN* and *long haul network*.

well-known port

A protocol port number used by TCP or UDP that is preassigned to a specific service (e.g., e-mail).

Wi-Fi

A consortium that verifies 802.11b wireless network products interoperate, and a marketing term vendors use to sell their products.

window

See *sliding window*.

window advertisement

A value used by TCP to allow a receiver to tell a sender the size of an available buffer.

Windows Sockets Interface

A variant of the socket API developed by Microsoft that is also called *WINSOCK*.

working group

A group of people in the IETF working on a particular protocol or design issue.

World Wide Web

The large hypermedia service available on the Internet that allows a user to browse information.

WRR

(*Weighted Round-Robin*) A packet scheduling mechanism used to accept packets from multiple queues and send them across a single transmission channel. WRR allows each queue to be given a guaranteed percentage of the channel bandwidth.

WWW

See *World Wide Web*.

XDR

(*eXternal Data Representation*) The standard for a machine-independent data representation. To use XDR, a sender translates from the local machine representation to the standard external representation and a receiver translates from the external representation to the local machine representation.

X-Window System

A software system developed at MIT for presenting and managing output on bit-mapped displays.

zero window

See *closed window*.

zone of authority

Term used in the domain name system to refer to the group of names for which a given name server is an authority.

Bibliography

ABRAMSON, N. [1970], The ALOHA System – Another Alternative for Computer Communications, *Proceedings of the Fall Joint Computer Conference,* Vol 36, 295-298.

ANDREWS, D. W., and G. D. SHULTZ [1982], A Token-Ring Architecture for Local Area Networks: An Update, *Proceedings of Fall 82 COMPCON,* IEEE.

ATALLAH, M., and D. E. COMER [June 1998], Algorithms for Variable Length Subnet Address Assignment, *IEEE Transactions on Computers*, vol. 47:6, 693-699.

BBN [1981], A History of the ARPANET: The First Decade, *Technical Report* Bolt, Beranek, and Newman, Inc.

BBN [December 1981], Specification for the Interconnection of a Host and an IMP (revised), *Technical Report 1822*, Bolt, Beranek, and Newman, Inc.

BERTSEKAS D., and R. GALLAGER [1992], *Data Networks*, 2nd edition, Prentice-Hall, Upper Saddle River, New Jersey.

BIAGIONI E., E. COOPER, and R. SANSOM [March 1993], Designing a Practical ATM LAN, *IEEE Network*, 32-39.

BIRRELL, A., and B. NELSON [February 1984], Implementing Remote Procedure Calls, *ACM Transactions on Computer Systems,* 2(1), 39-59.

BLACK, U., [1995], *ATM: Foundation for Broadband Networks*, Prentice-Hall, Upper Saddle River, New Jersey.

BOGGS, D., J. SHOCH, E. TAFT, and R. METCALFE [April 1980], Pup: An Internetwork Architecture, *IEEE Transactions on Communications,* Vol 28(4), 612-624.

BORMAN, D., [April 1989], Implementing TCP/IP on a Cray Computer, *Computer Communication Review,* 19(2), 11-15.

BROWNBRIDGE, D., L. MARSHALL, and B. RANDELL [December 1982], The Newcastle Connections or UNIXes of the World Unite!, *Software – Practice and Experience*, 12(12), 1147-1162.

CASNER, S., and S. DEERING [July 1992], First IETF Internet Audiocast, *Computer Communication Review*, 22(3), 92-97.

CERF, V., and E. CAIN [October 1983], The DOD Internet Architecture Model, *Computer Networks*, Vol. 7, 307-318.

CERF, V., and R. KAHN [May 1974], A Protocol for Packet Network Interconnection, *IEEE Transactions of Communications*, Com-22(5), 637-648.

CERF, V. [October 1989], A History of the ARPANET, *ConneXions, The Interoperability Report*, 480 San Antonio Rd, Suite 100, Mountain View, California.

CHERITON, D. R. [1983], Local Networking and Internetworking in the V-System, *Proceedings of the Eighth Data Communications Symposium*, 9-16.

CHERITON, D. [August 1986], VMTP: A Transport Protocol for the Next Generation of Communication Systems, *Proceedings of ACM SIGCOMM '86*, 406-415.

CHESSON, G. [June 1987], Protocol Engine Design, *Proceedings of the 1987 Summer USENIX Conference*, Phoenix, AZ, 209-215.

CHESWICK, W., S. BELLOVIN, and A. RUBIN [2003], *Firewalls And Internet Security: Repelling the Wiley Hacker*, 2nd edition, Addison-Wesley, Reading, Massachusetts.

CLARK, D., and W. FANG [August 1998], Explicit Allocation Of Best-Effort Packet Delivery Service, *IEEE/ACM Transactions On Networking*, 6(4), 362-373.

CLARK, D., M. LAMBERT, and L. ZHANG [August 1987], NETBLT: A High Throughput Transport Protocol, *Proceedings of ACM SIGCOMM '87*, 353-359.

CLARK, D., V. JACOBSON, J. ROMKEY, and H. SALWEN [June 1989], An Analysis of TCP Processing Overhead, *IEEE Communications*, Vol 27(6), 23-29.

COHEN, D., [1981], On Holy Wars and a Plea for Peace, *IEEE Computer*, Vol 14, 48-54.

COMER, D. E., [2004], *Computer Networks And Internets*, 4th edition, Prentice-Hall, Upper Saddle River, New Jersey.

COMER, D. E. and J. T. KORB [1983], CSNET Protocol Software: The IP-to-X25 Interface, *Computer Communication Review*, 13(2), 154-159.

COMER, D. E., T. NARTEN, and R. YAVATKAR [April 1987], The Cypress Network: A Low-Cost Internet Connection Technology, *Technical Report TR-653*, Purdue University, West Lafayette, IN.

COMER, D. E., T. NARTEN, and R. YAVATKAR [1987], The Cypress Coaxial Backbone Packet Switch, *Computer Networks and ISDN Systems*, vol. 14:2-5, 383-388.

COMER, D. E. and D. L. STEVENS [1999], *Internetworking With TCP/IP: Volume II: Design, Implementation, and Internals*, 3rd edition, Prentice-Hall, Upper Saddle River, New Jersey.

COMER, D. E. and D. L. STEVENS [2000], *Internetworking With TCP/IP Volume III – Client-Server Programming And Applications, Linux/POSIX Sockets Version*, Prentice-Hall, Upper Saddle River, New Jersey.

COMER, D. E. and D. L. STEVENS [1996], *Internetworking With TCP/IP Volume III – Client-Server Programming And Applications, BSD socket version*, 2nd edition, Prentice-Hall, Upper Saddle River, New Jersey.

COMER, D. E. and D. L. STEVENS [1997], *Internetworking With TCP/IP Volume III – Client-Server Programming And Applications, Windows Sockets version*, Prentice-Hall, Upper Saddle River, New Jersey.

COMER, D. E. and D. L. STEVENS [1994], *Internetworking With TCP/IP Volume III – Client-Server Programming And Applications, AT&T TLI version,* Prentice-Hall, Upper Saddle River, New Jersey.

COTTON, I. [1980], Technologies for Local Area Computer Networks, *Computer Networks* Vol. 4, 197-208.

DALAL Y. K., and R. S. PRINTIS [1981], 48-Bit Absolute Internet and Ethernet Host Numbers, *Proceedings of the Seventh Data Communications Symposium,* 240-245.

DEERING S. E., and D. R. CHERITON [May 1990], Multicast Routing in Datagram Internetworks and Extended LANs, *ACM Transactions on Computer Systems,* 8(2), 85-110.

DEERING, S., D. ESTRIN, D. FARINACCI, V. JACOBSON, C-G LIU, and L. WEI [August 1994], An Architecture for Wide-Area Multicasting Routing, *Proceedings of ACM SIGCOMM '94,* 126-135.

DENNING P. J., [September-October 1989], *The Science of Computing: Worldnet,* in American Scientist, 432-434.

DENNING P. J., [November-December 1989], *The Science of Computing: The ARPANET After Twenty Years,* in American Scientist, 530-534.

DE PRYCKER, M. [1995], *Asynchronous Transfer Mode Solution for Broadband ISDN,* 3rd edition, Prentice-Hall, Upper Saddle River, New Jersey.

DIGITAL EQUIPMENT CORPORATION., INTEL CORPORATION, and XEROX CORPORATION [September 1980], *The Ethernet: A Local Area Network Data Link Layer and Physical Layer Specification.*

DION, J. [Oct. 1980], The Cambridge File Server, *Operating Systems Review,* 14(4), 26-35.

EDGE, S. W. [1979], Comparison of the Hop-by-Hop and Endpoint Approaches to Network Interconnection, in *Flow Control in Computer Networks,* J-L. GRANGE and M. GIEN (EDS.), North-Holland, Amsterdam, 359-373.

EDGE, S. [1984], An Adaptive Timeout Algorithm for Retransmission Across a Packet Switching Network, *Proceedings of ACM SIGCOMM '84,* 248-255.

ERIKSSON, H. [August 1994], MBONE: The Multicast Backbone, *Communications of the ACM,* 37(8), 54-60.

FALK, G. [1983], The Structure and Function of Network Protocols, in *Computer Communications, Volume I: Principles,* CHOU, W. (ED.), Prentice-Hall, Upper Saddle River, New Jersey.

FARMER, W. D., and E. E. NEWHALL [1969], An Experimental Distributed Switching System to Handle Bursty Computer Traffic, *Proceedings of the ACM Symposium on Probabilistic Optimization of Data Communication Systems,* 1-3.

FEDOR, M. [June 1988], GATED: A Multi-Routing Protocol Daemon for UNIX, *Proceedings of the 1988 Summer USENIX conference,* San Francisco, California.

FLOYD, S. and V. JACOBSON [August 1993], Random Early Detection Gateways for Congestion Avoidance, *IEEE/ACM Transactions on Networking,* 1(4), 397-413.

FRANK, H., and W. CHOU [1971], Routing in Computer Networks, *Networks,* 1(1), 99-112.

FULTZ, G. L., and L. KLEINROCK, [June 14-16, 1971], Adaptive Routing Techniques for Store-and-Forward Computer Communication Networks, *Proceedings of The IEEE International Conference on Communications,* Montreal, Canada, pages 39-1 to 39-8.

GERLA, M., and L. KLEINROCK [April 1980], Flow Control: A Comparative Survey, *IEEE Transactions on Communications,* Vol, 28(4), 553-574.

HALL, M., M. TOWFIQ, G. ARNOLD, D. TREADWELL, and H. SANDERS [1993], *Windows Sockets: An Open Interface For Programming Under Microsoft Windows,* Microdyne Corporation.

HINDEN, R., J. HAVERTY, and A. SHELTZER [September 1983], The DARPA Internet: Interconnecting Heterogeneous Computer Networks with Gateways, *Computer,* Vol. 16(9), 38-48.

INTERNATIONAL ORGANIZATION FOR STANDARDIZATION [1996], Information processing systems — Open Systems Interconnection — *Transport Service Definition,* STD 8072, ISO, Switzerland.

INTERNATIONAL ORGANIZATION FOR STANDARDIZATION [1997], Information processing systems — Open Systems Interconnection — *Connection Oriented Transport Protocol Specification,* STD 8073, ISO, Switzerland.

INTERNATIONAL ORGANIZATION FOR STANDARDIZATION [2002a], Information processing systems — Open Systems Interconnection — *Specification of Basic Specification of Abstract Syntax Notation One (ASN.1),* STD 8824-1, ISO, Switzerland.

INTERNATIONAL ORGANIZATION FOR STANDARDIZATION [2002b], Information processing systems — Open Systems Interconnection — *Specification of Basic Encoding Rules for Abstract Syntax Notation One (ASN.1),* STD 8825-1, ISO, Switzerland.

INTERNATIONAL ORGANIZATION FOR STANDARDIZATION [1998a], Information processing systems — Open Systems Interconnection — *Management Information Service Definition,* STD 9595, ISO, Switzerland.

INTERNATIONAL ORGANIZATION FOR STANDARDIZATION [1998b], Information processing systems — Open Systems Interconnection — *Management Information Protocol Definition, Part 1: Definition,* STD 9596-1.

JACOBSON, V. [August 1988], Congestion Avoidance and Control, *Proceedings ACM SIGCOMM '88,* 314-329.

JAIN, R. [January 1985], On Caching Out-of-Order Packets in Window Flow Controlled Networks, *Technical Report,* DEC-TR-342, Digital Equipment Corporation.

JAIN, R. [March 1986], Divergence of Timeout Algorithms for Packet Retransmissions, *Proceedings Fifth Annual International Phoenix Conference on Computers and Communications,* Scottsdale, AZ, 174-179.

JAIN, R. [October 1986], A Timeout-Based Congestion Control Scheme for Window Flow-Controlled Networks, *IEEE Journal on Selected Areas in Communications,* Vol. SAC-4, no. 7, 1162-1167.

JAIN, R., K. RAMAKRISHNAN, and D-M. CHIU [August 1987], Congestion Avoidance in Computer Networks With a Connectionless Network Layer. *Technical Report,* DEC-TR-506, Digital Equipment Corporation.

JAIN, R. [1991], *The Art of Computer Systems Performance Analysis,* John Wiley & Sons, New York.

JAIN, R. [May 1992], Myths About Congestion Management in High-speed Networks, *Internetworking: Research and Experience,* 3(3), 101-113.

JAIN, R. [1994], *FDDI Handbook; High-Speed Networking Using Fiber and Other Media,* Addison Wesley, Reading, Massachusetts.

JENNINGS, D. M., L. H. LANDWEBER, I. H. FUCHS, D. J. FARBER, and W. RICHARDS ADRION, [February 28, 1986], Computer Networking for Scientists and Engineers, *Science* vol 231, 943-950.

JUBIN, J. and J. TORNOW [January 1987], The DARPA Packet Radio Network Protocols, *IEEE Proceedings,* Vol. 75(1), 21-32.

KAHN, R. [November 1972], Resource-Sharing Computer Communications Networks, *Proceedings of the IEEE,* 60(11), 1397-1407.

KARN, P., H. PRICE, and R. DIERSING [May 1985], Packet Radio in the Amateur Service, *IEEE Journal on Selected Areas in Communications,* Vol. 3(3), 431-439.

KARN, P., and C. PARTRIDGE [August 1987], Improving Round-Trip Time Estimates in Reliable Transport Protocols, *Proceedings of ACM SIGCOMM '87,* 2-7.

KAUFMAN, C., PERLMAN, R., and SPECINER, M. [2002], *Network Security: Private Communication in a Public World,* 2nd edition, Prentice-Hall, Upper Saddle River, New Jersey.

KENT, C., and J. MOGUL [August 1987], Fragmentation Considered Harmful, *Proceedings of ACM SIGCOMM '87,* 390-401.

LAMPSON, B. W., M. PAUL, and H. J. SIEGERT (EDS.) [1981], *Distributed Systems - Architecture and Implementation (An Advanced Course),* Springer-Verlag, Berlin.

LAMPSON, B. W., V. SRINIVASAN, and G. VARGHESE [June 1999], IP Lookups Using Multiway and Multicolumn Search, *IEEE/ACM Transactions on Networking,* Vol. 7(3), 324-334.

LANZILLO, A. L., and C. PARTRIDGE [January 1989], Implementation of Dial-up IP for UNIX Systems, *Proceedings 1989 Winter USENIX Technical Conference,* San Diego, CA.

McKUSICK, M., K. BOSTIC, M. KARELS, and J. QUARTERMAN [1996], *The Design and Implementation of the 4.4BSD UNIX Operating System,* Addison Wesley, Reading, Massachusetts.

MCNAMARA, J. [1988], *Technical Aspects of Data Communications,* 3rd edition, Digital Press, Digital Equipment Corporation, Bedford, Massachusetts.

MCQUILLAN, J. M., I. RICHER, and E. ROSEN [May 1980], The New Routing Algorithm for the ARPANET, *IEEE Transactions on Communications,* COM-28(5), 711-719.

METCALFE, R. M., and D. R. BOGGS [July 1976], Ethernet: Distributed Packet Switching for Local Computer Networks, *Communications of the ACM,* 19(7), 395-404.

MILLS, D., and H-W. BRAUN [August 1987], The NSFNET Backbone Network, *Proceedings of ACM SIGCOMM '87,* 191-196.

MORRIS, R. [1979], Fixing Timeout Intervals for Lost Packet Detection in Computer Communication Networks, *Proceedings AFIPS National Computer Conference*, Vol. 48, 887-891.

NAGLE, J. [April 1987], On Packet Switches With Infinite Storage, *IEEE Transactions on Communications*, Vol. COM-35:4, 435-438.

NARTEN, T. [Sept. 1989], Internet Routing, *Proceedings ACM SIGCOMM '89*, 271-282.

NEEDHAM, R. M. [1979], System Aspects of the Cambridge Ring, *Proceedings of the ACM Seventh Symposium on Operating System Principles,* 82-85.

NEWMAN, P., G. MINSHALL, and T. L. LYON [April 1998], IP Switching — ATM Under IP, *IEEE Transactions on Networking,* Vol. 6:2, 117-129.

OPPEN, D., and Y. DALAL [July 1983], The Clearinghouse: A Decentralized Agent for Locating Named Objects In A Distributed Environment, *ACM Transactions on Information Systems (TOIS),* Vol 1(3), 230-253.

PAREKH, A. K., and R. G. GALLAGER [June, 1993], A Generalized Processor Sharing Approach To Flow Control In Integrated Services Networks: The Single-Node Case, *IEEE/ACM Transaction on Networking,* Vol. 3:1, 344-357.

PAREKH, A. K., and R. G. GALLAGER [April, 1994], A Generalized Processor Sharing Approach To Flow Control In Integrated Services Networks: The Multiple-Node Case, *IEEE/ACM Transaction on Networking,* Vol. 4:2, 137-150.

PARTRIDGE, C. [June 1986], Mail Routing Using Domain Names: An Informal Tour, *Proceedings of the 1986 Summer USENIX Conference*, 366-376.

PARTRIDGE, C. [June 1987], Implementing the Reliable Data Protocol (RDP), *Proceedings of the 1987 Summer USENIX Conference*, 367-379.

PARTRIDGE, C. [1994], *Gigabit Networking*, Addison-Wesley, Reading, Massachusetts.

PELTON, J. [1995], *Wireless and Satellite Telecommunications,* Prentice-Hall, Upper Saddle River, New Jersey.

PERLMAN, R. [2000], *Interconnections: Bridges and Routers, Switches and Internetworking Protocols,* 2nd edition, Addison-Wesley, Reading, Massachusetts.

PETERSON, L. [1985], *Defining and Naming the Fundamental Objects in a Distributed Message System,* Ph.D. Dissertation, Purdue University, West Lafayette, Indiana.

POSTEL, J. B. [April 1980], Internetwork Protocol Approaches, *IEEE Transactions on Communications,* COM-28(4), 604-611.

POSTEL, J. B., C. A. SUNSHINE, and D. COHEN [1981], The ARPA Internet Protocol, *Computer Networks,* Vol. 5, 261-271.

QUARTERMAN, J. S., and J. C. HOSKINS [October 1986], Notable Computer Networks, *Communications of the ACM*, 29(10), 932-971.

RAMAKRISHNAN, K. and R. JAIN [May 1990], A Binary Feedback Scheme For Congestion Avoidance In Computer Networks, *ACM Transactions on Computer Systems*, 8(2), 158-181.

REYNOLDS, J., J. POSTEL, A. R. KATZ, G. G. FINN, and A. L. DESCHON [October 1985], The DARPA Experimental Multimedia Mail System, *IEEE Computer*, Vol. 18(10), 82-89.

RITCHIE, D. M., and K. THOMPSON [July 1974], The UNIX Time-Sharing System, *Communications of the ACM,* 17(7), 365-375; revised and reprinted in *Bell System Technical Journal,* 57(6), [July-August 1978], 1905-1929.

ROSE, M. [1993], *The Internet Message: Closing The Book with Electronic Mail,* Prentice-Hall, Upper Saddle River, New Jersey.

SALTZER, J. [1978], Naming and Binding of Objects, *Operating Systems, An Advanced Course,* Springer-Verlag, 99-208.

SALTZER, J. [April 1982], Naming and Binding of Network Destinations, *International Symposium on Local Computer Networks,* IFIP/T.C.6, 311-317.

SALTZER, J., D. REED, and D. CLARK [November 1984], End-to-End Arguments in System Design, *ACM Transactions on Computer Systems,* 2(4), 277-288.

SHOCH, J. F. [1978], Internetwork Naming, Addressing, and Routing, *Proceedings of COMPCON,* 72-79.

SHOCH, J. F., Y. DALAL, and D. REDELL [August 1982], Evolution of the Ethernet Local Computer Network, *Computer,* Vol. 15(8), 10-27.

SHREEDHAR, M., and G. VARGHESE [1995], Efficient Fair Queueing Using Deficit Round Robin, *Proceedings SIGCOMM'95,,* 231-242

SOLOMON, J. [1998], *Mobile IP: The Internet Unplugged,* Prentice-Hall, Upper Saddle River, New Jersey.

SOLOMON, M., L. LANDWEBER, and D. NEUHEGEN [1982], The CSNET Name Server, *Computer Networks* Vol. 6(3), 161-172.

SRINIVASAN, V., and G. VARGHESE [February 1999], Fast Address Lookups Using Controlled Prefix Expansion, *ACM Transactions on Computer Systems,* vol. 17(1), 1-40.

STEVENS, W. R., et. al. [2003], *UNIX Network Programming, Vol. 1: The Sockets Networking API, 3rd edition,* Prentice-Hall, Upper Saddle River, New Jersey.

SWINEHART, D., G. MCDANIEL, and D. R. BOGGS [December 1979], WFS: A Simple Shared File System for a Distributed Environment, *Proceedings of the Seventh Symposium on Operating System Principles,* 9-17.

TICHY, W., and Z. RUAN [June 1984], Towards a Distributed File System, *Proceedings of Summer 84 USENIX Conference,* Salt Lake City, Utah, 87-97.

TOMLINSON. R. S. [1975], Selecting Sequence Numbers, *Proceedings ACM SIGOPS/SIGCOMM Interprocess Communication Workshop,* 11-23, 1975.

WATSON, R. [1981], Timer-Based Mechanisms in Reliable Transport Protocol Connection Management, *Computer Networks,* Vol. 5, 47-56.

WEINBERGER, P. J. [1985], The UNIX Eighth Edition Network File System, *Proceedings 1985 ACM Computer Science Conference,* 299-301.

WELCH, B., and J. OUSTERHOUT [May 1986], Prefix Tables: A Simple Mechanism for Locating Files in a Distributed System, *Proceedings IEEE Sixth International Conference on Distributed Computing Systems,* 184-189.

WILKES, M. V., and D. J. WHEELER [May 1979], The Cambridge Digital Communication Ring, *Proceedings Local Area Computer Network Symposium,* 47-61.

XEROX [1981], Internet Transport Protocols, *Report XSIS 028112,* Xerox Corporation, Office Products Division, Network Systems Administration Office, 3333 Coyote Hill Road, Palo Alto, California.

ZHANG, L. [August 1986], Why TCP Timers Don't Work Well, *Proceedings of ACM SIGCOMM '86,* 397-405.

Index